THE PURSUIT OF LIBERTY

THE PURSUIT

A HISTORY OF THE AMERICAN PEOPLE

Wadsworth Publishing Company

Belmont, California
A Division of Wadsworth, Inc.

OF LIBERTY

VOLUME TWO/SECOND EDITION

R. Jackson Wilson
Smith College

James Gilbert
University of Maryland

Stephen Nissenbaum
University of Massachusetts

Karen Ordahl Kupperman
University of Connecticut

Donald Scott
The New School for Social Research

History Editor: Peggy Adams
Production Editor: Leland Moss
Interior and Cover Design: James Chadwick
Art Editor: Marta Kongsle
Art Assistant: Roberta Broyer
Photo Research: Pembroke Herbert
Print Buyer: Barbara Britton
Compositor: Jonathan Peck Typographers
Copy Editor: Anne Montague
Editorial Assistant: Karen Moore
Cover Art: A Social History of the State of Missouri, by Thomas Hart Benton, Missouri State Capitol Building, Jefferson City, Missouri. Courtesy Missouri Department of Natural Resources, Missouri State Museum.

Chapter opening photos are from the following sources: Chapter 12, Library of Congress, Brady Collection; Chapter 13, Culver Pictures; Chapter 14, Culver Pictures; Chapter 15, Library of Congress; Chapter 16, Culver Pictures; Chapter 17, Theodore Roosevelt Birthplace Association; Chapter 18, Library of Congress; Chapter 19, Culver Pictures; Chapter 20, Wide World Photos; Chapter 21, UPI/Bettmann Newsphotos; Chapter 22, Ralph Crane, *Life* Magazine, © 1958 Time Inc.; Chapter 23, © Burt Glinn/Magnum; Chapter 24, © Alex Webb/Magnum; Chapter 25, Bill Viggiano, Photographer.

Printed in the United States of America   **34**

1 2 3 4 5 6 7 8 9 10—94 93 92 91 90

**Library of Congress
Cataloging-in-Publication Data**

The Pursuit of liberty.

    Includes bibliographical references.
    1. United States—History. I. Wilson, Raymond Jackson.
    E178.1.P985   1990   973   89-16712
    ISBN 0-534-11694-9 (hardcover)
    ISBN 0-534-11697-3 (pbk. : v. 1)
    ISBN 0-534-11699-X (pbk. : v. 2)

CONTENTS

14   The Climax of the Industrial Revolution

15   A New West

16   The Gospel of Wealth

17   The Politics of Reform

18   Imperial America

19   Mass Culture and the "Jazz Age"

20   Capitalism in Transition

21   A Global Nation

∽

25   The Way We Are

∽

AUTHORS' PREFACE

When the oldest of the authors of *The Pursuit of Liberty* was in the eighth grade, he had to take his first course on the history of the United States. His teacher was a legend in the school, a tough, slightly forbidding woman, who was determined that her students were going to learn *something* about the history of their country.

She gave her roomful of fourteen-year-olds a demanding task. They had to memorize any 200 facts about American history, including dates. When the final examination came, they had to write down their list of facts in the correct chronological order. You could choose any facts, as long as there were 200 of them and they were in chronological order. You might start with "1492—Columbus discovers America." Or you could begin with "1607—First English colony in America at Jamestown, Virginia." (In both cases, you would be a bit wrong. But that didn't matter. These "facts" were in the textbook, and the important thing was that you had learned them.)

Nowadays, of course, everything about learning history has changed. The authors' own children come home from history classes in schools and colleges with their heads full of "concepts." They don't think "1607—Jamestown" (or even "1587—Roanoke," which is closer to the truth). Instead, they are taught to talk about large and abstract events, such as "The Confrontation of European and Native-American Cultures." They study grand processes such as "Industrialization," "Immigration," and "Urbanization." They seem to learn history in a more sophisticated and better way than memorizing some list of 200 facts.

But there is a problem. Students who study American history today seem to know something in general, but nothing in particular. They discuss abstractions and generalizations, but these are not connected with any firm grasp of relevant factual information. Have our best and most innovative teachers and professors simply replaced 200 facts with 20 vague concepts? The old problem was that history was a grab bag of names and dates and places. Students learned something in particular and nothing much in general. But the new problem, knowing the general but not the particular, is just as serious. Either way, studying history runs the risk of being a plain waste of time.

This dilemma is partly the result of the nature of history itself. There *are* large and general tendencies and there *are* particular facts. The difficult thing is to see how the two fit together. We tend to look at history the way we look at a painting. We focus on the foreground—the facts. Or we think about the background, about the general way the picture is structured and the kinds of claims it makes on our imagination. But when we study history, it is difficult to put the foreground and the background, the facts and the general concepts, together. We seem to choose between foreground and background, unable to see how each makes sense in terms of the other.

When most history textbooks try to bring specific facts and general concepts together, they do so by simply *telling* readers that this or that fact is an example of this or that general tendency. First comes a heading, something like "The Contact of European and Native-American Cultures" or "Industrialization." Then comes a sentence or two of generalization. A little further on come the facts, such as "1607—Jamestown" or "The first transcontinental railroad was completed in 1869."

Some important things are lost in this way of writing history. We are not asked to see or understand the relationship between fact and general concept at all. Did something called "industrialization" *cause* the first transcontinental railroad or did a host of facts, such as the building of that railroad, cause industrial development? Concrete facts and general concepts merely coexist in such textbooks, each of them inert and incapable of giving any sort of life to the other.

Perhaps worse, when students study history in textbooks of this sort, they get no sense of the human *experience* involved in either the specific events they find listed there or the generalizations they read and underline to study for next week's test. Most history textbooks contain no narrative, no stories, no accounts of the dramatic, sometimes triumphant, often shameful efforts and struggles of human beings. Human action is squeezed out of history and we are left with dead "events" and equally lifeless generalizations.

We have written *The Pursuit of Liberty* in the belief that we have found ways to solve these kinds of problems. We started with two convictions. First, we had to make it possible for students to see and *understand* the ways that specific sequences of human action were related to the general setting in which they took place. Second, historians ought not to keep a secret of the remarkably exciting and dramatic ways people actually acted in the past.

These two convictions have shaped our book, and they explain its unusual structure. Each chapter has two different parts. In the first, we tell the story of a very specific and concrete episode: a witchcraft hysteria in Salem, Massachusetts, in 1692, for example; or the massacre of a band of the Native American Sioux at Wounded Knee Creek in the Dakotas in 1890; or the rending struggle for custody of the infant known as "Baby M" in the 1980s. Episodes like these are the human material out of which history is made.

But history is more than stories. It involves coming to understand how the stories could have happened. To do this, we have to know something about the general context within which a specific episode took place. So the second part of each chapter is a discussion of the historical setting of the chapter's episode. The narrative of Salem witchcraft is followed by a discussion of seventeenth-century New England Puritanism; the Wounded Knee massacre by an examination of the westward expansion of European-American society into the territories of the Native Americans; the story of Baby M by a discussion of the tangled relationships between private morality and public politics that characterized American life in the 1980s.

And so we go through *The Pursuit of Liberty*, alternating between the specific and the general, between narrative and explanation. In the end we think our readers will have a much better grasp of the way history works, of the way that all the specific actions of people are shaped by the historical setting in which they take place. And we have faith, too, that some of our readers will learn the most important thing that history has to teach all of us: We all live in history, profoundly shaped by the society around us, by what it has been as well as by what it is now.

If this lesson is learned, then our readers will have learned what we already know, that learning history is a way of discovering our kinship with all those real people who have come before us, who have acted out their struggles, terrors, and occasional exaltations with the same anxiety and effort that go so deeply into all our lives. The past is inescapable, for everyone, whether one knows it or not.

It is better to know it.

R. Jackson Wilson
James Gilbert
Stephen Nissenbaum
Karen Ordahl Kupperman
Donald Scott

ABOUT THE AUTHORS

R. Jackson Wilson is a Professor of History at Smith College. He is a graduate of the University of Missouri and received his M.A. and Ph.D. degrees from the University of Wisconsin. He has taught at an unusually wide range of institutions, including the University of Arizona, the University of Wisconsin, Columbia University, the University of Massachusetts, Hartford College for Women, Yale University, the University of Pennsylvania, and the Flinders University of South Australia. He has been a fellow of the Woodrow Wilson Foundation, the National Endowment for the Humanities, the Charles Warren Center, Harvard University, and the National Humanities Center. He is the author of *In Quest of Community: Social Philosophy in the United States* and *Figures of Speech: American Writers and the Literary Marketplace, from Benjamin Franklin to Emily Dickinson*.

James Gilbert is Professor of History at the University of Maryland and a graduate of Carleton College and the University of Wisconsin. He has also taught at Teachers College, Columbia University; Warwick University in Coventry, England; the University of Paris; and Sydney University in Australia. His books include *Writers and Partisans* (1968), *Designing the Industrial State* (1972), *Work Without Salvation* (1978), *Another Chance: Postwar America* (1981), and *A Cycle of Outrage: America's Reaction to the Juvenile Delinquent in the 1950s* (1986). He has been a Fellow of the Woodrow Wilson Foundation, the National Endowment for the Humanities, and the Woodrow Wilson Center. Currently he is finishing a book on Chicago in the 1890s.

Stephen Nissenbaum is a Professor of History at the University of Massachusetts, Amherst, where he teaches intellectual and social history and directs The Center for New England Culture. He has held fellowships from the National Endowment for the Humanities and the American Council of Learned Societies. He has taught at Smith College, Hampshire College, and Mount Holyoke College. He has been the James Pinckney Harrison Professor of History at The College of William and Mary. He has served as president of his state humanities council, the Massachusetts Foundation for Humanities and Public Policy. He is the author of *Sex, Diet, and Debility in Jacksonian America* and (with Paul Boyer) *Salem Possessed: The Social Origins of Witchcraft*, which won the John H. Dunning prize of the American Historical Association. He is currently writing a book about Edgar Allan Poe, Nathaniel Hawthorne, and the social history of literature in the Jacksonian period.

Karen Ordahl Kupperman is Professor of History at the University of Connecticut. She is a graduate of the University of Missouri and holds an M.A. from Harvard University and a Ph.D. from Cambridge University. Her previous books include *Settling with the Indians: The Meeting of English and Indian Cultures in America, 1580–1640* (1980) and *Roanoake, the Abandoned Colony* (1984). She is also the editor of *Captain John Smith: A Select Edition of His Writings* (1988). In 1980, her essay "Apathy and Death in Early Jamestown" won the distinguished Binkley-Stevenson award of the Organization of American Historians. She has been a Mellon Faculty Fellow at Harvard, a fellow of the National Humanities Center, and senior associate member of St. Antony's College, Oxford.

Donald Scott is a Professor of History and Dean of Eugene Lang College of the New School for Social Research. He is a graduate of Harvard College and received his Ph.D. from the University of Wisconsin. He is the author of *From Office to Profession: The New England Ministry, 1750–1850,* and is co-author of *America's Families: A Documentary History.* He has been a fellow t the Davis Center for Historical Studies, Princeton University, and a National Endowment for the Humanities Fellow at the American Antiquarian Society. He is currently working on a book on democracy and knowledge in nineteenth-century America.

ACKNOWLEDGMENTS

We believe that everything that is said in *The Pursuit of Liberty* is true. Well, almost everything. But the book contains two unavoidable falsehoods, both of them on the title page. Both are formulas that are imposed by the powerful conventions that govern the publication of books in our society. The first is the suggestion that an abstract corporate entity named Wadsworth Publishing brought the book into existence. The second is that five individuals known as "authors" are responsible for all the words and ideas in the book. We would like to set the record straight on both these points.

The truth of the matter is that Wadsworth Publishing is really a set of very specific people who have generously invested efforts, care, and talent in this book. In particular, no one could have worked more diligently and effectively than Leland Moss, Margaret Adams, James Chadwick, Marta Kongsle, and Roberta Broyer. The book owes much to them.

The truth is, as well, that the writing of history is a collective enterprise. We owe an incalculable debt to generations of men and women who have labored to make the history of the American people comprehensible. We also owe a great deal to the people—many of them now mature men and women—who have been our students. We cannot repay them for all the history lessons they have given to us; we can only hope that some of *their* children may learn as much from our book as we have from them.

The Pursuit of Liberty is also the product of some fine advice from many extremely intelligent and dedicated people. We are grateful to them all, and particularly to: Katherine Abbott, John K. Alexander, Stephen L. Berk, David Bernstein, Lee R. Boyer, Thomas J. Boyle, John C. Chalberg, Lawrence Foster, Paula Franklin, William Graebner, Pembroke Herbert, James Henretta, Donald W. Hensel, William C. Hine, E. Rusten Hogness, Cornelia Hopkins, Marvin L. Jaegers, George L. Jones, Stephen Kneeshaw, Neil B. Lehman, Gerald McFarland, Frank Nation, Gary Nissenbaum, Gregory Nobles, Thomas C. Parramore, S. Fred Roach, Chris Rogers, Philip R. Royal, Alan Schaffer, Rodney Sievers, John Snetsinger, Dennis Thavenet, Stephen Weisner, Nancy Woloch, and Phyllis Zimmerman. Sometimes their suggestions have posed formidable tasks for us. Although their criticisms have not always been gentle, even their sternest comments have been useful because they were obviously motivated by a genuine concern for history and for teaching.

CHAPTER 12
"HIS TERRIBLE, SWIFT SWORD"

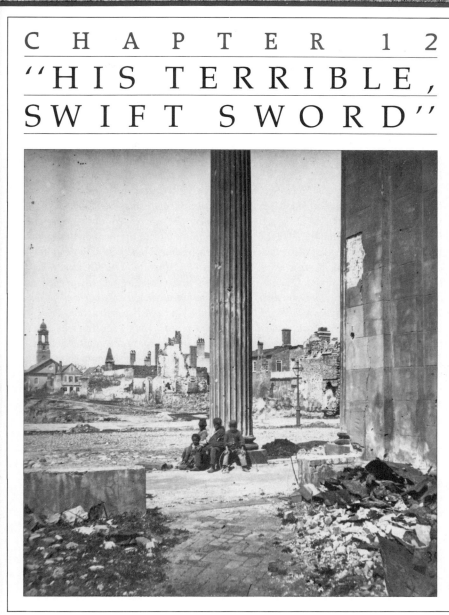

THE EPISODE: If the importance of historical figures can be measured by the amount of attention that historians and biographers pay to them, then Abraham Lincoln was surely the most important American. In this chapter, we look in some detail at several crucial moments and themes in his career as president.

The first is the secession crisis, which the new president confronted when he took office in March of 1861. The second is Lincoln's attempt to define the Civil War as the ultimate test of the principles of republican government, an attempt he began soon after the war started and that climaxed at Gettysburg, Pennsylvania, in 1863, when he said that the cause of the Union was the cause of "government of the people, by the people, for the people." The third is his halting, tentative effort to confront the question of slavery and the relationship between the preservation of the Union and freedom for African Americans. The fourth is his assassination and the public mourning that followed, which made it clear that he had become the symbol, in the North at least, of both Union and liberty.

We chose these moments and themes not only because they are intrinsically interesting and important, but because they also reveal much about a transformation in the man. When he ran for president in 1860, Abraham Lincoln was a folksy, practical, politically shrewd Illinois politician with a flair for words. If he had died then, nothing he had done would have made him more than a footnote to history. When he did die less than five years later, most Americans would agree that he was the nation's savior, the Great Emancipator, the embodiment of their highest national aspirations.

THE HISTORICAL SETTING: Abraham Lincoln did not cause the Civil War. In a sense, the war caused him—made him into the leader and the monumental memory he became. Understanding what happened to Abraham Lincoln after 1861 means understanding what happened to the nation during the decade and a half of Civil War and Reconstruction.

The momentous questions he confronted during every day of his two terms as president were the same questions that were also confronted by American men and women, North and South, white and African American. Would there be war? If the war came, who would fight and what would be the strategies of battle? Who would prevail, and how? And what would be the political, economic, and social fate of millions of African Americans held in slavery, not only in the states that formed the Confederacy but in several states that remained loyal to the Union? And when the war was over, if the Union did endure, how would the Confederate states be returned to their rightful place in it?

ABRAHAM LINCOLN: FROM POLITICS TO MARTYRDOM

As the winter of 1860–61 ended, the new president came quietly, even somewhat secretly, into Washington to take his oath of office. He was about to face a reality no other American president had had to face: a divided Union. And no one, not even men who had agreed to serve in his cabinet, not even the political friends who had helped engineer his nomination and win his election, knew what his strategies and policies would be. Most people who thought about Abraham Lincoln at all thought of him as a western lawyer, as a pretty good stump speaker, and—above all—as a shrewd politician. And they were, in the main, right. Lincoln had shown a remarkable ability to find moderate positions about slavery, positions he knew were not far from the opinions of the Northern voters who had elected him.

No one could have predicted that four years later, a murdered Abraham Lincoln would leave the capital as the greatest national hero since George Washington. When his body returned westward, back to Illinois, it was no longer the political figure, or even the political leader, that people mourned. It was a dedicated, heroic martyr to what Lincoln had managed to define as a national crusade. He had managed to transform an ugly civil war into a spiritual struggle for principles much higher than the political unity of a nation. His death put the seal on that transformation.

He began his presidency by playing a complicated political "game," as he sometimes called it. The game became war. And war changed Abraham Lincoln. The change was not complete: The shrewd politician remained always a part of him. But he began to see the war as something more than politics, more even than battle and suffering. Part of him began to think of it as a religious experience, in which a nation that seemed to have been chosen by God for special blessings was now being put through a special trial and punishment. He began to insist more and more that the war was a kind of blood sacrifice demanded by God as a payment for the long sin of slavery. And when, at the war's end, he paid with his own blood, dramatic proof seemed to be given that his redefinition of the war was correct.

As Lincoln prepared to take office, the political situation was so delicate and so dangerous that even his practical skills had only a slender chance. Seven states in the lower South had already seceded and had established a new federal government for

515

Abraham Lincoln, 1860 and 1865. The first portrait shows Lincoln in June 1860, at the opening of his presidential campaign. (Library of Congress) The second, taken just four days before his assassination, reveals the psychological and physical toll the Civil War had extracted from Lincoln. (McLellan Lincoln Collection, Brown University, John Hay Library)

themselves, the Confederate States of America. Several states in the upper South, particularly Virginia, Maryland, and Kentucky, were poised to join the new Confederacy. All the federal officials in the seceded states had either given allegiance to the Confederacy or had been replaced by secessionists. The Confederacy had taken over almost all the federal property within its borders—the post offices, the customs and land offices, even the forts and arsenals. All that remained of visible federal authority were two forts. One was Fort Pickens, far off in Pensacola, Florida; the other was Fort Sumter in Charleston Harbor, in the heart of secession country.

Then, as inauguration day approached, there was a strange lull. Everyone waited to see what Lincoln would do. He made no public statements. The only prediction anyone could hazard was that his actions would be—characteristically—cautious, secretive, and essentially political. In Lincoln's mind, the best direction things could go was clear: Secession would somehow be stopped without violence; the Union would be restored. And this would be done without compromising the basic Republican position on slavery in the western territories. The problem was, did he have the means and the power to work out such a political solution?

The answer would surely lie with Virginia. If he could manipulate events carefully enough so that Virginia stayed in the Union, then surely Maryland and Kentucky, probably Tennessee and Missouri, would follow Virginia's lead. Time would take its toll on the weak and isolated Confederacy. Good sense might win out, and one by one the seceding states could come back into the Union.

At this point, Lincoln saw the problem in terms that were legal, political, and constitutional. It was illegal for any state to secede. He had no doubt of that. But it was equally unconstitutional for the federal government to interfere at all with slavery in any of the states. The political bargain he wanted was for the upper South to accept this political settlement, remain in the Union, and keep their slave system as long as they could make it last.

But it was a tricky situation. If Lincoln did anything that even seemed hostile, he might provoke the border states and the upper South, especially Virginia, into joining the Confederacy, leaving the Union in a much more vulnerable position if and when war came. But he could not simply ignore secession: The people who had elected him expected Lincoln to stand up to the slave power, not give in to it. Should he try to get national institutions going again and send Republican postmasters, judges, and customs officials into the Confederacy? Should he try to reclaim federal property? What about Fort Pickens and Fort Sumter? There had already been one crisis over Fort Sumter. On December 26 Major Robert Anderson had moved his Union garrison out of Fort Moultrie, far out in the harbor into Sumter. But outraged South Carolinians had demanded the total evacuation of federal troops. After three days of vacillation, President Buchanan had rejected the Confederate demand and the first Sumter crisis had died down. But Fort Sumter had become an important symbol: To the North it was an emblem of the endurance of the Union; to the South it was a galling sign of Yankee aggression.

Lincoln announced his policy in his first act as president, his inaugural address. He began by reassuring the South. His administration would not "directly or indirectly interfere with the institution of slavery where it exists." Lincoln then flatly declared that the Union remained unbroken. "No state," he insisted, "can lawfully get out of the Union; and acts of violence within any state or states against the authority of the United States are insurrectionary." He warned that he would use "the power confided to me to hold, occupy, and possess the property and places belonging to the government." But then, his resolve to defend the Union unmistakable, he assured the South that there would be "no bloodshed or violence unless it be forced upon the national authority." He would deliver the mails only if the South wanted them delivered, and he would not "force obnoxious strangers into the South to carry out Federal business." Even though he had "the strict legal right" to do so, he would "forgo, for the time, the use of such offices" because any attempt to do otherwise "would be so irritating and so nearly impracticable."

Finally, Lincoln insisted again on his peaceful intentions. "In your hands, my dissatisfied fellow countrymen, and not mine, is the momentous issue of Civil War—the government will not assail you. You can have no conflict, without being yourself the aggesssors."

Lincoln was carefully walking a political tightrope, trying to avoid as long as possible any action that would set events on an irreversible course to war. His policy was designed to buy some political time to get his administration set up and to let Unionist sentiment in the South regroup. But the policy was also aimed toward making sure that if war *did* come, the responsibility for starting it would lie not with Lincoln but with "his dissatisfied fellow countrymen." It would be easier to rally the political support needed to wage war if the Confederacy rather than Lincoln was seen as the aggressor. Also, if Lincoln started the war, all the remaining slave states would probably join the Confederacy, and then Britain and France, leaping at the chance to split the American empire, might formally recognize the Confederacy as a separate nation.

Lincoln's policy of "masterly inactivity," as the *New York Times* dubbed it, rested on the assurance of his military advisers that Fort Sumter could hold out indefinitely and stand as a continuing symbol of the unbroken Union. But the day after Lincoln delivered his inaugural address, Major Anderson sent the surprising word that his provisions would last only four to six weeks. He would have to surrender Fort Sumter unless 70,000 troops were sent to relieve him.

So Sumter would have to be reinforced or evacuated. Neither alternative was very desirable in political terms. Sending military relief would certainly bring civil war. It would surely drive the upper South and quite possibly the border states as well into the Confederacy. But evacuation also had political risks. It would probably avoid war for a time and might help Southern Unionists. But it might push reunion ever further away by confirming the secessionists' claim that the North lacked the will to fight, thus strengthening their political grip on the Confederate states. The impact of evacuation on Northern opinion could be even more disastrous. Most Northerners, and especially the Republican majority that had elected Lincoln, would surely consider evacuation a betrayal of his pledge to "hold and possess" federal property. This might so discredit him as a political leader that his capacity to govern would collapse. And that, Lincoln feared, would lead to the collapse of the Republican party, the political force that had finally succeeded in wresting the federal government away from the slave power. Everything the Republicans had fought for during six long years would be lost forever.

Lincoln proceeded cautiously. He asked each of the members of his cabinet for a written response to the suggestion that provisions only, not fresh troops, be sent to Fort Sumter. Only one man, Postmaster General Montgomery Blair, urged that course. The others feared that even this would lead to war. Secretary of State William Seward argued most vehemently against sending provisions, insisting that the evacuation of Sumter was the only possible way, short of war, to end the crisis and restore the Union. Lincoln listened to the debate but did not express a firm position of his own. Those around him certainly thought he had accepted the overwhelming opinion of his cabinet that the fort would have to be surrendered. In fact (unknown to Lincoln), Seward privately assured some Confederate commissioners who had come to Washington to demand recognition of the Confederacy that Sumter *would* be evacuated. The commissioners knew that Lincoln could not possibly accept their demand for recognition, but they hoped to use his formal refusal to prove their contention that his real intent was hostile. Arguing that Sumter was about to be evacuated, Seward persuaded the commissioners to delay asking for an immediate answer to their demand. He himself favored evacuation and was dead certain that the inexperienced Lincoln would follow his seasoned advice.

But Lincoln had not decided to pull out of Fort Sumter. Seward and the others had misread his silence as an endorsement of evacuation. (Lincoln usually listened to advice, but he rarely revealed his own intentions until he was ready to act.) Though it seemed likely that Sumter would have to be abandoned, Lincoln was reluctant to take the step and played for more time. He had ordered the troops waiting aboard ship in Pensacola Harbor to move into Fort Pickens. This quiet, relatively unprovocative act might let him turn Pickens into the symbol of an unbroken Union. He sent Stephen Hurlbut, a Charleston-born friend, to South Carolina to find out how strong the Union sentiment there really was.

But the clamor for action was mounting. The rumors of an impending evacuation of Sumter were eroding Lincoln's support, and disillusionment over his "weakness" and "inaction" began to set in. "The country feels no more assurance as to the future than it did on the day Mr. Buchanan left Washington," the *New York Times* editorialized. "The people want something to be decided on—some standard raised—some policy put forward which shall serve as a rallying point for the abundant but discouraged loyalty of the American heart." Lincoln's old friend Senator Lyman Trumbull, of Illinois, introduced a resolution into the Senate declaring that it was "the duty of the President to use all the means in his power to hold and protect the property of the United States."

Hurlbut reported back that Unionism was utterly dead in South Carolina and all but extinct in other seceding states. He was sure that the Confederacy would accept nothing but "unqualified recognition of absolute independence," and he believed that nothing done "by the government will prevent the possibility of armed collision." Major Anderson in the meantime sent back word that he could hold out no longer than April 15. So on March 29 Lincoln ordered that an expedition to provision Sumter be prepared, "to be used, according to circumstance."

Still, the president hesitated. For weeks he had waited for word from Pensacola, but when it finally came, on April 6, it was not what Lincoln had hoped to hear. The order to garrison Fort Pickens, sent by sea rather than land, had taken a long time to get there. When it finally had arrived, it had not been obeyed! The captain of the troopship, acting on orders issued under Buchanan, would not take orders from the army and refused to act until a navy superior told him to. Now lack of supplies would force the surrender of Sumter before Pickens could be established as the symbol of the Union. And so, finally, Lincoln sent a message to Governor Pickens of South Carolina, informing him that "an attempt will be made to supply Fort Sumter with provisions only, and that if such attempt be not resisted, no effort to throw in men, arms, or ammunition will be made without further notice, or in case of an attack upon the fort." On April 9 the expedition, carrying provisions for a year, set forth with an armed escort.

Lincoln's message to Governor Pickens surprised and angered Southern leaders, who thought that Seward had spoken for Lincoln when he had promised the evacuation of Sumter. But secessionists were also becoming impatient with the inactivity of *their* leaders. The United States flag fluttering above the fort, in full view of Charlestonians, was a continuing affront to the idea of Southern independence. The Confederates acted. At 4:30 A.M. on April 12, 1861, before the relief expedition had time to arrive, shore batteries opened fire on Fort Sumter. The next day Major Anderson withdrew his forces, and on the following day, April 14, Lincoln, declaring that the South had fired the first shot, issued a call for 75,000 volunteers to put down the insurrection.

Lincoln's efforts to avoid the war had been political—naturally enough, for the situation *was* political until one side or the other began to shoot. And the political task had suited his personality and his talents. Now, confronted with a war that quickly became more deadly and more enduring than anyone on either side expected, what would Lincoln do? What was there in his character that would emerge under the intense pressure of armed conflict?

Initially, some of his work was still mainly political. He had to organize the government for war. He had to take full control of his party, which was as yet merely a loose electoral coalition. Few Republicans felt much loyalty to the "little Illinois lawyer," as Secretary of State William Seward had once called Lincoln. He had become president through a combination of adroit maneuvering and accident. Now he had

Mary Todd Lincoln (1818–82) encouraged her husband's political ambitions and fully supported his presidential aspirations. But her White House years were especially difficult. Born in Kentucky, she was suspected of disloyalty to the Union. Washington society condemned her as both a crude westerner and an excessively extravagant hostess. The death of her son Willie in 1862 and the assassination of her husband undermined her physical and mental health. In her last years, she was a desperate and pathetic woman bordering on insanity. (Lilly Library, Indiana University, Bloomington)

to spend enormous amounts of time handing out the favors and the offices that would create political loyalties.

But in the midst of the politics, a new Lincoln began to find his voice. He developed a special way of talking about the war—no longer as a war for the Union, or just as a combat forced on the government by a few hotheads in the South. In his language, the war gradually became a test of the principles of freedom and democracy—for white people, at least. On July 4, in a message calling Congress into special session, Lincoln stated the argument he was to use for the next four years: that the struggle was not between North and South, or between Union and secession, but a struggle for the rights of the people. The real issue, he declared,

> embraces more than the fate of these United States. It presents to the whole family of man the question whether a constitutional republic, or a democracy—a government of the people, by the same people—can or cannot maintain its territorial integrity against its domestic foes. It presents the question whether discontented individuals, few in number, can arbitrarily break up their government and thus practically put an end to free government upon the face of the earth.

These brief words summarized a brilliant rhetorical strategy. There were three interlocking steps. First, identify the Union cause as the cause of "the people," the cause of democracy. Second, make the outcome a test case of the cause of democracy not just in the United States but for the whole world, the "family of man." Third, make the outcome the *ultimate* test case: If democracy cannot survive here and now, then it can never survive anywhere.

From that July 4 address to the end of the Civil War in 1865, Abraham Lincoln continued to insist on these principles. They were somewhat illogical: There was no sound reason why democracy might not fail in the United States and still succeed in other places. And they were somewhat unrealistic: There was in fact little or no democracy for the "family of man" in the world. But neither logic nor realism was at stake for Lincoln. He understood the necessity of enabling his countrymen to believe they were embarked on an ennobling crusade. And he plainly came to believe it himself.

Lincoln's definition of the war got its most famous statement two years later, in November 1863. He traveled to Gettysburg, Pennsylvania, where the Union armies had turned back a Confederate advance in one of the bloodiest battles of the war just three months earlier. Lincoln's speech came at the end of a long ceremony dedicating a military cemetery. This short address came to represent his greatest performance as a writer, speaker, and ideological leader of his people. His strategy had not changed. He still defined the war as a war for democracy, for all the world, and for all time. But the tactics had become even more skillful.

First, Lincoln sanctified democracy by making it into an *inheritance*. "Four score and seven years ago," he began, "our fathers brought forth on this continent a new nation, conceived in Liberty, and dedicated to the proposition that all men are created equal." No more skillful sentence was ever written by an American president. "Four score and seven years" sounded much more ancient and more holy than "eighty-seven." And "our fathers brought forth . . . conceived . . ." was the language of procreation and birth. It stood in superb dramatic contrast to the place of death he had come to dedicate. Again, the logic and the accuracy were questionable. The United States was already heavily populated by immigrants whose "fathers" had not "brought forth" the nation at all. And it was equally true that the fathers who had "conceived" the nation included a great many slaveholding Virginians and South Carolinians. But once again, logic and realism were not what counted. Lincoln was making the war into an act of faith.

In his next paragraph—and the Gettysburg Address consisted of only two paragraphs—he began to make this religious message clear. The first sentence used the words *dedicate, consecrate*, and *hallow*: "But in a larger sense, we cannot dedicate, we cannot consecrate, we cannot hallow, this ground. The brave men, living and dead, who struggled here, have consecrated it." (Those brave men, of course, were all Union soldiers, for nothing in Lincoln's way of defining the struggle could admit Confederate dead to a share in the "unfinished work . . . so nobly advanced.") The issue was, in the end, dedication—not the dedication of a cemetery but the need for dedication of those who lived on to complete the work. And so Lincoln ended with a ringing plea that "we here highly resolve that these dead shall not have died in vain—that this nation, under God, shall have a new birth of freedom—and that government of the people, by the people, for the people, shall not perish from the earth."

∼∞

Lincoln had, by the force of his words more than by any other means, made the war into a crusade. But while he worked out the definition of the crusade as a struggle to defend democracy for all time, a nagging, often private dilemma would not go away. Lincoln's fine speech at Gettysburg did not mention the problem of slavery. Was that part of the crusade? Did "our fathers" include African-American fathers? Did "a new birth of freedom" include freedom and some measure of equality for slaves? This part of Lincoln's drama was never settled with anything like the clarity and coherence of his mighty assertion of liberty and democracy as the real stakes of war. But his halting, indecisive attempts to confront the issue of slavery are still a central thread in the story of his movement toward heroic martyrdom.

While Lincoln was defining the war as democracy's struggle for survival, other men around him wanted a different, more radical definition. For them, slavery *was* the issue. Charles Sumner, a Massachusetts senator and the leader of the abolitionist wing of the Republican party, insisted that Lincoln strike immediately at slavery—both as an act of justice and as a military measure to weaken the Confederacy. Frederick Douglass, the leading black abolitionist, declared that "the innermost logic of events will force it upon them in the end: that the war is a war for and against slavery." A leading white abolitionist, Wendell Phillips, spoke in even more demanding terms to the North: "Seize the thunderbolt God has forged for you, and annihilate the system that has troubled your peace for seventy years."

But Lincoln hung back. He knew that somehow slavery was the "root of the rebellion." And he knew he did not like it. He could not remember a time when he did not believe that "if slavery is not wrong, nothing is wrong." At the same time, he shared the view of most Northern white voters that black people were racially inferior to whites. Even if he considered fighting the war *against* slavery, he could not conceive of it as a war *for* black freedom and equality. He was also deeply convinced that the Constitution did not give him any power to interfere with slavery within the states.

Most of all, the idea of emancipating slaves by executive order went against Lincoln's political instincts. He knew that a leader who defied public opinion might lose his capacity to lead at all. He had not been elected on an abolitionist platform (and no Republican could have been elected that way). The support he enjoyed early in the war came to him as the friend of the Union, perhaps as the friend of democracy and liberty for whites, but not as the friend of black slaves. Most of all, Lincoln feared that the political outcome of any attempt to emancipate the slaves would be to drive the border states, especially Kentucky, into the Confederacy. "To lose Kentucky," he said, "is nearly the same as to lose the whole game. Kentucky gone, we could not hold Missouri, nor, as I think, Maryland. These all against us, the job on our hands is too large for us. We would as well consent to the separation at once, including the surrender of this capital."

But Frederick Douglass was right: The "innermost logic of events" did keep forcing the question of slavery to the surface. In the most practical way, military commanders operating in places like Missouri and Maryland had to deal with the status of slaves. Twice, in August 1861 and then again in May 1862, Union generals in the field issued orders declaring the slaves of rebels or slaves who had come within Union battle lines free. Lincoln quickly and unambiguously canceled both orders, to the dismay of abolitionists in the North.

Lincoln was in trouble. And he groped for a solution. He proposed the old idea of "colonization"—sending freed slaves out of the country. He even had agents scouting out suitable land in Central America. He promoted the idea of encouraging slaveholders to give up their slaves voluntarily, in return for federal government compensation.

Lincoln and his cabinet. Lincoln selected his cabinet carefully, making sure that the many factions of his party were represented. From left to right: Edwin M. Stanton, secretary of war; Salmon P. Chase, secretary of the treasury; Lincoln; Gideon Welles, secretary of the navy; Caleb Smith, secretary of the interior; William H. Seward, secretary of state; Montgomery Blair, postmaster general; Edward Bates, attorney general. (Gift of Mrs. Chester E. King, National Portrait Gallery, Smithsonian Institution, Washington, D.C.)

But he was beginning a private journey toward a new policy. During the spring of 1862, he slipped down into the telegraph room of the White House. It was the only place he could hide from the nagging politicians and office seekers who dogged his tracks all day. There he wrote out a draft proclamation of emancipation, which he put away to use in case he needed it.

It waited for two months, until July 1862. He continued to try to rally support for his plan for voluntary, gradual, and compensated emancipation followed by colonization. But the support did not come quickly enough nor in great enough strength. On July 13 Lincoln hinted to two members of his cabinet that emancipation might become a "military necessity." A week later, on July 21, he called the rest of the cabinet together to read them his draft of an emancipation proclamation. The cabinet was stunned by the policy change. They argued the question back and forth while the president listened. Finally, he was persuaded to wait again. The Union was still losing battle after battle. At home and in Europe, a proclamation might seem to be only a clumsy attempt to draw public attention away from the military blundering and defeats. Back into Lincoln's desk drawer went the draft, to wait for at least a Union victory.

While he waited, the president suffered, publicly and privately. In public, he was accused of being "an Ass for the Slave Power to ride." Horace Greeley, editor of the influential Republican paper the *New York Tribune*, printed an open letter to the president: "On the whole face of this wide earth, Mr. President, there is not one determined, intelligent champion of the Union cause who does not feel that all attempts to put down the Rebellion and at the same time uphold its inciting cause are preposterous and futile."

The *Tribune* letter gave Lincoln a chance to restate, in the clearest possible way, his continued analysis of the relationship between the war and slavery. He did wish, he wrote in reply, that "all men everywhere be free." But—and the "but" was the same one that had dogged him since his election—"My paramount object is to save the Union and is *not* either to save or to destroy Slavery. If I could save the Union without freeing any slave I would do it, and if I could save it by freeing all the slaves, I would do it, and if I could do it by freeing some and leaving others alone, I would also do that."

That answer might satisfy some, even most, Northerners. But the private suffering was harder to deal with. Lincoln had begun to brood over the meaning of the war—especially of the Union defeats—in a way that went far beyond politics and public opinion. After one particularly disastrous military failure, he sat in his study at night and thought about God. "We are whipped again." That much was clear. If God was all powerful, as Lincoln devoutly believed He was, then why did the slaveholders keep winning? Maybe God had something in mind that neither Union nor Confederacy could know. "God wills this contest, and wills that it should not end yet," he thought. "By His mere quiet power, He could have either saved or destroyed the Union without human contest." Alone, at night, Lincoln began to wonder whether he "might be an instrument in God's hands for accomplishing a great work." He even began to look for some kind of sign from God.

The sign—or something like it—came on the battlefield. The Confederates invaded Maryland at summer's end, in 1862. This time they were stopped cold. The Union commander wired that he had won a great victory, a statement Lincoln soon learned was somewhat exaggerated. But he proclaimed the victory anyway. Lincoln went to his cabinet and told them he had made a covenant with God that when victory came in Maryland, he "would consider it an indication of the Divine Will" that he should "move forward in the cause of emancipation."

The next day, September 22, 1862, Lincoln issued his Emancipation Proclamation. He had come only a little distance. The proclamation did not free a single slave until New Year's Day 1863, and then it declared only that the slaves in Confederate territory were to be freed. Since most of that territory was still very firmly in the hands of the Southerners, the proclamation could hardly be enforced. In fact, the proclamation suggested a very odd paradox: that slavery was illegal in rebel states but still perfectly all right in Union states like Kentucky or Missouri—in the city of Washington itself, if it came to that.

But Lincoln had done one decisive thing. He had settled one question firmly that no one had considered settled before. If the Union won the war, then slavery in the American South would effectively come to an end. Now the war was not just a war for the Union but against slavery. It was not yet a war *for* African-American rights—and it never would become quite that. But it was a very different thing from the intricate political "game" it had been when the president took office.

Abraham Lincoln's sense that the Civil War had some sort of deep, religious meaning deepened over the next year and a half. The casualty lists grew to appalling proportions on both sides. But the months and the battles favored the Union, whose armies now advanced in the unanticipated role of liberating armies for black slaves. No one, including Lincoln, had any clear idea what liberation might mean in fact and in practice. But Frederick Douglass's "logic of events" had done its work. When on March 4, 1865, Lincoln again climbed the steps of the Capitol to deliver his second inaugural address, the end was in sight. He knew everything he said would be studied with care by men and women, blacks and whites, in the North and in the South. And so he tried once more to say what the war signified, to give some explanation of the reasons he thought the nation had to endure what it was going through.

When the war had begun almost four years earlier, he began, no one on either side had guessed that it would last so long, or that it would be transformed into a war against slavery. But that had been God's will. He had given the Americans this long and "terrible war," perhaps as a punishment for the "offense" of slavery. "Fondly do we hope, fervently do we pray," Lincoln went on, "that this mighty scourge of war may speedily pass away." His language had the accents of the Old Testament prophets. And he did not hold back: "Yet if God wills that it continue until all the wealth piled by the bondsman's two hundred and fifty years of unrequited toil shall be sunk, and until every drop of blood drawn with the lash shall be paid by another drawn with the sword, as was said three thousand years ago, so still must be said, 'the judgements of the Lord are true and righteous altogether.'"

But in the religious world of Abraham Lincoln and of most of his countrymen, North and South, the Lord did not only judge, he forgave. So Lincoln ended with a plea that echoed more the New Testament than the Old. "With malice toward none; with charity for all; with firmness in the right as God gives us to see the light, let us strive to finish the work we are in; to bind up the nation's wounds, to care for him who shall have borne the battle, and for his widow, and his orphan—to do all which may achieve a just and lasting peace, among ourselves and with all nations." Here were the words so central to the New Testament: *charity, light, care, peace.* When he lay dead a few weeks later, the vocabularies of both testaments would echo back over him, and he would be compared to Moses, then to Jesus.

At Appomattox Courthouse in Virginia on April 9, 1865, Robert E. Lee surrendered his Army of Northern Virginia to Ulysses S. Grant. By April 14—which was Good Friday—it had all begun to sink in: Armed resistance in the South was practically over. The sadness that had seemed to weigh so heavily on Lincoln lifted a bit. That night, he and his wife would go to the theater. A new English comedy, *Our American Cousin,* had just opened at Ford's Theater, and the Lincolns were in just the right mood for such a play. During the third act, John Wilkes Booth, a member of the famous Booth family of actors, slipped into the president's box, pointed a derringer at Lincoln's head, and pulled the trigger. Lincoln slumped forward, with the bullet that had passed through his brain now lodged just behind his right eye. He probably never knew what had happened. He was carried, deeply unconscious, to a house across the street. All through the night, the hopeless vigil of the doctors, of high government officials, and of Lincoln's son, Robert, continued. Then, at 7:22 in the morning, Lincoln died. The secretary of war, Edwin Stanton, was heard to mutter, "Now he belongs to the ages."

Stanton was right. What now began was a drama of grief that seemed almost boundless. War and victory had made Lincoln a hero. Now death transformed him into a near-saint. "The heart grows sick and faint," wrote the *Washington National Republican* on this day before Easter. "The pen almost refuses to trace the details of the tragedy." Crowds had gathered in the rain outside the house where Lincoln lay dying. At 7:30 "the tolling of bells announced to the lamenting people that he had ceased to breathe. His great and loving heart was still." Immediately, the streets were crowded with "people, men, women, and children, thronging the thoroughfares. It seemed as if everyone was in tears." As the bells tolled, offices, government buildings, and stores all closed. The black crepe of mourning replaced the red, white, and blue bunting that only a few days earlier had been put up to celebrate Lee's surrender. It was the same everywhere. As the telegraph hurried the news over the land, people gathered in the streets to express and share their horror, bewilderment, and grief.

To many, the loss was personal—something that had happened directly to them, not just to the nation. Some could barely contain their rage and struck out at anyone who uttered anything against the fallen president. Black freedmen were numbed by the word that the president was dead. One young girl remarked that she thought she could "never love God anymore." Walt Whitman expressed his sense of loss in a poem. News of the assassination had come to him just as the lilacs, portent of spring, rebirth, and renewal, had come into blossom:

> When lilacs last in the dooryard bloom'd
> And the great star early droop'd in the western
>   sky in the night,
> I mourn'd, and yet shall mourn with ever-returning spring.
> Ever-returning spring, trinity sure to me you bring,
> Lilac blooming perennial and drooping star in the west,
> And thought of him I love.

The press and public orators struggled to find ways to comprehend and interpret the tragedy. What dumbfounded the people, wrote the *New York Herald*, was that such a thing could have happened to the American Republic. The real "horror of the deed," the *Boston Transcript* insisted, was "the fact that the victim was the kindliest and most magnanimous of great magistrates and seemed to fall martyr to his own goodness." In Lincoln's hometown, a newspaper that had not always supported the president described the event this way:

> Just in the hour when the crowning triumph of his life awaited him; . . . when he could begin clearly to see the promised land of his longings—the restored Union— the assassin's hand at once put a rude period to his life and to his hopes. As Moses of old, who had led God's people through the gloom and danger of the wilderness, dies when on the eve of realizing all that his hopes had pictured, so Lincoln is cut off just as the white wing of peace begins to reflect its silvery radiance over the red billows of war.

As the first shocked grief poured forth, plans for the funeral and burial were made. Several groups laid claim to the body. The City Council in Springfield, Illinois,

Lincoln lies in state. Lincoln's open casket lay in state for two days in the Capitol rotunda. (UPI/Bettmann Archives)

insisted that Springfield "should be the final resting place for all of him that remains mortal." New York papers urged construction of a monument that would contain his remains. The Commission of Public Monuments in Washington declared that the body ought to be deposited in the vault that had been prepared for George Washington under the rotunda of the Capitol. But the distraught widow insisted (as had Washington's family) that "his dust shall lie among his own neighbors and kin." Lincoln would be returned to Springfield for burial, but not directly and immediately as Mary Lincoln wanted. Her husband also belonged to the public. Secretary of War Stanton, in charge of the official arrangements, thought it was important that as many people as possible have a chance to take part in the farewell to Lincoln.

At noon on Wednesday, April 19, the official funeral service took place in the East Room of the White House. At the same hour, people all over the country gathered in their churches for simultaneous services. Lincoln's pastor eulogized the president and pointed to the belief in the "justness and goodness of God" that had been "an anchor to his soul" and had "emboldened him in his path of duty." Then a procession, led by an African-American regiment, followed by half a dozen other military units, thirty bands, and then another African-American regiment, carried the body past a vast crowd of blacks and whites, soldiers and wounded veterans, to the Capitol, where the open casket lay in state for two days. "The procession of saddened faces came pressing forward at the rate of three thousand persons per hour. The Rotunda, which

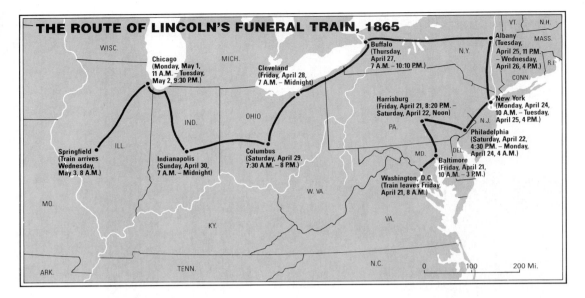

THE ROUTE OF LINCOLN'S FUNERAL TRAIN, 1865

Chicago (Monday, May 1, 11 A.M. – Tuesday, May 2, 9:30 P.M.)

Buffalo (Thursday, April 27, 7 A.M. – 10:10 P.M.)

Albany (Tuesday, April 25, 11 P.M. – Wednesday, April 26, 4 P.M.)

Cleveland (Friday, April 28, 7 A.M. – Midnight)

Harrisburg (Friday, April 21, 8:20 P.M. – Saturday, April 22, Noon)

New York (Monday, April 24, 10 A.M. – Tuesday, April 25, 4 P.M.)

Springfield (Train arrives Wednesday, May 3, 8 A.M.)

Indianapolis (Sunday, April 30, 7 A.M. – Midnight)

Columbus (Saturday, April 29, 7:30 A.M. – 8 P.M.)

Philadelphia (Saturday, April 22, 4:30 P.M. – Monday, April 24, 4 A.M.)

Baltimore (Friday, April 21, 10 A.M. – 3 P.M.)

Washington, D.C. (Train leaves Friday, April 21, 8 A.M.)

0   100   200 Mi.

Rotunda, which was lighted only by a sort of twilight hue, was filled with solemn stillness, unbroken save by the rustling of the dresses of female mourners, and occasionally a deep sigh from some of those passing the coffin."

Then, on April 21, a nine-car funeral train left Washington for the long journey back to Springfield. The train retraced the route that just four years earlier had carried Lincoln to his inauguration. It stopped in ten cities along the way. Everywhere it was the same: a procession through the city, ceremonies in a hall where the body lay in state, throngs of people filing past the coffin to get a last glimpse of the "face of our great friend." In Philadelphia 100,000 people joined the procession; 300,000 more looked on, as the hearse bearing the casket made its way to Independence Hall, "the Temple of American Liberty," to lie in state. When the body arrived at the hall, three women placed a cross of pure white flowers on the casket. It was, according to the silk streamer attached to it, "A Tribute to our Great and Good President Fallen a Martyr to the Cause of Human Freedom—'In my Hand No Price I Bring, Simply My Cross to Cling.'"

In every city, banners along the route that the procession took proclaimed their messages: "His Memory, like the Union he Preserved, is not for a day, but for all time"; "God's noblest work, an honest man"; "Weep, generous nation, weep; the sad, swift removal of him whom Heaven indulgent sent to man. Too good for earth, to Heaven art thou fled, and left the Nation in tears." At numerous ceremonies, Lincoln's second inaugural address was read again and again. Orators and clergymen tried to capture the meaning of the man and the tragedy. Lincoln's "death, which was meant to sever the Union beyond repair, binds it more firmly than ever," George Bancroft declared. "The country may need this imperishable grief, to touch its inmost feelings.

Lincoln's funeral train. This nine-car train carried Lincoln across the land to his grave in Springfield, Illinois. (Culver Pictures)

The grave that receives the remains of President Lincoln, receives a martyr to the Union, and the monument which arises over his body will bear witness to the Union."

Not only the cities mourned. As the train passed through hamlet, countryside, and town, it went through arches with banners and emblems, past bands playing requiems, and regiments of militiamen and Union soldiers. Everywhere, at every hour and in every kind of weather, people thronged to see the train. At midnight, in Syracuse, New York, 35,000 people stood in a drenching rain as the train passed by. During the nights, all along the way, a "pillar of fire" guided the cortege as "at every crossroads the glare of innumerable torches illuminated the whole population from age to infancy, kneeling on the ground, their clergymen leading them in prayers and hymns."

After twelve days and more than 1,600 miles, the funeral train reached Springfield, Illinois. At ten in the morning on May 3, the casket was closed, carried to the waiting hearse, and taken by one last procession to Oak Ridge Cemetery.

The long journey was over. Stanton had said that Lincoln belonged to the ages. As the funeral train had made its way across the nation, the people themselves had poured out on him the accumulated grief of four years of war and taken possession of him. "Give him place, oh, ye prairie," the Reverend Henry Ward Beecher had said as the cortege passed through New York. "Ye winds that move over the mighty prairies of the west, chant his requiem. Ye people, behold the martyr, whose blood pleads for

The execution of the conspirators. John Wilkes Booth, killed trying to resist capture, escaped trial for the assassination of Lincoln. But four others were tried and, on July 7, 1865, publicly executed. One of them, Mary E. Surratt, in whose boardinghouse some of the plotting had taken place, was probably innocent of any involvement in the crime, a victim of the hysteria and desire for revenge that Lincoln's assassination provoked. (Culver Pictures)

fidelity, for law, for liberty." From Lincoln's words and acts, out of their own needs, from historical myth and their religious traditions, they had transmuted the Lincoln many of them had once ridiculed and condemned into Lincoln the martyr—the good and pure Lincoln, who had befriended the lowly slave, and sacrificed himself for liberty and the Union. "Washington the Father, Lincoln the Savior of his Country" countless banners along the way proclaimed.

CIVIL WAR AND RECONSTRUCTION

When Lincoln summoned the North to combat, few people were really surprised—war talk had been going on for a long time. But neither side was at all ready for war. The United States scarcely had a military establishment: Its army existed mainly to fight Native Americans and consisted of about 20,000 soldiers scattered in remote frontier forts. Its navy was made up of about ninety ships, most of which were obsolete, out of commission, or in foreign ports. In addition, Americans were largely an agricultural people, living in a huge, sparsely populated, decentralized society.

Building and Equipping Armies

The first task was to create armies. There was no shortage of men willing to fight. Northerners and Southerners both greeted the call to arms with naive enthusiasm. All over the nation, men, many scarcely more than boys, rushed to volunteer. The big question was "not who shall go to the wars, but who shall stay at home." Local communities themselves organized companies, platoons, and regiments. With a motley assort-

ment of uniforms and weapons, with fiery speeches, and with knapsacks crammed with cakes and mementoes from wives, mothers, and sweethearts, the volunteers went off to war, flushed with idealism, eager to serve the sacred cause of Union or Southern independence. Death did not frighten them. Each side expected its valor in a righteous cause to bring quick victory. If death did come, it would be heroic: "And for life," wrote one young man in words many on both sides would have echoed, "if the Nation will take me, I do not see that I can put myself— experience and character—to any more useful use."

The flood of volunteers had to be turned into disciplined armies. There was not much to build on. Their only military experience was the musters of local militias, to which most able-bodied white men had gone each month for a little haphazard drill, a lot of speechmaking, and even more drinking. More serious was the lack of an adequate and experienced officer corps. Of the 1,000 officers with any formal military training (about three-quarters of whom joined the Confederacy), none had ever commanded more than a few battalions. At the company and regimental levels (and often even at higher levels), command was often conferred because of political connections or local prominence rather than military competence. Throughout the war, but especially in the first two years, the war efforts of both sides

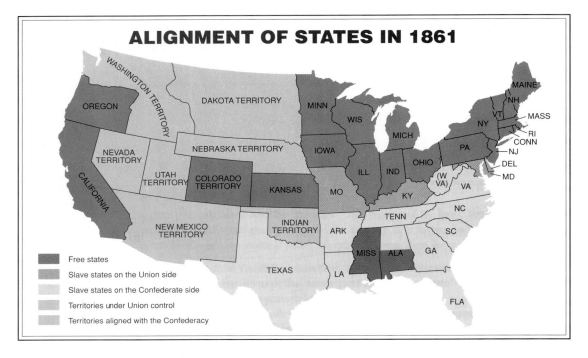

ALIGNMENT OF STATES IN 1861

Free states

Slave states on the Union side

Slave states on the Confederate side

Territories under Union control

Territories aligned with the Confederacy

Confederate volunteers. With the outbreak of hostilities both sides had to scramble to build armies from new volunteers and from any existing prewar militia companies. Both sides greeted the outbreak of war with confidence and enthusiasm. Here the Sumter Light Guards, which became part of the 4th Georgia Infantry Regiment, stand at review in April of 1861. (Library of Congress)

and particularly the North were plagued by wildly incompetent officers.

Creating and fielding armies also demanded kinds of economic and governmental organization that neither side had. Both sides and particularly the North possessed considerable resources, but in 1861 neither economy (especially the South's) was designed for feeding, equipping, and transporting large armies. The North's textile mills, for example, produced hundreds of thousands of yards of cloth each year, but this cloth was still turned into finished clothing (like uniforms) in small workshops. And the nearly 10,000 miles of Southern railroad (as much railway, in proportion to population, as the North had) did not constitute a genuine transportation system, since few of the railroads were hooked up to each other.

There was a similar lack of administrative machinery. Except for the postal service, the federal government played only a small role in people's lives. With a minuscule military establishment, no federal taxes or national banking system, and no educational or welfare agencies, the experienced officials or bureaucratic mechanisms needed to prepare for and conduct war did not exist. Near-chaos reigned for much of the first year. Leroy P. Walker, the Confederacy's first secretary of war (whose filing system consisted of piling papers on a chair), turned away tens of thousands of volunteers because he did not know what to do with them. The Union's first secretary of war, Simon Cameron, like Walker a political appointee with no relevant experience, was equally unable to cope with the flood of recruits and military contracts. As a result, corrupt profiteers had a heyday, getting exorbitant prices for often worthless equipment. One large lot of Northern uniforms, for example, was made of "shoddy," a cheap cotton fabric that disintegrated in a hard rain.

Not until well into the second year of the war did many of these problems begin to get worked out. Lincoln shipped Cameron off to a relatively innocuous ambassadorship in Russia and replaced him with Edwin Stanton, who ran the War Department from then on with incorruptible efficiency. Confederate President Jefferson Davis, too, found more competent personnel, and by 1862 the Confederacy had an ordinance chief who was able to procure 20 million cartridges for a 400,000-man army. (When the Confederacy declared war, it had only 20 cartridges per soldier.)

Jefferson Davis. Though a reluctant secessionist, Davis (1808–89) was a firm and unrelenting champion of the Confederacy. Like Lincoln, he was often vilified by opponents who objected to his handling of the war. Imprisoned for two years after the war, he remained a believer in the righteousness of the Southern cause to the end of his life. He refused to request official amnesty and never regained United States citizenship. (The Museum of the Confederacy, Richmond, Virginia. Photo by Katherine Wetzel)

Strategy—Theory and Practice

Economic strength and military power go hand in hand, and when war began, the North seemed to have an overwhelming economic advantage. Its population of 22 million was more than double that of the South; its industrial output and its overall wealth were more than ten times that of the South. It even outstripped the agricultural South in the production of food. Jefferson Davis (a West Point graduate who would have preferred to lead the Confederate armies rather than head its government) chose a defensive strategy to offset the North's enormous economic advantage. It would cost far less in men and resources to force the Union to fight in the South than it would to invade the North. Davis's strategy was to have the Confederate army fight close to its economic base and use the military advantages of defense, familiar territory, and short supply lines to win a few major battles. The North, Davis believed, would find the price of victory too high and would grant the Confederate States of America independence, just as a war-weary and frustrated

The battle of the ironclads. In an attempt to break the Northern naval blockade, the Confederacy devised the first "ironclad" vessel, a wooden ship plated with armor. In March 1862, the first battle of the ironclads took place, a standoff between the Confederate *Merrimac* and the Union *Monitor*. By the end of 1864, the Union navy had more than seventy ironclads in commission. (National Gallery of Art)

Britain had granted the American colonies their independence.

Northern strategy, not surprisingly, was almost the mirror opposite. By the nature of its paramount goal—to save the Union—the North had to go on the offensive. Only if the South was thoroughly defeated, Lincoln and his military advisers believed, could it be forced to give up its claim to independence. Lincoln knew that even with its economic superiority the North faced a task that would strain its will and resources to the utmost. And he recognized, too, the link between economic and military strength. To strangle the South economically, he declared a naval blockade, hoping to keep the Confederacy from importing the war materials it needed. On the military front, he planned a two-pronged attack. In the West, Northern armies would invade and try to cut the Confederacy in two, while in the East, they would strike at the Southern capital of Richmond.

These were the grand designs. But geography and the conventions of military doctrine shaped how they were put into practice. Until the last year of the war, almost all the fighting in the East took place in the narrow area between the Blue Ridge Mountains and the Atlantic Ocean and between the James and Potomac rivers, the narrow corridor between Richmond and Washington. In the thinking of the day, capital cities had great military, political, and symbolic significance. According to strategic doctrine, capturing the enemy's capital could itself bring victory, and loss of one's own might well bring defeat.

The war in the West was very different. There, the changing border between Union and Confederacy stretched for over a thousand miles. In this vast theater, warfare took many forms. The long border exposed both sides to quick strikes and raids. Along the Missouri and Kansas border, a marauding guerrilla warfare of the most brutal sort took place. (Indeed, Jesse and Frank James, the most notorious bandits in American history, got their start as members of William C. Quantrill's Confederate guerrilla band.) In the West, too, the Mississippi, Tennessee, and Cumberland rivers opened up avenues into the heart of the Confederacy.

THE FIRST BATTLE OF BULL RUN, JULY 21, 1861

The Struggle Begins

If the war could be won (or lost) quickly, as a lot of people on both sides expected it would be, then the decisive action would surely come in the East. If the war had to be fought in the heartland beyond the Appalachian Mountains—in Kentucky, Tennessee, or Mississippi—then it would be long and bitter.

During the first spring and early summer of war, 1861, not much happened on the battlefields. Both sides were getting ready. Then Lincoln decided to try for the quick victory that would end the war. He ordered General Irvin McDowell, who commanded about 30,000 inexperienced troops, to march south from Washington toward the Virginia town of Manassas, to do battle with a smaller Confederate army commanded by General P. G. T. Beauregard. In mid-July McDowell moved. Beauregard waited just south of a muddy little creek (or "run" as country people called it) named Bull Run. The two armies met on July 21. Several times the federal soldiers charged Beauregard's lines. Each time, they were driven back. Then Beauregard ordered a counterattack. The heat, the clamor, and the unexpectedly heavy casualties all took their toll on the

young and green federal soldiers. The Union forward units panicked and ran back across Bull Run. The panic spread, and before it was over, McDowell had to retreat all the way to Washington.

The retreating soldiers brought only a few of their dead and wounded. But they also brought a blunt, wordless message. The war would not be won and lost in a few weeks in northern Virginia. It would be long and bloody. The first force of Union volunteers had enlisted for three months. Now Lincoln set out to raise a force of hundreds of thousands, recruited not for a few weeks but for three years. The Confederate leaders began the same grim task.

The winter of 1861–62 was another season of regrouping, supply, and training on both sides. And when the war heated up again, it was in the West, and it was savage. The Confederate armies in Kentucky were grouped around Bowling Green in the east and Columbus in the west. A Union commander, Ulysses S. Grant, received permission to move south from Illinois to drive a wedge between the armies and try to gain control of the Tennessee River. He succeeded in capturing two Confederate forts just inside Tennessee before the Confederate commanders could get their armies in position to challenge his advance. Then he quickly headed southward up the river. By early April he had reached Pittsburg Landing, near the Mississippi border and a crucial rail junction at Corinth, Mississippi.

Meanwhile the two Confederate forces in the West, split by Grant's maneuver, had fallen back, abandoning the western half of Tennessee. The two armies, one commanded by Beauregard, the other by Albert Sidney Johnston, came together in northern Mississippi. Sooner or later they and Grant's force would have to meet. The Southern commanders decided to strike at Grant before Union reinforcements, racing down from Louisville, could reach him. They attacked near a Tennessee country church called Shiloh on April 6.

The struggle was ferocious. The Confederate generals had 55,000 troops to throw at Grant, who had about 40,000 men. The first day ended in stalemate, but the corpses piled up. Then Grant's reinforcements arrived, and after the second day, the Southerners had to break off their attack.

Neither army had been broken or destroyed at Shiloh. But two things were now clear. First, the Confederate forces had not been able to drive Grant's threatening army out of the Deep South. Second, the war was going to be more savage than even Bull Run had hinted it would be. On the fields and in the woods at Shiloh, 13,000 Union soldiers and 10,000 of the Confederacy's best troops lay dead. Many thousands of others on both sides were wounded. Victory was now a question of which side could stand the carnage longer, could continue to pour men and guns into one titanic battle after another, and could go on hauling away the wagonloads of the dead and wounded.

Strategically, the Union was very close to accomplishing a major goal: controlling the Mississippi. In April 1862, the same month as Shiloh, Flag Officer—soon to be Admiral—David Farragut captured Mobile and New Orleans for the Union. A little later, he had moved up the Mississippi to Baton Rouge. Grant took Corinth, Union forces occupied Memphis, and now most of the river was theirs, except for the strong Confederate fortress at Vicksburg.

While the Union attack in the West went forward, the war in the East became a bloody standoff. Neither the Union's failures nor the Confed-

THE WAR FOR THE MISSISSIPPI, 1862–63

eracy's successes were decisive enough to bring either side within sight of final victory or defeat.

The main Union army in Virginia, the Army of the Potomac, was now commanded by young George B. McClellan, who had convinced Lincoln to let him try to take Richmond, not by land this time but by sea and up the peninsula between the York and James rivers—that same peninsula where Charles, Lord Cornwallis, had surrendered to George Washington in 1781. Confederate armies led by a new commander, Robert E. Lee, and his ablest lieutenant, General Thomas J. "Stonewall" Jackson, met the threat and turned McClellan back. The major battles of the campaign lasted seven days and cost Lee 20,000 dead, McClellan 15,000. But Lee had won. The Army

THE "SEVEN DAYS,"
June 25–July 1, 1862

1. Fair Oaks
2. Mechanicsville
3. Gaine's Mill
4. Savage's Station
5. Frayser's Farm
6. Malvern Hill

THE PENINSULAR CAMPAIGN AND THE
SECOND BATTLE OF BULL RUN, 1862

THE BATTLE OF ANTIETAM, 1862

of the Potomac was driven back down the peninsula.

Lincoln ordered McClellan's army home to Washington, determined to attack Richmond overland. But Lee and Jackson now moved north, hoping to defeat other Union forces near Washington before McClellan's army could complete its withdrawal and regroup. And they succeeded. A second battle near Manassas, the Second Battle of Bull Run, August 29–30, 1862, was the most decisive Confederate victory yet.

Now Lee took the offensive. He moved his army into Maryland, knowing that the federal army would have to place itself between him and the capital, leaving Virginia's farmers free to take in the fall harvest without the presence of massive Union armies. McClellan moved out to meet the threat and threw an army of almost 90,000 at Lee's 50,000 near Sharpsburg, Maryland, at a stream called Antietam Creek.

On September 17 Lee's men and McClellan's fought three pitched battles on the same field. The Confederate lines bent under overwhelming

pressure. Then, when it was clear that one more Union assault would bring a massive defeat, Jackson rushed to Lee with reinforcements. Still, McClellan might have won with one more charge. But he held back and even gave Lee another day to withdraw.

Antietam was the bloodiest single day of the war. At its end, 13,000 men in Union blue and almost 11,000 in Confederate gray lay dead. Lincoln called it a victory and used it as the occasion for the Emancipation Proclamation. But he mourned McClellan's failure to follow up on his apparent advantage, and he relieved McClellan as commander. In the East, as in the West, some things had become clear, at least for the time being. Neither side had an overwhelming advantage in the field. The Union was not able to manage a successful offensive against Richmond. But neither was Lee able to operate successfully outside Virginia. Any Union commander who wanted to defeat Lee had to be prepared to accept appalling casualties and keep attacking, again and again.

Such an officer was the man Lincoln chose to replace McClellan, General Ambrose E. Burnside. Burnside shocked Lee and Jackson by driving his Army of the Potomac across the Rappahannock River, near Fredericksburg, Virginia, and attacking strong Confederate positions on the high ground near the town. The Confederates held. Burnside sent his men again up the heights. Again they failed. The bewildered general commanded another attack. Another failure. And by the end of the battle, Burnside had lost 12,000 men in his disastrous effort. The two exhausted armies dug in for a winter of waiting on the opposite shores of the Rappahannock.

The next spring, another new general, "Fighting Joe" Hooker, took charge of the Army of the Potomac. But his luck against Lee was no better than McClellan's or Burnside's had been. Hooker tried moving upriver, then across the Rappahannock, to outflank Fredericksburg. Lee and Jackson met him at Chancellorsville, in early May 1863, and defeated him decisively. But by now the Confederacy was so weakened that no Southern general could assemble the supplies and fresh troops necessary to take decisive advantage of any victory. Once more, Lee had won, but he had won only time and stalemate. And time and stalemate were now clearly the allies of the Union.

War, Diplomacy, and Northern Morale

The fortunes of war are not made only on the battlefield. From the perspective of long-range strategy, the Union's successes in the West put it in a fairly strong position. But it did not seem that way to the Northern people. The Civil War was the first American war to get vivid daily newspaper coverage, and it was in the eastern theater that the most dramatic, closely watched, and highly publicized fighting took place. There in the early years of the war the North took a pounding, and this was far more important than Union victories in the West at Shiloh and Corinth in shaping the politics and diplomacy that could determine the outcome of the war.

Diplomacy played an important part in the Confederacy's overall strategy. From the outset, Davis hoped to secure recognition and support from the European powers, especially England and France. The South's confidence that Britain would come to its aid lay in the importance of its cotton to the English economy. Nearly 20 percent of Britain's population was dependent on textiles for its livelihood; cotton goods made up over 40 percent of its exports, and it got more than 80 percent of its raw cotton (700 million pounds per year) from the South. This situation, and the fact that Britain's own imperial designs in the Western Hemisphere would be well served if the American Union fell apart, brought that country very close to recognizing the Confederacy. As it was, in thinly disguised fashion Britain supplied the South with blockade-running ships and, at the risk of provoking war with the North, had even taken orders for two ironclad rams that could easily have broken the Northern blockade. Still, prudence and certain hard economic facts—the fact that Britain, having stockpiled a great deal of cotton before hostilities, had not yet felt much of an economic pinch; the fact that its merchants were profiting handsomely from trade with both sides; the fact that it imported a great deal of Northern wheat—dictated caution. Though leaning heavily toward the Confederacy, the British government chose to look carefully before it leaped; it waited to see how the war was going before it did anything that might provoke the North's open hostility. Lincoln knew that the British had their eyes trained on the battlefield. That was one of the reasons he so hastily proclaimed Antietam a major victory and issued the Emancipation Proclamation. He hoped to swing British public opinion behind the Northern cause.

Those at home also watched the eastern theater with concern. Northern morale—the willingness of the people of the North to endure the suffering of war—was almost as important for Northern victory as what happened on the battlefield. Lincoln knew that one of his greatest tasks was to keep up support for the war, and he tried at every point to strengthen commitment to the Union as a cause worthy of any sacrifice. Moreover, Confederate strategy was aimed directly at Northern morale. Davis expected Southern independence to come from the Confederacy's ability to hold off defeat until a weary Northern public turned against the war. The strategic importance Lee attached to the destruction of a Northern army lay in the impact he hoped it would have on Northern and foreign opinion.

Lincoln was acutely aware of how precarious Northern morale was in the summer and fall of 1862. Enthusiasm for the war had waned with the end of any hope for a quick victory, and many people were beginning to wonder if there would be any victory. Discontent with the administration's conduct of the war was mounting, and the war weariness threatened to slip into opposition to the war itself. Already there were those who argued that the North should stop fighting and negotiate with the Confederacy about rejoining the Union. Lincoln issued his Emancipation Proclamation partly to line up antislavery fervor solidly behind the administration and to draw more blacks into the Union's war effort. He considered the organized opposition to the war to be a form of treason and jailed some of its leaders. If things in the East kept going as they were, the North's will to fight might well give out.

Leadership and Opposition in Wartime

As the war ground on inexorably, opposition to Lincoln and Davis mounted. Northerners and Southerners increasingly blamed the seeming weakness and incompetence of their respective leaders for the hardship, suffering, and frustration they had to endure. Throughout the war, opponents portrayed Lincoln as a well-meaning

but hapless bungler. To many Southerners, Davis seemed petty, aloof, bogged down in detail, and incapable of strong leadership. But oddly enough, Lincoln and Davis were also accused of being *too* forceful and were vilified as dictators and tyrants.

In large measure, the charge of tyranny reflected the fact that the war had led to an unprecedented centralization of government power on both sides. In 1863 the North reinstituted a national banking system. The Confederate and Union governments both levied new forms of taxation. The North imposed duties on most goods and adopted an income tax, while the South introduced a tax that required each planter and farmer to contribute 10 percent of his produce to the government. By early 1863 both sides had turned to conscription to help fill their armies. The opposition to the draft was intense, especially because the conscription acts contained exemption clauses that let the rich avoid the draft by hiring substitutes.

Finally, both presidents used executive authority in unprecedented ways. Lincoln used his authority as commander in chief to initiate limited emancipation, and Davis used executive authority to impress slaves for work on military projects. Both Lincoln and Davis at times suspended the right of habeas corpus so that those suspected of aiding the enemy could be arrested and detained without trial. (In the North, more than 13,000 were detained in this way.) From an administrative point of view, these were all pragmatic measures dictated by military necessity, but to the Northerners and Southerners who experienced them, they were forms of centralization and regimentation—tyranny—that went against long-standing traditions of local autonomy.

Lincoln and Davis also found it increasingly difficult to muster the unified support needed to carry out the policies necessary for victory. The Republican party itself was divided, and Lincoln constantly had to try to balance the conflicting demands of moderates and radicals in his own camp. Most Northern Democrats had initially lined up behind the war effort, but partisan politics quickly reasserted itself. The Demo-

Draft riot in New York City, 1863. Violent riots broke out in New York and other Northern cities in reaction against Abraham Lincoln's conscription policies. Most of the rioters were workers who were especially angered because men with enough money could buy their way out of being drafted. The riots were only one manifestation of widespread dissatisfaction with Lincoln's administration. In the South, Jefferson Davis also met with major resistance to his policies. (Library of Congress)

crats, even while supporting the war, subjected Lincoln's leadership and policies to unrelenting attack. Finally, the growing war weariness sapped support for the war effort itself. By the summer of 1864, the North, with its overwhelming economic and military strength, was on the brink of triumph. But war weariness was so strong that Lincoln thought it likely that Northern voters would repudiate him in the fall elections and elect General George McClellan on a Democratic "peace" ticket instead. Lincoln was rescued by the fall of Atlanta, his own political skills, and his ability to provide the Northern public with a sense of the higher, sacred meaning of the war. He won a solid victory, gaining the support he needed to see the cause through to victory.

There was far less opposition to the war effort in the Confederacy than in the Union. But Jefferson Davis had even greater problems getting the support he needed than Lincoln did. Many planters, though steadfastly loyal to the Confederacy, opposed Davis's policies and did all they could to evade or subvert them. Davis's efforts also ran afoul of the doctrine of states' rights. His own vice president, Alexander Stephens, led the opposition to Davis's alleged usurpations of state sovereignty, and the governors of Georgia and North Carolina continually obstructed Davis's efforts to develop and carry out a unified policy. This dissension and disaffection proved insurmountable, even for one as singlemindedly dedicated to Southern independence as Jefferson Davis.

The Struggle Climaxes

At the end of April 1863, Grant had put the Mississippi River town of Vicksburg under heavy siege. The situation was critical. If Vicksburg fell, as it must if not given massive support from the East, then Confederate communications with the states west of the river would be cut. Lee had to decide whether to send an army west to raise the siege. He decided on another, daring strategy, designed to try for a victory that might force the Union to move part of Grant's forces east. So once more Lee invaded, this time not just into Maryland, but into Pennsylvania.

As Lee moved north, Hooker moved too, keeping his army between the enemy and Washington. But Hooker did not attack. Chancellorsville had been a painful lesson. He finally asked Lincoln to remove him from command, and the hapless Army of the Potomac now received yet another new commander, George G. Meade. With Lee about ten miles inside Pennsylvania, Meade moved in on the rear of the advancing Confederates.

On July 1, 1863, Lee sent a brigade of infantry into the town of Gettysburg, hoping to seize shoes for his army. The infantry stumbled onto some Union cavalry units, and there was a brief skirmish. Messengers on both sides rode away toward their main armies, asking for quick reinforcements. Neither commander had chosen Gettysburg as a battlefield. But Lee could not keep moving northward once the Army of the Potomac had found him and was at his rear, able to cut him off from Virginia. The Union commander, Meade, could not give Gettysburg to Lee. The town was just too important. It was a junction for a dozen different roads, one of them leading straight into Baltimore.

All day long on July 1, both armies rushed men toward Gettysburg. Lee was a bit closer, so he managed to get 25,000 soldiers into action on that first day. Meade managed to move up about 20,000. The Union's forward units fought and fell

Ulysses S. Grant (Library of Congress)

back, then fought again. (One Northern unit, after ferocious fighting, retreated in a panic through the town of Gettysburg, to take up new positions on Cemetery Hill. As they rushed sweating and frightened past the gates of the town's cemetery there, some of them may have noticed a small sign, a memory of more peaceful days. It read, "All persons found using firearms in these grounds will be prosecuted with the utmost rigor of the law." The good citizens of Gettysburg wanted their dead to sleep in peace.)

At the end of the first day's fighting, Meade's soldiers had fallen back into tight and powerful defensive positions on the long hook-shaped ridge south and west of Gettysburg. Time was on his side. Every hour, he could expect fresh men and supplies. Lee was reluctant to attack because he did not know where the rest of the great Army of the Potomac was, or how long it would take it to fall upon him. But he was encouraged by the success of his men on that first day, when they had seemed able to drive the Union troops back toward the ridge top with ease. In fact, Lee was fighting a war of morale, hoping

Robert E. Lee (Cook Collection, Valentine Museum)

he could break the spirit of the Union soldiers at Gettysburg and that a victory here would damage the Union's will to continue the war.

So Lee decided to try to turn both Union flanks on July 2. He ordered General Richard Ewell to take Cemetery Hill, on the Union right, "if practicable." But Ewell, who commanded the corps that Stonewall Jackson had once led, was not willing to risk his men. He was certain that the enemy was securely dug in on the hill and had a lot of artillery ready to fire into his advancing troops. So he held back.

Lee also ordered a larger force, commanded by General James P. Longstreet, to attack the Union left and to try to take the hills, known as Little Round Top and Round Top, at the southern end of Cemetery Ridge. Longstreet's desperate charge fell short and only succeeded in driving some Union cavalry units off the forward slopes of the ridge.

Lee's hope had been that attacks by Ewell and Longstreet would tempt Meade to move forces out of the center of his line, to defend its open

flanks. Meantime, he was massing almost the entire Confederate artillery in the center, ready for an assault on the third day. Despite Ewell's decision not to attack Cemetery Hill, and despite Longstreet's bloody and costly failure, Lee decided to go ahead with his plan. In fact, given the state of battle and the state of the war, he probably had no choice but to launch an all-out attack.

By noon on July 3 the Confederates had everything ready. About 143 cannon were massed near the center of the field. At 1:00, Lee ordered them to fire. They were answered by a barrage of equal ferocity from the heights. It was the single heaviest exchange of artillery of the entire war. But as the exchange wore on, two things happened. The Confederate guns dug themselves more deeply into the earth on each recoil, pointing their barrels higher. Their shots began to fly above the Union positions, where the infantry crouched behind defenses they had dug for themselves the day before. Second, Union commanders, understanding that a massive infantry assault would soon be coming, ordered their artillery gradually to fall silent and wait. In fact, Meade had anticipated Lee's strategy, and was ready for the assault on his center. He had placed a lot of artillery there and had some of his best and toughest troops defending that part of the line.

Lee and his generals may have been convinced they had a good chance to break the Union's lines. Or Lee may have felt he had no choice but to continue his attack, no matter what. He could hardly take up a defensive position this deep into enemy territory. And he could not retreat without dooming Vicksburg to surrendering to Grant. Whatever the reason, Lee ordered 13,000 men, commanded by General George Pickett, to charge Cemetery Ridge. Pickett formed his men in parade-ground order and sent them forward. The Union artillery opened up, followed by a withering fire from a strong center held by some of the most seasoned troops in the Army of the Potomac. And still the Confederates came. A few of them actually reached Union breastworks along the ridge line. But only a few. The rest were dead or wounded on the field, and the few who did make it to Union lines had no choice but to die, surrender, or run back down the slope under the same deadly fire.

As the charge began, Pickett had had three brigade commanders. Two were now dead and the third badly wounded. The thirteen colonels

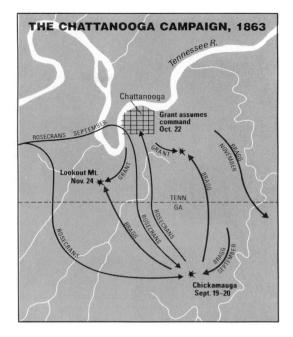

THE CHATTANOOGA CAMPAIGN, 1863

Tennessee R.

Chattanooga

Grant assumes command Oct. 22

ROSECRANS SEPTEMBER

GRANT

BRAGG NOVEMBER

Lookout Mt. Nov. 24

GRANT

BRAGG

TENN. GA.

ROSECRANS

ROSECRANS

BRAGG

ROSECRANS

BRAGG SEPTEMBER

Chickamauga Sept. 19–20

in his division were all dead. And three-fourths of his men were dead, wounded, or captured.

All in all, the Confederate armies had lost between 25,000 and 30,000 men at Gettysburg. (Lee had lost seventeen generals in the three days of battle.) Meade had lost about 23,000 men. But he had held. And on the day of Pickett's dreadful charge, the news came to both sides that Vicksburg had fallen to Grant.

The Struggle Ends

The end was all but inevitable, but still the fighting and dying continued. Union troops occupied Chattanooga, Tennessee, in August. Then a Union force moved down into Georgia. They were beaten there in the fierce battle of Chickamauga, one of the few fights in which the Confederates outnumbered the Union troops. But the

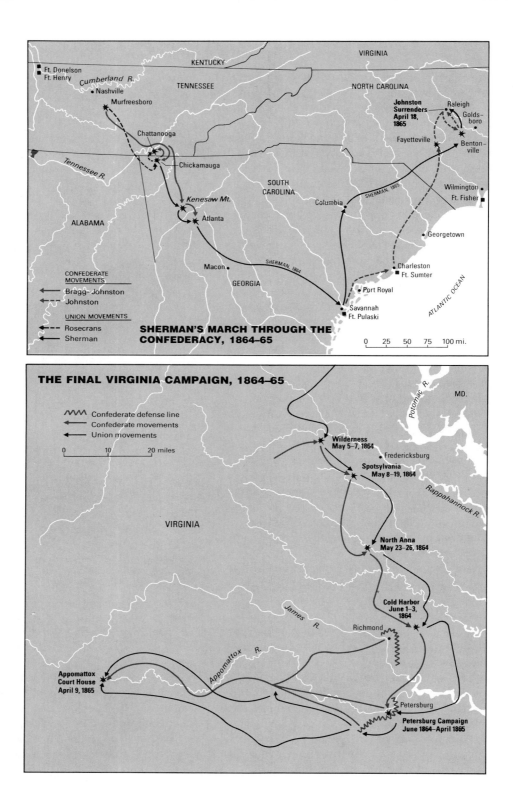

SHERMAN'S MARCH THROUGH THE CONFEDERACY, 1864–65

CONFEDERATE MOVEMENTS
→ Bragg–Johnston
⇢ Johnston

UNION MOVEMENTS
⇢ Rosecrans
→ Sherman

VIRGINIA
KENTUCKY
TENNESSEE
NORTH CAROLINA
SOUTH CAROLINA
ALABAMA
GEORGIA
ATLANTIC OCEAN

Ft. Donelson
Ft. Henry
Cumberland R.
Nashville
Murfreesboro
Chattanooga
Chickamauga
Tennessee R.
Kenesaw Mt.
Atlanta
Macon
Columbia
SHERMAN, 1864
SHERMAN, 1865
Savannah
Ft. Pulaski
Port Royal
Charleston
Ft. Sumter
Georgetown
Wilmington
Ft. Fisher
Fayetteville
Benton-ville
Raleigh
Goldsboro
Johnston Surrenders April 18, 1865

0 25 50 75 100 mi.

THE FINAL VIRGINIA CAMPAIGN, 1864–65

ᨏᨏᨏ Confederate defense line
→ Confederate movements
→ Union movements

0   10   20 miles

VIRGINIA
MD.
Potomac R.
Rappahannock R.
James R.
Appomattox R.

Wilderness May 5–7, 1864
Fredericksburg
Spotsylvania May 8–19, 1864
North Anna May 23–26, 1864
Cold Harbor June 1–3, 1864
Richmond
Appomattox Court House April 9, 1865
Petersburg
Petersburg Campaign June 1864–April 1865

victory counted for little. A month later, in the Battle of Chattanooga, Grant's army drove the South off its positions on the ridges and mountains around the city.

Once the Union armies had taken unchallenged control of Chattanooga, Atlanta lay before them, and then the sea. The South, already divided along the Mississippi, could now be split a second time by a line of soldiers stretching from Kentucky across Tennessee and Georgia to the Atlantic. This mission was not to be Grant's. Lincoln called him east to take command of the Army of the Potomac. The West was left under the command of William Tecumseh Sherman.

In the spring of 1864, the end drew nearer—though still it would not come. Grant embarked on the most vicious offensive of the war, attacking Lee day after day in May in a terrible struggle known as the Wilderness Campaign. The Southerners fell back, but they continued to kill with deadly skill. They cost Grant 55,000 casualties in a little less than a month. But they suffered 30,000 of their own, losses they could no longer afford.

Meanwhile, in May, Sherman had begun his move southeastward from Chattanooga. It took him three months to reach Atlanta, but reach it he did. Then he set off on one of the most remarkable military marches in history. He ordered his men to advance along a front fully sixty miles wide, feeding off the countryside and destroying civilian property as they went. By December he was in Savannah.

For nine months the armies of Grant and Lee had been entrenched around Richmond, Grant waiting, Lee unable to attack. Defeat for the Confederacy was becoming more and more obvious with every dispatch from Georgia. Then Grant finally moved to surround Lee's force. The Confederate army, now numbering only about 25,000, made a desperate lunge westward, trying to escape encirclement, but it failed. Lee surrendered his army at Appomattox Court House, Virginia, on April 9, 1865. There were a few days more of scattered fighting in the Carolinas. But the war had finally ended. So had the lives of 600,000 soldiers.

The Toll of Total War

In the North, there was an outpouring of jubilation, then a sense of completion and deliverance that was sealed in the ritual of mourning and transfiguration that carried Lincoln to his martyr's grave. To the ex-slaves, it was also time for jubilation—the day of deliverance longed for and promised in so many spirituals. Among the defeated whites of the South, especially those of the planter class, there was shock and disbelief, fear and uncertainty; their ordeal, it seemed, was far from over. All around them was chaos and destruction—no money, little food, a society and economy in shambles. Many wondered how or if they would survive and what might become of them. Would their lands be seized? Would they be tried and hanged as traitors, especially now that some Southern fanatic had killed the seemingly magnanimous Lincoln? Some also experienced an overpowering sense of loss. Not only had the Confederate armies been defeated, Southern civilization seemed also to have been destroyed. It was more than some could bear. On June 17 Edmund Ruffin, an early and vehement secessionist, who had been chosen to pull the lanyard that opened fire on Fort Sumter, made a final entry in his diary: "I here proclaim my unmitigated hatred to Yankee rule and the perfidious, malignant, and vile Yankee Race." Then he placed the muzzle of his gun in his mouth and pulled the trigger with a forked stick.

The final push to the bloody end had made clear what the decisive year of 1863 had already suggested. This was a war unlike any previous war. The Civil War has been called the first modern war, for good reasons. It was the first railroad war, with unprecedented quantities of troops and supplies transported over unprecedented distances. While Sherman conducted his siege of Atlanta, sixteen trains rushed him 1,600 tons of supplies each day. In addition, the huge armies—ten times the size of any previous units—using

Mary Boykin Chesnut

Mary Boykin Chesnut wrote one of the most revealing pieces of Southern literature to come out of the Civil War era, a book first published under the title *A Diary from Dixie* in 1905, nearly forty years after the events it described. Chesnut was in a particularly strong position to observe the Confederacy as it rose, fell in defeat, and disintegrated. Born into a well-known South Carolina family, she also married into one of the most prominent families of the South. As was customary for the scion of such a family, her husband, James Chesnut, Jr., entered politics, becoming a U.S. senator in 1858 and serving throughout the war as a chief aide to Jefferson Davis, whose wife was one of Mary Chesnut's closest friends. Stationed close to the heart of the Confederacy—she was in Washington as the nation divided, in Charleston for the firing on Fort Sumter, and in the Confederate capital of Richmond during much of the war—Chesnut kept an extensive journal filled with notations about the people and events that came to her attention.

Though a keen and often detached observer of her class and culture, Chesnut still held the attitudes of the planter elite. Her faith in the righteousness of the Confederate cause never wavered, and although she condemned slavery as a curse that had brought her society to its destruction, she viewed blacks with the paternalistic condescension common to her class. But

Mary Chesnut was only partly an insider. Intelligent, well-educated, and informed, she was nonetheless excluded from the masculine world of power and politics. Even while basking in the social attention her femininity bestowed on her, she resented her position on the periphery of things. Her journal gave her a vicarious sense of participation and superiority, as she gazed down on the masculine world and condemned and criticized its folly and hypocrisy.

A Diary from Dixie was fashioned in the 1870s and 1880s from a deliberate reworking of the original journals. Chesnut began to think of herself as a writer only after the war. She wrote partly to try to help recoup the family fortunes, partly to relieve the pain of the collapse of her world, and partly out of a compulsion to preserve the South that once had been. She first tried her hand at fiction, writing but never publishing three novels before turning to her Civil War journals as the source for her "big book" about the South and the Civil War.

Filled with gossip, romance, and the ordinary events that happen even in wartime, Chesnut's book retained the day-to-day randomness of a true diary. At the same time, it possessed the coherence and sense of theme and direction that only hindsight and Chesnut's conscious literary intentions could give it. The result was an extraordinary document about the Civil War but strongly shaped by Reconstruction. Her work kept alive the pain of the South's defeat. Throughout the *Diary*, life goes on, but the war keeps intruding, with its death, uncertainty, and destruction. A sense of sadness and loss begins to punctuate the book, a sense that in spite of the righteousness of its cause, the Confederacy is doomed and its civilization is ending.

Picture: National Portrait Gallery, Smithsonian Institution, Washington, D.C.

new technologies of destruction—trench warfare, repeat-loading rifles—had brought about an unprecedented mass slaughter. As Walt Whitman wrote in 1863, "The heart grows sick of war after all, when you see what it really is—every once in a while I feel so horrified and disgusted— it seems to me like a great slaughterhouse and the men mutually butchering each other."

But what more than anything else set the Civil War apart from earlier wars was its character as

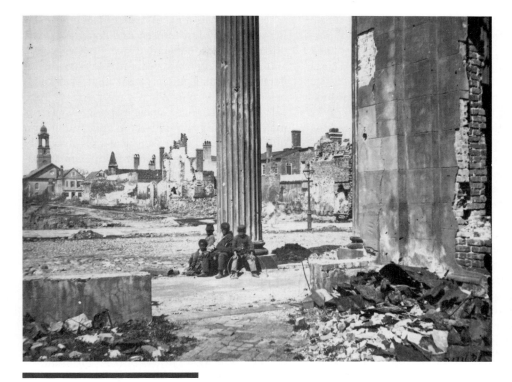

The destruction of Charleston, South Carolina. As the Union armies pressed into the South, they left much of it in ruins, visiting a destruction upon the civilian population that few other Americans have ever experienced. (Library of Congress, Brady Collection)

a total war. Wars traditionally had been fought by professional armies, which jockeyed for territory until some kind of negotiated settlement was reached. Partly because of the new technologies of war and partly because each side was fighting for a principle it would not compromise, the Civil War became the first total war in modern times. It pitted not just two armies, but two societies—each by the end fully mobilized for the effort—against each other. Victory came not with the taking of territory but with the destruction of the other society's capacity to fight. Sherman grasped the brutal logic of total war. As he put it, as he embarked on his march to the sea, "We are not only fighting hostile armies, but a hostile people. We must make old and young, rich and poor, feel the hand of war." And victory and defeat were themselves total: A destroyed South held on until it was forced into unconditional surrender. At the end, the Confederacy was in no position to negotiate a peace—it surrendered because it could no longer carry on.

The War and Slavery

After four long years, the war had once and for all determined that the American Republic could not be divided. But the society that had to be reunited was very different from the one that had split apart in 1861. As Lincoln had written to a Southern Unionist in early 1864, "The nation's condition is not what either party, or any man, devised or expected." The Emancipation Proclamation had formally ended slavery in the Confederacy, and the Thirteenth Amendment, proposed by Lincoln in 1864 and ratified in

December of 1865, had made freedom universal. But well before these acts and well before hostilities ended, the institution of slavery had started to fall apart, due to the "friction and abrasion" of war. By the end of 1861, runaways to the Union armies were treated as "contraband" of war, rather than returned to their masters. As early as 1862 the Northern fleet had captured the Sea Islands off the Carolina and Georgia coasts, and the slaves there had been freed.

Masters tried to keep news of the approach of the Northern armies and the progress of the war from their slaves, but slaves devised ways of finding out anyway. In Forsythe, Georgia, a slave who was responsible for bringing the newspaper to his mistress always showed it to the local black preacher before he delivered it. House servants often overheard their masters talking and returned to the quarters with information about the whereabouts of the Union armies. More than once, a master awoke to find that many if not all of his slaves had slipped away in the night to become "contraband." As it marched through Georgia, Sherman's army became a veritable army of liberation (somewhat ironically, since Sherman himself had not opposed slavery and was deeply prejudiced against African Americans). After the collapse of the Confederacy, actual freedom came by direct announcement to the slaves by former masters, the grapevine, or federal officials.

By the summer of 1865 most slaveholders had relinquished their slave property. But they still held onto the attitudes that had justified holding African Americans in bondage. They thought of blacks as childlike people, whom they had fed, clothed, housed, and cared for. And most had convinced themselves that their own slaves were loyal and happy, content with the lot to which their race had consigned them. The former masters thus had great difficulty even imagining blacks as anything but a dependent and subservient people. Masters were perplexed, angered, and even hurt when their slaves (often led by personal or house servants, who had been considered most loyal) left them, refused to work, or stole tools and food.

The response of the ex-slaves to their new status was similarly confused and complex. Word of emancipation penetrated many places slowly and often in a garbled way. A few slaves wondered if emancipation meant that they now belonged to Lincoln. When slavery ended, there was nothing definite to take its place. The freedmen possessed a number of agricultural and other skills, but they were a people suddenly released from bondage, with few personal possessions and no money, property, or housing. It was not at all clear what they should do, where they should go, or how they could feed, clothe, and shelter themselves. Some set off for places from which they had been sold, hoping to reunite with their families. Others stayed where they were, working for their former masters or for nearby planters. Others, essentially refugees of war, roamed about and flocked to Union encampments in search of food, shelter, and protection.

In spite of all the confusion and uncertainty, the ex-slaves possessed a clear and definite idea of the difference between slavery and freedom. They asserted their sense of freedom in subtle ways. A rural and agricultural population tied to land and place, most were reluctant to leave areas they regarded as home. But, refusing to stay in quarters that reminded them of their previous situation, they often moved to huts scattered around their former master's lands. Some moved to a neighboring planter's land to demonstrate that the tie to their former master had indeed been broken. For many, simply the act of moving, whatever the distance, was a gesture of liberation, a deliberate exercise of the choice and freedom that had been denied them under slavery.

Many blacks resisted contracting for their labor, a refusal many whites condemned as a sign of laziness and irresponsibility. But many freedmen were suspicious of anything that seemed to bind them and their labor to any white man. Possession of their labor had been one of the essential marks of their enslavement. Indeed, many thought themselves justified in taking food, tools, and mules from their former masters as payment morally due them for their previous labor. But land was probably the most important

Freed African Americans in Richmond, Virginia. A major problem after the war was the future of the former slaves. Slavery ended without any clear sense of what was to take its place. All over the South, freed men and women drifted to the cities in search of work or simply to test their newfound freedom. (Library of Congress)

token of freedom—a parcel of land that was their own. Again and again, blacks during Reconstruction pleaded for land, "forty acres and a mule," that would enable them to establish their independence and set up households where husbands and wives could work for themselves and rear and protect their children.

LINCOLN'S PLAN Reunion required more than just returning the seceded states to full and equal participation in the nation. It also meant reconstructing a society in which slavery no longer existed and determining what kind of freedom the ex-slaves would have. Lincoln had begun to plan for the aftermath of war well before the end of the fighting. He hoped to restore political relations as quickly and with as little animosity as possible. On December 8, 1863, he issued a proclamation specifying that whenever voters equal to 10 percent of the eligible voters of 1860 took an oath swearing future loyalty to the Constitution, the Union, and the acts freeing the slaves, a state could set up a republican form of government and resume ordinary political operations. (As blacks had not been eligible to

vote in 1860, Lincoln's proclamation excluded black suffrage.) The Republican leaders in Congress wanted a much tougher procedure, one that would guarantee what they considered true loyalty to the Union. In July 1864, Congress passed the Wade-Davis Bill, which Lincoln pocket-vetoed. The bill required action by 50 percent of the eligible electorate. More important, it contained provisions for an "ironclad" oath—a pledge of past as well as future loyalty—which was designed to bar all former secessionists and Confederate officeholders from political participation.

Lincoln was not unmindful of the troubling question of the freedmen, nor was he unaware of the tricky relationship between race and the politics of reunion. But just as he had initially subordinated slavery to the task of preserving the Union, he now placed highest priority on reestablishing normal political relations. He thought Reconstruction could be best achieved if the question of the freedmen was separated from the process of political reunion: If the ordinary political machinery was reestablished, the nation would be better able to work out what the freedman's place in American society should be. Lincoln had always been reluctant to push for civil and social equality for blacks, partly because of his awareness of the depth of American racism and partly because he shared some of that prejudice. Still, at the time of his death, he had begun to work on the problem of the freedmen and on the politics of that problem. When Louisiana drew up its constitution in 1864, he urged the governor to consider giving the vote to "some of the colored people," especially "the very intelligent and those who have fought gallantly in our ranks." (Altogether, nearly 178,000 black troops, many of them ex-slaves, served in the Union armies.) On March 3, 1865, he signed a bill creating a Freedmen's Bureau. The bill gave federal protection and aid to ex-slaves and contained a limited provision for giving them land, a provision that looked forward to the possible establishment of a landholding black yeomanry.

Reconstruction: 1865–77

PRESIDENTIAL RECONSTRUCTION UNDER JOHNSON Lincoln's successor, Andrew Johnson, fully intended to carry out the policy Lincoln had begun. But he operated at a severe disadvantage. As is the case with most vice presidents, Johnson was chosen with no expectation that he would ever be president. He was selected because he was a Democrat and a staunch Union man from the border state of Tennessee. These very attributes, plus the fact that he had once owned slaves, heightened Republicans' suspicion of him and made them all the more eager to keep control of Reconstruction in the hands of Congress. In addition, he lacked the political power Lincoln had amassed through his adroit dispensing of favors and patronage. Even more important, Johnson lacked the stature—the legitimacy—Lincoln had acquired as the head of state who had seen the Union through to victory and the first president since Andrew Jackson to win

Andrew Johnson. When Tennessee seceded in June 1861, Johnson—alone among Southern senators—refused to resign and join the Confederacy. Lincoln appointed him military governor of Tennessee. His staunch Unionism and his effectiveness in restoring civilian rule to Tennessee made him a logical choice as Lincoln's running mate in 1864. This political cartoon favorable to Johnson depicts him as the leader needed to repair the torn fabric of the Union. (American Antiquarian Society)

reelection. And even with all these assets, Lincoln had run into stiff opposition to his approach to Reconstruction.

Congress was not in session when Johnson took office, and he proceeded to carry out his own plan for Reconstruction by executive action, without consulting the Republican leaders of Congress. Here, too, he partly followed Lincoln's example. Lincoln had jailed opponents to the war, ended slavery in the Confederate states, and instituted a draft—all by executive action. He had launched Reconstruction by proclamation and vetoed the Wade-Davis Bill because he opposed its more stringent conditions and thought Reconstruction was properly an executive function. So Johnson charged ahead. He renewed the promise of amnesty to most ex-Confederates, and he set three conditions for a rebel state's reentry into the political system: The state had to nullify its ordinance of secession, accept the Thirteenth Amendment, and repudiate all Confederate debts. Johnson insisted that the states had never legally been out of the Union and hence retained the power to set their own rules on who could vote. He also assured Southern leaders that Congress was constitutionally bound to accept these governments. Under the leadership of many ex-Confederates, the South moved quickly. When Congress came back into session in December, it was presented with a fait accompli: All but Texas had set up state governments firmly under the control of former slaveholders and Confederate leaders and had sent senators and representatives to Washington to claim their seats in the new Congress.

Johnson and most white Southerners thought political reconstruction was substantially complete. Johnson's major goal was political reunion. He was unconcerned about the freedmen. He rescinded General Sherman's Special Field Order of January 1865, which had set aside a thirty-mile strip along the South Carolina coast to be distributed in forty-acre plots to the freedmen, and ordered the land returned to its previous white owners. But the planters also wanted to create a society as close as possible to the antebellum South, a goal in direct conflict with the freedmen's aspirations for land and independence. (After Johnson's reversal of Sherman's order, one freedman declared, "They will make freedom a curse to us, for we have no home, no land, no oath, no vote.")

As soon as the ex-slaveholders found themselves regaining local power, they moved rapidly to reestablish their economic and social dominion, to return the freedmen to a position of social subordination and keep them as a cheap source of plantation labor. Mississippi, South Carolina, and Alabama enacted Black Codes (the other states followed in early 1866), which severely restricted black freedom. In general, the codes were designed to do two things: to maintain white supremacy and to secure a black labor supply. Some codes barred blacks from jury service or testifying against whites; others restricted them to agricultural labor; still others forbade them from renting land or carrying firearms, or imposed curfews on them. The most far-reaching codes, however, were the vagrancy laws, under which unemployed African Americans who could not pay their fines for vagrancy could be bound out to work for whomever paid the fine.

To many in the North, the new South that Johnson's Reconstruction had ushered in seemed frighteningly similar to the old South. Most of the ex-Confederates seemed right back in power. They filled the state legislatures. And the former vice president of the Confederacy, six former cabinet members, nine generals, and more than fifty members of the Confederate legislature had been elected to the national Congress by the reconstructed states. Moreover, the Black Codes seemed to have reestablished slavery under another name. As the *Chicago Tribune* thundered, "We tell the white men of Mississippi that the men of the North will convert the state of Mississippi into a frog pond before they will allow any such laws to disgrace one foot of soil over which the flag of freedom waves."

Northerners were divided over what they wanted out of Reconstruction, and few were eager to grant equality to blacks. (Twelve Northern states still refused to give the franchise to blacks.) Still, they had opposed slavery, fought and won a war that had come about partly because of slavery, and they did not want to see it restored under some new guise. But most upsetting of all, those who had led the rebellion—those responsible for the terrible war—refused to acknowledge defeat. Mississippi had rejected the Thirteenth Amendment, South Carolina refused to nullify its ordinance of secession, and members of the old slavocracy demanded seats in Congress. It seemed as if Reconstruction was about to deprive the North of the victory for which so many of its men had died.

When the new Congress returned to Washington, it refused to seat the senators and representatives from the former Confederate states. It moved to take Reconstruction policy into its own hands and set up a Joint Committee on Reconstruction headed by two strong-willed radical Republicans, Representative Thaddeus

Stevens of Pennsylvania and Senator Charles Sumner of Massachusetts. They believed that the Reconstruction of the nation would not be completed until the revolution in Southern society brought about by the end of slavery was completed. For Sumner, this required granting full citizenship and political rights to the freedmen, while for Stevens it involved using government lands and confiscating the plantations of the old planter aristocracy to give the freedmen the land to establish themselves as independent farmers. Even the moderate members of Congress were alarmed by what was happening in the South: Unless there was "some legislation by the nation for his protection," Senator Trumbull of Illinois insisted, the ex-slave would be "abused and virtually re-enslaved."

Concern for the freedmen was certainly not the only thing that motivated Republicans in Congress. Johnson's Reconstruction threatened them with the loss of their political power, and many Republicans were more concerned with holding onto political power than with the rights of blacks. With the end of slavery, Southern representation in the House of Representatives would be increased by about twenty seats, since for purposes of apportionment a slave had been counted as only three-fifths of a person. Republicans feared that the exclusion of Southern blacks from the vote would ensure the election of unreconstructed rebels, who would join with pro-Southern Democrats to drive the Republicans from power. Black suffrage might be essential for the establishment of any real freedom for the ex-slaves, but it also seemed essential for keeping the Republicans in power. In fact, it was not until the Republicans began to lose power in the North in 1870 that they passed the Fifteenth Amendment, granting suffrage to African-American males in the North and South.

CONGRESSIONAL RECONSTRUCTION But Stevens and Sumner were not yet in control of Congress. Moderates like Senator John Sherman of Ohio were still in the ascendancy. They did not want to throw out the governments orga-

nized under Johnson, but they did want to give some protection to the freedmen. Congress enacted two pieces of legislation. It extended the Freedmen's Bureau, the agency that had been set up to help the transition out of bondage by providing relief, setting up schools, and helping freedmen find employment. It also passed the Civil Rights Act of 1866 that granted the rights of citizenship to the ex-slaves and gave federal courts jurisdiction over all cases involving those rights. President Johnson promptly vetoed both acts. The moderates then countered with the Fourteenth Amendment, a complex measure designed to give some basic protection to the ex-slaves in a form that the moderates hoped the South would accept. The amendment contained the basic features of the Civil Rights Act, but it also reduced the political power of the old Southern elite by barring from public office anyone who had ever sworn fidelity to the Constitution and then participated in rebellion. At the same time, the amendment did not directly require black suffrage; it only threatened to reduce Southern representation if blacks were not permitted to vote. Nor did it contain any provision for the confiscation or redistribution of lands. It was clear, however, that the Republican Congress would not accept any state back into the Union that did not ratify the amendment.

President and Congress were now at complete loggerheads. Johnson denounced the amendment and even urged Southerners to reject it. He decided to take the issue of Reconstruction directly to the voters in the upcoming congressional elections. Contrary to custom, Johnson went on the political hustings, denouncing the Republican Congress and further polarizing the issue. But his campaign was a disaster, and the voters overwhelmingly repudiated his policies. The Republicans, now increasingly under the influence of Sumner and Stevens, won more than two-thirds of the seats in both houses, enough to override any presidential veto.

Most of the members of the newly constituted Southern legislatures were firmly opposed to the Fourteenth Amendment, which would remove many of their members from office. But white

A Freedman's Bureau school. The Freedman's Bureau was the central federal agency set up to help former slaves make the transition to life after slavery. One of its main goals was to set up schools, often staffed with women from the North, many of whom had been active supporters of the antislavery movement. (Library of Congress)

Southerners were also angry and felt a deep sense of betrayal. Many had complied with Lincoln's and Johnson's requirements in good faith, only to have new and harsher conditions imposed on them in what seemed like an all-too-familiar resurgence of Yankee tyranny. Amid fiery denunciations of fanatical South-hating Republicans, all the Southern states except Tennessee rejected the Fourteenth Amendment, further infuriating the Republicans in Congress. "The last one of the sinful ten has flung back into our teeth the magnanimous offer of a generous nation" was how Representative John Garfield of Ohio saw it. It was now two years after the end of the fighting, and North and South were further from reconciliation than ever. In his last major speech, Lincoln had pleaded for Americans to "bind up the nation's wounds"; two years of Reconstruction politics had only poured salt on them.

RADICAL RECONSTRUCTION An aroused Republican Congress came to Washington in December 1866 determined to impose a harsh new style of Reconstruction on a dismayed and angered South. They moved quickly to consolidate their power and to ensure that neither the courts nor the president thwarted their will. When the Supreme Court issued a ruling that seemed to challenge the validity of the military courts of the Freedmen's Bureau, they reduced the size of the Court, depriving Johnson of the chance to make any appointments to it. When in 1868 the Court seemed about to challenge the Reconstruction Acts the radicals had passed, they took jurisdiction over such matters away from the Court. But it was Johnson's power that the Republicans were most determined to check. The election had given them the votes to nullify his veto power. The Republicans were equally determined to nullify his use of executive authority, especially his powers as commander-in-chief (the powers Lincoln had used so effectively during the war to bypass Congress). They enacted legislation that required all military orders, including those of Johnson, to go through General Grant. The Republicans were also worried that Johnson would try to use federal patronage to create a political machine that would be loyal to him. To thwart this possibility, they passed a Tenure of Office Act, designed to prevent Johnson from firing people opposed to his policies. They even used this act to try to remove Johnson from office. In August of 1867, Johnson suspended the secretary of war, Edwin Stanton (who worked closely with the radicals). When the Senate refused to agree to Stanton's removal, Johnson ordered Stanton to vacate his office. The Republicans responded by voting articles of impeachment in the House of Representatives. The subsequent Senate vote to convict him failed by one vote.

In the spring and early summer of 1867, the radical Republicans drew up a plan of military reconstruction. Lincoln and Johnson had argued that since secession itself was illegal, the Confederate states had never really been out of the Union. But the radicals insisted that by rebelling, the states had forfeited their statehood, committing "state-suicide," as Sumner called it. Congress accordingly declared the Johnson governments illegal and divided the conquered South into five military districts. The commander of each district, with the aid of the army, would prepare the states for readmission by registering all adult black males and all white males not disenfranchised under the provisions of the Fourteenth Amendment. All voters were required to take a stringent oath of loyalty. Once legitimate voters had been certified—approximately 700,000 blacks and 650,000 whites were registered under these provisions, and probably between 100,000 and 200,000 whites were disenfranchised—the usual steps for setting up a state would take place. Then, if Congress accepted the state's constitution and the state legislature passed the Fourteenth Amendment, the state would be readmitted to the Union. By June 1868, seven states, all clearly under the control of Republican-dominated "Reconstruction" governments, were accepted back into the Union; by early 1870 the remaining states were also admitted and the Union was formally restored.

For three years, much of the drama of Reconstruction had taken place in Washington. But as the states returned to the Union under the radical formula, the battle shifted to the South. The North finally had "reconstructed" states it could accept as legitimate, full-fledged members of the Union. But to many white Southerners these governments were never legitimate, and they were determined to do whatever it took to undermine them. To them, radical Reconstruction was an unmitigated nightmare, and it left a century-long legacy of bitterness. There was, first, the tyranny—the imposition by military force of governments and rulers that they themselves would never have chosen. It was a long-standing American axiom that government rested on the consent of the governed, and Southerners had certainly never consented to the kinds of governments that military Reconstruction forced on them. But to most white Southerners, the greatest of the horrors of radical Reconstruction was that it subjected them to "Negro rule."

The "Negro rule" of radical Reconstruction was a myth. In no state did blacks dominate or control the government. There was not a single elected black governor, and only in South Carolina was there ever a black legislative majority. Moreover, the range of ability, education, and competence among black officeholders was not wildly different from the range among most white officeholders in the North or South. The Reconstruction governments certainly contained corruption, but they were no more corrupt than their "lily-white" counterparts before or after the war. Although black suffrage was essential for keeping these regimes in power, their electoral base, especially in the beginning, extended beyond the ex-slaves. Many former Whigs, Southern Union men, and antisecessionists initially allied themselves with the new Republican governments. Many whites in nonslaveholding regions who had always resented the rule of the planter elite

"Of Course He Wants to Vote the Democratic Ticket." The efforts to "redeem" the South from Republican rule centered around attempts to neutralize the political effects of black enfranchisement. This Republican cartoon depicts the intimidation often used to keep blacks from voting or to get them to vote against the Republicans. (The Bettmann Archive)

voted for and participated in the Reconstruction governments. These governments were in many ways reform governments. But they spent comparatively little time trying to achieve social equality between whites and blacks. Instead, they concentrated on such things as public education and eliminating the undemocratic features of the antebellum political system, by which the planter elite had maintained its dominion—things that benefited poor whites as well as the freedmen.

"REDEEMING" THE STATES But this is not how the former slaveholders and old planter elite saw radical Reconstruction. Illiterate black field hands who could vote while former planters could not, blacks who held office, "uppity" ex-slaves who mocked their former masters, black soldiers who now patrolled whites—all these things in the eyes of the former slaveholders turned radical Reconstruction into "Black Reconstruction." "Negro rule" became the galling symbol of all the horrors of radical Reconstruction,

of all they had lost, of the defeat they had suffered and the degradation they now felt. They struck back against the Reconstruction governments with all the means at their disposal. They appealed to white supremacy to draw support of the poorer whites away from the Republicans, casting themselves as saviors who would "redeem" the South from the twin specter of black rule and Yankee domination. In states like Tennessee, Virginia, and North Carolina, where white voters held a clear majority, the "redeemers" gained control by 1871. For the most part they relied on the ballot box for victory, but in some areas they used intimidation and violence against blacks and their allies.

Where the racial balance was even or blacks held a majority, the battle for control was often violent. Carpetbaggers (whites from the North) and scalawags (white Southerners who collaborated with the Yankees) were ostracized and boycotted. Blacks were threatened with loss of jobs, credit, and access to lands for sharecropping. Secret organizations like the Ku Klux Klan were set up. Striking at night, dressed in robes and

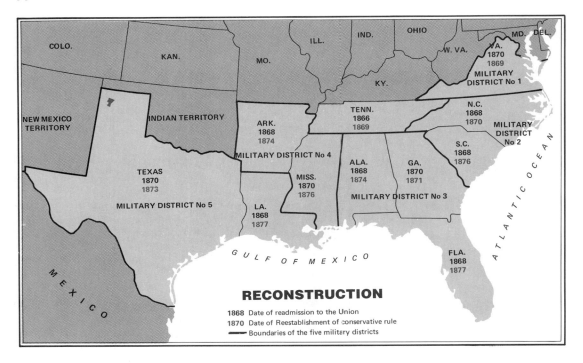

RECONSTRUCTION

1868 Date of readmission to the Union
1870 Date of Reestablishment of conservative rule
——— Boundaries of the five military districts

hoods, they beat, mutilated, and often murdered their victims. Directing their attacks mostly against scalawags and black leaders, they tried to terrorize blacks into withdrawing from political activity. The campaign of terror shocked Northerners and a number of Southerners. Two "force bills" and a Ku Klux Klan Act were passed by Congress, and in 1871 President Ulysses S. Grant initiated federal prosecutions in Mississippi. In South Carolina, Grant placed a few counties under martial law. But the laws were unevenly enforced and violence continued. "White legions," semimilitary organizations that intimidated whites into voting Democratic and forcibly kept blacks from voting, helped redeem Texas, Arkansas, and Alabama. As the 1875 Mississippi election approached, whites were determined to keep blacks and Republicans away from the polls, and the governor feared a bloodbath if he used black militia to oversee the elections. When he asked for federal help, the Grant administration refused, declaring that "the whole public are tired of these annual autumnal outbreaks in the South." The Democrats swept to power, aided by

the white legions, and Mississippi too joined the ranks of the redeemed.

THE END OF RECONSTRUCTION By 1876 only Louisiana, South Carolina, and Florida remained "unredeemed." Even there the hold of Reconstruction was precarious, dependent on the continuing presence of federal troops. The election of 1876 removed this prop, largely because most Northerners (at best minimally interested in the welfare of the ex-slaves) no longer cared very much about what was happening in the South. In his inaugural address of 1869, Ulysses S. Grant called for "peace," which most Northerners took to mean relief from the turmoil of Reconstruction politics. The election of 1872 indicated how rapidly Northern concerns were shifting. Many liberal Republicans who had been staunch in their concern for black rights, including Charles Sumner, turned against the Republican party and supported the Democratic nominee, Horace Greeley, himself an old Whig-Republican, who focused his campaign largely on the corruption of the Grant administration. By the mid-1870s, Northerners were more preoccupied with the politics of corruption and agrarian discontent, and with the problems of inflation, tariffs, and railroads, than with Reconstruction.

The election of 1876 resulted in a bizarre deadlock between Rutherford B. Hayes, the Republican nominee, and his Democratic opponent, Samuel J. Tilden. In exchange for the disputed electoral votes of South Carolina, Florida, and Louisiana, Hayes, who had narrowly lost the popular vote to Tilden, promised to remove all remaining federal troops from the South, thus putting a symbolic end to the Reconstruction that in all essential respects had already come to an end.

The end of Reconstruction did not mean a sudden end to all black gains or rights. African Americans continued to vote and even to hold a few offices, and they fought hard to preserve their schools and to hold onto whatever land they had. But continuing intimidation, white unity, and the indifference of the North isolated the ex-slaves politically and made their rights increasingly vulnerable. In his second inaugural address, Lincoln had linked the survival of the Union to the fate of the slaves. Slavery had ended and "the mighty scourge of war" was lifted, but twelve years of Reconstruction had made it clear that white Americans were far from ready to make good on the promise of emancipation.

Suggestions for Further Reading

ABRAHAM LINCOLN

The literature on Abraham Lincoln is voluminous. Benjamin Thomas, *Abraham Lincoln* (1952), is a good single-volume biography; it is somewhat surpassed by Stephen B. Oates, *With Malice Toward None: The Life of Abraham Lincoln* (1977) and *Abraham Lincoln: The Man Behind the Myths* (1988). Lawanda Cox, *Lincoln and Black Freedom* (1981), is a very useful study of the decision for emancipation. David Donald, *Lincoln Reconsidered* (1958), and Richard Current, *The Lincoln Nobody Knows* (1951), provide refreshing perspectives on Lincoln as a politician. Edmund Wilson, *Patriotic Gore* (1962), treats Lincoln's mystical attachment to the Union and his deepening religious sentiments during the war. David Potter, *Lincoln and His Party in the Secession Crisis* (1942), remains the best study of the subject. John Hope Franklin, *The Emancipation Proclamation* (1963), is a succinct history of how the document came about; Allan Nevins, *Lincoln and the Gettysburg Address* (1954), is a solid account of that famous oration. Ralph Borreson, *When Lincoln Died* (1965), is a detailed account of Lincoln's assassination and funeral. T. Harry Williams, *Lincoln: Selected Speeches and Letters* (1960), is an excellent sampling of the president's own writings.

CIVIL WAR

An excellent overview of the period is James McPherson, *Ordeal by Fire* (1982). The same author's *Battle Cry of Freedom* (1988) covers much the same ground, but in a somewhat more readable fashion. James G. Randall and David Donald, *The Civil War and Reconstruction* (2nd ed., 1961), is an older work but is still a useful survey. An excellent study of secession in one state is Michael P. Johnson, *Toward a Patriarchal Republic: The Secession of Georgia* (1977).

Two fine recent studies of the armies and battles of the war are Michael Barton, *Good Men: The Character of Civil War Soldiers* (1981), and Gerald F. Linderman, *Embattled Courage: Combat in the Civil War* (1977). William S. McFeely, *Grant: A Biography* (1981), is essential reading. Sherman's Georgia campaign is discussed in rich detail in *March to the Sea and Beyond* (1985). The causes of Northern victory and Confederate defeat are discussed in David Donald, ed., *Why the North Won the Civil War* (1960); Richard E. Beringer, Herman Hattaway, Archer Jones, and William N. Still, Jr., *Why the South Lost the Civil War* (1986); and Herman Hattaway and Archer Jones, *How the North Won* (1983). The life of the common soldier is the subject of Bell Irvin Wiley's pioneering works, *The Life of Johnny Reb* (1943) and *The Life of*

CHRONOLOGY

1861 Mississippi, Alabama, Georgia, Florida, Louisiana, and Texas secede.
Lincoln inaugurated president.
Firing on Fort Sumter.
Border states secede.
First battle of Bull Run (Manassas).

1863 Lincoln issues Emancipation Proclamation.
Battle of Chancellorsville.
Battle of Gettysburg.
Grant captures Vicksburg.
Draft riots in northern cities.
Lincoln begins planning a reconstruction program.

1865 Confederate government flees Richmond.
Lee surrenders to Grant at Appomattox.
Lincoln assassinated, Andrew Johnson becomes president.
Johnson institutes presidential reconstruction.
Congress creates a joint House and Senate committee to oversee reconstruction.
Thirteenth amendment ratified.

1867 Congress passes Military Reconstruction.
Congress passes Tenure of Office Act.

| 1860 | 1861 | 1862 | 1863 | 1864 | 1865 | 1866 | 1867 |

1860 Abraham Lincoln (Republican) elected president.
South Carolina secedes.

1862 Battle of Shiloh.
Robert E. Lee named commander of the Army of Northern Virginia.
Second battle of Bull Run.
Battle of Antietam.
Lincoln drafts preliminary Emancipation Proclamation.
Battle of Fredericksburg.

1864 Grant named Union general in chief.
Siege of Petersburg.
Sherman captures Atlanta.
Lincoln reelected president.
Sherman's march to the sea.

1866 Johnson vetoes Freedman's Bureau Bill and Civil Rights Act.
Congress passes fourteenth amendment.
Republicans win large majorities in both houses of Congress.
Ku Klux Klan established.

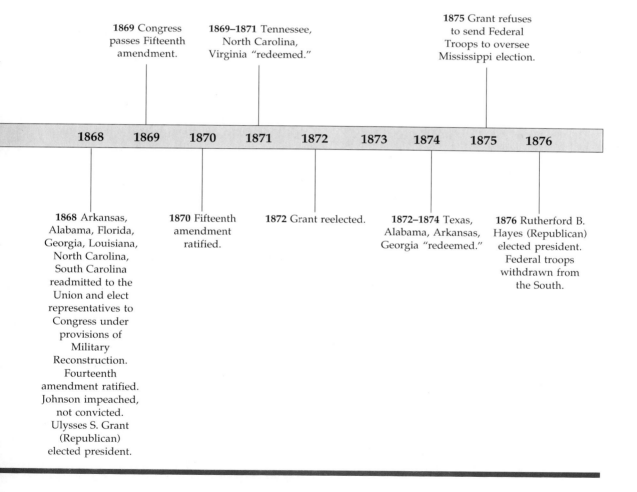

1869 Congress passes Fifteenth amendment.

1869–1871 Tennessee, North Carolina, Virginia "redeemed."

1875 Grant refuses to send Federal Troops to oversee Mississippi election.

1868   1869   1870   1871   1872   1873   1874   1875   1876

1868 Arkansas, Alabama, Florida, Georgia, Louisiana, North Carolina, South Carolina readmitted to the Union and elect representatives to Congress under provisions of Military Reconstruction. Fourteenth amendment ratified. Johnson impeached, not convicted. Ulysses S. Grant (Republican) elected president.

1870 Fifteenth amendment ratified.

1872 Grant reelected.

1872–1874 Texas, Alabama, Arkansas, Georgia "redeemed."

1876 Rutherford B. Hayes (Republican) elected president. Federal troops withdrawn from the South.

Billy Yank (1952). Allan Nevins, *The War for the Union*, 4 vols. (1959–71), Bruce Catton, *This Hallowed Ground* (1956) and *Centennial History of the Civil War* (1961–65), and Douglass Southall Freeman, *R. E. Lee*, 4 vols. (1934–35), provide full, readable accounts of the military history of the Civil War. T. Harry Williams, *Lincoln and the Radicals* (1942), argues that Lincoln and the radicals were in continuing opposition; whereas Hans L. Trefousse, *The Radical Republicans* (1968), stresses their cooperation. Emory L. Thomas, *The Confederate Nation* (1979), is a good single-volume treatment. Charles Ramsdell, *Behind the Lines in the Southern Confederacy* (1944), discusses the internal political conflicts within the Confederacy. The lives of African-American women are treated in Jacqueline Jones, *Labor of Love, Labor of Sorrow* (1985). Other valuable works on blacks and the war include Benjamin Quarles, *The Negro in the Civil War* (1953); James McPherson, ed., *The Negro's Civil War* (1965); and Dudley Cornish, *The Sable Arm: Negro Troops in the Union Army* (2nd ed., 1987). James L. Roark, *Masters without Slaves* (1977), describes the breakdown of the plantation system during the war and Reconstruction.

Politics and ideology in the North are the subjects of Earl J. Hess, *Liberty, Virtue, and Progress: Northerners and Their War for the Union* (1988); Eric Foner, *Politics and Ideology in the Age of the Civil War* (1980); and Dale Baum, *The Civil War Party System* (1984).

George Frederickson, *The Inner Civil War* (1965), and Edmund Wilson, *Patriotic Gore* (1962), provide superb discussions of the intellectual impact of the war. Ralph Andreano, ed., *The Economic Impact of the American Civil War* (1962), contains a number of important articles assessing the economic dimensions of the war. James L. Roark, *Masters Without Slaves* (1977), analyzes the plight of Southern planters during the Civil War and Reconstruction.

RECONSTRUCTION

John Hope Franklin, *Reconstruction After the Civil War* (1961), Kenneth M. Stampp, *The Era of Reconstruction* (1965), and W. E. B. du Bois, *Black Reconstruction* (1935), are valuable general treatments of Reconstruction. Herman Belz, *Reconstructing the Union* (1969), is a solid treatment of national policy; W. McKee Evans, *Ballots and Fence Rails* (1966), is a superb study of the politics of Reconstruction on the local level in North Carolina. Lawanda Cox and John Cox, *Politics, Principle, and Prejudice* (1965), and William Gillette, *The Right to Vote* (1969), treat race and politics in North and South during the period. Eric McKitrick, *Andrew Johnson and Reconstruction* (1966), is a thorough study of early presidential Reconstruction. William S. McFeely, *Grant* (1981), is the best study of Grant's presidency. William S. McFeely, *Yankee Step-Father: General O. O. Howard and the Freedmen* (1968), is a useful study of the Freedmen's Bureau. Allen Trelease, *White Terror* (1967), analyzes the role of the Ku Klux Klan and white terrorism in defeating Reconstruction. C. Vann Woodward, *Reunion and Reaction* (1951), and William Gillette, *Retreat from Reconstruction* (1980), describe the end of Reconstruction.

LIFE DURING THE CIVIL WAR AND RECONSTRUCTION

The story of blacks in Reconstruction is explored in several works. The most notable are Joel Williamson, *After Slavery* (1966); Thomas Hold, *Black over White* (1977); Willie Lee Rose, *Rehearsal for Reconstruction* (1964); and Leon Litwack, *Been in the Storm So Long* (1979). Other important books on Reconstruction and its impact are Paul D. Escott, *Many Excellent People* (1985); Eric Foner, *Nothing But Freedom* (1983); and Stephen Hahn, *The Roots of Southern Populism* (1983). Morgan Kousser and James McPherson, eds., *Region, Race, and Reconstruction* (1982), is a valuable collection of essays.

Collections of documents include Frank Moore, ed., *Rebellion Record*, a twelve-volume compilation put together in the 1860s and reprinted in a modern edition in 1977; Francis T. Miller, *The Photographic History of the Civil War*, 10 vols. (1957), is the most extensive of the many collections of Civil War photographs. Frank Freidel, ed., *Union Pamphlets of the Civil War* (1967), provides a valuable collection of Northern writings. See also Harold Hyman, ed., *The Radical Republicans and Reconstruction* (1967). C. Vann Woodward, ed., *Mary Chesnut's Civil War* (1981), and Robert Myers, *The Children of Pride* (1972), provide invaluable insight into Southern life during the war. Rupert S. Holland, ed., *The Letters and Diary of Laura M. Towne* (1970), is a superb collection of letters from a young woman who went to the South Carolina Sea Islands to teach the ex-slaves.

CHAPTER 13
THE POLITICS
OF RESTORATION

THE EPISODE: *In 1876, the United States passed through the most unusual presidential election in its history. What made the election unique was not the candidates. Republican Rutherford B. Hayes and Democrat Samuel J. Tilden were not remarkable men. The issue turned on disputed election returns from three states—Louisiana, Florida, and South Carolina—the only states where Union troops still enforced Reconstruction measures that protected the voting rights of African Americans.*

The Constitution was extremely vague about how electoral votes should be counted. It said only that the members of the electoral college in each state should send their votes to Washington. Then "the President of the Senate shall . . . open the certificates and the votes shall then be counted." What it did not say was exactly who should count the votes, or who should choose between competing votes when more than one set of men claimed they had been chosen as electors by the voters of their state. One candidate had won a clear majority of the popular vote. But the other party realized that if it could get the electoral votes of all three disputed states, it would win the electoral balloting by a bare margin of one.

THE HISTORICAL SETTING: *In normal political times, the way the disputed election was settled would not have been of such urgent importance. But the 1870s were not normal times. The Civil War had ended just eleven years before, and most*

of the nation's political leaders had taken part in that struggle. The contest between Republicans and Democrats still evoked extremely bitter memories. The fundamental issue in 1876 and 1877 was not who would be president, but how Reconstruction would be ended and national politics restored to the "normal" practices of the pre–Civil War period.

The twin political outcome was the end of Reconstruction and the restoration of competition between two very evenly matched political parties. But, for a generation after 1876, the parties tried to win elections by avoiding clear stands on issues. This had three important results: a shift of power to Congress; a failure to confront problems resulting from profound social and economic change; and the rise of protest movements that attempted to bypass an inert political structure.

This chapter—the first of four that deal with the last quarter of the nineteenth century—establishes a political framework. The three subsequent chapters will analyze the impact of the climax of the industrial revolution, the expansion of European-American society into the far-western territories of Native Americans, and deep changes in the lives of women and their families. Many basic features of modern American society were taking shape during these twenty-five years; looking at the period from four distinct angles can help us understand the world we inherited from our great-grandparents.

THE ELECTION OF 1876

About half a century ago, the novelist Thomas Wolfe thought back to the times of his own father. It was a dull past for him, that world of the 1870s and 1880s, a world of forgotten men: "Garfield, Arthur, Harrison, and Hayes . . . for me they were the lost Americans: their gravely bewhiskered faces mixed, melted, swam together. And they were lost. For who was Garfield, martyred man? Who had heard the casual and familiar tones of Chester Arthur? And where was Harrison? Where was Hayes? Which had the whiskers, which had the burnsides: which was which?"

The problem for Thomas Wolfe was not just one of time. Abraham Lincoln's career lay further back in the past, but Lincoln could never have seemed "lost." Or Andrew Jackson or George Washington either. The fog that settled over the history of the 1870s and 1880s was a fog of dullness and sameness, with no personalities, no drama, no profound causes won and lost. No Lincolns, Jacksons, or Washingtons.

Wolfe was a novelist, not a historian. But the historians have echoed his brooding. They have called the politics of the late nineteenth century the "politics of complacency" or the "politics of inertia." They have defined it as a period of "uncertainty" or "drift." Little wonder that the bewhiskered faces melt into one another.

But the odd fact is that this period of American political history began with an election that was extremely tense and dramatic. From election day in November 1876 down to dawn of March 2—less than two days before a new president had to be inaugurated—no one could be sure who would be sworn into office. It was even possible that no one would be, and that a new election might have to be held. Another possibility was that two men would claim the presidency and that the question might have to be settled by force of arms. Except for the crisis of secession following Lincoln's election in 1860, no four months of American political history have seemed more dramatic to the participants than that winter of 1876–77.

By midnight on election day, November 7, 1876, everything seemed over. In Ohio, the Republican candidate, Rutherford B. Hayes, passed the evening with a few friends and supporters in his home. The telegrams that came in made it clear he had lost. His wife, Lucy, tried to hide her disappointment. But she lost heart and went upstairs to bed, saying she had a headache. Sometime before 1:00 A.M., Hayes joined

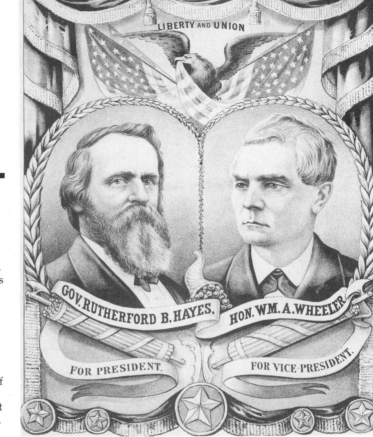

Hayes campaign poster. This engraving, done by the nation's most successful illustrating firm, Currier & Ives, is filled with the political symbolism of the day. The eagle and the axes are taken from the Great Seal of the United States. The slogan, "Liberty and Union," is from a famous speech by Daniel Webster and is meant to recall the Northern cause in the Civil War. The stars appear as they did on military uniforms during the war. And the horn of plenty at the center suggests that Hayes will bring renewed prosperity. In the midst of it all is Hayes, looking candidly at the voter with an expression meant to convey an incorruptible honesty. (Culver Pictures)

her, and they talked for a while the talk of losers: about how defeat was really a good thing, since it meant that their personal lives would be quiet and easy. Their sadness, they told each other, was not that Hayes had lost but that the "poor colored people" of the South would now be abandoned to an administration of Democrats dominated by the ex-rebels of the South. This said, Hayes wrote in his diary, "We soon fell into a refreshing sleep and the affair seemed over."

In New York, the home of the Democratic candidate Samuel J. Tilden, it had rained in the afternoon. But by nightfall, bonfires of celebration lit up the wet streets of lower Manhattan. At Democratic headquarters, the telegrams came in from state after state, promising victory. The politicians all knew the formula. If they could win the electoral votes of all the old slave states, and carry Tilden's own New York, then they only needed to win any two out of three promising states in the North: Indiana, Connecticut, and New Jersey.

By midnight, the Western Union machines had dotted and dashed the message into party headquarters: The Democrats had almost the whole South. They had New

York by more than they had dared hope for. And they had won in all three of the other Northern states they had needed. Now, even if two Southern states still under federal military "occupation"—South Carolina and Louisiana—were taken from them, they still had won. Tilden's campaign manager, New York Congressman Abram S. Hewitt, stepped onto the wet pavement just before midnight and bought a copy of the leading Republican newspaper, the *New York Tribune*. The headline was short and to the point: TILDEN ELECTED.

At Republican national headquarters in the Fifth Avenue Hotel, everyone except for one clerk had already gone home. A little before midnight, Republican Daniel Sickles, a Union general who had lost a leg at Gettysburg, stumped in, to find only a few gaslights still burning and the clerk putting away the records of defeat. Sickles studied the telegrams. They seemed at first to confirm what the party's chairman, Zach Chandler, had decided an hour or so before, when he gave up and went to his room with a bottle of consoling whiskey.

But Sickles was one of those Republican leaders to whom politics was deeply associated with the war. It was not just because of the Confederacy that men like Sickles had lost legs or arms or had suffered in prison camps. The Democratic party had also been their enemy. Sickles would surrender only when the enemy's victory was absolutely certain. As he shuffled the telegrams, they seemed to hold out one tiny hope. If Hayes could win Louisiana, South Carolina, *and* Florida, then he would have exactly the 185 electoral votes needed to claim the presidency.

Sickles knew—as every Republican did—that the vote in these three Southern states had been determined by force and fraud on both sides. Federal marshals and Republican election officials had done whatever they could to throw these states to Hayes. Democratic crowds and local officials had done whatever *they* had to do to keep black voters from the polls. If force and fraud were going to prevail on one side or the other, there might still be time to make sure that these states cast their final electoral votes for Hayes.

But if these three states were going to be "saved," the Republican election officials had to be warned to be alert. Sickles, on no authority, drafted telegrams to the three Republican governors: WITH YOUR STATE SURE FOR HAYES, HE IS ELECTED. HOLD YOUR STATE. He signed the name of Zach Chandler, who was asleep upstairs. But did he dare send the telegrams? Just then, Chester A. Arthur, a New York Republican office-holder, wandered in and offered to share responsibility for the decision. Sickles sent the telegrams, as Arthur went home to a sick wife. Then Sickles also left.

For the next few hours, only a handful of Republican leaders was still awake, and still clinging to their slender hope. Others, like Hayes's Ohio lieutenant, general and Congressman James Garfield, were sleeping the sleep of the defeated, convinced that they had been beaten. Only those were awake who had to be for some reason: William Chandler, a New Hampshire senator, was on a train from his home state to New York. About dawn, he called at the party headquarters to find only the clerk, who gave him the news of Hayes's apparent defeat. Another wakeful Republican was John Reid, who had been at work all night on the dawn edition of the *New York Times*. Reid had been a prisoner during the war, at a Confederate camp of horror known as Libby Prison in Virginia. Like Sickles, he did not forget. And like Sickles, he regarded the Democrats as the party of slavery and rebellion. Reid's determination had kept the *Times* from conceding the election to Tilden. The paper's morning edition bravely said: RESULTS STILL UNCERTAIN.

Now Reid rushed into the Fifth Avenue Hotel with a bit of news he thought might be important. He had just received a telegram from Democratic headquarters asking exactly what the *Times* thought the electoral count would be. If the Democrats were themselves not sure of the outcome, maybe there still *was* a chance to pull it out for Hayes.

At headquarters, Reid met William Chandler. Reid told his story, and together the two men decided to try to rouse Zach Chandler. They had to beat on the door for a long time, and when he finally appeared, he was in a nightshirt and was thoroughly befuddled. Sleepily, and probably a little drunk, he told the two men to do whatever was "necessary." Back downstairs, Reid and William Chandler sent out more telegrams. The messages to South Carolina, Florida, and Louisiana were about the same as Sickles had sent earlier: CAN YOU HOLD YOUR STATE?

Some hours later, around midmorning, Zach Chandler roused himself, dressed, and did his arithmetic. Leaving Florida, Louisiana, and South Carolina out, Tilden had certainly carried sixteen states, with a total of 184 electoral votes, just one short of the necessary 185. Hayes had clearly won nineteen states, with a total of 166, 19 short of victory. Tilden's forces were claiming all 19 electoral votes from the three disputed Southern states. (Even Hayes still believed that Tilden had surely won at least one of the three.) In the face of these facts, Zach Chandler did something audacious. He issued a brief and blunt statement saying, "Hayes has 185 votes and is elected."

The Democrats were astounded. Tilden had won a majority of the popular vote— about a quarter of a million more than Hayes, out of the 8 million votes cast. He had a sizable reported majority in Louisiana: around 9,000 votes. And he seemed clearly to have won in Florida. In South Carolina, things were closer. But Tilden could concede South Carolina if he had to.

There was only one chance for the Republicans to snatch the election from Tilden and the Democrats. The small election boards that had to certify election results in South Carolina, Louisiana, and Florida were still controlled by Republicans. And the states had Republican governors. If those officials threw out enough Democratic votes, they might report a victory for Hayes.

As both sides quickly understood, the first step that had to be taken was to complete the official count of the votes in the three disputed states. In this process, the election boards had the legal right to challenge and exclude votes where there had been evidence of fraud or coercion of voters. This meant days and days of taking testimony and reviewing sworn statements. And so both parties sent teams of "observers" to the three Southern state capitals, to make certain that the election officials behaved fairly. It was in this stage of things that something quiet but remarkable began to happen.

As the Republican "observers" went South, they encountered something that surprised them. They found that the Southern elected officials were, above all, professional politicians. And so two sets of men began to come together in New Orleans, Tallahassee, and Columbia (just as they had been doing in Congress increasingly for ten years). These were ex-officers of the Union and of the Confederacy, men who

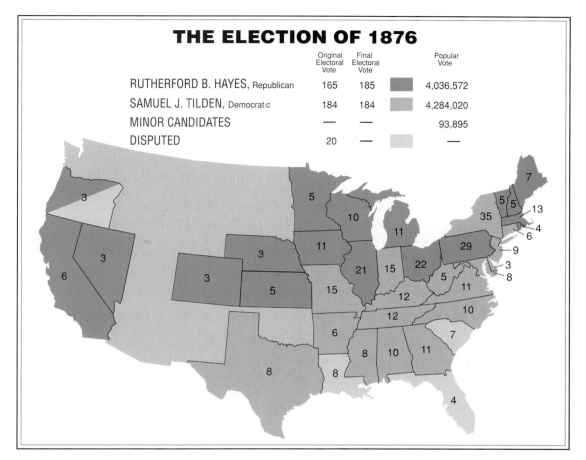

THE ELECTION OF 1876

	Original Electoral Vote	Final Electoral Vote		Popular Vote
RUTHERFORD B. HAYES, Republican	165	185		4,036,572
SAMUEL J. TILDEN, Democratic	184	184		4,284,020
MINOR CANDIDATES	—	—		93,895
DISPUTED	20	—		—

remembered all the violence and the passion of the war, and in whom old hatreds could be roused by a careless remark or discourtesy. But now they could not afford to look backward, for they were politicians and lawyers as well as ex-generals and ex-colonels. This newer role demanded order, courtesy, and decorum. And it was this professional side of their lives that began now to dominate the political maneuvering.

General Garfield, one of the Republican observers in New Orleans, scratched into his diary the story of a day in November when a curious group of men took a day off from the political struggle to take a boat trip down the Mississippi to its mouth. One member of the party was General Sherman, who had been the most feared and hated of all Lincoln's soldiers in the South. The leader of the excursion was the Confederate General P. G. T. Beauregard, who had commanded Southern troops at Shiloh, one of the bitterest battles of the war. Under Beauregard's courtly eye, the visiting Yankees marveled at the river's beauty, at the "vast plantations" and "great orange groves that made the shore beautiful with green and gold." Garfield, who had fought at Shiloh, talked with Beauregard: "He told me, quite fully, the history of the battle in which we were both engaged. It was curious to hear the history of the battle by the rebel commander."

The Democratic observers who went south met "reconciliation" of a different kind from Republican officials in Florida, Louisiana, and South Carolina. (At least they thought they did.) Various Democrats were met with apparent offers from the Republican members of electoral boards to *sell* their state's electoral votes to Tilden. Henry Watterson, a Kentucky Democrat observing in New Orleans, was visited by a man who claimed he had an offer from the two white and two black Republican members of the state's election board. They would sell the election for $250,000—$100,000 each for the two white members, and (as Watterson put it) "$25,000 each for the two niggers."

Watterson apparently did not take the offer seriously. But other Democrats did. Soon coded telegrams were flying back and forth between the three Southern states and Tilden's mansion in New York. They never reached Tilden, or even his campaign manager, Abram Hewitt. Instead, they went to Tilden's nephew, William Pelton. One, sent by New York editor Manton Marble from Florida, was decoded by Pelton to read:

HAVE JUST RECEIVED A PROPOSITION TO HAND OVER AT ANY HOUR REQUIRED TILDEN DECISION OF BOARD AND CERTIFICATE OF GOVERNOR FOR $200,000.

Pelton wired back, PROPOSITION TOO HIGH. Marble responded that he had another offer to help rig the vote for only HALF A HUNDRED BEST UNITED STATES DOCUMENTS—meaning $50,000.

All these "negotiations" failed. And the fact is that Marble and Pelton were probably being tricked into dealing with "intermediaries" who had no control over the votes anyway. As soon as Tilden found out about the telegrams, he put a stop to such dealings on Pelton's part. Marble and Pelton themselves explained that they were convinced the Republicans were stealing the election and were only trying to bribe them into doing the *right* thing. On their side, the visiting Republican observers were offering federal jobs to Republican election officials once their "duty" had been completed.

In the end, both sides concentrated their attention on the legal process of getting the votes counted and certified. No one said so, at least in public, but a kind of informal agreement was gradually being reached by the politicians: The election would be decided on the basis of a bundle of legal technicalities. It would be dealt with by lawyers and by politicians, using the quiet skills and devices of their trade. In all three Southern capitals, the spirit of inducement, legality, and courtesy prevailed. One by one, and in peace, the Republican election boards turned their results over to Republican governors, to be certified and returned to the Republican president of the U.S. Senate. In each case, the result was the same: All nineteen disputed electoral votes in the South were recorded for Hayes. And in each state, Democratic officials refused to recognize the result and sent in contesting results: nineteen electoral votes and the presidency for Tilden.

But the first of many practical compromises had been made: Voters and officials in the three Southern states had in effect agreed to leave the final solution in the hands of officials in Washington. During the month between the election and the official casting of the electoral votes of the states, there was no violence in the South, no

mobs, no hangings or beatings of visiting Yankees, no challenges to the federal troops
that were still posted in the three state capitals.

A curious villain now entered the scene: English grammar—more precisely, the
passive voice. The Constitution contains no more cumbersome and creaking piece of
machinery than the electoral college, an institution that never meets and exists only
as an abstraction every four years. But the framers must have been in an especially
wry frame of mind when they prescribed what was to be done with the electoral votes
once they were cast. According to Article II and the Twelfth Amendment, the electoral
votes "shall be transmitted to the seat of the government of the United States, directed
to the President of the Senate" (who is normally the vice president). Then "the President of the Senate shall, in the presence of the Senate and House of Representatives,
open all the certificates and the votes shall then be counted." There it was, the insidious
passive voice: "the votes shall then be counted."

But by whom? By the president of the Senate? He was a loyal Republican. By
the members of the House and Senate, sitting together? The Democrats outnumbered
the Republicans in Congress as a whole.

The dilemma was acute. And it could not be resolved on any clear constitutional
ground. But such puzzles provide a field day for professional politicians. Where the
rules are not clear, outcomes can be determined by negotiation and compromise. The
talents of bluff, swap, and deal now become paramount. The only question was, could
some sort of compromise be reached before Inauguration Day? If not, the possibilities
would become even more dizzying. President Grant might try to decide who had been
elected, and somehow use the army to enforce his choice. The Democratic House
might name Tilden president and the Republican Senate might name Hayes. Then
whom would the army obey? For men who had lived through secession and Civil
War, such possibilities, though remote, were real enough, especially when some politicians were publicly calling for 100,000 men to come to Washington to settle the matter.

At this point, the personalities and strategies of Hayes and Tilden themselves
became crucial. Would either of them *demand* the presidency and exhort their followers
to action?

On the face of it, Tilden was the least likely leader of any kind of revolutionary
movement. He was a soft-spoken lawyer (but a lawyer whose soft speech had won
him a fortune of around $10 million), a scholarly bachelor who seemed to love the
great library in his Gramercy Park mansion more than the arena of politics. Like Hayes,
he had followed American custom by not campaigning personally. Unlike many politicians in both parties, he had not been in the war. His quiet habits had been reinforced
by a mild stroke he had suffered in 1875. The Republican chairman, Zach Chandler,
had assembled a drawerful of signed statements by various nurses and doctors who
had treated Tilden, statements that claimed that Tilden was physically "sexless." In a
Victorian world where "manliness" was an obsession, there could have been no more
profound suspicion.

During the weeks after the election, Tilden played the role of lawyer and scholar.
He spent a month doing detailed research on the history of presidential elections. He
ignored the pleas of his supporters that he issue a strong statement claiming that he

Samuel J. Tilden. Tilden's face was hardly likely to inspire passionate support among his followers. It did suggest a capacity for worry or concern. But its most striking feature, given the fashions of the day, was what it *lacked*, for Tilden sported no beard, no moustache, not even elaborate sideburns. And even his hair was much more closely cut than most men's in the post–Civil War decades. (Library of Congress)

had won. He forbade any mass meetings in his name. He sent telegram after telegram in which the first word was "Wait," or "Delay," or "Procrastinate." Democratic leaders who came to him looking for instruction, advice, or practical wisdom on how to handle the crisis went away shaking their heads in disappointment.

Tilden gave his blessing to only one practical action. In Oregon, one of the Republican electors had been a postmaster. The Constitution forbade any federal officeholder from serving as an elector. So, working with the Democratic governor of Oregon, Tilden's campaign manager Abram Hewitt devised a scheme to replace the Republican elector with a Democrat: a hole card to play against the inside straight the Republicans were trying to put together in the South. For the rest, Tilden contented himself with quiet, legalistic preparations, making it clear that he wanted no hint of force, fraud, or a mobilized public opinion. In this attitude, Tilden was consistent from beginning to end.

Hayes, on the other hand, was a man divided against himself. In many ways, he was quite different from Tilden. He was a lawyer and a man of some cultivation, but far from being scholarly. He was married and had several children. He had fought for the Union and had even been seriously wounded. He was something of a self-made man and, though very well-to-do, had nothing approaching Tilden's fortune. Above all, Hayes was a man who was deeply committed to being decent and moral. And it was this commitment that established an initial division in his mind about what to do in the disputed election.

On one side, Hayes was convinced that a fair election, with blacks permitted to vote all over the South as the Fifteenth Amendment provided, would certainly have given him a victory. On the other side, however, he had felt all his life that politics was a dirty business, full of fraud and deception. He had managed to avoid being "soiled," and his first reaction to his apparent defeat was to let the election go rather than risk getting involved in a sneaky strategy. His diary recorded his puzzlement.

> November 12—We shall, the fair-minded men of the country will, history will, hold that the Republicans were by fraud, violence, and intimidation, by a nullification of the Fifteenth Amendment, deprived of the victory which they fairly won. But we must, I now think, prepare ourselves to accept the inevitable.

> November 27—A fair election would have given us about forty electoral votes in the South. But we are not to allow our friends to defeat one outrage and fraud by another. There must be nothing crooked on our part. Let Mr. Tilden have the place by violence, intimidation, and fraud, rather than undertake to prevent it by means that will not bear the severest scrutiny.

As late as December 3, Hayes believed that Louisiana would probably be decided for Tilden. But he had gradually come to think more realistically. He was looking for a way to have Congress investigate the Louisiana vote, to throw out Democratic ballots: "Should not the whole case be gone into?" (But when Louisiana finally went Republican, Hayes steadfastly maintained that Congress had no *right* to investigate the vote in any state.)

Two days later, a group of Republicans who had been in New Orleans came to Columbus to assure Hayes that he had won Louisiana fairly, without bribery or trickery. The assurances were bland and pious, and Hayes was a little suspicious. He went around the room asking each man in turn to promise that the result had been "lawful" and "honest." Congratulations began to pour in by telegram and letter. Hayes began to feel more "presidential." He would act, he wrote in his diary, "as Washington would have acted under similar circumstances." From this point onward, he made it clear to his supporters that they were free to make strategies (honest ones, of course) and pursue them in a concerted effort to win the presidency by political means as well as legal. In contrast to Tilden, Hayes gave his party an important advantage. The question was, how could they use it?

Hayes's men began to work on a strategy. The Congress whose authority would last until inauguration day in March was divided. In the Senate, the Republican majority was 46 to 29. In the House, the Democrats held the majority: 181 Democrats, 107 Republicans, and 3 who called themselves independents. If 36 Southern Democrats could somehow be persuaded to break with their party in the House and vote with the Republicans, then Hayes could become president with the consent of both houses of Congress.

The idea was bizarre. Why would Southern Democrats suddenly forsake the hatreds of a generation and help elect a Union general as their president? But against the apparent absurdity of such a notion, Hayes and his strategists could weigh an increasing number of very tempting facts.

First, soon after the election stalemate became clear, Hayes began to be visited by Southern politicians and journalists assuring him of their "good will." They claimed to represent large numbers of Southern political and business leaders.

Second, a plain majority of Republicans were tired of Reconstruction and convinced that it had ended in corruption and failure. Many Southerners understood this. So a congressman from Mississippi or Tennessee might well be ready to make peace with a changed Republican party.

Third, the Southerners made it clear in everything they said and did that their main concern was to put an end to Reconstruction in the South: to get rid of the hated "carpetbagger" governments that still claimed to rule South Carolina and Louisiana; to see the Union soldiers taken out of the Southern capitals and never returned; and to be free to "handle the color problem" their own way. This goal was much more important to them than the question of who had won the presidency.

Fourth, the Republicans remembered all too well that before 1860, the South had been anything but "solid" for the Democrats. There had been a vigorous opposition party there until 1850, led by the same sorts of urban, national-minded businessmen who had now become the backbone of the Republican party in the North. A tantalizing vision began to form in Hayes's mind: Maybe a real Republican party could be built in states like Tennessee, Texas, and Arkansas.

But what did Hayes and his supporters have to offer? The answers to this question provided the basis for one of the most famous attempted bargains in American history: the Compromise of 1877.

The bargainers for Hayes were initially a group of journalists and newspaper publishers, headed by three men who were convinced that they might be real kingmakers: William Henry Smith, an old friend of Hayes and the head of the Western Associated Press; Confederate colonel and ex-Whig William Kellar, a Memphis publisher; and Henry Van Ness Boynton, who was the Washington correspondent of a Cincinnati newspaper. With Hayes's apparent blessing, these men began to cultivate contacts with Southern politicians and to work out—or to think they were working out—a monumental deal.

On his side, Hayes would promise to order federal troops in the South to their barracks and keep them there. He would recognize Democratic governors and state legislatures in the "unredeemed" states of Louisiana and South Carolina. And he would appoint at least one Southerner to his cabinet.

On their side, the Southerners would quietly accept the Republican count of the contested ballots from Louisiana, Florida, and South Carolina, and they would "promise" that African Americans in the South would be given their political and civil rights as the constitutional amendments required.

The difficulty with the deal, taken this far, was that it offered nothing to the Southerners that Tilden would not also give them. He would withdraw the troops. He would recognize Democratic governments everywhere. He would appoint Southerners to the cabinet.

Something more was needed.

The Southern politicians were talking a good deal about "internal improvements": federal money for reopening harbors that had been ruined during the war, for repairing wrecked levees on the Mississippi that had left 28 million acres of prime cotton land exposed to vicious floods. For sixteen years, the Northern states had sucked at the federal treasury. Now, with the South back in the Union, would it get its share? Would the difference be made up? Would the old Confederate states be "reconstructed" in a way their white leaders wanted: with expensive road, harbor, and flood control projects paid for in Yankee dollars? During the war, the North had even begun a railroad to the Pacific, with more than $100 million worth of federal government support—a sum greater than all the federal expenditures for transportation facilities before 1860 combined. Was it now to be the South's turn?

Here Hayes's strategists had a card worth playing. Tilden and the Democratic party were strongly opposed to spending federal money for internal improvements—and had been since the days of Thomas Jefferson. The Republicans, on the other hand, had an impressive record of opening the federal treasury for improvements. And so Boynton, Kellar, and Smith began to propose that Hayes commit himself to a strong program of federal projects of construction and reconstruction in the South. This, they believed, would lure in the thirty-six Southern congressmen they needed.

The confidence of the negotiators was high because they had a specific project in mind: the railroad to the Pacific that had long been a dream of many Southerners. It so happened that one of the most restless railroad promoters in the nation, Thomas Scott, vice president of the powerful Pennsylvania Railroad system, had already secured a land grant of 16 million acres for building a road from Texas to the West Coast. Companies had already been formed to promote a system of branch lines connecting Fort Worth to New Orleans, Vicksburg, Memphis, and St. Louis. (In fact, William Kellar was an officer of one of these companies. And numerous other Southern politicians were officers and board members of the companies.)

Thomas Scott had built a huge reputation as a successful lobbyist. Hayes's journalist friends were awed by the possibility that they might set Scott's forces in motion, divide the Democrats, and make Hayes president with little further ado.

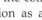

What Hayes understood but his negotiators did not was that the Republicans themselves were no more "solid" than the Democrats. Grant had told his cabinet that he believed Tilden had won. A key Republican senator, Roscoe Conkling of New York, had never supported Hayes. And there were the Republican senators and congressmen from the South—"carpetbaggers" all—whose careers would be ruined if Hayes came in as a result of a bargain with the South. The Republican majority in the Senate was slender. If six men refused to support Hayes, the Senate would be lost. Paradoxically, all the Republican efforts to win the Democratic House would then be defeated in the Senate they supposedly controlled.

And so the bargainers bargained, and Hayes's forces worried about whether they could keep the Republican senators in line. But meanwhile, a quiet process had been going forward that would eventually decide who was to be president. During the first two weeks of December, both houses of Congress had passed motions to create special committees to study the problem of the election. From the House came four Democrats—including Tilden's manager, Hewitt—and three Republicans. From the Senate came a committee of four Republicans and three Democrats.

Hayes's path to the presidency. In the cartoonist's view of things, Hayes had a very difficult acrobatic feat to perform before he could mount the presidential throne. He has come this far only by walking on the bayonets of the federal troops still in the South. His balance pole has the corruptions of "Grantism" at one end and the weight of his own electoral minority at the other. And the uncomfortable chair he is trying to reach is held together only by cannon and balls, supported by very doleful-looking dogs. (Library of Congress)

From the middle of December to the middle of January the two committees hammered away at their problem, sometimes meeting together and sometimes separately. Their votes were usually along party lines, and it was clear to all of them that they would have to devise a scheme they could all support, or no scheme at all.

What gradually emerged from these committee meetings was the idea of handing the question of the election over to a special body, an Electoral Commission. The committees proposed plan after plan, but what finally won their approval was a cumbersome idea that would, in effect, leave the decision up to one man whose identity could only be guessed at. On January 15, the committees agreed to propose an Electoral Commission made up of five members of the House, five senators, and five Supreme Court justices. The House, clearly, would send three Democrats and two Republicans. The Senate would balance off with three Republicans and two Democrats. The committees chose two Supreme Court justices whose past records were clearly Republican and two others with equally clear Democratic loyalties. These four justices were to agree on which remaining member of the Court was to be the fifteenth member of the commission—the deciding vote.

Perhaps the most important feature of the proposal was that the commission's findings would be final unless *both* houses of Congress rejected them. In effect, the House and Senate were about to surrender their separate power over the decision. Hayes was upset. Tilden was as close to anger as he came during the entire crisis. But the members of Congress were calm. The politicians in Congress, professionals all, understood that whoever became president now would come in with the weakest possible mandate. The system of power would tilt away from the presidency and back toward Congress, where it had firmly rested during the generation before the Civil War. Control over budgets, patronage appointments, and policy would lie with the senators and the congressmen, not with either Tilden or Hayes. It had simply become more important to name *a* president peacefully than to name any one man.

For the professional politicians, the important thing was to be able to pursue political interests in an atmosphere of compromise and customary horse trading. To win this, they were prepared to leave the question of the presidency to fate. (At one point, the House and Senate committees had strongly favored letting the fifteenth member of the electoral commission be chosen by *lot!*)

This attitude became sharply clear when Hewitt went up to New York to explain the proposal to Tilden. Tilden complained that it was a bit late in the day for the Democrats in Congress to consult him. Hewitt's reply was short, but it spoke volumes about the way Congress had begun to look at the presidency: "They do not consult you," he said. "They are public men with their own responsibilities."

Of course, each side could still hope to win, even if the question had been handed over to fate. And the Democrats' hopes were probably higher.

Everyone supposed that the fifth justice, and deciding vote, would be Justice David Davis, who called himself an independent but leaned toward the Democratic side. Then, just as the electoral commission was being passed by Congress, came astounding news from Illinois, Davis's home state. The Illinois legislature had just elected him to the Senate. He would resign from the Court and refuse to serve on the electoral commission. (Ironically, Davis had been elected to the Senate with over-whelming Democratic support. Neither Tilden nor his supporters had paid any attention, even though they knew that Davis, their best hope for the deciding vote, was a candidate.)

Now the four justices did their duty. They named the least partisan of the remaining justices, Joseph Bradley of New Jersey. Bradley was a Republican, but he had a reputation for fairness.

~≈⁊

The electoral commission was, in essence, a judicial body. It even held its sessions in the chamber normally occupied by the Supreme Court. Both parties hired the most talented and famous lawyers they could find. The lawyers presented arguments that lasted day after day on each of the disputed states.

A cynical observer might have supposed that everyone except Bradley would simply vote along party lines, and that it would be simpler for that one justice to announce *his* decision. But the commission did not function that way. The arguments were learned. The galleries of the courtroom were crowded to overflowing with the rich, the famous, and the powerful. The commission's members kept an anxious watch over each other. Bradley kept a scrupulous silence.

The first state to be considered was Florida, and the first question was technical but all-important. Congress had left the commission itself to decide one key question: Could the commission investigate the *people's* voting in the contested states? Or were its powers confined to examining the procedures by which the *electoral* votes had been arrived at and certified? The Democrats, of course, wanted a full inquiry into what had happened in Florida, South Carolina, and Louisiana on election day. The Republicans wanted to examine only what had happened after the election.

On February 6 and 7, after four days of public arguments, the commission met in secret to decide the case of Florida. One by one the members read their opinions—for seven hours on the first day, and five more on the second. One after another, they voted on party lines, until the Republicans and Democrats each had seven votes. Finally, it was Bradley's turn. Garfield, who was a member of the commission, wrote in his diary, "All were intent, because B. held the casting vote. . . . All were making a manifest effort to appear unconcerned."

Bradley made this crucial ruling: The commission could not investigate the actual voting. It could only determine whether all legal rules had been followed in the certifying and casting of the state's vote in the electoral college. Two days later, the commission ruled that Florida's Republicans *had* followed the rules, and that the votes of the state would go to Hayes.

There was less than a month to go before the scheduled inauguration of a new president. One by one, the commission took up the states in question. One by one, they decided each case for Hayes. Even Hewitt's Oregon ace in the hole failed. The commission simply ruled that the Democratic elector from Oregon had been appointed through a faulty procedure, and that Hayes was entitled to all three Oregon votes. Every vote was the same: Eight for Hayes, seven for Tilden, with Justice Bradley casting every tie-breaking vote.

～♊

The game was up. But there were two political instincts still alive that wanted to keep it going until the bitter end. One was the instinct of pure partisanship, best put by a Tilden adviser: "God damn them, they will beat us and elect Hayes, but we shall give them all the trouble we can."

The second and more practical instinct was Southern. It was clear that Hayes would win. But it was equally clear that he would like to win gracefully and come into office on a wave of good will that was as truly national as possible. This opened a tactical possibility. If the Democratic House could delay by filibuster and adjournment until the very dawn of inauguration day, then Hayes would be kept on tenterhooks, practically imprisoned out in Columbus, unable to adopt the grand style of the president-elect, unable to make the fine speeches calling for national unity. Perhaps some practical concessions could still be won.

Now, *after* the decision had been made, the Democrats in the House began to reject the commission's findings. It made no practical difference, for the Senate naturally voted to accept them all. But the House Democrats began a war of nerves, adjourning from day to day. In corridors and in the hotel suites of senators and congressmen around Washington, Southern politicians and Hayes's spokesmen began to deal and trade.

Finally, on February 26, a conference took place of a type that Hayes's journalist-strategists had dreamed of in early January. At Wormsley's Hotel, five Ohioans close to Hayes met with four Southerners who spoke for the Democratic parties of Louisiana and South Carolina. A curious bargain was struck. Hayes's people made general commitments on his behalf: that there would be a Southerner in the cabinet, that the president would be "liberal" on the question of internal improvements in the South. The Southerners made promises that were equally vague, especially that the political and civil rights of the African Americans in the South would be protected by the Democrats, once they were granted "home rule." Hayes's spokesmen then made it clear that they would return the army to its barracks and that they would allow the Republican governments in Louisiana and South Carolina to fall and would recognize Democratic governors there.

(The Texas and Pacific railroad scheme was not mentioned. Tom Scott had already presented his request for a subsidy to Congress, and the total bill was too high—a staggering $200 million. The plan died in committee, with two of Hayes's closest supporters voting against it. It would have to wait for a new Congress, where it had no real chance.)

Here was the most famous back-room deal in the political history of the United States. It was known for generations as the bargain that put an end to Reconstruction and preserved the political stability of the nation. But as a bargain, it was meaningless. Hayes had already decided to confine the army to its barracks in the South. Indeed, Grant had already drawn up an order making this last "magnanimous" gesture to the South. Hayes had already decided on a Southerner for the cabinet, and the politicians all knew it. The Southern Democrats' promise to "protect" black rights could be believed by only the most absurdly naive—though Hayes stubbornly chose to believe it, since it was the only real alternative to thinking of himself as a traitor to the memories of Lincoln, the war, and the crusade against slavery.

Then what were nine experienced, tough, and even cynical men doing in that hotel room? Why were they sealing a bargain that exchanged nothing for nothing? And why did their deal become monumentally famous overnight and for a century afterward?

The answer is that they were doing what their careers required. They were professional politicians, all. Hayes's representatives hoped for future cooperation from Southern Democrats in the House and Senate. To get it, the new administration had to keep up the appearance of being approachable and ready to compromise. The Southern Democrats, on their side, needed to convince their supporters back home that they had not simply knuckled under, that they had shrewdly won last-minute concessions from the victorious Republicans. They had done their job and had, by a spectacular bluff, achieved "home rule" for the South. Or so they wanted it to appear, no matter what the realities were.

For the next five days, the Democrats in the House walked a tightrope. They put up enough opposition to delay the completion of the official count of the electoral votes to the last minute. But they moved along just fast enough to make it clear that the count could be finished on time. They manufactured an atmosphere of crisis that

Philadelphia centennial. Somewhat ironically, in light of the stalemated election of that year, 1876 was the centennial year of the Declaration of Independence. The center of national celebration was a great fair, or exposition, in Philadelphia, where independence had been proclaimed. This crowd is waiting patiently for the doors to open on the first day of the exposition, watched over by the ever-present eagles that were such a favorite symbol of the day. (Culver Pictures)

allowed their supporters to believe that they had held out to the last, used every weapon, fought every battle, and lost only to superior force. In fact, they held out until dawn on March 2, when Hayes was finally declared the winner. But the struggle, like the bargain at Wormsley's Hotel, was by now more show than reality. Hayes was president. Reconstruction was ended. But the real victor was politics. What had been restored was not so much the Union, but a "normal" political practice, in which the arts of the professionals mattered much more than any ideological commitment to policies or programs.

GOVERNMENT IN AN AGE OF INDUSTRIAL CAPITALISM

The political maneuvers and compromises of 1876 and 1877 preserved the Republican control of the presidency, which already had lasted for sixteen critical years. When the Civil War had ended and Abraham Lincoln was assassinated, the Republican party was wracked by internal dissent and beset by a very vigorous Democratic opposition. In 1868, the candidacy of Ulysses S. Grant had brought the party into harmony—at least during the election. Grant's majority of the popular vote was only 600,000, and that majority was made up of the votes of free blacks who cast their ballots under the protection of Union troops still in the South. But the Republican electoral majority was still an impressive 214–80. Four years later, the Democrats ran newspaper editor Horace Greeley, who died between Election Day and the official counting of the votes of the electoral college. Even though one wing of the Republican party, calling themselves Liberal Republicans, bolted and supported Greeley, Grant won another smashing victory, 286–66. The president and his party seemed to be riding very high indeed.

So did their policies—the three constitutional amendments giving African Americans freedom, citizenship, and the right to vote; civil rights acts and strong measures to enforce them; continuing Republican control of several state governments in the South; and high tariffs and other subsidies for business, industry, and railroads in the North.

But four years later, when the 1876 campaign opened, Grant could not even win the nomination of his party for a third term, though he badly wanted it. And both parties nominated candidates who pledged to *end* Reconstruction. Something profound had happened, something that would affect not only Grant's career, and not only the 1876 election, but that would shape the history of American politics for a generation. The Republican party, which had begun as a movement with a strong sense of ideological mission, had become a "normal" American party, less concerned with ideology and mission than with elections and offices. In fact, it had suddenly become a party that was difficult to distinguish from the Democratic party. For the next quarter of a century, the two parties would struggle for control of the presidency, Congress, and state governments. But the contest between them would be one that offered voters no real choice between differing policies or programs.

Of course, the Republican party had always had its political side. Many of its leaders, including Lincoln, had been professional politicians, with careers that linked them to the Whig party of the 1840s. But during the Civil War and Reconstruction, the party professionals had driven to power with a definite program. They might differ among themselves in degree, some more radical than others. But there had been something to be radical *about*. After Grant's presidency, there was simply no Republican position on which any politician could have taken a radical stance, even if he had wanted to.

The Slide from Ideology

THE GRANT SCANDALS   Signals of the change had begun to emerge during Grant's administration. Perhaps the clearest sign was the revelation of a string of corrupt deals that reached into the White House itself. Grant had maintained a public friendship with two of the most notorious speculators in the United States, Jay Gould and Jim Fisk. During 1869 they staged a daring attempt to corner gold—that is, to buy it up—driving its price higher and higher (and the price of corporate stocks correspondingly lower). The solution would have been simple. The president could have begun to sell government gold, flooding the market and bringing the price down. But Grant held off, convincing many people that he was part of the cornering strategy. Only a panicky day on the stock market, known as "Black Friday," in September 1869, finally forced Grant's hand.

Then in 1873 came clearer proof of corruption in the administration—though none of the proofs ever touched Grant directly. The Union Pacific Railroad, which had heavy federal subsidies, had been involved for years in a fraudulent arrangement with a construction company known as Crédit Mobilier. Crédit Mobilier was owned by a number of financiers who also owned stock in the Union Pacific. They arranged for contracts between the railroad and the construction company that simply milked the railroad. Since they owned a minority of the shares of Union Pacific, and almost all of Crédit Mobilier, the financiers

were the clear winners. The losers were the federal government and the other stockholders of the railroad.

One of the officers of Crédit Mobilier was a congressman from Massachusetts, Oakes Ames. He began to peddle Crédit Mobilier stock to his colleagues in the House at giveaway prices, buying their support. Among those who took the bribes was Grant's vice president, Schuyler Colfax.

Then, a few months later, another scandal broke. A ring of whiskey distillers had been cheating the government of tax money by submitting false reports. The distillers had bought off several politicians by making large contributions to their state organizations. They had even involved Grant's own private secretary, Orville Babcock.

Everyone seemed to be on the take. New scandals in one cabinet department after another were revealed in the press. And because the Republicans controlled Washington, they were most deeply damaged.

THE STALWARTS   A second sign of change in the Republican party was the rise of leaders in state organizations whose sole interest in politics seemed to be office and power, and for whom political ideas were a nuisance or a joke. Matt Quay in Pennsylvania, Nelson Aldrich in Rhode Island, and Mark Hanna in Ohio were typical. (The Republicans called such men "Stalwarts.") They controlled tightly disciplined party organizations in their states. These organizations in turn controlled the state legislatures. And the state legislatures elected United States senators. So the Senate became the key to and the reward of power.

From the Senate, party leaders managed patronage appointments at all levels and kept watch over federal appropriations for "internal improvements" that might benefit their supporters and contributors back home. To such men, the notion that political parties ought to have a mission or purpose higher than power belonged to the old days of the Civil War. One of the most powerful Republican senators, Roscoe Conkling, spoke for them all—Republicans and Democrats alike—when he said, "Parties are not built by deportment, or by ladies' magazines, or gush."

THE MUGWUMPS A third signal that the Republican party had undergone a profound change was the split that developed in it in 1872. Worried about corruption in Grant's administration, a group of Republican politicians met in a separate convention to nominate their own candidate and write their own platform. They called themselves Liberal Republicans, and they were led by high-minded reformers, journalists, and scholars. Their most prominent member was the old radical, Charles Sumner, who now wanted a quick end to Reconstruction, which he felt Grant had transformed into a party-building machine.

Sumner and the other Liberals had, in reality, only one common belief: Government ought to be "clean"—controlled not by party patronage but by a civil service system that would make it immune to influence and bribery. They nominated Horace Greeley, the old fire-eating editor of the *New York Tribune*. The Democratic convention also endorsed Greeley.

The movement failed. Greeley won in only a handful of states. But the emergence of the Liberal Republicans put a marked stamp on presidential politics for the next twenty years. They were independents without a mass base or party organization. In fact, the leaders of the two main parties caricatured the reformers as "Mugwumps"—a curious sort of political animal, straddling a fence, with its face (or "mug") on one side and its rump (or "wump") on the other. But the Mugwump politicians of the 1870s and 1880s were men of considerable influence. Through reformist editors like E. L. Godkin of the *Nation*, they controlled important magazines and newspapers. Their leaders included men like Charles Francis Adams, who had been Lincoln's

ambassador to Great Britain. And they could reach an important segment of the Republican elite through books like *Chapters of Erie*, exposing railroad mismanagement and political corruption, written by Adams's brilliant sons, Henry and Charles Francis, Jr.

Mugwump independence was a threat to Republicans, a promise to Democrats. It pushed both political parties toward a consistent policy of nominating a special kind of presidential candidate: a man of supposedly spotless moral character and record, who could promise the electorate "good government." The politicos in effect weakened their chances of personally holding the presidency, unless they might come in the side door, through the vice presidency. In return, they maintained control over the Senate, the party machinery, and the all-important system of patronage appointments.

In this respect, the two parties became mirror images of each other. There were some differences during the 1870s and 1880s. The Democrats came to control a solid base in the South, the Republicans in the Middle West. Republicans appealed more to Protestant, native-born Americans, the Democrats to urban Catholic immigrants. The Republicans consistently nominated Union officers as presidential candidates. The Democrats almost always ran governors of New York, certain that that state held the key to their political fortunes.

But underneath these differences lay a crucial sameness. Both parties were very conscious of the need for organization, from the ward and precinct level up to the Senate. Both were acutely sensitive to the need for money to mobilize more and more voters. Both succeeded in mustering larger voter turnouts than in the pre–Civil War period. At the presidential level, elections became desperate struggles to win a slim victory. In fact, only one president between 1872 and 1896 won the office with a majority of the popular vote. And this forced both parties into a struggle for swing voters. Democrats and Republicans both tried to occupy a noncontroversial center on major issues at election time, so both had to avoid any position that might generate any sort of division in party ranks.

The Powerless Presidents

The net result of all these political factors was to make the presidency an office for men who did not control their own parties and had not been elected on any sort of program they might press through Congress, men whose position was almost that of a figurehead. They might have very strong personal character, as several of them did, but in political terms their situation was almost impossible. They entered office to find all the important positions in their administration already sold to win the nomination or the election, all the important legislation controlled by the Senate leadership, and Congress usually divided between a Democratic House and a Republican Senate.

The grave questions posed by industrialization could hardly find their way onto the political stage, where the only issue seemed to be control of the government itself. Politics had become a kind of serpent, devouring itself, concerned not with economic and social questions, or even questions of diplomacy and war, but only with the political process. Government had become its own object. A twentieth-century president, Calvin Coolidge, once remarked, "The business of America is business." Any of his predecessors from the 1870s and 1880s could aptly have said that the politics of America was politics.

HAYES VS. HIS OWN PARTY Soon after his election in 1876, Rutherford B. Hayes announced that he would not run for another term. This, taken together with the way he had won, made

him almost powerless. When the Democrats won the Senate in 1878, the administration was even further weakened. Hayes did end Reconstruction—which the Democratic Congress would have done anyway, through its control over appropriations for the military. But for the rest, he confined himself to trying to make decent appointments and to institute a merit system of civil service in some of the federal departments, particularly in the astonishingly corrupt Post Office and Treasury.

In fact, Hayes's worst enemies turned out to be not Democrats but the Republican party leaders. The party was divided into the Stalwarts, headed by Conkling, and the "Half-Breeds," who were very much like the Stalwarts but wanted a few concessions to the small "good-government" Mugwump wing of the party. The Half-Breeds were led by a curiously charismatic senator from Maine, James G. Blaine, whose career had been besmirched by the revelation of railroad fraud. Blaine had written several letters to a colleague in corruption named Mulligan, letters that often ended "Burn this letter!"—an instruction that Mulligan did not obey. For Conkling and Blaine and their followers, Hayes's concern for clean government and for appointments based on merit were the worst kind of nuisance.

The president vainly attempted to get an appropriation through Congress to fund the modest Civil Service Commission that had been created during the Grant administration. Finally, in frustration, Hayes removed two of Conkling's New York supporters, Alonzo B. Cornell and Chester A. Arthur, from their lucrative federal offices. Conkling fought back by persuading the Senate not to approve replacements for the two men. Hayes could do nothing but submit name after name, waiting for the Senate to turn each of them down, until finally even the senators grew weary and allowed two names to pass.

1880: GARFIELD AND ARTHUR When the Republicans met to choose a nominee in 1880, Conkling and his Stalwart faction supported

George Washington Plunkitt

In the late nineteenth century, especially in major cities, elections turned not on issues or even on the personalities of candidates, but on the careful efforts of men whose lives were devoted to two things: getting out the vote on election day and distributing patronage and favors between elections. The most famous political organization in the United States was Tammany Hall, the Democratic "machine" in New York City.

The Tammany Society was founded in 1789 as a social club for businessmen and bankers. But by the mid-nineteenth century, Tammany had become the city's Democratic party organization. It controlled the elections of the city's aldermen and representatives to the state legislature. It managed the appointments of the city's bureaucrats. It beat back periodic efforts to reform the city government. And in the process, it profited. Tammany's leaders became rich. Some of them, like the infamous "boss" William Marcy Tweed, went to prison for bribery or theft.

But a more typical Tammany leader was George Washington Plunkitt. He was born in 1842 in an Irish shantytown in Manhattan. He worked his way up in the organization to become an alderman, a state legislator, and a state senator. He died at eighty, a rich man—mostly from investments in real estate. He helped finance construction of the George Washington Bridge and the American Museum of Natural History.

This was the real Plunkitt of Tammany. A man who knew how to turn inside knowledge of politics into shrewd real-estate deals that made him wealthy, but probably never stole anything directly from the public treasury. A man with superb knowledge of the ethnic basis of urban politics, who knew how to organize not just the Irish who were Tammany's original strength but the newer groups of Jews and Italians. A man who knew, above all, how to deliver the many favors his constituents expected.

But there was another Plunkitt, half-fictitious, who fascinated millions of American readers. This Plunkitt was the creation of a journalist named William Riordon, who hung around Plunkitt's "office," a shoeshine stand in the city courthouse, and listened to Plunkitt talk. Riordon then published, in 1905, *Plunkitt of Tammany Hall, a Series of Very Plain Talks on Very Practical Politics*. The book was a masterly blend of cracker-barrel humor, political cynicism, biography, and inside dope. In it, Riordon's readers discovered a man who was a surprising combination of their image of an Irish political hack and their own middle-class moralism.

Plunkitt's "plain talks"—or at least Riordon's version of them—really constituted a book of advice to young men on how to get ahead, how to go from rags to riches in politics. And his rules were unexpectedly familiar to Riordon's middle-class audience. Don't drink, Plunkitt warned, for it takes a clear head to run a political organization. Be loyal to your friends and to the party. Be modest. Dress plainly. Live in the neighborhood where you work. Be absolutely tolerant of ethnic and religious differences. Work hard: The ward boss must be up early and late, taking care of the legitimate needs of the voters. Never steal: There is plenty of opportunity for "honest graft," so no politician ever needs to take money from the public treasury. Don't be befuddled by moralistic abstractions: A young man must learn to "rise above principle" sometimes.

Riordon's achievement—and we will never know how accurately he represented the real Plunkitt—was to weld the prevailing myths of the self-made entrepreneur to the image of the political boss. The result was a charming portrait of a man who wanted his epitaph to be one that could have fitted any rags-to-riches hero of the period: "He seen his opportunities and he took 'em."

Grant. Blaine and his Half-Breeds, with Mug-wump help, were able to deny Grant the nomination for thirty-five ballots, until the convention finally turned to a noncontroversial dark horse, James A. Garfield, a man of pure character, a tried veteran of the House of Representatives from Ohio—and, of course, a former Union officer. The Stalwarts contented themselves with the vice-presidential nomination for the model party professional Chester A. Arthur. The Democrats chose to play dead—or to try to beat the Republicans at their own game. They made the uninspired choice of their own Union general, Winfield Scott Hancock, a man whose military record had created no political following. The result was a Republican victory but a narrow one, in which Garfield and Arthur won 4,454,000 votes as against 4,444,000 for their opponents.

Garfield was a study in rags to riches, a self-made man. He had been born in a log cabin—a real one—and had managed to become a teacher, then a lawyer and a politician. He had served in Congress since the war years and was apparently a man of honesty. His postmaster general, with Garfield's strong support, unearthed a major fraud in the postal service, and the stage seemed set for another struggle between a reasonably clean president and the barons of the Senate. But before the struggle could reach a climax, Garfield was assassinated. On July 2, 1881, after four months in office, he was shot by an obscure, ambitious, and clearly insane man named Charles Guiteau, who shouted as he shot: "I am a Stalwart, and Arthur is president!" Garfield clung to life for three months before Arthur was indeed president. The new chief executive surprised everyone by continuing to press the fraud cases in the Post Office, and by making independent appointments, as though he were trying to live down a career as a consummate spoilsman of the Stalwart faction. He even got a modest civil service law, the Pendleton Act, through Congress in 1883. The law put only about one federal job out of ten on a merit system, but it did allow for future expansion of the number by executive

James A. Garfield. Garfield won the Republican nomination for the presidency in 1880 not because of any groundswell of support among voters but as a compromise designed to prevent the nomination of Grant. Here he is shown as a model political leader of the period, staring into the distance with an expression that is concerned but determined and confident that the future can indeed be conquered. Surely, the photograph suggests, such a man could not have been involved in the Crédit Mobilier scandal, even in a minor way. (Library of Congress)

order. (In fact, it put every future president in the position of being able to appoint supporters to non–civil service jobs, and then, once they were in place, extending the blanket of protection to them so they could not be removed. Through this process, by the 1940s, a bare majority of

Republican poster, 1884. In 1884, after years of trying, Senator James G. Blaine of Maine finally won the Republican presidential nomination. Blaine looks much less fierce here than he was described in a famous speech at the 1876 Republican convention: "Like an armed warrior, like a plumed knight, James G. Blaine marched down the halls of the American Congress and threw his lance full and fair against the brazen foreheads of the defamers of his country and the maligners of her honor." (Culver Pictures)

federal jobs were brought under the Civil Service Act.)

1884: GROVER CLEVELAND Arthur made no one happy, not Stalwarts, Half-Breeds, or Mugwumps. The Republican convention of 1884 simply ignored him, and turned instead to the prince of the Half-Breeds, James G. Blaine. The Mugwumps announced they would not support Blaine if the Democrats were to nominate a "good-government" man, and the Democrats

obliged them by choosing Grover Cleveland, a reform mayor of Buffalo and governor of New York. The resulting campaign was heavily financed on both sides, and consisted mainly of attacks on the personal character of the candidates. For his part, Blaine was vulnerable because of the Mulligan letters, and the Democrats could chant:

> Blaine! Blaine! James G. Blaine,
> Continental liar from the state of Maine!
>   (Burn this letter!)

But Cleveland proved to have an unexpected weak spot. He had accepted responsibility for an illegitimate child in his youth, so his opponents could come back with a chant of their own:

Ma! Ma! Where's my Pa?
Gone to the White House, Ha! Ha! Ha!

In November, Cleveland got the better of the chantings. The election may in fact have been thrown to him at the last minute. Blaine, at a reception in New York City, was called on by a delegation of Protestant ministers. One of them made a brief speech, in which he accused the Democrats of being the party of "Rum, Romanism, and Rebellion." Blaine, who had a Catholic mother, either did not hear the remark or chose to ignore it. But when it became public, he was stuck with it. And this slender bit of chance may have moved enough immigrant and Catholic voters in New York City to swing the election to Cleveland. Almost 10 million men voted, and Cleveland received only about 20,000 more votes than Blaine. New York State could have given either man the necessary electoral votes for a victory.

Grover Cleveland believed staunchly in laissez faire. The government, he thought, should be a minimal institution, whose main purposes were maintaining law and order and conducting foreign policy. He once vetoed a relief bill to aid farmers who had been stricken by drought, with the observation that the people should support the government, but the government should never support the people. He even did what no president before him had done: He actually read the applications that Union veterans submitted to Congress when they asked for special relief and pension legislation. He vetoed hundreds of such requests—to the fury of the congressmen whose constituents' loyalty was heavily dependent on their ability to get such government favors. Congress responded with a bill granting general pensions to *all* disabled veterans—no matter when or how their disability had come

about. Cleveland provoked an even more serious storm by vetoing this law.

The president's laissez-faire attitude even extended to one of the sleeping giants of American politics, the tariff. For twenty years or more, the country had had a high Republican tariff, and a system had been worked out for buying support from agricultural states by putting their products—sugar or wool, for example—on the protected list along with manufactured goods. But Cleveland, in the middle of his administration, went to Congress to ask for substantial reductions in tariffs. He was, among other things, embarrassed by a large surplus in the treasury, a surplus that made it clear no tariff was necessary for revenue. For him, the meaning of the surplus was plain and outweighed all the justifications for a high tariff that scholars might produce: "It is a *condition* that confronts us," he said, "not a theory."

1888: BENJAMIN HARRISON The Democrats in the House managed to push through a bill making some reductions in tariff schedules, but the measure stalled. For the first time in years, the presidential contest coming up in 1888 would have a stateable issue—though a minor one when measured against the more serious questions being posed by industrial development. The Democrats chose Cleveland again. The Republicans turned to Benjamin Harrison of Indiana, who was as unknown as Hayes and Garfield had been, and just as respectable and easy to identify with the cause of clean government. He was the grandson of William Henry Harrison, the Whig president of the 1840s.

But if the parties had a clear issue—high tariffs or low—the voters were not ready with a verdict. Cleveland won the popular vote, though by less than 100,000 out of 10 million. In fact, he was the only presidential candidate of the period to win a clear majority of the total popular vote. But he lost the election. The vote of the electoral college was 233 for Harrison, 168 for Cleveland.

Grover Cleveland. Grover Cleveland, shown here in a studio photograph, was a shortish, heavy man whose political reputation was built entirely on an honest willingness to say no—to both corrupt party organizations like Tammany Hall and small appropriations meant to relieve farmers ruined by drought. The photographer managed to capture some of Cleveland's determination, along with the conventional brave stare into the distance. On the floor is what appears to be a brass spittoon of modest size. (Library of Congress)

Harrison rode into office on a very frail horse. But his Republican Congress behaved as though the party had won a mandate for a great cause.

They set out to write the highest protective tariff law in United States history, and they won. The resulting McKinley tariff—named for its sponsor in the House, William McKinley of Ohio—established a level of protection that satisfied every tariff lobby in the nation. But the initiative had come almost entirely from Congress; Harrison himself was as hamstrung by his lack of control over his party as his predecessors in office had been. In fact, after he left office he complained, "When I came into power, I found that the party managers had taken it all to themselves. I could not name my own Cabinet. They had sold out every place to pay the election expenses." And if that were not enough, he was soon to face a Congress in which his party was crippled. When the results of the congressional elections of 1890 came in, the Republicans had only 88 of the 323 seats in the House.

To some extent, the congressional elections of 1890 may have been a referendum on the McKinley tariff. If it was, the answer was clear: McKinley himself was defeated in his home district, and his political career seemed to be over. But the tariff itself was less the issue than it was the symbol of a range of issues that were struggling to the surface of American political life, issues that focused on the general problem of "monopoly" capitalism and the failure of governments to take any effective measures to control or regulate it. A few Democrats—even some who had supported the tariff where it protected economic interests in their home states—began to play on the problem of monopoly and to argue that the tariff was designed to protect trusts from overseas competition. They hit a responsive chord. The electorate had become increasingly concerned and frustrated over the apparent inability of their political leaders to do anything about the power of the giant corporations over American life.

1892: CLEVELAND AGAIN In the presidential election of 1892, the Republicans ignored the danger signs and renominated Harrison. The Democrats countered with Cleveland. Once again, as in 1888, the two parties' platforms were almost identical—except for the tariff. The Republicans once more promised to maintain the kind of "protection" provided by the McKinley tariff. The Democrats promised tariff reductions. This time, the swing that had been clear in the congressional voting of 1890 bore fruit for the Democrats. Cleveland won almost twice as many electoral votes as Harrison, and almost a 10 percent edge in the popular voting. More important, the Democrats won majorities in both the House and the Senate. For the first time in a generation, they controlled the executive and legislative branches of the federal government.

The result was disappointing to anyone who had voted for a significant change in policies. Cleveland stood more firmly than ever for his laissez-faire policies, his belief that the government should not "support" any of the people by intervening in their economic life in any significant way. Cleveland did try to push a lowering of the tariff rates through Congress, but even here he failed. The Democrats in Congress would give him only about a 10 percent reduction in the average duties that had been voted a few years earlier. On the surface, at least, the Democrats' surge to power had produced little or nothing in the way of an important shift in major government policies.

The Rise of the Populist Party

But there were straws in the political wind suggesting that some sort of challenge to the prevailing political order of things was building toward a climax. The new tariff included the first peacetime income tax in the history of the United States. The rates were mild—2 percent on all incomes over $4,000, a formula that meant a sizable majority of Americans would pay no tax at all. But the income tax had been a clear concession to a new and highly visible element in politics, a movement of protest demanding changes that were, from the point of view of the normal politics of the preceding twenty years, almost revolutionary. The political challenge took its clearest form in the South and the West as an organized movement of farmers, and it finally resulted in the formation of a new political party.

The movement, whose roots went well back into the 1870s, focused on questions of policy on which the major parties had either taken a weak and tentative stand or no stand at all.

THE GRANGE   Farmers during the early 1870s—times of prosperity for most of them—had begun to organize themselves into local chapters of the National Grange of the Patrons of Husbandry. The word *grange* was from a medieval term for a building on a manor where grain was stored. In England, *grange* was a name sometimes given to the farmhouse and buildings of a well-off, "gentleman" farmer. The Americans who first became "Grangers" and "Patrons of Husbandry" were adopting a terminology that suggested farming was in fact a gentleman's occupation. They met primarily for cultural and social purposes, and used a somewhat elaborate secret ritual. (In these respects, they were very much like the early "Knights" of labor; see p. 641.)

But in 1873 the nation entered the most serious depression in its history, and farmers suffered even more than other Americans. They began to join the Grange in massive numbers—800,000 by 1875—and to redefine its purposes. They formed cooperative grain elevators, stores, milk-processing plants, even factories to make farm machinery and stoves—all in the hope of freeing themselves from the grip of what they clearly understood to be "monopolies." Most of all, they turned to politics at the state level, to attack what they felt were the cruel and monopolistic practices of the railroads.

Beginning in 1871, then with even greater success after 1873, the Grangers were able to muster enough votes in the state legislatures of Wisconsin, Illinois, Iowa, and Minnesota to impose rate regulations on railroad companies. (These attempts at regulation were at first endorsed by federal courts, then increasingly struck down. See pp. 547–49.)

The return of prosperity in the late 1870s reduced both the size and the effectiveness of the Granger movement. By 1880 it had lost 700,000 of its 800,000 members, and it would remain small and inconsequential.

THE ALLIANCE MOVEMENT As the 1880s wore on, however, the farmers who raised staple crops—wheat and cotton especially—began to experience a steady and serious drop in the market price for their crops. They began to organize into farmers' alliances. In the plains states, they formed the National Farmers' Alliance. By 1890 the National Alliance had a membership of over 3 million.

In the South, the rise of the Alliance movement created the possibility of the first large-scale collaboration between poor farmers, black and white. A society in which race had been the main way of maintaining social divisions seemed, for a time at least, to be dividing along lines of class and status, rather than along the "color line." Black and white farmers joined parallel alliances, the Colored Farmers' Alliance and the Southern Farmers' Alliance. By the middle of the 1880s the two organizations had over a million members. And the movement continued to grow. By 1890 the Southern Farmers' Alliance claimed over 2 million members, and the Colored Farmers' Alliance more than a million. (Both claims were probably exaggerated. But even if the Colored Farmers' Alliance had only 250,000 or so active members, that was still an astonishing number, since these men faced harassment, threats, and even death from their white neighbors.)

Never before in the history of the South had the pent-up frustrations of so many farmers found organized expression. And never before had political activism posed such an obvious threat to the established order of Southern society. Tom Watson of Georgia, who was one of the most radical and eloquent white political leaders of the farmers' movement, summed up the situation of the farmers in a way that bluntly made class interest more important than race. The "crushing burdens which now oppress both races," he said, could only be overcome if blacks and whites alike took action to win a "similarity of remedy." Calling for "remedies" that would treat black and white people the same way was a serious departure from Southern white traditions. But Georgia voters sent Watson to Congress in 1890, a definite sign that economic hardship might create a solidarity that cut across the color line.

The Alliance movement was even more political than the Grangers had been. The western group ran candidates under its own party label for state and national offices. In the South, the Alliances tried a different tactic: They attempted to gain control of the securely entrenched Democratic party. In fact, in 1890—the year the Republicans suffered their massive defeats in congressional elections—the Alliances managed to win varying degrees of control over eight legislatures in the South and four in the West. From the South came forty congressmen who had been endorsed by the Alliances against conservative Democrats.

During the next two years, the Alliance leaders planned an even more active challenge to the standing political order. They founded a new party, the People's, or Populist, party. In 1892, delegates representing the Alliances, the Knights of Labor, and other antimonopoly groups gathered at an exultant convention in Omaha to write a platform and nominate a candidate to oppose Cleveland and Harrison.

The Populist platform was a radical document, in the sense that it addressed political and economic questions that had been either kept off-stage entirely or dealt with by the federal government in a hesitant and reluctant way. The Populists had three main concerns: public finance, monopoly, and the conduct of politics. They confronted these concerns much more directly than either Republicans or Democrats had been able or willing to do.

CURRENCY AND CREDIT For the Populists, public finance boiled down to two questions: the currency and credit. The federal government, under both Republicans and Democrats, had been pursuing policies that led to a restricted supply of currency, or "tight" money, and to equally restricted credit. Both currency and credit had been eased during the Civil War. The Lincoln administration had printed paper "green-backs"—about $450 million worth. At the end of the war, some $400 million worth were still in circulation. The government had also built up a large debt by selling bonds. Most of the bonds were owned by national banks, which had been allowed to make loans to their customers in return for the bonds, to be held by the banks as their "reserve" to pay off depositors. These two policies had resulted in higher prices and easy credit for most farmers.

After the war, the federal government had decided to keep a fixed amount of greenbacks in circulation but to back them with gold. This policy did not create a currency large enough to feed the tremendous economic expansion of the postwar period. So the volume of money in circulation actually was decreasing in proportion to the size of the economy. In addition, Congress in 1873—in what many Populists saw as the "Crime of '73"—removed the silver dollar from the list of money to be coined.

No one had objected at the time, but over the next twenty years the idea took root that the solution to the currency problem was the "free and unlimited coinage" of silver. Cleveland and all the Republicans were "sound money" men—in effect, gold standard men. And so the Populist plank demanding free and unlimited coinage was a direct challenge to the dominant groups of both major parties.

As for credit, the Populist platform of 1892 included a program that would have moved the federal government much further into the credit system. The platform asked for savings banks operated by the Post Office, to give people an alternative to private banking institutions. And it asked the federal government to create storage warehouses for grain and cotton, where farmers might keep their crops when the market price was low. The scheme would have allowed farmers to receive interest-free loans worth 80 percent of the current market price of the crops while they were in storage.

MONOPOLIES The credit scheme was, when compared with policies then existing, a radical one. But the platform took an even more radical attitude toward the great monopolies the Populists thought were oppressing them. Corporate combinations of all sorts—pools, trusts, holding companies, and mergers—had become a major fact of American life. But Democratic and Republican politicians had responded very little to the growing uneasiness of many of their voters. In a few states, there had been attempts to regulate railroads. But the prevailing attitude of politicians had been one of benign neglect toward, or even support for, corporate growth and integration.

During the late 1880s some members of Congress had recognized the necessity of making at least a token gesture toward controlling corporations. The result had been two laws that seemed to discourage monopolistic practices—one by regulating them, the other by forbidding them.

The first was the Interstate Commerce Act of 1887. This law created an Interstate Commerce Commission, charged with regulating the railroad industry. The commission was, in theory, to make certain that all railroad rates were "reasonable." The railroads were forbidden to create market "pools" or to discriminate among shippers by giving a lower price to some than to others.

The second was the Sherman Antitrust Act of 1890. In its language, the act was an affirmation of the idea that the best economy was one in which there was pure competition. It forbade every "combination" that acted to "restrain" trade, or competition, in interstate commerce.

These two laws had seemed to move in the direction the Populists wanted. But in practice, both turned out to be virtually meaningless. It was clear by 1892 that neither was going to provide an effective check on the power of corporations. And so the Populists wrote their most radical plank to deal with the monopolies they believed oppressed them most: the railroads. They demanded, simply, government ownership of all railroad and telegraph companies. As a challenge to the power of other corporations, the platform proposed that the eight-hour workday be made standard in all industries—though this would have been a marked extension of federal power to regulate private businesses and industries.

Experience had taught the Populists that they had no hope but to try to win control over the political process itself. So their platform included demands for significant reforms to the system. They wanted a secret ballot. They asked for a system of initiative and referendum, through which voters could pass laws or repeal them. And they sought to break the stranglehold of the two major parties over the system by providing that senators be elected directly, instead of by the state legislatures.

To run on this platform, the Populists nominated James B. Weaver, who had been a Democrat before the Civil War, then a Republican, now a Populist. In the election of 1892 Weaver won twenty-two electoral votes, and the Populists won over a million popular votes. About a dozen members of Congress now called themselves Populists.

Defeat of the Populists

The stage seemed set for a mighty contest in 1896 to determine whether the People's party would gain full access to federal power for their reform challenge. The drama was intensified by a depression that began in 1893 and was in some ways the most serious the nation had ever experienced. Well over a hundred railroads and 400 banks failed. Even more important, probably as many as 20 percent of the nation's workers were unemployed—in an era when no programs of relief or unemployment compensation existed. If the Populists could tap the discontent growing out of the depression and add it to the older and still smoldering complaints that had created their party, they might expect to play a profoundly important role in the future of American politics.

On their side, the Republicans had just as much reason to expect victory. The depression was, as usual, blamed on the current administration. The elections of 1894 had seemed to confirm both Populist and Republican hopes. Taken altogether, Populist candidates collected almost 1.5 million votes—a sharp increase over 1892. And the Republicans came out of the election in full control of the House of Representatives, something they had had only twice in the preceding twenty years.

1896: McKINLEY VS. BRYAN So the parties approached 1896: the Republicans confident, the Populists excited, the Democrats divided between those who wanted to nominate another Eastern conservative (as the party had done for a generation) and those who wanted to move South or West, to tap the energies of the Populists.

The Republicans nominated William McKinley, author of the McKinley tariff, who after losing his seat in Congress had become governor of Ohio. Behind McKinley stood the man who was, in effect, the head of the party, Marcus A. Hanna, who would manage to raise somewhere between $4 million and $15 million for the campaign. (No one probably will ever know the full amount, but it is clear that McKinley's run for the presidency was the first "modern" campaign in terms of the dollars spent. Standard Oil alone contributed $300,000—almost as much as the Democrats spent on their entire effort.) For a platform, Hanna and his party decided on even higher tariffs, solid support for the gold standard, and a vague promise of "prosperity." Nothing was said about the problem of the trusts, regulation of railroads, or the income tax.

At the Democratic convention in Chicago, there was nothing but confusion. The party was divided. On one side was a Cleveland faction that was predominantly Eastern, favored gold, and rejected most of the Populist program. On the other side were Southerners and Westerners who demanded the endorsement of free silver and

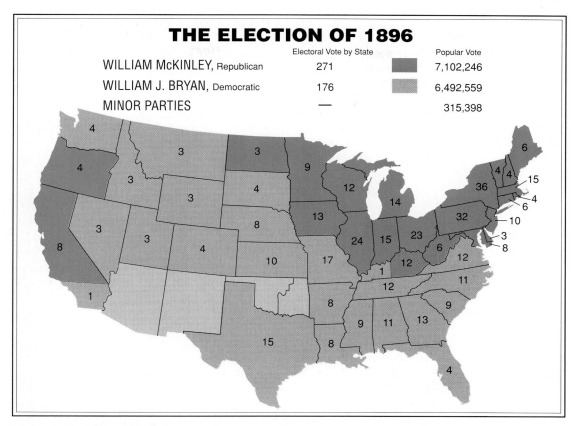

THE ELECTION OF 1896

	Electoral Vote by State		Popular Vote
WILLIAM McKINLEY, Republican	271		7,102,246
WILLIAM J. BRYAN, Democratic	176		6,492,559
MINOR PARTIES	—		315,398

wanted the party to support at least some of the Populist program—the income tax, for example, and a stronger federal attempt to regulate railroads and corporations. This faction wanted, in effect, to repudiate Cleveland, who had led the party into all three presidential elections since 1884.

To settle the question of the Democrats' position on gold, a debate was arranged, with three men speaking for the gold standard and three for "bimetallism." Surely none of the politicians expected the party to resolve such a problem with speeches. But for once they were surprised. The final speaker for silver, William Jennings Bryan, gave such a masterly address that the convention, swept by something approaching political hysteria, nominated him for president the next day.

Bryan's strengths were his words and his voice. He could roll out sentences that schoolchildren would be forced to memorize for decades. He ended his address to the convention with a dramatic challenge to the Republicans, a challenge that attempted to identify free silver with the cause of the common man:

If they dare to come out into the open and defend the gold standard as a good thing, we will fight them to the uttermost. Having behind us the producing masses of this nation and the world, supported by the commercial interests, the laboring interests and the toilers everywhere, we will answer their demand for a gold standard by saying to them: "You shall not press down upon the brow of labor this crown of thorns; you shall not crucify mankind upon a Cross of Gold."

McKinley campaigns (more or less). While his opponent Bryan traveled and spoke more than any candidate ever had before, William McKinley stayed home in Ohio, speaking occasionally from his own front porch to carefully chosen crowds. His was a cautious campaign in which the greatest risk was to put the candidate on a rug covering an unstable wicker basket that substituted for a speaker's "stump." But from the Republican point of view, it all worked splendidly. (Ohio Historical Society)

Bryan was a Nebraskan with only two terms in the House of Representatives to his political credit. But he had managed to steal the party and to steal, in the bargain, one of the main planks of the Populists. The Democrats also endorsed the income tax and railroad regulation. This created a painful dilemma for the Populists. Bryan was almost certain to win every state where a Populist would have had a chance against a traditional Democrat. They seemed to have no option but to endorse him and the principle of "fusion" with the Democrats. And so a majority of Populists voted in their convention to accept Bryan as their candidate, preserving a fiction of independence by choosing Tom Watson of Georgia as their vice-presidential nominee.

Bryan campaigns (more). William Jennings Bryan's strongest political weapon was his ability as a speaker. And his only real hope of victory was to use that skill as often as possible. He traveled and spoke tirelessly but nevertheless failed to carry most of the states he visited. Here in a rare photograph of him in 1896, he is talking to a crowd in Union Square in New York City. (Brown Brothers)

The Democrats' problem was, in part, lack of money—a problem Bryan attempted to offset by traveling almost 20,000 miles and making more than 600 speeches to audiences that finally totaled in the millions. (In this way, Bryan's campaign was as modern as McKinley's. But McKinley stayed at home and campaigned from his front porch. It would be some time yet before a candidate would conduct a race using both money *and* speeches on an enormous scale.)

But money was only part of the problem. Bryan defined the campaign almost from the beginning as a contest between rural and urban Americans. "Burn down your cities," he said, "and leave our farms, and your cities will spring up again as if by magic; but destroy our farms and grass will grow in the streets of every city in this country." The result was that Bryan won little support from urban workers, even from those who were unemployed or embittered. Hanna, on the other hand, had 120 million pamphlets printed in half a dozen languages, aimed specifically at the urban-industrial-immigrant work force.

Bryan, to no one's surprise, carried the South. He also won much of the electoral vote of the Great Plains and the mining states of the Rockies. But he could not carry states where the Granger movement had been popular in the 1870s: Iowa, Wisconsin, Minnesota, or Illinois. He failed in California and Oregon. And, most important, he did not win a single state north of the Ohio River and east of the Mississippi. The cities, including most workers, went for McKinley, gold, and high tariffs.

Twice more Bryan would attempt to lead the Democrats to victory, in 1900 and 1908. But he would fail decisively. And with his failure would go the failure of the Populists as a party. They had staked their political future on Bryan and on fusion, and it had failed. They had mounted a serious challenge to corporate power, to laissez faire, and to the political system. They had cried, in effect, "conspiracy" between government and private wealth. (They had even, some of them, blamed "Jews," but in this their attitudes were no more anti-Semitic than those of the leaders of the two principal parties.) They had won a victory of a kind: The Democratic party would never again be quite the same. But the victory had cost them their chance at national power over the long run. The voters and the system of government had returned a negative answer.

In the wake of the Populist defeat lay another dreamlike possibility, the possibility of political unity among poor Southern farmers, black and white. It was a dream that a clear majority of Southern whites had always rejected, but one that thousands of white and black people in the South had dared to believe in for the first time. Racism, however, not racial or social democracy, triumphed in the South in the 1890s.

As the Southern and the Colored Farmers' Alliances had grown in the 1880s, Democratic politicians had begun to put more and more restrictions on black voting rights. Literacy tests were one method used in many states. Another was the requirement that in order to vote, a man had to prove he had paid a per capita tax known as a poll tax—a flat dollar amount each year. But many blacks did pay the poll tax, and an increasing number every year were literate. So as the Populist movement neared its climax, the conservative Democratic establishment in the South responded with sterner measures.

Mississippi took the lead in 1890 with a provision that every voter had to be able not only to read but to "interpret" the state's constitution. And it was up to the supervisors at the polling place—who were always white—to decide whether the voter's "interpretation" was acceptable. Black college graduates were turned away, and watched while white men who had not finished elementary school were allowed to vote. The Mississippi law became a model for other Southern states. In states like South Carolina, black voting fell from about 70 percent of eligible voters in 1880 to about 10 percent in the election of 1896.

But white voters knew perfectly well that a strategy like this could be used to prevent poor whites from voting—especially if they were known to be Alliancemen or Populists. The question for the Democratic party regulars was how to devise a voting statute that would drive a wedge between blacks and whites and still get around the Fifteenth Amendment, which forbade any state to deny a citizen the right to vote because he was black or had once been a slave. On this delicate question, Louisiana took the lead. In 1898 the state's Democratic party invited the defeated white Populists back into the fold with a voting-rights law built around the first "grandfather clause." According to this law, if a man—literate or not—could prove that either of his grandfathers had ever voted, then he could vote. Since almost every black's grandfather had been a slave, the law clearly favored whites and denied all but a few blacks the vote.

The net effect of the threat that the Southern and the Colored Farmers' Alliances had posed to the political supremacy of the Southern white elite was, in the end, that racism in the South became more intense and vicious. The white establishment rose up in full wrath against the threat. And many white Populists, embittered by failure and lured on by demagogic politicians, came out of the experience more deeply committed than ever to white supremacy. It is no coincidence that the decade of Populist and Alliance agitation in the South was the same decade in which the ultimate expression of racism—lynching—reached terrifying heights. A mass lynching helped bring the Colored Farmers' Alliance to an end. In 1891 some black cotton pickers in western Tennessee carried out a strike during the picking season. Like all seasonal field workers, they had only one powerful weapon: to refuse to work during the short, crucial period when the crop was ready. For the white land-owners of the area, this was the ultimate challenge to the system of racial exploitation that had replaced slavery, and they responded with great force. A "posse" was sworn in to hunt down the strikers. They resisted, and in the end fifteen blacks were hanged.

During the rest of the 1890s about a hundred blacks were hanged every year. (These were the *known* lynchings; many other blacks may have perished deep in woods or swamps, silently and without trace.) The victims were almost always male, and their bodies were often mutilated, before and after their deaths. Whatever promise of a new kind of social and racial democracy Populism had held, for the South or for the nation as a whole, it had failed. And the federal courts were making that failure even more ringing and definite.

A Judicial Defense of Privilege

In the courts, particularly in the Supreme Court, the new industrial capitalism found an endorsement that was sure and powerful.

The Constitution did not mention corporations, or labor unions, or trusts. It had been drawn up by men who would hardly have been able to imagine the scale of Standard Oil or of Andrew Carnegie's steel works, and certainly not the billion-dollar realities of the great railroad corporations. And the decisions of the courts affecting corporations during the pre–Civil War period had been about small bridge companies or shipping companies—or even incorporated colleges.

The question now was, how could the Constitution be adapted to the astonishing industrial and corporate developments of the second half of the nineteenth century? What powers did state and local governments have to control and regulate the gigantic new enterprises of the period? How would the brief statement in the Constitution that the federal government had the power to "regulate" interstate commerce be interpreted in an industrial age?

When judges had to decide on the validity of state and local regulation of business, the new legal problem they had to come to terms with was the Fourteenth Amendment, which guaranteed that no state could take away any of the privileges of citizens of the United States. And it extended to the states an old provision—from the Fifth Amendment, in force since 1791—that no person could be deprived of "life, liberty, or property, without due process of law." On the other hand, the courts had long recognized that state and local governments had general "police" powers to control the "persons" in their jurisdictions—including corporations. The question now was, did the Fourteenth Amendment cut into the police power of the states and municipalities?

This question was put to the Supreme Court very directly in what were known as the Slaughterhouse Cases, decided in 1873. A Louisiana law of 1867 had given one slaughterhouse a monopoly of business in New Orleans by simply ordering all competing meat processors to stop doing business in the city.

The Court ruled—by a bare majority—that Louisiana was in the right. The state had followed all the legal forms in creating the law, and so had satisfied the "due process" requirements of the Fourteenth Amendment. To be sure, the justices admitted, the complaining slaughterers had been deprived of the right to do business. But so long as the state had not violated any legal *procedures,* the law was a valid exercise of the police power. For the moment, the power of governments to intervene drastically in the conduct of business had been upheld, and the application of the Fourteenth Amendment had been confined to the protection of the rights of the ex-slaves.

RAILROAD CASES The efforts of railroads to prevent state regulation of their rates had a similar outcome in the 1870s. In several Midwestern states, farmers' movements gained control of state legislatures and pushed through laws controlling the charges of railroads and grain elevator companies. The railroads went to court, and the question eventually reached the Supreme Court, in 1877, in the case of *Munn* v. *Illinois*.

The companies argued, in effect, that the states were depriving them of rights and property without due process of law. But the Court refused to go along. The justices made a distinction between types of property and ruled that a railroad or a grain elevator was a special kind of property, devoted to a "public use." This "public use" created a "public interest" in the property, so the railroads had to "submit to being controlled by the public for the common good."

For the moment, the railroads had no option but to go back to the legislatures to try to get the rate regulations repealed—which they were able to do in the long run. But there had been dissenting votes—four in the Slaughterhouse Cases. And in the next decade, seven new justices would be appointed. Gradually but certainly, the Court would work its way to a new vision of property rights and of "due process of law."

In 1886, in the case of *Stone* v. *Farmers' Loan and Trust Co.*, the Court examined a Mississippi law that had set up a commission with the power to establish railroad rates and fares. The Court upheld the statute but added an important new caution—one that had been absent from the Slaughterhouse Cases and from *Munn* v. *Illinois*: The regulation must set rates that would allow the railroads to make a profit. The problem of regulation was coming to a clear focus on two questions: What was a fair profit for a corporation to expect on its property? And who was going to *decide* what was fair—the legislatures and their commissions? The railroads and other companies? The courts?

The answers came in 1890, in a complicated case known as *Chicago, Milwaukee, and St. Paul Railway Co.* v. *Minnesota*. Corporations, the Court now decided, were not only entitled to *hold* their property, they were entitled to *use* it to make a profit. But the profit had to be "reasonable." And the legislature could not be allowed to decide what was reasonable. "Due process of law" required a *judicial* finding of the reasonableness of regulation.

In 1898 this opinion received a ringing confirmation in the case of *Smyth* v. *Ames*. The Court set aside a Nebraska law that had set railroad rates directly by enactment and not through any commission. The Court made a very lengthy examination of the company's records and found that the rates set by the legislature were "unreasonable" and so constituted a taking of property without "due process of law." The Court had become something new: a type of regulating agency in itself, which would review state and local regulations to determine whether they met the requirements of the "rule of reason."

The occasional efforts of Congress to control corporations and commerce met a similar fate. The Sherman Antitrust Act had outlawed all "combinations in restraint of trade." And if there was a combination that seemed clearly devoted to restraining competition, it was the Sugar Trust, a holding company that controlled more than 90 percent of all sugar refining in the United States. But when a federal suit against the company, E. C. Knight, reached the Supreme Court, the Sherman Act was sliced neatly in two. The Court, in *United States* v. *E. C. Knight* (1895), reached the conclusion that the company was not engaged in commerce at all, but in "manufacturing." And since the Constitution did not give the federal government the power to regulate "manufacturing," the company was not subject to federal power. Indeed, according to the Court, "production" of all kinds—in agriculture, mining, and manufacturing—was beyond the reach of congressional legislation.

The Interstate Commerce Act, Congress's second tentative exercise in regulation, was attacked in a slightly more piecemeal way, but the result was no less clear. In 1898, in *Cincinnati, New Orleans, and Texas Pacific Railway Co.* v. *Interstate Commerce Commission*, the Court ruled that the commission did not have the power to establish railroad rates. The justices had already found that rates on interstate shipments could not be controlled by the states. Now they were in effect deciding that such rates could not be set by *any* governmental authority. The force of the Interstate Commerce Act was reduced to two provisions: that the railroads publish their rate schedules, and that they charge all shippers the same prices. The commission itself was becoming, in the words of a dissenting justice, "a useless body for all practical purposes."

In all the important cases of the 1880s and 1890s, the Court had consistently ruled in favor of the arguments of corporations, and against the regulation of business by either federal or state governments. Later judges and historians would come to call the decisions "conservative," even reactionary. But there was nothing conservative about them. The Court was not defending any sort of status quo, or protecting legal tradition against innovation. It was *making* innovations, and it was doing so not to protect the past but to accommodate to the present, a present whose main characteristic was change.

SOCIAL CASES In the process, the Court was endorsing a set of social arrangements in which distinctions of wealth and status were becoming more obvious and extreme. This endorsement was clearly expressed in two landmark decisions of 1895 and 1896. In the first, *Pollock* v. *Farmers' Loan and Trust Co.*, the justices struck down the primitive income tax Congress had passed as part of the tariff law of 1894. In the second, *Plessy* v. *Ferguson*, the Court gave its approval for the first time to legal racial segregation.

In the income tax case, the judges were presented with an argument that the tax law violated a constitutional provision that all taxes be apportioned among the states by population. But the argument went further and pictured the income tax as an attempt on the part of the poor to take the property of the rich. The tax exempted all incomes under $4,000. This amounted, according to the argument, to a decision on the part of three-fourths of the people—who would pay no tax—to tax the other fourth. From this, the lawyers argued, would inevitably result "communism" and "anarchy." The opinion of the justices was less emotional, but they did reject the principle of the income tax outright—and so took away the one shred of legislative success for which the Populists could claim full credit.

The next year the Court took up what may have been the most radical possibility of Populism in the South: the challenge to racism. The Court had already ruled, in 1876, that the Fifteenth Amendment should be interpreted narrowly. In *United States* v. *Reese*, the justices said that state restrictions on voting rights were invalid only if they clearly and explicitly based those restrictions on race or color or "previous condition of servitude"—meaning enslavement. Then, in *Williams* v. *Mississippi*, the Court had upheld the Mississippi law of 1890 providing that voters must not only be able to read but to "interpret" the state constitution. The effect and purpose of the law was simple, and obvious to everyone: It was meant to prevent black men from voting. But the Court approved the law because it did not *mention* race or color. Now the question before the Court was to be much more straightforward. What about a state law that did use race or color as the basis of a social distinction? Did such laws, by segregating people by race or color, violate the Fourteenth Amendment's guarantees of equal access to "privileges and immunities"?

In *Plessy* v. *Ferguson*, the issue involved a Louisiana law that required railroads to provide "equal but separate accommodations for the white and colored races" and required white and "colored" passengers to obey the designations. The question was simple. Did this state law deprive citizens—white *or* black—of the equal

CHRONOLOGY

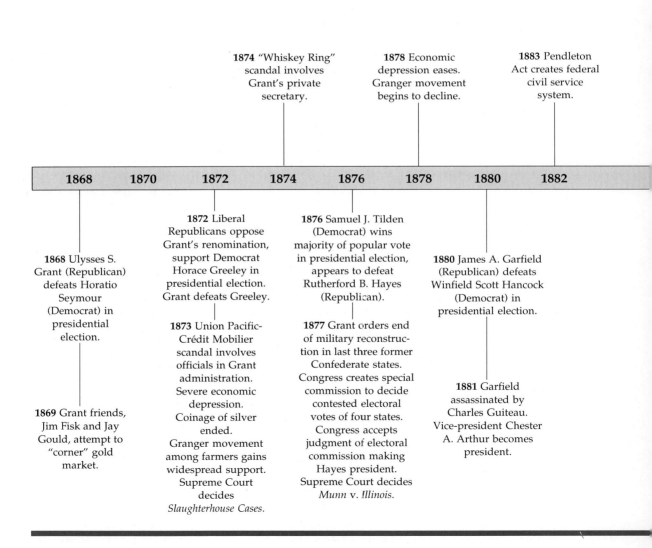

1874 "Whiskey Ring" scandal involves Grant's private secretary.

1878 Economic depression eases. Granger movement begins to decline.

1883 Pendleton Act creates federal civil service system.

| 1868 | 1870 | 1872 | 1874 | 1876 | 1878 | 1880 | 1882 |

1872 Liberal Republicans oppose Grant's renomination, support Democrat Horace Greeley in presidential election. Grant defeats Greeley.

1876 Samuel J. Tilden (Democrat) wins majority of popular vote in presidential election, appears to defeat Rutherford B. Hayes (Republican).

1868 Ulysses S. Grant (Republican) defeats Horatio Seymour (Democrat) in presidential election.

1880 James A. Garfield (Republican) defeats Winfield Scott Hancock (Democrat) in presidential election.

1873 Union Pacific-Crédit Mobilier scandal involves officials in Grant administration. Severe economic depression. Coinage of silver ended. Granger movement among farmers gains widespread support. Supreme Court decides *Slaughterhouse Cases*.

1877 Grant orders end of military reconstruction in last three former Confederate states. Congress creates special commission to decide contested electoral votes of four states. Congress accepts judgment of electoral commission making Hayes president. Supreme Court decides *Munn* v. *Illinois*.

1869 Grant friends, Jim Fisk and Jay Gould, attempt to "corner" gold market.

1881 Garfield assassinated by Charles Guiteau. Vice-president Chester A. Arthur becomes president.

1886 Supreme Court decides *Stone* v. *Farmers' Loan and Trust.*

1887 Interstate Commerce Act.

1890 Supreme Court decides *Chicago, Milwaukee, and St. Paul Railway Co.* v. *Minnesota.* Farmers' Alliance movements claim several million members, black and white, in South and West. Alliance candidates win many seats in state legislatures. Mississippi enacts first "literacy" test designed to exclude African-American voters. Sherman Antitrust Act. Democrats win landslide victory in congressional elections.

1891 Mass lynching ends strike of black cotton-pickers in Tennessee.

1894 Populist candidates receive 1.5 million votes in congressional elections. Republicans gain control of House of Representatives.

1895 Supreme Court decides *United States* v. *E.C. Knight* and *Pollock* v. *Farmers' Loan and Trust Co.*

1898 Louisiana enacts first "grandfather clause," designed to lure poor whites back to Democratic party. Supreme Court decides *Smyth* v. *Ames* and *Cincinnati, New Orleans, and Texas Pacific Railway Co.* v. *Interstate Commerce Commission.*

1884	1886	1888	1890	1892	1894	1896	1898

1884 Grover Cleveland (Democrat) defeats James G. Blaine (Republican) in presidential election.

1885 Farmers' Alliance movements begin to gain strength in South and West.

1888 Benjamin Harrison (Republican) defeats Cleveland in presidential election.

1889 McKinley tariff raises import duties.

1892 Populist party founded. Cleveland defeats Harrison and James B. Weaver (Populist) in presidential election. Democrats gain control of both houses of Congress. Populist-supported candidates win approximately 10 percent of congressional seats. Tariffs on imports reduced by approximately 10 percent. First peacetime income tax enacted.

1893 Severe economic depression begins.

1896 Supreme Court decides *Plessy* v. *Ferguson.* Populist party endorses Democratic candidate for president, William Jennings Bryan. William McKinley (Republican) defeats Bryan in presidential election.

protection of the laws guaranteed by the Fourteenth Amendment? Plessy, a man who had
seven white great-grandparents and one black,
had been arrested for refusing to leave a "white"
railroad car.

In its decision, the Court made a distinction
between "political equality" and "social equality."
The Fourteenth Amendment, clearly, required
that the states respect "political" rights absolutely, without regard to race or color. But the
Constitution could not—in matters of race or any
other area of ordinary human life—require
"social equality." In "social" areas, the legislature
was free to pass laws that enforced "the customs
and traditions of the people."

A year later, the judges would decide that education, like seating arrangements on trains, was
a "social" fact and not a "political" one. And so
it would endorse segregated public schools as a
proper way to prevent the "comingling of the two
races upon terms unsatisfactory to either."

The message was clear. An act of Congress
that attempted to make wealthier citizens pay a
tax that ordinary citizens did not pay had been
struck down. The right of the dominant race to
segregate private and public facilities and schools
was secure. A string of decisions had turned back
even modest attempts to regulate railroads and
prevent the formation of trusts and other forms
of monopoly. All this, combined with the clear
failure of the Populists, seemed to make it certain
that the United States could look forward only to
a continuation of politics that accepted the privileges of wealth and the power of corporations
as an established fact, above any sort of serious
challenge.

There still were voices demanding change,
demanding that economic and social and political
privilege be spread more equally. During the two
decades since Reconstruction had ended in the
election of 1876, feminists were organizing and
working for a greater measure of equality and
participation. Socialist and labor leaders were lis-
tening to the complaints of workers, and held out
hope that the future might be different. Native
Americans on the Great Plains were resisting the
destruction of their society and culture. And
black leaders still spoke their eloquent dreams of
a new day and a new kind of society. In the year
of *Plessy* v. *Ferguson*, a Nashville college professor
with the appropriate name of John Hope gave
voice to the passion for equality in words that
other oppressed Americans might have understood very well indeed:

> Rise, Brothers! Let your dissatisfaction break
> mountain-high against the walls of prejudice.
> . . . Then we shall not have to plead for justice,
> nor on bended knee crave mercy; for we shall be
> men.

The major political parties and the court system had turned deaf ears to such voices. But the
drama of American history often takes place outside politics and government, and this was
emphatically the case during the period between
the end of Reconstruction and the turn of the
century. The next three chapters will examine the
efforts of workers and immigrants to find their
way to decent lives in a new industrial order; the
efforts of Native Americans to maintain their culture and society against the white advance into
the West; and the ways women of different
classes and colors tried to come to terms with a
society that hemmed them in behind John Hope's
"walls of prejudice."

Suggestions for Further Reading

THE ELECTION OF 1876

The classic work on the Compromise of 1876–77 was published in 1951 by C. Vann Woodward as *Reunion and Reaction: The Compromise of 1877 and the End of Reconstruction*. It should be read alongside the more Northern-oriented work of K. I. Polakoff, *The Politics of Inertia: The Election of 1876 and the End of Reconstruction* (1973). A third important study is William Gillette, *Retreat from Reconstruction, 1869–1879* (1979). The lives of Tilden and Hayes can be studied in A. C. Flick, *Samuel Jones Tilden* (1939), and Harry Barnard, *Rutherford B. Hayes and His America* (1964).

PARTIES AND PRESIDENCIES

A thoughtful overview is Morton Keller, *Affairs of State: Public Life in Late-Nineteenth-Century America* (1977). Good discussions of politics are also available in Robert Wiebe's influential *The Search for Order, 1877–1920* (1967); H. Wayne Morgan, *From Hayes to McKinley* (1969); R. Hal Williams, *Years of Decision: American Politics in the 1890s* (1978); and Richard J. Jensen, *The Winning of the Midwest: Social and Political Conflict, 1888–1896* (1971). A useful study of elite reformers in politics is Gerald McFarland, *Mugwumps, Morals, and Politics, 1884–1920* (1975). Three good studies of the election of 1896 are Paul W. Glad, *McKinley, Bryan, and the People* (1964); Robert Durden, *The Climax of Populism: The Election of 1896* (1965); and Stanley Jones, *The Election of 1896* (1964).

POPULISM

Lawrence Goodwyn, *Democratic Promise: The Populist Movement in America* (1976), stresses the radical egalitarian side of the movement. A different view can be found in Stanley B. Parsons, *The Populist Context: Rural Versus Urban Power on a Great Plains Frontier* (1973), and Robert C. McMath, *Populist Vanguard: A History of the Southern Farmers' Alliance* (1975). Two important biographies of Populist leaders are Peter Argersinger, *Populism and Politics: Alfred Peffer and the People's Party* (1974), and C. Vann Woodward's beautifully written *Tom Watson* (1938). For the story of the disenfranchisement of blacks in the South, see J. Morgan Kousser, *The Shaping of Southern Politics: Suffrage Restriction and the Establishment of a One-Party South* (1974). But no student should miss a chance to read C. Vann Woodward's elegant little book, *The Strange Career of Jim Crow* (1974, 3rd edition).

CHAPTER 14
THE CLIMAX OF
THE INDUSTRIAL
REVOLUTION

THE EPISODE: *In 1886, workers at the McCormick Harvester Works in Chicago went on strike. They managed to shut down the huge factory that manufactured machinery for reaping grain. But the McCormick family and management were determined to break not only the strike but the unions that had organized it. They brought in a force of armed "detectives" and tried to replace their union workers with strikebreaking "scabs."*

During the same spring, thousands of other Chicago workers organized a general strike, asking their employers for an eight-hour working day. These strikers were very attentive to what was happening at the McCormick company. A violent incident at the main gate of the McCormick factory provoked a workers' evening protest meeting at a square in Chicago known as The Haymarket. Again there was violence. Someone planted a bomb, which killed or wounded a number of policemen. The bombing set off a police riot, in which several civilians were killed and many others injured. Some public authorities in the city were convinced that they were facing a revolutionary conspiracy led by "foreign anarchists." They were determined to restore "order" and put down labor "unrest." Their efforts produced one of the most spectacular trials in American history, a trial that pitted the power of the state against those who had tried to organize workers to resist the system of industrial capitalism.

THE HISTORICAL SETTING: *This is the second of four chapters that focus on the period between the end of Reconstruction and the beginning of the twentieth century. In the preceding chapter, the political history of the period was established as a chronological framework. This chapter examines the nature of the climactic phase of the nineteenth-century industrial revolution and the ways it affected how Americans lived, worked, and came into conflict with each other.*

Many of the six main themes of this chapter had a direct bearing on what happened in the Haymarket episode: (1) a rapid introduction of heavy machine technology in agriculture, manufacturing, and transportation; (2) the growth of large corporations and the formation of trusts and other kinds of monopolies; (3) a rapid increase in immigration from areas of the world that had not supplied much of the American population before the Civil War; (4) increasing prejudice among Americans who thought of themselves as "natives" against "foreigners" of all sorts; (5) the rapid growth of cities, most of them with immigrant slums and racial ghettos; and (6) a heightening conflict between labor and capital. The political system that was described in the preceding chapter proved unable or unwilling to find ways of dealing with the problems produced by these deep and important changes.

THE HAYMARKET: STRIKE AND VIOLENCE IN CHICAGO

April 15, 1885

My Dear Virginia,

We have had a week of trial and anxiety on the great subject of disturbances in our main factory—the serious labor troubles we have encountered—a great "strike," and all the resulting derangement of our relations—old and pleasant as they were—with our workmen.

Trouble has come to hundreds of families in consequence; hatred and fierce passions have been aroused; and an injury has resulted to our good name.

It began with a few molders and went on, one force operating on another, until 1,200 men went out, part of them by intimidation and part of them led by ignorant and blind passion. It ended by our conceding the terms demanded.

What a sore heart I have carried these days!

Your Devoted Mother

This letter was written by a bewildered woman in her early seventies to her daughter. The writer, Nettie Fowler McCormick, was the widow of Cyrus Hall McCormick. An ambitious and ingenious Virginia farm boy, McCormick had made millions of dollars from the invention and manufacture of the reaper, a machine that harvested crops mechanically. He opened his Chicago factory, the McCormick Harvester Works, in the 1840s. It was the largest producer of harvesting machines in the world.

Nettie McCormick had always paid close attention to the family business. Now, just a year after her husband's death, a stable and profitable enterprise seemed to be falling to pieces before her eyes. At first, her husband had known all the original 23 workmen by name. He had worked alongside them in the little Chicago factory. Even when, after a few years, there were about 200 workers producing over 1,000 reapers a year, he could still name those who had been with the company for any length of time.

As the business grew, relations with the workers had become more difficult. During the Civil War, when labor had been scarce and prices had jumped every week,

Cyrus Hall McCormick. McCormick invented the first successful reaping machine in 1834. He turned his invention into a booming business in Chicago by using sales techniques like installment credit. (Navistar Archives)

there had been many strikes or threats of strikes. McCormick had been forced to agree to one wage increase after another. But after the war ended, McCormick was able to cut wages in the plant five times in five years.

During the two decades after the Civil War, the McCormick company had grown rapidly. In 1884, when Cyrus McCormick died, the main factory covered dozens of acres. Its modern machinery, including two huge steam engines that supplied power for the whole factory, covered twelve acres of floor space. On these floors, about 1,300 men put in six 10-hour days a week. They turned 10 million feet of lumber and thousands of tons of iron into about 50,000 reapers a year. And these machines were making possible an agricultural miracle in the United States.

For the McCormicks, the result was money and status. In 1884 the company showed a profit of 71 percent. The family lived in a great mansion staffed with servants. They had invitations to the "best" Chicago homes, counted other wealthy people among their friends, sent their sons to Princeton, traveled luxuriously, and supported carefully selected philanthropies. Nettie Fowler McCormick had ample reason to be concerned about "our good name."

She had some reason to carry a "sore heart," too. The McCormick workers had always seemed content enough. Nine out of ten of them were Germans, Norwegians, or Swedes, and most lived in the neighborhoods just west of the factory—neighborhoods built by the McCormicks—with Swedish and German street names. All this made the strike of 1885 difficult for Nettie Fowler McCormick to understand. Perhaps her husband's death was part of the problem. But McCormick's was still a family business. Her son, Cyrus McCormick II, had taken over the presidency, and other members of the family had always held important positions in the company. What had happened, then, to the "old and pleasant" relations with the workmen?

Nettie Fowler McCormick. The wife of the McCormick company's founder had trouble grasping the reasons for the discontent of the workers at the plant in the 1880s. (Navistar Archives)

The problem had to lie, the McCormicks believed, with some small, misguided minority within the plant. And the most likely candidates for this role were clearly the molders. Ethnically, the molders were a distinct group. Almost all of them were Irish—"fighting Irish," as one plant official called them. And they had a tight, successful craft union, Molders Local No. 233. This union had been making trouble for the McCormicks for twenty years. There were only about ninety molders, but their operation was crucial to the manufacture of reapers. They could bring production to a complete standstill, and they had successfully used the power of this threat several times. Every time old Cyrus McCormick had tried to cut wages, the molders had been the first to resist.

The strike of 1885 had its origins in a decision by the new young president of the company to cut wages again. In December 1884 he had announced a 10 percent pay cut throughout the work force—except for the molders, who were to be cut by 15 percent. At first, there was quiet. Even the molders appeared to accept the reduction. But they were only biding their time until production reached its annual peak in the spring. In March 1885, the molders demanded that the wage cut be restored to them. When McCormick refused, the molders went out on strike. And, to the McCormicks' alarm, some of the other workers followed them out.

McCormick was anxious to prove himself. To break the strike, he sent telegrams to McCormick salesmen all over the Midwest, asking them to send strikebreaking molders to Chicago. He even had these workers listed on the company payroll as "scabs"—the union term of insult for nonunion workmen who replaced striking members. The newcomers were housed inside the plant in a barracks listed in the company records as "scab house."

But McCormick's efforts to break the strike did not work. The "scabs" could not be trusted. Early in April, these two revealing telegrams were sent from company headquarters to salesmen in Iowa and Illinois:

> To Tom Braden, Agent, Des Moines, Iowa: Out of the lot of men you sent us yesterday, but two of them showed up in Chicago. We find it not safe to ship these critters at our expense unless nailed up in a box car or chained.

> To J. F. Utley, Agent, Sterling, Illinois: The gentleman you sent to us as a molder did not remain over an hour or two until he packed his valise and skipped. We took special pains to get him into the Works by his riding with Mr. McCormick in his buggy. If you are able to do so, try and collect back his Rail Road fare.

Just a week after Cyrus McCormick had sneaked this unreliable scab into the plant, hidden in the president's own buggy, the strike reached a climax. On April 14, with the police scattered all over the city to patrol a local election, strikers attacked McCormick workers outside the plant. McCormick, like many other companies of the period, had hired a small private army of the Pinkerton "detective" agency to maintain peace. A wagon loaded with Pinkerton men and a case of Winchester repeating rifles tried to enter the plant gate. The strikers attacked the wagon and burned it, and the rifles disappeared into the crowd. The captain in charge of the few Chicago police still in the area did nothing. His name, O'Donnell, was as obviously Irish as that of any molder.

The violence confirmed the McCormick family's opinion of the "fighting Irish" molders. If twenty years' experience were not enough, the Pinkerton agents' secret reports confirmed what the family had long suspected: They were the victims of an ethnic "conspiracy." Just after the violent episode of April 14, one Pinkerton man submitted this report:

> The assault on the Pinkerton police during the strike of last week was urged by Irishmen, who are employed at McCormick's as molders and helpers. These Irishmen are nearly all members of the Ancient Order of Hibernians [an Irish social fraternity] who have a bitter enmity against the agency.

To the Pinkertons, it seemed clear that the molders were actually supported by their fellow Irishmen on the police force:

> It looks somewhat strange that these men at McCormick's could have police protection. On each occasion, the police stood by during the assaults and made no effort to stop the outrage.

Once, during the strike, a group of molders had attacked a group of nonunion workers outside the plant gate. The police, according to Pinkerton reports, had this time not merely stood by but had actually chased and arrested the Pinkerton men who were trying to restrain the molders:

> The police made the utmost speed in calling a patrol wagon, which followed the Pinkerton men and arrested them! The men who made the arrests were treated by the strikers in saloons, and from their talk and insinuations, the police urged the mob to more violence by saying the Pinkerton men were sons of bitches, no better than scabs, there to take the bread out of women and children's mouths.

After the molders' triumphant April 14 attack on the Pinkertons, Cyrus McCormick went looking for help and advice. He appealed first to the mayor, Carter Harrison. But Harrison remembered full well that the McCormicks had consistently opposed him in local politics. He politely advised the young industrialist to give in to the molders' demands. McCormick then turned to what he hoped would be a more sympathetic listener, old Philip Armour, head of a large meat-packing company and a veteran of many labor troubles. But even Armour told McCormick that the molders had won. There seemed to be no choice. McCormick offered to give back to the molders 5 percent out of their original 15 percent pay cut. But they refused this, and he ended by restoring the whole 15 percent.

To both Cyrus McCormick and his mother, their defeat at the hands of a few Irishmen was a painful mystery. But it was a mystery that had to be solved. Cyrus wrote to his mother as he mulled over the problem:

> The whole question of these labor troubles is vast and important and throws more new light on a department of our manufacturing interests which we have not hitherto studied with sufficient depth and understanding.

But to this twenty-five-year-old, who had only two years earlier been taken out of Princeton to run the plant, "depth and understanding" were limited to one fact and one conclusion. The fact was that a handful of disaffected molders could bring the entire McCormick enterprise to a standstill. The conclusion was that such a situation must be avoided in the future by making the skills of the molders unnecessary. He wrote his mother:

> I do not think we will have a similar trouble again because we will take measures to prevent it. I do not think we will be troubled if we take proper steps to weed out the bad element among the men.

McCormick went to work at once to "weed out" the offending Irish molders. He focused his efforts on a daring technological gamble. During the summer of 1885, the summer following the strike, the McCormick company bought a dozen new "pneumatic molding machines." They were supposed to perform mechanically most of the foundry tasks that the skilled molders had always done by hand. The machines were expensive, and they were experimental. No one knew whether they would work. McCormick hoped that they would enable the company to rid itself once and for all of the troublesome molders.

In August the McCormick foundry closed for two months so that the machines could be installed. The closing was not unusual, since reapers were manufactured seasonally—much as automobiles are today, with a new model season every fall. August and September were always light months at the harvester works. But when the foundry reopened for fall production, the new machines were in place. Not one molder who had participated in the spring strike was back on the payroll.

McCormick seemed to have won a complete victory. All he had done was spend a vast sum of money on the new machinery. A few months after the machines went into operation, he wrote his mother triumphantly that the machines

> are working even beyond our expectations and everybody is very much pleased with the result. Two men with one of these machines can do an average of about three

The reaper works. This company picture of the McCormick plant exaggerated the factory's size a little. But it did suggest the strategic location of the city at the junction of railroad, lake, and river transportation. In the nineteenth century, smoke was a symbol of progress and a national blessing—the thicker and blacker, the better. (Navistar Archives)

days work in one. Add to this fact that we have only nine molders in the whole foundry (the rest are all laborers), and you can see what a great gain this will be to us.

But McCormick was being more optimistic than he should have been—probably to reassure his anxious mother. Actually, there were troubles with the machines. In October the McCormick company complained to the manufacturer that the castings turned out by the pneumatic molding device were too brittle to use. And in November, Cyrus McCormick was called home from a trip to New York because of a crisis in the foundry. He wrote in his diary for November 11: "Telegram from mother urging come home at once about molding machines—probably failure. Critical situation."

The machines were fixed, but even when they worked they seemed to require an endless amount of labor to keep them functioning. Before the machines were installed, the total wage bill in the foundry was about $3,000 a week. After the machines had been in operation for about six months, foundry wages totaled $8,000 a week. Most of the labor was common, unskilled work. But gradually the company had to hire additional new molders to supervise the work. Economically, the machines were a complete failure.

Still, the new technology had broken the molders' union at McCormick. And the union was unhappy. The leader of the molders was a veteran union man named Myles McPadden. He devised a new scheme that was much more dangerous to the

McCormicks than the old union, with only ninety members. If there was to be no molders' union, then McPadden would simply organize all the other workers in the plant into one union or another. The workers were discontented, so the time was ripe. By February 1886 he had succeeded in organizing every major group of workers in the plant. The skilled workers—blacksmiths, machinists, and so on—joined the Metalworkers Union. McPadden encouraged the others to join the Knights of Labor, a general, nationwide union. Only 300 of the 1,400 McCormick workers remained nonunion. The lines of a new strike battle were shaping up clearly.

During this time McCormick, too, was busy. After his frustrated attempt to enlist Mayor Harrison's help, McCormick had gone to some lengths to make peace with the powerful political leader of the city. In every election before 1885 the McCormicks had opposed Harrison. After that year they supported him. As a result, Captain O'Donnell, the Irish police official who had been sympathetic to the workers in the spring of 1885, was replaced. The new man in charge of the area where the works were located was Police Inspector John Bonfield.

Bonfield had a reputation as a tough antilabor cop. He had once literally beaten his way through a crowd of strikers, shouting a slogan for which he became famous: "Clubs today spare bullets tomorrow." If there was going to be trouble in 1886, McCormick could count on the police in a way impossible a year before.

In mid-February 1886 a union committee representing all three unions—the Knights of Labor, the Metalworkers, and the Molders—presented McCormick with a series of demands:

> First, that all wages of laboring men be advanced from $1.25 to $1.50 a day. Second, that all vise hands[1] be advanced to $2.00 a day, and that blacksmith helpers be advanced to $1.75. Third, that the time the men spend in the water closet [the toilet] not be limited as heretofore. Fourth, that, inasmuch as the molding machines are a failure, the preference should be given the old hands. The scabs in the foundry must be discharged, and a pledge given that no man would be discharged for taking part in a strike.

The company offered to meet some of the demands, but not the fourth, which was one that must have made Cyrus McCormick furious. The unions rejected the offer and called a strike.

Before the strike was scheduled to begin, however, the company announced a complete shutdown of the plant for an indefinite period of time. Union pickets started marching near the plant, but they were kept away by 400 city policemen, now under Bonfield's command. To show its gratitude, the company served free hot meals to the police, with Cyrus McCormick sometimes personally pouring the coffee.

After two weeks the works were reopened, but only to nonunion employees. There was a loyal holdover force of only 82 men. The company furnished them with pistols. McCormick hoped they would lead an enthusiastic rush for jobs, but only 161 men showed up the first day. The second day was not much better. Once again the

---

[1]"Vise hands" were workers who used a vise, a tool for holding metal being worked. They had a skill and were, therefore, to receive higher wages than the "laboring men," who were unskilled workers.

company's agents scoured the region for workers. Gradually, the company's situation improved a little. McCormick was willing to sacrifice almost half a year's production in order to settle the union question once and for all.

For the men on strike the situation was just as important. If they lost, their future at McCormick (or any other manufacturing plant in the city) was dim. As March turned into April, families got hungrier and tempers hotter. The explosion McCormick had avoided the year before by giving in to union demands now looked inevitable.

The situation at McCormick was complicated by the fact that during the spring of 1886 strikes were taking place all over Chicago. On May 1 all the unions in the city began a general strike for the eight-hour day, one of the largest and most heated labor actions in American history. The strike at McCormick merged with the more general agitation, involving thousands of skilled and unskilled workers from plants all over the city.

Then, on May 3, two days into the general strike for an eight-hour day, a lumber workers' union held a mass meeting to hear an address by August Spies, a radical labor agitator. The meeting took place on Black Road, just a short distance from the McCormick factory. Some McCormick men were at the meeting, even though none was a lumber worker.

The McCormicks had been so desperate for workers that they had already granted the eight-hour day (with ten hours' pay) to their scab workers. So at 3:30, two hours before the former 5:30 closing, the bell at the plant rang, and the strike-breaking workers streamed out of the plant. The striking union men at the meeting watched the scabs leave the plant on their new short schedule.

Here were union men, on strike for an eight-hour day, watching scabs who were *working* an eight-hour day. The sight proved too much. Several hundred men, some of them McCormick strikers and some of them lumber workers, mobbed the scabs leaving the plant, driving them back inside the gate. The strikers began to smash windows, unleashing anger that had been building for months. About 200 policemen, under Inspector Bonfield, were there. Suddenly, they began firing their revolvers into the crowd, forgetting Bonfield's slogan about using clubs to spare bullets. When the noise died away, two workers lay dead and several others had been wounded.

August Spies, who had been addressing the meeting, followed the crowd and witnessed the violence that occurred. The next day, in the newspaper office where he worked, he heard that a mass meeting was scheduled at Haymarket Square to protest the shootings at McCormick. A circular announcing the meeting was being printed in both German and English when Spies arrived at the paper.

Spies agreed to address the meeting, but he insisted that the final line in the circular be omitted. About 200 of the circulars had already been printed, but the line was removed from the rest. Few of the 20,000 circulars that were finally distributed on the streets of Chicago contained the words "Workingmen Arm Yourselves."

Spies was not, strictly speaking, a workingman. He might best be described as a radical journalist. At the time of the Chicago troubles he was thirty years old and

Attention Workingmen!

GREAT

MASS-MEETING

TO-NIGHT, at 7.30 o'clock,

AT THE

HAYMARKET, Randolph St., Bet. Desplaines and Halsted.

Good Speakers will be present to denounce the latest
atrocious act of the police, the shooting of our
fellow-workmen yesterday afternoon.

Workingmen Arm Yourselves and Appear in Full Force!

THE EXECUTIVE COMMITTEE.

The call to the Haymarket. This poster was prepared to call a meeting to protest the shooting at the McCormick factory. August Spies insisted that the final line, calling on the workers to come to the square armed, be omitted before the poster was circulated. (Chicago Historical Society)

the editor of the *Arbeiter-Zeitung,* a German-language newspaper with a radical viewpoint. He was also the business manager of an organization called the Socialist Publishing Society, a propaganda organization of a small political party known as the Socialist Labor Party.

From time to time Spies had been in trouble with the police. Only a year before, during the McCormick strike of 1885, he had angered the police by intervening in the case of a poor German servant girl who had been arrested by the police and held in jail for several days. When Spies and the girl's mother went to the jail, they discovered that the girl had been sexually molested repeatedly. Rather than keep quiet, Spies swore out a warrant for the police sergeant in charge of the jail. He lost the case for lack of evidence, but he became well known to the Chicago police.

Spies was, in short, a politically active radical who did not hesitate to condemn people in positions of authority. He was also a committed socialist politician. He hoped that the rally at Haymarket would attract enough people to fill the square, which could hold about 20,000.

Spies reached Haymarket Square late, at about 8:30 on the night of May 4. He must have felt disappointed. No meeting was in progress, and there were only about a thousand people scattered around the square. The other main speaker, a socialist named Albert R. Parsons, was nowhere in sight. Spies climbed on a wagon, sent someone to look for Parsons, and began his talk. He was a good speaker, and soon the small crowd became enthusiastic:

> The fight is going on. Now is the chance to strike for the oppressed classes. The oppressors want us to be content. They will kill us. The day is not far distant when we will resort to hanging these men. [Applause, and shouts of "Hang them now" came from the crowd.] McCormick is the man who created the row on Monday, and he must be held responsible for the murder of our brothers! [More shouts of "Hang him!"]

Spies went on in the same vein for about an hour, trying to rouse his working-class audience to anger and a sense of solidarity against their "oppressors." Then someone announced that Albert R. Parsons had been found. Spies turned over his wagon rostrum to the second speaker.

The crowd had been waiting for Parsons, for he had a reputation as a spellbinder. Unlike Spies and many other Chicago socialists, he was a native American. Born in Alabama in 1848, Parsons came from a family whose ancestry went back to 1632 in New England. He was a self-trained printer in Texas before the Civil War. During the war he fought for the Confederacy in a Texas artillery company. After the war Parsons became converted to socialism and moved to Chicago, the center of working-class politics in the United States.

Like Spies, Parsons was not a worker at all but a political journalist. He edited a radical workingmen's paper called the *Alarm*. The Haymarket rally was just one more in a long series of political speeches for him. His speech was much like that of Spies but slightly stronger in tone:

> I am not here for the purpose of inciting anybody, but to speak out, to tell the facts as they exist, even though it shall cost me my life before morning. It behooves you, as you love your wife and children—if you don't want to see them perish with hunger, killed or cut down like dogs in the street—Americans, in the interest of your liberty and independence, to *arm*, to *arm* yourselves!

Here again there was applause from the crowd and shouts of "We'll do it! We're ready!"

What Parsons and Spies did not know was that the crowd was full of police detectives. Every few minutes one or another ran back to a nearby station house to report what the speakers were saying. Waiting in the station were almost 200 policemen, fully armed, and under the command of none other than John Bonfield.

Parsons and Spies probably did not notice Mayor Carter Harrison in the crowd, either. Only the mayor's presence had kept Bonfield from breaking up the meeting. As Parsons finished, the mayor left; it was obvious to him that everything was peaceful. It was almost ten o'clock and rain was in the air. Most of the crowd, too, began to drift off as the third speaker, Samuel Fielden, began to speak.

Suddenly, 180 policemen (a group almost as large as the crowd itself) marched into the square and up to the wagon where Fielden was speaking. One of the captains turned to the crowd and said: "In the name of the people of the State of Illinois, I command this meeting immediately and peaceably to disperse." After a moment the

The Haymarket tragedy. Newspapers and magazines had a field day with events in the Haymarket. This engraving was published with the title "Anarchist Riot." It shows the workers and their leaders as a wild-eyed mob, firing into the police ranks. And it pictures the police advance as resolute and orderly. In truth, there was no mob, and the police had no discipline. (Library of Congress)

police captain repeated his order. The crowd was already starting to melt away (it was almost 10:30 by now). Fielden had stopped speaking and was climbing down from the wagon platform. "We are peaceable," Fielden said to Bonfield.

At that moment, without any warning, a dynamite bomb was thrown (it is not known from where or by whom) at the police. The fuse burned for a second or two after the bomb struck the ground. Then it went off with a deafening roar. Screams split the air as people ran in all directions. A number of policemen lay on the ground, one dead and the others wounded. Quickly, the police re-formed their ranks, and some of them began to fire into the crowd. Other policemen waded into the confusion swinging their clubs. The uproar lasted only a minute or two. Then suddenly the square was empty.

In addition to the dead policeman, seventy-three of his colleagues were wounded, six of whom died later. Four civilians were killed, and the official reports listed twelve as wounded. The twelve were those who had been too badly hurt to leave the square. Probably several times as many limped or struggled home and never became official statistics.

The Haymarket tragedy: Another view. This representation of what happened in Chicago in 1886 is probably more accurate than the one on page 617. It shows workers fleeing, none firing at the police. And it shows the bomb killing both workers and the policemen who were beating them with nightsticks. (Library of Congress)

Like most such incidents, the Haymarket affair had been short. And considering what could have happened, very few people were hurt. But it occurred on the heels of trouble at the McCormick plant, in the midst of the strike for an eight-hour day, with 80,000 Chicago workingmen off the job. Thus the Haymarket bomb touched off a near-panic in the city and much of the rest of the nation. Thousands of respectable citizens convinced themselves that a dangerous conspiracy of anarchists, socialists, and communists was at work to overthrow the government and carry out a bloody revolution. One of the leading business magazines of the day, *Bradstreets'*, spoke for thousands of Americans when it said of the Haymarket incident:

> This week's happenings at Chicago go to show that the threats of the anarchists against the existing order are not idle. In a time of disturbance, desperate men have a power for evil out of proportion to their numbers. They are desperate fanatics who are opposed to all laws. There is no room for anarchy in the political system of the United States.

Also important was the fact that many people had been frightened and angered by a recent flood of immigration from Europe to America—and many of the "anarchists" were also foreigners. Not only in Chicago but all over the nation, newspaper editorialists and public speakers demanded the immediate arrest and conviction of the alien "radicals" who had conspired to murder honest policemen and subvert law and order. The result was a swift and efficient series of illegal raids by the Chicago police. They searched property without warrants. They imprisoned people without charging them and threatened potential witnesses. All in all, the authorities arrested and questioned about 200 "suspects"—probably none of whom had anything at all to do with the bombing.

In this heated atmosphere, fueled by journalists who whipped up unreasonable fears of an anarchist conspiracy, a jury met to determine whether indictments could be brought against anyone for the violence. It decided that although the specific person who threw the bomb could not be identified, anyone who urged violence was a "conspirator" and was as guilty of murder as the bomb thrower. On the basis of this decision, another jury met and indicted thirty-one persons on counts of murder. Of the thirty-one, eight were eventually tried, all of them political radicals. Most had not even been present at the Haymarket bombing.

The effect of the Haymarket affair had now become clear. What had begun weeks before as an ordinary strike at the McCormick works had been transformed into a crusade against political radicalism, most of which was said to be foreign in origin. Only Parsons and Samuel Fielden were not German or of German descent. The names of the other six would have been as natural in Berlin or Hamburg as in Chicago: August Spies, Michael Schwab, Adolph Fischer, George Engel, Louis Lingg, and Oscar Neebe.

In one way or another, all the defendants had some connection with the labor movement and with political agitation for revolution. Several of them were anarchists, though their ideas about anarchism as a philosophy were vague. They might as well have called themselves socialists, as several of them did at one time or another. In general, they were intellectuals. Their jobs were connected with radical journalism in either the English- or German-language press. They did not all know one another, but by the time their trial was over, most of them were probably "comrades," a word they used more and more in the months ahead.

On the other side of the battle were all the forces of law, order, and authority. True, some agreed with Mayor Harrison that the Haymarket meeting had been peaceful, that the whole idea of a conspiracy was a false and legally incorrect notion. But most of Chicago society (including even many elements of the labor movement) favored a quick conviction and the hanging of all eight defendants. The judge who tried the case, the prosecuting attorney, most business leaders, almost all the local clergymen—almost everyone who had anything to say in Chicago—were convinced even before the trial began that the defendants were guilty. Moreover, most of Chicago's leading citizens, and their counterparts in the rest of the country, agreed that the trial was a struggle to the death between American republicanism and foreign anarchism. The entire established order of American society, with very few exceptions, was determined to make an example of the "conspirators."

The Haymarket trial began June 21, 1886. The first three weeks of the seven-week trial were spent selecting a jury. Under Illinois law, the defense had the right to reject a total of 160 jurors on peremptory challenges—that is, without having to discuss a juror's qualifications and abide by the judge's decision. As one prospective juror after another was called, it became clear that most of them were extremely prejudiced against the defendants. The defense attorneys quickly used up their 160 challenges. They then had to show cause for turning down a juror and depend on the judge, Joseph Gary, to rule fairly. Again and again, plainly biased jurors were accepted by the judge—whose own prejudice against the defendants became apparent as the process went on. The result was a jury composed of twelve citizens who obviously wished to hang the defendants.

In his opening statement, prosecuting attorney Julius Grinnell set the tone of the entire trial:

> Gentlemen, for the first time in the history of our country people are on trial for endeavoring to make anarchy the rule. I hope that while the youngest of us lives

this will be the last and only time when such a trial shall take place. In the light of the 4th of May, we now know that the preachings of anarchy by these defendants, hourly and daily for years, have been sapping our institutions. Where they have cried murder, bloodshed, anarchy, and dynamite, they have meant what they said. The firing on Fort Sumter was a terrible thing to our country, but it was open warfare. I think it was nothing compared with this insidious, infamous plot to ruin our laws and our country.

It was obvious that this would not be an ordinary murder trial. The defendants would be judged by their words and beliefs. A ninth "conspirator," Rudolph Schnaubelt, had fled. The prosecution would try to prove that he had thrown the bomb. The next step would be to convict the other eight of conspiracy, which would carry the same penalty as murder itself. And they would be convicted by the fact that they had made speeches and written newspaper articles urging violent revolution. Day after day the prosecution offered evidence about the defendants' beliefs, their writings, and even pamphlets they had not written but supposedly helped to sell.

The prosecution had weak cases against the individual defendants. They were able to prove that one, Lingg, had actually made bombs. But Lingg was a stranger to most of the others, and he had not even been at Haymarket Square. Parsons, Spies, Fischer, and Schwab had left the square before the bomb was thrown. George Engel proved that he had been home drinking a glass of beer with his wife. In the end the prosecution's case rested on a theory of "general conspiracy to promote violence." No evidence of a single violent act was brought into court that could withstand even the mildest cross-examination by the frustrated defense attorneys.

After four weeks of testimony the jury retired. The jury members had been instructed by Judge Gary in such a way as to make conviction almost inevitable, and they needed only three hours to discuss the matter. After this short deliberation the jury filed solemnly back into the courtroom. It was ten o'clock, August 19, 1886, when the foreman read the verdict.

> We the jury find the defendants Spies, Schwab, Fielden, Parsons, Fischer, Engel, and Lingg guilty of murder in the manner and form as charged, and fix the penalty at death. We find Oscar Neebe[2] guilty of murder in the manner and form as charged, and fix the penalty at imprisonment in the penitentiary for fifteen years.

Years later Judge Gary recalled that "the verdict was received by the friends of social order with a roar of almost universal approval."

Before they were sentenced, each of the defendants made a speech to the court. Spies spoke for all of them when he said, in the German accent he had never lost:

> There was not a syllable said about anarchism at the Haymarket meeting. But "anarchism is on trial," foams Mr. Grinnell. If that is the case, your honor, very well; you may sentence me, for I am an anarchist. I believe that the state of classes—the state where one class dominates and lives upon the labor of another class—is doomed to die, to make room for a free society, voluntary association, or universal brotherhood, if you like. You may pronounce the sentence upon me, honorable judge, but let the

---

[2]Neebe was the youngest defendant; almost no evidence had been presented against him. Most of the jury's three-hour deliberation was devoted to this case.

"The voices you strangle today." On November 11, 1886, three months after one of the most unfair verdicts in American history, Albert Parsons, August Spies, George Engel, and Adolph Fischer were hanged by the state of Illinois. Victorian refinement required that the victims be put into robes to hide two things: that they were tightly tied up and that most people who are hanged lose muscular control and soil their clothing. (Chicago Historical Society)

world know that in A.D. 1886, in the state of Illinois, eight men were sentenced to death because they believed in a better future.

There were appeals, of course, first to state courts and then to the Supreme Court of the United States. One by one the appeals failed. Then there were pleas to the governor of Illinois for mercy, and the sentences of Fielden and Schwab were commuted to life. Lingg, the bomb maker, who was probably half mad, committed suicide in jail—using dynamite set off by a fuse that he lit with his jail-cell candle. The other four condemned men—Engel, Spies, Parsons, and Fischer—were hanged on November 11. As the four stood on the scaffold, ropes around their necks and hoods over their heads, Spies broke the deep silence by shouting: "There will come a time when our silence will be more powerful than the voices you strangle today!"

At the McCormick works the situation had returned to normal months earlier. On May 7, 1886, three days after the Haymarket bombing, Cyrus McCormick was able to write in his diary: "A good force of men at the works today, and things are resuming their former appearance." Three days later, taking full advantage of the public outrage over the "devilish plot," as McCormick called it, at Haymarket Square, the McCormick works quietly resumed the ten-hour day. On Monday, May 10, McCormick wrote: "Things going smoothly. We returned to 5:30 closing hour today, instead of 3:30."

FACTORIES, WORKERS, AND A NEW SOCIAL ORDER

This chapter is about the creation of a new social and economic system in the United States: the system of industrial capitalism. In a sense, industry is as old as human society. People have always made things—tools, weapons, clothing, and so on. But beginning in the eighteenth century, their ability to make goods began to increase rapidly. This so-called industrial revolution originated in England and spread quickly to the rest of western Europe and to the United States. By the time of the Civil War, this revolution was well under way in North America, fed by inventions like the steam engine, the cotton gin, and the reaper. After the war, industrialization altered the basic patterns of life in the United States even more drastically.

Everything had to be changed, since every element of this new system had to hang together. Raw materials, like coal and iron for making steel, had to be found and developed. Cheap transportation, like railroads, had to be available to bring these materials to factories and to take finished products from them. Workers had to be hired to operate the factories. And agriculture had to be improved so that fewer and fewer people would be needed to grow more and more food. More and more machines were needed to provide a livelihood for more and more factory workers, who would in turn make still more machines. Nothing could happen at all unless everything else happened—and in the proper order. Every factory functioned as part of a chain of invention, materials, transportation, and workers.

The McCormick Harvester Company, for example, was only part of a complicated series of events and machines. The reapers made at the McCormick works enabled farmers on the Great Plains to produce unheard-of quantities of grain. Some of this grain was milled into flour for bread eaten by people like McCormick's molders. Other farm products fed cattle, which were slaughtered in big cities at factories owned by men like Philip Armour.

The new transcontinental railroads were necessary to take the reapers west and bring the flour and beef east. Since there were not enough workers to lay the new rails, Irish and Chinese were encouraged to immigrate. The McCormick plant, too, was tended by more than a thousand immigrants. And it was German immigrants who were the main victims of the Haymarket riot. The city of Chicago itself was a new kind of city, built around railroads and factories in a way that no other American city had ever been built—a great barracks for the workers at dozens of factories like the McCormick works.

The United States was transformed. It had once been a nation in which nine out of every ten people lived on farms or in rural communities. By the end of the nineteenth century, it was the world's most productive industrial nation, and one of the most urban. The landscape had been remade. The people had been changed, too. There had always been immigrants to the United States, but new industries attracted different types of immigrants in greater numbers. In the end, the daily lives and even the language of Americans were changed. New words like *telephone, subway, scab,* and *millionaire* became common speech. They signaled just how deep and complete the change had been.

Technological Change

Few of the men and women who made or watched the industrial revolution understood its complexity. Most of them probably regarded it as a product of new types of machines. Certainly one of the most obvious changes of the nineteenth century was that many things that had once been done slowly by hand were now being done rapidly by machine. But technological change touched more than machinery. It transformed every sector of economic life, including the way food was produced.

AN AGRICULTURAL REVOLUTION   Agriculture was a prime example of the replacement of hand labor by machine power. The most striking introduction of new agricultural technology took place on the Great Plains. On these flat and treeless expanses, plowing, planting, and harvesting could be done on a scale that would have stunned colonial settlers and even most plantation owners of the Old South. But what happened on the plains was just an extreme version of what went on in all areas of American agriculture: the industrialization of the farm.

At first, the new machinery was fairly simple. McCormick's earliest reapers, built before the Civil War, were small. They were drawn by one horse and worked by one or two men. Another invention, a steel plow that could cut deeper and faster than the old iron plow, was a further small step. But gradually the new technology gained force and speed. Reapers were soon equipped with automatic binders that could fasten grain into bunches mechanically. The single steel plow was soon modified into a multiple, or gang, plow that could cut several furrows at one time.

Soon other new machines appeared. One could plow and plant at the same time. Another, the combine, added to the reaper a mechanical thresher, which could separate grain from stalks. A combine could move quickly through a wheat field, gathering wheat, separating the grain, and leaving behind only waste to be plowed under in the spring. The machine accomplished its work without a single human hand touching the earth, the wheat plants, or the finished grain.

During most of the nineteenth century, new machinery was still driven primarily by animals. Some steam engines were used, but the final mechanization of farms had to await the gasoline-driven tractor in the twentieth century. Still, even before the tractor, the life of the American farmer had been fundamentally altered by technology. Farming gradually came to resemble the running of factories, in which a product for sale was processed and made ready by machinery. Sooner or later, almost every step in all but a few kinds of agriculture was mechanized.

The result of the mechanical changes in agriculture was to double and redouble the volume and pace of food production. In 1840 it took more than three hours of human work time to produce a bushel of wheat. By the 1890s the time had been cut to ten minutes. In 1840 a bushel of corn required almost five hours of labor, from planting to final processing. By the 1890s the time had been cut to forty minutes.

The area of land under cultivation doubled between the Civil War and 1900. And the new lands were usually well adapted to the use of machinery. The net result of the agricultural revolution was an enormous abundance of food.

An agricultural vista. Even without steam engines or gasoline motors, giant commercial farms were able to harvest wheat fields with industrial efficiency. These machines, sometimes drawn by as many as thirty mules, cut and threshed the wheat, hauling the grain away and leaving a field of stubble at day's end. Here each machine is tended by only two men, plus a third to drive the mules. (Washington State Historical Society)

Hand in hand with the reduction of hours was a marked decrease in the number of farmers needed to produce food. Mechanization made it possible for a tiny minority of Americans to feed all the rest. Those who left farms were then free to work for the railroads and in oil fields, iron mines, factories, and offices—hurrying the process of industrialization along.

IMPROVING RAIL TRANSPORT   The agricultural revolution depended not only on new technology on the farms but also on new methods of carrying food from the farms to the cities— that is, railroads. It was railroads that brought Wyoming beef, Kansas wheat, and Louisiana rice to the table of a McCormick molder. Without the new railroad network built after the Civil War, the mechanization of agriculture would have had much less impact.

Railroads, like farms, benefited from new technological developments. The principle of the steam engine remained the same, but almost every other mechanical aspect of railroading changed drastically during the generation after Appomattox.

The old railroads had used iron rails, small and dangerous wood-burning engines, and tiny, rickety coaches and freight cars. The new lines used steel rails that would last for many years without cracking or rusting. Steel rails could support almost twenty times as much weight as iron, so larger engines and cars could be used. Freight cars increased in weight from 10 tons to over 100 tons. The typical pre–Civil War engine had weighed about 20 tons. By 1900 some locomotives weighed as much as 300 tons. The coal-burning locomotive became a giant source of power that could pull huge freights over the most difficult grades efficiently and safely.

Railroad mileage increased dramatically. In 1870—even after the completion of the first transcontinental line—there were only about 40,000 miles of track in the United States. By 1900 there were almost 200,000 miles. This total was greater than the entire railroad mileage of Europe, including Russia. Other inventions like the telegraph and the electric signal made it possible to control complicated traffic patterns and freight yards.

The trains and tracks of 1900 were as dramatically different from those of 1850 as today's jet plane is from the wobbly aircraft of the 1920s. Railroads were the new giants of the landscape, transforming the process of moving food, objects, and people from one place to another.

Manufacturing

Taken by themselves, the technological changes in agriculture and the railroads would have meant little. They were important only in their relation to other parts of the new industrial system. In this system, manufacturing was the crucial center.

By 1900—a little more than a century after George Washington had taken the presidential oath—the United States was the leading manufacturing nation in the world. Many factors made this possible. Americans found new beds of coal. They discovered iron ore in Michigan and Minnesota. They opened oil fields in Pennsylvania, the Ohio Valley, and the southern Great Plains. These raw materials and new energy sources fed the new factories of Pittsburgh, Chicago, and dozens of other cities. Mechanized agriculture made it possible for millions of people to move to cities to work in industrial plants. A high tariff kept down competition from foreign manufactured goods. Most important of all were the new machines and processes that enabled Americans to produce so much so quickly.

THE STEEL INDUSTRY Steel was very close to the heart of the new economy. It is stronger than iron, more resistant to rust, and easier to shape or mold. People had been making small quantities of steel for centuries, but the process was slow and difficult, since it depended on hand labor. In the 1850s an Englishman, Henry Bessemer, invented a converter that could turn iron into steel by blowing a blast of hot air through the molten iron. The process was spectacular to watch, sending a brilliant shaft of sparks and smoke skyward. The economic results were just as startling. For the first time it became possible to produce steel cheaply and in massive quantities.

The combination of the Bessemer converter, the demand for steel from the railroads and other industries, and the discovery of additional sources of iron ore and coal created a new industry. In 1870 the United States produced only about 77,000 tons of steel. By 1900 production had increased to over 10 million tons a year—an increase of more than 1,300 percent. Pittsburgh became the first of the steel towns. But eventually, cities like Birmingham, Alabama, and Gary, Indiana—built almost entirely around the steel industry—sprang up in what had until then been open countryside.

OTHER INDUSTRIES What happened in steel was repeated in dozens of other industries. The sewing machine and other inventions made it possible to manufacture shoes and clothing on a mass scale. Steam-powered mills using steel equipment could cut lumber, or grind wheat, or print newspapers with a speed and efficiency no one had dreamed of earlier.

Another new industry grew up based on electricity. The foremost American in this field was the versatile Thomas A. Edison. Throughout the late nineteenth century, a stream of inventions poured from his laboratories: the phonograph, the first practical electric light bulb, the storage battery, the dynamo, the electric voting machine, and the motion picture camera.

An industrial vista. For millions of Americans, industrial growth was not a miracle but a misery. The steelworkers who lived in these crowded houses and walked along these dirt streets to the Pittsburgh mills often worked twelve hours a day, seven days a week. (International Museum of Photography, George Eastman House)

An industry also developed rapidly around the discovery of oil and new ways of refining it. Oil yielded kerosene for lamps and stoves. Heavier oils lubricated the motors of the new technology. Beginning around 1900, it became important as a source of gasoline for the internal combustion engine (see Chapter 19). This vast new industry simply had not existed in 1800.

A revolution in communications began in 1876, on the hundredth anniversary of the Declaration of Independence. In that year a young inventor named Alexander Graham Bell exhib-ited the first working model of the telephone. At first, the telephone was purchased only by individuals who wanted to communicate between two specific locations, like a house and a factory or office. But soon there were enough phones in use to create the first telephone exchange. It was opened in New Haven, Connecticut, in 1878. Other cities and towns followed suit.

Soon cities began to link up with one another. The first intercity telephone line joined New York and Boston in 1884. New York and Chicago were connected in 1892. By 1915, when a line opened

Alexander Graham Bell was probably the most inventive man of his age. Here he is demonstrating his telephone for an attentive, if somewhat grim, audience. The other striking nineteenth-century invention involved in this photograph is the camera. (Courtesy AT&T)

between New York and San Francisco, it was possible to place calls between any two major cities in the nation.

The magnitude of what was happening to the United States can be measured only in statistics. In 1869 the value of American manufactured goods was about $1.5 billion. By the end of the century the figure was more than $4.5 billion. In 1869 about 2 million workers ran American shops, mills, and factories, and the market value of the average person's yearly output was about $940. By 1900, when almost 5 million men and women worked in industry, the market value of their average yearly product had almost doubled, to nearly $1,800.

By the 1890s the United States had more steel, more rails, more electric trolleys, more telephones, and more electric lights than any other nation in the world. To accomplish all this, Americans mined more metal, cut more lumber, dug more iron ore, and pumped more oil than any other country.

The Growth of "Big Business"

Technology and manufacturing were crucial in making the United States an industrial nation. But new methods of organizing industry and business were also vital.

THE FACTORY SYSTEM At the beginning of the Civil War, most Americans who worked in industry were employed in small mills or shops— a tailor shop, for example, or a blacksmith's or harnessmaker's. In 1870, when the revolution in industry was already under way, the average industrial plant still had only 8 employees. A median plant (one halfway between the largest and the smallest) had 30 workers. By 1914 the average plant had 28 workers, and the median 270. In 1870 no factory in America employed over 1,000 workers. By 1914 several had over 10,000 workers.

What was occurring, in other words, was a change that went beyond the technology of production. The change was nothing less than a parallel revolution. The factory was replacing the traditional small shop.

In a traditional shop (or in the home manufacture of items like cloth or soap), work centered on the person. Power was supplied mainly through human toil. The same worker was involved in all stages of production, from spinning thread, for example, to weaving the final cloth.

The idea behind a factory (first introduced in England in the late eighteenth century) is very different. Work in a factory centers on a machine. Power is mechanical, not human. Parts are nearly identical, and so they are interchangeable. Most important is the division of labor. Each worker specializes, performing only one step in a chain. He or she may never touch or see the raw material. He or she may never see or handle the final product. The result is mass production—manufacturing large numbers of articles in standard shapes and sizes.

Factories are inevitably larger than shops. They cost more money to build and equip with machinery. And more capital is needed in order to enter and compete in almost any line of business. As the factory system grew, then, so did the size of companies.

CHANGES IN ORGANIZATION
Growth in turn demanded changes in the organization of business. Mass production required a sizable investment. This made it difficult for family firms to be truly competitive. So large corporations gradually replaced companies owned by one family or a few partners.

The corporation is an old idea. The Virginia Company and the Massachusetts Bay Company were both seventeenth-century corporations. The idea is as simple as it is old. If many people invest in an enterprise by buying stock in it, the company can grow much larger than if it is funded by only a few individuals. If the company fails, each investor has lost only the value of his stock. He cannot be held personally responsible for any of the corporation's debts.

Just as there had been a few American factories before the Civil War, so had there been corporations. But their number increased greatly after the war. The corporation became the standard way of organizing business, just as the factory became the characteristic method of organizing production.

Mass production required not only corporate investment, but that each firm market its product efficiently on a broad regional or national scale, instead of selling just locally. To remain in business, a corporation had to create effective distributing and selling divisions. It also had to buy raw materials on a large scale. Ideally, in fact, it would purchase its own source of materials—for example, a forest for a paper company, or an iron mine for a steel mill.

In other words, mass production made it profitable for a company to invest in all the stages of its industry, from original materials to final sales. Economists call this phenomenon *vertical integration*. It involves a firm not only in manufacturing but in all the other stages and phases relating to the business. An oil company that owns wells, pipelines, and refineries and has its own sales force is fully integrated. It is freed from dependence on any other economic unit—except, of course, customers.

COMPETITION AND CONSOLIDATION
The new industrial order brought a new kind of competition into the American economy. Before the era of mass production, small shops and mills had catered to limited territories. They competed only where one territory bordered on another. But large corporations needed large markets to absorb their massive outputs. Thus a number of companies might find themselves competing for the same customers.

To win a big market, a corporation might advertise heavily. It might hire high-pressure salesmen and reward them with big commissions. But the most obvious way to win a market was to cut prices. A large company with efficient factories and lower production costs could force competitors into bankruptcy simply by lowering prices beyond the point where the smaller firms could stay in business.

In one industry after another, a few corporations gradually emerged as the leading firms. Each was too large, efficient, and powerful to be driven out of business by the others. Each was too small to be able to control the whole market. When this happened—and it happened sooner or later in most industries—the firm usually entered a period of intense competition. But most American businesses did not welcome such competition and tried to find ways to avoid it.

Railroads led the way. Railroad owners had witnessed the havoc and ruin that could be created when one railroad waged a price war with another. By a process of trial and error, the railroads worked out private agreements among themselves to control freight rates. Railroads also developed a system of grouping their customers in "pools," with each line "entitled" to a certain share of the total market. Gradually, too, the railroads had become consolidated into a few major lines, each one absorbing dozens of smaller companies. The Pennsylvania and New York Central railroads dominated the Northeast. The Southern Railway controlled much of the South. The Louisville and Nashville line was supreme in the Ohio Valley.

The agreements and consolidations of the railroads became the models for other businesses. Other industries soon copied what railroad leaders had learned and used the economic devices they had developed. Consolidation became the order of the day.

No matter what industry was involved, the process was the same. First, a few large, competing firms would emerge. A period of intense and costly competition would follow. Then firms would consolidate as a way of avoiding competition. During its period of rapid growth, the McCormick Harvester Company was competing with a handful of other large manufacturers of agricultural machinery. In the years after the Haymarket affair, however, the McCormicks began to realize that competition was wasteful and unnecessary. Early in the twentieth century, McCormick merged with its competition to form the huge International Harvester Company, which since then has produced practically all the harvesting machinery manufactured in the United States.

A similar development occurred in the steel industry, which was dominated for almost half a century by a Scottish immigrant, Andrew Carnegie. Carnegie was a classic example of the rags-to-riches success story. At thirteen he came to America with his family and immediately went to work. At eighteen he was a telegraph clerk for the Pennsylvania Railroad. During the rapid railroad expansion of the Civil War years, Carnegie realized that iron and steel for rails and bridges were the key to the railroads' future, and that railroads, in turn, were the key to an expanding economy. He saved every cent and invested daringly but successfully. By 1872 he was able to build his own steel plant near Pittsburgh.

Carnegie's company grew with the industry. By 1890 he was producing almost a third of a million tons of steel. By 1900 this amount had nearly tripled. At the same time, Carnegie worked to achieve vertical integration. He bought iron ore deposits, steamers to transport ore on the Great Lakes, and railroad cars to carry it overland—in fact, everything he needed for making steel.

In the meantime, the process of competition had eliminated all but a few other steel companies. In 1892 the Carnegie company was reorganized to combine seven other corporations in which Carnegie had acquired a controlling interest. In 1901 the largest steel concerns in the nation were all merged into one great new corporation, the United States Steel Corporation. The power behind this consolidation was another dominant figure of the period, J. Pierpont Morgan, a New York banker and financier. Morgan spent nearly half a billion dollars to buy out Carnegie and set

Andrew Carnegie

The most captivating idea in late-nineteenth-century American culture was the image of the "self-made man." And of all the industrial magnates of the day, the man who best fitted the picture was Andrew Carnegie. His life contained all the right ingredients: poor but honest parents, a daring willingness to gamble on innovations, and dazzling financial success.

The full picture, of course, was a little more complicated. Carnegie *was* the son of poor Scottish immigrants. But his parents were skilled weavers who were poor because their craft was already being destroyed by technological innovation when Carnegie was born in 1835. This family of skilled craftsmen had for generations been articulate and politically active. When his parents immigrated to the United States in 1848, Carnegie had the fair beginnings of an education in literature and politics.

Carnegie started as a bobbin boy in a cotton factory in Allegheny, Pennsylvania, where his parents settled. By the time he was thirty, he had made what was then classed as a great fortune: $400,000. The fortune derived from hard work, yes; but it was helped along by a powerful patron who was president of the Pennsylvania Railroad. When this patron was appointed assistant secretary of war in the Lincoln administration, Carnegie accompanied him to Washington as an aide. There he was in a superb position to learn the crucial role that railroads and iron and steel would play in the new, industrialized economy.

Carnegie's first fortune came from railroading, bridge building, oil, and a series of clever speculations. He had a somewhat ambiguous attitude toward his success. He sometimes seemed to fear that money might destroy his character. In 1868, in a remarkable memorandum to himself, he listed his assets and the income they could produce:

An income of $50,000 per annum! . . . Beyond this, make no effort to increase fortune. . . . Man must have an idol—the amassing of wealth is one of the worst species of idolatry—no idol more debasing than the worship of money. . . . To continue much longer overwhelmed by business cares and with most of my thoughts wholly upon the way to make more money in the shortest time, must degrade me beyond hope of permanent recovery.

Within five years, in spite of such thoughts, Carnegie was embarked on the creation of Carnegie Steel, which he made into a model of vertical integration and efficiency. When he finally sold his interest in the company to the new trust, United States Steel, in 1901, it was worth $250 million.

But Carnegie did try to rescue himself from "idolatry" in a variety of ways. He wrote five volumes of books and essays—a remarkable accomplishment for a man of affairs. He cultivated literary and philosophical friends in both England and America. He also embarked on a program of "scientific philanthropy" that eventually totaled about $350 million, dotting the landscape with what came to be called "Carnegie libraries." Carnegie was not a typical entrepreneur of the period. But his articulateness and his rhetoric of benevolence made him a model for people who wanted to believe in individual struggle, success through fair competition, and enlightened capitalism as the basis of American democracy.

up this supercorporation. Like International Harvester, the giant company dominated its industry. It produced almost all of some forms of steel and three-fifths of the total steel made in the United States.

An even more stunning example of consolidation brought John D. Rockefeller into control of the oil industry. Rockefeller started out as a poor boy, like Carnegie. He too saved every cent (except for the 10 percent tithe he regularly gave to his Baptist church). Starting with one refinery in Cleveland, Rockefeller by 1872 had created the giant Standard Oil Company.

THE TRUST Rockefeller also created a new device that made it even easier to consolidate an industry: the trust. A business trust is an arrangement in which several companies "sell" themselves to a group of trustees. The companies are paid for with shares in the new trust itself. Only paper changes hands, but the result is a single group of directors who control the operations of several companies.

Through the Standard Oil trust, the Rockefeller interests acquired almost total control of the oil industry. The trust could phase out unnecessary plants. It could take full advantage of mass production and distribution techniques to provide most of the kerosene that lighted American lamps and the oil that lubricated American machines. Rockefeller himself summed up adequately the reasons for the trust.

> It has revolutionized the way of doing business all over the world. The time was ripe for it. It had to come, though all we saw at the moment was the need to save ourselves from wasteful conditions [of competition]. The day of combination is here to stay. Individualism has gone, never to return.

One by one, the main American industries passed from competition to consolidation. It might occur through giant corporations created by mergers, like International Harvester or United States Steel. Or it might result from the

Capital and its champion. One of the favorite subjects for nineteenth-century cartoonists was the trust. Here Capital brings its newest gladiator to the edge of the ring to introduce the victor. The vanquished at the rear include the "small dealer" and the traveling salesman. (Culver Pictures)

formation of trusts in various industries, from cottonseed oil to sugar to whiskey. By 1900 a few large concerns controlled almost all the major facilities of production and distribution in the United States.

The New Americans

Industry has always needed people, and the new industrial order needed hordes. The growth in agriculture, railroads, and industry demanded millions of people—both as workers and as consumers.

The American population kept pace with industrial growth. For every 100 people living in the United States in 1870, there were 126 in 1880, 158 in 1890, 190 in 1900, and 230 in 1910. In one generation, the population more than doubled, from about 40 million in 1870 to over 90 million forty years later.

These were the millions who moved into the Great Plains and the Rockies, bringing about the final defeat of the Native Americans. These were the millions who made or bought McCormick's harvesters, who built the railroads that carried his reapers into every flat corner of the country where grain could be planted and harvested by machine.

SHIFTING TRENDS IN IMMIGRATION

These millions, however, were not just more of the same kinds of Americans who had lived here in Jacksonian times. Many of them were "new" people—with different languages, different religions, and different ways of life. Andrew Jackson's "common man" was, most likely, born in America; he was white, Protestant, and a farmer. His parents or grandparents might have been immigrants, but they would probably have come from England or Scotland. When they arrived here, they would have found the language, the ways of worshiping God, and the customs familiar and comfortable.

But the "common man" in New York in 1900 was more likely to be a Jew from Poland or a Catholic from Italy. He lived in a great city and probably had a job in a factory or a business. His English might be poor. His memories of the "old country" would be at least as important to him as his hopes for the new. He represented a social revolution that had accompanied the revolutions in technology, industry, and business—the creation of an urban immigrant working class.

There have been immigrants in America for thousands of years, since people began to cross over from Asia into Alaska. In the hundred years following the American Revolution, the actual proportion of immigrants to the total population did not change much. Two other things happened instead. First, the nature of the immigrant population changed. Second, the immigrants (along with other Americans) began to congregate in great urban centers. These two changes made industrial cities like Chicago the gathering places for a new kind of American: the poor immigrant from a country where English was not spoken and where an Anglo-Saxon Protestant was a rarity.

In 1790, when the United States took its first census under the new Constitution, nine out of ten Americans (except for the black slaves in the South) had English or Scottish ancestors. This pattern changed somewhat with the immigration of the 1840s and 1850s—the "old" immigration—when large numbers of German, Scandinavian, and Irish immigrants began to arrive. Although their languages might be strange to American ears, most of the Germans and Scandinavians were at least Protestants. And although many native-born Americans resented the Catholicism of the Irish, these immigrants at least spoke English. In 1865 the United States had only about 200,000 inhabitants who had been born in southern or eastern Europe. They were easily absorbed in a total population of about 40 million.

By 1914 this picture had changed dramatically. A "new" immigration—mainly from Italy, Russia, and Austria-Hungary—flooded into the United States. Poverty drove many of these people from their home countries. Some men left to avoid the military draft, which discriminated against the poor. Jews wanted to escape the official anti-Semitism of Russia and Poland. Armenians fled from persecutions carried out by the Turkish government. The new immigrants were drawn to the United States by advertisements of cheap steamship transportation, by rumors of free land and golden opportunity, and by a massive propaganda campaign conducted by railroads anxious for workers and for customers to buy up their lands.

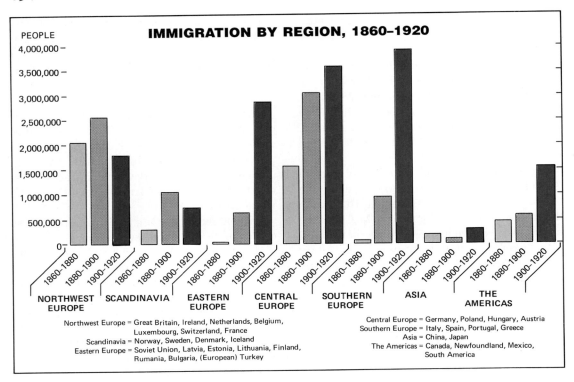

IMMIGRATION BY REGION, 1860–1920

Northwest Europe = Great Britain, Ireland, Netherlands, Belgium,
Luxembourg, Switzerland, France
Scandinavia = Norway, Sweden, Denmark, Iceland
Eastern Europe = Soviet Union, Latvia, Estonia, Lithuania, Finland,
Rumania, Bulgaria, (European) Turkey

Central Europe = Germany, Poland, Hungary, Austria
Southern Europe = Italy, Spain, Portugal, Greece
Asia = China, Japan
The Americas = Canada, Newfoundland, Mexico,
South America

Immigration from southern and eastern Europe amounted to only a trickle in the 1860s and 1870s. But by the 1890s over half the immigrants to America were from southern and eastern Europe. Between 1901 and 1910—the peak decade for immigration in the history of the United States—the proportion of new immigrants rose to over 75 percent, as over 6 million Italians, Russian Jews, Hungarians, and other immigrants from southern and eastern Europe poured into the country.

REACTION TO THE NEWCOMERS The McCormick strike and the Haymarket affair occurred just before the new immigration into the United States reached its peak. But prejudice had already been aroused by the entry of Irish and Germans, and by the beginnings of the influx from eastern and southern Europe. Both the McCormick strike and the trial of the Haymarket

Eight occurred in an atmosphere of fear and bigotry. The Pinkerton report on the "fighting Irish" molders and the newspaper comments on foreign "anarchists" make it clear that events in Chicago would probably have been different if they had not taken place at the time of this bewildering flood of immigrants.

The new immigrants were not only different in culture, language, and religion, they behaved in ways different from those who had preceded them. They moved into a society that was no longer predominantly agricultural and rural, but urban. So they did not fan out onto farms as many of the old immigrants had done. Instead, they followed the lead of millions of other Americans and settled into cities. Two thirds of foreign-born residents in the United States lived in towns and cities by 1900.

Bewildered and often victimized in America, new immigrants clustered together in their own city neighborhoods, or "ghettos." People from a particular province or even a particular village would move into buildings on the same block, re-creating much of the culture of their Old World homes. As the new immigration swelled, so did antiforeign sentiment. Ghetto dwellers earned a reputation among "native" Americans for being clannish, dirty, superstitious, and generally undesirable. They were considered strange, chattering in their old languages, and somehow suited only for city life. Actually, of course, they were no more "natural" city dwellers than were the English who had come to Virginia and Massachusetts in the seventeenth century. They were simply caught in a phase of the industrial revolution—the creation of an urban society.

Immigrants from Asia—almost all from China and Japan—were among the most ghetto-bound of the newcomers, rigidly segregated in their "Chinatown" communities. And for generations, neither the Asian Americans nor native-born whites believed that they ever could or should become integrated into American life. Most of the Asian immigrants believed that Western civilization was a form of barbarism, something to be resisted in every possible way. Few American officials paid any attention to whether Asian-American children attended public schools. No one thought it necessary for them to learn English. They were the victims of harassment, cruel jokes, and vicious cartoons. The state of California had special taxes for "foreign miners." Murderous riots against the Chinese took place in every major Western city during the 1870s and 1880s. The Asians' subtle and sophisticated way of cooking attracted some favorable attention, but even their food came into the American diet and language as "chop suey," an unkind culinary joke.

In California, especially, the Chinese immigrants were the objects of a double discrimination. Almost every American of European ancestry believed Asians were racially inferior. But white workers also resented competition in the labor market, especially during times of economic depression and high unemployment. In the 1870s the California Workingman's Party

began to agitate for a law forbidding any person from China to hold a job. The effort succeeded. In 1879 a clause was added to the state constitution of California that forbade any employer to hire Chinese workers. But no state had a constitutional right to forbid immigration. That was up to the national government. In 1882 an act of Congress put a ten-year prohibition on Chinese workers entering the United States as immigrants.

And so the new society that grew out of the industrial revolution was an intensely segregated society. As a result of the railroads and the rush of pioneers to the West, Native Americans were confined to their shrinking reservations. Blacks, Asians, and European immigrants in the towns and cities were just as confined to their ghettos. The very meaning of the word *American,* as it was normally used, reflected these racial and ethnic segregations. Being an American meant, to most people, *not* being "colored," *not* being Catholic or Jewish, *not* having Slavic or Greek or Polish ways and words. The two most intensely debated questions of the day among "native" Americans—that is, Protestant white people whose ancestry was British or northwest European— were: What could be done to slow down or stop the "foreigners" from coming? Who among them (if any) had a chance to become "Americans"?

BECOMING "AMERICAN" In the era of the new immigration, the goal of many was still assimilation—to take on the traits of the new society so as to blend with it. But becoming an "American" was not an easy process for most European immigrants in the late nineteenth century.

Real assimilation meant knowing the language. Many immigrant parents made enormous sacrifices to bring their families to a country where education was free and easily available. Mary Antin, a Jewish immigrant, remembered it this way:

> Education was free. It was the one thing that my father was able to promise us when he sent for

Open-air restaurant. This pair of Chinese Americans have established their restaurant in a lumber camp in the West. Chinese cuisine made its way into the European-American diet only slowly in the nineteenth century. Guidebooks routinely described Chinese restaurants as the haunts of the Chinese themselves, the European-American poor, "outlaws," and African Americans. It never occurred to the authors of the guidebooks that poor people might not be quite as bigoted as the American-born middle class (and that they might have more flexible tastes, too). (Bancroft Library, University of California, Berkeley)

us; surer, safer than bread or shelter. On our second day in the country a little girl across the alley came and offered to conduct us to school. We five children between us had a few words of English by this time. We knew the word "school." We understood. This child, who had never seen us till yesterday, who was not much better dressed than we were, still was able to offer us the freedom of the schools of Boston! No application made; no questions asked; no examinations, rulings, exclusions; no fees.

Learning the language was only one step toward assimilation. Many immigrants joined some kind of voluntary association that brought them contacts with native-born Americans. In cities, the most obvious associations were political parties. They could provide favors, food, and jobs.

"Boss" Richard Croker of Tammany Hall in New York described the work of his machine as dealing with people who

do not speak our language and do not know our laws, yet are the raw material with which we have to build up the state. [The Tammany machine] looks after them for the sake of their vote, grafts them upon the Republic, makes citizens of them, in short; and although you may not like our motives or our methods, what other agency is there by which so long a row could have been hoed so quickly or so well?

Another powerful influence on the new immigrants was those who had preceded them. Some of the earlier arrivals learned English and helped recruit workers from Europe. They sometimes even paid the newcomers' transportation and helped them settle in the cities.

One popular name for such men was *padrone* (an Italian word meaning "patron"). A padrone might be paid by an employer for supplying cheap labor, by a political machine for delivering immigrant votes, or by the immigrants themselves for favors. Often the padrones, who existed among almost every immigrant group, were ward leaders in political machines, serving as links between the newcomers and the city organizations.

Urbanization

In the ancient world, only two great cities—Rome and Alexandria—had populations of over half a million people. By the time of Christopher Columbus, Rome and Alexandria had long since declined. The only European cities to have reached a comparable size were London and Paris. At the time of the Haymarket affair, however, Chicago had already become a great city. In fact, by 1900 the United States had six cities with more than half a million inhabitants.

The process of urbanization was not confined to the United States. All the industrializing nations of western Europe experienced it too. The factory system demanded high concentrations of workers, and the agricultural revolution made it possible for millions of people to leave their farms—whether in Germany or in Maine.

The United States experienced three great migrations in the generation after the Civil War. One was from the East to the Great Plains and the Far West. Another was from Europe to America. The third was from the country to the city.

Of the three, the movement from farm to city was the most extensive.

In 1800 only about 3 Americans out of every 100 lived in cities larger than 8,000. By 1900 this proportion had grown 1,000 percent; almost a third of the nation lived in cities of over 8,000. In 1800 there had been only 6 cities larger than 8,000; by 1900 there were over 400.

This increase was not gradual and smooth. Most of it came in the half-century after the end of the Civil War. During this period, at least 15 million native Americans moved out of farming areas and into cities, and their number was swollen by an almost equal number of new immigrants who settled in cities instead of on farms. Statistics tell the story. Between 1870 and 1900 the total population of the United States increased by about 35 million people. During the same period the urban population increased by about 24 million. The cities had absorbed more than two-thirds of the total increase.

TECHNOLOGICAL FACTORS A city is not just a collection of people in a small area. Like industry, modern cities were made possible by technological change. In the centuries before the industrial revolution, the size of a city had been determined mainly by the available transportation. It could not be too big, because a person had to be able to walk or travel by wagon or carriage to a marketplace or job and back home again. After about 1880, however, cities began to experience a transportation revolution. The introduction of electricity made it possible to replace slow and awkward horse-drawn transport with fast, clean trolleys, elevated trains, and subways. These improvements meant that people could live many miles from their place of work and still be part of a vast city.

Electricity also made it possible to light city streets. Cleveland, in 1879, became the first city to have electric street lighting. Similarly, the introduction of the telephone in the 1880s meant that homes, offices, and factories could be tied together in an almost instantaneous communications network.

An urban vista. This was a relatively prosperous, predominantly Jewish neighborhood in lower Manhattan at the end of the nineteenth century. The pedestrians and shoppers are comfortably dressed, and the pushcarts and storefronts offer a bewildering variety of goods and services, including a public bathhouse, an important institution in urban Jewish communities in Central and Eastern Europe. (Natural History Museum of Los Angeles County)

At first, city buildings themselves were a limiting factor. Even with the thickest walls, a stone or brick building could not extend higher than fifteen stories. To build a structure even this high, builders had to reduce the size of windows, because glass could not support the weight. A second problem was that human legs could tolerate only so many flights of stairs. The first problem was solved by the invention of the skyscraper in the 1880s, pioneered by a Chicago architect, Louis Sullivan. Skyscraper construction, in which walls were hung on steel frames, made structures as tall as a hundred stories possible. Thus more people could be concentrated, level upon level, on smaller parcels of land. The second problem was solved at about the same time by the invention of the electric elevator, which made the tall buildings usable.

The Industrial System

The new industrial system, with its machines and its factories, had some obvious economic advantages. It could produce more goods, with less labor, and at a lower cost. There were some equally obvious disadvantages. The factories were dirty, noisy, and dangerous. And so were the cities where they were built. Factories could

An early Chicago skyscraper. One of the break-throughs of the nineteenth century was the steel-frame technique that made possible construction of skyscrapers, like this one in progress in Chicago in 1894. Once the frame was up, the walls could simply "hang" on the outside of the building, since they no longer had to support the structure. (Culver Pictures)

produce only standardized goods, lacking the mark of individual craftsmanship. They undercut the skilled worker's control over the pace and intensity of work. And they drove small producers, using simpler methods, out of business.

Many Americans—perhaps even a majority—were convinced that the advantages outweighed the disadvantages. In fact, most Americans seem to have believed that there was something almost inevitable about industrial "progress."

CONDITIONS OF LABOR On the other hand, the new system did exploit and oppress many of those who worked in the factories and mills, on the railroads, in the mines, and on the farms. And they knew it. It took no sophisticated economic analysis for a man or woman who worked at a quickened pace from seven in the morning until six at night to understand fatigue. And seven out of ten Americans worked just such a sixty-hour, six-day week—collecting an average of about ten dollars a week in wages. For others, the situation was worse. In the steel industry, the norm was an eighty-four hour, seven-day week.

The average American worker at the end of the nineteenth century was earning about $450 a year. Everyone understood that a family needed about twice that much to live decently. In fact, about $600 a year was necessary to keep out of deep poverty. The difference, of course, had to be made up with the labor of children and, increasingly, women—all pooling miserable wages to try to put together a passable life.

In addition, the character of work itself was changing. In earlier times, the pace and nature of work had been adjusted primarily to people—to their arms, hands, and tools. But in factories, machinery set the pace, and people had to follow. Skilled workers, especially, understood that the factory threatened their control over the tone and atmosphere of the workplace, and that industrial work tended always to become dull, routine, speeded, and intensely bossed.

Workingmen and women—and even some of the children—responded to these conditions with complaints, protest, and resistance. On the simplest level, they argued and complained in their factories, challenging their bosses' authority and control. They agreed silently among themselves to slow down their efforts, until the machines themselves had to be adjusted to a more relaxed pace. When they could, they quit jobs and moved on to other towns and other factories. They brought effective emotional pressure to bear on foremen, who often shared their ethnic and religious identifications. They managed to insist, in a dozen different ways and in

Child labor. Working-class families were usually unable to support themselves on a father's earnings, so others had to take jobs. In many ethnic communities, there was a much stronger prejudice against women working than against children, so boys and girls found themselves in mills and mines. (Often, though, working-class families had no choice but to put women *and* children to work.) One result was the haunting faces of children like this scratched and dazed boy, whose ten-hour-a-day job was to carry mats bigger than he was. (George Eastman House Collection. Photograph by Lewis W. Hine)

the most desperate situations, on the simple dignity and independence of the working person.

Increasingly, however, it became clear that individual resistance and sabotage were not going to work, and that something more systematic and organized was necessary. And so working people began a generation-long quest for a method of action that would get results; one that would give them shorter hours, better pay, an increased degree of control over work itself, and perhaps even a larger voice in the way the new industrial society was shaped and managed.

EARLY ATTEMPTS TO ORGANIZE LABOR

One possibility was direct political action: entering party politics, either to support one of the major parties or to find labor candidates. Before the 1890s neither of the two principal parties was much interested in courting the support of organized groups of workers. So the most active workingmen experimented with parties of their own. In 1872 a National Labor Reform party tried to nominate a Supreme Court justice, David Davis, for president. But the candidate refused to run on their ticket. In 1876, labor leaders in

Knights of Labor. The Knights of Labor held out the hope, for a brief time, of racial integration in the labor movement. Here, at an 1886 annual convention of the Knights in Richmond, Virginia, an African-American delegate, Frank J. Farrell, has just finished introducing the visionary leader of the Knights, General Master Workman Terence Powderly. The artist has carefully shown the audience looking and gesturing enthusiastically toward Farrell, not Powderly. (Library of Congress)

the East helped to create a National Independent party, but their candidate won few votes, even among workers. A similar experiment in 1880 brought the same result. Just two years before Haymarket, an Anti-Monopoly party, created in part by labor leaders, was crushed.

With both the Democratic and the Republican parties turning a deaf ear, and with third-party politics offering no hope, it was clear that the only possible path was to organize labor itself, not to engage directly in politics.

In 1866, on the initiative of an iron molder who belonged to the same kind of trade union that was so active in the McCormick strike, the National Labor Union was formed. Its leader, William Sylvis, conceived it as a reform union. It included temperance groups and woman suffrage groups as well as trade union organizations.

And it repudiated the traditional last resort of workers, the strike. This union made little or no headway and lasted only about seven years.

A much more promising organization was the Noble Order of the Knights of Labor, created in 1869 by a tailor in Philadelphia. Its plan was to organize all workers—skilled and unskilled, farm and factory, male and female, even black and white—in one grand union. In fact, the Knights specifically excluded only four types of people, whom they labeled "parasites": liquor dealers, bankers, professional gamblers, and lawyers. Like the National Labor Union, the Knights of Labor officially discouraged strikes and favored, instead, the "education" of workers and owners.

For a decade, the Knights grew slowly. Then leadership passed to an extraordinarily hand-some and magnetic machinist from Pennsylvania, Terence V. Powderly. Powderly dropped an old rule making the Knights' ritual, rules, and membership a fraternal secret. In turn, the Catholic church dropped its official opposition, and membership began to increase. Still, Powderly opposed strikes and talked as though he did not represent workers at all but men who were anxious to become small capitalists: "I shudder at the thought of a strike," he said. "We must give men the chance to become their own employers."

It was, ironically, a strike that skyrocketed the Knights to prominence and to a fantastic rise in membership. Some of the local assemblies decided to stage a wildcat strike against the Texas and Pacific Railroad in 1885. Surprisingly, the railroad settled, and within a year the Knights suddenly had 700,000 members—a tripling of their rolls.

The Knights of Labor was not involved in the McCormick strike of 1886, and only indirectly in the Haymarket affair. But the organization was one of the principal victims of the public hysteria that followed the bombing and shooting in Chicago. Membership began to fall, and when the railroad assemblies were soundly beaten in a second strike against the Texas and Pacific in the same year, the disaster was complete. By 1890, 600,000 men and women had deserted the Noble Order, and it was, for all practical purposes, dead.

Meanwhile, another type of labor organization was building, one that would eventually become the most successful and characteristic in American society. In 1881 a group of craft unions formed the Federation of Organized Trades and Labor Unions. The principles of this organization were clear from the outset. First, it was concerned with skilled workers, not with trying to organize the industrial masses. Second, though reluctantly, they would use the strike as a weapon. Third, they were concerned strictly with wages, hours, and working conditions—not with politics, social reform, or other kinds of "utopian" schemes.

Here was unionism "pure and simple," as the members liked to say. Under the leadership of an immigrant cigar maker, Samuel Gompers, and

under a new name, the American Federation of Labor, the organization made steady gains. By the end of the century, it had half a million members (and a dozen years later, it would boast of 2 million).

STRIKES AND STRIKEBREAKERS   Large national unions were destined to be part of American life. But for most people, the "labor question" focused not so much on unions as on a series of spectacular outbreaks of violence that rocked a society which had never witnessed anything of the sort on such a scale. For a generation—from the 1870s until after the turn of the century—it seemed possible that society might actually be divided between rich and poor, owners and workers, in an increasingly desperate class struggle. This was, in fact, the atmosphere that fed the hysteria of Haymarket. And it was an atmosphere that intensified in every decade.

In 1877, just a year after the nation's centennial celebrations, four large railroads in the East announced a 10 percent cut in wages. The result was a sudden strike that paralyzed rail traffic all over the country. Crowds of workers stopped trains and occupied railroad buildings and roundhouses. In Pittsburgh, especially, the strikers' control seemed to be almost complete. Finally, in July, a frightened federal administration sent troops to "restore order"—that is, to break the strike. There was resistance. Nervous soldiers fired. Angry workers burned. In Pittsburgh a three-mile-long fire destroyed 160 locomotives and hundreds of freight cars.

Nine years later came Haymarket, less violent and destructive, but just as frightening to those Americans who feared that "radicals" were out to destroy "order."

Then, in 1892, six years after Haymarket, a Carnegie Steel plant at Homestead, Pennsylvania, was struck after the company announced pay cuts. The management asked the Pinkerton company to bring in several hundred armed guards— "goons" and "gun-thugs," the strikers called them. The Pinkerton men came on barges, down the river that ran next to the Homestead plant. The striking workers met them, as heavily armed. Someone fired, and before the guns had stopped several hours later, seven men were dead and many more wounded. In response, the governor of Pennsylvania sent in the entire state national guard, some 8,000 troops, to "restore order." The strike was broken. The men who had remained anonymous enough drifted back to work. The others simply drifted.

Two years later, in Illinois, a similarly angry and violent strike occurred, bringing back memories of Haymarket on both sides. George Pullman, who held a monopoly on the manufacture of Pullman coaches and parlor cars, had built what he boasted was a "model" industrial town near Chicago. Workers lived in company houses, bought in company stores, attended churches built and controlled by the company, and—mostly—worked for the company.

Most of the Pullman workers were members of the militant American Railway Union, led by the greatest of American union leaders, Eugene Victor Debs. A confrontation was almost certain when, in response to a depression, Pullman announced a 25 percent cut in wages, but with no cuts in the rents of company houses or the prices in company stores. The workers struck, and Debs called on all 150,000 members of his union to refuse to move any train with a Pullman coach. Railroads everywhere fired any of Debs's men who refused to handle Pullmans. When this happened, the union called a strike against the offending railroad. In a few days, railroads from Chicago to the West, as well as many in the East, were paralyzed.

Once again, the "solution" was military. President Grover Cleveland sent federal troops into Chicago to "protect the mails," even though Governor John Peter Altgeld—who had pardoned the surviving Haymarket defendants—objected. The strike collapsed. Debs went to prison. And Americans on both sides of the struggle seemed to have new evidence that industrial revolution might have more revolutionary consequences than they had at first imagined.

American Culture, 1875–1900

Economically and socially, the most important facts about American society in the period following the Civil War were industrialization, urbanization, and immigration. These facts together brought about a change in the landscape that was almost brutally obvious—the crowded, dirty, smoky city, with its "alien" working class. But people very often did not or *would* not see or acknowledge what was most plain. In their art and architecture, their novels and magazines—in all the areas of their culture—native, white, middle-class Americans seemed determined to ignore the realities of their age. At both the popular and the sophisticated level, middle-class culture seemed almost serene in its lack of awareness of industrial capitalism and its social consequences. To some extent, of course, the practice of ignoring, evading, or denying reality is a characteristic of culture in any society. But Americans in the 1870s and 1880s were abnormally, almost absurdly, consistent in their unwillingness to come to terms culturally with the actualities around them.

LITERATURE This characteristic of American culture was not confined to the sentimental and quaint books and essays published for a middle-class, primarily female readership. It was evident in the most talented and sophisticated intellectuals, too. Henry James wrote great novels and stories, as great as any ever published in English. But they were about the elegant and complicated lives of wealthy Americans and were usually set in Europe. Even when one of James's heroes was a businessman, as in *The American* (1876), he appeared in the novel only *after* he had made his fortune and arrived in Europe in pursuit of "culture" and an aristocratic French bride.

Henry James was born to wealth, cultivated society, and European travel. Samuel Clemens was born in Missouri into a modestly well-to-do family and spent much of his life scratching for a living as a journalist. As Mark Twain, he wrote about plain people. But his plain people were not immigrants or factory workers. And his settings were the small towns of the Mississippi, where boyish and innocent characters like Huckleberry Finn and Tom Sawyer had their "adventures." *Huckleberry Finn* (1885) was a great novel by almost any standard. But it was hardly a novel that confronted American realities. Clemens lived in Hartford, Connecticut, a modern city; he was married to the daughter of a coal baron. But the closest he came to an examination of such realities was when he fantasized about the experience a technologically inventive Yankee might have if he suddenly woke up in medieval England, as in *A Connecticut Yankee in King Arthur's Court* (1889).

What was true of Mark Twain and Henry James was equally true of lesser talents. Even when novels were about businessmen—as in William Dean Howells's *The Rise of Silas Lapham* (1884)—the real subject seemed to be not business but high society and romance, and the action occurred *after* the fortune was acquired. Edward Bellamy's *Looking Backward* (1888), one of the most popular novels of the period, was a utopian romance about Boston in the year 2000. The utopia was, in theory at least, highly industrialized, urbanized, and socialistic. And the response of middle-class readers was enthusiastic. But beneath its appearance of relevance to nineteenth-century realities, *Looking Backward* really described a small, pleasant Boston, from which the factories, the poor, and the immigrants had disappeared as though by magic.

In the 1890s a few books did try to deal with the more sordid aspects of factory and slum life. Jacob Riis's *How the Other Half Lives* (1890) described a slum in vivid language that alarmed his primarily middle-class, native audience:

Cherry Street. Be a little careful, please! The hall is dark and you might stumble over the children pitching pennies back there. Not that it would hurt them: kicks and cuffs are their daily diet. They have little else. Here where the hall turns and dives into utter darkness is a step, and another, another. A flight of stairs. You can feel your way, if you cannot see it. Close? Yes! What would you have? All the fresh air that ever enters these stairs comes from the hall-door that is forever slamming, and from the windows of dark bedrooms.

Stephen Crane's *Maggie: A Girl of the Streets* (1893) was a dark account of the way slum poverty turned innocent girls to sordid lives. But such books came only after decades of industrialization. And they created almost as much scandal as if they had been about sexual perversion. For the most part, native-born writers and other intellectuals provided no insight whatever into the lives and difficulties of the new, immigrant, urban working class.

On the level of popular culture, the picture was much the same. A revolution in printing technology had made inexpensive books and magazines easily available, and a flood of popular fiction poured off the new steam-driven presses. But most of the stories and books dealt with rural life or with the doings of chaste and sentimental small-town girls; or they had as their heroes idealized Western cowboys, romantic sailors, or heroic figures from ancient history.

A new type of popular fiction did emerge after the Civil War: the tale of business success. The most notable promoter of the rags-to-riches formula was a Harvard-educated former clergyman, Horatio Alger. His *Ragged Dick: Or, Street Life in New York* (1867) was a sensational best-seller. For the next thirty years Alger sold over 200 million copies of his stories, with titles like *Jed the Poorhouse Boy* and *Struggling Upward*.

Superficially, at least, the Alger stories reflected important economic realities. But the reflection was indirect and distorted. Alger did not deal with the adult, business careers of his heroes. Instead, he wrote coy exercises in moralism, designed to show how Ragged Dick or Tattered Tom or Poorhouse Jed overcame orphan-hood and poverty by saving the drowning daughter of a wealthy, sonless merchant. The books always ended just as their heroes were about to embark on adult careers in commerce. The reader was left to assume that, in their adult lives, Alger's heroes would continue to thrive through a steady application of "pluck."

ART AND ARCHITECTURE The practice of turning away from economic and social realities that was so central to the literature of the 1870s and 1880s was equally characteristic of the art and architecture of those decades. The greatest American artist of the period, James McNeill Whistler, painted mostly portraits and nocturnal landscapes. When Whistler did depict a scene of contemporary social or economic activity, the subject was more likely to be European than American.

Most artists confined themselves to painting scenes of nature, domestic life, or portraits of the wealthy in which the sources of wealth were carefully ignored. Winslow Homer, who probably was the second most talented American painter of the period, used his muscular and vivid style primarily on seascapes. When he did paint men at work, they were almost always fishermen in aged boats—an ardently preindustrial subject.

Architecture was even more flagrantly systematic in denying the actualities of industrialism. The expanding society of the period required an enormous number of new buildings—campuses for colleges and universities; buildings for banks and corporations; homes and summer houses for new millionaires; railroad stations; and so on. But even the most talented architects were mired in a contest to restore ancient styles. The familiar, reliable Greek and Roman styles that had been so popular since the Revolution were pressed into service again. There was an astonishing revival of Gothic and Georgian, especially in campus architecture. And anyone could stare for days at the largest of the new railroad stations, with their Greek columns or baroque decorations, without

The lure of success. More than any popular writer of his time, Horatio Alger captured the essence of the dream of success that attracted many American youths from the countryside into the cities. This was the cover for one of Alger's many novels, *From Farm to Fortune*. It is a "before and after" depiction of the sudden rise of a farmer's son to urban wealth. He has exchanged his hunting rifle for a business document, but the artist is careful to suggest that the transition need not endanger the innocent virtue of a young man of good character. (Library of Congress)

gaining any clue as to what the function of the building actually was. In their buildings, as in their novels and paintings, Americans seemed more intent on disguising the industrial revolution than in celebrating it.

1869 Two-term administration of Ulysses S. Grant begins. Knights of Labor founded in Philadelphia.

1872 John D. Rockefeller founds Standard Oil company. Andrew Carnegie builds steel plant near Pittsburgh, Pennsylvania. National Labor Reform Party attempts to nominate Supreme Court Justice David Davis for president; he refuses.

1876 Alexander Graham Bell exhibits working telephone. Eastern labor leaders form National Independent party. Henry James publishes *The American*.

1877 Administration of Rutherford B. Hayes begins. Railroad strike paralyzes eastern lines; President Hayes uses military to restore "order."

1880 "New" immigration from central, eastern, and southern Europe begins rapid acceleration. Terence Powderly assumes leadership of Knights of Labor. Labor leaders form Anti-Monopoly party.

1881 Administration of James A. Garfield and Chester A. Arthur begins. Federation of Organized Trades and Labor Unions, forerunner of American Federation of Labor, founded.

1866	1868	1870	1872	1874	1876	1878	1880	1882

1866 William Sylvis founds National Labor Union.

1867 Horatio Alger publishes *Ragged Dick: Or, Street Life in New York.*

1870 Railway track mileage in United States reaches 40,000. Two decades of mob violence against Asian Americans begin.

1878 First working telephone system installed in New Haven, Connecticut.

1879 California constitution forbids employers to hire Chinese workers. Cleveland, Ohio, becomes first American city with electric lighting system.

1882 Federal law places ten-year prohibition on immigration of Chinese workers to the United States.

1886 McCormick workers join Metalworkers Union and Knights of Labor. Strike at McCormick, and general strike in Chicago for eight-hour day. Haymarket bombing and police riot. Four men hanged for Haymarket "conspiracy"; strike at McCormick broken. Knights of Labor membership begins rapid decline after failed strike against Texas and Pacific railroad.

1890 Jacob Riis publishes *How the Other Half Lives.*

1894 American Railway Union strike at Pullman railway car company near Chicago; President Cleveland orders federal troops to Chicago; strike broken and its leader, Eugene Victor Debs, imprisoned.

1884	1886	1888	1890	1892	1894	1896	1898	1900

1884 Chicago architect Louis Sullivan begins to pioneer "skyscraper" architecture. First intercity telephone line opened between New York and Boston. McCormick Harvester Works shows 71 percent profit; cuts workers' wages 10 to 15 percent. William Dean Howells publishes *The Rise of Silas Lapham.*

1885 Administration of Grover Cleveland begins. Strike at McCormick works; 1884 pay cuts restored. McCormick installs new molding machinery. Knights of Labor holds successful strike against Texas and Pacific railroad. Samuel Clemens ("Mark Twain") publishes *Huckleberry Finn.*

1888 Edward Bellamy publishes *Looking Backward.*

1889 Administration of Benjamin Harrison begins. Mark Twain publishes *A Connecticut Yankee in King Arthur's Court.*

1892 Telephone connection completed between New York and Chicago. Strike at Carnegie steel plant at Homestead, Pennsylvania, broken by National Guard troops.

1893 Second administration of Grover Cleveland begins. Beginning of severe economic depression. Stephen Crane publishes *Maggie, a Girl of the Streets.*

1900 Railway track mileage in United States reaches 200,000; United States is world's leading manufacturing nation.

1901 United States Steel company founded.

Suggestions for Further Reading

THE McCORMICK STRIKE AND
THE HAYMARKET BOMBING

The most recent study of the Haymarket affair is Paul Arvich, *The Haymarket Tragedy* (1984). But Henry David, *History of the Haymarket Affair* (1936), is still worth reading. The strike at the McCormick plant is discussed in Robert Ozanne, *A Century of Labor and Management Relations at McCormick and International Harvester* (1959).

TECHNOLOGICAL CHANGE

The most curious and interesting study of technological change during this phase of the industrial revolution is an aging book by Lewis Mumford, *Technics and Civilization* (1934). A breezier book is Roger Burlingame, *The Engines of Democracy* (1940). Matthew Josephson, *Edison* (1959), is a fine biographical study of one of the most important innovators of the period, as is Robert V. Bruce, *Bell: Alexander Graham Bell and the Conquest of Solitude* (1973). The best places to begin the study of railroads are Alfred Chandler, *The Railroads, the Nation's First Big Business* (1965), and Robert Fogel, *Railroads in American Economic Growth* (1964). Chandler stresses the significance of railroad development; Fogel casts doubt on it. See also Oscar Winther, *The Transportation Frontier: The Trans-Mississippi West, 1865–1890* (1964), and John F. Stover, *American Railroads* (1961). The best general book on agriculture in the Middle West is still Fred A. Shannon, *The Farmer's Last Frontier* (1963).

MANUFACTURING

The basic industries can be approached through these special studies: Peter Temin, *Iron and Steel in Nineteenth-Century America: An Economic Inquiry* (1964); J. F. Wall, *Andrew Carnegie* (1971); Harold Livesay, *Andrew Carnegie and the Rise of Big Business* (1975); Alfred D. Chandler, *Strategy and Structure: Chapters in the History of Industrial Enterprise* (1962); Ralph W. and Muriel E. Hidy, *Pioneering in Big Business, 1882–1911: A History of Standard Oil* (1955); and John Ingham, *Iron Barons: A Social Analysis of an American Urban Elite* (1978).

IMMIGRATION

A very readable introduction to the general problem of immigration is Philip Taylor, *The Distant Magnet: European Immigration to the U.S.A.* (1971). Humbert Nelli, *The Italians in Chicago, 1880–1930* (1970), and Thomas Kessner, *The Golden Door: Italian and Jewish Immigrant Mobility in New York City, 1880–1915* (1977), are two of the better studies of particular immigrant experiences. Josef Barton, *Peasants and Strangers* (1975), treats the experiences of Italians, Slovaks, and Rumanians in an urban setting. Andrew Rolle, *The Italian Americans* (1980), is excellent, as is Helen Znaniecki Lopata, *Polish Americans* (1976). On Asian Americans, see Jack Chen, *The Chinese of America* (1980), and William Peterson, *Japanese Americans* (1971).

URBANIZATION

The transformation of Boston from a small center with a number of outlying towns into a major city is a model of what happened to American cities during this period. The process can be followed in Sam Bass Warner's fine book, *Streetcar Suburbs: The Process of Growth in Boston, 1870–1900* (1962). The same author's *The Urban Wilderness* (1972) is a good introduction to urban history. These general books are also extremely useful: Howard Chudacoff, *Evolution of American Urban Society* (1981); Zane Miller, *The Urbanization of America* (1973); Constance M. Green, *The Rise of Urban America* (1965); and Raymond Mohl, *The New City* (1985). Thomas L. Philpott, *The Slum and the Ghetto* (1978), provides an excellent treatment of black and immigrant life in Chicago. Martin Melosi, *Garbage and the Cities* (1982), is a fascinating and important book. An excellent study of urban politics is Jon C. Teaford, *The Unheralded Triumph: City Government in America, 1870–1900* (1984).

THE INDUSTRIAL SYSTEM

Two fine places to begin are Herbert Gutman's collection of essays, *Work, Culture and Society in Industrializing America* (1976), and David Montgomery, *Workers' Control* (1979). David Brody's study of the steelworkers, *Steelworkers in America: The Nonunion Era* (1960), is one of the best of the works on particular industries. The shaping of the Pullman world is sympathetically treated in Stanley Buder, *Pullman: An Experiment in Industrial Order and Community Planning, 1880–1930* (1967). A different view of the matter is Ray Ginger's very readable *The Bending Cross: A Biography of Eugene Victor Debs* (1969), which should be supplemented by the more recent study by Nick Salvatore, *Eugene V. Debs, Citizen and Socialist* (1982). A good brief survey is Joseph Rayback, *A History of American Labor* (1959). The contest between the industrial unions and the craft unions is detailed very nicely in Gerald N. Grob, *Workers and Utopia* (1961). Labor radicalism is discussed in John Laslett, *Labor and the Left* (1970). Two other important books are Peter Shergold, *Working-Class Life* (1982), and Roy Rosenzweig, *Eight Hours for What We Will* (1983). For women as workers, see the Suggestions for Further Reading for Chapter 16.

AMERICAN CULTURE, 1875–1900

Gunther Barth, *City People* (1980), is a good introduction to the leisure-time activities of urban Americans during the period. Perry Duis, *The Saloon* (1983), and John Kasson, *Amusing the Millions: Coney Island at the Turn of the Century* (1978), are also important. Henry F. May, *The End of American Innocence* (1959), contains a very readable survey of the cultural life of the last decades of the nineteenth century. On writers, a good introduction is Jay Martin, *Harvest of Change: American Literature, 1865–1914* (1967). One of the most interesting ways to approach the culture of the Gilded Age is through Lewis Mumford, *The Brown Decades: The Arts in America, 1865–1895* (1931). On art and architecture, see Oliver W. Larkin, *Art and Life in America* (1949), and John Burchard and Albert Bush-Brown, *The Architecture of America: A Social and Cultural History* (1966).

CHAPTER 15
A NEW WEST

THE EPISODE: *A few days before the year 1890 ended, near the banks of a small creek deep in the Dakotas, occurred the last major armed struggle between Native Americans and the army of the United States. Some people called what happened that morning at Wounded Knee Creek a battle. Others called it a massacre. It was really some of both. Sioux warriors and the men of the Seventh United States Cavalry began shooting at the same time. That began what might be called a battle. But the Sioux had their women and children with them, and the cavalry rifles and cannon made no distinctions of age or sex. When the shooting finally stopped, only about half the Sioux dead were men, many of them unarmed. The other Sioux bodies were women and children. And some cavalrymen had lost discipline during the combat and pursued fleeing, unarmed Sioux of both sexes and cut them down with bullets or sabers. So Wounded Knee can fairly be called a massacre. But the exact word for it does not matter much. What had really happened was the end of a long, sometimes heroic, and often tragic struggle by the Sioux people to maintain their civilization and culture against the advance of the European Americans into the far-western frontier.*

THE HISTORICAL SETTING: *The Sioux were only one of many Native American groups who, during the closing decades of the nineteenth century, had their lands taken, their cultures severely damaged, and their people herded onto reservations that were sometimes hundreds of miles from their original homelands. Whites were moving into the Pacific Coast, the Sierras, and the Rockies, and onto the Plains with explosive speed and energy. The lures were many: gold in California, Colorado, and Nevada; traces and rumors of gold and silver in other areas like the Dakotas' Black Hills; a cattle bonanza in the Southwest; seemingly endless stretches of farm and timber land that could be had for next to nothing under federal land policies designed to promote westward migration.*

The drama of Wounded Knee was a moment in the long and unhappy story of the systematic attempt of European Americans to destroy a civilization they did not understand and to take for their own uses the lands that had sustained it. The Native Americans had little chance to keep their cultures intact. One by one the western tribes were forced to choose between accepting a miserable half-life on the reservations or attempting a futile and usually deadly resistance.

This chapter is the third that deals with the last decades of the nineteenth century. It shows how the political system discussed in Chapter 13 did little to control westward expansion. It also shows that the industrial revolution, discussed in Chapter 14, had consequences that reached far beyond the manufacturing cities of the East and hastened the brutal suppression of Native American ways of life.

MASSACRE AT WOUNDED KNEE

There was a confusion about names—there almost always was when Native Americans were involved. Most whites called the tribes the Sioux. But this name was just a French abbreviation of what some of the tribes' enemies had called them. They called themselves the Dakota.

There was more than one Indian name for what whites called Wounded Knee Creek, on the Pine Ridge Reservation in South Dakota. Also, whereas some people called what had happened at Wounded Knee Creek a battle, others called it a massacre. Even the man who rode out from reservation headquarters to Wounded Knee had two names. One was a Native American name, Ohiyesa. One was a white man's name, Charles Eastman. He was a Sioux, but he had been educated in white schools in New England. In fact, he was a doctor of medicine—white medicine.

But there was no confusion about what Charles Eastman saw on that bright New Year's Day morning in 1891:

> On the day following the Wounded Knee massacre, there was a blizzard. On the third day it cleared, and the ground was covered with fresh snow. We had feared that some of the wounded Indians had been left on the field, and a number of us volunteered to go and see.
>
> Fully three miles from the scene of the massacre, we found the body of a woman completely covered with a blanket of snow, and from this point on we found them scattered along as they had been hunted down and slaughtered. When we reached the spot where the Indian camp had stood, among the fragments of burned tents and other belongings, we saw the frozen bodies lying close together or piled one upon another. I counted eighty bodies of men, who were almost as helpless as the women and babes when the deadly [gun] fire began, for nearly all their guns had been taken from them.
>
> Although they had been lying in the snow and cold for two days and nights, a number had survived. Among them I found a baby of about a year old, warmly wrapped and entirely unhurt. Under a wagon, I discovered an old woman, totally blind and helpless.

82412

Big Foot. The body of Big Foot, the leader of the Sioux band that was massacred at Wounded Knee, waits, frozen, for the burial party of whites shown in the background. He is wearing mostly white man's clothing, and his body has wrenched itself into a half-sitting position, partially covered with the snow that fell after the massacre. (The Bettmann Archive)

Eastman began to load the few survivors into wagons to return to the agency (reservation headquarters), where he had set up a small hospital. Two groups of white men stayed behind at Wounded Knee. One was a troop of the U.S. Seventh Cavalry. The other was a group of about thirty white civilians who had agreed to bury the dead, at a charge of two dollars a body. They found the body of the chief of the band, an old man named Big Foot, frozen half sitting, half lying down. Ill with pneumonia, he had been lying on a blanket on the frozen ground when the shooting started.

It took until the next day to dig a big, open grave. Then the bodies were gathered. Under an unusually strong January sun, the gravediggers sweated; many worked in their shirtsleeves. They stacked 146 dead Indians—128 men and women and 18 children—in the pit. Then, while the cavalrymen stayed out of sight, the civilians gathered in a half-circle around the grave to have their photograph taken. For the photographer, they held their rifles, not shovels. Then they shoveled dirt over the bodies. When the diggers and the cavalry rode away, nothing was left at Wounded Knee but the fresh dirt of the grave and the charred poles of the tepees that had been put up only a few days before. The battle or massacre (it was really some of both) was over.

Wounded Knee was the last and most tragic moment in a long, difficult, and often ugly process: the conquest of the Sioux Indians. The conquerors were the white citizens and blue-coated soldiers of the United States. The process began before the

Civil War. At that time the Sioux were a powerful tribe, probably numbering well over 20,000. They hunted on thousands of square miles of the plains west of the Missouri River.

The Sioux had resisted the invasion of white miners, farmers, and ranchers. They fought often, and they usually won. In the summer of 1876 they had won two astonishing victories. At Rosebud Creek, in what is now Montana, they had attacked a large column of cavalry and infantry and forced the soldiers into a retreat. Then, just a few days later, the Seventh Cavalry, with General George A. Custer commanding, attacked a large Sioux camp on the Little Bighorn River, just a few miles from Rosebud Creek. Custer divided his force, and the Indians killed Custer as well as most of the Seventh, which was one of the most experienced cavalry units operating in the West.

But there were too many soldiers. Though the Sioux were never defeated, their surrender was inevitable. In 1877, just a year after "Custer's last stand," the great war chief Crazy Horse led many of his followers onto a reservation that had been recently set aside for the Sioux. Crazy Horse was murdered a short time later. Some of his people fled to Canada to join the other outstanding Sioux leader, Sitting Bull. About 2,500 Sioux then tried to survive in Canada. But hunger and cold—and the fact that white people had slain most of the buffalo—finally drove them to the reservation. In 1881 Sitting Bull surrendered—"came in," as it was said. This was the end of a golden age for the Sioux, one that had lasted more than a century.

Originally, before white Europeans had come to North America, the Sioux had lived very much like the Native Americans of the eastern seaboard. Their territory was not the open plains of the Dakotas but the woods and lakes of Minnesota and Wisconsin. There they had built permanent bark houses, used canoes, and hunted only small game. They had also farmed. This life was disturbed by indirect contact with white civilization. The Sioux were driven out of their woodlands and onto the Great Plains by another tribe, the Chippewas, who had come into contact with the French in Canada and had obtained guns in trade for furs. The guns gave the Chippewas an overwhelming advantage, and the Sioux had had to retreat to the west and south, out onto the Great Plains.

But what began as a painful retreat soon turned into a triumphant new life. Gradually, the Sioux themselves obtained guns. They also discovered another European import, the wild horses descended from the mounts the Spanish had brought into Mexico and the Southwest. Together, these European tools, the horse and the rifle, transformed the Sioux culture. For the first time, they could hunt buffalo. The plains were transformed from a barren, hostile environment into a hunting paradise. The buffalo herds became a source of meat, clothing, and shelter. The old bark houses gave way to hide-covered tepees that could be moved from one hunting area to another. This nomadic life brought the Sioux into contact (and conflict) with other Plains tribes. Hunting and warfare became the central focus of the Sioux economy and culture. For men, status in the tribe became dependent on skill and bravery in hunts and skirmishes. To a Sioux man, the tools of the hunt—his ponies, his rifle, his bow and arrows—were everything. The rituals of hunting and warfare gave meaning to his life. Any work that was not part of hunting, like preparing hides or drying meat or gathering berries, belonged to women. By the early part of the nineteenth century, the new society the Sioux had built on the plains was confident, prosperous, and expanding. They hunted all the way from the Missouri River to the valleys of the Big Horn Mountains on the eastern edge of the Rockies.

But almost as soon as this civilization was established, it was challenged. The whites, with their cannon, their railroads, their plows, and their reservations, eventually destroyed the Sioux way of life. The whites slaughtered buffalo by the thousands, until practically none were left. Then the whites insisted that the Sioux live again in permanent houses. Government rations of beef, flour, and beans were substituted for the hunt. It did not help much if a kindly agent sometimes allowed the men to "hunt" their twice-monthly ration of cattle. Games like this could not replace the old life. The authority of warriors and chiefs had depended on their skill in violent and dangerous activities. Reservation life was, above all, peaceful. The white agents even forbade the most holy annual ritual of the Sioux, the Sun Dance. And they insisted, too, that the men of the tribe could have only one wife.

What was happening was simple and, from the Sioux point of view, tragic. They had been defeated by a much more powerful and complex society. Some of them—the ones the whites referred to as the "nonprogressives"—might resist in a few ways. They could reject the cotton shirts and trousers of the white man and continue to wear Indian clothing. They could insist on wearing their hair in the traditional long braid. But resistance could not revive the old life. They had long ago accepted some of the white ways and tools. The horse and the rifle had been useful in the old life. But the government, with the "Great Father" president at its head, had plans for the Sioux that were utterly at odds with the old ways.

American policy was aimed at one long-range goal: to make each Native American family into a self-supporting farming unit. In the old life, the tribal band, not the family, had been the basic social unit. The band moved, hunted, ate, and worshiped together, and families tended to merge imperceptibly with the common life of the band. The white vision saw each family gathered in its own log house, wearing white people's clothes, huddled around its own, private fire (the white man's stove), and, preferably, worshiping the white God instead of the old Sioux god, Wakan Tanka. To well-intentioned reformers in the East, this meant "raising the Indian to civilization." To many whites in the West, it meant a final end to the Indian as a barrier to westward expansion.

For the Sioux, it all meant a divided world. Even those who wanted to cooperate most, the so-called "progressives," lived a double life. A man might put on white clothes, might plow and harvest, have only one wife, and send his children to white schools. But the old life was still alive in memory. George Sword, for example, was a progressive. He was even a member of the Indian police force the agents used to help keep order. But George Sword's description of his religious beliefs captures the painful division of loyalty that existed in the minds of even the most "civilized" Sioux:

> When I believed that Wakan Tanka was right, I served him with all my powers. In war with the white people, I found their Wakan Tanka superior. I then took the name of Sword, and have served their Wakan Tanka according to the white people's manner.

I became chief of the United States Indian police, and held the office until there was no trouble between the Sioux and the white people. I joined the church and am a deacon in it and shall be until I die.

But all this Christianity and "progress" had not erased the old ways in George Sword. He was still a member of the Ogalalla band of the Dakota tribe, and his spirit might find itself in the Sioux's heaven, not the whites':

> I still have my Wasicun [ceremonial pouch] and I am afraid to offend it, because the spirit of an Ogalalla may go to the spirit land of the Dakota.

This divided consciousness, unable to choose finally between the old and the new, the Native-American way and the European-American way, touched every area of life for the reservation Indians. To the whites who watched them, the Indians seemed almost like "children" in their confusion. In fact, the Sioux men, especially, had been deprived of their adult roles in the hunt and battle. So their maturity *was* at stake.

One of the whites' main hopes for destroying the old Sioux culture was to educate a new generation in white schools. They took numbers of Sioux children away from their parents and put them in distant boarding schools. The Sioux reaction was mixed. They could hope that this process would make their children's lives better. But there was the inevitable resentment, too, the feeling that their children had been, in effect, kidnapped by the whites.

Even when the white schools were close to home, the Sioux sent their children to them reluctantly. When a new school was opened at Pine Ridge, Sioux parents brought their children in on the first day, but they stayed outside the building, milling about, curious and frightened. Their fears were increased when the white teachers pulled down the shades, so no one could see what was happening inside. Suddenly, a gust of wind blew one of the blinds aside for a moment. The parents got a glimpse of something that filled them with horror. A white woman was holding one Sioux boy while another woman cut his hair. The whole meaning of the reservation experience came quickly into focus. In the old life, a Sioux male's long braids were a symbol of his manhood. Here were white women scissoring away, symbolically, the tribal badge of masculinity. The parents, alarmed and outraged, charged into the school and took their children out.

Only at odd moments and in ineffective ways did the Sioux resist the relentless white pressure on their old customs. The whites controlled the Indians' sources of food, blankets, fuel, housing. The whites even controlled the ownership of an Indian's individual plot of land. The Sioux, like other Native Americans, did not have a clearly defined concept of private property—especially private ownership of land. But they could see plainly that their survival depended on the mysterious white concept of land ownership. To lose the land would be to lose everything.

The deep conflict between Indian and white ways came to the surface in 1883, when a Senate investigating committee visited the Sioux. Sitting Bull, who had been one of the Sioux leaders at the Battle of the Little Bighorn, came to testify. But the chairman would not recognize Sitting Bull as chief. Sitting Bull got up and left, and all the Indians followed him out. But several of the progressive Indians returned to plead with the committee to use its influence with the Great Father to get better treatment for the Indians. Soon even Sitting Bull swallowed his hurt pride and returned to apologize.

Then Sitting Bull gave a remarkable account of what defeat had meant to the Sioux. They had been wealthy in their own terms, with land, ponies, and buffalo aplenty. In one lifetime the white man had reduced them to poverty.

> Whatever you wanted of me I have obeyed. The Great Father sent me word that whatever he had against me in the past had been forgiven and thrown aside, and I accepted his promises and came in. And he told me not to step aside from the white man's path, and I am doing my best to travel in that path. I sit here and look around me now, and I see my people starving. We want cattle to butcher. That is the way you live, and we want to live the same way. When the Great Father told me to live like his people, I told him to send me six teams of mules, because that is the way the white people make a living. I asked for a horse and buggy for my children; I was advised to follow the ways of the white man, and that is why I asked for those things.

Sitting Bull's ideas were a little confused, at least by white standards. But he summed up neatly the dilemma of the Sioux. He was still proud of himself and his tribal ways. He resented the whites' failure to understand this pride. But another side of him recognized defeat and was prepared to plead with the whites not for less civilization but for more. In Sitting Bull, and in almost all the other reservation Indians, pride, resentment, hunger, and begging were so intermixed that a meaningful pattern of life was almost impossible. The Sioux were gradually becoming "civilized." But anger was just below the surface. Some crucial event or idea was all that was needed to bring conflict with the whites back into the open, tip the scales one way or the other, and offer the Indians a clear choice between the old life and the new.

A new idea did come, and from an unpredictable direction. In the summer of 1889—about a dozen years after Crazy Horse had surrendered his band of "hostiles"—the Sioux began to hear rumors of an Indian Messiah (or savior) who had come to earth in the West. They had learned enough of Christianity on the reservation to understand the alien notion of a Messiah. If it were true that one had come to save the Indians from the whites, surely it was worth investigating.

The Messiah was said to be at the Paiute reservation at Walker Lake, Nevada. The Sioux selected important men to make the trip west. It was about a thousand miles away—farther than almost any of the Sioux had ever traveled. Pine Ridge Reservation sent eight men, including Kicking Bear, who was to become the most effective disciple of the new Messiah. One of the men from Rosebud was Short Bull. The Cheyenne River Reservation, with a smaller population than either Pine Ridge or Rosebud, sent one man.

The eleven Sioux started west by train. Railroads had by then penetrated all the major Western areas, and Indians hopped freight cars with little or no opposition from the white railroad men. When the Sioux reached Wyoming, they found that other tribes—Cheyennes, Arapahoes, Bannocks, and Shoshonis—had also sent wise men to seek the Messiah. The whole group then traveled south to Walker Lake. There the

Wovoka. Wovoka, or Jackson Wilson, was the Paiute who apparently originated the Ghost Dance religion. His ideas were a blend of Native-American legends and Christianity. He asked his followers only to dance the Ghost Dance and to await the resurrection of their dead ancestors. (Smithsonian Institution/ National Anthropological Archives)

Paiutes gave them wagons to complete the pilgrimage. Soon they were in the presence of the Messiah.

His Indian name was Wovoka, his white name Jackson Wilson. He was about thirty-five years old. He was Paiute, but he had grown up close to a white ranching family named Wilson, who gave him his English name. The Wilsons were a religious family. From them Wovoka had learned in some detail how Jesus had controlled the wind and the seas, how he had promised eternal life to his followers, and how other whites had crucified him. Wovoka was apparently the son of a Paiute shaman, or medicine man. One day in 1889, when he was ill (and perhaps delirious) with a high fever, there was an eclipse of the sun. This led him to believe that he had been taken up to heaven. After talking with God, he had been returned to earth to bring salvation to the Indians.

Wovoka's doctrines were a fairly straightforward Native-American version of some of the basic teachings of the New Testament. In a sermon to some visiting Cheyennes he summarized his new faith:

> You must not hurt anybody, or do harm to anyone. You must not fight. Do right always.
>
> Do not tell the white people about this. Jesus is now upon the earth. The dead are all alive again. I do not know when they will be here; maybe this fall or in the spring. When the time comes there will be no more sickness and everyone will be young again.

Wovoka was telling his disciples that the dead would be resurrected soon. The earth would tremble; a new earth would cover the old. But true believers need not be afraid, because they would soon enjoy perfect life, youth, and health. In the meantime, the Indians should live in peace with the whites.

Do not refuse to work for the whites, and do not make any trouble with them until you leave them. When the earth shakes, do not be afraid, it will not hurt you. That is all. You will receive good words from me again some time. Do not tell lies.

Wovoka gave the visiting Cheyennes some clay for making the sacred red paint of the Paiutes. Symbols drawn with it were signs of their salvation. Then he advised them: "When you get home, you must make a dance to continue five days. You must all do it in the same way."

This was the Ghost Dance from which Wovoka's new religion soon took its name. During the five days it lasted, men and women sang certain songs and went into hypnotic trances. During the dance they were supposed to be able to visit their departed relatives in heaven.

When Short Bull returned to South Dakota, he gave his version of the Ghost Dance religion to his excited Sioux audience. The tone was much more militant than Wovoka's. Short Bull promised punishment for those who refused to be converted— just as the Christian missionaries promised damnation for those who rejected their Messiah. He also promised victory over the hated and feared soldiers for those who wore holy shirts into battle. The shirts were supposed to protect wearers from the whites' bullets.

> If the soldiers surround you, three of you, on whom I have put holy shirts, will sing a song around them, then some of them will drop dead. Then the rest will start to run, but their horses will sink into the earth. The riders will jump from their horses, but they will sink into the earth also. Then you can do as you desire with them. Now, you must know this, that all the soldiers and that race will be dead. There will be only five thousand of them left living on the earth. The guns are the only things we are afraid of, but they belong to our father in heaven. He will see that they do no harm.

Short Bull was not the only one who brought back this interpretation from the visit to Wovoka. A militant version of the Ghost Dance faith emerged on all the Sioux reservations during the summer of 1890. The Sioux were offered a new ritual, the Ghost Dance, and a new faith, which held that the whites would soon be buried in the earth and the Indians would once again own the plains. There is no way of knowing how sincere Short Bull was. Nor is there any way of knowing whether Sitting Bull, who soon became a disciple of the Ghost Dance, really believed in the coming resurrection. Most of the Sioux probably rejected the Ghost Dance and decided to continue along the whites' path. For many, though, the religion of Wovoka offered great hope for the return of the old life and the end of their humiliating captivity. There can be no doubt that large groups of Sioux did accept the Ghost Dance.

Agents on all the reservations tried to stop the dances, using Indian police. But time and again, the dancing Sioux refused to be intimidated. They threatened their own police with rifles, insulted the agents, and began to behave like the Sioux of the 1870s. The agents reacted in various ways. When the police failed to make the Sioux obey, some of the agents refused to issue rations to those Indians who were active

A Ghost Dance. During a Ghost Dance, which might last up to five days, the Sioux were apparently able to enter into a type of trance. Believers in the new religion thought they actually could visit their dead during these trances. The complicated relationship between white and Indian cultures in the lives of these people is suggested by the fact that the women dancers are wearing factory-made print dresses. (Smithsonian Institution/National Anthropological Archives)

Ghost Dancers. At least two of the agents asked for federal troops. One, a new agent at Pine Ridge, was so incompetent that the Indians named him Young-Man-Afraid-of-Indians. White newspapermen, always hungry for a sensational story, began to write about "hostile" Sioux. And white settlers in the Dakotas began to demand protection from the government.

Finally, after a tug of war between the Department of the Interior and the Department of War in Washington, the government authorized the army to send infantry and cavalry onto the reservations. This move brought about the first real confrontation since 1876 between the Sioux and the dreaded bluecoats. On November 20, 1890, cavalry and infantry units occupied the Pine Ridge and Rosebud reservations. A few days later the entire Seventh Cavalry arrived at Pine Ridge. This had been Custer's unit, and it included many veterans of the Little Bighorn.

The effect on the Sioux of the appearance of the troops was overpowering. Instead of retreating to the outer edges of the reservations, most of the Indians at Pine Ridge and Rosebud immediately left their cabins and camps and gathered around the agency buildings. They pitched their tepees in rambling confusion and hoped that they would not be suspected of any wrongdoing. It was as though the only way to be safe from the rifles and cannon of the army was to be right under the noses of the officers and agents.

Thus the arrival of the army segregated the Indians. Those who wanted peace with the whites had gathered at the agencies. Only the most militant of the Ghost Dancers, led by Kicking Bear and Short Bull, decided to hold out. They were gathered along the creeks not far from the Pine Ridge agency—at Medicine Root, Porcupine, and Wounded Knee.

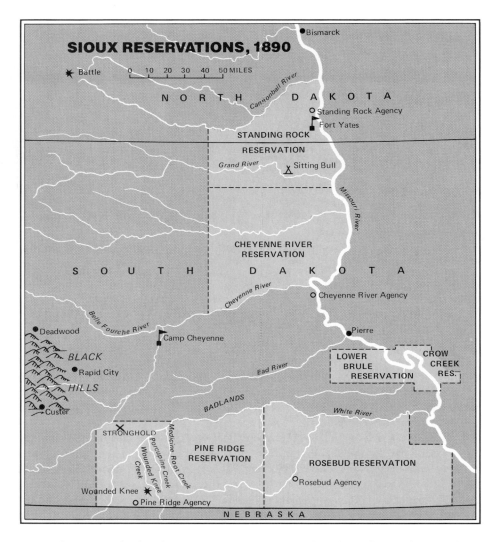

SIOUX RESERVATIONS, 1890

About a week after the cavalry's arrival, several hundred of the militant Indians broke for open country. They plundered the farms of the "peaceful" Indians who had fled to the agencies, and they raided the agency cattle herds for beef. Then about 600 warriors and their families struck out for a low plateau at the northwest corner of Pine Ridge. This was known as the Stronghold. Here the Indians had grass, water, cattle, ponies in large numbers, and plenty of guns and ammunition. They announced that they intended to stay all winter, dancing, and then see what the spring brought.

Fortunately, the officer in command at Pine Ridge decided to be cautious. He sent one messenger after another to the Stronghold, promising that there would be no punishment if the militants surrendered and returned to the agency. In turn, the Indians had to agree to give up the Ghost Dance and return the cattle and other things they had taken. The messengers were badly treated, but some of the men at the Stronghold wanted to surrender. It seemed clear that sooner or later the militants

Kicking Bear. Kicking Bear was one of the Sioux who traveled to California to seek out the prophet Wovoka. He gave the Ghost Dance doctrine a much more militant interpretation than Wovoka had, creating divisions among Indians and alarm among some whites. (U.S. Signal Corps/National Archives)

would disagree among themselves and the threat of uprising would be broken. The situation at Pine Ridge settled into a stalemate, with neither side ready to force a confrontation.

Now the scene of the action shifted north to Standing Rock reservation, where Sitting Bull kept his camp. The nonprogressive Indians regarded Sitting Bull almost reverently. He was probably not as great a war chief as Crazy Horse had been, but Sitting Bull had held out against the whites longer than any other Sioux leader. And his people believed that he had extraordinary powers as a medicine man.

The agent at Standing Rock was James McLaughlin, a tough and experienced agent. For years he had struggled to gain moral leadership of the Indians, and for years Sitting Bull had stood in his way. McLaughlin had been looking for a way to break Sitting Bull's hold over the nonprogressive Sioux at Standing Rock. When Sitting Bull took up the forbidden Ghost Dance, McLaughlin decided that arresting him would be the best course. McLaughlin wanted to delay the arrest until winter, when the Indians stayed indoors to avoid the bitter cold and to rest. The agent also believed that the arrest should be made by the Sioux police, not by the cavalry units stationed near the agency at Fort Yates.

In November 1890, McLaughlin began to enlarge the force of Indian policemen that the Sioux called "metal breasts," because of their badges. He ordered them to keep a close watch on Sitting Bull's camp and make certain that the old chief did not leave.

In mid-December McLaughlin learned that Sitting Bull had been invited to the Stronghold, where he would join the Pine Ridge and Rosebud Sioux under Short Bull and Kicking Bear. The agent was determined to stop Sitting Bull from taking his group to Pine Ridge. He knew that a stalemate had developed there, and he felt that Sitting Bull's presence might be enough to tip the scales toward open warfare between the Sioux and the cavalry. So McLaughlin ordered Sitting Bull's arrest. He commanded the Indian police, who were led by an experienced lieutenant, Bull Head, to sneak into Sitting Bull's camp at dawn on December 15. They were to arrest the chief and bring him into the agency.

Bull Head and the police met the order with mixed feelings. Most of them were progressives. They prayed to the white man's God before starting their mission. But the thought of Sitting Bull still brought back memories of the great days of the Sioux. One of the police, He Alone, whose white name was John Lone Man, later remembered how he felt when the orders were read and translated to the police. (The English here is the work of an educated relative of his.)

> I'm simply expressing my viewpoint as one who had reformed from all the heathenish ways, formerly one of the loyal followers of Chief Sitting Bull. But ever since I was about ten years of age, I had participated in a good many buffalo hunts and fought under Sitting Bull. But the most important fight I took part in was the Custer fight. After this fight I still went with Sitting Bull's band to Canada. Even after Sitting Bull was returned to Standing Rock Reservation, I remained in his camp, where I tamed down somewhat. We all felt sad.

The police gathered in the early evening of December 14 and passed the night telling war stories. Then, just before dawn, Bull Head ordered He Alone and the thirty or so other police to get ready.

Sitting Bull's camp stood on the north bank of the Grand River. The police, circling from the east, crossed the river to cut off any possible escape southward toward Pine Ridge. Soon they could see Sitting Bull's log cabin. In front of it stood the very tall tepee that was the headquarters for the Ghost Dance. Sitting Bull's two wives, his son Crow Foot, and several other children and relatives lived in the cabin. Other tepees were scattered around it. The police paused for a moment, then crossed the river again. The policeman named He Alone recalled:

> We rode up as if we attacked the camp. We quickly dismounted, and while our officers went inside we all scattered around the cabin. It was still dark, and everybody was asleep, and only dogs greeted us.
>
> Bull Head knocked at the door, and the Chief answered, *"How, timahel hiyu you."* [All right, come in.]
>
> Bull Head said, "I come to arrest you. You are under arrest."
>
> Sitting Bull said, *"How.* Let me put on my clothes and go with you."
>
> When Sitting Bull started to go with the police, one of Sitting Bull's wives burst into a loud cry which drew attention. No sooner had this started, when several leaders were rapidly making their way toward Sitting Bull's cabin. Bear That Catches, particularly, came up close saying, "Now, here are the metal breasts just as we had expected. You think you are going to take him. You shall not do it."

Sitting Bull: two views. The photograph on the left shows Sitting Bull dressed in the costume he wore in traveling circuses. His face is that of a brave warrior and leader of his people. His eyes are unflinching and his expression grave, but his costume is a purely white version of Indian dress. The second photograph, of Sitting Bull and his family and a white woman, was taken on the Dakota reservation, not in a white circus. It shows the other side of Sitting Bull's personality—frightened, confused, and shy of the camera. This is a family that has been very nearly broken in spirit by defeat and reservation life. (left: Library of Congress; right: National Archives)

By now the entire camp was up and angry. The police might still have been able to arrest the sleepy Sitting Bull if Crow Foot, his seventeen-year-old son, had not intervened. Sitting Bull had been grooming Crow Foot to be a chief, filling his youthful head with tales of courage in battle. As He Alone described it, Crow Foot upset the delicate balance of fear and anger in the cabin:

> Just about this time, Crow Foot got up, moved by the wailing of his mother and the remarks of Bear That Catches, and said to Sitting Bull, "Well, you always called yourself a brave chief. Now you are allowing yourself to be taken by the metal breasts."
>
> Sitting Bull then changed his mind, and said, *"Ho ca mni kte sni yelo."* [Then I will not go.]
>
> Lieutenant Bull Head said to the chief, "Come now, do not listen to any one."
>
> I said to Sitting Bull, "Uncle [Native Americans often used words like *Uncle* and *Father* as terms of respect, not kinship], nobody is going to harm you. Please do not let others lead you into any trouble."

But the chief's mind was made up not to go, so the three head officers laid their hands on him, pulling him outside. By this time, the whole camp was in commotion. Bear That Catches pulled out a gun from under his blanket and fired into Lieutenant Bull Head, wounding him. I ran up toward where they were holding the chief, when Bear That Catches raised his gun. He pointed and fired at me, but it snapped [misfired]. I jerked the gun away from his hands and laid him out. It was about this moment that Lieutenant Bull Head fired into Sitting Bull while still holding him, and Red Tomahawk followed with another shot which finished the chief.

There was more shooting, and soon the Ghost Dancers ran for a line of trees. After a time the police took shelter in Sitting Bull's cabin. The inner walls of the cabin were hung with strips of brightly colored sheeting, sewn together and tacked to the walls. Suddenly, one of the policemen noticed a movement in a corner, behind the sheeting. He Alone raised the curtain:

> There stood Crow Foot, and as soon as he was exposed to view, he cried out, "My Uncles, do not kill me. I do not wish to die." Lieutenant Bull Head said, "Do what you like with him. He is the one that has caused this trouble." I do not remember who fired the shot that killed Crow Foot—several fired at once.

Just after Crow Foot was killed, the cavalry units from Fort Yates arrived. The remaining members of Sitting Bull's band scattered toward the south.

He Alone and the rest of the police went home filled with the confusion that was so much a part of reservation life. He Alone performed a Sioux ritual. He built a small shelter and dropped hot stones into water to create a steam bath "that I might cleanse myself for participating in a bloody fight with my fellow men." Then he burned all the clothes he had worn to Sitting Bull's camp. Next, He Alone set out to perform a white man's ritual:

> The next day, I took my family into the agency. I reported to Major McLaughlin. He laid his hand on my shoulders, and said, "He Alone is a man. I feel very proud of you for the way you have carried out your part in the fight with the Ghost Dancers." I was not very brave at that moment. His comment nearly set me acrying.

Four Indian policemen died at Sitting Bull's camp. Two more (including Lieutenant Bull Head) would soon be dead of their wounds. One of them, Shave Head, asked McLaughlin, "Did I do well, Father?" McLaughlin nodded. Shave Head went on:

> Then I will die in the faith of the white man, to which my five children already belong. Send for my wife, that we may be married by the Black Gown [priest] before I die.

Shave Head's wife came, but too late. The next day, the six dead police were buried. A squad of bluecoats fired honorary volleys over the graves, and taps was blown.

At least eight of Sitting Bull's followers had died. Their bodies were left where they had fallen. Only Sitting Bull was buried. A few moments after the ceremonies for the Indian police, Sitting Bull's body, in a plain coffin, was lowered into a grave in the Fort Yates cemetery. The only people who watched were three officers, serving as official witnesses, and the four guardhouse gravediggers.

None of Sitting Bull's followers was present at his burial. Most of them—about 400—had fled south and west from the Grand River camp. The authorities at Standing Rock had a number of nightmarish ideas about what might happen next. The Standing Rock Ghost Dancers might join Chief Big Foot on the Cheyenne River, where the dance had been in full swing for weeks. On the other hand, the frightened Sitting Bull group might strike out for the Stronghold, where Short Bull and Kicking Bear still held out. Or they might set Big Foot in motion toward the Stronghold too, with terrible results. News of the death of Sitting Bull, likely to spread like prairie fire, could ignite the entire Sioux reservation system.

Agent McLaughlin immediately sent friendly scouts to Sitting Bull's band. The scouts were able to persuade over half to return to the Standing Rock reservation. Some of those who simply scattered sooner or later went back to their homes around Grand River. The rest—fewer than a hundred—headed south to join Big Foot.

They reached a camp that was already nervous and confused. Big Foot had been a great chief. But he was old now, in his seventies, and his control over his band was slipping. The band's medicine man, Yellow Bird, was a fanatical Ghost Dancer. Many of the young braves were ready to bring about their hoped-for victory over the whites. There were about 200 in the band, and all of them were aware of mounting pressure from the white soldiers.

The War Department had ordered Big Foot's arrest, on the false theory that he was almost as large a source of potential trouble as Sitting Bull had been. An observation camp, Camp Cheyenne, had been established by the cavalry just a few miles up the Cheyenne River. Infantry units from the east were trying to cross the Missouri River, which was partially ice-covered.

For several days Big Foot wavered among various alternatives. At one point he was convinced by messengers from the cavalry to go to the Cheyenne River agency. But many of his young men wanted to go to the Stronghold instead. Big Foot had also been invited by the Pine Ridge chiefs to go there to help settle the troubles. He had a great reputation as a diplomat, and he was offered a hundred ponies to heal the split between the "friendly" Sioux and the Ghost Dancers at Pine Ridge. Most of the time, however, Big Foot seemed to want only to stay put at his own camp and wait.

Finally, for reasons that are difficult to guess, Big Foot made his decision. He would go to Pine Ridge, make peace, and accept the gift of ponies. What he did not realize was that leaving his reservation when the whites were so frightened of a Sioux "uprising" would make him a fugitive "hostile" in the eyes of the military. Almost immediately, new orders went out for Big Foot's arrest. His band was to be disarmed and their horses taken. Then they would be marched to the railroad and sent to Omaha—far away from their own reservation lands. Big Foot never understood that this was the army's plan. He assumed that he was going to Pine Ridge on a mission of peace.

Big Foot's band left camp December 23, under the cover of night. As soon as the officers at Camp Cheyenne realized the old chief had gone, cavalry units started patrolling the line between Big Foot's camp and the Stronghold, looking for him. But the chief passed east of the patrols. The band moved very slowly, for Big Foot had caught pneumonia. He rode in a wagon without springs. Soon Big Foot was bleeding from his nose. And it was bitterly cold for the old man. At one point, in a pass through a steep wall along the Bad River, Big Foot's men had to dig out a road for the wagon. Big Foot managed to reach Porcupine Creek, only about thirty miles from the Pine Ridge agency, without being sighted by the army. He sent men ahead to tell the Sioux he was coming.

On December 28, five days after starting south, Big Foot's band was finally "captured" by the Seventh Cavalry. When the Indians and cavalry met, there was a tense moment. The cavalry formed a skirmish line and brought up cannon. Big Foot's braves formed a battle line in front of his wagon. But then the cavalry commander came forward. He and Big Foot shook hands, and the chief accepted an "escort"—going, he thought, to Pine Ridge. Together, the cavalry and the Indians made their way to a trading post at Wounded Knee Creek.

The officer in charge had wisely not tried to disarm the Sioux, and he let them keep their horses for the trip. He even transferred Big Foot into an ambulance wagon. When the two groups reached Wounded Knee, the Indians were issued rations. The rest of the Seventh Cavalry came from Pine Ridge to join the patrol. The Indians pitched their tepees in a low hollow near a ravine that led into the creek. There were 102 men and 230 women and children. The soldiers, a total of about 500, camped on a rise just to the north. Armed sentries surrounded the Indians, but on the whole everything seemed peaceful enough.

Soon the Indians settled down and the cavalry—except for the ring of sentries around the Indian camp—went to sleep. Only a few officers, veterans of the Little Bighorn disaster, stayed up late. They celebrated over a keg of whiskey someone had brought from the agency.

The next morning Colonel James Forsyth, commander of the Seventh Cavalry, asked all the men of Big Foot's group to gather in a council between the tepees and the cavalry encampment. The sentries remained in place. The rest of the cavalry units drew up, mounted, around the Sioux men and their camp. Forsyth asked the Indians for their weapons.

Big Foot tried diplomacy. From his ambulance bed he quietly advised his men to give up their bad guns but hide the good ones. Soon Forsyth sent twenty of the Sioux to the tepees to bring the guns. Meanwhile, however, the Sioux women (who understood the value of a weapon) had hidden the rifles that the Sioux had bought, stolen, or taken in battle. The Sioux returned to the council with only two old, broken cavalry carbines.

Forsyth heightened his search. He placed a line of troops between the Sioux braves and their camp and sent his own men into the tepees. But this search uncovered only thirty rifles, most of them old and useless. This left one other real possibility: Some of the Sioux were hiding rifles under the blankets they kept draped over their shoulders against the cold.

By now the situation was very delicate. Forsyth ordered Big Foot brought out on his blanket. The medicine man, Yellow Bird, was dancing around, chanting Ghost Dance songs, urging the young braves to be firm. In the tepees women were hastily packing, ready to run.

Suddenly, one Sioux man, Black Coyote, pulled a rifle from his blanket and began to shout, holding the weapon over his head. He was probably deaf and, by the Indians' testimony, a little insane. Two soldiers grabbed him and struggled for the rifle. It went off, firing overhead. In what may have been a signal, Yellow Bird threw a handful of dust into the air. Several braves pulled rifles from their blankets and aimed at the cavalry. "By God, they have broken," an officer shouted. The Indians fired, and at about the same moment came the command "Fire! Fire on them!"

No one could stop what happened next. Big Foot was quickly killed. Cavalry carbines ripped into the group of Sioux men. The bullets that did not find a Sioux body passed on across the ravine into the tepees. Women ran this way and that, followed by children. Some of the Sioux broke toward the creek, where they were cut down by waiting cavalrymen. Others ran into the ravine.

Corporal Paul Weinert manned one of the Seventh Cavalry's small, rapid-firing cannon on the hill. Like the other cavalrymen, he was surprised when the shooting started. But within a moment or two, he was caught up in the battle, pumping shots angrily wherever he saw moving Sioux:

> All of the Indians opened fire on us. Lieutenant Hawthorne ran toward me and was calling, when suddenly I heard him say, "Oh, my God!" and then I knew he had been hit. I said: "By God! I'll make 'em pay for that," and ran the gun into the opening of the ravine. They kept yelling for me to come back. Bullets were coming like hail from the Indians' Winchesters. I kept going in farther, and pretty soon everything was quiet at the other end of the line.

Corporal Weinert was a veteran soldier with a sophisticated weapon. The experience of Catching Spirit Elk, a Sioux who had surrendered his rifle, was almost the opposite of Weinert's:

> Then followed firing from all sides. I threw myself on the ground. I then jumped up to run toward the Indian camp, but was then and there shot down, being hit on my right leg, and soon after was shot again on the other leg. When the general firing ceased, I heard an interpreter calling out, saying the wounded would be kindly treated. I opened my eyes and looked about and saw the dead and wounded all around me.

Some officers did what they could to prevent women and children from being shot down. But the Sioux (at least those who still had weapons) were fast and accurate with their repeating rifles, so the soldiers sometimes fired at anything that moved. When the artillery on the hill opened up on the Indians in the ravine, the shells exploded on all without regard to age or sex. Apparently, too, some of the raging soldiers broke ranks and chased down fleeing Indians. These were the bodies Charles Eastman found miles away from Wounded Knee.

The battle lasted only a few minutes. About 150 braves rode out from Pine Ridge, too late and too few to help their comrades. The cavalry gathered their own dead (25) and wounded (39) and returned to the Pine Ridge agency. They took some

Burying the dead at Wounded Knee. Several days after the massacre, a party of about thirty white men, armed with shovels and rifles, went to Wounded Knee to bury the Sioux dead. They were paid $2 a body, a total of a little less than $300, for their work. But they also got to pose for publicity photographs like this one. (Nebraska State Historical Society)

of the wounded Sioux with them and left the rest on the field. There were at least 146 Indian dead—about half of them men. Some bodies were probably taken away during the next two days, before Eastman's party arrived to rescue the living and bury the rest. All in all, probably 200 Sioux and whites had died.

Wounded Knee was followed by a few small skirmishes. But soon Pine Ridge was "pacified." The Stronghold Indians had given up while Big Foot's band was on the march. The Ghost Dance was over. Spring came and went, but the earth did not cover the white man, as Wovoka had promised. Paul Weinert, the cannoneer, received a Congressional Medal of Honor for his part in the action at the edge of the ravine. A small white church was later built at the Sioux mass grave, on what came to be called Cemetery Hill. In 1903, with the help of missionaries, the Sioux put up their own small monument, burying Wounded Knee in the past:

This monument is erected by surviving relatives and other Ogalalla and Cheyenne River Sioux Indians in memory of the Chief Big Foot Massacre, Dec. 29, 1890. Col. Forsyth in command of U. S. troops. Big Foot was a great chief of the Sioux Indians. He often said, "I will stand in peace till my last day comes." He did many good and brave deeds for the white man and the red man. Many innocent women and children who knew no wrong died here.

THE LAST FRONTIER

There is nothing unique about the history of the Sioux. It is true they resisted the whites longer and more fiercely than some other Native Americans, East or West. And they were the only tribe that, inspired by Wovoka's new religion, developed a militant resistance to reservation life. But despite these differences, they were finally defeated in a manner typical of the way white Americans subdued all the Indians.

The defeat of the Sioux and the other Plains Indians was just one chapter in the history of continental expansion. White Americans had begun moving across the Mississippi in the 1830s. In the decades after the Civil War, this movement increased both in speed and recklessness.

The Last West

Until the 1840s, America had a clearly drawn frontier. It was possible at each census before then to draw a zigzag line from north to south showing how far settlement had advanced in each decade. But after the Mexican War this was no longer true. The drift of pioneers into Oregon, the settlement of Texas and Utah, and the discovery of gold in California created isolated pockets of white settlement thousands of miles beyond the old frontier line near the Mississippi.

672

By the early 1850s, it was evident that the Pacific Coast would be settled fairly quickly, organized into territories, and carved into states. California had already been admitted to statehood as part of the Compromise of 1850. Oregon entered the Union nine years later.

Between the Pacific and the old frontier in eastern Kansas and Nebraska lay a vast stretch of plains and mountains. It formed an area larger than the whole territory over which George Washington had governed as president. This region was the last frontier, the last region to be settled by white Americans.

The Great Plains begin in the first tier of states west of the Mississippi River and extend west to the Rockies. In 1836 the Senate Committee for Indian Affairs declared that the Great Plains were an "uninhabitable region." The Indians there "are on the outside of us, and in a place which will forever remain on the outside." In fact, the plains were given an official name, "The Great American Desert." The weather was dry. There was no water in many of the rivers during most of the year. The land was covered not with trees but with stubborn grass. Only the Native Americans and the buffalo seemed able to thrive. The Rocky Mountain region also seemed to offer little to encourage settlement. For many years its great peaks and high valleys were the home only of small Indian bands and a few American fur traders.

through the West to California. The North and the South, however, had not been able to agree on the western part of the route. The North wanted a line to run from Chicago to San Francisco. The South insisted on a route through Texas to southern California.

The Civil War ended this competition. By seceding, the South lost its right to participate in the decision making. In 1862 Congress settled on a route between Council Bluffs, Iowa, and San Francisco. The same law provided for enormous financial support from the federal government. There would be two companies. The Central Pacific would build east from San Francisco. The Union Pacific (a patriotic name suited to wartime) would go west across Nebraska and Colorado. They were to meet somewhere in the middle. Each railroad would be given a right-of-way 400 feet wide. In addition, the government would lend the railroads up to $48,000 for each mile of track laid—less for flat country, more for mountain track. Most important, the railroads would be *given* 6,400 acres for every mile of track completed. In 1864 this land allowance was doubled.

The Central Pacific started building toward the east, but the work went slowly for two reasons. First, the company did not have enough capital. Second, labor was scarce in California. The first problem was eased when the Lincoln administration allowed the Central Pacific to claim flat-country miles as mountain miles, which entitled the company to the largest possible federal loans. The labor problem was "solved" by the brutal importation of thousands of Chinese laborers. Many of them were unwilling immigrants, and all of them were exploited as gang labor. They lived in extremely crude conditions, with poor food and almost no housing. And when the tracks were laid and their work was finished, they would be cast loose to try to earn their livings in the cities and towns of California, in a society whose European-American majority was at least as bigoted toward them as toward Native Americans or African Americans. But the Chinese workers endured, and their endurance was translated into rail mileage. In the first year of construction, 1864, the Central Pacific had completed only twenty miles of track. But by 1867 the pace was up to twenty miles per month, largely as a result of Chinese-American labor.

At the other end of the proposed route the Union Pacific also built slowly, at first. But it picked up speed by bringing in thousands of Irish immigrants to lay rails. In 1868 alone the Union Pacific laid 425 miles of track, well over a mile a day.

In May 1869, after only five years of construction, the two work gangs met at Promontory Point, Utah, just east of the Great Salt Lake. The last crosstie put down was coated with silver; the last spike was gold. A telegraph operator cabled east and west: "Hats off—prayer is being offered." Then there was a wait of almost fifteen minutes. Again the telegraph clicked. "We have got done praying. The spike is about to be presented." Railroad officials took turns with the hammer; the first blow was a bad miss, but the work was done. Two locomotives eased forward until they touched. The nation celebrated almost as wildly as it had at the end of the Civil War. Chicago's parade was seven miles long. The nation was joined, east to west, across a "desert" that an earlier generation had believed would never be settled.

During the next fifteen years three more routes were opened across the Rockies. Iowa, Missouri, Kansas, and Nebraska were crisscrossed by rails. In the process, the government gave the railroad companies almost 180 million acres of public land, and it lent them over $100 million. Because of complicated regulations that allowed railroads to delay choosing the land they wanted to keep along their rights-of-way, they were able to keep great stretches of land for years, waiting for its price to rise.

At one point the railroads controlled—at least on paper—almost all of Iowa and Wisconsin. The Northern Pacific, whose route crossed the northern tier of states between Lake Superior and the Pacific, controlled a strip of land larger in area than many European nations. The same kind of situation developed in Arizona and New Mexico. By 1885 the railroads held land totaling almost a sixth of the entire country.

East meets West. In the years after the Civil War, American railroad companies imported thousands of Chinese workers to help finish the rail network in the mountains and deserts of the West. Here, Chinese workers use hand labor to complete a graceful and impressive trestle on the Central Pacific Railroad in the Sierra Nevada of California. (Library of Congress)

Many of the congressmen and senators who voted these huge grants to the railroads did so in the belief that most of the land in the "Great American Desert" was of little value. The motive behind the first transcontinental lines was not to build a transportation network for the Great Plains and the Rockies but to build a link to the Pacific Coast. It took a generation's experience to make clear that the intervening territory was valuable, that it would be settled and farmed. As things turned out, the railroads may have been a very efficient mechanism for disposing of the public lands, at least in some areas. The government's own land policy was confused and often corrupt, and the "public interest" may, on balance, have been served about as well by the railroad grants as by the government's direct land grant practices. But the public whose interest was at stake was, of course, solely a white public.

From Buffalo to Cattle

In any case, the first important effects of the railroads on the Great Plains had less to do with land ownership and cultivation than with animals. The railroads created a new industry on the plains: ranching. Building the railroads not only hastened the destruction of the buffalo herds, it made possible the systematic exploitation of another set of resources: grass and cows.

The Great Event. In 1869 the Union Pacific Railroad advertised the first passenger service from Omaha to San Francisco. The trip took only four days and avoided "the Dangers of the Sea." The railroad's artist emphasizes a handsome buck in a forest, as though the railroad did not destroy but merely passed through nature. (Union Pacific Railroad Museum Collection)

Early in the sixteenth century the Spanish had begun importing European cattle into America. Over the years the cattle had multiplied. Some had escaped and become wild, especially in southern Texas around the Nueces River. These were the famous Texas longhorns—lanky, tough, and too dangerous to be captured or herded on foot. They roamed at will over the open range, a huge expanse of grass that was part of the public domain. By 1860 there were probably 5 million head of longhorns in Texas.

The Civil War sent beef prices soaring in both the North and the South. The beef herd in the Northern states was smaller at the end of the war than it had been at the beginning. At the same time, the population had grown by more than 20 percent. Thus the demand and price for beef had increased. A man could buy a longhorn steer in Texas for as little as three dollars. The same steer in Chicago was worth ten times as much, if he could just get it there.

THE LONG DRIVE   By 1866 the Missouri Pacifc Railroad had pushed its line west to Sedalia, Missouri, just east of Kansas City. That same year the first large group of Texans drove enormous herds north across Indian Territory to reach the rail line. The men ran into many difficulties. Part of the route passed through dense forests. The longhorns, unaccustomed to woods, panicked and refused to be driven through the trees. The Indians (whose treaty gave them control of all white travel across their land) harassed the cowboys. This early attempt showed, however, that it was possible to herd cattle safely over hundreds of miles to the railroad—and thereby to Eastern markets.

Thus began the twenty-year era of the "long drive." As the years passed, the railroads extended farther west. New cattle towns replaced Sedalia. Among them were Abilene (probably the most successful), Wichita, and Dodge City. Between 1866 and 1888, Texans drove as many as 6 million head of cattle over the grasslands to Kansas.

For those who succeeded, the profits of the long drive were enormous. Cattlemen claimed that as much as 40 percent profit per year was not unusual. Like the miner's frontier, the cattleman's bonanza soon attracted thousands of eager Easterners. Each usually had a few hundred dollars and a dream of running a vast ranch. Like the prospectors, most of the would-be ranchers were disappointed. Many of them either returned home or switched to another line of work such as running a store or saloon.

The long drive, despite the romantic myth of the cowboy it fostered, was a business. It required capital if it was to succeed on a big scale. In the end, only the lucky few who had been there first (like the prospectors in California or Nevada) became "cattle barons." It was Eastern and European investors, with enough capital to buy and move large herds, who controlled most of the industry.

The men (and occasional women) who rounded up the herds and drove them to the "cowtowns" along the railroads have become the most romanticized figures in American culture. In truth, they were workers. On the drives, they put in brutal, dangerous, fourteen-hour days. Although they had to learn highly specialized skills, and managed herds that were worth hundreds of thousands of dollars, they typically earned less than ten cents an hour. And when they finally reached Sedalia or Dodge City, what they found was not a roaring, adventurous scene where gunfighters might face off at any moment in a saloon or on a dirt street. In reality, the homicide and crime rates in the cattle towns were probably no higher than in Eastern towns and cities. Cattle ranching was an industry that, like most industries of the day, made many owners rich. But the workers in the cattle industry earned little, labored hard, and lived quiet and usually dull lives.

A considerable number of the cowboys were African Americans. But the trail and ranch foremen were always white. One black cowboy, who had been born into slavery, claimed to be the

Nat Love. This African-American cowboy was born a slave in Tennessee during the 1850s. He eventually made his way west to Deadwood, South Dakota, where he claimed to have won a contest in 1876 to determine who could become known as "Deadwood Dick." The mythic American cowboy was less a western reality than the creation of eastern journalist and dime-novel writers, whose audiences were mainly city folk. (Library of Congress)

original "Deadwood Dick"—although the popular hero of pulp fiction was transformed into a white man. Another black ranch hand, well known for his steady nerves and great skill, said bitterly that he would have been a boss if it had

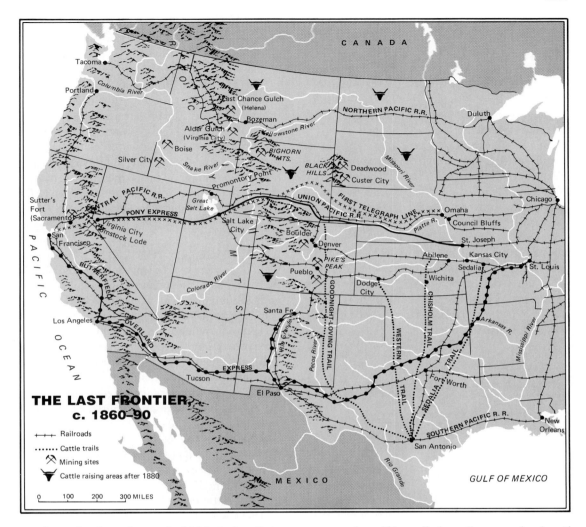

THE LAST FRONTIER
c. 1860–90

|—|—|—| Railroads

.... Cattle trails

Mining sites

Cattle raising areas after 1880

0   100   200   300 MILES

not been for "my damned old black face." An even larger number of cowboys, probably a third or more, were of Mexican ancestry. In fact, the Mexican counterparts of the American cowboys, the vaqueros (from the Spanish word *vaca*, cow), had mastered their trade long before Anglo-Americans reached Texas or the plains. If an American cowboy called his pony a pinto, it was because that Spanish word meant "painted." If he roped with a lariat, it was because the Spanish term for such a rope was *la reata*. If he preferred to say *lasso*, he was using the Spanish word for

a snare, *lazo*. If he called another man *hombre*, if he said *vamoose* instead of *leave*, or *savvy* instead of *know*, it was because the Spanish *hombre*, *vamos*, and *saber* meant "man," "we're going," and "to know," respectively.

THE END OF THE OPEN RANGE The long drive had a brief existence. Gradually, people north of Texas realized that as the railroads came closer, it made sense to breed and feed cattle nearby instead of driving them up from Texas.

During the 1880s the long drive from Texas was replaced by an even wilder cattle bonanza in other plains territories to the north. In 1860 there were no cattle at all in the northwestern plains, and there were only a few in Kansas and Nebraska. By 1880, Montana, the Dakota Territory, Wyoming, and Colorado had great herds, totaling almost 4 million head.

But the days of the open range, when cattle wandered on public land from one spring to the next, could not last long. The cattle industry soon found itself in a situation faced earlier by tobacco and cotton growers: overproduction. Rapid expansion led to an overstocked range. The grass could not support so many cattle. The increased supply also caused prices to fall. Between 1885 and 1886 the Chicago price of a steer dropped from thirty dollars to ten. The following winter on the plains was the bitterest in memory. Thousands of cattle starved and froze to death. The cattle bonanza was over.

The Defeat of the Native Americans

The miners, railroaders, and cattlemen brought about the final chapter in the conflict between whites and Indians. It was a conflict older than Jamestown and as tragic as any aspect of American history. The whites cloaked their actions with high-sounding expressions like "civilization against savagery" and "Manifest Destiny." But the facts were simple: The whites came and took the Indians' lands.

White people in the New World had always regarded the Native Americans as a "problem." Most whites—whether they were French, Spanish, or English—saw the Indians either as a people to be exploited through trade or slavery or as a barrier to westward expansion. A few whites sympathized with the Indians and did what they could to protect them from the worst aspects of white civilization. But even to those who were sympathetic, helping meant teaching the Indians to "adjust to civilization."

The Indians might be a "problem" for the whites, but for the Indians the whites meant disaster. At stake for the whites was only the delay of continental expansion for a generation or so. The stakes for the Native Americans were much higher. They were in danger of losing their culture, their freedom, their identity as human beings, and, in many cases, their lives. This was true from the time Cortes invaded Mexico to the final conquest of the tribes of the West.

ADVANTAGES OF THE WHITES   White people's ways were overpowering to the Indians. In the first place, the whites' methods of dealing with the environment were unlike those of the Native Americans. Some Indians farmed a little. But the whites were able to cultivate vast stretches of land, first with teams of mules or oxen, then with machinery. Some Indians, like the Navahos, made ornaments out of silver or gold. But the whites came for gold and silver in droves. Big new towns and frightening machines and explosives changed the face of the mountains and valleys of the Rockies. The Indians hunted wild animals, which seemed numerous enough to last forever. But the whites killed off the wild animals, fenced in the range, and raised great herds of cattle instead.

These were the main weapons of the whites: farming, mining, and ranching. Along with these the whites brought strange powers and "medicine" that made the Native Americans' situation hopeless indeed: the railroad, machine guns and cannons, and the telegraph.

Another weapon of the whites against the Indians was something they only rarely used on purpose—indeed, the whites feared it themselves. This was disease. Smallpox, measles, and other sicknesses may have wiped out as many as half the Western Indians before any significant number of whites even arrived in their territory. The germs traveled with traders and so preceded

Gulliver's Travails. This 1886 cartoon was adapted from Jonathan Swift's *Gulliver's Travels*. It shows a helpless Cherokee nation, tied down, like Gulliver, by Lilliputian Americans. The courts cut his hair, the missionaries drain his brains, the railroads steal his shoes. In the background, the government is shown trying to "discipline" other tribes. But it is like the old woman who lived in a shoe and had so many children she didn't know what to do. (The Bettmann Archive)

actual white migrations by decades. The Indians had no inherited resistance or immunity to many diseases of the whites, because the germs had been "imported" from Europe. Indians died by the band and even by the tribe from sicknesses that only made most whites uncomfortable.

Finally, the whites had an advantage that probably counted more than anything else: numbers. They poured west by the thousands. In one change of seasons, between one Sun Dance and another, the whites seemed able to throw up towns like San Francisco, Denver, or Deadwood—towns with populations larger than the whole Sioux nation.

One by one, the tribes of the Great Plains, the California-Intermountain area, and the northwest coast were made to realize that the whites were a force they could neither understand nor control. Some groups, like the Sioux, the Kiowas, and the Apaches, fought back. They were sustained by their myths, their magic, and their hatred of the cavalry that invaded their villages, shooting men, women, and children. But in the end, all the tribes were defeated. Only something as unusual as Wovoka's Ghost Dance could convince the Indians—and only a few at that—that there was any way to combat the enveloping white civilization.

DEALING WITH THE TRIBES From the beginning, United States policy toward the Native Americans had been contradictory. On the one hand, the government treated tribes as independent nations with whom it could make treaties. On the other hand, Indians were not citizens but wards of the government, subject to federal control. In addition, the American nation was growing with incredible speed. Again and again, government aims that seemed practical in one decade were obsolete ten years later.

In California and Oregon, and in the frontier regions of the Rockies, relations between whites and Indians were poorly controlled by the government. Groups of whites simply drove the Indians out, murdering many of them in the process. The Indians of California suffered especially. They had settled around Spanish missions and learned farming and various crafts. After the Spanish missions were closed down in the 1830s, the Indians were defenseless against the greedy whites. In the ten years after the gold rush of 1849, some 70,000 of these mission Indians died from starvation, disease, and outright murder.

On the Great Plains, whites might band together to attack Indians. But the government and its army played a much larger role in keeping the peace there than it did farther west. After 1850 the history of Indian-white relations settled down to a fairly steady rhythm of treaties, "uprisings," war, and new treaties. The Native Americans were always the losers. Even when they won the battles, they lost in the making of the treaties.

This process began in 1851 at Fort Laramie on the Oregon Trail. To protect the trail, the government called hundreds of Indian leaders together and persuaded them to agree not to bother the wagon trains crossing their territory. Each tribe accepted boundaries to its hunting grounds. In return, the government promised to leave them in peace.

These agreements left the Indians in possession of almost all of the Great Plains. But accepting boundaries laid out by Washington opened the door to a new government tactic: getting each tribe, by a separate treaty, to give up part of its lands. By 1865 the Indians had given up all of Kansas, most of Nebraska, the central half of Utah, and almost all of Texas.

THE SAND CREEK MASSACRE Much Native American land was surrendered peacefully, in return for promises of peace and annual shipments of government supplies, called annuities. But in 1861 in Colorado, a government attempt to move Cheyennes and Arapahoes onto a small reservation at Sand Creek resulted in the Indians' waging a three-year guerrilla war. In 1864 the leader of the warring Indians, Black Kettle, tried to make peace with the whites. The army and the territorial government refused. The unyielding commander of the Colorado militia, Colonel John Chivington, told Black Kettle: "My rule for fighting white men or Indians is to fight them until they lay down their arms and surrender."

Black Kettle led his people to a camp at Sand Creek, where he hoped to be left in peace. But the Indians woke on November 29, 1864, to find 1,000 of Chivington's militia surrounding them. The militia rushed the camp, shooting at everything that moved. When the "fight" was over, 450 Indians were dead. Only about 50 had escaped the massacre. The next year the Cheyennes and Arapahoes had to sign a new treaty. It forced them to leave their Colorado plains for a barren corner of Indian Territory.

NEGOTIATIONS WITH THE SIOUX The Sioux fared better, at least for a time. Their agreement at Fort Laramie in 1851 gave them one of the largest hunting areas in the West: most of the Dakota Territory and the region around the Powder River in eastern Wyoming and southern Montana. But by 1865, miners had crowded into Montana at Bozeman, Virginia City, and Helena. These towns soon demanded a road connecting them with the Oregon Trail. This road would cross the Yellowstone River, skirt the Sioux hunting areas around the Big Horn Mountains, and cross directly over the valley of the Powder River.

Chief Joseph

Hinmaton-Yalaktit was his name—"thunder coming out of the water and over the land." Joseph was his white man's name. He was a chief in the Sahaptin tribe, which the whites called Nez Percé—"pierced nose"—because of their habit of wearing nose ornaments made of shells. Before he was taken captive he did two things. He fought the most brilliant and sustained military campaign against the United States Army ever waged by any Native-American leader. And he made the most poignant and famous surrender speech any American Indian ever delivered.

In 1863 the Nez Percé ceded most of their lands to the United States and agreed to live on a small reservation in Idaho. A "renegade" portion of the tribe, however, refused to recognize the treaty. For ten years, the government did not try to enforce the treaty, and all the Nez Percé had to do was fend off individual white squatters. This was the situation when Joseph, at age thirty-three, became chief after his father's death in 1873.

In 1876 the government decided to enforce the treaty and move the "renegade" Nez Percé onto the Idaho reservation. A group of Joseph's warriors, almost certainly without his blessing, went on a rampage and killed twenty or so white settlers. Reluctantly, Joseph was drawn into a situation in which he knew final victory was impossible. He decided to strike out for Canada.

The force Joseph led into the mountains contained fewer than 200 fighting men, who had to protect and care for about 600 women and children. But Joseph was able to lead this group on a superb retreat that covered more than a thousand miles of difficult wilderness. He ran when he could and fought when he had to. In August 1877 he defeated the cavalry in a desperate struggle on the Big Hole River in Montana. Finally, Joseph got his people into the Bear Paw Mountains, only thirty miles from Canada.

Joseph thought he had won, and stopped to allow his dozens of wounded and helpless followers to rest. But he was overtaken by a force of cavalry, and had to decide, and quickly, whether to run, to surrender, or to fight. He chose to fight, and kept the cavalry at bay for five days. On October 5 he surrendered his beaten force: 87 men, almost half of them wounded, and about 350 women and children. To this broken remnant of the Nez Percé, Joseph made his speech:

I am tired of fighting. The old men are all dead. [My brother] who led the young men is dead. It is cold, and we have no blankets. The little children are freezing to death. My people, some of them, have run away to the hills. No one knows where they are. I want to have some time to look for my children and see how many I can find. Maybe I shall find them among the dead.

Hear me, my chiefs. From where the sun now stands, I will fight no more forever.

Joseph and his people were taken first to Kansas and then to Indian Territory, where many of them died of disease. A few were eventually returned to Idaho. But Joseph never went home. He was moved to a reservation in Washington State, and he lived to visit a new "Great Father" in Washington, D.C., Theodore Roosevelt, in 1903. Joseph died in 1904, at the age of sixty-four. The official cause of death was entered as a broken heart.

In the summer of 1865 the cavalry moved into the area to construct forts and begin work on the road. A Sioux chief, Red Cloud, led his people in a two-year attack on the road and the forts. And in 1868 the government made a new treaty that seemed to give the victory to Red Cloud. The road was abandoned. But the Sioux, in return, had to agree to a reservation that included only the Dakotas west of the Missouri—the so-called Great Sioux Reservation. According to the treaty, they could still hunt in the Powder River country. For the first time, however, they had accepted a reservation to replace the large domain that their 1851 treaty had recognized.

The commission that made the 1868 agreement with the Sioux dealt with other Plains tribes in the same way. Reservations were created in Indian Territory for the southern groups: the Kiowa, Comanche, Arapaho, Cheyenne, Osage, and Pawnee tribes. Between 1868 and 1874 the northern tribes—Crow and Blackfoot, Shoshone and Mandan—also accepted new, restricted reservations. By 1876 the Plains Indians had given up over three-fourths of the land they had held under the Fort Laramie Treaty just twenty-five years before.

THE BATTLE OF THE LITTLE BIGHORN
The policy of concentrating Indians on reservations was applied once again in the Black Hills area of South Dakota. The treaty of 1868 guaranteed the Teton Sioux complete possession of the Black Hills. But in 1874, rumors of gold led to a reconnaissance of the area by a military column of the Seventh Cavalry under Colonel George Custer. Custer's men found gold, and the resulting rush into Deadwood and other mining towns made conflict between the Sioux and the whites inevitable.

The Grant administration tried for a time to hold the prospectors back. The army even removed some of them. But finally the government gave in and allowed the prospectors to enter the Black Hills "at their own risk." The next step was as cruel and illegal as any the government ever took against the Sioux. To prevent clashes between the miners and the Indians, Washington ordered all the Sioux to report to reservation agencies. Any who remained outside would be considered automatically "hostile" and liable to attack. Many of the Sioux obeyed the order. But about 8,000 of them defied the government and gathered in the area of the Big Horn Mountains for their annual summer encampment and Sun Dance.

In June 1876 the army launched powerful forces of infantry, cavalry, and artillery against these Indians. One column, marching north from the Platte River, met Crazy Horse at Rosebud Creek on June 17. The army was beaten back in fierce fighting. Crazy Horse returned to the Sioux camp at the Little Bighorn River, where 8,000 Teton Sioux had gathered—the most powerful single force of Indians the army would ever face. Another army column advanced from the east. On June 25 the Seventh Cavalry, again under Custer's command, rode foolishly to the attack. The Sioux killed Custer and most of his troopers in the most famous (and, from the white point of view, perhaps the most stupid) Indian battle in American history.

Another cycle of treaty, war, and new treaty was about to be completed. Within a year, the Sioux were forced to give up their important Black Hills area. They were now herded onto a reservation covering only the central part of South Dakota, between the Missouri River and the Black Hills. But their troubles were not over. A railroad was pushing toward the reservation, and the remaining Sioux stood in its path. Farmers and ranchers were also beginning to look longingly at the land that the Sioux still held.

A CHANGING POLICY The idea of private property is so deeply rooted in white society that it is sometimes difficult to grasp the Native Americans' concept of land "ownership." Most Western tribes looked on the land in more or less the same way that fishermen look on the sea—as a place to hunt. No Indian thought of himself as owning a piece of the land. He might own his horses, his weapons, his tepee. But the land itself

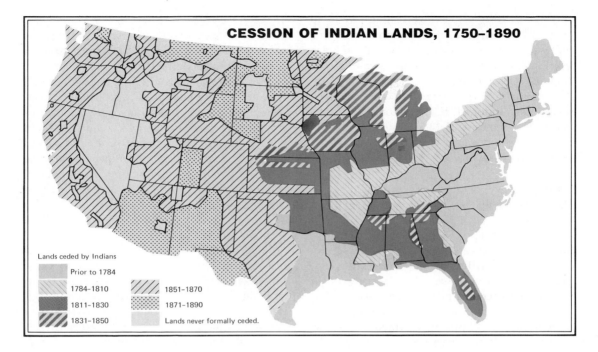

CESSION OF INDIAN LANDS, 1750–1890

Lands ceded by Indians
Prior to 1784
1784–1810   1851–1870
1811–1830   1871–1890
1831–1850   Lands never formally ceded.

was the "property" of the whole tribe, to be used communally and protected from other tribes.

When the various tribes of the plains agreed to give up their land, they did so as tribal units, not as individuals. When they accepted the reservations, too, they accepted them as tribes, not as individual property owners.

Reformers, most of whom lived in the East, believed that private property was an essential feature of "civilization." To break the Indians' old, communal concept of land, the reformers proposed that the reservations be divided into lots and given to the Indians in "severalty"—that the Indians be treated as several, or separate, individuals. Westerners, anxious to exploit the Indians, agreed with this proposal. Their enthusiasm was a result of some simple arithmetic. If every Indian family was given an individual farm, a lot of reservation land would be left over. There simply were not enough Indians, in most tribes, to "fill" the reservations. The remaining land could become available to whites.

This new policy became law in 1887 in the Dawes Severalty Act. The next year, after much

argument, some trickery, and probably some bribery, the whites persuaded the Sioux to accept the new plan. The one big Sioux reservation could then be broken down into five smaller ones that were, all together, less than half as large in area as the original. The same policy was applied to the other Plains Indians. One after another, the tribes settled for 160 acres per family. One after another, they realized this meant giving up about half their tribal lands. The resulting demoralization provided fertile ground for the new Ghost Dance religion. No matter what the intentions of the whites who wrote and supported the Dawes Severalty Act, it was a disaster for the Indians. In 1887, Indians had held about 130 million acres of land in the United States; by 1930, after forty-three years of the Dawes Act, the total had been reduced to less than 50 million acres.

With the new policy came even stronger efforts to convert Native Americans to white civilization—to make them "walk the white man's road," as Sitting Bull put it. These efforts hardened the conflict in attitudes between the progressive Indians, who accepted the new ways, and the nonprogressives, who clung to the old ones. The division was dramatized when Sitting Bull was arrested by Indian police from his own tribe. Even after the "reforms" of the 1880s, American policy toward the Indians was a calamity. They were reduced to a condition in some ways worse than that of the freed slaves in the South. The stage was set for Wounded Knee.

Farming on the Plains

Mining, railroads, and cattle ranching had created a scattered pattern of settlement on the Great Plains and in the Rockies. Miners gathered in towns that were separated by hundreds of miles. Railroads created towns, but only along their rights-of-way. And ranchers needed only a few cowhands to handle even very large herds. The actual white settlement of the plains had to await the slower migrations of farmers away from the Mississippi and onto the dry grasslands.

THE HOMESTEAD ACT The pace and pattern of settlement depended very much on government encouragement. In its youth, the Republican party had been the party of "free soil," which meant both agriculture without slavery and free land for any American. One of the first measures promoted by the Lincoln administration was the Homestead Act of 1862. According to this law, any citizen (or any immigrant who had taken the first step toward becoming a citizen) could claim 160 acres of public land, just by paying a fee of $26–$34. If he "lived upon or cultivated" the land for five years, the land became his, free and forever. If the homesteader did not want to wait five years, he could pay for the land at $1.25 an acre and own it after only six months.

The Homestead Act resulted in over a half million claims, totaling 80 million acres. But if its purpose was to award most of the public lands of the West to simple farmers, it was a failure. Much more land was given to railroads and states or sold directly to speculators than was ever acquired by small farmers.

Moreover, many of the homestead claims were phony. By law it was possible to transfer ownership at any time to any other person or corporation. So, for example, a rancher could have each of his hands claim a homestead and then (for a small bribe) transfer ownership to the ranch. Any land speculator could do the same, just by paying a bribe to a stranger passing through.

OTHER LAND ACTS Congress made the situation worse by passing several more laws that promoted corruption and the robbery of public land. First, in 1873, came the Timber Culture Act, which allowed a homesteader (or a rancher or speculator) to claim an additional 160 acres if he would plant trees on 40 of the acres. In 1877, Congress passed the Desert Land Act, which allowed an individual to claim 640 acres of land if he would begin irrigation. Under the law, ranchers took up section after section of land, especially in the Southwest, since they needed it for grazing cattle. They had their friends swear that it was irrigated (even if they had only poured a bucket of water on it in the presence of their "witnesses").

Even more corruption resulted from the Timber and Stone Act of 1878. This law applied to forest land that could not be farmed but that was highly profitable for timber. Under this law, any citizen or immigrant could purchase up to 160 acres of Western forest for $2.50 an acre. Lumbermen used the same tricks that ranchers and other speculators used. They imported sailors, prospectors, and others to buy land and then sign it over to a company for a small fee. And since one good log sold for about $2.50, every tree after the first from any acre of land was pure profit. Under these laws, over 20 million more acres of potentially valuable public land fell into the hands of corporations and speculators.

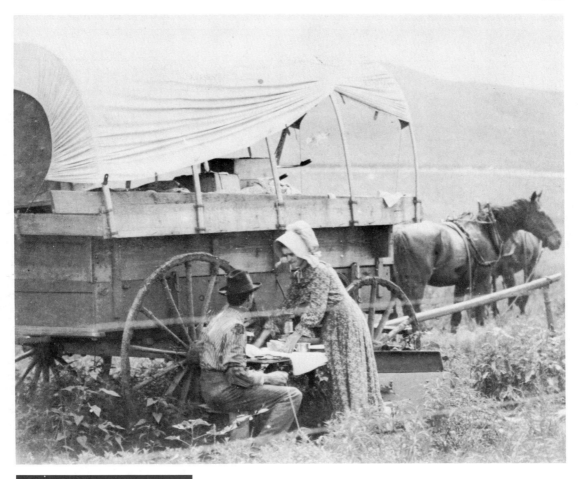

Kansas rest stop. People moving west took as much with them as their covered wagons could haul. And this included as much of their old life as possible. This woman has brought along a symbol of the home she has left behind, a clean white tablecloth. Somewhere on a treeless Kansas plain, the couple has paused for a meal, which she is spreading on a make-shift table set up in the grass. (Kansas State Historical Society)

HARDSHIPS AND SOLUTIONS Despite the fact that many of the profits went to land speculators and big corporations, Western lands were opened to the American people. Though they might have to pay ten dollars an acre to a speculator instead of getting homestead land virtually free from the government, farmers moved out onto the plains anyway. The majority came from the states bordering the Mississippi. Most of the rest were immigrants. Almost no workers from Eastern cities made the trip west. But the men and women who did settle on the plains performed a monumental task. In the thirty years after 1870 they brought more land under cultivation than had been cleared and plowed by all the generations of farmers from the settlement of Jamestown to the Civil War.

These farmers confronted problems that they had not met farther east. They found that their old ways of plowing and planting would not

CHRONOLOGY

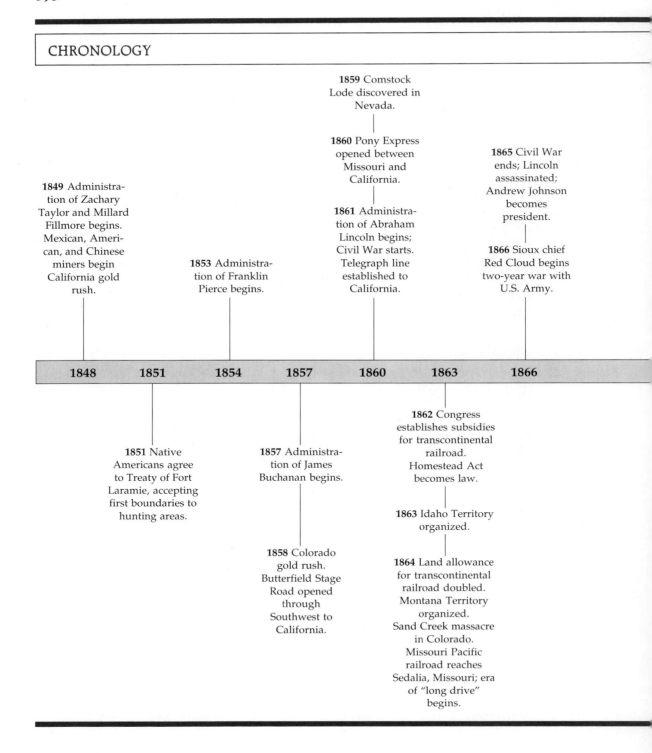

1859 Comstock Lode discovered in Nevada.

1860 Pony Express opened between Missouri and California.

1865 Civil War ends; Lincoln assassinated; Andrew Johnson becomes president.

1849 Administration of Zachary Taylor and Millard Fillmore begins. Mexican, American, and Chinese miners begin California gold rush.

1853 Administration of Franklin Pierce begins.

1861 Administration of Abraham Lincoln begins; Civil War starts. Telegraph line established to California.

1866 Sioux chief Red Cloud begins two-year war with U.S. Army.

| 1848 | 1851 | 1854 | 1857 | 1860 | 1863 | 1866 |

1851 Native Americans agree to Treaty of Fort Laramie, accepting first boundaries to hunting areas.

1857 Administration of James Buchanan begins.

1862 Congress establishes subsidies for transcontinental railroad. Homestead Act becomes law.

1863 Idaho Territory organized.

1858 Colorado gold rush. Butterfield Stage Road opened through Southwest to California.

1864 Land allowance for transcontinental railroad doubled. Montana Territory organized. Sand Creek massacre in Colorado. Missouri Pacific railroad reaches Sedalia, Missouri; era of "long drive" begins.

1873 Hinmaton-Yalaktit (Chief Joseph) becomes leader of Nez Percé tribe. Timber Culture Act becomes law.

1877 Administration of Rutherford B. Hayes begins. Chief Joseph and his Nez Percé band surrender. Crazy Horse surrenders, enters Sioux reservation. Desert Land Act becomes law.

1878 Timber and Stone Act becomes law.

1883 Senate investigating committee visits Sioux reservation.

1885 First administration of Grover Cleveland begins. Rapid collapse of Chicago price for steers.

1889 Administration of Benjamin Harrison begins. Bitter winter severely damages cattle bonanza. Sioux learn of Wovoka Ghost Dance religion.

1890 Massacre at Wounded Knee. United States Bureau of the Census officially declares that the frontier no longer exists.

1869	1872	1875	1878	1881	1884	1887	1890

1868 Great Sioux Reservation established in Dakotas.

1869 Administration of Ulysses S. Grant begins. Transcontinental railroad completed.

1874 Gold discovered in Black Hills of South Dakota.

1876 Battles of Rosebud Creek and Little Bighorn. Nez Percé "renegades" strike out for Canada.

1881 Administration of James A. Garfield and Chester A. Arthur begins. Sitting Bull returns from Canada, enters Sioux reservation.

1887 Dawes Severalty Act becomes law.

work. For one thing, rainfall was scarce, rivers often ran dry, and the water table was deep. Farmers had to haul water from long distances or collect it in holes when it did rain. New well-digging machinery, invented in the 1880s and 1890s, however, enabled people to dig deeper wells to reach the water table. And steel windmills made it easier to pump the water up. Plains dwellers also developed dry farming. This technique, by which a farmer covers a plowed field with a blanket of dust, conserves the moisture in the soil.

Another problem on the plains was lack of wood. Farmers living there often made their first homes from cakes of sod. For fuel they burned old hay or dried cow dung. Fencing was a special problem until the invention of barbed wire in the 1870s.

A farm family soon learned that, while sixty acres of land could support them back east, five times as much was needed on the plains. Nature seemed to do things on a grand scale there. In summer the wind blew hot, and twice as hard as in the East. In winter, blizzards howled down out of the mountains, burying homes and killing livestock. Tornadoes, dust storms, and plagues of locusts and grasshoppers were frequent.

Dry years drove thousands of farmers back east. Many of those who stayed barely survived.

In the end, though, farmers turned the plains into the world's most efficient area for producing wheat, corn, and other grains. By 1880, American flour—like American beef and pork from the same area—was being exported in great quantities all over the world.

In all this the Native American was, of course, the great loser. The whites' successes on the plains seemed to prove what white Americans had always believed—that the Indians could not make "proper" use of their environment because they lived too much *with* it and not enough *from* it.

Whites were able to exploit even the tough plains environment, to draw from it enough food to feed not only most of the United States but part of the rest of the world, too. The Indians, in contrast, had used only what they needed to maintain their way of life. A full century was to pass before white Americans began to ask themselves seriously whether the Indians' way was not somehow at least as good as theirs. Only one thing was certain: In their "primitive" way Native Americans had respected nature more. They had never viewed their world as an object to be owned, changed, and exploited. This, at least in part, was what the battle at Wounded Knee was all about.

Suggestions for Further Reading

WOUNDED KNEE

Robert M. Utley, *The Last Days of the Sioux Nation* (1963), is a scholarly, balanced, but readable story of the gradual collapse of Sioux society under white pressure. Also important is Utley's more recent book, *Frontier Regulars: The United States Army and the Indian* (1973). Stanley Vestal's biography *Sitting Bull* (1957) is important, as is C. M. Oehler, *The Great Sioux Uprising* (1959). James Mooney was an anthropologist who did extensive fieldwork among Western Indians during the period. He collected his

observations and many of the Ghost Dance songs in his classic *The Ghost Dance Religion and the Sioux Uprising of 1890* (republished in 1965).

THE MINING AND CATTLE FRONTIERS

A great beginning is to read Mark Twain's uproarious but informative *Roughing It* (1872). A nice discussion of the astonishing development of mining cities is Gunther Barth, *Instant Cities* (1975). The same author's *Bitter Strength* (1964) deals with the experiences of Chinese immigrants in the Far West.

The unhappy social history of the Spanish-speaking natives of California is the subject of Leonard Pitt, *The Decline of the Californios* (1966). On the gold-mining areas, a somewhat dated but still usable book is G. C. Quiett, *Paydirt: A Panorama of American Gold Rushes* (1936). More modern discussions of the various mining frontiers are available in R. W. Paul, *Mining Frontiers of the Far West* (1963), and William S. Greever, *Bonanza West: Western Mining Rushes* (1963). Useful treatments of the origin and development of the cattle frontier are E. E. Dale, *The Range Cattle Industry* (1930); Lewis Atherton, *The Cattle Kings* (1961); Terry Jordan, *Trails to Texas* (1981); Robert Dykstra, *The Cattle Towns* (1968); and J. M. Shagg, *The Cattle Trading Industry* (1973). J. B. Frantz and J. E. Choate, *The American Cowboy, Myth and Reality* (1955); David Day, *Cowboy Culture* (1981); Roger McGrath, *Gunfighters, Highwaymen, and Vigilantes* (1984); and Philip Durham and E. L. Jones, *The Negro Cowboy* (1965), are careful and realistic treatments of the highly romanticized culture that grew up around the cattle industry.

THE DEFEAT OF THE NATIVE AMERICANS

Dee Brown, *Bury My Heart at Wounded Knee* (1955), is a sometimes moving and not always precisely accurate book. But it is still an excellent place for the student to begin reading. F. G. Roe, *The Indian and the Horse* (1955), discusses the most intimate and important relationship of the Western Indians to a new animal "tool." The most general and reliable scholarly discussion of the gradual ruin of Native American civilization and culture on the Great Plains is R. K. Andrist, *The Long Death: The Last Days of the Plains Indians* (1964). Two general studies by Wilcomb Washburn, *The Indian in North America* (1975) and *Red Man's Land / White Man's Law* (1971), have useful information on this period. Federal policy toward the tribes is the subject of Francis Paul Prucha, *American Indian Policy in Crisis* (1976).

FARMING ON THE PLAINS

Two accounts of the way the public lands of the United States were made available for settlement and exploitation are R. M. Robbins, *Our Landed Heritage* (1942), and Paul W. Gates, *The History of Public Land Development* (1968). On farming on the plains, F. A. Shannon, *The Farmer's Last Frontier* (1945), Gilbert C. Fite, *The Farmer's Frontier* (1966), and Allen G. Bouge, *From Prairie to Corn Belt* (1963), are the basic studies. J. A. Malin, *The Grasslands Agriculture of North America* (1947), is a technical but important book. The impact of the railroads can be followed in G. R. Taylor and I. D. Neu, *The American Railroad Network* (1956).

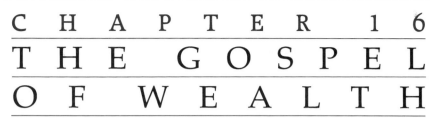

CHAPTER 16
THE GOSPEL OF WEALTH

THE EPISODE: *On August 4, 1892, two wealthy inhabitants of the industrial city of Fall River, Mass., were brutally murdered in their home—hacked many times about the head with an axe. All the evidence pointed to a most improbable suspect—Lizzie Borden, the victims' own daughter. Lizzie was arrested and put on trial. Throughout the United States the case was headline news. Most Americans found it difficult to believe that Lizzie Borden was guilty. But the prosecution mounted a provocative case, arguing that beneath the calm, respectable surface of the Borden household lay a deep well of conflict and anger. As the trial developed, both the jury and the public followed in fascination as the prosecution and the defense presented two profoundly contrasting pictures of life in the Borden family.*

THE HISTORICAL SETTING: *Whether or not Lizzie Borden was guilty, the two competing pictures of life in the Borden household reflected two different sides of life in late nineteenth-century American cities and towns. For the well-to-do and the middle classes, life was good—on the surface. Benefiting from the great increase in national prosperity over the decades following the Civil War, these people proudly (even frantically) displayed their new wealth by building bigger houses, wearing fancier clothing, and behaving with ever more elaborate rituals of "good manners." Through their family life they found the greatest opportunity to display the signs of their public status.*

But their families were also designed to provide refuge and comfort from the tensions of life in the outside world of business and moneymaking. Women, above all, had to play both roles at once. They had to display—with their clothing, their manners, and their "leisure"—all evidence of family prosperity. But they also had to act as selfless sources of kindness and emotional support for their husbands, children, and parents. Playing both these roles demanded that women remain at home, away from the sordid business world where money was actually made.

Women in poorer families, however, lacked the choice of remaining at home. For these women (many of them recent immigrants or African Americans), it was necessary to earn money to supplement the meager incomes of their husbands or fathers. Usually, that meant taking menial, dead-end jobs for very low wages. So for many Americans, rich and poor alike, the family was unable to become the deep source of inner satisfaction and peace it was expected to be. The burden of this failure fell especially hard on women. Few responded the way Lizzie Borden may have done, but the tensions hidden within the Borden household were commonplaces of late nineteenth-century American life.

THE LIZZIE BORDEN MURDERS

Thursday, August 4, 1892. The summer morning was hot and sultry in Fall River, Massachusetts. It was uncomfortable everywhere—out in the city's streets and inside its textile mills, its tenements, and even its mansions.

In the house at 92 Second Street, Bridget Sullivan, the live-in Irish servant, was at work, washing the downstairs windows. At exactly 10:40 A.M. her employer, Andrew J. Borden, arrived home from his daily business rounds downtown and started to open the front door. There were two separate locks on the door, and even after Mr. Borden opened both of them, he was still faced with a metal bolt, which could be opened only from the inside. Bridget Sullivan knew what was happening, so she stopped her work and walked over to the entrance in order to help Mr. Borden. For a moment, Bridget had trouble releasing the bolt. As she fumbled with it she muttered in frustration—a sound she later reported to be "Pshaw." Her expletive was overheard by the only other person known to be in the house, Lizzie Borden, Mr. Borden's thirty-two-year-old daughter. Lizzie, standing on the top of the stairs leading up from the front hall, laughed.

Andrew Borden walked into the house without speaking to Bridget, and the maid resumed her window washing. Lizzie joined Mr. Borden, and father and daughter spoke briefly with each other. From the next room, Bridget was sure she heard Lizzie tell Mr. Borden that his wife "had a note and had gone out."

After a few minutes, Andrew Borden got up, took the key to his room from its accustomed spot on the dining room mantelpiece, and went upstairs. A few minutes later, he came down again to take a nap. Still dressed in his tie and jacket, he lay down on the couch in the sitting room, his feet resting on the carpet.

As Mr. Borden lay down, Bridget moved discreetly into the dining room, to wash the windows there. After a few moments, she was joined by Lizzie, who was carrying an ironing board and who now began to iron a stack of handkerchiefs. Quietly, Lizzie began a conversation with the servant:

> "Maggie, are you going out today?" Lizzie asked. (Maggie had been the name of a previous Borden family servant, and Lizzie Borden always addressed Bridget by that name.)

"I don't know," Bridget answered. "I might and I might not. I don't feel very well."
(Bridget had been vomiting earlier in the morning.)

"If you go out, be sure and lock the door, for Mrs. Borden has gone out on a sick call [to visit a sick person], and I might go out, too."

"Miss Lizzie, who is sick?"

"I don't know. She had a note this morning. It must be in town."

Soon, Bridget finished washing the dining room windows and returned to the kitchen to clean up. She was feeling ill, and she needed to rest. She climbed upstairs to her room in the attic, and without undressing, lay down on her bed. Soon Bridget heard the clock at city hall, two blocks away, strike eleven. It was too hot to sleep. Andrew Borden had now been home for twenty minutes. Bridget Sullivan continued to lie on her bed for ten minutes more. All this time, she heard nothing at all from downstairs, no doors opening or closing, no voices talking or arguing, no sound.

Until 11:10. That was when Lizzie Borden hollered up to her: "Maggie, come down!" Bridget could tell something was wrong. "What is the matter?" she called down.

"Come down quick!" Lizzie yelled back. "Father's dead! Somebody came in and killed him!"

Bridget ran downstairs and headed toward the sitting room—but Lizzie stopped her. "Oh, Maggie, don't go in," she warned. Then she said, "I have got to have a doctor, quick. Go over. I have got to have the doctor." The doctor was Seabury Bowen, who lived diagonally across the street. But Dr. Bowen was out on his rounds, so Bridget blurted the news of the murder to the doctor's wife, then quickly returned to the Borden house.

Once again, Lizzie asked Bridget to go out—this time to find her some companionship. "Go and get Miss Russell. I can't be alone in the house." (Alice Russell was Lizzie's best friend; Lizzie had visited her just the previous evening.) As Bridget went out to fetch Miss Russell, she was observed by a next-door neighbor, who noticed that Bridget was walking fast and looking pale. The neighbor, a woman named Adelaide Churchill, knew that something must be wrong. She looked out through her kitchen window and peered into the Borden house, where she spotted Lizzie Borden standing by the side door. Opening the window, Mrs. Churchill yelled across: "Lizzie, what is the matter?"

"Oh, Mrs. Churchill, do come over," Lizzie replied. "Someone has killed father!"

Mrs. Churchill rushed over and found Lizzie sitting on the inside stairs. Placing her hand on Lizzie's arm to comfort her, she asked, "Oh, Lizzie, where is your father?"

"In the sitting room."

Then Mrs. Churchill asked Lizzie a key question: "Where were you when it happened?"

Lizzie's response was the basis of the story she would continue to tell, with variations, over the next year: "I went out to the barn to get a piece of iron. I heard a distressing noise and came back and found the screen door open."

But Mrs. Churchill was more worried about the rest of the Borden family than suspicious of Lizzie's story. She realized that Lizzie's stepmother, Abby, might be in danger. Where was Abby? she asked.

"I don't know," Lizzie replied. "She had got a note to go see someone who is sick." And she added: "But I don't know but she is killed, too, for I thought I heard her come in."

Now Lizzie changed the subject, and spoke once again of her dead father: "Father must have an enemy, for we have all been sick, and we think the milk has been poisoned. I must have a doctor."

As it turned out, Dr. Bowen had just returned home, learned of the horrifying event, and headed to the Borden house. He went straight to the sitting room to examine the body, which was lying face up on the sofa. He later reported what he had seen.

> His face was very badly cut, apparently with a sharp instrument. His face was covered with blood. I felt of his pulse and satisfied myself he was dead. I glanced about the room and saw there was nothing disturbed—neither the furniture nor anything at all. . . . His face was hardly to be recognized by one who knew him.

His brief examination complete, Dr. Bowen moved into the dining room. He kept repeating: "He is murdered, he is murdered." Then Dr. Bowen returned to question Lizzie Borden. Had she seen an intruder? he asked. She repeated her story that she had been out in the barn looking for a piece of iron. And she mentioned the fear she had expressed a few minutes earlier about some "enemy." But now she offered an explanation of that fear: "She said she was afraid her father had had trouble with tenants, and she had overheard loud conversations several times recently."

Meanwhile, Bridget Sullivan had found Lizzie's friend Alice Russell, and the two women returned to the house. Bridget, too, had begun to be concerned about her mistress, Abby Borden. Bridget knew there was only one person who would have been likely to ask Abby Borden to come visiting when she was sick: That was Abby's younger sister, Mrs. Sarah Whitehead. So Bridget offered a suggestion:

"Oh, Lizzie, if I knew where Mrs. Whitehead was, I would go and see if Mrs. Borden was there, and tell her that Mr. Borden was very sick."

But now Lizzie repeated her hint that Mrs. Borden might not be out after all, but might be somewhere in the house that very minute. And if she was, then why had she not come downstairs to see what was the matter? "Maggie," said Lizzie Borden, "I am almost positive I heard her coming in. Won't you go upstairs to see?"

Bridget knew very well what it was she might see, so she refused to do what her mistress asked. She said simply: "I am not going upstairs alone."

The next-door neighbor, Mrs. Churchill, said she was willing to accompany Bridget to the second floor, and the two women started upstairs together. Bridget led the way, so she was the first to spot the second body. It was in the guest room, lying face down, resting on its knees where it had fallen. The two women did not stay very long—they knew who it was and that she was dead. They headed right back to the first floor. Now Lizzie was lying down, as if expecting the dread news. But it was her friend Alice Russell who spoke first, her words tactful, almost delicate: "Is there another?" Mrs. Churchill answered: "Yes, she is up there."

The police made efforts to find a crazed intruder—but they never found a serious suspect. In fact, the possibility of such an intruder almost had to be excluded: Too

The murder scene. This photograph of Andrew J. Borden's body was taken by the Fall River Police Department within a few hours of his murder. Examine the furnishings—comfortable, but shabby and out of fashion. (Courtesy Fall River Historical Society)

many people had been abroad on Second Street that morning, or watching the street from their windows. If there had been an intruder, he had somehow escaped everyone's notice. So they also pursued another avenue of investigation, trying to discover whether anyone had sufficient reason to *want* to kill Andrew Borden. And they could come up with no such hypothetical person, either. Andrew Borden may have had trouble with his tenants, as Lizzie had said, but extensive investigation revealed no "enemy" with any real reason to slaughter him and his wife. Finally, robbery could be excluded as a motive: Nothing at all had been taken from the house, and there were not even signs of a search.

What was troubling was the extreme brutality of the murders. Each victim had been hacked in the skull some twenty times—well after the killer must have known they were already dead. Whoever killed them was crazy—or else filled with consuming rage.

Most unsettling of all, perhaps, was the fact that the two victims had been killed at least ninety minutes apart—Mrs. Borden around 9:30, and her husband shortly after 11:00. This had to mean one of two things: Either the murderer had killed Mrs. Borden and then hidden himself without detection somewhere in the house from 9:30 until after 11:00, waiting first for Andrew Borden to return home (whenever that might be) and then waiting for him to fall asleep so that he would not put up a struggle or raise an outcry, or else the murderer had sneaked into the house, not once but *twice*, totally unseen by neighbors or passersby. But the house had been locked and bolted all morning. And there were no signs of a forced entry.

Every one of these problems and improbabilities simply disappeared with a single alternative hypothesis: that the murderer was not an outsider at all, but a member of the household. Inevitably, then, even as the police dutifully tried to track down all other possibilities, their attention turned toward Lizzie Borden. And they found that the pieces fitted perfectly—almost. Lizzie's guilt could explain the time that passed between the two murders and also the absence of any sign of forced entry or of struggle on the part of either victim. Furthermore, her own account of her actions on the morning of the murders—which she told first to her father, and then to Bridget Sullivan, Mrs. Churchill, and a variety of police officers—simply failed to hold together. Abby Borden had *not* left the house earlier in the morning and then returned. In fact, none of her acquaintances was sick that day or had sent a note asking her to come visit. No such note was found in the Borden house. Finally, despite extensive and repeated inquiries, nobody ever came forward (either within Mrs. Borden's circle of acquaintants or outside it) to acknowledge having written one. The conclusion became inescapable: There was no such note. Lizzie had invented the story and told it to her father simply in order to prevent him from looking for his wife—and dis- covering her bloody corpse.

There were also contradictions in Lizzie's account of her actions between the time her father returned home and the discovery of his murder half an hour later. She claimed to have gone out to the barn loft soon after her father's arrival—that was the reason she had not witnessed the murder. But she was unable to keep her story straight. To her neighbor Mrs. Churchill, she said she had visited the barn "to get a piece of iron." To another person, she specified that the iron was intended to repair a broken screen on a window. But later, and under oath, Lizzie testified she had gone to the barn because she was planning to go fishing in a few days and wanted "to find lead for a sinker." Most damning of all, a policeman who examined the barn shortly after the discovery of the murders reported that the loft was coated with dust so thick that his own footprints were like tracks in the snow—yet there were no other prints to be found in the place!

The evidence was clear: Lizzie Borden had not been in the barn at all. She had remained in the house the whole time. She must have witnessed her father's killing— or committed it herself.

Lizzie was arrested, charged, and tried for the murder of her parents, in the most famous American criminal case of the nineteenth century.

Although the evidence against Lizzie Borden was powerful, there were some equally powerful problems that the prosecution faced if it was to put together a case strong enough to gain a conviction. To begin with, the evidence against Lizzie was entirely circumstantial: She had neither confessed to the crime nor been seen by any witness to have committed it. Circumstantial evidence was perfectly valid from a legal point of view; however, jurors would have to be persuaded not only that the evidence was airtight but that the defendant was capable of committing murders of such bru- tality. So the prosecution had to deal with *image* as well as evidence—and that was its most difficult challenge.

Lizzie Andrew Borden. This photograph of a fashionable Lizzie Borden was taken in 1890, when she was 29 or 30. Those people who came to believe two years later that Lizzie was guilty of double murder made their point with the following ditty, first sung in the streets of Fall River's textile mill district: "Lizzie Borden took an axe / And gave her mother forty whacks; / When she saw what she had done / She gave her father forty-one." (Courtesy Fall River Historical Society)

In the first place, Lizzie Borden was female. As her minister put it, "To my mind, it is an impossibility for this girl to have committed the deed." (The minister was not alone in referring to Lizzie as a girl rather than a woman, even though she was thirty-two years old.) She was a woman of established character—a church member, a Sunday school teacher, and an active member of the Women's Christian Temperance Union, or WCTU. In fact, the Fall River branch of the WCTU voted to "declare our unshaken faith in her, as a fellow worker and sister tenderly beloved." Even the *Woman's Journal*, a feminist magazine, declared: "The citizens of Fall River who have known Miss Lizzie Borden from childhood are unanimous in their belief of her innocence. She is a solid, substantial young woman of gentle disposition and quiet habits, much beloved by her friends."

Added to the fact that Lizzie was a woman who had lived a respectable life was a closely related point: Her family was extremely wealthy. By any standards, her father was a rich man—a member of the single wealthiest and most powerful clan in the city of Fall River. A local newspaper reporter described Andrew Jackson Borden's position in these words:

> He was one of the family of Bordens whose name has always been identified with the growth and business enterprises of the city. No one knows how much money he was worth, but persons who are as well acquainted with his affairs as he would allow them to be, do not hesitate to say that his estate was worth $300,000. He was president of the Union Savings Bank, a member of its Board of Trustees and Investment, a director of the Merchants Manufacturing Company, the B. M. C. Durfee Safe Deposit and Trust Company, the Globe Yarn Mills, the Troy Cotton and Woolen Manufactory and other manufacturing concerns.

It was difficult enough to believe that any woman—even some poor, working-class, immigrant woman—was capable of committing such a hideous crime. But a Fall River jury had recently been persuaded to convict a local woman of a brutal murder. That woman, however, had not been from a respectable old family. What the jury that would soon sit in judgment of Lizzie Borden would have to decide was whether a woman whose family held such a high position could have committed a murder so foul. Lizzie Borden was not only a woman, she was a "lady."

The final difficulty in persuading a jury of Lizzie's guilt was the simplest, and perhaps the most powerful, of all. Lizzie Borden was not accused of murdering some stranger but of killing her own parents. She was not only a woman, not only even a "lady," she was also the victims' own daughter. As her defense attorney put it: "To foully murder her stepmother and then go straight away and slay her own father is a wreck of human morals. Such acts as those are morally and physically impossible for this young woman."

That was the issue, then. The evidence pointed to Lizzie Borden, and to nobody else. But the evidence was all circumstantial, and Lizzie was not the kind of person who seemed capable of committing such a crime. That fact alone might be grounds for "reasonable doubt."

There was only one strategy for the prosecution to follow. It had to convince the jury that Lizzie Borden had a clear and powerful motive to commit the crimes—a motive powerful enough to overcome the doubts inevitably raised by her sex, her background and social status, and her familial role. Lizzie's past history precluded the possibility that she was demented or prone to fits of sudden rage or violence. The second murder had been committed such a long time after the first one that the killings could not have been a sudden act of unpremeditated emotion. The crime had been planned in advance. This meant the prosecution had to convince the jury that Lizzie had some reason to want her family dead—a reason so long-standing, so deep, that it could overcome all the circumstances that made it so hard to believe she could do such a thing.

The prosecution therefore attempted to undermine with a single stroke all the favorable feeling that had built up around Lizzie Borden. It did so by insisting that she was not the tender woman or the dutiful daughter she was made out to be, and

Master Bedroom

Locked Door

Lizzie's Bedroom

2nd Floor

Locked Door

Bedroom

Pantry

Kitchen

Sitting Room

Sink Room

1st Floor

Entry

Dining Room

Front Entry

Parlor

FLOOR PLAN OF THE BORDEN HOUSE

that her family was not a haven of cordial affection. Instead, the prosecution argued, the Borden household was pervaded by a venomous hostility that ran so deep the family had turned into a "murderous" unit and had settled into a kind of silent warfare that divided the two generations into armed camps, each eyeing the other with constant suspicion. As the district attorney put it, "Although they occupied the same household, there was built up between them an almost impassable wall."

It was easy to show that Lizzie had remarkably little to do with her parents. She spent much of her time outside the house, and when she was at home she usually stayed in her bedroom—with the door shut. She rarely bothered to greet her parents when she entered the house. In fact, she hardly ever joined them even at mealtime— instead, she waited until they were finished, and then she ate alone.

Abby Durfee Gray Borden. On the morning of the murders, Lizzie Borden claimed that her stepmother had been about to go shopping for food, clothed in a housedress. "Won't you change your dress before you go out?" Lizzie allegedly asked, and Abby Borden replied: "No, this is good enough." This trivial exchange reveals the conflict between a fashion-conscious "lady" and a woman who did not need to parade her status by a display of "conspicuous consumption." (Courtesy Fall River Historical Society)

But the "impassable wall" that ran through the Borden house was more than a figure of speech. Lizzie and her parents had divided the house up by an elaborate series of locks and bolts and bars. The guest room (the room where Mrs. Borden was murdered) was right next to Lizzie's bedroom, and there was even a door connecting the two rooms. But Mrs. Borden used the guest room for sewing, and Lizzie made sure that the connecting door could not be used. As she reported at the inquest, "It has been locked and bolted, and a large writing desk in my room kept up against it." When Lizzie was asked how she could get from her room to the guest room, she replied: "I have to go to the front hall." (In any case, she said, she was "not allowed in that room.") In the same way, Lizzie could not get to her bedroom by walking up the back stairs—that was her father's territory. "Father's bedroom was kept locked, and his door into my room locked and hooked, too, and I had no keys."

Such arrangements affected the whole household, and the prosecution suggested that they stemmed from the particular hostility that Lizzie felt toward Mrs. Borden. There even seemed to be a plausible explanation for the hostility. Abby Borden was not Lizzie's mother at all, but her stepmother. Lizzie's own mother had died when Lizzie was only two years old, and Andrew Borden had married Abby two years later. Abby had now been living in the Borden household for twenty-eight years. Even so, when a policeman on the scene routinely asked Lizzie "if she had any idea who could have killed her father and mother," Lizzie had said: "She is not my mother, sir; she is my stepmother. My mother died when I was a child."

Just a few months before the murders, a seamstress who made clothing for the women of the Borden household had made the mistake of referring to Abby as Lizzie's mother. Lizzie quickly shot back: "Don't say that to me, for she is a mean good-for-nothing thing." That was strong language, and the dressmaker had tried to give Lizzie a chance to take it back (or, perhaps, to say even more):

> "Oh, Lizzie, you don't mean that?"
> "Yes, I don't have much to do with her. I stay in my room most of the time."
> "You come down for your meals, don't you?"
> "Yes, but we don't eat with *them* if we can help it."

The pattern of hostility was clear. But what was its basis? The prosecution came up with an incident it argued was an important piece of family history.

Five years earlier, in 1887, Andrew Borden had given a piece of real estate to his wife and his wife's sister—the same Mrs. Whitehead who was supposed to have written Abby Borden the "sick note" on the morning of the murders. It was an open secret that Lizzie resented this gift. And there was another open secret about the episode: It was at this very time that Lizzie began to address Abby Borden as "Mrs. Borden." Until then, she had called her "mother."

Behind Abby—behind it all—loomed the figure of Andrew Jackson Borden. It was Andrew who had married Abby, who ran the household, and who more than any other person dominated the life and the imagination of Lizzie Borden. Andrew was a well-known man around Fall River, and something of a local character. He had earned the reputation of being tight-lipped, iron-willed—and notoriously stingy. He was known as a man who loved to make money, but who hated to spend it. And his tastes determined the shape of Lizzie's life—a life she had come to loathe.

It was not that Lizzie was short of money. Several years earlier, her father had given her and her sister Emma one of the other houses he owned, and the rent from this property had provided Lizzie with plenty of spending money—enough money to buy the nineteen dresses that hung in her closet, and more. When she went out, Lizzie could dress as she wished. But in the house to which she always had to return, she was forced to live in the dark shadow of her father.

The house itself was one of Lizzie's problems. Over the previous forty or fifty years, most of the bankers and mill owners of Fall River had sold their old houses downtown and had moved to an elegant section of the city, known as the Hill, where they could look down on the factories that had made their fortune—and also on the thousands of laborers (most of them Irish or French-Canadian immigrants, and many of them children) who worked ten hours or more each day, six days a week, in those factories, and who lived crowded in nearby tenement houses that were owned by those same wealthy capitalists. Most of Lizzie Borden's wealthy cousins lived in lavish new mansions on the Hill, and so did many people with far less money. But Andrew Borden had never chosen to move up to the Hill. He and his family continued to live downtown, just two blocks away from the bank he owned (and only a few blocks from one of the largest factories in the city). Second Street was one of the busiest streets in the city. Andrew Borden's neighbors were a mixed lot of shopkeepers and professional men, many of whom took in unmarried working-class boarders to help make ends meet. One house on the street contained as many as nine boarders. The immediate neighborhood was respectable enough (even though, just a block down the street, a brothel operated openly). But Andrew Borden was its wealthiest resident—by far.

What made the situation even odder was the appearance of the Borden house. It was a modest building even for the Second Street neighborhood. The house was relatively small, and it was more than fifty years old. (There was even a barn in the backyard.) And its two stories were constructed in a style that seemed strangely out-of-date by the year 1892. The house contained no halls or corridors. The only way to reach most rooms in the house (even the bedrooms) was by walking through another room. That was the reason for all the locked doors in the house: Because of the structure of the building, there was simply no other way for Lizzie or her parents to ensure privacy.

The house was old-fashioned in other ways as well. For one thing, it lacked most of the modern amenities. Fall River had dug an underground water and sewer system during the 1880s—but Andrew Borden had never chosen to have his house connected up with it. There was no indoor plumbing at 92 Second Street. The household got water from a well in the backyard (that was where Bridget Sullivan had filled her pail to wash the windows on the morning of the murders). They urinated into "slop jars" kept in their bedrooms, and defecated in a water closet down in the cellar. A decade or two earlier these had been the standard arrangements. Even in 1892 they would not have seemed unsanitary—merely out of fashion.

The house was furnished in a style that was a generation or more out of date. Police photographs of the bodies of Mr. and Mrs. Borden show some of these furnishings (see p. 700). The glossy black horsehair of the sofa on which Andrew Borden was murdered would have been replaced long ago in more fashionable households by decoratively printed cotton or velvet plush. Mrs. Borden's body lay beside a heavy wooden bedstead with a tall, elaborately carved headboard. It should by now have been replaced by a more modern metal bedstead. And the carpets in both rooms, running wall-to-wall to cover the wide, uneven floorboards, would have been replaced by smaller throw rugs over narrow, evenly joined, polished floorboards.

The house was so embarrassingly old-fashioned that Lizzie Borden's defense attorney felt obliged to confront the issue in his concluding speech to the jury, out of fear that it might provide his client with the necessary motive for murder:

They say she killed her stepmother and father because that was a house without any comforts in it. Well, gentlemen, I hope you all live in a better way than the Borden family lived, so far as having good furniture and conveniences. Are *your* houses all warmed with steam? Do *you* have pictures and pianos and a library, and all conveniences and luxury? Do you? Well, I congratulate you if you do. This is not a downtrodden people. There are lots of comforts in our country homes. I know something of them, but I remember back in my boyhood *we* did not have gas and running water in every room.

The lawyer's argument was clever. He knew that the jury members were all "old-fashioned" men from the small towns around Fall River, and he was trying to persuade these men that Andrew J. Borden was basically one of them—not a miser, but a man who had remained true to solid, old-fashioned country ways. The lawyer summed up his point simply and effectively:

Andrew Borden was a simple man, an old-fashioned man. He did not dress himself up with jewelry. He carried a silver watch [not a gold one]. He was a plain man of the everyday sort of fifty years ago.

The Borden house. Andrew Borden moved here at the age of fifty-one, in 1872, after he had become wealthy enough to retire from the undertaking business. Until then, he and his family had lived with his father in an old and seedy section of Fall River. The new house was modest, even by the standards of its own neighborhood, but it was exactly what Andrew Borden wanted. Note the barn in the background at the left. (Courtesy Fall River Historical Society)

Gradually, Lizzie Borden's guilt or innocence had become tied to her father's character. The prosecution wanted the jurors to perceive Andrew Borden as a mean-spirited miser who systematically deprived his household of the most ordinary comforts. The defense wanted the jurors to see him as a conservative man who had courageously refused to surrender to the fads of the day. The ambiguity was deep and real, and it lay at the heart of the bitter feeling that pervaded and divided the Borden family, and that finally destroyed it. To understand the problem, it is necessary to probe deeper into the inner history of the family—deeper than either side in the trial cared to go.

The Borden clan had seen Fall River grow from a tiny farming village of a few hundred people in 1800 to a dynamic city of 75,000 in 1890. In 1890 more cotton textiles

FALL RIVER, 1812

MOUNT HOPE BAY

North Watuppa Lake

Thomas Borden's Saw Mill

Quequechan River

South Watuppa Lake

— Street
• House
▣ House owned by Thomas or Richard Borden

MASS.
R.I.

FALL RIVER, 1892

MOUNT HOPE BAY

North Watuppa Lake

The Hill

Downtown Industrial and Commercial Area

Lizzie Borden's House

Quequechan River

Housing

Mills and Mill

South Watuppa Lake

MASS.
R.I.

— Street

These two maps reveal the intensive growth that Fall River experienced during the nineteenth century. In 1812 it was a small, quite rural settlement—though even then the Bordens were a prominent family. By 1892 it had become a densely populated and industrialized city, with well-defined districts. Industrialization and expansion even altered the topography of the area. The Quequechan River, crossed by a single bridge in 1892, had been integrated into Fall River's downtown center seventy years later.

were manufactured in Fall River than in any other city in the entire world. And the Bordens had played an important part in the city's industrial transformation.

At the beginning of the nineteenth century, a farmer named Borden had owned the rights to operate a sawmill and a gristmill along the powerful stream that gave Fall River its name. With the beginning of industrialization around 1820, these mills had been replaced by the first cotton factories—and farmer Borden's children owned and controlled most of them. As the community began to grow in size and wealth, the Borden brothers took the capital they earned from these factories and shrewdly used it to organize a variety of other economic activities. By 1850 the Borden brothers controlled the banks that regulated the city's credit system and the new factories that produced the dyes and patterns used in the cotton factories, as well as the complex machines that powered those factories. The Borden brothers even owned the steamboats and railroads that soon connected Fall River to the commercial centers of Boston and New York City.

Over the thirty years between 1850 and 1880, the Borden brothers consolidated the family grip on Fall River by carefully passing their power into the hands of their own children—nearly twenty of them—and by engaging in a systematic pattern of arranged marriages between those children and the members of another wealthy Fall River clan, the Durfees. The *New York Times* sarcastically described the situation:

> Fall River has been more or less controlled by Durfees and Bordens, who appear and reappear as officers in most of the corporations. Of the Fall River Bleachery, Jefferson Borden is President, Spencer Borden is Treasurer, and Jefferson Borden, Spencer Borden, Richard B. Borden, Philip D. Borden, and George B. Durfee are Directors. Of the American Print Works, Jefferson Borden is President, George B. Durfee is Clerk, Thomas J. Borden Treasurer, and Jefferson Borden, Thomas J. Borden, George B. Durfee, and W. B. Durfee are Directors. Bordens and Durfees have put their sons, brothers, uncles, sons-in-law, and cousins into office, and permitted them to do nearly as they chose. This is the way the Bordens and Durfees continually break out, like small-pox, in all the industrial enterprises of that city.

From Andrew J. Borden's point of view, one fact about this *New York Times* story would have been particularly striking: His own name did not appear in it even once. Andrew would have known exactly why not. It was because he was not one of the sons of the wealthy Borden brothers. In fact, he belonged to a different branch of the family. The family had many branches. In 1892 there were no fewer than 128 heads of households in Fall River named Borden—including *four* named Andrew Borden. Andrew J. Borden's grandfather, a farmer, was the *brother* of the man who owned the original sawmill and gristmill. Andrew's father, an unskilled worker who never cared to make anything of himself, was only a cousin of the Borden brothers who "held everything commercial and industrial in their grasp." And Andrew J. Borden himself was only a second cousin of those twenty-odd children whose names "continually break out, like small-pox."

Andrew J. Borden therefore found himself in a curious situation. In a technical sense, it was accurate to describe him (as the local newspaper writer did on the day after his murder) as "one of the family of Bordens whose name has always been identified with the business enterprises of the city." But in real terms, he was not a member of that family at all; he was a classic self-made man. He had earned his fortune on his own, without any assistance from his unambitious father on the one hand or his wealthy Borden cousins on the other. A local obituary summed up his career like this: "When he started in life, his means were extremely limited, and he made his money by saving it."

Andrew J. Borden got his start by entering the funeral business, as a casket maker and undertaker. With a single partner and a small gift of cash from his father, Borden opened the business in 1844, as a young man of twenty-three. The population of Fall River was beginning to increase rapidly in those years of dynamic industrial growth. And a larger population in turn meant that there were more people to die. In this indirect way—and in this way only—Andrew Borden prospered on account of his cousins' banks and cotton mills.

Andrew Jackson Borden. A few months before he was murdered, Andrew J. Borden discussed his future and that of his neighborhood. "Second Street will eventually become an overflow business highway, but it won't be in my time," he told an acquaintance. "I don't like to move off the street in my lifetime." (Courtesy Fall River Historical Society)

A dozen years after he went into business, Andrew Borden began to invest some of his profits in local real estate and, later, in mill and bank stock. By the time he was fifty, in 1871, he had accumulated enough capital to leave the undertaking business and spend all his time in managing his various investments, which now included a downtown office building that bore his name, and a bank and a cotton mill of which he was president, along with other real estate in and around Fall River. By the time of his violent death at the age of seventy-one, the local newspaper was able to claim that Andrew J. Borden was "regarded as one of the wealthiest men in town."

Borden did all this on his own. To be sure, his luck was good—he lived at a time of opportunity. But he worked long and hard to take every possible advantage of that opportunity. Long before his death, he had a reputation for good judgment and impeccable honesty. His creditors acknowledged that he was "safe and reliable," a "good, honest" businessman who stuck to his word and undertook no risky enterprises. His customers and tenants knew him as a man who always drove a hard bargain, but who was "scrupulously upright in all his dealings, and expected the same fairness in others." In his later years, he invariably chose to pay for investments in hard cash, and shortly before his death he told an acquaintance that "the man who didn't borrow lived the most contented life." He believed that it was his character that had made his fortune. He also stressed the contrast between himself and his wealthy Borden cousins, who had inherited their positions with no effort of their own. He had received no help from them, and he steered clear of them. He remained a loner to the end.

It is not hard to see why. Despite all the money he made, Andrew Borden remained an outsider to the Fall River industrial aristocracy. The fact that this aristocracy was dominated by his own cousins and namesakes made his own alienation even more acute. His cousins were the children and grandchildren of wealthy men. They had been raised with all the advantages (disadvantages, Andrew Borden might have said) of inherited wealth. They had been sent to prestigious colleges like Harvard, Yale, and Brown, and early in their lives they had developed fashionable and expensive tastes. One of Borden's cousins was an accomplished yachtsman. Another bred prize thoroughbred horses. A third was a collector of paintings and rare books. Almost all of them traveled widely, and several owned lavish vacation homes in places like Newport, Rhode Island. They took fully as much pleasure in spending their money as in making it.

In contrast to these industrial aristocrats, Andrew Borden never went to school at all, and to the end of his life he never developed any hobbies or outside interests. As his local obituary tactfully put it, he was "domestic in his tastes, and, although he had considerable leisure time, was rarely to be found where men are accustomed to congregate"—at their clubs or in fancy restaurants. According to the same newspaper, Borden had only a single interest in life: "money getting." To the end of his life, he remained a poor man who had made a lot of money. No wonder that when his cousins chose to build expensive mansions on Fall River's fashionable Hill, Andrew Borden never cared to follow them. No wonder that he chose to live out his days in an old-fashioned downtown house without hallways or indoor plumbing.

Lizzie Borden's aspirations were different because her youth was different. Lizzie was Andrew's daughter—but she inhabited a different world. Unlike her father, Lizzie never grew up poor. By the time Lizzie was born in 1860, her father's business was thriving, and when she entered her teens he was already a rich man. By then, Fall River was an industrial city, and people who had money were living on the Hill. It would have been hard for Lizzie Borden to avoid feeling that that was where she belonged, too. She rarely talked about it (being able to keep her mouth shut was one trait she did pick up from her father), but it seems apparent that she deeply craved to live in the kind of style her father could afford. The nineteen dresses that hung in her closet on the day of the murders provided a vivid display of the deep gulf that divided daughter and father.

The money for Lizzie's dresses came from her father. He did give her gifts of cash and a steady source of income of her own. By his own lights, he was extremely generous toward her and tried to indulge her in satisfying needs he could hardly understand. In the summer of 1890 he even treated Lizzie to a long vacation in Europe. She had a splendid time abroad, but ironically, this taste of elegance and freedom only intensified her revulsion for the household to which she had to return. As the ocean liner approached New York harbor in November 1890, Lizzie confessed to her cabinmate that "she regretted the necessity of returning home after she had had such a happy summer, because the home she was about to return to was such an unhappy home." Leaving the house on Second Street altogether was the only thing that would have relieved Lizzie Borden's dread. But her father had no intention of ever doing that.

The silent anger that filled the air at the Borden house reflected something more complex than a gulf between generations. It was also a conflict between social classes.

~⁓

What could Lizzie do? How could she escape from the prison of her parents' house? The simplest avenue of escape was simply to move out. But Lizzie did not have the money to purchase a house on the Hill. And in any event, moving into a place of her own was utterly unthinkable as long as her parents were alive and she was unmarried. By taking such an unrespectable step, Lizzie would have lost all chance of ever being accepted into the homes and parties of the Fall River upper class.

There was only one way for Lizzie to enter that world—by marrying a man who lived in it already. Only such a marriage would be able to provide her, in a single stroke, with a better house in a better neighborhood, and with the companionship of a person who shared her own values. In short, only marriage could bring her real membership in the class she aspired to join, and real independence from her family.

But now, still single at the age of thirty-two, Lizzie Borden was forced to confront the ever-increasing likelihood that she would never get married. And, with it, she had to confront the likelihood that she would remain in the grubby house on Second Street until her father's death. (Lizzie knew that the Borden males were usually long-lived. Andrew's own father, her paternal grandfather, had died only six years earlier, in 1886, at the ripe age of eighty-eight. Andrew Borden himself was in fine health at seventy-one; who knew how long he might survive?) By then, Lizzie would be past her prime—it would be too late to marry, too late to enjoy the life that was left to her.

It was not that Lizzie had lacked the opportunity to get married. She was not unattractive, and in any case her father was the richest man in her neighborhood. But that was part of the problem: The young men who lived on Second Street were shop clerks and laborers, hardly in a position to give Lizzie the kind of life she craved. On the other hand, it would have been difficult for her (maybe even impossible) to find more desirable suitors. Even if she did make the acquaintance of a proper young gentleman, how could she invite him to visit her Second Street home and be entertained by her family? What would her suitor think about a stepmother who might not even bother to change out of her housedress for the occasion? About a neighborhood filled with boardinghouses and immigrants? About an out-of-date house that lacked even a toilet and running water? Lizzie Borden was in a bind, and whichever way she looked at it, her parents were the cause. And now, in the summer of 1892, the hopelessness of her situation, and of her future, was becoming impossible to deny. Lizzie was reaching a point of quiet but total desperation.

~⁓

On Wednesday, August 3, 1892—the evening before the murders—Lizzie Borden left her house to visit her old friend Alice Russell, an unmarried woman in her forties. For many years Alice Russell had been a neighbor of the Bordens on Second Street, but she had recently moved a few blocks away. She was probably

Lizzie's closest friend, and Lizzie was visiting her to confide her confused and desperate feelings.

Much later, at Lizzie's trial, Alice Russell testified for the prosecution about some of the ominous and revealing things Lizzie had said to her. It was a confusing story that Lizzie had told, but also an extraordinary one—the closest she ever came to disclosing her state of mind on the day just before the death of her parents.

> I feel depressed. I feel as if something was hanging over me that I cannot throw off, and it comes over me at times, no matter where I am.

Lizzie did not (or could not) explain the cause of her depression, but she was vaguely aware that her feelings were affecting her behavior. A few weeks earlier, for example, she had turned down an appealing invitation to join a group of her friends who were planning to spend a few weeks on vacation at a seaside cottage in the resort town of Marion, Massachusetts. This was just the kind of opportunity Lizzie would ordinarily have welcomed, since it would allow her to escape from the oppressive midsummer urban heat as well as from the equally oppressive atmosphere of her family. But Lizzie had refused to join the vacationing party, offering her friends the feeble excuse that she "ought to stay home to see that everything went all right." Circumstances seemed to be getting more and more out of control, and she was not sure what was going on. Certain things were happening within the household, she confided to Alice—things that upset her profoundly, in ways she could not explain.

Lizzie reported these things to Alice Russell in rambling, half-coherent fashion. It was unclear to Alice (and perhaps also to Lizzie herself) just which statements described real events and which were simply expressions of Lizzie's fears or fantasies.

Lizzie talked about an occurrence that seemed simple enough, however unpleasant: "Mr. and Mrs. Borden were awfully sick last night," she said. "They were awfully sick, and I wasn't sick. I didn't vomit, but I heard them vomiting, and stepped to the door, and asked if I could do anything, and they said, 'No.'" Was it something Mr. and Mrs. Borden had eaten? Alice asked. Lizzie acknowledged that it might have been the household bread or milk. Then Lizzie offered a bizarre explanation of her parents' illness: "Sometimes," she said, "sometimes I think our milk might be poisoned."

Alice Russell was startled, and she tried without success to convince Lizzie that the Borden family milk could not possibly have been poisoned. But Lizzie would not hear her out. She went on to make an even more bizarre suggestion: The "poisoning," she hinted darkly, was only the latest in a series of scary events in the household. For example, she now revealed, "the barn has been broken into twice." Alice Russell, trying hard to calm her friend, reassured Lizzie that the break-in must have been nothing more than petty vandalism—nothing to worry about. "Well," Lizzie went on, "they have broken into the house in broad daylight, with Emma and Maggie and me there." And one night not long before, Lizzie had even seen a strange man "run around the house."

Lizzie was almost certain that these were not random events at all, that they were part of a pattern of conscious hostility on the part of some person who was determined to do nothing less than destroy the entire household: "I feel as if I wanted to sleep with my eyes half open—with one eye open half the time—for fear they will burn down the house over us."

Lizzie seemed unaware that the hostility she was describing was actually her own. But at this point, she unconsciously made a revealing shift in her emphasis. Up to now, she had been speaking of her parents as if they were the innocent victims of some incomprehensible malevolence. But now she began to suggest that the trouble might not be incomprehensible after all—that her father had actually *provoked* it by his behavior and manner.

"I feel afraid sometimes that father has an enemy," Lizzie began, and told a story (which she would repeat several times the next day, after the murders) of how her father had lost his temper at a prospective tenant who spoke to him in a "sneering" voice about his reputation for money grubbing.

Lizzie was unable to face her own hostility. She simply could not grasp a fact that might conceivably have saved the lives of Andrew and Abby Borden: Her father's "enemy" was Lizzie herself. "I think sometimes—I am afraid sometimes that somebody will do something to him. *He is so discourteous to people.*" For a few moments, Lizzie came close to acknowledging that her father made *her* feel embarrassed, threatened, and enraged.

As if to explain something about her feelings, Lizzie began to go into detail about what had happened earlier that very day, after Andrew and Abby had gotten sick and vomited. Mrs. Borden had felt concerned, and she told her husband she wanted to send for a physician—Dr. Bowen, who lived across the street (and who would examine her dead body the next day). Andrew Borden did not see the need for professional help, and he scolded his wife for her wastefulness. He told Mrs. Borden, as Lizzie recalled, "Well, *my* money shan't pay for it." But Abby had called Dr. Bowen anyway, and when he came over to examine her, Andrew had treated the physician with characteristic rudeness. When she told the story to Alice Russell, Lizzie did not report her father's exact words—but, for once, she directly expressed something of her own feelings toward her father. What Lizzie told Alice Russell was this: "I am so ashamed, the way father treated Dr. Bowen. I was so mortified." It was as close as Lizzie would ever come to identifying *herself* as her father's "enemy."

Never again would Lizzie Borden expose so much of her feelings. Barely twelve hours after her conversation with Alice Russell, Andrew Borden and his wife were lying dead, and their deaths seemed somehow to restore Lizzie's characteristic poise— and her silence. In the hours after the murders were discovered, and in the days and months of public exposure that followed, the people who observed Lizzie Borden were struck by her extraordinary emotional control. Newspaper reporters often used words like "cold" to describe her manner. She rarely broke down and cried (although at one point during her trial, she fainted—when her father's skull was displayed to the jurors).

Some people even suggested that Lizzie's composure was "unfeminine" and was evidence that she was capable after all of having committed the crimes of which she stood accused. But Lizzie's composure was her characteristic style, developed in years of hiding her feelings behind a facade of cold civility. Throughout the trial, the defense tried—and failed—to offer evidence that the Bordens had been affectionate with each other (the word they used was "cordial"). Similarly, the prosecution could not show that life in the household had been tempestuous. Even Bridget Sullivan, the servant who had lived in the house for almost two years, said that she had never seen or heard "any trouble with the family, no quarreling or anything of that kind." This kind of testimony was damaging to the prosecution's case. But the fact was that Lizzie and her parents had learned to avoid expressing their feelings—just as they had learned to avoid each other in the flesh. There were not only physical locks and bolts that kept the family from invading each other's space, there was also an elaborate, unspoken series of emotional locks and bolts that prevented Lizzie and her parents from expressing either love or hatred, and possibly from even *feeling* the hatred that was always there. Perhaps if these emotional locks had been opened, and if explosions of anger had been tolerated in the Borden household, Lizzie might have been able to express her hidden rage in some fashion less deadly than the form it took on the morning of August 4, 1892. The cold composure that Lizzie displayed to the world at her trial was the hard veneer of lethal civility that pervaded her life. It was almost as if she had found it easier to confront her parents with an axe than with sharp words.

When Lizzie Borden came to trial in June 1893, she never took the stand in her own defense. The only time she ever testified for the record was ten months earlier, at the private inquest hearing. Her defense lawyers realized that if she were to testify at her trial, she would probably make a poor impression on the jury—and she would be forced to acknowledge the contradictory testimony that she had given at the inquest. Fortunately for the defense, the judges refused to admit Lizzie's inquest testimony into evidence at the trial. (They decided that she should have been offered the opportunity to have a lawyer present during the inquest, so that anything she said on that occasion was therefore legally inadmissible.) The exclusion of Lizzie's inquest testimony dashed any hopes for a conviction that the prosecution might have entertained. So did the presiding judge's final charge to the jury, which was so biased in Lizzie's behalf that one newspaper called it "A PLEA FOR THE INNOCENT."

The jury was out little more than an hour. When it returned, the verdict was "Not guilty." A newspaper described the scene that followed:

> A cheer broke the stillness of the courtroom. Everybody sprang to their feet, and the greatest excitement prevailed, but the woman on whom all eyes were turned sank to the rail, with her face buried in her hands. Lizzie Borden wept as she had not for many months.
>
> Then, in a calm and kindly tone, Judge Mason announced that Lizzie Borden was a free woman at last. The jury came forward to shake hands with Miss Borden.

A few minutes later, Lizzie held a brief press conference in the judge's chamber. She refused to say a word about the verdict, but she did talk about her immediate plans. Her words were so conventional that they must have sounded startling, and they would be proven false soon enough. Lizzie Borden said: "I want to go home: take me straight home tonight. I want to see the old place and settle down at once."

MONEY, CLASS, AND WOMEN

The reporters who interviewed Lizzie Borden a few moments after she was found innocent must have been astonished to hear her say that all she wanted was to go home, "to see the old place," and settle down. In fact, she did not settle down in the "old place." Two years later, after the excitement had subsided and she received her share of her father's estate, she bought a mansion on the Hill and named it, grandly, Maplecroft. Then she changed her name from Lizzie—which was no nickname but her legal given name—to the fancier Lizbeth. She began to buy nice things. Maplecroft got a set of fine china, elegant furniture, the oil paintings that had been so absent from the old house on Second Street. She also bought five diamond rings and a lot of other expensive jewelry.

Still, her father's investments in real estate and industrial stock continued to grow. Lizbeth Borden died quietly in 1927, at the age of sixty-seven, a rich woman. (She left only one small bequest, to the Fall River Animal Rescue League. "I have been fond of animals," her will explained, "and their need is great and there are so few who care for them.")

Lizbeth Borden got some of the things Lizzie Borden must have wanted. But there were other things she did not get. She never married. She lived a more or less isolated life, with few friends and no invitations to balls or parties, no memberships in fancy women's clubs. She had won

her way into the physical world of the Hill, but the murder trial had cost her whatever chance she might have had for access to the Hill's society. She even lost contact with her sister. Her little bequest to the Animal Rescue League was a pathetic testament to her isolation from the social world of human beings.

What Lizbeth Borden did escape was tackiness. She got out of a shabby house, with its slop jars and its basement privy. She acquired flush toilets and running water. She got away from the embarrassing, old-fashioned horsehair sofa, the barn, and the well on Second Street. Had Andrew Jackson Borden shamed her by carrying a silver watch and not a gold one? She would have diamonds and gold aplenty.

The question of Lizzie Borden's guilt or innocence was settled legally by the jury. Most historians have decided the question the other way. She may well have killed her parents. But, on a deeper level, her legal guilt or innocence is irrelevant. What matters most is that her behavior before and after the murders says a great deal about American society at the end of the nineteenth century, particularly about the lives of middle- and upper-class Americans.

Murder, especially one like the brutal axe murder of the elderly Bordens, is a bizarre event that may have little historical significance. But the preoccupations with social class and social status that set the scene for the murder and the trial can

717

tell us a lot about the kinds of ambitions and stresses that "normal," nonmurderous American families labored under. That is what one man suggested in a letter to a Fall River newspaper:

> A striking feature of this case is the picture it gives of life in the Borden household, and presumably in other households in Fall River—and elsewhere. I dare say that this life is so familiar to many people that they are unable to appreciate the meanness and sordidness of it.

Whether Lizzie Borden killed her father and mother might interest a jury or a novelist looking for a plot. *Why* Lizzie Borden might have wanted to kill her parents is a question that takes the case out of the realm of the bizarre and into the realm of history.

The Gilded Age

The steel baron Andrew Carnegie, one of the richest men in the world, once visited an American Indian village on the Great Plains. He noticed that the tepee of the chief looked very much like the tepees of all the other men, and he drew what he believed was the compelling lesson. In the modern world of industrial capitalism, Carnegie said, the home of the millionaire was drastically different from the home of the farmer or factory worker. The glaring extremes of wealth and poverty might seem to signal a much more severe exploitation of the poor by the rich than in a "primitive" society like that of the Indians. But the opulent life of the modern millionaire was really a sign of social progress. He lived a fantastically rich life. But his riches were the result of production. And that same production had made the average citizen wealthy, too. An ordinary family under industrial capitalism lived in a style that Carnegie believed would have made any tribal chief, or even any ancient king or emperor, envious.

Carnegie's meditation, which he made famous in a popular essay of 1888 entitled "The Gospel of Wealth," was typical of the attitudes of both wealthy and middle-class Americans in the 1880s and 1890s. One of the most obvious features of their world was wealth. And their awareness of wealth only increased their consciousness of poverty. They were not heartless people. They could pity the poor, especially the "deserving" poor and the children of poverty. They might even try to relieve suffering through philanthropy. But they seldom doubted what they believed were the inevitable twin consequences of industrial capitalism: the creation of fortunes for a small fraction but of a much better life for everyone else.

THE MONIED CLASS In 1877, when Lizzie Borden was a teenager, Cornelius Vanderbilt died. His will, when it became public, astonished a society that was not yet accustomed to fabulous fortunes. He left an estate worth a staggering $100 million. But by the time Lizzie Borden went to trial, fifteen years later, Americans had become used to seeing newspaper stories about single donations made by men of fortune that almost equaled Vanderbilt's entire estate. By the 1890s the wealth of men like Carnegie, Rockefeller, and a dozen or so other multimillionaires had become public and legendary. Even more important, there were a hundred millionaires for every well-known multimillionaire. By the 1890s the United States had, by conservative guesses, well over 3,000 men whose holdings were worth over a million dollars. And there were even more with "moderate" fortunes of several hundred thousand dollars.

Every American city of middling size had its tight cluster of wealthy families. Around these rich people, in every town and city, were grouped a growing number of others who would have described themselves as "well-to-do" or "respectable." Like the truly wealthy, this class of Americans was increasingly a fact of urban life. In 1880 the total value of all rural and urban real estate in the United States was still about equal. Just

Newport mansions. Every American city in the late nineteenth century had its fashionable neighborhoods, like the Hill in Fall River, Massachusetts, where Lizzie Borden moved after her trial. But no single place in America was as fancy or as pretentious as Newport, Rhode Island, where many wealthy Americans built summer homes—vast Victorian "cottages" like these along Cliff Walk. At the same time, yachting became a popular sport—and means of display—among the rich. And so began a continuing contest for the American shoreline between the wealthy and the rest of the population. (Culver Pictures)

ten years later, the value of urban real estate had increased twice as much as rural. Even more striking was the fact that city dwellers owned almost three times as much of other kinds of property—furniture, jewels, stocks, bonds, and bank accounts—as rural people did. The average farm family owned about $3,000 worth of such property in 1890, but the average city family owned about $9,000 worth. Since a lot of city people had no money, the average wealth of those who had any at all was far above $9,000.[1]

THE PREOCCUPATION WITH WEALTH, DISPLAY, AND STATUS This new money was not quiet, discreet, and invisible. The style of the wealthy, from the 1870s through the end of the

century, was one of display. For the very rich and the moderately well-to-do, the purpose of life seemed to be to mount exhibitions of opulence. For the multimillionaire, this meant building "cottages" like Marble House at Newport; or houses with palatial dining rooms like that of the Astors in New York; or imposing mansions fronting on Central Park, like the home of Henry Clay Frick, Carnegie's partner in steel.

But even for people of moderate income, in smaller cities and towns, the new style permitted dramatically larger and more pretentious houses. The typical middle-class house of the period was a vast affair, with eight, ten, or even twelve rooms. Cheaper lumber and labor made its vastness possible. New methods of power milling and carving wood gave it opulent woodwork and elaborately decorated mantels and staircases. It had eleven-foot ceilings, central steam heat, running water, and gaslights. Soon it would have

[1]These figures can be translated into today's dollars by multiplying them by at least seven, perhaps even ten.

Pennsylvania Station, New York. Opulence, grandeur, and display—these were the values expressed not only in the private homes of the wealthy but in the public and semipublic architecture of the late nineteenth century. This was the waiting room of the station of the Pennsylvania Railroad in New York. Architects of the time were also careful to design buildings that disguised the purposes for which they were intended. This great room could have served any number of ceremonial functions, but nothing suggests that below the floor was a network of railroad tracks. (Culver Pictures)

electricity and a telephone. But the Victorian house of the period, with its turrets and its wrought-iron fences, had one obvious purpose: to be imposing. It was to declare to the world that the family who lived within had achieved the sweet dream of success. This was exactly what the Borden house on Second Street did *not* declare.

The determination to display opulence and grandeur controlled the design and size not just of houses but of all the places the new middle and upper classes might frequent or pass through. Their hotels and restaurants were leg-endary for their elaborate gilding and marble, their ornate mirrors and high ceilings. Railroad stations, like the new Pennsylvania Station in New York, were designed to dwarf many a European palace—and many an American government building from the early days of the Republic. The Pullman "Palace" cars, in which rich and near-rich Americans traveled, were fantastic studies in conspicuous display.

For the first time, the rich became celebrities—not because of some achievement in war or politics, but simply because of their wealth. To give a dinner at the fabled Delmonico's restaurant in

New York, with seventy-two guests and a total tab of $10,000, was enough to make a rich man into a famous one, with pictures and headlines not only in New York newspapers but others around the country. Simply to have and to display money seemed enough to attract attention—and, of course, envy. To return from a ride in Central Park, on beautiful horses, to a mansion facing the park was enough to draw an admiring crowd. The clatter of hooves, the men in fancy dress, including perhaps a polished top hat, the women in elegant riding costume, with brilliantly colored silk scarves trailing almost to the street—this was the stuff of which the sweet dream of success was now made. And the public attention was as important as actually having the horses, the clothes, and the mansion in the first place.

Wealthy Americans not only flaunted their money, they tried hard to consolidate their position as an upper class—and to make it clear to those who wanted to join them that there were certain definite steps and initiations that had to be passed through. Especially for young men, college now became an important rite of passage. Before the middle of the century, poor boys studying for the ministry had constituted the primary student body of many American colleges. But by the time the century drew to a close, three things had happened. First, there was a great expansion in the number and size of colleges and universities—from about 60,000 students in the 1870s to almost 200,000 twenty years later. Second, beginning in the 1870s, a number of private colleges for women were established, and many state universities began to admit women. Third, the students were now from a more homogeneous social class, almost all sons and daughters of middle- and upper-class families. Within the colleges and universities, the students heightened class consciousness even further through an array of secret societies, Greek-letter fraternities and sororities, and dining clubs—organizations that had not been a part of college life a generation earlier.

The students' parents were doing the same sorts of things. A number of institutions took root in every American town, institutions whose main purpose was to segregate people along class lines. The country club became a regular feature of the lives of the urban middle and upper class. Indeed, most cities of any size would have two or three country clubs, each precisely distinguished from the others along fine but definite lines of status. The same was true of the yacht clubs that seemed to dot every usable harbor on the coasts and lakes. Men joined downtown clubs and women formed an astonishing variety of social clubs of their own. The lodge movement, with its Masons, Moose, Odd Fellows, and the like, served many of the same functions for middle-class men. There had always been clubs, of course. The Masons was an organization much older than the American Republic. The difference now was that the clubs and lodges were not only much bigger, and consisted of many more members, they were more subtly and elaborately graded signs of class membership.

THE PREOCCUPATION WITH MANNERS
The preoccupation with wealth, display, and status gave a peculiar intensity, even desperation, to Americans' concern with "manners." A flood of manuals of etiquette poured from the presses during the decades after the Civil War. These were reinforced by regular columns in the high-circulation magazines of the day, many of which were aimed especially at women: *Ladies' Home Journal*, *Cosmopolitan*, and *Harper's Bazaar*. Major newspapers (whose circulation was now leaping into the millions each day), also employed women to write daily columns of advice on good form and "personal" problems.

This tremendous volume of avidly read material was all based on two assumptions. The first was clear and explicit: There was a correct way of doing everything—eating, dressing, talking, dancing, courting—and that correct way was very likely to be something complicated, unnatural, and slightly European in tone. The manuals were littered with French expressions, as though to convey ideas that were a little too subtle or too

College women. During Lizzie Borden's lifetime, American women began to attend colleges and universities, mostly small private colleges for women only or coeducational state universities. Here, obviously posed for the camera, a class of young ladies in Washington, D.C., all dressed in black, shows how they study even such scientific subjects as geography and physics without losing their "femininity." (Culver Pictures)

elegant to be expressed in English. Some things were *très distingué*, which lent them an air of mystery not conveyed by the English "distinguished." Readers were warned of *faux pas*, as though a simple misstep were a dark and disgraceful thing indeed. People who were planning dinner parties might be pleased to learn that host and hostess were no longer expected to carve and serve at the table, that food should be brought to the table by servants. But that information was given an even greater air of elegance when the reader learned that this practice had originated with the Russian aristocracy and was called service *à la Russe*.

The second, somewhat hidden, assumption behind all the books and columns was that a failure to know the right fork or the proper way to invite a lady to waltz was a failure of class. The individual whose manners were not in good style—or *bon ton*—had to worry not just about a revealed weakness of personality, or even a lapse of morals, but about being betrayed in class terms, about being pegged as part of what was now called "the other half."

The world that Lizzie Borden inhabited was a world preoccupied, even obsessed, with wealth and with displays of elegance and manners. Her father was certainly rich enough to afford service *à la Russe*. But he insisted on just keeping plain Bridget. Lizzie, and thousands of other young men and women, pored over newspaper stories of the doings of the wealthy, and over books that laid out impossibly fancy designs of behavior for the proper. In one person, the response might be heightened ambition to have the money and the grand house that lay at the center of the dream of success. In another person, the response might be shame or disgust with the extent to which his or her manners and lifestyle fell short of what was considered correct. In many, the response was a simple fear of exposure of their rudeness or vulgarity, their lack of "respectability."

One book of manners gave its readers the following example of an elegant conversation. A gentleman has just offered his arm to a lady, to lead her in to table at a fine dinner party.

> The gentleman may say, "We must be careful not to step on that elaborate train," referring to the costume of a lady preceding the pair.
>
> "Yes, indeed, that would be a mishap. But trains are graceful in spite of their inconvenience."
>
> Her companion must answer: "Oh! I admire them, of course. Only I have such a dread of stepping on them and bringing down the wrath of the fair wearer on my devoted head."

The proposed conversation may appear comic. But it would have seemed a little bitter to Lizzie Borden, who lived in a house where a dinner party was simply an impossibility. It also suggests something of the discomfort that even the "lady" and "gentleman" had to labor under. She acknowledges that the train is an inconvenience that has to be endured because it is "graceful." He in turn reveals his dread of the wrath that will come down on him if he causes a mishap. If even the men and women in manner-book examples felt this way, their readers can only have been even more anxious.

Much of the fiction of the period explored this anxiety. William Dean Howells's 1885 novel *The Rise of Silas Lapham*, for example, dramatized a family situation that mirrored that of Lizzie Borden in some striking ways. Like Andrew Borden, the title character was a wealthy self-made man. Like Borden, too, he was an unpolished boor who did not much worry about whether his neighborhood was fashionable or his conversation elegant, and who did not easily recognize that his behavior provoked the disdain of those more refined than he. (One of these men explained the situation with supreme elegance when he asked whether the Laphams "had knowledge enough to be ashamed of their ignorance.") Silas Lapham's behavior also embarrassed his socially ambitious daughters, eager to marry into polite society. Once, when Lapham boasted openly of his wealth—a taboo subject in society—one of his daughters squirmed, muttering: "Oh, I wish Papa wouldn't brag so!" She later confided, *"I thought I should die."* Many young Americans, Lizzie Borden among them, would surely have understood.

In the novel, things came out all right, because Silas Lapham had a wife who was quick to grasp all the "right" things to do, and who could be counted on to coax her husband into doing them—and even to show him how. The lesson was clear: A young woman needed a mother who could and would bridge the awkward gap between an economically ambitious father and his socially ambitious children—the gap between two classes as well as two generations. It was exactly here, of course, that the parallel between the fictional Laphams and the real-life Bordens broke down. Lizzie Borden was painfully aware that her stepmother cared just as little as her father did about helping her enter polite society. If Lizzie Borden ever read *The Rise of Silas Lapham*, she would have found it a profoundly depressing book.

ETIQUETTE OF The Street.

RULES OF CONDUCT TO BE OBSERVED.

LADIES and gentlemen, when meeting on the sidewalk, should always pass to the right. Should the walk be narrow or dangerous, gentlemen will always see that ladies are protected from injury.

Ladies should avoid walking rapidly upon the street, as it is ungraceful and unbecoming.

Running across the street in front of carriages is dangerous, and shows want of dignity.

The gentleman should insist upon carrying any package which the lady may have, when walking with her.

Before recognizing a lady on the street, the gentleman should be certain that his recognition will meet with favor.

No gentleman should stand on the street-corners, steps of hotels, or other public places, and make remarks about ladies passing by.

A gentleman may take two ladies upon his arms, but under no circumstances should the lady take the arms of two gentlemen.

Upon the narrow walk, for her protection, the gentleman should generally give the lady the inside of the walk (Fig. 21), passing behind her when changing at corners.

Allowing a dress to trail on the street is in exceedingly bad taste. Such a street costume simply calls forth criticism and contempt from the more sensible people.

A gentleman walking with a lady should accommodate his step and pace to hers. For the gentleman to be some distance ahead, presents a bad appearance.

Should protection on the street be necessary, it is customary for the gentleman to give his right arm to the lady; but if more convenient, he may give the left.

It is courtesy to give silent, respectful attention as a funeral procession passes. It shows want of respect to pass between the carriages while the procession is moving.

Staring at people, spitting, looking back after they pass, saluting people across the street, calling out loudly or laughing at people as they go by, are all evidences of ill-breeding.

The gentleman accompanying a lady should hold the door open for the lady to enter first. Should he be near the door when a lady, unattended, is about to enter, he will do the same for her.

In the evening, or whenever safety may require, a gentleman should give a lady his arm. It is not customary in other cases to do so on the street, unless with an elderly lady, or the couple be husband and wife.

A gentleman will assist a lady over a bad crossing, or from an omnibus or carriage, without waiting for the formality of an introduction. When the service is performed, he will raise his hat, bow, and pass on.

In a street car or an omnibus, the passengers who are seated should strive to give seats to those who are standing, rendering such accommodation as they would themselves desire under similar circumstances.

When crossing the pavement, the lady should raise her dress with the right hand, a little above the ankle. To raise the dress with both hands, is vulgar, and can be excused only when the mud is very deep.

No gentleman will smoke when walking with, or standing in the presence of, a lady on the street. He should remove the cigar from her presence entirely, even though permission be granted to continue the smoking.

A gentleman should give his seat to any lady who may be standing in a public conveyance. For this favor she should thank him, which courtesy he should acknowledge by a slight bow. In an omnibus he will pass up the ladies' fares.

A true lady will go quietly and unobtrusively about her business when on the street, never seeking to attract the attention of the opposite sex, at the same time recognizing acquaintances with a courteous bow, and friends with pleasant words of greeting.

Swinging the arms when walking, eating upon the street, sucking the parasol handles, pushing violently through a crowd, very loud and boisterous talking and laughing on the streets, and whispering in public conveyances, are all evidences of ill-breeding in ladies.

A lady should have the escort of a gentleman in the evening. A gentleman at the house where she may call may return with her if she goes unattended; gossip and scandal are best avoided, however, if she have some one from her home call for her at an appointed hour.

On the narrow street-crossing the gentleman will allow the lady to precede him, that he may see that no injury befalls her.

Should a lady stop in the street, when meeting a gentleman, it is courtesy for him to stop also. Should his business be urgent, he will apologize for not continuing the conversation, and ask to be excused. Should it be desirable to lengthen the interview, and the lady resumes her walk in the midst of her conversation, it is courtesy for him to turn and accompany her. Should she desire to end the conversation, a slight bow from her will indicate the fact, when he should bid her "good day" and take his leave.

Fi. 21. The street-promenade. The gentleman gives the lady the inside of the walk. *

* Some authorities claim that it is most sensible for the lady to walk always at the right of the gentleman, whether on the street or indoors; her right hand being thus free to hold trail, fan, or parasol.

The lady and the gentleman. This page from an etiquette book—clearly meant for those people who needed elementary instruction—laid down some quite fastidious rules. It advised the ladies, for example, to lift the hem of the skirt when crossing a street, but only with one hand, for "To raise the dress with both hands is vulgar." The manual is uncertain on one point, however. It recommends in general that gentlemen give ladies the inside of the sidewalk when they "promenade" together. On the other hand, it admits some authorities recommend that the lady walk on the gentleman's right, so as to leave her right hand free to carry a parasol. If the lady in the picture had adopted that rule, she would have spared the gentleman from being jabbed in the chest by her parasol. But such were the valiant sufferings demanded of the gentlemen of the day. (Culver Pictures)

AMERICAN IMAGES

Status for Sale

Horatio Alger, the tireless storyteller of the self-made man—or, more precisely, the self-made boy—once had his hero, Ragged Dick, pass by the Palace Hotel in New York. It was magnificent, more magnificent even than the palaces of European nobles. But it was a great "democratic" palace, Alger insisted. Anyone could walk into the lobby, and anyone who had the modest price of a room could luxuriate in its grand, Victorian opulence. Here, to Alger and to his readers, lay the magic of American society. The "average" citizen had open access to elegance, style, and pretension—to all the visible badges of social class.

But how could the truly rich and the well-to-do deal with the fact that people of very modest resources could dress themselves like the wealthy and learn "refined" manners from cheap manuals? One way was to make the clothing of the rich more and more elaborate, their houses larger and more ornate, their furniture hopelessly grand and gilded. Something like a race developed between the attempts of the wealthy to monopolize the marks of caste and the capacities of manufacturers and marketers to provide inexpensive facsimiles of these marks at prices many ordinary citizens could afford. No matter how complicated and absurd the clothes of wealthy women became, factories and retailers seemed able to run off and sell cheap versions of them. No matter how shiny gentlemen's top hats were, or how elegant their cotton or linen jackets for the seashore, a man with a dollar to spare could own something very much like them.

Some people were simply out of the contest, of course. No one could mistake the social status of blacks. No one could be confused about the class identity of an immigrant arriving in the United States with a great bundle of possessions. But for a mass of other Americans, even for

Plate 1. All photos on these pages are from Fred L. Israel, ed., *1897 Sears Roebuck Catalogue* (New York: Chelsea House, 1968).

Plate 2.

domestic servants and poor store clerks, the possibility of simulating wealth and status—and the darker possibility that one might not succeed in simulating it—was a central fact of life.

One of the clearest expressions of the dreams and pangs of class anxiety at the end of the nineteenth century was the catalog—the Consumers Guide, they called it—of "Sears, Roebuck and Co., Cheapest Supply House."

The two main business notions of the Sears and Roebuck operation, from its beginning in 1895, were low prices and high volume. But these business notions were heavily reinforced with a guiding principle of promotion.

The goods being offered for sale, the clothing and the furniture, the canes and the carriages, all were "fine" and "elegant," the "best that money can buy," and "the equal of any available." Page after page of the 1897 catalog repeated the message. Fine was probably the most often used adjective. Then came choice, elegant, and even nobby—a new bit of slang for belonging to the upper "crust." Even a gentleman's "suspensory" was described as being "for elegance the best in the world" (Plate 1). And the Consumers Guide followed the practice of the manuals on manners: It suggested that its products were somehow royal or French, to emphasize their refined

Plate 3.

character. The "bust developer" offered in one of the largest
displays of the catalog was called the "Princess." The cream
that was part of the treatment had been produced by an
"eminent French chemist," and the tonic sent along to be
taken internally was called the "Fleur de Lis" (Plate 2).

But it was in its sections on clothing that the Consumers Guide insisted most passionately on the capacity
of modern manufacturing and marketing to obliterate the
visible lines of class and caste. Two elegant gentlemen are
posed in casual costume (Plate 3). In the background,
people are playing lawn tennis and sailing—both the rec-
reations of the very rich. But the dapper sporting jacket,

dashingly striped in black or blue and white could be had
for 35 to 95 cents. (This was roughly the price of the work
jacket for railroad engineers that was shown on the next
page.) A "Prince Albert Suit," in black worsted, sold for
about $10. It came lined in "fine Italian cloth" (Plate 4).
For something more up-to-date, there was a suit of fine
"cassimere," for as little as $6.50—guaranteed to be "the
latest in style for this season . . . fine tailor made . . .
fancy velvet arm shields under sleeves . . . very dressy"
(Plate 5). A man's fancy dress shirt cost a mere 50 cents—
the exact price of a work shirt (Plate 6).

Mens Black Prince Albert Suits

We make and sell more Prince Albert Suits direct to the consumer than all other mail order houses combined and we are prepared to offer values that will mean a saving to you of 25% to 50%. **We can furnish you a double breasted Prince Albert suit,** perfect fitting and equal to anything your local tailor can make, at a saving to you of at least 50%. **We are anxious to get your order** for one of these suits to show you that it is possible for us to furnish the highest class goods at prices within easy reach of all. **Our Prince Albert suits** are made in the very highest style of the art on the latest patterns, cut by expert cutters to fit perfectly, and made by the best tailors we can employ. The linings and trimmings are all of the very finest, and we guarantee every suit to give the best satisfaction. **Sizes run regularly from 34 to 42 inches chest measure,** but larger sizes can be furnished at 20% extra.

Our terms are liberal. Any suit will be sent to any address on receipt of $1.00 as a guarantee of good faith, balance and express charges payable at express office. A discount of 3% allowed if cash in full accompanies your order. ☞ **Samples of cloth will be sent free on application.**

Men's tailor made Clay Worsted Double Breasted Prince Albert Suits at $9.80 surely should interest all careful buyers, for a Clay Worsted Prince Albert suit was never before offered at anything like the price.

We offer a line of Double Breasted Prince Albert Suits at $9.80, $12.00, $14.00, $16.00, $18.00, and $20.00, and we know that the sale of one suit in a neighborhood will result in the sale of many more.

No. 4342. Our $9.80 Men's Clay Worsted Prince Albert Suit, a suit that would retail at nearly double our price. Made from a good quality imported **All Wool Black Clay Worsted Cloth,** well lined, trimmed and finished and guaranteed in every respect. **Our Special Price......... $9.80**

No. 4343. Our $12.00 Men's Clay Worsted Prince Albert Suit, made from 14 oz. imported all wool black English clay worsted cloth, guaranteed for wear, nicely lined, trimmed and finished and guaranteed in every respect. **Our Special Price.... $12.00**

No. 4344. Our $14.00 Black Clay Worsted Prince Albert suit, made from an imported all wool 16 oz. black English clay worsted cloth, finely lined, trimmed and finished and guaranteed in every respect. **Our Special price.$14.00**

No. 4345. Our $16.00 Black Clay Worsted Prince Albert Suit, made from 18 oz. imported all wool black English clay worsted, coat lined throughout with fine imported Italian cloth, elegantly trimmed and finished, and guaranteed in every respect. **Our Special Price......................$16.00**

No. 4346. Our $18.00 Black Clay Worsted Prince Albert Suit, made from a very fine imported all wool English 18 oz. black clay worsted cloth. This is one of our finest Prince Albert suits. The coat is lined throughout with fine imported black Italian cloth, nicely trimmed and finished, and gotten up first-class in every respect. **Our Special Price...............$18.00**

No. 4347. $20.00 for our very finest Black Clay Worsted Prince Albert Suit. The suit is made from our 19 oz. imported all wool black English clay worsted, one of the best English weaves, a goods that we guarantee will never wear smooth, has a very nice soft surface finish. Every suit is made by expert tailors, the coats are lined throughout with fine imported black Italian cloth, nicely trimmed and guaranteed in every respect. **Our Special Price..$20.00**

Plate 4.

MEN'S SIX-DOLLAR CASSIMERE SUITS.

N° 1   N° 2

Our $6.00 line is a leader this season. Very Fine, Stylish, All-wool Fabrics, All fine tailor made. You would pay others $10.00 to $12.00 for such Suits, and then consider you had a rare bargain. We only ask that you send us $1.00 with your order, balance, $5.00, and express charges to be paid at your express office when received. One quality of material in our $6.00 line. They differ only in the color and pattern. The cassimere is the product of one of the oldest and most reliable woolen mills in America, a manufacturer with a reputation for the production of only first-class goods. The cloth is closely woven, good weight, guaranteed strictly all-wool and unexcelled for wearing qualities. Very latest in style for this season, guaranteed fine tailor made, made only by our best tailors and cut by expert cutters to fit perfectly. Coats are lined throughout with fine Italian cloth in shades to match the cloth, satin piped as shown in cut. Fancy velvet arm shields under sleeves. Sewed throughout with silk and linen, nicely padded, trimmed and finished. Sizes run from 34 to 42. Extra sizes, $2.00 extra. They come in Styles 1, 2 or 3, round cut sack, square cut sack or double breasted square cut sack, as desired. Style 3 is always 50 cents extra. Samples of cloth free on application.

No. 4360. This beautiful $6.00 all-wool Cassimere Suit is made in a medium gray with very neat hair line stripe and invisible cross weave. It is very stylish and will make up very dressy.

Our price, Style 1 or 2 .... $6.00   Style 3 .... $6.50

No. 4361. This $6.00 tailor made suit comes in a very neat brown and gray check with invisible plaid, the very latest thing for this season and a goods that will make up very stylish.

Our price, Style 1 or 2 .... $6.00   Style 3 .... $6.50

No. 4362. This $6.00 tailor made suit comes in a gray and white check invisible whip cord stripe, one of the latest patterns for this season.

Our price, Style 1 or 2 .... $6.00   Style 3 .... $6.50

No. 4363. This $6.00 tailor made suit comes in a very neat medium brown with very small check and large modest invisible plaid effect.

Our price, Style 1 or 2 .... $6.00   Style 3 .... $6.50

No. 4364. This $6.00 tailor made suit comes in a brown with small white check and large modest invisible plaid, a very stylish pattern.

Our price, Style 1 or 2 .... $6.00   Style 3 .... $6.50

Plate 5.

Plate 6.

Women were promised even more. Their union suits—sold with the slogan "In Union There Is Strength"—had "an air of refinement" (Plate 7). The underskirt that might be put on next was "rich in appearance" (Plate 8). Then came the Venus, "the very latest improved French Corset . . . made of finest Zanella cloth" (Plate 9). After an ornate blouse that might cost as little as 25 cents, or perhaps 47 cents (Plate 10), came the grand suits—"smart . . . magnificent . . . fancy . . . rustling . . . very fine." The cost of such a suit, all in wool and taffeta and velvet, was between $4.50 and $8.50 (Plate 11).

It is tempting to smile at the clothes. Nothing seems quite so ludicrous as the costumes of a former generation. But there was a deadly serious point behind it all—a point that Lizzie Borden, and her stepmother, and the servant Bridget would all have grasped instinctively. Whatever might be the facts about wealth, income, class, and mobility in the United States, the appearance of things was plainly fluid, mobile, and in a certain sense democratic. It was possible (and perhaps even necessary for many people) to go to extraordinary lengths to display wealth. But it was equally possible (and perhaps equally necessary to millions of others) to imitate those displays at discount prices.

Plate 7.

No. 23678. A Skirt built for wear, of a fine quality muslin, the embroidery is 10 inches wide and is headed by a cloister of five tucks. The pattern of embroidery is neat and quiet, but nevertheless rich in appearance. Realizing that there are a great many women who still want the class of reliable merchandise on the market years ago, we make a special feature of this skirt. If you want a well wearing skirt order this number. Each......**$1.20**
  Two for... 2.30

Plate 8.

No. 23653 French Coutel Corset; extra long waisted; sateen striped; fitted with unbreakable French wire; trimmed with handsome silk embroidery and heavily flossed, and produces an elegant appearance equaled only by corsets costing double the money. Colors: White, drab or black. Sizes, 18 to 30 only. Price............**95c**
  Extra size in black only; size 31 to 36. Price............**$1.20**

No. 23654 The Very Latest Improved French Corset, very highest grade workmanship and material; made of finest Zanella cloth, extra long waisted, medium size bust and hips, cross boned, high back, beautifully embroidered and finished in every way equal to any corset retailing for $2.65 each; colors, drab or black; size, 18 to 30. ....**$1.89**

Plate 9.

Ladies New Spring and Summer shirt waists

24393
58¢

24390
50¢

24391
50¢

24392
85¢

Plate 10.

LADIES TAILOR MADE SUITS

STYLES 1897

24959 $4.50

24965 $6.75

24966 $7.50

24961 $4.50

24967 $8.50

24960 $4.50

24959
24960   24961
Very fine ladies'
suit made of imported
repellant cloth in black,
navy or tan. We make the
suit 24959 Bolero, 24960 Blazer,
24961 Reefer styles. The skirt is
very full; lined throughout with rustling taffeta and bound with velvet. **$4.50**
24962 Same style as 24959 made of fine serge
in black, blue or green. Jacket all lined with
fine fancy serge. Price....................................**$5.50**
24963 Same style as 24960 made as 24962. Price....**$5.50**
24964 Same style as 24961 made as 24962. Price....**$5.50**
24965 Smart Blazer suit made of imported ladies cloth, in
either black or navy, trimmed with braid and small buttons, full
skirt, lined throughout with rustling taffeta, bound with velvet,**$6.75**
24966 A magnificent Eaton style ladies suit of fancy Scotch mixture, trimmed with fine Hercules braid around bottom of waist and on
sleeves, fancy horn buttons in front, waist lined with changeable silk
serge, full sweep skirt interlined with crinoline and lined with rustic
taffeta, bound with velvet. A fine $15.00 suit for....................**$7.50**
24967 **Very Stylish Ladies' Suit.** Bolero style, made of blue or black
serge cheviot, newest sleeves, outer jacket trimmed all around with
black mohair and silk, mixed gimp and lined with changeable silk.
Very full skirt trimmed as illustrated. Skirt lined with rustling
taffeta and interlined with crinolino, bound with velvet. Very
rich. Price....................................**$8.50**

SPECIAL OFFER.
WE WILL SEND ANY of these fine tailor-
made suits C. O. D., **SUBJECT TO**
EXAMINATION, on receipt of
$1.00, balance with express
charges to be paid upon examination and approval.

3 PER CENT. OFF
for full cash
with order.

SOLD ONLY BY SEARS ROEBUCK & Co. incorporated Chicago.

Plate 11.

A prosperous African-American family. Eleven family members (four men, seven women) posed for this formal portrait, taken sometime between 1880 and 1900. Everything in the photograph points to the family's worldly success: the rich tapestry and the artwork adorning the wall, the ornamental rug on the floor, and the expensive organ that sits in the very center of the group. This was the kind of "conspicuous consumption" that Lizzie Borden could only envy from a distance—until 1893. (Schomberg Center for Research in Black Culture, The New York Public Library)

Utopian Vision of the Family

Americans usually remember the last decades of the nineteenth century as the age of "rugged individualism," when men (almost exclusively *men*) competed in a no-holds-barred contest for individual success. But the sweet dream of success was not really an individual dream. Men experienced life as members of families, and success meant the success of the *family*—clothes and social standing for the wife, education for the children, fine careers for the sons (and increasingly the daughters). The specter of failure was a horror the entire family had to face, a fear not so much of poverty as of losing the vague but urgent sense of being "respectable."

In fact, the American dream of success was in many ways a family dream. It was a dream that money might buy enough ease and comfort, enough space and privacy within the home, to make the family a place of harmonious refuge from a world of striving, competition, and ambition. If people could get enough money, the dream promised, then their personal problems within the home might be solved. Strife between husbands and wives, anger and resentment between generations—all might disappear once there were goods enough, rooms enough, servants enough. For wealthy and well-to-do Americans, the ideal family had gradually become a truly utopian vision of sanctuary from a lonely, dangerous, and corrupt world.

This utopian vision of family life lay behind the astonishing support Lizzie Borden got from middle-class and wealthy Americans during her trial. In Fall River, "respectable" people immediately assumed that she was innocent, that she could not have committed such a deed, since she was a *lady*—not just a woman. As Lizzie Borden became a celebrity in newspapers and magazines around the country, this kind of support broadened and became even more insistent. The reasons had little to do with the facts of the case. They had to do with the profound commitment that "respectable" Americans had made to the relationship between wealth and family happiness. They had assumed that money, honestly earned, could lead only to the good life, to family circles that were quiet and loving. In a very real sense, this *was* the American dream. For the men and women who read about the Borden murders, Lizzie *had* to be innocent. To admit otherwise was to admit that the dream was false, that even Andrew Jackson Borden's wealth could not buy the kind of family they wanted.

The jury that acquitted Lizzie Borden did so not only because its members had trouble believing that a woman was capable of such a crime (a Fall River jury had already convicted a woman of a sensational murder before). The jury's real problem was that its members found it threatening to believe that a woman like Lizzie Borden—who was, after all, "a Borden"—could have done such a thing. To believe this would have undercut the jury's cherished hope that wealth and prominence could produce families that would be havens of security from the troubles of the world. Convicting Lizzie Borden would have been an admission that wealth offered no sanctuary from social disaster and family nightmare.

THE MIDDLE-CLASS WOMAN'S BURDEN

The utopian vision of family put a great deal of emotional pressure on all those Americans who entered the struggle for "respectability." But it probably bore most heavily on middle-class women. Some of them were interested in political causes like getting the right to vote. A small but increasing number were looking for professional careers, attending one of the new women's colleges or one of the state universities that had become coeducational. Various kinds of jobs were becoming "respectable" options for young middle-class women: nursing, teaching, being a librarian or a stenographer or even a clerk in a fancy city store. But for a large majority of women in the white middle class, "respectability" meant staying at home, being a mother, and perhaps—cat most—getting involved in church work, women's clubs, or a reform movement like temperance.

These were the women who carried the difficult burden of translating money into comfort, decorum, and elegance at home. And their task was defined in ways that made it extremely trying. For one thing, they were expected to present themselves to the world as models of purity and innocence. Even their clothing seemed designed to shut them off from contact with the world. In the 1870s the heavily corseted "wasp" waist, which enclosed women in an armor of bone or spring steel, became fashionable among the middle class. Then, about a decade later, came the bustle, heaping layer upon layer of heavy cloth between women and the world. In fact, the most marked characteristic of women's dress was becoming its heavy, complicated, encasing nature. A standard "walking costume" of the 1880s required a strip of cloth two feet wide and forty-five feet long—a total of ninety square feet. Lizzie Borden, before her parents were murdered, had many elaborate dresses hanging in her closet—as though clothes were the one way she could break through her father's determination to be old-fashioned. And she had sometimes quarreled with her stepmother because the older woman seemed as indifferent to clothing as Mr. Borden was to his house.

But even when they were properly dressed, women had to worry even more than men did about doing all sorts of things the "right" way. For men, in their working lives, there was a simple test of what was right: Did it help get and keep a job? Did it increase profit in the long run?

Ladies' wear. During the period between the Civil War and World War I, wealthy women—and many who were not so wealthy—dressed themselves in more and more ornate costumes. Here two women promenade at an elegant summer garden party in fashionable Newport, Rhode Island. The woman on the left is wearing an outfit that probably weighed some twenty pounds or more. But the sight of the photographer has apparently cheered her up a bit. (Culver Pictures)

But women were more at sea in a world where social standing seemed to depend on elegance and etiquette, where every detail of life was prescribed, and where a single misstep might lead to disgrace. One manual of manners for the period even tried to dictate the precise replies a woman ought to make to every kind of letter or note. In a "Letter Refusing a Donation to an Old Ladies' Home," one should write "I am compelled to contribute only to such objects as have my warmest sympathy." Then there was a "Letter Congratulating a Friend upon Finding a Lost Child": "God Bless Essie." Social care and caution seemed to know no limits, with every conceivable situation demanding a rule. There was even a proper "Answer to a Letter of Condolence on the Loss of a Limb": "Hoping to see you soon, maimed as I am." The book was published in 1888. One can only speculate what its author

might have suggested a few years later as the proper way to answer a "Letter of Condolence upon the Axe Murder of One's Aged Parents."

Of course, for most women, most of the time, such detailed prescriptions were unnecessary. But there was no way to escape the sense that there were rules governing what was proper in "good society" for every kind of occasion, and that failure to know those rules doomed a woman and her family to being cast down into "the other half."

Even more important was the fact that the doings of the very rich were relentlessly written up in newspapers and magazines, and paraded as models of "taste." There had always been prominent ladies, members of one kind of aristocracy or another. But now they had become public celebrities. With what mixture of awe, envy, and confusion could a young woman of

Lizzie Borden's social class read the *New York Times* description of the costume Mrs. William Kissam Vanderbilt wore to a very famous ball she held in 1883?

> Mrs. Vanderbilt's irreproachable taste was seen to perfection in her costume as a Venetian princess. The underskirt was of white and yellow brocade. The figures of flowers and leaves were outlined in gold and lined with Roman red. Almost the entire length of the train was caught up at one side forming a large puff. The waist was of blue satin covered with gold embroidery; the dress was cut square in the neck, and the flowing sleeves were of transparent gold tissue. She wore a Venetian cap, covered with magnificent jewels, the most noticeable of these being a superb peacock in many colored gems.

It is difficult to measure the emotions of even a single individual, much less of an entire social class or group. But the levels of tension and anxiety among middle-class women in the 1880s and 1890s must have been extremely high. One of the most popular woman writers of the day asked, in 1880, "What is this curious product of today, the American girl or woman?" Her answer was tentative, but a little frightened: "She does not yet understand herself. The face of today is stamped with restlessness, wandering purpose, and self-consciousness." Isabel A. Mallon, who wrote a phenomenally successful advice column in the *Ladies' Home Journal*, put the problem this way ten years later, in 1890: "The great fault of the girl of today is discontent. She calls it by the more magnificent sounding name of ambition, but in reality she is absolutely restless and dissatisfied with whatever may be her position in life."

Two serious writers of the period wrote brilliant and chilling stories of the plight of middle-class, middle-aged women. The first was *The Awakening*, published in 1899 by Kate Chopin. The second was *The Yellow Wallpaper*, by Charlotte Perkins Gilman, which was first printed in 1892.

Kate Chopin's heroine is Edna Pontellier, a woman of intelligence and acute sensitivity, married to a wealthy Creole businessman in Louisiana. The social and physical setting in which she moves is lush, picturesque, and even interesting. But she has a vague, powerful sense that her life is incomplete. She considers leaving her husband for another man but discovers that her lover thinks of her as "his" just as much as her husband does. She ponders the possibility of simply having an affair with some experienced, gentlemanly rogue. But that prospect galls. She talks to friends and to a doctor, but no one has any sort of workable advice. Edna Pontellier becomes increasingly despondent. Even the children she wants to love come to seem a trap and a burden to her. Finally, in a curiously indecisive way, she swims naked, out too far to survive, and dies with pink memories of innocent girlhood floating through her mind.

The nameless heroine of *The Yellow Wallpaper* shares Edna Pontellier's vague and powerful sense that she is trapped in an unsatisfying life. She too is married, and to a man of obvious "breeding" and success, a doctor. But she is being gnawed at by depression and anxiety. Gilman paints a classic picture of the way insanity creeps into the life of a woman who feels imprisoned by her marriage, her family, her social position. She begins to imagine that a strange woman is trapped in the vines that decorate the yellow wallpaper in her room. She starts refusing to leave the room, and as the story ends, she is convinced that *she* is the woman in the wallpaper, where she can now hide forever, creeping invisibly around and around the room.

Both of these stories are about women who, superficially, have nothing to complain of. Both seem to have satisfied every conventional ambition for success. Both are married to men who are far from cruel, and who are rich or near-rich. Both women have "help" aplenty and well-behaved children. But both are cut off from any serious use of their intelligence or their talent. They are suffocating in a world that reduces them to social ornaments, a world ruled by a stifling decorum. And for both heroines, life becomes intolerable. One chooses suicide, the other is pictured as actively choosing insanity. Lizzie Borden would have understood.

The exercise break. These 60 women—some young, others middle-aged—worked for the National Cash Register Corporation. In this photograph, taken around 1900, they stand in twelve rows behind the tables at which they sit and work all day, which is why the management wanted to picture them doing healthy physical exercise. The woman standing second from the right in the front row seems to be their supervisor: She is the only member of the group not dressed in an apron, and she alone wears a wedding ring. During regular worktime, this woman probably observes the others from the point where the camera has been placed. (National Cash Register Corp.)

The Other Half

The heroines of *The Awakening* and *The Yellow Wallpaper* were women for whom the domestic ideal had become a stifling, suffocating nightmare. And it is probably true that some middle-class and wealthy women experienced marriage and motherhood as a frustrating round of tedium and despair. But the domestic ideal was kept vital by one simple, inescapable fact: For most women, there was no acceptable alternative.

WOMEN'S WORK There was one possible alternative, of course: paid work. Lizzie Borden and other women like her could have escaped the confinements of home and marriage by getting jobs. But the alternative was simply not socially acceptable. The jobs to which women had access in the nineteenth century were even more degrading and poorly paid than the jobs most men could find. For most women, a job was an unpleasant and temporary alternative to domestic life. For some others, it was an inescapable necessity, not a freely chosen way to avoid marriage, home, and children.

Women had always worked in ways for which they were not paid. Before the Civil War, about 2 million African-American women had worked as slaves, harder than most men. Women worked in their homes, whether they were wives, widowed aunts, or daughters. They cooked, they cleaned and sewed, they planted and harvested. But neither slave women nor "homemakers" were counted as part of the work force, because they were not paid. On the record, at the time of the Civil War, only about 10 percent of American women held paid jobs, and they constituted only about 10 percent of the work force.

After the war, the unpaid work done by women increased in at least three ways. First, many ex–slave women began not only to keep house for themselves and their families, but also to "take in" washing, sewing, and other work. They also entered into informal arrangements with white families, coming in to take care of children or to cook. These arrangements were usually not recorded, so such women did not show up on official records of who "worked" and who did not. Second, the practice of "boarding" increased, especially in American cities. By the end of the century, one out of every five Americans was a lodger in someone else's home. This meant that the women who kept all these houses had additional work to do, work that did not count as a paid job, even though it earned family income. Third, as cities grew, so did prostitution. Tens of thousands of women earned livings in this trade, most of them working now and then for brief periods. But their work did not count as part of the public record of women's employment.

The amount of unpaid work that many women had to do kept them from seeking paid jobs. Still, more and more women did find the opportunity—or, more often, the need—to work outside the home for money. In 1870, women constituted about 15 percent of the total paid work force, an increase of about 50 percent from the proportion in 1860. And the figures climbed steadily. By 1910, despite the vast immigration of male workers from Europe and Asia, women made up 20 percent of the paid labor force. And fully 25 percent of all women worked for money.

For a few of these working women, a job *was* an attractive and hard-won escape from the pressures of marriage and motherhood. But for most of them—as for most men—work was a grinding necessity. The plain fact was that most men, whether they were native-born, immigrants, or blacks, could not support a family on the wages from their jobs. Because almost all Americans lived in families, the difference had to be made up somehow, and when it could not, people had to go hungry. The difference was made up, more often than not, by women. (In immigrant families, particularly, child labor also supplemented family income.)

WHICH WOMEN WORKED? The fact that women who worked did so not because the jobs were more attractive than home, or because they wanted "careers," created a female working population with a peculiar profile. The women who worked were not typical. They were women for whom the domestic ideal was unreached or unreachable. They were black women. They were daughters of immigrants living in urban ghettos. They were native-born women who were still unmarried and who would quit work as soon as they could.

Black women were probably the women who were most forced to work for wages, even after they married. In 1900 only about 3 percent of the white married women in America earned wages (and this percentage included many women who lived in poor, immigrant families). But among married black women (most of whom lived in stable, two-parent households), more than 25 percent held paying jobs. And the jobs were unfailingly poor. African-American women worked in about equal numbers as agricultural laborers in the South and as domestic servants in Northern and Southern cities. Their ability to find work as servants caused black women to migrate to Northern cities much more often than black men. A careful and probably accurate census in New York in 1890 found ten black women living in the city for every eight black men.

In most of the families of the new immigrants living in the cities, cultural pressures against wives and mothers working were very powerful. In these families, some of the slack in family income was taken up by children. By 1900 fully a quarter of Americans under the age of fourteen worked for wages. But an even more typical solution to the problem was to send older unmarried daughters into the labor market. In New York in 1880, the women who held jobs were, typically, young, unmarried, native-born daughters of recent immigrants from Europe. In fact, fully 90 percent of the city's working women over the age of fourteen were single. Seventy-five percent were not yet twenty-five years old. And 90 percent were the daughters of an immigrant father or mother.

Nurses. At the turn of the century, there was a concerted effort to transform nursing from a branch of domestic service into a profession. One clue to the transformation was the development of a uniform. But the uniform shown here in a photograph taken just after the turn of the century bore the indelible marks of nursing's past. The apron and the striped dresses could have been worn by any Victorian servant whose work kept her distinct from the family who employed her. And the woman holding the batch of keys could have been any head housekeeper. (Culver Pictures)

WOMEN'S JOBS What did they do, these women who "chose" jobs? How did they earn the incomes that would almost invariably put them below the poverty line if they had been trying to support themselves, let alone a family?

A few women did manage to have careers as scientists, social scientists, doctors, lawyers, or writers. And for such women, a career was an authentic alternative to being a wife and mother. When the census takers in 1920 asked professional women—most of whom had begun their careers in the nineteenth century—whether they were married, nine out of ten answered no. But such women were only a minuscule part of the total female population of the United States. The

lives of an overwhelming majority were far removed from any recognized or prestigious profession.

During the nineteenth century, two occupations had opened up to women, nursing and teaching. But nursing was still classified as "domestic service" in most areas. And as women moved into teaching, the status of the occupation fell. Salaries had dropped, and very few middle-class men were willing to take teaching jobs. As a result, most women who taught did so in exactly the same way that most white women worked at other jobs; temporarily, until they married. But teaching was not, in reality, a job that could attract middle-class women for even the

CHRONOLOGY

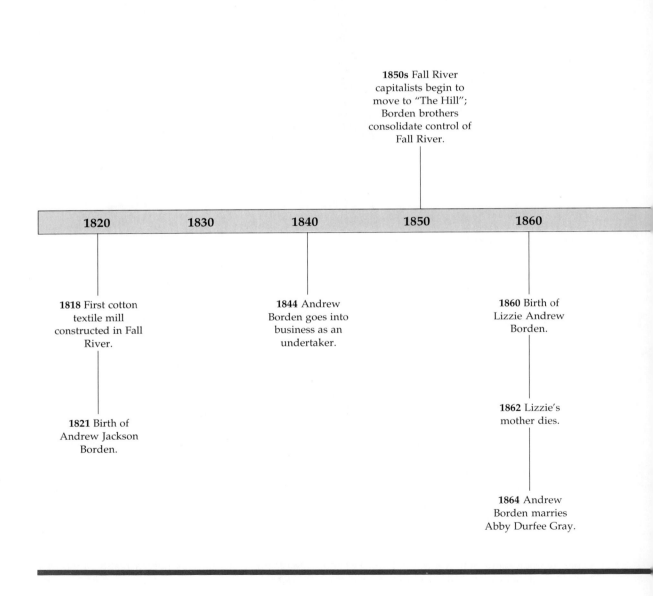

1850s Fall River
capitalists begin to
move to "The Hill";
Borden brothers
consolidate control of
Fall River.

1820   1830   1840   1850   1860

1818 First cotton
textile mill
constructed in Fall
River.

1844 Andrew
Borden goes into
business as an
undertaker.

1860 Birth of
Lizzie Andrew
Borden.

1821 Birth of
Andrew Jackson
Borden.

1862 Lizzie's
mother dies.

1864 Andrew
Borden marries
Abby Durfee Gray.

1870 Heavily corseted "wasp waists" begin to come into fashion; several private colleges for women are established.

1871 Andrew Borden retires from the undertaking business.

1872 Andrew Borden moves his family to Second Street.

1877 Cornelius Vanderbilt dies.

1890 Lizzie Borden vacations in Europe.

1892 Andrew and Abby Borden murdered; Lizzie Borden arrested.

1892 Charlotte Perkins Gilman writes *The Yellow Wallpaper*.

1893 Lizzie Borden tried and acquitted.

1895 Lizzie changes her name to Lizbeth Borden, moves to "The Hill."

1895 Sears and Roebuck begins operation.

1899 Kate Chopin writes *The Awakening*.

1870	1880	1890	1900	1910	1920

1880s Indoor plumbing comes to Fall River.

1885 Wiilliam Dean Howells writes *The Rise of Silas Lapham*.

1887 Andrew Borden gives his wife a piece of real estate.

1888 Andrew Carnegie writes "The Gospel of Wealth."

1927 Death of Lizbeth Borden.

short term. As late as 1911, the average woman teacher came from a family, usually headed by a skilled worker or a farmer, that earned only about $800 a year. Teachers and nurses may have yearned for gentility, but in economic terms they were no better off than most other Americans who worked for a living.

An increasing number of women went to work in manufacturing. They were an important part of the work force in a few selected industries, like cigar making, clothing, shoes, and bookbinding. But even at the end of the century, only a small number of the industrial workers of the United States were women. And here, too, women tended to work for a few years, until marriage, at only the worst, most unskilled, and most poorly paid jobs. Industrial work did not provide a reasonable, permanent choice for middle-class women. And even working-class women left the factories as quickly as they could and returned only under the most severe economic pressure.

More women earned their wages as domestic servants than at any other job. In the last decades of the century, about a million women were working as maids, cooks, or laundresses. (So there were about half as many female "domestics" in 1900 as there had been female slaves in 1860.) They lived at home with parents when they could. But more often they had to accept miserably paid "live-in" jobs. A few of them may have developed affectionate relationships with the families in whose homes they worked. But only a few. The rest were like the Borden household's Bridget: a little resentful, and dreaming of the day they could put away their uniforms and aprons.

The statistical records tell a clear story. The domestics were almost all single (unless they were black). They were young. About half of them were either immigrant women or the daughters of immigrant parents. Another quarter of them were black. And they did not like their work. Around the turn of the century, social scientists—mostly women—began to survey domestic servants, asking them about their working conditions and their attitudes toward their jobs. The answers were plain. Mostly, the servants testified, they missed "respect" and "freedom." As one young woman put it in an interview in the 1890s, freedom was "as dear to women as to men, although we don't get so much of it."

Lizzie Borden knew all these things. She knew that working for a living was not an acceptable alternative to marriage—especially at her advancing age. Marriage was ruled out, at least to a suitable partner, for the simple reason that a well-mannered courtship was impossible. She had no place to go, no home of her own to look forward to, and no other kind of career. Lizzie Borden probably committed murder for reasons that were partly personal and private. But she was also pushed to violence by inescapable facts about the kinds of things a respectable woman could and could not do outside the home.

American women, like American men, lived in a country where faith that hard work would lead to the good life was widespread. For women, this faith was merged with another dream—that economic success would lead to an idealized home and family. But for most workers, men and women, neither the faith in the gospel of wealth nor the vision of a gentle and "refined" family would alter grim reality. And middle-class women probably clung to the ethic of domestic refinement not so much because they wanted to as because they could not reach for that other ethic of work and career. Most of the men who dreamed of becoming "self-made" successes failed. But most women did not even have the chance to fail.

Suggestions for Further Reading

LIZZIE BORDEN

Edmund Pearson, *The Trial of Lizzie Borden* (1937), is an abridged version of the transcript of the inquest and trial. A good analysis of the case is Robert Sullivan, *Goodbye, Lizzie Borden* (1974), written by a modern lawyer and Massachusetts judge, who attempts to prove her guilt. Victoria Lincoln, *A Private Disgrace* (1967), is written by a Fall River native who believes that Lizzie committed the murders in an epileptic fit. Edward Radin, *Lizzie Borden: The Untold Story* (1961), argues that Lizzie was innocent—the murderer was Bridget Sullivan, the family maid. Ann Jones, *Women Who Kill* (1979), shows how murders committed by women—Lizzie Borden's among them—were treated by contemporaries as products of feminine passion.

WEALTH AND DISPLAY

Irvin G. Wyllie, *The Self-Made Man in America* (1954), examines the myth of rapid upward social mobility. Stephen Thernstrom, *Poverty and Progress* (1967), tests the reality of upward mobility in one Massachusetts community during the nineteenth century. Harold C. Livesay, *Andrew Carnegie and the Rise of Big Business* (1975), is a biography of one of the most famous self-made men in U.S. history. Frederic C. Jaher, *The Urban Establishment* (1982), is about the upper classes in five major American cities. William Dean Howells, *The Rise of Silas Lapham* (1885), is a novel of the period about social mobility and a family

that somewhat resembled the Bordens. Thornstein Veblen, *The Theory of the Leisure Class* (1899), is a classic critique of "conspicuous consumption" by a man who probably shared many of Andrew Borden's values. Arthur M. Schlesinger, *Learning How to Behave* (1946), traces the development of etiquette through American history. Ann Douglas, *The Feminization of American Culture* (1976), is an analysis and criticism of consumer culture in the nineteenth century.

WOMEN AND THE FAMILY

Sheila M. Rothman, *Woman's Proper Place* (1978), traces changing ideas and practices from 1870 to the present. Alice Kessler-Harris, *Out to Work* (1982), is a history of working women. A more specialized study of maids like Bridget Sullivan is David M. Katzman, *Seven Days a Week: Women and Domestic Service in Industrializing America* (1978). Ellen Dubois, *Feminism and Suffrage* (1978), is a good account of feminism in the same period. Richard Sennett, *Families Against the City* (1970), deals with the family as a "utopia," and the tensions between private and public lives in the late nineteenth century. Arthur M. Schlesinger, *The Rise of the City, 1878–1898* (1933), provides a panoramic overview of middle-class life, with a very good chapter on the domestic world of urban women. Ellen Rothman, *Hands and Hearts* (1985), is a history of American courtship practices.

CHAPTER 17
THE POLITICS
OF REFORM

THE EPISODE: *In the first two decades of the twentieth century, American political life was illuminated by two brilliant and forceful leaders: Theodore Roosevelt and Woodrow Wilson. Both were self-conscious leaders, aware of their impact on others, and able students of the science of politics. Woodrow Wilson, in particular, consciously sought higher office in order to exert influence for what he believed to be the public good. However, Wilson was an unlikely possibility for higher office. Born a Southerner, the son of a minister, he scorned ordinary politics to devote himself to statesmanship and history. Earning a doctoral degree and rising to the presidency of Princeton University, he suddenly found his political ambitions realized in a flash. Yet the story of this success is anything but a straight line of accumulating accomplishments. Indeed, the psychological dynamic that drove Wilson often seemed embedded in failure and weakness and the remarkable force of personality he marshalled to transform adversity into what he called leadership.*

THE HISTORICAL SETTING: *The Progressive Period, from the 1890s through World War I, was noteworthy for the number of remarkable men and women who affected American political life. No doubt many of them were inspired by a sense of impending crisis. The end of the century was ushered in with vivid scenes of violence and exploitation, strikes and industrial warfare in the new manufacturing centers of the Midwest and East. In 1893, a chilling economic depression stilled factories and businesses throughout the nation. Great businessmen, happy with their enormous profits and protected by political influence, often generous with gifts for civic enterprises, conducted their lives in extraordinary splendor. They constructed urban castles, suburban mansions, and country estates that shamelessly borrowed ideas from the homes of European nobility. At the same time, vast numbers of immigrants pressed into squalid tenements, where they continued to speak foreign languages, read newspapers in their native language, and attend Catholic churches or synagogues. It appeared as if America might become permanently divided by social class, by ethnic origin, by occupation.*

This ominous situation also presented opportunities. Reform movements sprang up across the nation, powered by people deeply concerned about the evolution of American society; intrigued by new ideas about the function of government, administration, and bureaucracy; empowered by the status of new institutions devoted to social science; and inspired by a rejuvenated social Christianity. Their movement greatly changed America, founding the institutions of government and the ideas of social welfare that are, recognizably, part of our modern world.

WOODROW WILSON: PROGRESSIVE MODERATE

Why may not the present age write, through me, its political autobiography?

WOODROW WILSON, 1889

Beyond the main reading room of the Princeton library, with its marble busts of Presbyterian ministers and college benefactors, the meeting in the Trustees' Room had just begun. The dark oak paneling of the room deepened the solemnity of the occasion. The trustees cast their eyes downward momentarily while Woodrow Wilson, president of the university, delivered a short prayer. Jaw firmly set and eyes flashing, Wilson finished his invocation and turned to the business of the morning—his resignation. Wilson asked for a suspension of the normal agenda of such meetings, which the assembly quickly granted. He requested release from his duties at once, asking only that "the University may go forward without halt or hindrance in the path of true scholarship and thoughtful service to the nation."

Picking up his hat and coat, while the trustees looked on in silence, he strode from the room. The assembled members voted to accept the resignation. Their victory and Wilson's defeat were total. Dispute over the direction of the university, its graduate program, and more important, its tone and commitments had finally flared into the open. By this morning in 1910, Wilson had lost a struggle that had been smoldering for several years.

Wilson's morning defeat, however, was more than matched by victory that evening. Addressing an overflow crowd at the Opera House in Flemington, New Jersey, a town noted for peaches, applejack, and rock-ribbed democracy, Wilson told an enthusiastic assembly: "I feel as if I am between sizes in occupation." Indeed he was. He had resigned from Princeton to run for governor of New Jersey on the Democratic ticket. As so often in the past, Wilson had turned a personal defeat into a practical and moral victory. Frustrated by opposition to his educational plans, he had set his ambitions and goals higher. More than ever, he felt sure of the slogan that beat in him like a moral pulse: "To be right is the only happiness in this world."

This was the sort of bittersweet moment he had reflected on in a hundred ways before. As he wrote in an unpublished manuscript (doubtless with himself in mind):

Men of strenuous minds and high ideals come forward with a sort of gentle majesty as champions of political or moral principle. They wear no armour; they bestride no chargers; they only speak their thoughts in season and out of season. But the attacks they sustain are more cruel than a thousand keen arrows of obloquy. Friends desert them and despise them. They stand alone.

At the same time, Wilson foresaw:

Masses come over to the side of reform. Resistance is left to the minority, and such as will not be converted are crushed.

In his imagination he thus accepted defeat as an overture to triumph.

In 1917, essayist Randolph Bourne described the "Puritan" personality in America in very unflattering words—a portrait that Wilson's enemies were fond of invoking to describe him. "Not until we become *proud* of our self-control do we get satisfaction," wrote Bourne. "To the true puritan the beauty of unselfishness lies in his being able to enforce it on others." Although Bourne was describing a whole generation of political and intellectual leaders, his words raise important questions about Wilson. What forces shaped this unusual man who at one moment seemed sophisticated and worldly and at other times rigid and moralistic? How did his strong moral vision and his ambition to be a leader come to symbolize the progressive reform spirit of America in the second decade of the twentieth century?

Woodrow Wilson was the first Southerner to win the presidency of the United States since before the Civil War. He was a politically inexperienced intellectual in an age of rough-and-tumble practical politics. But he was also a man who could rebound from defeat: from the defeat of the South, the shock of his thwarted Princeton presidency, the persistent and threatening illnesses he suffered. At every such point he refused to face failure; instead, he reset his aims and purposes on a higher plane. This was a reflex of self-mastery he had learned early in his youth, and it remained a defining characteristic of his personality. As he preached in a baccalaureate sermon during his last year at the university, a man's purpose in life was the successful "mastery of himself, of circumstance, of physical forces, and of human relations, of the spirit that is within him." Only self-interest, narrow greed, or cowardice could defeat him.

Thomas Woodrow Wilson (Tommie to his parents and young friends) was born December 28, 1856, in the small city of Staunton, nestled in the Shenandoah Valley between the Blue Ridge and the Allegheny mountains in western Virginia. His father, Joseph Ruggles Wilson, had moved there in 1855 to accept a call to preach at the First Presbyterian Church. The move was a serious displacement for both parents, for it tore up their roots in the North and planted them in the very different culture of the antebellum South.

As the Civil War approached, Joseph Wilson emerged as a prominent leader in splitting the Presbyterian church into Northern and Southern wings. So important had he become in encouraging this schism that in 1861, Southern separatists favoring slavery held their first assembly in his church in Augusta, Georgia, where he had moved.

The early years of Woodrow Wilson's childhood in Augusta left memories of devastation: His father's church became a hospital, and his home scarcely shut out the agonies and destruction of civil war. His education postponed, Woodrow did not learn to read adequately until the age of eleven, in part because he suffered from dyslexia. Nonetheless, family life was warm and intellectually animated. One of four children, he was his father's favorite: "You are my alter ego," the elder Wilson told him once. "You are assuredly my second edition." At the same time he developed a deep dependence on his mother. From these surroundings, he absorbed paternalism toward slaves, chivalry to women, and the tone and tenor of his father's faith.

In the Wilson family, religious instruction was reserved primarily for Sunday afternoons, but family relationships were awash in moral sentiment. Jospeh Wilson, a fine-speaking, impressive man with a sharp wit that he often aimed at his son, taught a Christianity of stewardship and service. Emphasizing the Presbyterian notion of covenant—God's agreements with mankind that underlay religion and the social order—Joseph Wilson instilled in his son a need to find religious justification for all his activities. Ambition, hard work, and success in this formula became stages in the struggle to do God's work on earth.

If Joseph Wilson drew out and encouraged ambition in his son, it was partly because he increasingly brooded over his own limitations. As friend and confidant, the elder Wilson often confessed his own frustrations to his son. Writing in 1880 to Woodrow, he spoke of his mistakes: "My life might have been greatly stronger by being greatly happier. But mistakenly, I have nearly always chosen the dark sides of probabilities at which to look. It will not do. It is irrational. It is sinful even." The senior Wilson advised his son to resist such self-indulgence and choose a purpose: "Make your mind like a needle of one eye and a single point. Shoot your words straight at the target."

Initially, both parents hoped Woodrow would follow his father into the ministry. In 1873 that seemed a possibility. After experiencing a religious conversion, Woodrow enrolled in Davidson College in North Carolina, a Presbyterian institution for training young boys for the ministry. But separation from his family proved too painful. Woodrow was, he remembered, "a laughed-at mama's boy til I was a great big fellow." Suffering from exhaustion, he returned home during the spring semester to resume old, comfortable habits.

The following fall, Wilson struck out once more for college, this time Princeton University in New Jersey. Correspondence with his parents continued apace over the next several years. "Write me freely, my darling," his father said in an 1878 letter, "as to all your feelings, and trust us both, in the future as in the past, with all your secret desires—being *sure* that we are your truest friends." Wilson responded to their plea.

One subject that both chose to discuss was ambition. For example, in 1877 Joseph warned his son: "Dearest boy, can you hope to jump into eminency all at once?" A year later, the father wrote somewhat ambiguously:

Self-consciousness is a torment: was mine at your age; has, often since then, been such. Go out from your personality. Do not regard ego as the Centre of this universe. Reflect: I am not charging egotism upon you.

In 1880 his words of caution became more pointed:

> One of the dangers of a young man like yourself—thoughtful, aspiring, conscious of certain stirring of ambition, and anxious to succeed even where success is hardest—one of your dangers arises from the tendency to *look in* too much and too far: to become too subjective: in short to be too self-conscious.

A better method, he continued, "is to grapple with things outward—is to attack and conquer . . . to learn to defy circumstances, even those that seem most adverse."

Wilson seemed to have heeded these words. While at Princeton, he cast off the confines of parental hopes for the ministry and increasingly expressed his interest in a political career. Thirty years later, addressing the General Theological Seminary of New York, he explained his reasons for abandoning the ministry. He could not judge others according to the uncompromising principles of the church and still love them. This, he confessed, "is one reason why I have kept out of the ministry." Yet the political ideals he adopted remained anchored in the bedrock of religion, far from the deals and smoke-filled rooms of Gilded Age politics. Indeed, what Wilson thought of as politics was, in his mind, a process like religion and education, in that it thrust the most righteous and upstanding men into positions of leadership. It had very little to do with politics as it was practiced since the Civil War.

In the 1880s there was little evidence that politics would ever tolerate the sort of moral vision Wilson had in mind. Party strife, regionalism, factionalism, and self-interest blocked the emergence of the sort of leadership Wilson envisioned. But then, Wilson's view of politics had always been idealized. He was especially attracted to the British House of Commons and contrasted its tradition of formal debate with the American Congress and its reliance on wheeling and dealing.

Very early on, Wilson dreamed of ways he might transform American government into an institution of high ideals and serious debate. In his first published article (aside from several sermons printed in his father's paper), he proposed to change the Constitution to accommodate a cabinet system. By making the president and cabinet members of Congress, he hoped to encourage free and serious debate on large issues. "Only a single glance," he wrote, "is necessary to discover how utterly Committee government must fail to give effect to public opinion." This emphasis on words, debate, and communication was a striking choice for a young man who still read with some difficulty.

At Princeton, Wilson experienced a quickening of ambition and development of his oratorical skills. His first and greatest love was debate. He joined the Whig Society, one of the university's two debating clubs. These clubs, encouraged by the administration, were important institutions to prepare students as lawyers, ministers, and politicians. Although he did not always win "first mention" in contests, Wilson impressed his fellow students. But he wanted to institute his own program of debates, something closer to the House of Commons, where young men could dispute the political questions that concerned them. Unsatisfied with the university-sponsored clubs, he founded a smaller society, the Liberal Debating Club—a more or less secret society that considered such issues as the Civil War and the ideal length of terms for congressmen.

The Alligator Club at Princeton. Woodrow Wilson (with his hat in hand) joined the Alligator Club while a student at Princeton. Later as president of the university, he attempted to abolish the social clubs for engendering an undemocratic spirit. (Library of Congress)

Wilson also learned about molding public opinion during his stint as editor of the *Princetonian* in 1878. As well as writing most of the editorials himself, he contributed football stories, accounts of baseball games, and book reviews. Religious ideas and points of theology rarely preoccupied him, but he nonetheless crusaded against two Victorian phobias: impropriety and vulgarity. Students in physical education class, he wrote, "wore too scanty shirts in the gymnasium." Rowdiness, noise, and unseemly conduct by Princeton students drew his disapproval. But more than anything, Wilson urged baseball and football teams on to better organization, coaching, and performance. For these efforts he was elected president of the Baseball Association and a director of the Football Association, formed to oversee the institution of the new sport at Princeton.

At the same time, young Wilson's political views began to emerge with some force. As a loyal Southerner and devoted Democrat, he supported a low tariff on foreign manufactured goods. When he found himself chosen to defend universal suffrage (including votes for blacks) during a final debate between the two leading societies, he refused. He would not compromise his principles by supporting this proposition.

Yet Wilson did not consider entering politics when he graduated from Princeton. There was nothing in vote getting, bargaining, and party caucuses that inspired him, even though he longed for a political career. So he decided to devote himself to the law. Here, perhaps, his interest in the structure of the government could find honest expression.

Wilson's decision was something of a compromise between the need to find an occupation and his widening ambition for leadership. He began his studies at the University of Virginia in 1879. This was a wise choice. Virginia boasted a fine faculty, a commitment to hard work, and a tradition that reached back to Jefferson, founding father of the university. Wilson worked hard, but he nonetheless succumbed to the enticements of extracurricular activities. He entered the Jefferson debating society, sang in the choir, joined Phi Kappa Psi fraternity, and spent much of his time courting Harriet Woodrow, his first cousin. But when Hattie realized his intentions were serious, she broke off the liaison.

Much of the time, Wilson was thinking about the nature of government and outlining the arguments he later put into *Congressional Government*, published in 1885. Other ideas began to emerge, notions that appeared in his first historical work, *Division and Reunion*, published in 1893. A series of brilliant speeches before the Jefferson society won him Virginia's Orator's Medal—in effect a second prize, behind William Cabell Bruce, a budding young politician who went on to a distinguished career in Maryland politics. Wilson, discouraged and perhaps angered by the choice, nevertheless accepted his prize.

The following fall term was to be his last. The young law student returned to classes and an active round of debating and club activities, but declining health and spirits discouraged him. Bored with law, now fancying a literary career, and distressed over the thwarted romance with Hattie, he left Virginia abruptly and returned home. It was a pattern he had established at Davidson earlier, and one that renewed his spirits.

During the year at his parents' home in Wilmington, North Carolina, Wilson continued to study law and worked on improving his literary style and speech with his father, an ever-ready critic and adviser. Restless and much improved physically, Wilson decided to try law again, and he obtained his degree from Virginia in 1881.

Quickly tiring of the law, however, Wilson abandoned his new profession before he had proved himself. "In a word," he wrote, "my ambition could not be fulfilled at the bar; the studies for which I was best fitted, both by nature and by acquired habit, were not legitimate in a law office." Recognizing his mistake, he struck out in a new direction and enrolled at Johns Hopkins University in 1883 in history. At the same time, he was stirred by a new romance with Ellen Louise Axson, a "demure little lady" who was the daughter of a local pastor. She encouraged his attention, and the two engaged in a long and friendly correspondence. In his letters, Wilson confessed his ambitions and his strong passions. Ellen had begun to replace his parents as his principal confidant.

Wilson chose Johns Hopkins at a time when that university was becoming a model of national scholarship. Its revolutionary new forms of graduate education and its brilliant young faculty made it a pioneer in developing new notions about the origins of American institutions. Wilson joined a founding generation of historians who set the style, methods, and interpretations of the new profession. He worked diligently but chafed at the boredom and small scope of his studies. This was hardly the public forum he sought.

Politics still fascinated him most, and he began to construct his book *Congressional Government*. Not always original and sometimes laboriously written, the book still marked a new facility with language. Wilson's public presentation of ideas was beginning to acquire force. Moreover, the argument he made favoring parliamentary government had become an appeal for the kinds of literary and debating skills at which he excelled. If the American government had a cabinet system, Wilson could imagine playing a major role in it.

Yet a month after this book appeared, Wilson was despondent. A successful author and only twenty-nine years old, he judged himself a failure. As he wrote to Ellen: "I do feel a very real regret that I have been shut out from my heart's *first* primary ambition and purpose which was to take an active, if possible, a leading, part in public life and strike out for myself, if I had the ability, a *statesman's* career." He had an unfulfilled "passion for interpreting great thoughts to the world; I should be complete if I could inspire a great movement of opinion."

Once more Wilson decided to abandon his studies. This time, however, he did not return home but considered a teaching position at Bryn Mawr College. His father encouraged this move and urged him to see it as a first small step: "How greatly I wish it had pleased God to open for you a door very different and much larger than this. Yet perhaps you need the discipline of such narrowness, to enable you to show the stuff of which you are made." Wilson accepted the position and pressed Ellen to marry him. On June 24, the couple were wed in Augusta, Georgia. Loosening the bonds of his parents, he now found a new source of comfort in his wife.

The fledgling women's college at Bryn Mawr, Pennsylvania, founded in 1885, hired Wilson to lecture in history and political science. While at Hopkins, he had written to Ellen that he could best express "whatever influence I might be able to exercise . . . through literary and non-partisan agencies." Bryn Mawr was a bitter disappointment. But during his three years there, he saw his family expand with the birth of two daughters, he continued to publish works on political science, and he completed his Ph.D. at Hopkins. When an offer came to move to the men's college of Wesleyan in Middletown, Connecticut, he seized it.

The next two years were momentous, with a widening scope of influence and national attention. Wilson taught history, but his book *The State*, published in 1889, and articles in prestigious academic journals and influential magazines like the *Atlantic Monthly* focused on politics. In 1890 he received a call from his alma mater, Princeton, to teach jurisprudence and political science, and moved there with his wife and three daughters.

Quickly establishing himself on campus—students flocked to his courses—Wilson began to realize some of his dreams of leadership. He idealized Princeton. It was a perfect society to him, democratic in the sense that those who gained admission could rise, carried by their abilities, to the heights of influence and success. Its gradations and distinctions indicated merit, not privilege. Professors and seniors were "the leading citizens of the little community. They are self-selected," he wrote. In Wilson's mind, this was a vision that never dimmed, even in moments when he knew it was not accurate.

Politics also began to interest Wilson more. No longer so attentive to theories of government reorganization, he had begun to shift his interest to questions of administration and public policy. By the beginning of the great depression of 1893, he spoke more warmly of reform—on a limited scale. Although his political instincts were still conservative, Wilson responded to the chaos of unemployment, bankruptcies, and strikes by developing a more fluid approach to political problems.

Wilson's private world also took a new shape during this time. Dependence now shifted from his parents to Ellen. Increasingly absent for speaking engagements, he wrote passionate love letters to her. This private side would have surprised most casual acquaintances, who assumed that the stern, flashing eyes and studied speech reflected an interior of the same austere design. In one of his few moments of public introspection, Wilson discussed the distinction between his inner and outer lives. As he told the National Press Club in 1914: "You may not believe it, but I sometimes feel like a fire from a far-from-extinct volcano, and if the lava does not seem to spill over it is because you are not high enough to see the cauldron boil." He spoke truly.

Home provided relief from a public life that demanded repression of such drives. In the shelter of his house, Wilson unbent. He loved limericks, poetry, and nonsense rhymes, and he entertained close friends and family with parodies and imitations of characters. "He would, in fact," one friend remembered, "enjoy telling jokes on himself, but never liked to have them told about him by other people."

Wilson also suffered recurrent episodes of what were probably psychosomatic illnesses: nervous stomach, depression, and headaches. A robust man who enjoyed bicycle riding, Wilson nonetheless drove himself beyond his capacities. In May 1896, at the age of forty, he suffered a slight stroke, the first evidence of the vascular disease that would ultimately kill him. Although the episode was mild, he suffered numbness in the first and second fingers of his right hand which did not disappear until the next spring.

Wilson's reaction to this secret weakness was (after a European vacation) to rededicate himself to work of even greater seriousness and scope. His denial of fragile health fitted a boyhood pattern of rejecting defeat or frailty by finding and attaching himself to a higher, selfless cause, following his father's advice to "grapple with things outward." To many observers, he turned more serious, more dedicated, more committed. If anything, Wilson's disease strengthened his need to find a forum for moral leadership and statesmanship.

At about this time, Wilson wrote an essay titled "When a Man Comes to Himself." He spoke of the moment of self-recognition that comes to every man as he moves from self-interest to belief in a higher cause:

> He comes to himself after experiences of which he alone may be aware; when he
> has left off being wholly preoccupied with his own powers and interests and with

Woodrow Wilson and family, 1912. Despite his great love of public life, Wilson relished privacy and the comfort and good spirits of his wife and three daughters. (Library of Congress)

> every petty plan that centers in himself; when he has cleared his eyes to see the world as it is, and his own true place and function in it.

The forsaking of private, narrow interests, he continued, and acceptance of a cause brought rebirth as a public man, almost in the manner of a religious conversion.

> It is for this reason that men are in love with power and greatness: it affords them so pleasurable an expansion of faculty, so large a run for their minds, an exercise of spirit so various and refreshing; they have the freedom of so wide a tract of the world of affairs.

Clearly, Wilson had begun to think of himself in a larger leadership role and of leadership as a vocation elevated beyond defeat and frustration. He had submerged his self-concern in ambitious dreams of a larger cause. At the same time, he had begun to think of commitments beyond the classroom and a scope wider than the volumes of history he wrote. As one faculty member described him, "His driving force would brook no opposition."

From 1890 to 1902, he traveled across the country giving over 100 inspirational addresses on democracy, patriotism, religion, liberty, and leadership. "I can't imagine why I consent to do this sort of thing," he wrote to his wife, "but such is your husband—hungry—*too* hungry—for reputation and influence." He sometimes fretted about his narrow and constricted profession, hoping for more adventure and responsibility. These emotions undoubtedly inspired him to write glowingly of young American men in 1899 "who prefer dying in the ditches of the Philippines to spending their lives behind the counter of a dry goods store in our eastern cities. I think I should prefer that myself."

By the turn of the century, Wilson had emerged as a candidate to replace the current Princeton administration. Wilson first clashed with Francis Patton, president of the university, in 1893, over the honor system. Patton criticized the system, which he said was unworkable and open to abuse. At a faculty meeting, Wilson rose to the challenge and defended the practice as the very heart of the university. His eloquence persuaded the assembly, and the system stood. By 1902 other issues had arisen. Dismayed at the decline of academic standards and obstacles to several of his pet projects, Wilson allied himself with younger faculty members and sought support from the Princeton board of trustees. Together, this opposition ousted Patton. Wilson was appointed in his place.

Granted wide powers to reorganize the university, Wilson moved to change instruction and raise standards. He was determined to make Princeton the ideal intellectual and moral community he dreamed it could be. His basic program was a preceptorial system based partly on the British tutorial system at Oxford and Cambridge. This and other schemes were expensive but adventurous. He called for new buildings, an endowment for tutors' salaries, and general staff salary increases. To finance these projects, he had to raise over $12 million. Important as he knew it was, he found great difficulty and embarrassment in approaching alumni or corporation directors. He could not bear to lobby, hat in hand, for gifts from the wealthy. Fortunately, his plans were saved by a special fund-raising committee of board members. By 1905 the preceptor plan had been accepted and implemented, and Wilson hired an outstanding group of young men to live and work closely with students.

With such reforms, Princeton grew in national prestige, although admissions fell because of more selective standards. Wilson believed that his mission was to make Princeton a national university. In his inaugural speech to the university, he had declared: "We are here to serve our country and mankind, and we know we can put selfishness behind us." Princeton would provide the nation with training in "practical religion." Somewhat later, Wilson put it this way:

> The whole Princeton idea is an organic idea, an idea of contact of mind with mind—no chasms, no divisions in life and organization,—a grand brotherhood of intellectual endeavor, stimulating the youngster, instructing and balancing the older man, giving the one an aspiration and the other a comprehension of what the undertaking is,—of lifting, lifting, lifting the mind of successive generations from age to age.

Despite this succession of achievements, these were not entirely happy years. Family illnesses, the death of Ellen's brother and his wife in 1905 in a freak accident, and overwork may have contributed to Wilson's second serious stroke in 1906. Awakening one morning in late May, he found he had become blind in his left eye. Doctors advised immediate and permanent rest—even retirement. Disguising his infirmity,

Wilson spent the summer recuperating in England. He gradually regained some of the vision in his affected eye. And he rejected thoughts of resignation and invalidism. He returned to Princeton a transformed man, more committed to work and leadership than ever, and less tolerant of opposition.

When Wilson returned, he plunged into a fight that he believed would save the soul of the university. He had by now completely submerged private setback in a cause of public regeneration. Ambition and reform merged. Princeton had long had eating clubs, to which most students belonged. During his years as a student, Wilson had joined the Alligators, one of the more exclusive of these establishments. Recently, however, the clubs had moved into large, elegant quarters. Wilson was shocked by the frivolity, the drinking, and the luxury of these student organizations. The clubs, he concluded, diverted students to think only of the "social question." They introduced factionalism and degraded university life. Social ambition had become "too strong for individual honour." Nothing could be more remote from Wilson's educational philosophy, and he determined to replace the clubs with more democratic, on-campus activities.

Wilson's solution, called the quadrangle plan, proposed to divide the campus into "quads" resembling the colleges of Oxford and Cambridge. The freshman, sophomore, junior, and senior classes would each live together, rather than mixing in exclusive clubs. "The fight is on," he declared in 1907, "and I regard it not as a fight for the development, but as a fight for the restoration of Princeton. My heart is in it more than it has been in anything else, because it is a scheme of salvation."

Wilson's plan stirred powerful opposition. Wealthy alumni who fondly remembered their club days opposed the plan. They found sympathetic allies, like ex-president Grover Cleveland, on the board of trustees. This opposition plus the estimated costs of the plan made the whole board pause. Wilson, when he saw that his plan might be rejected, reacted angrily. He believed that wealth and privilege were blocking fulfillment of his most cherished educational ideals. Finding the opposition well entrenched, he took his case to the Princeton alumni. Again he traveled around the country, making his case in a series of rousing speeches against the narrow-mindedness and selfishness that he believed were standing in his way. But the board remained unmoved by his efforts.

Nonetheless, Wilson's speeches and his growing prestige attracted national attention and promoted rumors on campus that he might seek high political office. Princeton seniors sang a satiric verse on the subject in 1908:

> Here's to Woodrow, King Divine,
> Who rules this place along with [Dean] Fine,
> We hear he wants to leave the town
> And try for Teddy Roosevelt's crown.

One of the principal enemies to the quad plan had been Andrew West, dean of the graduate school. A portly, elegant man with fine manners and a good instinct for infighting, West emerged as leader of the opposition to Wilson. He too had a plan to transform Princeton. But unlike Wilson, he carefully nurtured a base of power among the trustees. West wanted to relocate the graduate school off campus, where students might, in the midst of leisure and comfort, continue their studies. Wilson fought this

Wilson and Carnegie at Princeton, 1906. The great industrialist and philanthropist Andrew Carnegie was one of many wealthy patrons whose contributions Wilson solicited while president of Princeton. A university of the importance and prestige of Princeton depended heavily on the generosity of such men to undertake innovations in graduate and undergraduate education. (Culver Pictures)

notion. It was, after all, a plan that would effectively turn the graduate school into a social club. Wilson had an alternative. He wanted to keep the graduate school on the campus, subject it to his administrative control, and integrate its students into the intellectual life of the university.

In various ways, the graduate school fight between Wilson and West merely continued the quad system struggle. West organized a major segment of the trustees and found wealthy outside benefactors to finance his plan. Wilson made several efforts to raise funds for his plan, even visiting the industrial pioneer Andrew Carnegie in his castle in Scotland. But to no avail; West proved to be the better organizer. Working from the inside, he blocked Wilson's efforts, operating in the way traditional politicians smoothed the passage of controversial legislation. Attempts at a compromise between the two plans failed, for there was no way to merge the philosophies, the styles, or the power struggle behind them.

Realizing that he had been rebuffed on campus, Wilson transformed his fight into a national campaign among Princeton alumni. In his speeches, he reached out to castigate his enemies in harsh terms. The men of great industrial and banking fortunes who served on the board of trustees were acting like a "House of Lords," he railed. The struggle, he maintained, had larger overtones: It involved a national crusade for democracy and against privilege.

Wilson made these points especially sharply in a speech to a bewildered gathering of Princeton alumni in Pittsburgh in April 1910. The *Pittsburgh Dispatch* reported that the alumni gathered to sing college songs, toast the college and old friends, and relive school days. But Wilson, the last speaker at the affair, jolted "the jolly grown-up college boys" with his stern remarks. He had come to raise questions about the survival of Princeton, American society, and religion. Striking a tone of high seriousness, he declared:

> The colleges are in the same dangerous position as the churches. I hope that the last thing I will ever be capable of will be casting a shadow on the church, and yet the churches—the Protestant churches, at least—have dissociated themselves from the people. They serve the classes, not the masses. They serve certain strata, certain visible uplifted strata, and ignore the men whose need is dire.
>
> The colleges are in the same class, looking to the support of wealth rather than the people.

This intolerable situation, Wilson continued, had evoked an outcry for the moral regeneration of American society from top to bottom. It even extended to the political parties, which were "going to pieces." Inevitably, the forces of regeneration, he told his shocked audience, would come from the

> mass of obscure men, not from the handful of conspicuous men; it is to that mass of obscure men that it [the nation] must look if it is to live. And we should cry out against the few who have raised themselves to dangerous power, who have thrust their cruel hands into the very heartstrings of the many on whose blood and energy they are subsisting.

Wilson's radical-sounding speeches won him no converts among Princeton alumni. Indeed, they sounded like the inflammatory rhetoric of the old Midwest Populists. His strategy could not overcome the clever politicking of Dean West, who by early 1910 controlled the votes of most of the trustees. And while Wilson had turned his cause into a larger crusade—to save Princeton and the nation, to create an "absolute democratic regeneration in spirit"—he had also risked losing everything, including his presidency of the university.

By late spring Dean West had won. The trustees decided that the graduate school would be off campus. But by this time Wilson's thoughts had turned elsewhere—to state politics. Already mentioned as a possible candidate for governor in 1908, Wilson

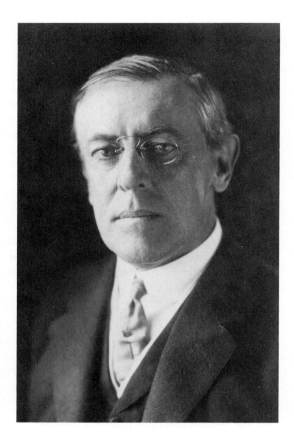

Wilson as governor of New Jersey, 1912. Woodrow Wilson's meteoric rise to the presidency was aided by his widely noted victory in the New Jersey governor's race of 1910. Although he held public office for only two years before he was elected president in 1912, he had learned leadership in the bitterly fought academic politics of Princeton University. (Library of Congress)

seemed even stronger to state Democratic bosses in 1910. In June, several leaders visited him and offered him the nomination. They also spoke of a possible presidential bid two years later.

After a week of consideration, Wilson consented, and the machine kicked into operation. Crushing any opposition, party leaders secured his nomination over the objections of several reform groups. But Wilson hastily mended his fences. He campaigned for electoral reforms and began to speak of his support for labor unions. He won election in November and began the most reform-minded administration in New Jersey in decades. His presidential race was just two years away.

Much had changed in Wilson's political ideas since he first expressed them as a youth in his early debates and articles. Still an unreconstructed Southerner, he retained his belief in a low tariff, his commitment to economic individualism, and his sense of racial superiority. Despite his fiery rhetoric, he was still a conservative, ambiguous about labor unions. He was hostile to large corporations and monopolies, but he remained suspicious of too much government regulation of the economy. Nevertheless, he was poised to plunge into the mainstream of reform. He had begun to change his mind about William Jennings Bryan, the Populist-Democratic candidate for president in 1896, whom he had once considered a dangerous radical. He shared two key principles with other reformers: He increasingly agreed about the need to shape public opinion to bring it to bear upon large social and economic questions of the day, and he increasingly thought of the executive branch as the focus of an activist national government. Here was the best locus for his concept of inspired leadership.

In fact, Wilson's political philosophy had come to rest on one key question: the worth of the leader. It was an old question in a new guise:

> He stands for himself. And the final verdict with regard to him will be based upon the answer to this question: is he serving himself alone, or is he serving the public interest?

Thrust into national leadership by special circumstances, Wilson had by an odd route come to prepare himself for this position. At every crucial point in his life he had rejected defeat and limitation, turning to a larger, more extensive cause of moral and national regeneration. The nation had come to accept and expect this definition of its progressive politicians, as men whose moral vision outweighed the problems they faced. Wilson had nourished this ideal since childhood. He was also the sort of man demanded by the political fashion of the day: stern, moralistic, reformist, and a shaper of public opinion.

Shortly after he had been forced out of Princeton and been elected as governor of New Jersey, one of the Princeton preceptors he had appointed came across him, sitting deep in thought at the Princeton Junction railway station. "You appear to be revolving a deep problem in your mind," said the young man. Indeed, he was. "I am thinking about leadership," Wilson replied.

IN SEARCH OF THE PUBLIC INTEREST

The movement that thrust Woodrow Wilson into the White House in 1913 and followed his leadership for eight years had begun almost two decades before in the moral and political awakening of a broad group of reformers called progressives. This diverse coalition of men and women emerged primarily from the ranks of the new urban middle class. Drawing on traditional ideas of democracy and an intense but secular Protestantism, they worried deeply about the contradictions of their society. They puzzled over the contradictions between self-interest and social interest, between progress and poverty. Steeped in nineteenth-century concepts of self-help, stewardship, and the work ethic, they were surprised and troubled by the unexpected byproducts of industrial growth. The obvious success of the capitalist economic system—its productivity, invention, and urbanization—had a threatening, dark side: poverty, exploitation, and violence. Industrial development degraded work and initiated cycles of economic boom and bust, violent strikes, and political instability. Ironically, the Victorian economic ethic, based on saving, investing, and individualism, had spawned a generation of business leaders whose greed made a mockery of the precepts they invoked to justify wealth and success.

In a justly renowned article published in 1889 (see Chapter 16), Andrew Carnegie, self-made millionaire and steel and iron entrepreneur, reflected on his society that had grown rich and poorer at the same time. Competition, he wrote in his essay "The Gospel of Wealth," made a few men like himself very rich, but many other people poor. Because competiton also stimulated the marvels of productivity, he would certainly not oppose it. But its social effects demanded attention. As he put it, finding "the proper administration of wealth" would "bind together the rich and poor in harmonious relationship." But could it be done? Carnegie had raised the question that most worried progressives: Could industrial progress and economic individualism continue without degenerating into violence and class warfare? Was a social gospel possible?

The depression of 1893 helped precipitate the forces that created progressivism as a national movement. This deep economic downturn shook millions of workers from their jobs. Unemployment rose from around 3 percent in 1892 to over 18 percent two years later. The gross national product (the estimated sum of goods and services produced by the economy) fell by 12 percent in 1894 and did not recover until 1897.

A measure of the depression's seriousness was the social unrest to which it gave rise. In the spring of 1894, this burst into an angry disturbance in Washington, D.C. Led by Jacob S. Coxey, an Ohio businessman, a small army of supporters dubbed the "Commonweal of Christ" marched to the capital to ask for a public works bill to end unemployment. Although it posed no threat, the group was attacked by police and Coxey was jailed.

A far more threatening labor incident began in May 1894 with a strike at the Pullman Palace Car Company in Chicago. Sparked by falling wages and management opposition to unions, the strike took on national significance in June (see Chapter 15). Alluding to these events later that summer, Woodrow Wilson remarked: "Every one knows that the relations—even the legal relations—now existing between capitalists and laborers are seriously amiss."

Why were these relations frightening to so many observers in the 1890s? There are, essentially, two answers. The industrial system encouraged the organization of powerful private institutions: corporations and labor unions that seemed pitted against each other in a ruthless struggle for power. Surely, it was assumed, society itself would be the loser in such strife. Second, the private, unregulated industrial system had created untold hardships for millions of Americans through unemployment and injury.

Corporations vs. Unions

CORPORATIONS ORGANIZE   The most powerful economic institutions of the early twentieth century were corporations. Many of them were assembled in the waning days of the 1893 depression and in the first few years of the twentieth century. Their objective was to control markets, raw materials, and labor. By 1900 about two-fifths of total American manufacturing capital and two-thirds of railroad trackage were concentrated in the hands of large combines and corporations. Ten of the largest holding companies (that is, corporations that owned other operating companies)

had assets of more than $100 million; the greatest of these, U.S. Steel, controlled over $1 billion. Such concentrations of power touched off controversy from almost the moment they appeared. In 1890, Congress passed the Sherman Antitrust Act, intended to prevent monopolies from restraining trade and competition. But business circumvented the act and, aided by the courts, turned the Sherman Act against labor unions.

Some capitalists ignored the adverse publicity. But others believed they had to act to deflect criticism of their private power and fortunes. Some, like Andrew Carnegie, also recognized a larger social responsibility. The successful businessman, Carnegie suggested, should administer his wealth for the good of society. Carnegie acted on his own advice and endowed over 2,000 free public lending libraries during his lifetime.

Carnegie's charitable gifts exemplified the development of professional philanthropy. But this money was not intended for the unemployed or the poor. Instead, most was given to encourage culture or to fund scientific or social research or educational projects. As Carnegie put it, his gifts provided "ladders upon which the aspiring can rise." During the first half of the twentieth century, universities also acquired large endowments from such wealthy donors. Several important institutions, such as Stanford, started by railroad magnate Leland Stanford in 1885, were founded by men with large fortunes. Universities hired professional fund raisers and used fund drives to expand their educational offerings. It was this process that snagged Woodrow Wilson in a bitter fight over the disposition of gifts to Princeton in 1910.

Indeed, the manipulations that Wilson encountered in his fight with the Princeton trustees revealed the shortcomings of modern philanthropy. In many cases, philanthropists wished to control the use of their gifts even after their own death. In others, philanthropy became a device to deflect criticism from questionable business practices. John D. Rockefeller, whose reputation for ruthless competition was national, used charitable giving to improve his public image. In 1889 he began a series of large donations to the new University of Chicago. In 1891 he hired Frederick T. Gates, a Baptist clergyman, to oversee his donations. But such philanthropy did not prevent criticism; instead, it made the very act of giving suspect. Journalists and politicians denounced Rockefeller's motives, calling him a "robber baron" and "spoiler of the state," and his gifts "tainted money." Obviously, philanthropy itself was not enough.

In response to the 1893 depression and mounting public sympathy for labor unions, corporations formed two important new organizations: the National Association of Manufacturers (NAM) in 1895 and the National Civic Federation (NCF) in 1900. The NAM, especially after 1903, pushed the "open shop" movement—a movement devoted to preventing unions from forming. Particularly directed against the American Federation of Labor (AFL), this drive gathered strength in the West, where affiliated organizations sprang up to defeat union drives or prolabor legislation.

The NCF adopted a much less confrontational approach to industrial strife. Reformer and journalist Ralph Easley, its driving force, had been deeply affected by the Pullman strike of 1894. He believed that business had to negotiate with unions to prevent class warfare. Persuading Samuel Gompers of the AFL and John Mitchell of the United Mine Workers to join Ohio Republican political boss Mark Hanna and a group of financiers, businessmen, and academics, Easley created an organization devoted to moderate labor legislation.

UNIONS ORGANIZE Unions were obviously the weaker force in the struggles of the 1890s. The problems they sought to overcome were legion: poverty, industrial accidents, strikes and lockouts, exploitation. For almost all factory workers, wages were low and industrial accidents frequent. Average wages for nonfarm employees hovered around $500 a year in this period. Jobs not only paid poorly, they were dangerous, particularly in the key railroad sector.

Because of lax safety standards and poor maintenance in the deadly year of 1907, 610 passengers, 4,534 railroad employees, and 6,695 workers in railroad shops lost their lives.

Before they sought to unionize an industry, labor organizers knew they would confront tough employer opposition. Employers possessed an arsenal of legal tactics to discourage unions. They could demand a "yellow-dog" contract, allowing dismissal of any worker who joined a union. They assembled blacklists of workers who sympathized with unions, and they hired scabs to cross picket lines. Often they could persuade a friendly court to declare a strike illegal. As a last resort, employers could hire small armies of detectives, spies, and bodyguards to break up union gatherings.

Other obstacles to unionization arose from the nature of the American working class. Increasingly, industrial workers were immigrants from eastern and southern Europe. Divisions by language and national origin made organization difficult—a circumstance that employers often exploited.

Despite these factors, substantial unions emerged toward the end of the nineteenth century. The most important and lasting of these was the American Federation of Labor (AFL), founded in 1886 by Samuel Gompers of the Cigar Makers Union. Consisting primarily of skilled craft unions, the AFL grew rapidly in the 1890s. Gompers, an English immigrant and one-time Marxist, guided his union through thirty-five years of strife and conflict. Although he gave up his belief in class struggle, he remained deeply suspicious of politicians and legislation. Gradually he developed a philosophy of voluntarism, or union independence from political parties and government intervention. Anxious to avoid the socialist unionism sweeping Europe, he devoted the political energies of the AFL to rewarding its friends and punishing its enemies. By 1900 the union had increased its membership to 400,000.

The dangers and exploitation in industrial work also bred radical organizations. The most important of these, the Socialist Party of America, was formed in 1901. Eugene Debs, of Terre

Haute, Indiana, leader of the American Railway Union, epitomized the movement. Enormously popular, Debs addressed audiences across the country in speeches laced with discussions of class struggle and promises of the coming Christian brotherhood, under which the people, not the capitalists, would own the means of production.

The Socialist party, along with the revolutionary Industrial Workers of the World (IWW), also known as the "Wobblies," which it helped to found, grew rapidly during the progressive era up to World War I. In 1912, when it presented a serious challenge to Wilson, the party had 118,000 dues-paying members, 1,200 public officials, and 300 socialist periodicals. With strength in old Populist strongholds of the Southwest, socialists created a movement dedicated to an "international socialist commonwealth—God's Kingdom." Although it eventually broke with the Socialist party, the IWW also grew rapidly. It achieved important, though temporary, successes in widely noted strikes such as the textile strike in Paterson, New Jersey, in 1913.

Middle-Class Reformers

Facing substantial industrial turmoil and large new power blocs in the economy, middle-class reformers tried to develop a program and philosophy of national public interest. They believed government could solve the problems raised by unregulated competition and industrial struggle. As reformers, they were critical of both sides, owners and unions. They intensely disliked the selfish moneyed interests and feared the organized power of monopolies. Perhaps even more, they distrusted the industrial labor force of newly arrived immigrants. Many worried that labor unions or socialist organizations would challenge the basic tenets of American capitalism. Like Woodrow Wilson, they proposed to create a reformed society, guided by moral principles, in

which all of the contending interests would share the benefits.

The forerunners of the progressives, the Mugwumps (see Chapter 13), appeared first in the sedate halls of Harvard University and the gentlemen's clubs of Boston. These genteel reformers bolted the Republican party in 1884 to vote for Grover Cleveland, the Democratic candidate. They put principle above party and supported changing the electoral system and, above all, honesty in government enforced by civil service reform. On issues of labor rights, they remained conservative; to them, reform began and ended with good government. However, they did will to the next generation of reformers a commitment to national change and an invitation to the respectable classes to enter politics.

CHURCHES AND COLLEGES The Mugwumps also bequeathed a tone of moralism and high-mindedness that progressives like Woodrow Wilson shared. The Protestant churches in particular paid special attention to the developing evils of the industrial system. Led by Baptist minister Walter Rauschenbusch and Congregationalist Washington Gladden, ministers and churchmen advocated a new social Christianity. This "Social Gospel" proclaimed that Jesus had taught a social ethic, not individualism as conservative theologians preached. Proposing social salvation through good works, these men sought greater and greater social cooperation. Many of them entered local good-government campaigns and crusades to regulate industry.

The intellectual climate in American universities and colleges also lent itself to new ways of thinking about society and government. Much as Princeton had done under Wilson, other prestigious American universities like Johns Hopkins, the University of Chicago, Harvard, and the universities of Wisconsin and Michigan hosted new intellectual movements that swept away the cobwebs of nineteenth-century conservative individualism. The development of the new profession of sociology, which underscored the importance of social engineering as the legitimate function of the state, was one such movement.

Fiery speaker Elizabeth Gurley Flynn addresses a crowd of workers during the I.W.W. strike at Paterson, New Jersey, in 1913. Note that she is the only person in the picture not wearing a hat, as if to emphasize the singularity of a woman exhorting an assembly of unionists. (Archives of Labor and Urban Affairs, Wayne State University)

VEBLEN AND DEWEY Perhaps the most profound thinker of the era was Thorstein Veblen. A difficult writer and an eccentric personality, Veblen wrote several remarkable sociological works. The best known was *The Theory of the Leisure Class* (1899), in which he satirized the "conspicuous consumption" of the American middle and upper classes. In its stead, he called for the cultivation of the "instinct of workmanship," which he deemed a more natural and creative human impulse.

Veblen's attack on wastefulness and class consciousness was seconded in the philosophical and educational writings of John Dewey. Dewey belonged to a group of important American philosophers, called pragmatists, who stressed the effectiveness and efficiency of ideas rather than their religious or traditional origins. Dewey constructed a philosophical system that emphasized the possibilities for growth, change, and increasing control of the environment. In education, he emphasized the importance of work and experience. To him, education meant placing the child in an environment where he or she could understand the process of change and social evolution. Hence the school, in Dewey's educational plans, became the center of society and a force to rejuvenate the community. It would, he hoped, help narrow distances between social classes and strengthen American democracy.

THE GOOD-GOVERNMENT MOVEMENT Civic reformers also provided an important practical ingredient of progressivism. These city dwellers were often appalled by the powerful coalitions of urban politicos and immigrant voters, and they organized to wrest cities like New York, St. Louis, and Minneapolis from the control of the bosses. The good-government movement received national attention with the founding of the National Municipal League in 1894.

The achievements of this movement were exemplified by Tom Johnson of Cleveland, Ohio. Johnson had earned a fortune as an inventor, steel mill owner, and operator of streetcar rail-

John Dewey. John Dewey's writings provided a philosophical foundation for the progressive faith in institutional reforms. His theories of education also profoundly altered teaching practices, particularly in urban schools. (Library of Congress)

A key instrument in conveying this terrible reality was the photograph. Although photography had been possible before the Civil War, its potential for persuasion—for propaganda—was scarcely realized until the 1890s. Jacob Riis in *How the Other Half Lives* (1890) recorded a grim vision of the urban immigrant world. But it was Lewis Hine who probably most evoked pity and outrage through his photographs of working children in the first two decades of the new century. Newsboys, girl mill workers, oyster shuckers, cranberry pickers, and a legion of other working children were the subjects of his camera. Published in national journals and displayed by reform organizations, these poignant, brave children's faces made the reality of exploitation and child labor inescapable. Camera in hand, Hine helped transform poverty from private suffering into a public cause.

Women and Progressivism

Women contributed to progressivism in a variety of ways. Roused by a fear of disease and shoddy products, and desiring to protect their families, middle-class women organized consumer groups in the 1890s. The General Federation of Women's Clubs (1890), the National Congress of Mothers (1896), and the Consumers League (1899) hoped to safeguard American homes by improving conditions in the factories where products were made.

THE SETTLEMENT HOUSE MOVEMENT
Women were also heavily represented in the settlement house movement, which began in 1886 with the establishment of the Neighborhood Guild (later the University Settlement) on New York's Lower East Side. Probably the most famous settlement was Jane Addams's Hull

ways. Elected mayor of Cleveland in 1901, he pushed through several impressive municipal reforms: a new garbage disposal system for the city, a low-cost municipally owned electric company, meat and milk inspection, and the construction of broad streets and parks to provide open spaces and uncongested throughways for all the city's residents. He also attacked organized gambling. Johnson quickly earned a national reputation. In the words of journalist Lincoln Steffens, Cleveland was the "best governed city in the United States," and Johnson's was "the greatest movement in the world today."

Other urban reformers focused on overcrowded living conditions, poor diet, and the ravages of poverty. Tuberculosis, typhoid fever, influenza, and other contagious diseases were sweeping American cities, fueled by overcrowding, poor sanitation and hygiene, and contaminated food.

Settlement house workers. Julia Lathrop, Jane Addams, and Mary McDowell (left to right) were three important settlement house workers in Chicago. Besides ministering to the needs of slum residents, they worked to secure national reforms such as women's suffrage. (Library of Congress)

House, opened in Chicago in 1889. Addams expressed many of the ideals of the late Victorian reformers who peopled the progressive movement. Well educated, with a sensitive social conscience, she rejected the roles open to her: marriage, teaching, or nursing. Instead, she helped create something new: the profession of social work. Hull House, a mansion near the slums of Chicago, became a residence for women who, like herself, sought a useful profession. Addams and her fellow workers plunged into daily life in the slums, agitating for local garbage disposal, public education, and child labor laws. (The 1910 census reported that hundreds of thousands of children between the ages of ten and fifteen were employed, many of them in factories

and mines.) Hull House also offered a distinctive program to nearby immigrants. The residents taught nutrition and cooking, art and literature. By the turn of the century, the settlement included a gymnasium, boys' club, auditorium, and library, making it an institution almost as large as the University of Chicago.

SUFFRAGE But a large segment of women reformers felt that their own rights were as much at stake as the welfare of immigrants and child laborers. Although women organized many of the important reform movements that constituted the larger progressive mood, they were still unable, by law, to vote in elections, except in

Frederick Winslow Taylor

The change from rule-of-thumb management to scientific management involves . . . not only the study of what is the proper speed for doing the work and a remodeling of the tools and the implements in the shop, but also a complete change in the mental attitude of all the men in the shop toward their work and toward their employers. The physical improvements in the machines necessary to insure large gains, and the motion study followed by minute study with a stop watch of the time in which each workman should do his work, can be made comparatively quickly. But the change in the mental attitude and in the habits of the three hundred or more workmen can be brought about only slowly.

These words, written by Frederick Winslow Taylor in his book *The Principles of Scientific Management*, represent a curious variant of progressive reformism. Taylor, who was both a hero and a villain to the public, was an enthusiast for corporate and industrial reorganization. He was one of the first—and certainly the most notorious—of modern efficiency consultants. His works were cited by some as a bible for industrial reorganization. To others, his writings appeared to be evidence of a management conspiracy to speed up production and lower wages.

Born in 1856 in Germantown, Pennsylvania, Taylor was educated in Europe and at private schools before entering Harvard Law School. Finding study and preparation too strenuous for his eyes, he shifted to engineering. While working as a manual laborer for Midvale Steel Company, he took a mechanical engineering degree from Stevens Institute of Technology. Over the next decades, he secured scores of patents for inventions, primarily in machine tool development.

Taylor was intrigued, and not a little distressed, by the organization of work at Midvale, and he set out to change it. He developed a system of work time and motion study. Quite literally this meant observing and timing (with a stopwatch) the individual motions of a worker, then studying ways to economize effort and eliminate all unnecessary motions, thus speeding production. In addition, Taylor designed new tools and suggested new minimum production quotas, new shop arrangements, and incentive wages. The whole system was designed to increase efficiency. But it required complete cooperation from workers and management—something that Taylor generally failed to achieve.

Taylor's emphasis on efficiency and increased wages, plus his own reform intentions, placed him within the ranks of the progressive movement. Nonetheless, he was bitterly criticized for his exaggerated claims and, most particularly, for his treatment of workers as if they were no more than robots. When he died in 1915, his fame was widespread. Motion studies had become common in industry. But his hoped-for revolution in mental attitudes toward work had not occurred.

Picture: Bettmann Archive

some statewide contests. The women's movement in America had a long and varied history. Beginning in the mid–nineteenth century, the movement pushed a variety of aims, from the abolition of slavery to the prohibition of alcoholic drinks. But in the early twentieth century, it concentrated on obtaining the right to vote.

Many reformers—men and women—believed that extension of the vote was essential to a responsible public spirit. By adding the moral weight of women to the electorate, they assumed it would be easier to legislate national reforms. Some suffragists, like Mrs. George Bass when she appeared before the Senate in 1915, declared that

The *Holbrook* carries the suffrage torch. The campaign for women's suffrage took many forms designed to attract public attention and support. Civil disobedience and hunger strikes were eventually added to more traditional spectacles and parades. (Library of Congress)

women's duty to family should be expanded to become a sort of social motherhood: Women wanted the vote because they required it to continue "the business of being a woman."

For those women opposed to the vote, the logic was reversed. Mrs. A. J. George of the National Association Opposed to Woman Suffrage told Congress that suffrage would destroy women's special character. She explained: "The Woman-suffrage movement is an imitation-of-man movement, and, as such, merits the condemnation of every normal man and woman." The vote, she concluded, would condemn women to jury duty, protection of life and property, and quite possibly, military service.

Like other reformers of the progressive era, the suffragists turned to the national government for remedies. They sought an amendment to the Constitution. Finally, toward the end of the progressive period, they persuaded Congress and the president to support their initiative. The Nineteenth Amendment was passed by Congress and three-quarters of the states during World War I. It was declared in effect in 1920.

Progressivism as a Movement

Like Jane Addams's social workers, urban reformers and Social Gospel ministers shared a feeling of identity with the victims of society. As Woodrow Wilson put it in 1909, a man of the people "felt beat in him, if he had any heart, a universal sympathy for those who struggle, a universal understanding of the unutterable things that were in their hearts and the unbearable burdens that were upon their backs."

Progressivism became a movement by establishing a national audience for reform ideas and a program that stressed social and political solutions to individual misfortune. In other words, it pushed onto a national reform agenda social problems and solutions defined by local and state reformers. It clearly relinquished the older notion of effective charity as individual stewardship in favor of the idea that society itself, as represented in government, must actively protect and promote the welfare of its most vulnerable citizens. Men like Woodrow Wilson became expert in gathering public support for their reforms. But much of the attention to reform came from a new sort of journalism, called *muckraking*. The technological revolution in printing that occurred in the 1890s enabled large-circulation magazines to lower prices to a dime an issue and begin printing photographic features. Newspaper chains owned by William Randolph Hearst adopted an aggressive investigative journalism. Vying for public attention, journals such as *Cosmopolitan, Munsey's Magazine*, and especially *McClure's* began to expose corruption and corporate ruthlessness. For example, *McClure's* in late 1902 published the first installment of Lincoln Steffens's attack on urban corruption, "The Shame of the Cities." At the same time, it included the first of several articles by Ida Tarbell on the history of Standard Oil. Almost overnight, the company became a symbol of corporate greed and monopoly.

Other journalists, taking their cue from these successful articles, began investigations of other sordid elements of modern life: poverty, corruption, and exploitation. In 1906 reporter David Graham Phillips even attacked the Senate in his series "Treason of the Senate." Phillips's accusations aroused the ire of Theodore Roosevelt, who believed the journalist had gone too far. In an April speech, Roosevelt denounced journalists who raked the muck and never lifted their eyes from it. The name "muckraker" stuck.

By the early twentieth century, progressivism had begun to emerge as an important although divided political force stressing industrial regulation and a new social ethic. The problems of industrialism, immigration, poverty, social violence, and corruption were widely recognized. And middle-class reformers had begun to advocate a larger role for government to balance the contending interests of capital and labor. They had begun to articulate a vision of society controlled by men and women of good faith who had an acute sense of the public interest. At every level, in countless organizations, they clamored for an about-face in social ethics, stressing the need for social intervention to correct ills that individuals and families, by themselves, could not resolve. In the process they helped transform local and national priorities—and themselves. But the shape of public interest would depend partly on Woodrow Wilson and partly on the other leading political progressive of the era and his great rival: Theodore Roosevelt.

Theodore Roosevelt

Everything in Theodore Roosevelt's background seemed to have prepared him for his aggressive and expansive years in the presidency, which he sometimes called the "bully pulpit." Roosevelt brought a keen mind, unexcelled vigor, a talent for publicity and writing, and a love of politics to the office. He also displayed a Victorian sense of social duty, manliness, and culture.

He was born October 27, 1858, into a wealthy and established New York family. His father, whom he admired immensely, was a gentleman banker with broad interests in social reform and charities. Suffering from delicate health, asthma, and poor vision, young Theodore evoked his parents' concern. They planned long trips to the country and European vacations, and hired tutors to educate their son at home. But it was a strenuous body-building regimen begun after the age of twelve that enabled Teddy to overcome his physical weaknesses. This success dramatically affected his personality. In a sense, it made him a "self-made" man, despite his wealth. It added energy to his efforts and confidence to his ambitions. At the same time, however, it tinged him with excess. Too much self-confidence sometimes became arrogance. And failure could be devastating.

Roosevelt resembled other men of his class who entered politics during the progressive era. Educated at a private preparatory school and then at Harvard, he believed firmly in laissez-faire economics, charity for the poor, and ethical government. Like Woodrow Wilson, he tested other careers before he entered politics. Like the Mugwumps, he had an upper-class background, but unlike them, he made the transition to progressivism, developing and changing with the clash of events.

THE PATH TO THE WHITE HOUSE Roosevelt rose through the ranks of the Republican party by loyally supporting party candidates and pursuing modest reforms. He earned a reputation as a civil service commissioner and later as police commissioner of New York City. In 1896, when William McKinley won the presidency, the Republicans rewarded Roosevelt with the position of assistant secretary of the navy, an appointment he relished.

Roosevelt pushed enthusiastically for a larger navy. When war broke out in April 1898 between the United States and Spain, he quit his position and rushed to organize a cavalry regiment. Telegraphing Western governors for men, he assembled and outfitted a band that became known as the Rough Riders. His major enemy was time. Spain was so weak it might crumble before he could reach the battlefield. The Spanish obliged, however, and held on long enough for Roosevelt to lead a frantic charge up Kettle Hill near San Juan Ridge in Cuba on July 1, 1898. As he wrote in his *Memoirs*, "I waved my hat and we went up the hill with a rush."

Roosevelt's exploits delighted the newspapers and helped win him the nomination for governor of New York. The hero of San Juan Hill squeaked through to victory by about 18,000 votes. In his first term as governor, he pushed through civil service reform and a tax bill on corporations. And he promoted an investigation of a state insurance scandal. When the Republicans renominated McKinley in 1900, Roosevelt stood in line for the vice presidency. Republican bosses who disliked him helped steer him into this position. They reasoned that Roosevelt could do no damage in this powerless and dead-end job. Stumping the country for his ticket, Roosevelt helped deliver a huge majority for the Republicans: 292 electoral votes to 155 for William Jennings Bryan.

The bosses were right. At first, Roosevelt had little to do. But on September 6, 1901, while visiting the Pan-American Exposition in Buffalo, New York, McKinley was struck down by two shots fired by anarchist Leon Czolgosz, and he finally succumbed on September 14. Roosevelt was president. At age forty-two, he was the youngest man yet to assume the presidency. With a command of American and European history, widely read in American fiction, and with a speaking knowledge of French and German, he was one of the best educated men ever to occupy the office.

Roosevelt immediately announced that he would continue McKinley's policies. But in fact, he moved first to ensure his own position in the party. He also initiated a series of steps to consolidate power in his office, dramatically increasing its influence and importance. Thus, as progressivism moved into the White House, Roosevelt began a transformation of the executive branch. During his presidency, Roosevelt actively campaigned and lobbied for legislation he favored and increasingly acted as a broker among the organized national interest groups that were clamoring for or resisting reform, attempting to create what he called a "Square Deal" for the American public.

BUSINESS POLICY Roosevelt's first administration established new guidelines for the behavior of American corporations. In 1903 Congress passed the Elkins Anti-Rebate Act, which prevented railroads from charging special low rates to favored customers. Congress also established a Bureau of Corporations under the new cabinet-level Department of Commerce and Labor. This agency perfectly fitted Roosevelt's philosophy of business regulation. The bureau could control business behavior through its power to investigate and publicize its findings about corporate concentration and monopoly.

The president took other unusual steps to intervene in the economy in the public interest.

President Theodore Roosevelt in Asheville, N.C., 1902. Part of Roosevelt's skill as a politician was his ability to sway crowds of voters. A masterly campaigner, he, as well as other progressives, took their reform message to the people. (Theodore Roosevelt Birthplace Association)

The first occasion came in 1902 during the long anthracite coal strike. In this bitter clash between mine workers and coal operators, Roosevelt leaned toward the miners. The nation demanded action as winter came. The president pushed for arbitration, against the stubborn opposition of the operators. Labeling them unreasonable, he fought to save them "from the dreadful punishment which their own folly would have brought on them if I had not acted."

Roosevelt finally persuaded the owners to accept arbitration. Workers returned to their jobs, and in early 1903 a commission granted some but not all of their demands. The judgment raised wages by 10 percent and established a conciliation board. But the miners did not win union recognition. In fact, the biggest winner was Roosevelt. He had helped end the strike and had moved labor relations to the level of federal responsibility.

Roosevelt earned the reformer's mantle in another well-publicized action. In 1902 his attorney general, Philander C. Knox, instituted a lawsuit under the Sherman Act to dissolve the Northern Securities Corporation. The company typified what Roosevelt considered a "bad" corporation. Certainly he did not oppose bigness or consolidation, but a corporation that existed only to secure a monopoly was another matter. The Northern Securities Corporation resulted from a compromise between two giant railway systems (the Union Pacific–Northern Pacific and the Great Northern) fighting to control rail access to Chicago. The courts decided that the consolidated company must be dissolved, and in 1904 the Supreme Court upheld this decision. Roosevelt was elated by this and other successful trust-busting suits. Thus Roosevelt could be considered either a conservative who staved off more fundamental change or a liberal who forced through a radical reorientation of government policy. Whatever the point of view, however, Roosevelt would occupy center stage of American politics for almost eight years.

With a reputation for activism and good marks earned for his intervention in the coal strike, Roosevelt won the Republican nomination in 1904. He soundly defeated Democrat Alton B. Parker in November and then began a more aggressive legislative program. The railroads continued to be a special concern. They were the nation's biggest business and the favorite target of muckrakers.

Roosevelt actively supported a new regulatory law, the Hepburn Act, named for its sponsor, Congressman Peter Hepburn of Iowa. Passed into law in 1906 after a difficult fight, the act expanded the federal Interstate Commerce Commission and added to its authority. Congress granted the commission power to regulate express companies, sleeping car companies, bridges, ferries, terminals, and oil pipelines. Most important, the agency was granted the power to lower shipping rates that it considered excessive.

Roosevelt also responded to calls to regulate consumer products. Two pioneering measures were passed by Congress in 1906: Spurred by a broad campaign against adulteration of drugs and cosmetics and shocked by the gruesome details of the meat-packing industry revealed in Upton Sinclair's novel *The Jungle*, Congress agreed to the Pure Food and Drug Act in June, which established the Food and Drug Administration, and the Meat Inspection Act in July. The second of these acts, championed by progressive Senator Albert J. Beveridge of Indiana, provided federal inspection for meat sold in interstate commerce. Together, the acts set up the structure to regulate a wide variety of consumer products. In many cases, the affected industries supported this legislation, which, in effect, meant a government stamp of approval for their products. The result was reform that satisfied many activists, consumers, and businessmen. It was a model of Roosevelt's commitment to executive intervention, compromise, and reform in the national public interest in a manner that would not hurt business interests.

OTHER ACHIEVEMENTS The president's other substantial accomplishments came in the withdrawal of public lands from unregulated exploitation. No preservationist or sentimentalist about wildlife, Roosevelt believed in conserving land for a variety of uses: parks, hunting, timbering, and mining. Working with Gifford Pinchot of the U.S. Forest Service (a part of the Agriculture Department), Roosevelt set aside about 150 million acres of public land for restricted use. And he supported reclamation legislation that created dams and irrigation projects. (But when Congress canceled executive power to set aside land in 1907, Roosevelt quickly withdrew a final 16 million acres.) He called this policy of preserving resources the "principle of stewardship."

From 1906 through 1908 in particular, Roosevelt supported other important progressive reforms: establishment of the eight-hour day for railway workers, termination of child labor in the District of Columbia, and a minimum wage. Although Roosevelt was not able to persuade Congress to act on these measures, they reveal his deepening commitment to federally sponsored social reform and his greater adherence to progressive goals.

Yet in other areas that deeply affected millions of Americans, Roosevelt was inactive. The progressive era saw racial tension, sweeping attacks on the voting rights of black Americans, and rigid segregation in the South. Even some black leaders, most notably educationist Booker T. Washington, publicly embraced a strategy of racial separation. Sympathetic to Washington's theories of gradual black self-improvement, Roosevelt appointed several black politicians to patronage jobs early in his presidency. He personally opposed lynchings and disfranchisement, and he even invited Washington to dine at the White House in 1901. But he did little to improve race relations generally. As he told students at Tuskegee vocational school in Alabama in 1905: "The race cannot expect to get everything at once. It must learn to wait and bide its time."

William Howard Taft

In 1908 Roosevelt initiated a course of action that ended with his bitter split from the Republican party in 1912: He kept his promise not to run again for president in 1908 and selected William Howard Taft as his successor. Only superficially was Taft a good choice to follow Roosevelt. A staunch party man with few political debts to pay—except to Roosevelt—Taft would have preferred an appointment to the Supreme Court (which he eventually got in 1921, serving as chief justice until his death in 1930). He was an able administrator but an unimaginative leader. Taft was also unsure about his legislative goals and unsympathetic to the growing band of progressive congressmen in his own party. He lacked their commitment to using government as an arbitrator between contending economic interests. During his four years in office, he relied more and more on conservative Republicans, with whom he shared a natural affinity.

Taft's victory in 1908 came partly because of Roosevelt's aggressive campaign for him. But the presidency became his own. Roosevelt, in a gesture of self-advertisement, sailed off after the inauguration on an African safari to stalk "dangerous game." The new president had to find his own way in the political jungle of Washington.

Taft's cabinet appointments disappointed progressive senators but pleased House Speaker Joseph Cannon, a stalwart Republican conservative. With Senate leader Nelson Aldrich, Cannon and Taft agreed to seek a lower tariff. The president called Congress into special session in March 1909. The House managed to pass a somewhat lower tariff bill, but the Senate actually proposed increases. In a conference committee meeting the two houses compromised. When Taft signed the law in August, there were 654 decreases in rates and 220 increases. The legislation also raised a tax of 1 percent on corporate

Presidential equestrian pose. President William Howard Taft sits astride a horse in front of the Executive Office Building in Washington, D.C. (Culver Pictures)

profits above $5,000. Although Taft proclaimed the legislation a victory—the best revision ever passed by Republicans—progressive congressmen complained that the president had caved in to special manufacturing interests.

Progressives supported other presidential initiatives, however. For example, Congress passed the Mann-Elkins Act in 1910 placing telephone, telegraph, and wireless companies under the jurisdiction of the Interstate Commerce Commission. Congress also established a postal savings bank system. In addition, Taft's administration initiated ninety antitrust suits against large corporations. One of these secured the breakup of Standard Oil. Another, however, against U.S. Steel, seemed an indirect attack on Roosevelt: Roosevelt had given tacit approval to a giant merger of U.S. Steel and the Tennessee Coal

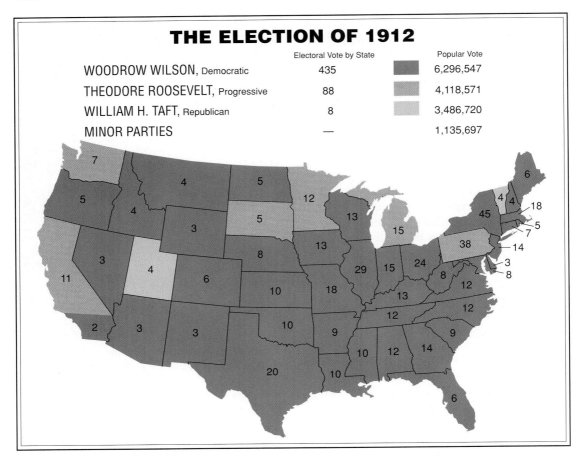

THE ELECTION OF 1912

	Electoral Vote by State		Popular Vote
WOODROW WILSON, Democratic	435		6,296,547
THEODORE ROOSEVELT, Progressive	88		4,118,571
WILLIAM H. TAFT, Republican	8		3,486,720
MINOR PARTIES	—		1,135,697

and Iron Company during the deep recession of 1907; Taft's action implied that Roosevelt had done wrong. Other presidential initiatives helped establish administrative reform: a new Children's Bureau and a separate Department of Labor. Taft also supported the Sixteenth Amendment to the Constitution, legalizing the income tax, and the Seventeenth Amendment, establishing the direct election of senators.

This was an impressive legislative record but no proof of leadership among Republicans. In fact, Taft's hold on the party gradually weakened. Opposition came from two sources: congressional progressives and Roosevelt. By the midterm election of 1910, the Republicans were badly split. Taft encouraged conservatives to challenge

progressives. But the effort backfired. Democrats won the House, and together with Republican progressives, they also controlled the Senate. Early in January 1911, progressives meeting at Wisconsin senator Robert La Follette's Washington residence formed the National Republican Progressive League—with the assumption that La Follette would be their candidate in 1912.

La Follette's chances dimmed, however, when Roosevelt bounded back on stage. Never content to sit on the sidelines, the ex-president was furious at Taft's "betrayal." Taft, he said, had taken a narrow view of the presidency: "Most able lawyers who are past middle age take this view," he added disparagingly. Worse, Taft had forced Gifford Pinchot, Roosevelt's ally, out of office in 1910 in a fight over conservation policy: Taft's secretary of the interior, Richard A. Ballinger, had approved the transfer of several federal sites to private development. Pinchot, still in the Forest Service, had opposed the transfer and taken his case to the public. Forced to choose between the two men, Taft had fired Pinchot.

The Election of 1912

The 1912 election brought progressivism to center stage in American politics, and reoriented both principal parties. The groundswell of progressivism split the Republican party. The Democrats shifted away from their Western leader, William Jennings Bryan, to choose the urban progressivism of Woodrow Wilson. And Eugene Debs challenged conservatives and progressives with his socialist proposals.

In some respects the election tested two competing philosophies of progressivism developed by two extraordinary contemporary thinkers, Louis Brandeis and Herbert Croly. Brandeis, a lawyer who both influenced and advised Wilson and whom Wilson later appointed to the Supreme Court, believed deeply in an economy based on small competing units. The power of government, he argued, should guarantee such a fair contest. But perhaps even more important, in a series of legal briefs Brandeis developed powerful arguments for the constitutionality of social reform legislation. In *Muller* v. *Oregon*, in 1908, he told the Supreme Court that the state of Oregon had the right to limit the workday for women to ten hours. The law, he asserted, had to take account of the conditions of real life. And the facts, he persuaded the justices, made the law compelling.

Herbert Croly, author of *The Promise of American Life* (1909) and editor of the influential journal the *New Republic*, approached the large questions

of government from a different direction. Convinced of the importance of expert guidance of the Republic, he accepted what repelled Brandeis: bigness in industry. Croly admired the growth of huge industries, although he rejected the antisocial, selfish, and ruthless exploitation characteristic of some companies. The solution, he believed, was government regulation, not competition. A revived national spirit meant giving up the old and inappropriate Jeffersonian dream of a nation of small, competing farms and accepting the modern condition of large-scale enterprise. It meant, too, accepting the rights of unions to organize and bargain. These ideas appealed to Roosevelt, who saw them as a justification for many of his actions as president and as a plan for the future.

By February 1912, Roosevelt had stormed into the presidential race. Entering Republican primaries where he could, he piled up significant convention votes, but not enough to control the party machinery. Taft's forces engineered a narrow—but hollow—victory. Roosevelt's delegates withdrew and called for a new party. Meeting in Chicago in August, the new Progressive party nominated Roosevelt at a meeting that joined shrewd politics and revivalism. The delegates, with banners flying, broke into hymns.

Roosevelt's platform promised direct primaries, legislative initiative and referendum, recall of judges, woman suffrage, an end to child labor, the eight-hour day, and a federal trade commission. The candidate's "New Nationalism" was designed to centralize control of the economy in the executive branch. And Roosevelt received important financing from wealthy capitalists like George Perkins, a power in the National Civic Federation.

Taft, the incumbent president, was odd man out. He defended his administration but did little active campaigning. The race pitted Roosevelt against Wilson. But Roosevelt could not overcome the effects of the Republican split. Wilson won more than 6 million votes, Roosevelt more than 4 million, Taft about 3 million, and Debs almost 1 million.

Wilson's Progressivism

Woodrow Wilson brought a special kind of leadership to the White House. His sense of purpose and commitment was unyielding. He believed that his cause was also the nation's. Sympathetic to the plight of the "masses of men," and distressed by the arrogance of wealth, Wilson supported many of the progressive causes. But the new president's vision also had its bounds. His progressivism spoke nominally for the underprivileged. And his vision of government—like his ideal of Princeton—consisted in the exercise of leadership by meritorious gentlemen.

Having proclaimed a "New Freedom" in the election, Wilson set about to institute it. Congress, both houses now firmly Democratic, prepared to help him. Wilson aimed first at eliminating corporate monopoly and other obstacles to free market competition. He strongly believed that the restoration of competition would liberate business talent and prevent the excesses of the greedy few. But proposing competiton was easier than establishing it. Quickly, Wilson accepted reform projects more in tune with Roosevelt's New Nationalism. By the end of 1916 he had begun to advocate centralized executive power and federal economic regulation. And he put these ideals into practice after 1917. When America entered World War I, Wilson began a limited experiment in national economic and social planning.

Wilson appointed a cabinet to represent the various geographic and ideological wings of the Democratic party: Bryan as secretary of state, William B. Wilson, former official of the United Mine Workers, as secretary of labor, and William G. McAdoo, from Georgia, as secretary of the treasury. Like Taft, Wilson began with the tariff and a special session of Congress. But Wilson worked skillfully for lower tariff rates. When lobbyists and conservatives tried to stop him, he took his case to the public. Wilson relished the fight; as so many times in the past, he was con-

vinced that it pitted principle against special narrow interests. He won the struggle. The new law, the Underwood tariff, lowered rates by about 15 percent and attached a small income tax to make up for lost revenues.

Banking also demanded reform. Ever since the financial panic of 1907, Congress had debated the issue. Two solutions emerged. The first, proposed by Arsene Pujo, representative from Louisiana, attacked private banks. The second called for a national banking system controlled by private banks. Wilson steered toward the second position. The resulting Glass–Owen Act of December 1913 established a new federal banking system consisting of twelve regional banks controlled by a Federal Reserve Board appointed by the president. Local banks that joined the system could borrow from the Reserve banks. And the Federal Reserve system could expand or contract credit by lowering or raising the discount rate it charged member banks for loans. This new banking tool of the federal government supplied the power to create a national monetary policy. By expanding or contracting interest rates and the money supply, it could theoretically shrink or increase economic activity. Although this was not a precise tool—and it was only as effective as the wisdom of its board of governors—the Federal Reserve system represented a major step in creating an institution that could potentially guide and protect the economy from the repeated shocks of recession, inflation, and overexpansion.

Trusts, monopolies, and corporations were also a primary concern of the new president. Wilson's New Freedom had promised decisive action to unclog competition. But the problem was not simple. Wilson recognized this and gradually moved away from trust busting to a regulatory approach. Passed in September 1914, the Federal Trade Commission Act, which he supported, incorporated features of Roosevelt's Bureau of Corporations. The commission of five members, appointed by the president, could investigate business combinations and issue "cease and desist" orders where combinations acted illegally. Another law, the Clayton Antitrust

Act, passed a month later, defined antitrust policy more sharply and assured labor that it would not be prosecuted under the Sherman Act.

The second half of Wilson's first term saw reforms aimed at curbing the excesses of labor exploitation. Adoption of these progressive reforms marked a significant (and often controversial) expansion of federal power. Wilson was under considerable pressure from progressives, and he acted. In 1916 he supported the Keating-Owen child labor bill, which banned child labor under the age of fourteen in interstate commerce. (But in 1918, the Supreme Court declared the law unconstitutional.) Wilson also supported the Adamson Act, which set an eight-hour day for railway workers and established, by example, a standard for other industries to follow. He supported a workmen's compensation bill for federal employees. He also signed the Federal Farm Loan Act of 1916, which provided loans for farmers using their land and improvements as security— thus enacting legislation similar to proposals long supported by the Populists.

One of Wilson's most controversial acts endeared him to progressives but drew the ire of conservatives. He nominated Jewish lawyer and activist Louis Brandeis to the Supreme Court in 1916. The American Bar Association and influential political and social leaders were outraged partly because of his ethnic heritage and partly because of his social views. Nonetheless, working with congressional progressives, Wilson secured the appointment. Acts such as these demonstrated the power of Wilson's leadership.

Although Wilson broke important ground by making the first appointment of a Jewish American to the Supreme Court, he followed the inclinations of his Southern heritage when it came to black Americans. Wilson did nothing to defuse the explosive racial situation in the South. By this time, racism in the South, where most African Americans lived, had reached an extraordinary crescendo. In the late 1890s the South was ravaged by hundreds of lynchings, mostly of black men accused of rape or alleged insults to white women. Mob rule executed as many as 156 in 1892 alone. Although the number fell by Wilson's

Louis D. Brandeis. Brandeis's appointment to the Supreme Court in 1916 was noteworthy for several reasons. He was Jewish—the first person of his faith to attain this high office. And he was widely known for his successful advocacy of progressive social reform legislation. (Culver Pictures)

first administration, conditions for blacks did not improve. Indeed, the reorganization of the Ku Klux Klan in 1915 was an ominous sign. The popularity of a 1915 film, *The Birth of a Nation*, shown at the White House and seen throughout the nation, pictured the Klansmen as heroes who saved the South from ruthless exploitation by former slaves during Reconstruction. The acceptance of this brilliant but morally flawed film proved that blacks could count on little understanding in the North for their plight. Even the organization of the National Association for the Advancement of Colored People (NAACP) in

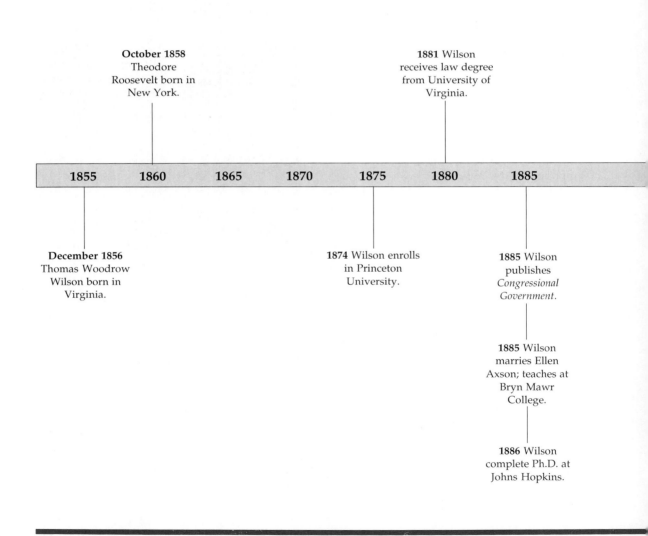

October 1858
Theodore
Roosevelt born in
New York.

1881 Wilson
receives law degree
from University of
Virginia.

| 1855 | 1860 | 1865 | 1870 | 1875 | 1880 | 1885 |

December 1856
Thomas Woodrow
Wilson born in
Virginia.

1874 Wilson enrolls
in Princeton
University.

1885 Wilson
publishes
*Congressional
Government.*

1885 Wilson
marries Ellen
Axson; teaches at
Bryn Mawr
College.

1886 Wilson
complete Ph.D. at
Johns Hopkins.

1889 Jane Addams opens Hull House in Chicago
Andrew Carnegie publishes "The Gospel of Wealth."

1890 Jacob Riis publishes *How the Other Half Lives*. Wilson accepts teaching position at Princeton.

1893 United States enters severe depression period.

1899 Thorstein Veblen publishes *Theory of the Leisure Class*.

1900 McKinley-Roosevelt slate wins presidential election.

1901 Theodore Roosevelt becomes president. Robert LaFollette elected governor of Wisconsin.

1902 *McClure's* magazine begins muckraker articles. Wilson becomes president of Princeton.

1907–1910 Wilson fights for quadrangle plan at Princeton.

1910 Wilson elected governor of New Jersey. Gifford Pinchot fired by President Taft.

1912 Woodrow Wilson elected president over Taft, Roosevelt and Debs.

1913 Glass-Owen Act passed. Wilson appoints Louis Brandeis to the Supreme Court. Sixteenth Amendment ratified confirming right of Congress to collect income taxes; Seventeenth Amendment ratified providing for direct election of senators.

1920 Nineteenth Amendment ratified, giving women the right to vote.

1890	1895	1900	1905	1910	1915	1920

1894 Coxey's "army" marches on Washington; Pullman workers go on strike.

1895 Booker T. Washington delivers his "Atlanta Compromise" speech.

1895 National Association of Manufacturers formed.

1896 Theodore Roosevelt becomes assistant secretary of the navy. Wilson suffers a slight stroke.

1898 Theodore Roosevelt forms the Rough Riders.

1903–1906 Roosevelt's progressive measures enacted by Congress.

1904 Roosevelt reelected president.

1906 Wilson suffers second stroke.

1908 William Howard Taft elected president.

1914 Federal Trade Commission established. Clayton Antitrust Act passed.

1916 Keating-Owen Act passed. Wilson reelected over Charles E. Hughes of New York.

1918 Eighteenth Amendment ratified, imposing Prohibition.

1910 was only a first, small step in a battle against enormous odds.

Wilson did nothing to prevent the disfranchisement of Southern blacks by means of poll taxes or literacy tests. Indeed, his record was worse than the benign neglect of the Republicans. A firm believer in segregation, he allowed his cabinet to segregate federal jobs and downgrade or fire black employees. Wilson's defense of his actions suggests the serious limitations of his progressivism. Writing in 1913, he said:

> It is true that the segregation of the colored employees in the several departments was begun upon the initiative and at the suggestion of the heads of departments, but as much as in the interest of the negroes as for any other reason, with the approval of some of the most influential negroes I know, and with the idea that the friction, or rather the discontent and uneasiness, which had prevailed in many departments would thereby be removed. It is as far as possible from being a movement *against* the negroes. I sincerely believe it to be in their interest.

By 1916 Wilson had achieved party unity around his program of regulation and reform. The Republicans, still smarting from the split of 1912, nominated Charles Evans Hughes for president. Roosevelt supported him. Despite numerous advantages, Wilson won only a close victory. Progressives and peace advocates had probably provided the margin of victory.

Ironically, although the issue of peace had helped carry the election of 1916, it was the issue of war that preoccupied Wilson's second term. Europe exploded in 1914, as the major powers rushed into battle. When the United States was drawn into the conflict in 1917, Wilson turned to progressive ideas of regulation, creating an unprecedented system of planning and control of the economy. The demands of war accelerated the tendency of the executive branch to oversee the American economy. And Wilson gained considerable power to effect such changes through such legislation as the Overman Act of 1918, which allowed the president to reorganize executive agencies.

During the war, Wilson also extended his commitment to progressivism by advocating, as he had previously refused to do, votes for women. In September 1918, he urged the Senate to approve a constitutional amendment to grant suffrage to all Americans regardless of sex. He cited the "unusual circumstances of a world war."

Yet by supporting restrictions on free speech and empowering a vast public relations campaign to sell the war to Americans, Wilson extended government into controversial areas. In doing so, he kindled doubts about his leadership. Did he not see that others might have a valid, if different, sense of the public's interest? Was it sufficient to be confident in a righteous cause? This singlemindedness had long been a potential problem. Now it provoked a major crisis.

Quite possibly political writer Walter Lippmann was right about Wilson—and progressivism—when he said:

> The inner contradiction of Woodrow Wilson [is that he] knows that there is a new world demanding new methods, but he dreams of an older world. He is torn between the two. It is a very deep conflict in him between what he knows and what he feels.

Suggestions for Further Reading

PROGRESSIVISM

The literature on progressivism is both extensive and fascinating. One fine and very readable general account in Robert Wiebe, *The Search for Order, 1877–* 1920 (1967). A very different view of progressivism that stresses corporate interest in reforming the most flagrant and dangerous social injustices is James Weinstein, *The Corporate Ideal in the Liberal State,*

1900–1918 (1968). Geoffrey Blodgett examines the politics and ideology of the forerunners of the progressives in *The Gentle Reformers: Massachusetts Democrats in the Cleveland Era* (1966). Progressivism on a state level is skillfully reconstructed by David Thelen in *Robert M. La Follette and the Insurgent Spirit* (1985). As a national movement, progressivism developed because of publicity and journalistic exposés. Louis Filler, *The Muckrakers* (1976), is a revised edition of the classic work on reform publicists.

MOVEMENTS

In some respects, progressivism was the sum of contemporary social movements. One of the most important of these was Prohibition. Jack S. Blocker, Jr., *Alcohol, Reform, and Society: The Liquor Issue in Social Context* (1979), discusses this very significant movement in relation to other reform programs. Women played a key role in Prohibition, but, increasingly during the era, they also concentrated on securing the vote. Aileen Kraditor, in *The Ideas of the Woman Suffrage Movement* (1981), recounts the arguments for and against woman suffrage. An essential element in this turbulent era of reform was widespread interest in socialism. James Green's fine work, *Grass-Roots Socialism* (1978), documents the extensive socialist movement that grew up in the American Southwest during the progressive era. Reform inside the factory was, in many respects, as extensive as social reform at large. Daniel Nelson in *Frederick W. Taylor and the Rise of Scientific Management* (1980) examines Taylor's management ideas and

their relationship to progressivism. Intellectuals as well as workers, managers, and politicians were deeply affected by the swift changes of the opening century. Christopher Lasch, *The New Radicalism in America, 1889–1963* (1965), contains an outstanding discussion of new attitudes toward the self and society. For another view of the culture of progressivism, see Robert M. Crunden, *Ministers of Reform* (1982). Nick Salvatore, *Eugene V. Debs* (1982), is a crucial biography of this popular socialist and union leader.

PRESIDENTS

The two commanding political figures of the progressive era were Theodore Roosevelt and Woodrow Wilson. George E. Mowry, *Theodore Roosevelt and the Progressive Movement* (1946), is a fine older work and a good starting place for the study of the Roosevelt presidency. A fast-paced, very readable biography of Roosevelt's early years is David G. McCulloch, *Mornings on Horseback* (1981). On Roosevelt and Wilson see John Milton Cooper, *The Warrior and the Priest* (1983). Of all the political leaders of the era, Wilson has received the closest scrutiny. Arthur S. Link set the standard for this scholarship in his excellent *Woodrow Wilson and the Progressive Era, 1910–1917* (1954). John M. Mulder, *Woodrow Wilson: Years of Preparation* (1976), is a careful and fascinating study of Wilson's early years. An ingenious medical and psychological study of Wilson is Edwin Weinstein, *Woodrow Wilson: A Medical and Psychological Biography* (1981).

CHAPTER 18
IMPERIAL AMERICA

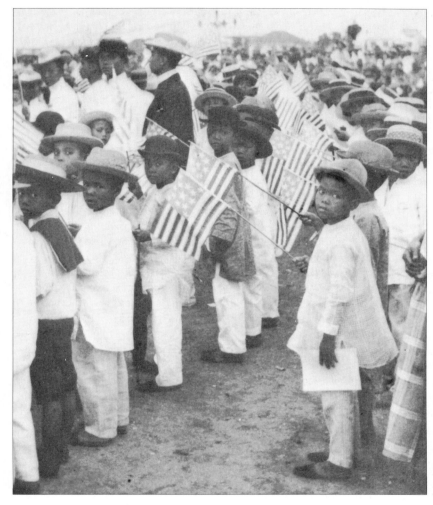

THE EPISODE: *In 1901, thousands of miles away from home, American soldiers were locked in a bloody war against an entrenched and popular guerrilla army in the former Spanish colony of the Philippines. Frustrated by a hostile population, deceived by local politicians playing on both sides, and impeded by terrible weather, jungle, and mountains, the American army vented its anger on the local population. The events on the island of Samar were among the worst aspects of this attempt to make the Philippines an American possession. The political presence of the United States, led by William Howard Taft, pursued hegemony in other ways: by improving social services and fiscal stability in government and by financing improvements such as schools and medical clinics. These two policies of force and persuasion reflected a divided and uncertain command. The result was disastrous.*

THE HISTORICAL SETTING: *By 1900 the United States had for some time been an important nation in world politics and, increasingly, a power in international economics. With a revolutionary tradition that faced inward and a policy that tried to avoid European wars and colonial expansion, the United States was, nonetheless, an active, expansive nation on the North American continent and in Latin America. By the end of the century, this isolation from Europe's politics was ending, partly to preserve the role of the*

United States as the dominant power in the Western Hemisphere. But a strong sense of moral superiority also convinced leaders like Woodrow Wilson that the United States could transform the old, tired European balance of power and lead others into a new world order based upon the American experience of democracy.

The Philippine war was an important step in the development of American internationalism. In the late 1890s the United States surveyed a world increasingly divided by cutthroat competition for trade and influence. European nations pursued expansionist policies that led to a scramble to conquer the remaining area of the world lying outside established colonial empires. After the United States went to war with Spain in 1898, American leaders found themselves with important choices to make about the spoils of victory. Should they keep the islands of the Caribbean to maintain an exclusive trade and defensive zone or should they release these nations to their own devices? Should the army seize the Philippines as an American colony or grant them independence? Suddenly, the United States found itself with a colonial empire and the possibility to acquire even more. Yet by the time of World War I, the nation's leaders were determined not to become another imperialist power along the lines of European nations. Thus, the United States kept itself aloof even as it plunged into one of the most brutal European wars.

THE CONQUESTS OF THE PHILIPPINES

The month of October, in the year of 1901,
Eventful in its history for the bloodshed it had run;
Soldiers and marines received orders to proceed without delay,
And avenge a nation's honor in the blood that passed away.

The memory of those comrades, who in China side by side
Did share our tribulation with courage and with pride,
And it was in the town of Balangiga, where those martyrs at their post
Were soon despatched by bolos, for there they gave up the ghost.

PRIVATE PATRICK CATHSEM, C Company of
9th Infantry, United States Marine Corps

The eighty-eight American troops of company C, 9th Infantry, gathered in the scorching early-morning sun of September 27, 1901, to eat breakfast. Some were eagerly reading or rereading mail that had arrived just the day before, after a long delay. Because it was Sunday, they skipped their usual duty of mustering out the larger group of Filipino workers who had been rounded up to clear the town of Balangiga, on the island of Samar, of garbage and jungle undergrowth that might conceal revolutionary troops. But it was not just any Sunday for the Marines. In fact, the American soldiers, who had just learned the terrible news of the assassination of President William McKinley, were expected to form at 8 A.M. for a eulogy and memorial Mass at the local Catholic church.

This break in the routine was not the only extraordinary event planned for that morning. The night before, the local priest had suddenly disappeared; Captain Thomas W. Connell, in charge of Company C, could not locate him to make arrangements for the eulogy service. Indeed, none of the clergy, normally found at the church, could be located.

About midnight the previous evening, a group of women had slipped into the area bearing small wooden caskets. To a suspicious American sentry, the women had explained that they were mourners, carrying the pitiful corpses of children struck down by a cholera epidemic in the countryside. The sentry ordered one casket opened,

American soldiers relax at a typical thatch-roofed mess hall in the Philippines. (Library of Congress)

but a quick glance confirmed that a child lay inside, so he ordered the box resealed and carried into the church. Had he looked further, he would have discovered, beneath the child, a bed of bolos (deadly machetes used by Filipino revolutionaries in close combat). And he also might have realized that many of the mourners were actually men in disguise.

So Sunday morning began with the Americans preparing to commemorate a fallen leader and the whole Filipino community anticipating an attack. It began by prearranged signal. The local chief of police, strolling by, stopped to chat with an American sentry. Suddenly, he seized the sentry's rifle, turned it around, and shot the American. At the same moment, armed revolutionaries poured out of the church, racing for the officers' headquarters, the mess, and the arsenal that held the company weapons. Filipinos working in the cleanup project joined in with the attackers. Captain Connell leaped out of his room, but the charging bolomen cut him down in the street. Most of the American soldiers fought with whatever weapon they could improvise: baseball bats, shovels, tent poles, and the few rifles snatched out of the arsenal before it was overrun. There were enough rifles and ammunition for one withering stand against charging bolomen. But the Americans had to retreat.

With all the other officers dead, Sergeant Frank Berton led the remaining thirty-eight men toward three dugout canoes. Leaping in, the men rowed along the island's coast until they reached the nearby town of Basey, where Company G was head-quartered. All along the route they were harassed by gunfire from Filipinos shooting

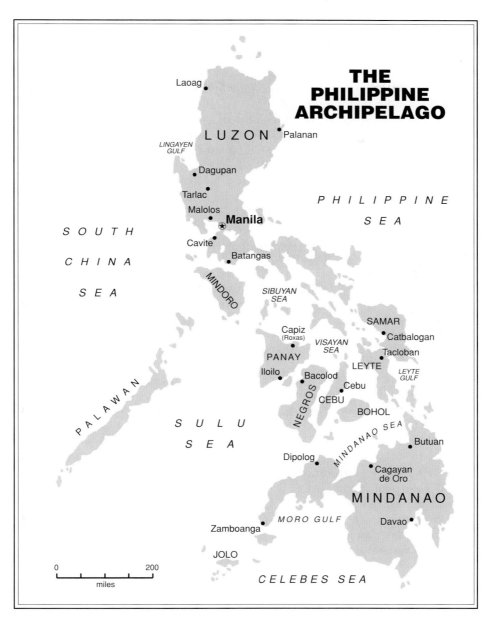

THE PHILIPPINE ARCHIPELAGO

Laoag

LUZON

Palanan

LINGAYEN GULF

Dagupan

Tarlac

Malolos

Manila

Cavite

Batangas

PHILIPPINE SEA

SOUTH CHINA SEA

MINDORO

SIBUYAN SEA

Capiz (Roxas)

VISAYAN SEA

PANAY

Iloilo

Bacolod

Cebu

CEBU

NEGROS

SAMAR

Catbalogan

Tacloban

LEYTE

LEYTE GULF

BOHOL

MINDANAO SEA

Butuan

SULU SEA

Dipolog

Cagayan de Oro

PALAWAN

MINDANAO

MORO GULF

Davao

Zamboanga

JOLO

CELEBES SEA

0   200

miles

newly captured American rifles. When they reached their destination, only six men remained unscathed. Of the total force of eighty-eight, fifty-nine men had died and twenty-three were wounded.

Immediately, the commander at Basey assembled a troop to return to Balangiga on a revenge mission. Over fifty volunteers quickly came forward, including the six uninjured soldiers from Company C. Rushing back in the gunship *Pittsburgh*, the troops turned their cannon and Gatling guns on any movement in the jungle. When the *Pittsburgh* stopped at the shoreline, its angry American troops rushed into the town with bayonets drawn. The few Filipinos discovered were shot on the spot, although the town seemed eerie and empty. But the horrifying evidence of the attack was everywhere: weapons stolen, food stores opened and carried off, and the bodies of fallen American troops mutilated.

As the soldiers pushed on to the edge of town, they came upon an enormous common grave freshly dug for the bodies of the Filipinos killed in the attack. Captain Bookmiller, the new American commander, halted the funeral in progress. Some of his sentries had discovered about twenty Filipino men, probably gravediggers, hiding nearby and marched them to the grave site. The commander then ordered them to pull the bodies of the Filipinos out, and bury the dead Americans in their place. This finished, the American troops held a short service. The dead Filipinos were piled together, soaked with kerosene, and burned in a huge pyre. The commander then ordered the gravediggers to face a firing squad made up of the six survivors of Company C. As the men of Company C moved back to their ship, they burned what remained of Balangiga.

When news of the attack reached the United States, the press, an active though divided player in the dramatic debate over what to do with the Philippine Islands, burst into accusations, blaming political and military leaders for coddling the Filipinos, for failing to realize that the islands had not been pacified, and for ignoring the ability of the Filipino independence movement to deliver such swift, punishing, and brutal action.

In the Philippines, General Adna Chaffee, commander of the American forces there, blamed Governor William Howard Taft and his civilian Philippine Commission for indecisiveness and for impeding a swift, decisive military victory. Taft, for his part, feared that Balangiga represented the inevitable consequences of an iron-fisted military policy. Although originally opposed to keeping the island colony as the spoils of war with Spain in 1898, he became convinced that once dominating them the United States should win over the hearts and minds of the Filipino people. To persuade them, he advised a program of firmly guided democracy and a reform policy of "benevolent assimilation," which was President McKinley's phrase. But two years of bloody warfare had proved that many Filipinos preferred their own self-government, whatever its character, to American democracy installed at the end of a rifle.

While the press and Congress clamored for an explanation of the surprise attack on Balangiga, the American occupation army planned to recapture the arms lost in the battle, to suppress the Filipino rebel army still controlling the island of Samar, and to avenge their fallen comrades. General Chaffee sanctioned new orders governing the behavior of American troops. Filipino attacks on Americans were redefined as murder, in which case a prisoner of war could face execution. Populations living outside the main towns in Batangas, an unpacified province south of Manila on the island of Luzon, were ordered into relocation centers, then towns, villages, and crops were burned and livestock dispersed. As news of this policy reached the United States, opponents and supporters of the war focused their attention on Balangiga and other examples of brutality in Senate hearings on the war chaired by Senator Henry Cabot Lodge.

These residents of Samar, obviously dressed in their best, pose for a visiting cameraman. Much of what Americans knew about the Philippines came from such photographs. (Library of Congress)

In the Philippines, the Army command concentrated on a strategy to crush the remaining rebellion in Samar. Samar was sparsely populated and lay halfway down the archipelago of the Philippines. With a spine of rugged, jungle-covered mountains, it had few towns other than Balangiga and Basey. Most of its usable land was devoted to raising hemp. The population was intensely loyal to the Philippine independence movement; the local leader, General Vincente Lukban, was the mastermind of the surprise attack on Balangiga. He and his men had become doubly dangerous because they now possessed an important store of captured American weapons and ammunition.

To suppress this pocket of insurrection, General Chaffee called on General Jacob Smith, a leader of the pacification of Batangas province and an experienced Indian fighter and veteran of Wounded Knee. Known to his men as "Hell Roaring Jake," Smith inspired fear and respect despite his diminutive stature. He organized a special force of 300 Marines, led by Major Littleton Waller, an officer with considerable experience in China and Egypt. Smith gave Waller clear and deadly orders: "I want no prisoners. I wish you to kill and burn; the more you kill and burn the better it will please me. I want all persons killed who are capable of bearing arms in actual hostilities against the United States." When Waller asked for clarification, Smith said that these orders applied to any male over "ten years of age."

Waller planned three operations for the fall of 1901: local search-and-destroy missions, a surprise attack on General Lukban's headquarters, and a forced march across the island to split the remaining rebel strongholds. Private John H. Clifford recalled the first operation in his diary:

> I never will forget this experience. I had just been taken off the sick report on Sunday, a bright November morning. A detachment went on a hike, with Second Lieutenant in charge. The first thing we got was wet feet in the rice fields; then a big hill to climb and through the woods we discovered a lonely shack built near a lot of trees. An investigation was made by the picket [an advance detachment], and the result was he found a knapsack, blanket, clothing, and the company chest. They all belonged to Company C. The boys divided the goods amongst themselves. We killed pigs, hens and cattle and destroyed the plantation, and then proceeded on our way as though nothing had happened. About a mile from this place we burned six fishing boats, a large pile of hemp, and we helped ourselves to the coconuts. It was getting late, so we returned on another trail. We discovered a shack of nipanipa [made of palm fronds] between some coconut trees and a man jumped out of the window. Several shots were fired, but we never knew whether we hit him or not. In the house there was a crippled old man and a young girl, probably his daughter. She was sitting on the floor. The house was surrounded by guards; I was one of them. We found a soldier's blue shirt, trousers, shoes, and a photo of a young man in civilian dress. There were also bloodstained bolos. Evidently they had been implicated in the massacre of Company C. When the boys saw these things, it made them mad, so they put the people to death and destroyed the place.

Returning to their base camp, the Americans made their way through the jungle in the dark, walking single file to avoid the deep pits dug by Filipino revolutionaries and filled with pointed stakes. When they finally returned home, the troops were exhausted: "We were hungry, wet and tired, and several of the men had chills and fever, while many were under the doctor's care with swelling of the feet caused by long hikes, and sore eyes."

The second campaign, against General Lukban, required guile and surprise. Waller located the general's headquarters on the Sohoton Cliffs overlooking the Caducan River in the interior of Samar. On November 15, 1901, he prepared a two-pronged attack. Placing a heavy gun on a raft, he assigned a first group to move up the river. Meanwhile, he ordered a second squad to set out overland to approach the rebel headquarters from the rear. Unable to penetrate close enough along the river to bring his guns into play, Waller's naval maneuver could do little to dislodge Lukban. But his other troops reached high terrain above the camp, from which they laid down a withering machine gun barrage that forced the terrified Filipinos to flee through a hail of bullets.

Lukban was routed and his headquarters destroyed, but his organization on Samar still remained powerful. Waller now moved into his third operation. To dislodge the organization's remnants, the commander decided to split the interior of the island. Thus he began sketching plans for his fateful march from the American base at Lanang to the town of Basey, about forty miles across the southern part of the island.

In some respects, Waller's decision is deeply puzzling. Perhaps he was reacting to a note from his commanding officer General Smith, urging him to turn the interior of Samar into a "howling Wilderness." But there was undoubtedly more to his rash

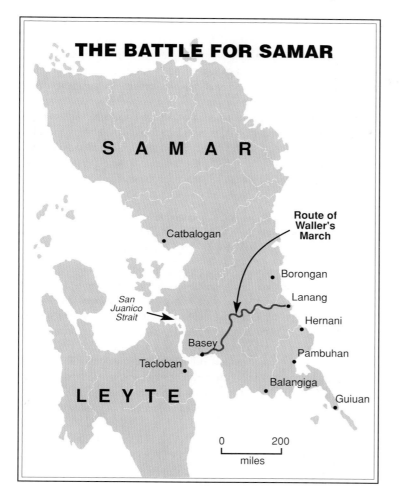

THE BATTLE FOR SAMAR

S A M A R

Catbalogan

Route of Waller's March

Borongan

San Juanico Strait

Lanang

Hernani

Basey

Pambuhan

Tacloban

Balangiga

L E Y T E

Guiuan

0   200
miles

decision than this cryptic biblical reference. Waller may well have believed that the march would be easy and that he could demonstrate to the Filipinos the mobility and power of his troops. Whatever his reasons, it was a mistake.

Waller and his men set out in December 1901 with only four days' supply of field rations but a full store of unwarranted optimism. The American troops and their Filipino bearers soon confronted torrential rains, swirling streams, and steep terrain. After three days, Waller realized that many of his troops were too weakened to continue, so he split his forces. He placed Captain David Porter in charge of the weaker men and instructed them to build rafts to float downstream, back to Lanang. Waller proposed to continue forward with his remaining group overland to Basey.

As instructed, Porter ordered his Filipino bearers to cut trees and fashion them into rafts. But these makeshift boats sank into the torrent. Desperate, fatigued, and low on supplies, Porter unwisely set out by foot, trying to retrace his steps to Lanang. He dispatched two messengers to catch up to Waller and inform him of his decision.

When Waller learned of Porter's move, he was shocked at the dangerous turn of events. Nonetheless, he continued forward toward Basey, hoping that common sense would force Porter either to stop or turn around again. When he finally reached Basey, Waller was sick with jungle fever and growing increasingly suspicious that his Filipino bearers were plotting against him. But he gathered fresh troops and plunged back into the jungle to rescue Porter and his men.

Unfortunately, Porter had neither stopped nor turned around. Instead, he pushed on toward Lanang, abandoning first one group of thirty-three men and eighteen bearers and then four more Marines who could not keep up. Finally, on January 11, 1902, with three other Marines he staggered into Lanang and collapsed. A relief column was immediately dispatched to rescue the two groups of men remaining in the jungle. As one survivor recalled:

> Our company got lost; we were without food, and in a terrible condition. Every man had sore feet, fever and was weak from lack of food and blind from leeches. We could not carry our belts or rifles, but just barely drag ourselves under a tree.

Facing these dire physical conditions, the thirty-three Marines who remained behind, commanded by a Lieutenant Williams, discovered another danger: a possible insurrection by their bearers. Increasingly nervous about the stock of bolos used by the Filipinos to cut through the jungle, Williams demanded that the weapons be kept under American guard at night. But several disappeared. Suddenly one evening when Williams ordered the bearers to gather some firewood, the missing bolos reappeared in Filipino hands. Several of the bearers attacked Williams, but failing to kill him, fled into the jungle. Furious, the lieutenant decided that next morning all the bearers should be shot. At this point, the relief column from Lanang appeared and escorted the exhausted men back to the American base. Ten of the bearers straggled into Lanang shortly thereafter.

Waller, now desperately ill and delirious from fever, returned to Basey, only to receive messages of the disaster that had befallen Porter and Williams. Worse, he heard rumors of a plot by Filipinos in Basey to repeat the massacre of Balangiga. The accused ringleaders, a merchant and the local mayor, were shot by a military firing squad. Waller then ordered two more conspirators to be executed and their bodies placed in a public square as a visible lesson to others.

At this point, a ship from Lanang arrived, carrying the ten Filipino bearers in chains. When he heard of the attack on Williams in the jungle, Waller became enraged and ordered the men shot. Survivors of the march crawled out of their sickbeds to volunteer for the firing squad. Without trial or a moment's hesitation, the Filipinos were dispatched, with their bodies left in the square of Basey to impress other would-be opponents of the Americans. As standard procedure Waller informed his commander, General Smith, who in turn relayed the information to the Army commander of the Philippines, General Chaffee.

When Waller's outfit was finally relieved on February 26, 1902, he and his men sailed back to the main U.S. naval base at Cavite in Manila Bay, heroes to the American soldiers who had heard of his dangerous trek and his vengeance against the Filipinos. Few questioned the reasoning behind his strategically inept traipses back and forth through the jungles of Samar. And certainly few sympathized with the surprise greeting that awaited Waller in Cavite: a summons to appear at a court-martial trial.

Philippine prisoners of war, held in a makeshift camp. The lounging, relaxed attitude of prisoners and their guards, posed for the photographer, misrepresents the ferocity of the war. (Library of Congress)

The shocked Marine commander appeared before his fellow officers on March 17, 1902. After some initial sparring over procedure, the court began its deliberations, with the astute Waller overseeing his own defense. At first, he claimed justification for all his decisions in the guidelines set out in the Army General Orders #100, a handbook outline of field practices. But when the prosecution convinced his commander, General Smith, to testify against him, Waller switched his defense. He produced written orders and confirmations of the verbal instructions he had received from Smith to burn, kill, and destroy. The court had little choice but to acquit him. Now the deflected guilt fell on Smith, who was ordered before the court.

In May, Smith began his testimony, defending himself and his orders also on the basis of the General Orders #100. Unrepentant to the end, he refused to acknowledge that he might have spoken metaphorically: He meant literally what he had told Waller. The only way to win the war was to shoot and burn out the "treacherous savages," he declared. Almost without choice, the court convicted the general of "conduct to the prejudice of good order and military discipline." This admonition was his only sentence.

The ordeal of Samar did not end with the conviction and mild reproof to Smith. For a time it threatened to engulf General Chaffee, Secretary of War Elihu Root, and Theodore Roosevelt, the new president of the United States and an enthusiastic and early proponent of seizing the Philippines as an American colony. Democratic party newspapers, as well as groups and journals associated with the anti-imperialist movement (opposed to keeping the Philippines), proclaimed that Samar and other American examples of brutality and torture proved their case against colonialism. America, in setting out on a course of empire, ran the risk of betraying its first principles.

Imperialism incurred more costs than any of its eager supporters had anticipated. The war against Spain that had brought the United States sovereignty over the Philippines had inflicted only a few hundred casualties (many more were lost to disease); it ended in 1898 almost as soon as it was declared. But the war to control the once-Spanish colony of the Philippines lasted three bitter years. Over 4,000 American lives were lost, with 20,000 Filipino combatants killed and an estimated 250,000 other Filipino civilians dead from starvation, disease, and combat. A deeply divided American nation, with a curious set of crossed purposes and conflicting aims, had stumbled into a policy that had enormous consequences.

The situation was also filled with ironies. At almost the same time that Samar and other holdout areas of the Philippines were crumbling under the military offensive, the U.S. Congress, on July 2, 1902, passed the first organic act of the Philippines. This comprehensive bill, designed to confirm the relationship between the United States and its new colony, defined that relationship in terms of American law, culture, and political power. It signaled benevolent intentions. For example, all Filipino citizens would be protected by a bill of rights to guard against arbitrary government. Following a census, the United States would establish an elected assembly that could pass laws (subject to the approval of the U.S. Congress). But the islands would not be independent.

The United States arrived at this position after several years of military intervention and a protracted argument over policy. The ordeal on Samar was a final, bitter incident in the unexpected guerrilla war that the United States had fought for three years. But this had never been the American intention. The United States had acquired title to the Philippines as a result of the short war and treaty with Spain in 1898. However, the actual dispute and the war between Spain and the United States had nothing to do with the Philippines.

The Spanish-American War began and ended auspiciously; in fact, it lasted barely three months. After a naval victory in Santiago, Cuba, and two widely reported and publicized Army victories in the hills around that city, including Theodore Roosevelt's celebrated charge up San Juan Hill, there were few important engagements except in the Philippines. There, on May 1, 1898, the United States fleet cornered and destroyed the Spanish fleet in Manila Bay. The war for the independence of Cuba ended. Now the war for the conquest of the Philippines was about to begin, although at this point it was not clear who the enemy would be: the remaining Spanish colonial troops or the Filipinos themselves.

By the end of the first week in May 1898, President McKinley acknowledged the confusing situation in the Philippines, although he had not developed a clear policy. From Admiral Dewey he learned that about 10,000 Spanish troops still held Manila and other Philippine cities. He also discovered that Filipino revolutionaries opposed to the Spanish had massed as many as 30,000 troops around Manila. McKinley quickly ordered Major General Wesley Merritt to gather an American expeditionary force in San Francisco. The first troops arrived in the Philippines on June 30, 1898, 7,000 miles from home and without a clear purpose other than to eliminate the Spanish army.

Awaiting American troops, Admiral Dewey, operating out of the naval base at Cavite across the bay from Manila, decided to employ the Filipino revolutionaries against the remaining Spanish army forces. He had invited their leader, Emilio Aguin-

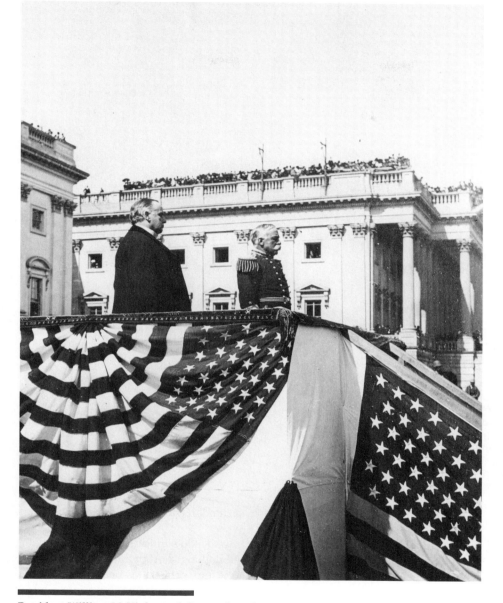

President William McKinley and Commodore George Dewey: Two of the principal decision-makers in the Spanish-American War. (Library of Congress)

aldo, in exile in Hong Kong, China, to join him as soon as possible. Aguinaldo and his aides arrived at Cavite on May 19 and immediately set out to reinvigorate the Filipino rebellion against the Spanish. Very quickly, local Filipino militias and revolutionary groups joined Aguinaldo, so that by mid-June, even before the American troops arrived, Spanish power on the central island of Luzon and in other parts of

Emilio Aguinaldo dons a western-style uniform. Although this dress gives the impression of a European leader (and that was, no doubt, its purpose), Aguinaldo was forced, by circumstances, to lead a guerrilla army. (Library of Congress)

the nation was crumbling. Town after town surrendered to the Filipino revolutionaries, many without even a struggle.

Perhaps to an uninformed outsider, Aguinaldo's quick success in organizing military and civil support would have seemed nothing short of miraculous. But then, few outsiders knew that the revolution against the Spanish was persistent and deep among Filipinos or that Aguinaldo was one of its tested leaders. Born into a mixed Chinese-Filipino family of moderate wealth, Aguinaldo was an important nationalist leader in a tradition that extended well back into the nineteenth century.

There were various threads of independence movements in the Philippines by the 1890s, but the most important one was the Katipunan, a secret society combining both intense revolutionary and religious sentiments. When the Spanish discovered the society, members were forced to declare independence prematurely, then turned to armed struggle on several of the largest islands. Aguinaldo was a latecomer to the Katipunan, but he quickly rose to leadership because of his military and administrative skills. He also wrote a Philippine framework for government based on the American Constitution.

Despite some early successes in 1896 against the Spanish, Aguinaldo's forces were defeated, so he retreated to a mountainous region near Manila to pursue a guerrilla war. Finally, a peace treaty of sorts was signed. In exchange for Aguinaldo going into exile, the Spanish promised reforms and the payment of damages. But by 1898, peace had broken down again as both sides reneged on their promises. In March 1898 the insurrection burst forth again and Aguinaldo prepared to return to the Philippines. When escorted to Luzon by the Americans, the Filipino leader was returning to an established, ongoing revolutionary struggle, with a long history and a developing sense of nationhood.

As Spanish power declined, Aguinaldo stepped in to build a revolutionary government in its place. On May 24, 1898, he proclaimed himself dictator and promised to institute a civilian government as soon as the islands were completely liberated. In late June he issued proclamations calling for local and municipal elections. Effective control of the islands, in all but a few areas, principally Manila, now lay in the hands of the revolutionaries. While they waited for troops, the Americans in the Philippines recognized two major forces to contend with: the remnants of the Spanish army holed up in Manila, and Aguinaldo's revolutionary Filipino government.

Understandably, relations between Aguinaldo and the American commander worsened. Aguinaldo presumed that the Americans supported Philippine independence; after all, they had summoned him to organize his revolutionary army and allowed him to increase his hold on the areas outside of Manila. At the same time, however, American military men treated Aguinaldo with growing hostility. In part, they were guided by instructions from Washington. On May 26 the Secretary of the Navy cabled Dewey, warning him against any permanent arrangements with Filipino forces that might limit future U.S. actions. By mid-June, messages from Washington instructed Dewey to avoid any agreement with Aguinaldo that might appear to legitimize the power of the revolutionaries. Finally, the American expeditionary force began to arrive.

When they took up their positions, the American soldiers found that Filipino revolutionaries had the Spanish pinned down in Manila. Aguinaldo reluctantly allowed American forces to station themselves around the city, in effect replacing some of his own troops. Then on August 1 General Merritt arrived to take command. With a total contingent of 10,000 men, the Americans considered that an assault on Manila was now possible.

American preparations for an assault dramatically increased tension with Aguinaldo's forces. Two armies, in effect, planned to attack Manila. Each of these "allies" regarded the other as an intruder. But because of his superior firepower, Merritt insisted on the sole right to attack and occupy Manila. When the strike finally came on August 13, American forces advancing into the city met almost no resistance. Spanish power in most of its colony had already faded. Now in control of the capital, Merritt insisted that Aguinaldo and his forces retreat to the outskirts of the city; joint

General Arthur MacArthur's headquarters and telegraph station outside Manila, August 13, 1898, the day of the American attack on that city. (Library of Congress)

occupation was not possible. In one day, with the miserable remnant of Spanish power crushed, the two uneasy allies became enemies. The American and Filipino armies now turned their guns on each other.

Four days later the U.S. commander received a message from Washington suggesting that the assault on Manila had probably been unnecessary. Spanish and American representatives had signed a protocol on August 12 ending the war. Among other things, Spain granted the United States the right to occupy Manila until a formal treaty would settle all the unresolved issues between the two nations. The message also ordered Merritt to insist that the Filipino insurgents recognize the legitimacy of American occupation. Furthermore, Merritt was commanded to enforce this order with "whatever means in your judgment are necessary to this end."

Thus the fate of the former Spanish colony now lay with Washington, although the administration ducked taking a clear stand. Over the summer, pressure on McKinley grew as senators, the press, and other groups urged him to keep the Philippines. Of many justifications, Britain's reasoning was particularly persuasive. Fearing the rise of German and Japanese naval power and imperial adventurism, Britain urged America to keep the entire nation, not just Manila or even a naval base.

In late August, General Elwell S. Otis replaced Merritt as commander of the Philippines, while Merritt embarked for Paris, where peace negotiators from Spain and the United States were gathering. He assured all parties that Aguinaldo's rebellion was limited; there would be no violence if the Americans took over administration of the islands.

While he was making these unfounded claims, sporadic fighting had already broken out between American troops and Filipinos. Some incidents resulted from drunkenness or insults to natives by American soldiers. But more serious clashes occurred as Filipino and American armies jockeyed for position around Manila. After a tense standoff in early September, Aguinaldo drew his troops back away from American lines. But in October, General Otis demanded that Aguinaldo pull back even further. The Filipino general agreed because at the moment he was concentrating on extending his power over the rest of the islands. By fall he had largely succeeded. The Americans controlled the seas, Cavite, and Manila. Aguinaldo's government assumed power elsewhere.

Although President McKinley generally understood the military situation in the Philippines, neither he, General Otis, nor his advisers fully realized the consequences of annexing the island nation. Furthermore, the president had to make his decision within an increasingly furious fight in Washington about imperialism. A real calculation of the costs in lives and money was rarely visible as the press and congressmen debated their fantasies about the potential role of the Philippines.

The "imperialist" side of the debate was led by such stalwarts as Senator Henry Cabot Lodge of Massachusetts and prodded by enthusiasts such as Theodore Roosevelt, supported by a skilled chorus of journalists whose ability to invent reasons to embark on overseas ventures was as brilliant as their knowledge of conditions in the islands was vague.

Four main arguments in support of keeping the islands emerged. Economically, the Philippines would protect and enhance a trade route to China. Strategic reasons centered on keeping the islands as a buttress against Japanese and German expansionism. A third rationale was promoted by Protestant missionary groups, who saw the islands as fertile ground for conversion (a great many Filipinos were already Roman Catholics). The fourth reason was vague but still compelling: It was America's destiny to conquer and hold the Philippines, to dominate the Pacific, and push the march of its civilization westward.

And yet Americans were not united at all. A powerful group of public figures led by William Jennings Bryan of Nebraska joined a group of distinguished writers, journalists, and intellectuals in opposing imperialism. Their arguments against imperialism warned of violence to American tradition in ruling over a subjected people. What would happen, these anti-imperialists asked, to sacred documents like the Declaration of Independence and the Monroe Doctrine? Would anything remain of the unique American civilization if the nation joined the unseemly European scramble for empire? Would acquiring territory compromise the American Republic? Might Americans be dragged down into the whirlpool of imperialist struggles with the aging empires of Europe? And what fate did Americans intend for the brown-skinned Filipinos, who would never be accepted as equals in a segregated American society?

Senator Beveridge had a chilling answer to all these objections. There was no compromise of tradition if one thought about the treatment of the Indians as a precedent. Furthermore, there was even an important lesson to be learned in the comparison:

> Our Indian wars would have been shortened, the lives of soldiers and settlers saved and the Indians themselves benefited, had we made continuous and decisive war; and any other kind of war is criminal because ineffective. . . . We acted toward the Indians as though we feared them, loved them, hated them—all at the same time—with a mingling of foolish sentiment, inaccurate thought, and paralytic purpose.

Yet the senator's desired clarity and decisiveness were the very qualities missing from Philippine policymaking. Even those who opposed acquisition of the Philippines failed to agree on reasons for their opposition, nor did they ever unite into a single-purpose political group. They raised questions about acquiring colonies that may now seem remarkably farsighted, but they lost the argument at the time. Debate, dispute, vagueness of purpose, contradictory reasoning, and outlandish claims determined the outcome. This confusion defined the context in which President McKinley decided his policy toward the Philippines.

The president was a cautious man. In moving toward war with Spain and then asking for colonies as a part of the peace treaty, he had appeared passive and vague. The United States in 1898 had been reluctantly belligerent against Spain. During peace negotiations in September, the president wrote (somewhat disingenuously) to his negotiating team in Paris that the United States had no intention of seizing the Philippines. Nevertheless, he reasoned:

> We cannot be unmindful that without any desire or design on our part the war has brought us new duties and responsibilities which we must meet and discharge as becomes a great nation in whose growth and career from the beginning the ruler of Nations has plainly written the high command and pledge of civilization.

Still somewhat reluctant, but leaning more and more toward acquisition, McKinley turned to prayer, as he explained, "for light and guidance from the 'ruler of nations.'" The inspiration he received strengthened his growing inclination. It was, he decided, America's duty to take the islands, to "educate the Filipinos, and uplift and Christianize them." On October 23, 1898, the president wired his commissioners in Paris. The United States, he declared, now demanded not just a naval base in Manila Bay; not even the central island of Luzon would be sufficient; the United States insisted on acquiring the whole archipelago. In return, he tendered the Spanish $20 million. Having little choice or desire to resist, Madrid agreed on December 10, 1898.

McKinley still faced two important obstacles. The first was the U.S. Senate, which had to consent to the treaty. Several strong and vocal members promised a bruising battle. Thus the struggle became a fight for American public opinion. The second impediment was Aguinaldo and his Filipino army, which already controlled most of the Philippine Islands except Manila and the nearby naval base at Cavite. Would he and his army exchange independence and self-rule to become an American colony?

Before the bar of American opinion, McKinley won his case easily. In elections in early November, Republican candidates, touting victory over Spain and promising the annexation of the Philippines, defeated the Democrats in key congressional races. They also gained the governorship of New York, where Theodore Roosevelt, charging into electoral politics, won an important victory by whipping up patriotism. "If you choose to vote for America," he declared bluntly, "if you choose to vote for the flag for which we fought this summer, then vote Republican." The Democrats, fearing the challenge, did not oppose annexation strongly, but the issue hurt them anyway.

Weeks of political maneuvering in the Senate followed the election with promises, pork-barrel agreements, and strident speeches. Finally, a vote was scheduled for February 6, 1899. Immense pressure focused on a few wavering anti-imperialist senators from the South and West. In the final tally, the treaty passed by a margin of two. Why the Senate approved this way is a complex question of party loyalty, opportunism, and response to public opinion. Perhaps more than anything, the issue had become one of patriotism and national unity. Having acquired the Philippines almost by default, it seemed easier in terms of domestic politics to keep them than to establish an informal protectorate to block German or Japanese encroachment or allow Aguinaldo's revolutionaries to take over.

Yet few Americans realized that keeping the Philippines committed the United States to conquering them first. There had been some warning, but it came too late. On February 5, 1899, just before the crucial Senate vote, war broke out. General Otis, continuing his pressure on Aguinaldo to retreat from Manila, insisted that the Filipino army abandon more of its positions close to the city. When the Filipinos refused, he alerted his men to fire on any military personnel approaching disputed territory. On February 4, U.S. troops opened fire on a group of revolutionary soldiers. The next day, Otis launched a general attack, backed up by heavy guns from Admiral Dewey's warships, anchored within easy range of the Filipino lines.

Charging through the Filipino lines, shouting the "Montana Yell," American troops decimated the ill-equipped and startled revolutionaries. Trapped by charging cavalry, as many as 3,000 Filipino soldiers died. There were only about 60 American casualties. The pattern of war was set. Otis marched out to engage and destroy Aguinaldo's army, then returned to the safety of the Manila area. This first phase of the war to conquer the Philippines resembled traditional warfare. Although the Filipino forces had few weapons or trustworthy artillery, they sought, at first, to engage the American force in pitched battles.

Despite efforts to negotiate a peace, Aguinaldo refused to give in; consequently, American troops extended their control over major cities on Luzon and some of the other islands. At the same time, McKinley initiated plans for a civilian government, sending the first Philippine Commission to the islands. On April 4, 1899, the commission (including Dewey and Otis as members) proclaimed eleven "regulative principles," establishing the outlines of colonial government. In matters of sovereignty, the United States would be supreme. The regulations guaranteed civil rights and liberties and promised maximum local self-government, improved education and economy, and speedy and fair justice. But there would be no Philippine independence.

Enforced by unrelenting military pressure, this policy was designed to win the allegiance of the Filipinos, particularly the elite groups who dominated the social, cultural, and economic life of the islands. Thus pacification proceeded along two lines: military and civilian. But time and again, just when the Americans believed they had

The gentlemen of the First Philippine Commission in 1899 include Jacob G. Schurman, Admiral George Dewey, Charles Denby, and Dean C. Worcester. (Library of Congress)

won the allegiance or cooperation of local officials, their trust proved premature as Filipinos cast their lot with Aguinaldo.

As a result, General Otis concluded that he must destroy Aguinaldo's army and capture the revolutionary general. During the summer of 1899 Otis succeeded in the first of these aims. At the same time, the commission's pacification policies proceeded. The Army distributed $100,000 worth of texts on arithmetic, geography, U.S. history, and English, and school supplies, including American flags. Roads were repaired and other public works undertaken. A vaccination program against smallpox began. Proud of these efforts, Otis assured Washington that he had won the war for the Philippines.

But while clashes between Aguinaldo's forces and the U.S. Army diminished over the summer of 1899, this did not mean the country had been pacified. The Filipino general had the loyalty of a great many of his people even if he could not field an army. Nonetheless, the United States government proceeded as if pacification was complete. In March 1900 the second Philippine Commission landed at Manila. Its purpose was to assume power in civilian matters from the Army. Secretary of War Elihu Root instructed the commission to collect taxes, appropriate public funds, and establish courts. The commission was to act as the legislative power of the colony. Root also replaced General Otis on May 1 with General Arthur MacArthur, who promised that the islands would be "submerged immediately under a tidal wave of education."

William Howard Taft led the second commission. A man of immense girth and talent, who had a close and valuable friendship with Theodore Roosevelt, Taft had once opposed taking the Philippines because, according to his wife, they "would only add to our problems and responsibilities without increasing in any way the effectiveness and usefulness of our government." But he now believed that America could

Young Filipinos dress up and carry flags to celebrate America's independence (not their own). By their looks, these children seem more interested in another American importation: the camera. (Library of Congress)

offer the islands efficient and businesslike reforms. Taft, unlike many military men—especially enlisted men—viewed the Filipino situation with optimism. It was widely believed in the islands that he had coined the phrase "our little brown brothers" to describe the Filipinos. But soldiers recited a bit of broken verse that recorded more hostile feelings:

> I'm only a common soldier-man in the blasted Philippines
> They say I've got Brown Brothers here, but I dunno what it means
> I like the word Fraternity, but still I draw the line;
> He may be a brother of William H. Taft, but he ain't no friend of mine.

A month after arriving in Manila, Taft confided his impressions of the Filipino people in a letter to Root: "The population of the Islands is made up of a vast mass of ignorant, superstitious people, well-intentioned, light-hearted, temperate, somewhat cruel, domestic and fond of their families, and deeply wedded to the Catholic church." Although this statement shows a paternalistic view of the Filipinos, it also suggests that the commissioner suffered from what might be called culture shock or an extreme misunderstanding of the customs of another society. Mrs. Taft was obviously amused by her husband's sensitivity to Filipino characteristics. As she noted in her diary: "The first conclusion he [Taft] reached in Manila was that the people knew nothing about the value of time, and it must have been a strain on his temperate-zone nervous system to watch a squad of men at work in his garden."

While Taft designed a policy of benevolence, General MacArthur increased military pressure. Not surprisingly, divergent U.S. civilian and military interests hardened into a dispute over how to pacify the Philippines. The behavior of American civilians and soldiers underscored the differences. Military men frequently referred to Filipinos as "gugus" or "niggers." The soldiers' bad handling of debts, drunkenness, and rude behavior increased tensions between them and Filipino citizens, despite the polite reception that Taft and his wife gave to the elite Philippine families of the capital city.

This contradictory policy reflected the profound division in the United States over the Philippines that continued throughout 1900. The debate became an issue in the election of 1900, which pitted the Republican President McKinley and his new vice presidential candidate, Theodore Roosevelt, against the Democrat William Jennings Bryan. Imperialism was a highly visible issue that divided the parties.

Although this issue may not have decided the election, newspapers returned again and again to the debate. Republicans publicly doubted the patriotism of Democrats who opposed the war; Democrats accused imperialists of undermining the Constitution. Yet Bryan proved to be a poor crusader for anti-imperialism. Considered unreliable on the issue, he lost the support of some of the most vocal opponents of the war.

The overheated rhetoric of the campaign did nothing to clarify Philippine policy or justify continued U.S. occupation of the islands. But it did convince Aguinaldo and his forces that a Bryan victory might lead to American evacuation and Philippine independence.

Partly to influence the election, Aguinaldo's army increasingly shifted to active guerrilla tactics over the summer of 1900. In a certain sense, they had no choice; superiority in men, arms, and mobility meant the Americans could win any direct, pitched battle. Against lightning strikes, ambushes, and surprise attacks carried out by citizen soldiers who then melted back into the population, the American army of occupation had far less success.

Partly out of frustration, the Americans responded with antiguerrilla tactics that carried warfare to the population harboring the revolutionaries. MacArthur's men burned barrios near the scenes of attacks, destroyed crops, and killed work animals. Because secrecy and surprise were the weapons of guerrilla warfare, the troops commonly relied on torture to extract information from prisoners. The approved method was the "water cure." Water was forced into the mouth of a suspect held on the ground, until he talked. The sensation was like drowning, and, if not stopped in time, could lead to death.

While conditions in the Philippines deteriorated and relations between MacArthur and Taft grew more hostile, the decisive electoral victory of McKinley and Roosevelt in November squelched the last hopes of the Filipino revolutionaries. MacArthur immediately toughened his policy after the election. He increased censorship of the news, announced that captured revolutionaries would henceforth be treated as criminals, not soldiers, making them susceptible to the death penalty. He initiated a policy of population concentration, gathering peasants into monitored areas where they could not support the guerrillas. In certain respects this policy resembled the treatment of Native Americans in the final struggle for control of the West after the Civil War.

Although this tough policy seemed to bear fruit—more weapons and taxes were collected—MacArthur was replaced in February 1901 by Brigadier General Adna R. Chaffee. Secretary of War Root declared that civilian authorities, led by William Howard Taft, would now exercise increased power. In part, this victory of Taft over MacArthur indicated that the United States government believed the war was coming to a close.

Further evidence of victory came in March 1901 with the capture of General Aguinaldo in northern Luzon. Aguinaldo had sent secret correspondence to his brother asking for more troops, but the U.S. Army intercepted the message. General Frederick Funston devised a ruse to enter Aguinaldo's headquarters. Filipino troops loyal to the United States disguised themselves in revolutionary uniforms while Funston and four other American officers posed as their prisoners. Welcomed into rebel headquarters during the celebration of Aguinaldo's birthday, the troop of conspirators opened fire.

Most of Aguinaldo's men panicked. The Americans seized the leader and rushed to the coast to a waiting ship.

A month later, in captivity and persuaded of the futility of continued resistance, Aguinaldo issued a proclamation from prison urging the Filipino people to lay down their arms and accept American rule. But the movement headed by the Filipino general lived on without him. The guerrilla war continued, particularly in the southern area of Luzon and on the island of Samar. Important pieces of the revolutionary government remained intact, although the ordinary people and even elected officials hid their loyalties to the rebels.

In most respects, Chaffee continued MacArthur's tough policy of carrying the antiguerrilla war to the civilian population. Under his command, final plans were drawn up to subdue Samar. He ordered American troops to occupy Balangiga, where the September 1901 attack on Company C took place.

The ordeal of Samar had far-ranging effects. A Senate investigation of the Philippine pacification revealed bungling, torture, atrocities, and the population concentration policy but did not change U.S. policy toward the Philippines. General MacArthur defended the suspicious casualty ratio among Filipinos. Explaining why there were fifteen dead to only one wounded (when in the U.S. Civil War there had been about one dead to five wounded), he denied that the Army had killed prisoners and wounded men. The general simply said that "inferior races" died more easily than Anglo-Saxons.

Although such harsh statements did not force practices to change, they may well have contributed to the growing sentiment that the occupation was a mistake and that the United States should grant independence to the Philippines as soon as self-rule became possible. A number of Americans remained uneasy about the intervention. *The Sultan of Sula*, a successful spoof of imperialism that played in Chicago and other cities in 1902, expressed some serious second thoughts about the whole endeavor. In the play, a chorus of American soldiers sings ironically about "benevolent assimilation."

> We want to assimilate if we can
>   Our brother who is brown
> We love our dusky fellow-man
>   And we hate to hunt him down.
> So when we perforate his frame,
>   We want him to be good.
> We shout at him to make him tame,
>   If he but understood.

Promises of changes in policy came rather quickly. The Jones Act of 1917 officially guaranteed independence as soon as the nation achieved "a stable government." Even superimperialist Theodore Roosevelt soon concluded that the islands were our "Achilles heel."

In the Philippines, MacArthur and Chaffee's tough tactics finally convinced most of the populace that struggle was futile. Taft successfully negotiated an arrangement

Pageant at Manila. Shortly before they left the Philippines in 1904, the Taft family, pictured here with two aides (left and right standing), held a costume ball. There could scarcely have been a more incongruous celebration, to imagine Manila as Venice and Taft as the cultured Doge who helped inspire the Renaissance. (William H. Taft National Historic Site)

with the Catholic church to pay for large tracts of land confiscated from it. And the Filipino elite recognized that they had nothing more to gain and much to lose by supporting the revolutionaries.

As the fighting diminished, Taft and the commissioners paid more attention to new government institutions and health and social reforms. Whether these improved the lives of the Filipino people significantly has been widely debated. Furthermore, traditional Philippine institutions proved more resilient (and resistant) than anyone anticipated. For example, despite an influx of missionaries, Protestantism made little headway in the largely Catholic population. Only about 3 percent of Filipinos in 1980 could trace their religious beliefs back to the efforts of these proselytizers. Political corruption, wide class differences, inefficiency, and slow economic growth continued. The islands benefited only marginally from special tariffs that allowed their products to enter the United States at lower rates than foreign goods.

Ultimately, confusion of purpose, indecision at home, and squabbling between American military and civilian authorities probably worsened the conflict with Filipino revolutionaries. Left without clearly formulated policies or instructions, local commanders fell back on their own experiences, improvising their response to the bitter guerrilla warfare. Because a great many of the officers had recent experience in fighting Native Americans, almost inevitably their actions and their attitudes recalled that bitter conflict. That is what Senator Joseph R. Burton of Kansas had in mind when he compared the antiguerrilla warfare tactics to the extermination of Indians at Wounded Knee. Both were, he noted, "entirely within the regulations of civilized warfare." After all, he told his fellow senators, "You cannot fight a barbarous foe in the same way you can a civilized enemy."

PROGRESSIVE FOREIGN POLICY, FROM EMPIRE TO WORLD WAR

Nationalism, benevolence, dreams of manifest destiny, economic self-interest, and a missionary zeal to spread Protestantism and Western civilization—these different notions lay behind U.S. involvement in the Philippines after the Spanish-American War. If it is true that foreign policy reflects domestic circumstances, it should be no surprise to find that during a period of striking transition in American society between an agrarian past and an industrial future, such deep contradictions and uncertainties of purpose appeared in foreign affairs.

Led by dynamic leaders who held strong opinions, with nationalism burgeoning, the United States confidently, but cautiously, stepped into a competitive and dangerous world. Problems at home seemed difficult but surmountable. A reform movement that preached efficiency, organization, and professionalism promised to solve domestic economic and social problems by applying the right combination of compassion and expertise. This also became the policy of America toward a world in the last throes of colonialism and bracing for its first wave of modern revolutions. The United States would offer progressive reform to the world.

In some respects, the war in the Philippines tested this offer. Its frustrating results anticipated much that happened in the next two decades of foreign policy. The same pattern seemed to repeat itself: The best intentions of policymakers brought unpleasant and often dangerous involvement with other nations. Facing this predicament, Americans were assailed by doubts about the aptness of trying to export institutions. The conflicting purposes that underlay policy reemerged. As a result, the nation turned toward isolationism again in the 1920s, skeptical that American ideas could be exported, suspicious of the motives of reformers, and with renewed worries about entangling alliances and colonial wars. There appeared to be a lesson in this: In a turbulent world, events had a way of flying out of control, whatever the objectives of policymakers. But there was also a profound question: Did America really stand for principle in a world of cutthroat economic and political competition?

The Myth of America's Destiny

After about 1896 the United States increasingly looked outward, toward the acquisition of an empire and then, warily, toward active participation in the conflicts between European nations. Every step of the way was accompanied by questions and debate over two issues: How should Americans treat the peoples of the undeveloped countries they encountered? And should the United States become permanently involved in alliances and covenants with European nations? If America was to remain the unique civilization that so many writers had proclaimed it to be, then these problems demanded a resolute answer.

The architects of a more engaged and activist foreign policy often found justification in their unusual interpretations of history. A great many Americans at this time were influenced by the idea of American "exceptionalism," the theory that America had a special destiny in the world born out of a combination of its European, principally Anglo-Saxon, racial and cultural heritage and its experience as a frontier civilization. Their ideas about the mission of the United States were similarly born out of the feeling of belonging to a unique society. It is these ideas that convinced Americans they were duty-bound to try to set the world right.

The words of journalist William Allen White capture the intense spirit of this idea: "It is the Anglo-Saxon's manifest destiny to go forth as a world conqueror. He will take possession of the islands of the seas. . . . That is what fate holds for the chosen people. It is so written. . . . It is to be." Ambrose Bierce, another journalist, whose biting realism vividly rendered the terrible battlefields of the Civil War, was a late convert to imperialism. Speaking of the gift of Western civilization to be granted to the Filipinos, he wrote:

> Of all it may safely be said that their only hope lies in subjugation by a master race. Such advancement as they may be capable of is not to be effected by suggestion or advice. Like all backward peoples, they fight against the light and will accept it, if at all, only when it is flashed upon them by the sword.

Indiana Senator Albert J. Beveridge, much given to hyperbole and handsome turns of phrase, justified taking the Philippines on all these grounds—and then some. Having visited the islands himself, he described the natives as a "barbarous race." America had a destiny to transform the world: "Of all our races He [God] has marked the American people as His chosen Nation finally to lead in the regeneration of the world." Climbing down from religious to patriotic metaphors, he called the flag the emblem of this movement: "That flag has never paused in its onward march." Beveridge's use of the term *race*, which meant something akin to "cultures" or "civilizations," had a certain urgent appeal to it. It could satisfy Americans who were increasingly puzzled by a dangerous and competitive world where history appeared to have chosen the nation to play a grand role.

The United States picked up the burden of empire after some reluctance. The nation was a late entrant in the expansion race. It quickly acquired a string of colonies and protectorates, but then withdrew from the contest. However, it did not retire from the scene; its overseas ambitions merely assumed a different form. In the Western Hemisphere, Americans began a series of interventions in the affairs of Latin American countries that continued, sporadically, for several decades. And by 1917 the United States could tip the balance of power in one of the gravest conflicts in human history.

These events inspired a new national self-consciousness. They gave rise to new ideas about national power, to a belief that because of its history and culture the United States was uniquely fitted to guide the destinies of other nations. Yet these events also aroused doubts. Would America's new activist role in the world forever compromise the special and unique qualities of life in the New World?

Such questions found their way into serious political discourse. Indeed, a great many Americans were talking about the nation's destiny in terms of world leadership. Of course words like *leadership*, *destiny*, and *mission* had always been part of the American political vocabulary. In the mid–nineteenth century, writers and politicians often spoke of the nation's manifest destiny to populate a continent bounded by two vast oceans, on the east and the west, and by two different cultures, to the north and the south. But with that geographic destiny fulfilled in the 1890s, with most of the fertile land already occupied and millions of new immigrants pouring into the cities of the East and Midwest, the idea of manifest destiny acquired a new meaning. American institutions of political democracy and economic mobility still seemed superior to the class-conscious societies of Europe, but many Americans wondered how this superiority could survive.

Frederick Jackson Turner, a historian at the University of Wisconsin, in a celebrated and influential essay about the American spirit, summed up the effects of the frontier on American society and offered a vision of continued expansion. Turner asserted that American democratic institutions came from the frontier experience. As settlements pressed across the continent, civilization and wilderness repeatedly intermingled. Savagery refreshed society, and civilization tamed the wilderness. Thus had Americans progressed in a westward trek for almost 300 years.

When he described his "frontier thesis" at the World's Columbian Exposition in 1893 in Chicago, Turner used the language of popularized evolutionary theory. Struggle and competition on the frontier, he declared, created a survival ethic of individualism and democratic cooperation. But the historian issued a warning. The frontier, he said solemnly, "has gone and with its going has closed the first period of American history."

Would there be a second, equally rich period of American history? Movement, restlessness, and a desire for opportunity still remained the essence of the American spirit. The lure of the West had not died. It drew thousands of young men onto what remained of the frontier. Many failed to make their fortune, but the dream of fleeing the workaday cities of the East remained irresistible. Perhaps some Americans could find escape in the fictional heroism and new frontier worlds of popular fiction: Westerns, science fiction, and adventure tales. But could the nation survive the loss of energy and creativity that had once come from opening up new frontiers?

Turner did not think so. Nor did he believe that the nation could prosper unless it continued to grow economically. So he advised continued expansion in world trade. In effect, the world was to become America's economic frontier. Many of his contemporaries agreed with Turner that the 1890s represented a watershed in American history. With the frontier officially closed and westward expansion blocked by natural and cultural boundaries, the only feasible economic expansion lay overseas in trade or empire. But there were dangers. Could America avoid falling into the traps that ensnared Spain, Britain, and France in costly colonial ventures? Would America's new activism in the world economy mean entangling alliances with European powers?

Those American policymakers who advised a new activism—a new foreign policy—believed American society would flourish because of its cultural superiority. They believed America was a nation of Englishmen purified by the encounter with the frontier. Long implicit in American thinking, this theory of Anglo-Saxon supremacy emerged full-blown in the early twentieth century. Many Americans believed that an English background bestowed a special racial heritage. America would survive world competition because of its superior racial stock, culture, and high principles. Nor was this thinking confined to a few diplomats or politicians. It was a myth that found a huge audience among all classes of Americans.

American cultural supremacy was the argument Theodore Roosevelt used to justify America's policy of Indian removal in his book *The Winning of the West*. "It was wholly impossible," he wrote, "to avoid conflicts with the weaker race unless we were willing to see the American continent fall into the hands of some other strong power." Progressive Senator Albert Beveridge, speaking of America's destiny, called the nation "the purest race of history." "Fellow Americans," he proclaimed in 1898, "we are God's chosen people." Even William Jennings Bryan, who opposed acquiring colonies, solemnly spoke of the nation's mission "to liberate those who are in bondage."

The Reality Behind the Myth

The men who developed America's new foreign policy at the turn of the century subscribed to this notion that the nation had a special destiny. Most believed in the superiority of the Anglo-Saxon "race." Some based their position on social Darwinism, a popular translation of evolutionary theory into a proclamation of the right of the "fittest" individuals and the strongest nations to rule over others. Many were influenced by the ideas that Turner had enunciated in his "frontier thesis." But they were also hardheaded realists who recognized the political and economic benefits of an activist foreign policy. They realized that the United States had to begin to exercise more power in the world because its economic position among nations had become preeminent.

The profoundest changes in America's world position were economic. In 1877 the United States struck a favorable balance of trade (more exports than imports). Forty years later, during World War I, the nation became a world creditor, owing less to other nations than it had lent out. This evolution toward financial independence reflected a dynamic economic growth. Rapid development in the 1880s and 1890s greatly increased the percentage of manufactured goods in American exports. This, in turn, focused the interest of American industrialists on maintaining and increasing overseas markets.

Much of the increased American economic activity abroad came in the form of investments, especially in underdeveloped nations. In Mexico, for example, by 1910 about 1,100 American firms held about $500 million worth of assets. In effect, American capital controlled most of Mexico's railroads and a large share of its ranching, lumber and paper industries, and banking. United States companies also dominated Mexican mining and oil extraction.

During the progressive era, exports constituted only between 6 and 7.5 percent of total American production, but this was a vital part of the nation's commerce. From 1890 to 1914 the share of trade with Latin American and Asian countries increased dramatically. The potential for even larger sales was alluring. Yet success bred worries. Power shifts in Europe and instability in Asia, South America, and Africa in-

American Exports by Value and Destination: 1896–1924

Year	Total*	Canada	Cuba	Mexico	UK	France	Germany	China
1896	$ 883	$ 60	$ 8	$ 19	$ 406	$ 47	$ 98	$ 7
1900	1,394	95	26	35	534	83	187	15
1904	1,461	131	27	46	537	84	215	13
1908	1,861	167	47	56	581	116	277	22
1912	2,204	329	62	53	564	135	307	24
1916	5,483	605	165	54	1,887	861	2	32
1920	8,228	972	515	208	1,825	676	311	146
1924	4,591	624	200	135	983	282	440	109

*Millions of dollars.

Source: U.S. Department of Commerce, Bureau of the Census, *Historical Statistics of the United States: Colonial Times to the Present*, bicentennial ed. (Washington, D.C.: Government Printing Office, 1975), Vol. II, p. 903.

Singer in South Africa. The caption to this advertising card from Singer read, "This is a fertile, well-watered country of South Africa, on the Indian Ocean, and forms a part of the region known as Kafraria. The native Zulus are a fine warlike people of the Bantu stock, speaking the Bantu language. The language extends over more than half of Africa and is one of great beauty and flexibility. The Zulu bids fair to be as forward in civilization as he has been in war. Our group represents the Zulus after less than a century of civilization. Worth wins everywhere. Our agent at Cape Town supplies both the European and native inhabitants of Zululand, The Transvaal, and Orange Free State with thousands of Singer Machines." (Library of Congress)

creased the aggressiveness of leading European powers. The rapid industrialization and armament of Germany and Japan threatened the dominance of Great Britain. After a scramble for colonies in Africa during the 1880s and 1890s, the major powers looked covetously on the weak Spanish empire in Asia. China appeared to be tottering. Even the unruly Latin American republics seemed in danger of intervention by European powers.

After many years of relative isolation, the United States suddenly had to rethink its foreign relations. Thus the new American foreign policy at the turn of the century was defined in the context of serious challenges as well as opportunities. If industrial nations divided the world into competing, closed empires protected by high tariff walls, United States trade and influence would collapse. If the European nations and Japan insisted on expanding their empires, the United States might be shut out from the world economic frontier. To make matters more urgent, many American business and political leaders concluded during the severe depression of the 1890s that agricultural and industrial overproduction were permanent American problems. They could be solved only by exporting more.

A New Foreign Policy

The men who formulated the new American foreign policy of the progressive era were in fundamental agreement: They insisted that the

The Singer Sewing Machine

It will doubtless surprise some readers of this article to learn that the serviceable and homely product of Yankee ingenuity, the sewing machine, is one of the things which has helped to spread the fame of America abroad, or that the symbol of the red S [for Singer] so familiar at home, is one of the things which, wherever his wanderings abroad may take him, is sure to confront the American expatriate with its reminder of the country he has left behind. . . . At whatever places men, in their meetings for trade, have set up their markets; in whatever places the cutter and fashioner of cloth or leather or fur, plies his calling, there the American sewing machine has made its way and is welcome, whether it be in the tent of the desert Arab, the Kaffir's hut in South Africa, or the Norwegian fishing village near the Arctic circle.

To quote another traveler's words, this time those of an American missionary speaking of his labors among the tribesmen of Arabia: "I have never yet been in an Arab town without finding Singer sewing machines among people who have never seen the word of God and who have never heard the gospel of Jesus Christ."

Sewing Machine Advance
Chicago, September 1908

The Singer Sewing Machine Company, founded in Boston by Isaac Merritt Singer in 1850 was by the first decade of the twentieth century an extraordinarily successful American enterprise. In 1913 it had almost 6,000 branches in the United States and abroad, with over 60,000 salesmen. Besides its special marketing program, it operated branch factories in Canada, Scotland, Germany, and Russia. Although other nations manufactured sewing machines, American companies dominated the world market, with Singer taking the largest share. Its machines seemed to be everywhere. As John Reed, an American war correspondent during the Mexican Revolution (see p. 826), wrote of a Mexican home: "In one corner was a big iron bed, and in the other a Singer sewing machine, as in every other house I saw in Mexico."

The Singer company prided itself on its aggressive salesmanship and favorable publicity. It offered a wide range of manually operated machines and attachments, and easy access to repair and replacement parts. Company employment policy stressed paternalism. Singer instituted a "civil service" so that "every workman knows he can rise if he has merit." The company paid a family man a slightly higher wage and encouraged young men of good character to apply for work. There were also company sports programs and social activities. Singer did not, however, tolerate labor unions.

A slogan picturing the sewing machine as "the great civilizer" reiterated the company belief, and the American assumption, that the export of Yankee know-how would transform the world.

There were, however, other views of this American dominance of world markets. During the Spanish-American War in 1898, newspapers in Madrid called for a boycott of Singer products. One paper accused Singer of being an "immense octopus whose tentacles encircle Spain and crush it, snatching from it the savings of its workers in order to aggrandize the miserable, iniquitous, cowardly, disgusting North American nation." During World War I, Germany placed Singer's branch companies under government control. And in 1919 the communist government in Russia nationalized the large Singer plant and sales outlets in that country.

United States pursue a more active role in the world. They were deeply influenced by ideas and worries about America's destiny. They realized the opportunities and problems created by rapid industrial development. But they disagreed sharply about how far the United States should go toward acquiring a formal empire of naval bases and colonies. This practical question dominated debate over foreign policy at the turn of the century.

The major shift toward a new, activist foreign policy began during the second presidency of Grover Cleveland, in the depths of a depression. Three unsettling events pushed the president toward new policy initiatives. The first was a revolt in the Hawaiian Islands in January 1893. Dominated by American planters, the islands became increasingly important because of the fine port at Pearl Harbor and their strategic position along trade routes to the Far East. Immigration of Chinese and Japanese settlers in the 1880s plus the growing economic importance of Americans led native Queen Liliuokalani to assert her powers. But the white settlers in Honolulu, led by sugar planters like Sanford Dole and supported by the U.S. minister to the island, John L. Stevens, overthrew the queen and asked for American annexation.

When Cleveland entered office in 1893, he faced a decision to accept or reject annexation. He refused, angrily saying that the revolt was "dependent for its success upon the agency of the United States." Cleveland desired trade and influence in Hawaii, but he was reluctant to annex the islands as a colony of the United States.

A second crisis developed in South America in a dispute between Great Britain and Venezuela that challenged the Monroe Doctrine of 1823, which had provided a motto for American foreign policy: no further encroachment by Europeans in the Americas. The British navy had generally supplied the shield for this policy. Now, suddenly, the British themselves threatened a Latin American republic.

The dispute was a long-standing one about the boundary between Venezuela and the British colony of Guiana. At stake was the Orinoco, a large navigable river whose upper reaches tapped trade and gold prospecting areas of Venezuela. Cleveland supported Venezuela's claims and pressed Britain to submit the dispute to international arbitration. On July 20, 1895, Secretary of State Richard Olney demanded that the British negotiate. In his message he reminded Britain of America's power: "Today the United States is practically sovereign on this continent."

Queen Liliuokalani of Hawaii. Queen Liliuokalani ascended the throne of the Hawaiian Islands in 1891. Her attempts to assume wider powers persuaded American residents on the islands to demand annexation by the United States in 1893. (Library of Congress)

When the British response came, it was curt and inflammatory. No arbitration and no Monroe Doctrine. Cleveland's next move edged the United States toward war. He sent a message to

Congress on December 17, 1895, calling upon the nation to resist the "willful aggression" upon Venezuelan rights. Talk of war flared but then subsided quickly. Already overextended elsewhere, the British agreed to arbitration.

The Spanish-American War

No sooner had the Venezuelan crisis ended than a rebellion flared in Cuba that quickly became the center of American attention. One of the last outposts of the crumbling Spanish empire, Cuba had gravitated into the U.S. economic orbit. American exports to the island reached $24 million in 1893, larger than to any other Western Hemisphere nation save Canada, and larger than all of America's Asian trade. In February 1895, Cuban rebels demanded independence. Too weak to enforce order, Spain nonetheless insisted that the rebels surrender. As fighting spread, American-owned sugar plantations and mills suffered from arson and looting. The whole structure of American investments on the island—$50 million worth—hung in the balance.

At first, Cleveland sympathized with the Spanish, and he never wavered from his desire to see the rebellion end. But continued violence eroded his patience. Moreover, Cuban rebels gathered significant support in the United States. Many Americans became openly sympathetic to their cause after Spanish General Valeriano Weyler introduced martial law and his "recon-centration" policy. Begun in October 1896, this policy pushed thousands of peasants into the cities to depopulate the countryside. But Weyler miscalculated, and thousands of Cubans died of starvation and disease in crowded city quarters. Newspaper publishers William Randolph Hearst and Joseph Pulitzer, who knew how to provoke sympathy (and circulation), played up the bru-

tality of this policy. Like their progressive counterparts, the muckrakers, these "yellow journalists" discovered the importance and malleability of public opinion.

Under the circumstances, Cleveland could only increase pressure on Spain to end the rebellion. He was not prepared to go to war over Cuba, yet he defined peace in the rebellious colony as key to American interests. Thus when he left office in 1897, he passed on to William McKinley, the new president, the task of protecting America's interests in this explosive situation.

McKinley's inauguration brought a new group of foreign-policy makers to power. They were more willing to push ahead in places where Cleveland had been reluctant. The most prominent of these new men was Theodore Roosevelt, the new assistant secretary of the navy, although other members of the group were also important: Senator Henry Cabot Lodge of Massachusetts, diplomat John Hay, historian Brooks Adams, and Admiral Alfred Thayer Mahan.

Although their views differed somewhat, most of the new men agreed with the strategic proposals outlined by Mahan in his book *The Influence of Sea Power upon History* (1890). Mahan proposed an export and investment network based on naval power. His tactics centered on building a Panama canal, acquiring protective bases around it, and then colonial stepping-stones across the Pacific to Asia. This would ensure American trade and influence in Latin America and the Orient. These goals, Mahan proclaimed, were far greater than mere national self-interest. "Every expansion of a great civilized power," he wrote, "means a victory for law, order, and righteousness." Overseas empire was America's destiny.

Spain was the major obstacle in America's route to empire when McKinley entered office in 1897. Senator Henry Cabot Lodge expressed what many in the administration, as well as many other Americans, believed about Spain, writing that the Spanish were a people who "stood for bigotry and tyranny as hideous in their action as any which have ever cursed humanity." Spain

Anti-American propaganda. A Spanish journalistic view of America during the war of 1898. The American pig courts the Lady of Spain with flowers and a handy money bag. (Memorial Library, University of Wisconsin)

Anti-Spanish propaganda. Portrayals of Spanish authorities as brutal murderers in journals and newspapers in the United States helped incite American public opinion in favor of war against Spain in 1898. (Library of Congress)

also held the important islands of Puerto Rico, Guam, and the Philippines.

The new president hoped to avoid direct intervention in Cuba. But unlike Cleveland, he committed himself to a more expansionist foreign policy, including acquisition of the Virgin Islands in the Caribbean, and Hawaii, and eventually removal of all vestiges of European colonialism from the Western Hemisphere. His first priority was to end the divisive pressure on domestic politics and the economy caused by the Cuban rebellion. So he stepped up pressure on the Spanish. In June 1897 he called on Spain to end its "uncivilized and inhumane conduct." Again in the fall, he warned the Spanish not to seek allies among the European powers.

As Spain moved from one inept policy to another, the United States pressed its case harder. By the end of 1897 the two nations were on a collision course. The Spanish minister to Washington, Enrique De Lôme, in a letter to a friend in Cuba referred to McKinley as "weak and a bidder for the admiration of the crowd." The letter was intercepted and published February 9 in the *New York Journal*. Sensationalists needed no more evidence of Spanish duplicity.

A far more serious event on February 15 almost ignited war. The U.S. battleship *Maine*, anchored in Havana harbor in Cuba, exploded mysteriously. Of the 350 officers and seamen aboard, 260 perished. Although the perpetrators of the act (if indeed there were any) were never captured, many Americans blamed the Spanish authorities. Once again, the sensationalist press resounded with cries of war.

As pressure on Cuba increased, the United States flanked the Spanish empire in the Pacific. Assistant Navy Secretary Roosevelt ordered Ad-

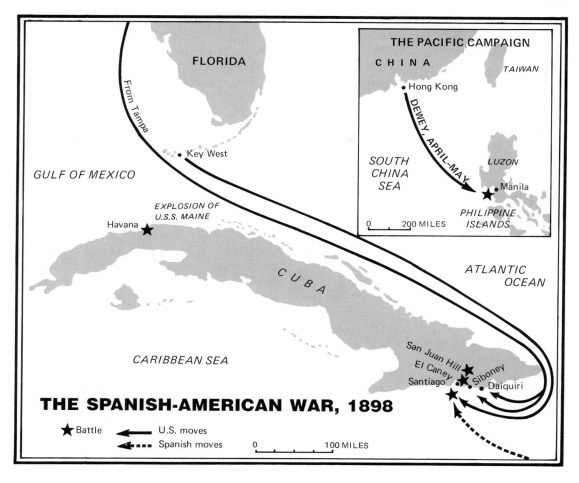

THE PACIFIC CAMPAIGN

CHINA   TAIWAN

• Hong Kong

SOUTH
CHINA   LUZON
SEA

DEWEY, APRIL-MAY

• Manila

0   200 MILES   PHILIPPINE
                          ISLANDS

FLORIDA

From Tampa

• Key West

GULF OF MEXICO

EXPLOSION OF
U.S.S. MAINE

Havana ★

CUBA

ATLANTIC
OCEAN

CARIBBEAN SEA

San Juan Hill ★
El Caney ★ Siboney
Santiago • • Daiquiri
★

THE SPANISH-AMERICAN WAR, 1898

★ Battle   ⟵ U.S. moves
          ⟵••• Spanish moves   0   100 MILES

miral George Dewey to anchor his fleet at Hong Kong. In the event of war, he was to destroy the Spanish navy in the Philippines. In late March, McKinley again demanded an end to hostilities in Cuba, proposing an immediate six-month armistice and American mediation. Spain accepted part of the proposal and hedged on the rest. Both nations prepared for war.

McKinley decided to ask Congress for a declaration of war on April 11, 1898. He gave a number of reasons, but they all revolved around one assumption: Peace in Cuba was necessary to the domestic tranquility of the United States. As he said, there was an "intimate connection of the Cuban question with the state of our own Union." In what became a rehearsal for policy in the Philippines, the president refused to side with the rebels; his intent was to end the rebellion. "Final military victory for either side seems impracticable," he concluded. America's purpose, in other words, was to preserve order in an area where U.S. interests were involved. On April 19, Congress declared war; one day later it proclaimed the Teller amendment renouncing any intention to annex Cuba.

Enthusiasm for the war ran high. After voting, congressmen burst into song, harmonizing "Dixie" and the "Battle Hymn of the Republic." Much of the popular poetry of the day underscored this feeling of enthusiasm and unity. The opposing sides of the Civil War were reunited in a splendid struggle against decadent Spain. As a *Baltimore News* poet rhymed in 1898:

> Those who wore the blue and gray,
> And they'll fight for common country,
>   And they'll charge to victory
> 'Neath the folds of one brave banner—
>   Starry banner of the free!

For many Americans this was a romantic war, a chance for a man to prove his heroism and courage. But the conflict was over in less than four months. American casualties were slight— only 385, although deaths from disease, accidents, and other hazards pushed the total to 2,446.

In Asia the war began as a naval operation. Dewey, as ordered, steamed to the Philippines in late April and discovered the Spanish fleet huddled under shore batteries in Manila Bay. Dewey ordered an attack on May 1. Passing before the harbor and pouring fire into the motionless ships, Dewey's forces devastated the Spanish fleet. The Americans sustained no casualties at all. The city of Manila surrendered on August 13. Elsewhere in the Pacific, U.S. forces took the island of Guam on May 10. And Congress annexed Hawaii in early July.

By the time Spain sued for peace in August, the outlines of an American empire existed: a protectorate over Cuba, with claims to Puerto Rico, Guam, and the Philippines. Hawaii and the port of Pearl Harbor now belonged to the United States. The question that remained was, should the United States annex the Philippines? The islands lay thousands of miles east of America. Here was a problem that required rethinking the whole history of American foreign relations. To take the islands meant embarking on colonialism. McKinley weighed these factors carefully. He agreed that a naval station at Manila was highly desirable. But he doubted it could be defended without holding the island of Luzon and perhaps all of the Philippines. If the United States moved

out, on the other hand, European powers such as Germany seemed prepared to move in. McKinley made his decision. The president forwarded his demands for the peace negotiations; Spain had no choice but to cede the islands to the United States in the Treaty of Paris, signed in December 1898. The treaty was sharply contested and barely passed the Senate, largely because of its provisions on the Philippines. America had, reluctantly, picked up the "white man's burden."

RESULTS OF THE WAR America plunged deep into colonialism when it took the Philippines, and this decision touched off a furious debate about the meaning of the new foreign policy. Two major groups emerged: the imperialists and the anti-imperialists. But these designations are somewhat misleading. Both sides agreed that America should intervene in areas of American interest. Both wanted a dynamic international trade. But there were real differences.

The imperialists generally favored acquiring colonies. They believed that these new territories could be administered by the United States without any serious compromise of tradition or the Constitution. The anti-imperialists, led by Grover Cleveland, William Jennings Bryan, Andrew Carnegie, civil service reformer Carl Schurz, together with a host of reformers, argued against keeping the Philippines. They drew a dividing line through American history. In the first period—up to 1899—they praised legitimate continental and territorial expansion. But taking the Philippines meant European-style colonialism. How, asked Schurz, could the United States absorb populations "incapable of becoming assimilated to the Anglo-Saxon"? For Bryan, principle overshadowed questions of race. America's mission was to liberate, "not place shackles upon those who are struggling to be free."

Most of the anti-imperialists believed that trade could be increased without colonies. They wanted a limited number of bases—a strategic empire—but not the Philippines. As many as 30,000 Americans joined the Anti-imperialist League and almost prevented passage of the peace treaty with Spain. And by 1913, they had reversed the initial victory of the imperialists regarding the formal possession of colonies. The new president, Woodrow Wilson, agreed that the Philippines should eventually be granted independence.

The Spanish-American War had other serious effects. It moved the United States closer to the sort of entangling alliances it had traditionally avoided. In the late nineteenth century, Great Britain faced a loss of its world predominance and looked around for new friends. The swift rise of Germany in Europe had upset the balance of power. Britain moved to court the Americans. After the near-collision in Venezuela, Britain strongly supported U.S. claims against the Spanish. In return, the United States expressed sympathy for England in its bitter colonial war in South Africa with the German-backed Boers.

The new informal alliance of Anglo-Saxon nations paid off handsomely. Britain supported American efforts to retard Japanese, German, and Russian efforts to carve protectorates out of the Chinese empire. Secretary of State John Hay's brash "Open Door" notes of September 1899 and July 1900 demanded that European powers stop partitioning China and that they treat all nations equally in their spheres of interest. This, he hoped, would prevent the collapse of China and the exclusion of American commerce. The British agreed in principle. Other nations were far less compliant, but China did manage to avoid being partitioned by the contending European nations.

Probably more significant, Britain agreed in 1901 to the Hay-Pauncefote Treaty, which canceled prior agreements for joint U.S.–British construction of a canal across the Isthmus of Panama. The treaty freed the United States to dig the canal alone. As Hay wrote of it, the developing American-British friendship was "a sanction like that of religion which binds up to a sort of partnership in the beneficent work of the world."

U.S. Foreign Policy, 1901–16

ROOSEVELT AND THE PANAMA CANAL

When an assassin's bullet brought Roosevelt into the White House in 1901, it elevated to power America's leading advocate of an activist foreign policy. But Roosevelt's actions disclosed that even he believed foreign policy had important limitations. By 1901 most of the pieces of an American empire had already fallen into place; only the Panama Canal remained to be built—"by far the most important action I took in foreign affairs," wrote Roosevelt.

By securing the independence of Panama and an American monopoly for a canal, Roosevelt reached into someone else's yard and plucked the ripest fruit. Panama had been the northernmost—and most troublesome—province of Colombia. Its greatest natural asset was favorable terrain for a shipping canal. Roosevelt encouraged Panamanian rebel leaders, who declared their independence in late 1903. Roosevelt ordered U.S. naval vessels to protect the fledgling government, and almost immediately afterward the United States signed a treaty with Panama. The new nation granted the Canal Zone to the United States plus exclusive rights to construct a canal. In exchange, the United States paid $10 million to the new republic.

Ownership of the Canal Zone and a network of bases and possessions focused American attention on the perennial instability of Latin America. In December 1904, Roosevelt issued his corollary to the Monroe Doctrine. The situation of economic chaos and potential foreign intervention he described in Central America was acute. Speaking of the need to preserve "civilized society," the president declared that he would intervene in any country to restore order and decent government. If a nation "keeps order and

This huge and intricate construction site of the Atlantic Ocean locks at Gatun reveals why the building of the Panama Canal was so difficult and took from 1904 to 1914 to complete. (Bettmann Archive)

pays its obligations," it need not fear the United States, he said. But if chaos invited foreign interference, America would intervene. Roosevelt backed up his statement with action in 1905, when he sent troops to the Dominican Republic to force it to pay its international debts.

On a very different front, Roosevelt played the role of arbitrator in the Russo-Japanese War of 1904–05. This bitter conflict between two rising forces in Asia brought huge casualties, civil unrest in Russia, and the shocking defeat of a European power by Japan. Roosevelt skillfully negotiated a peace treaty that called for Russian evacuation of portions of Manchuria and their withdrawal from Korea. It divided Sakhalin Island between Russia and Japan. To careful observers, this struggle portended an emerging new world in which Japan would become a leading participant and in which older European empires would be challenged. The war also confirmed the importance of naval power. For his efforts, Roosevelt won the Nobel Peace Prize. But perhaps most significant from the American perspective, he negotiated a settlement that prevented either Japan or Russia from becoming the dominant power in east Asia.

A portentous group of dignitaries in top hats, led by William Howard Taft, on an inspection trip of Panama Canal construction. (William H. Taft National Historic Site)

TAFT AND "DOLLAR DIPLOMACY" As president from 1909 to 1913, William Howard Taft continued most of Roosevelt's policies but under a new name: Dollar Diplomacy. He did not use this term to sound crass; he merely wanted to play down the use of force. But like so much else in his administration, good intentions tripped over a bad choice of words. Taft left much of his policymaking to Philander C. Knox, the new secretary of state. Knox reorganized the State Department into more efficient regional and topical divisions. Overt interventions in Latin America continued—in the Dominican Republic again, and in Honduras and Nicaragua. The purpose was to enforce order and security in areas around the Canal Zone. Taft's other purpose was to increase American economic dominance in the area. As he told Congress in 1912, he intended to support "every legitimate and beneficial enterprise abroad." He also worked hard to open European development consortiums in China to American investors.

Taft pursued this policy because he was convinced that foreign capital remained the only practical way to engineer progress in the undeveloped world and because he wished to aid

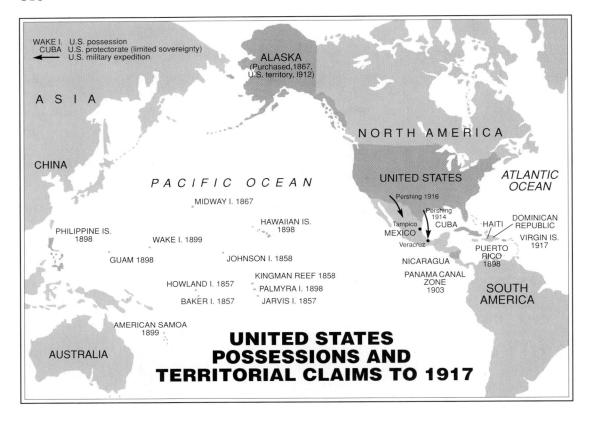

WAKE I. U.S. possession
CUBA U.S. protectorate (limited sovereignty)
← U.S. military expedition

ALASKA
(Purchased,1867,
U.S. territory, 1912)

ASIA

NORTH AMERICA

CHINA

PACIFIC OCEAN

UNITED STATES

ATLANTIC
OCEAN

MIDWAY I. 1867

Pershing 1916

HAWAIIAN IS.
1898

PHILIPPINE IS.
1898

WAKE I. 1899

Pershing
1914
Tampico   CUBA
MEXICO

HAITI

DOMINICAN
REPUBLIC

VIRGIN IS.
1917

GUAM 1898

JOHNSON I. 1858

Veracruz

PUERTO
RICO
1898

KINGMAN REEF 1858

NICARAGUA

HOWLAND I. 1857

PALMYRA I. 1898

PANAMA CANAL
ZONE
1903

SOUTH
AMERICA

BAKER I. 1857

JARVIS I. 1857

AMERICAN SAMOA
1899

UNITED STATES
POSSESSIONS AND
TERRITORIAL CLAIMS TO 1917

AUSTRALIA

American investors. Based on his experience in the Philippines and also in dealing with Cuba and Panama, he concluded that American institutions and investments would help bring enlightenment to the nonindustrialized areas of the world. Taft's legacy was, therefore, continued activism and intervention in support of American economic, political, and strategic interests without Roosevelt's rhetoric and daring.

WILSON AND MISSION DIPLOMACY

Taft's administration bridged the empire-building years of McKinley and Roosevelt with the mission diplomacy of Woodrow Wilson beginning in 1913. Wilson's assumption of the presidency brought leading anti-imperialists to power. With William Jennings Bryan as secretary of state, Wilson invoked a high moral tone in foreign relations. But much had changed since the debate over the Philippines. The United States had

acquired an empire and the Panama Canal. It had established an informal alliance with the British. Involvement in the affairs of Latin American republics had increased. Wilson did not intend to undo any of these developments, but he did commit his administration to what he believed was a more responsible exercise of power.

When Wilson assumed office, ideas about America's world destiny were very much in the air. Anglo-Saxon cultural consciousness, based on pseudoscientific theories of racial superiority, combined with traditional notions of moral mission to create a special American sense of purpose. At the same time, Americans were beginning to develop a view of the world as filled with social rebellion, insurrection, and imperial struggle.

Under Woodrow Wilson, the United States pursued a diplomacy that the president believed would confront these dangers and set new stan-

The U.S. campaign against Pancho Villa, 1916. In order to retaliate against Mexican revolutionary leader Pancho Villa for his raids across the American border, General John J. Pershing led an expeditionary force 300 miles into Mexico. Pershing never did capture Villa, but the American presence in Mexico greatly complicated U.S. relations with that country. (Library of Congress)

dards for international behavior. The next eight years proved the possibilities and limitations of this hope. When Wilson became president, the problems that had launched America's new foreign policy had grown more complex. The balance of power in Europe had continued to swing away from Britain; there were new rebellions in the nonindustrialized world; and American economic and political interests abroad had increased significantly. By 1917 these problems had helped draw the United States into World War I.

At first, Wilson hoped to wean American foreign policy away from the interventionism of his two predecessors. But he did not give up the idea that it was America's responsibility to act to sup-

press chaos. Nor did he wish to retard the growth of American trade and investment. This placed him in something of a dilemma. For example, he sympathized with the goals of the social revolutionaries in Mexico, but he intervened in that nation when he thought events were headed in the wrong direction. Although he found Dollar Diplomacy distasteful, he nonetheless worked to protect American trade and investments abroad. He desired to prove America's right to moral leadership, but he convinced some critics that such aims were delusive or, worse, hypocritical.

In October 1913 Wilson proclaimed a new Latin American policy: "Human rights, national integrity, and opportunity," he declared, "as against material interests—that, ladies and gentlemen, is the issue which we now have to face." In China, he terminated Taft's attempts to bring Americans into investment consortiums with European powers. And he supported Secretary of State Bryan's efforts to win international treaties of arbitration to prevent war. As a gesture, Bryan had several old swords belonging to the War Department melted down and fashioned into miniature plowshares, which he presented to the president and his cabinet.

The symbolism was clear, but the policy proved more difficult to shape, particularly in the Western Hemisphere. From the first days of his administration, Wilson faced increasing problems with Mexico. Under the friendly regime of Porfirio Díaz up to 1910, American capital streamed into Mexico. This had had two important effects: It gave control of much of the Mexican economy to Americans. And economic development increased the social strains, which in turn precipitated the Mexican Revolution. When it broke out in 1910, therefore, the revolution had serious implications for U.S. policy.

Although Wilson wanted the revolution to pursue democratic goals, he could not guide or control it. At first he tried nonrecognition as a means of convincing Mexican revolutionaries to moderate their policies. When this failed, Wilson intervened militarily. Responding to what he interpreted as an insult to the nation, Wilson ordered the seizure of the Mexican port of Vera Cruz in April 1914. Eventually, General John Pershing led an American expeditionary force into Mexico during the spring and summer of 1916 to capture a Mexican troop led by Pancho Villa that had attacked across the U.S. border. At this point, however, Wilson backed off and withdrew American soldiers. But for dire events in Europe, Wilson might have intervened further. Nevertheless, considerable damage had been done. American-Mexican relations suffered for many years. Anti-Americanism became a strong element in Mexican politics. With the best of intentions, Wilson had made a bad situation worse.

World War I

The increasingly desperate war in Europe curtailed Wilson's Mexican adventure. World War I began in late July 1914. Like the gears of a giant machine, the alliances of Europe engaged the British, French, Italians, and Russians (the Allies) against the Germans, the Austro-Hungarian empire, and Turkey (the Central Powers). Other nations joined the struggle, but the key battlefields developed in northern France and western Russia.

The outbreak of hostilities occurred in the Balkans, the most politically volatile area of Europe; it infected two tottering empires, Russia and Austria-Hungary; and it quickly spread to the most advanced industrial nations. Since the 1870s and the swift industrialization of Germany, Europe had embarked on an arms race, with each side fearing isolation and encirclement. Germany formed the Triple Alliance with Austria-Hungary and Italy. France signed an agreement with Russia and then an *entente cordiale* ("friendly understanding") with Great Britain. Competition between these two groups of nations had worldwide ramifications. Germany sought to overcome Britain's predominance in international trade and to acquire the colonies and naval bases befitting a modern imperial nation. Rivalry between these two powers inevitably came to involve other industrial nations, including the United States.

The war broke out along the explosive boundaries of Austria-Hungary and Russia. Austria-Hungary sought to repress Slavic nationals, who were supported by Russia in areas bordering the Ottoman empire (present-day Turkey), Greece, and Rumania. On June 28, 1914, a member of Black Hand, the Serbian nationalist group, assassinated Archduke Francis Ferdinand, heir to the Austro-Hungarian crown. Austria declared war, the Russians (supported by France) mobilized, and Germany declared war on Russia August 1 and on France August 3. Britain entered the war against Germany August 4.

EUROPE BEFORE WORLD WAR I (1914)

ICELAND

ATLANTIC OCEAN

NORWAY

SWEDEN

NORTH SEA

BALTIC SEA

DENMARK

RUSSIAN EMPIRE

GREAT BRITAIN AND IRELAND

NETHERLANDS

GERMAN EMPIRE

BELGIUM

LUX.

FRANCE

SWITZ.

AUSTRIA-HUNGARY

RUMANIA

ITALY

SERBIA

BULGARIA

MONTENEGRO

ALBANIA

OTTOMAN EMPIRE

GREECE

PORTUGAL

SPAIN

MEDITERRANEAN SEA

MOROCCO (FR.)

ALGERIA (FR.)

TUNISIA (FR.)

LIBYA (IT.)

EGYPT

☐ Allies   ■ Central Powers

Even before its official declaration of war, Germany had initiated what it planned to be a rapid, fatal blow to France. On August 1, German troops, in accordance with the Schlieffen plan (named after the former chief of staff), attacked. Disregarding treaties, Germany poured troops through neutral Belgium and toward northern France, hoping to trap the bulk of the French army up against heavy German defenses that lay along the northeastern borders of France. Then, with France knocked out of the war, the German armies could shift rapidly by railroad to battle the Russians.

To the dismay of the French and the British, the Schlieffen plan worked well. Belgium reeled and collapsed under the hammer blows of the advancing German armies. British troops rushed to northern France. By early September, German armies had occupied important areas of northern France. The Allies chose this moment to counterattack along the Marne River. The battle raged from September 5 to 12, resulting in 500,000 casualties. Despite its indecisive result and lack of a clear winner, the German advance now stalled; France was spared. German plans had not anticipated the resilience of the French and British armies nor the logistical difficulties of supplying and commanding an extensive force over long lines of communication. Now the war settled down to a stalemate, disrupted by intermittent bloody thrusts to secure limited territory. Both sides constructed elaborate networks of trenches and defensive positions ringed with barbed wire and separated from each other by a "no-man's-land."

The relative immobility of the forces in France was dictated by the technology available to each side at the time. The principal weapons, artillery and the machine gun, exacted a terrible price in manpower but could not, in themselves, turn the tide of battle. Mounted cavalry, which had always been important in earlier wars, proved ineffectual. New weapons like tanks and airplanes were too few to be decisive. Understandably, each side sought tactics or new weapons that might tip the balance. The Germans developed and employed poison gas, which they first used in 1916. And

to overcome their inferior naval position, the Germans deployed submarines, which effectively attacked British shipping.

On the eastern front, the Germans were more effective because they excelled in equipment, training, and command. Joined by the Ottoman empire and Bulgaria, Germany and Austria inflicted huge losses on the Russians. Despair, disorganization, starvation, and revolution stalked Russia. The czar was deposed in March 1917, and the Bolsheviks, led by V. I. Lenin, took power in November. In mid-December, Russia signed an armistice with Germany, whose troops were now freed for a final push on the western front.

Despite this victory, Germany was still badly overextended. Its allies, the Turks and the Austro-Hungarians, suffered discouraging defeats. More serious was the tight economic blockade around Germany enforced by the British navy. Consequently, the German general staff decided in the winter of 1917 to try one last, decisive assault. In the spring of 1918 the Germans initiated a massive ground offensive, hoping to win the war before the entrance of the United States into the conflict could turn the tide.

THE UNITED STATES: FROM NEUTRALITY TO WAR From the very beginning of the war, American economic power and trade became a major prize in the contest between the Allies and Germany. Both sides hoped to use American economic resources to their own advantage. In such a world it was extremely difficult for Wilson to maintain American neutrality, but he tried despite his Anglophilia. On August 19, 1914, the president appealed to Americans to remain "impartial in thought as well as in action." He promised that the United States would not be drawn into the conflict. Inevitably, his stance enraged war enthusiasts Theodore Roosevelt and Henry Cabot Lodge.

Try as he might, Wilson could not control events, nor did most Americans remain neutral. Many believed that Germany had ruthlessly

The face of modern warfare. Hidden in trenches, looking across no-man's land, a German soldier prepares to throw a grenade into Allied lines. (Bayerisches Hauptstaatsarchiv, Munich)

crushed neutral Belgium. They despised German militarism and feared their new weapons such as submarines and poison gas. On the other hand, the British had angered the United States with their attempts to control American policy. And much of the large American-Irish community rooted for defeat of the English.

Wilson's greatest problem became protection of American trade and commerce, an exchange that was more and more oriented to the Allies. In late August 1914 the British navy initiated an economic blockade of the Central Powers and announced it would search ships for contraband. Most of the goods that the Germans wished to import and the Americans hoped to export were on the banned list. Strict enforcement of the blockade caused periodic breaches between Britain and the Wilson government, particularly in the fall of 1915 and the summer of 1916.

The British tried to appease American objections while they vigorously pressed their economic strangulation of Germany. Skillful diplomacy and a large increase in British purchases of American goods made the policy work. For example, when the British placed cotton on the contraband list in 1915, they simultaneously bought American cotton to make up for the lost trade. In 1914 the value of American trade with Britain was about $600 million annually. By 1917 it had increased to over $2 billion. Smaller to begin with, German trade fell to almost nothing in 1917.

In effect, Wilson accepted the British blockade. The Germans, therefore, had to choose. They could let British-American trade flourish, or they could block it and risk sinking American ships. Germany tried at first to impose a blockade against the British Isles. Its only effective weapon was a fleet of submarines. Although no match for naval vessels on the surface, these U-boats (from *unterseeboot*, meaning submarine) wreaked havoc on undefended merchant ships.

For two years the Germans pursued an intermittent policy of sinking merchant ships. But they dared not use their full powers for fear of forcing the United States into war. This possibility loomed in May 1915 when, without warning, a German U-boat sank the British passenger ship *Lusitania*. Although carrying some war materiel, the ship had 2,000 passengers aboard. Struck by a torpedo, the ship sank; 1,200 people, including 128 Americans, perished.

Rejecting any excuses or explanations, Wilson demanded that the Germans immediately end their attacks on merchant ships. William Jennings Bryan, rather than send this ultimatum (which he believed betrayed American neutrality), resigned as secretary of state. His successor, Robert Lansing, was far more antagonistic to the Germans. But the crisis died down by summer, when the German government promised to refrain from attacking passenger ships.

The next serious confrontation occurred in the spring of 1916, when a U-boat sank the *Sussex*, an unarmed Channel steamer. This time Lansing sent an ultimatum to Germany. Either stop attacking "passenger and freight carrying vessels" he warned, or the United States would break diplomatic relations. Germany retreated. In the meantime, America and the Allies moved closer, as Wilson allowed the British and French to borrow large sums of money from American bankers.

WAR AND PEACE Wilson had always made it clear that in or out of the war, the United States desired a hand in settling the peace. This was the essence of his mission diplomacy. On January 22, 1917, he informed the Senate of his goals: peace without victory, the spread and support of self-government in Europe, freedom of the seas, and world disarmament. He also outlined an organization that would later become the League of Nations. Thus when German attacks on U.S. shipping forced the nation into war early in the spring of 1917, Wilson had already anticipated how the final peace treaty might be drawn.

By the winter of 1916–17, the Germans had decided they must win the war quickly by attacking all shipping to the Allies. In effect, they had

opted for war with America. An exacerbating factor was an intercepted note from Alfred Zimmermann, the German foreign secretary, that spoke of an alliance with Mexico—with recovery of Texas, New Mexico, and Arizona as part of the agreement—which helped persuade Wilson of the necessity for war. Then on February 1, 1917, Germany declared unrestricted submarine warfare against shipping. Three days later the United States severed diplomatic relations.

The declaration of war was passed by an overwhelming majority of Congress: 82 to 6 in the Senate and 373 to 50 in the House. American troops did not reach the front until the latter part of 1917, but the navy and merchant marine rushed to protect trade routes to England and France. In 1918, before American soldiers could make a difference, the Germans tried for a quick, decisive victory. They struck five times between March and July. Successful in some respects, these moves ultimately exhausted and disheartened the German troops. Over the summer and fall, the Allies struck back. By this time, fresh American troops had entered the contest. After a final offensive in September, the Allies advanced sharply and the Germans retreated. By November, Germany had been routed. On November 11, 1918, the two sides signed an armistice and maneuvering for a peace settlement

Defense Expenditures by Service: 1895–1920		
Year	Army	Navy
1895	$51,805,000	$28,798,000
1899	229,841,000	63,942,000
1903	118,630,000	82,618,000
1907	149,775,000	97,128,000
1911	197,199,000	119,938,000
1915	202,060,000	141,836,000
1919	9,009,076,000	2,002,311,000

Source: U.S. Department of Commerce, Bureau of the Census, *Historical Statistics of the United States: Colonial Times to the Present*, bicentennial ed. (Washington, D.C.: Government Printing Office, 1975), Vol. II, p. 1114.

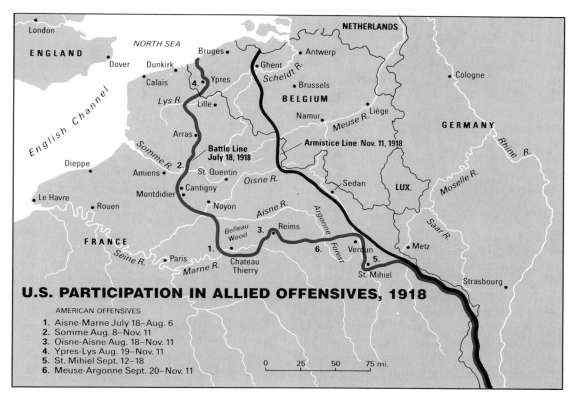

U.S. PARTICIPATION IN ALLIED OFFENSIVES, 1918

AMERICAN OFFENSIVES
1. Aisne-Marne July 18–Aug. 6
2. Somme Aug. 8–Nov. 11
3. Oisne-Aisne Aug. 18–Nov. 11
4. Ypres-Lys Aug. 19–Nov. 11
5. St. Mihiel Sept. 12–18
6. Meuse-Argonne Sept. 20–Nov. 11

began. Germany, Austria-Hungary, and the Ottoman empire watched helplessly as the Allied powers redrew the maps of Europe and the Middle East. Europe, meanwhile, lay devastated, with transportation, industry, and agriculture in shambles, governments in turmoil, and over 14 million dead. These were Wilson's most glorious and tragic moments.

Early in January 1918 Wilson had publicized his peace proposals, the Fourteen Points. Some of these—such as the return to France of Alsace-Lorraine and independence for the peoples of the Austro-Hungarian and Turkish empires—coincided with Allied aims. But others did not. For example, freedom of the seas and removal of trade barriers could be construed as an attack on the British empire. Among all the points, the proposed League of Nations to guarantee world peace was most important to Wilson, although some Allies viewed it with indifference.

The president traveled to Europe in early 1919, a hero to the huge crowds who greeted him. But in the peace negotiations he had no real power to impose his demands on the Allies. Thus he compromised: punitive territorial and economic measures to be exacted from the Germans; the German protectorate of Kiachow in China to be transferred to the Japanese. He did, however, win on the League of Nations. On June 28 the Germans, under duress, signed the treaty in the splendid Hall of Mirrors at the palace of Versailles outside Paris. Although something of a personal victory for Wilson, the negotiations had taken a heavy toll. One observer remarked: "I found him looking utterly worn out, exhausted, often one side of his face twitching with nervousness." In fact, he was very ill.

Wilson brought the treaty back to a deeply divided and war-weary America. The Democratic party had lost control of Congress in 1918, and

Henry Cabot Lodge, an opponent of the treaty and the League of Nations, now headed the Senate Foreign Relations Committee. To such opponents, the treaty, and especially the League of Nations, seemed destined to entangle the United States forever in the machinations of European politics. To some, this appeared not to be a fitting culmination of a war to end wars and make the world permanently safe for democracy; it seemed, instead, to risk recurring wars. Moreover, the war had caused enormous strains in American society.

WAR AT HOME Organizing for war was a test of Wilson's progressivism. Because of long-standing hesitations, the president only acceded to a cautious and temporary experiment in executive-branch centralization. Financing the war was accomplished largely through the sale of government bonds, dubbed "Liberty" loans, rather than increased taxes. Besides training and deploying troops, the federal government's greatest tasks included coordination, supervision, and stimulating production of war goods and food. This it conducted largely through the activities of the War Industries Board, the Railroad Administration, and the Food Administration created in the spring of 1917.

Given the immense problems and the minimal coercive powers granted to these agencies, much was accomplished that had lasting effects. One notable example was the standardization by size, weight, and shape of American industrial commodities, which helped create a national market of interchangeable parts and products. In many industries, employment and wages went up, while increased demand raised farm profits. There were also huge profits to be made by companies engaged in war production.

War profiteering was only one risk of the new intimacy between government and business. The close relationship that prevailed during the war remained afterward to undercut the broad premise of the progressive hopes for a pluralistic public interest. Moreover, Wilson's reluctance to use the power of government to regulate and guide the economy during the war opened the way for—perhaps even required—ideological coercion. This was inspired by an enthusiastic and occasionally excessive nationalism that was sometimes misdirected against unions and immigrants.

Wilson's strategy of persuasion was to encourage support for the war and compliance with his economic programs through advertising and public agitation. Consequently, in 1917 he appointed progressive reformer George Creel to head the Committee on Public Information. Creel took to his job energetically, overseeing a nationwide speaking campaign of 75,000 "Four-Minute Men" (so named to recall Revolutionary War Minute Men). The committee also published 75 million pieces of prowar literature. But its strident, all-or-nothing tone led to a rigid definition of patriotism. Clearly, some of these strains must be blamed on Wilson. He had allowed the overzealous Creel to wage a vociferous propaganda campaign in favor of the war. Unfortunately, the committee had oversold its case.

Attacks on civil liberties also soured Wilson's efforts. The Espionage Act of June 1917 and the Sedition Act of May 1918 effectively outlawed criticism of the American government, its leaders, and its national symbols. Intolerance was also aimed at German-Americans. In areas of large German immigrant populations in the Midwest, local authorities tried to suppress the German language and German culture. Popular writers depicted Germans as degenerate beasts in their fiction. Suddenly, ethnic identity and nationalism became a dividing line. Racial intolerance also flared in this charged atmosphere, in part because African Americans moved north to fill war production jobs. One of the worst incidents was a violent race riot in 1917 in East St. Louis, Illinois, in which thirty-nine blacks and nine whites died.

Attacks on radical political groups were also intense. This "red scare" drew energy from fears of the Russian Revolution of 1917, whose new government signed a separate peace with the

"Vive Wilson!" This electric sign in Paris (which translates as "Long live Wilson!") was part of the hero's welcome accorded to President Woodrow Wilson when he traveled to Europe in 1919 to negotiate a peace treaty. Despite his personal popularity, Wilson won only a compromise from America's European allies when he asked for a less harsh and punitive treaty against Germany. (U.S. Signal Corps, in The National Archives)

Germans. The organization of revolutionary communist organizations in the United States, which changed the face of American radicalism, and a series of widespread strikes aroused fears that revolution might spread to America. Socialist leaders like Eugene Debs who spoke against the war were imprisoned. And the government attacked the Industrial Workers of the World, seized their records, and deported many of their members. In this atmosphere of fear and suspicion, it was easy to conclude that America's active participation in the war—its pursuit of the new foreign policy—had resulted in contaminating the nation with the class struggle and the disorders of Europe. It seemed to threaten to compromise American uniqueness.

For a nation worried about such questions, the Versailles treaty was both too full of idealism and too riddled with compromises. Worse, it tied the United States to a permanent world organization. Wilson demanded its acceptance. Trying to arouse public support, to work around strong and articulate opposition in the Senate, he embarked on a futile speaking tour in late summer in 1919. On September 25, 1919, in Pueblo, Colorado, he renewed his vision of America's destiny: "We have accepted [the truth of America's moral vision] and we are going to be led by it, and it is going to lead us, and through us the world, out into pastures of quietness and peace such as the world never dreamed of before."

These were the words of a man who saw not just a dream of world peace but perhaps also his own final peace. The next day he collapsed, and he never fully regained his old vigor. The Versailles treaty languished in Congress; Wilson

John Reed

Soon we were near the battle. In the east, across the vast level country, a faint gray light appeared. The noble alamo trees, towering thickly in massy lines along the ditches to the west, burst into showers of bird-song. It was getting warm, and there came the tranquil smell of earth and grass and growing corn—a calm summer dawn. Into this the noise of battle broke like something insane. The hysterical chatter of rifle fire, that seemed to carry a continuous undertone of screaming—although when you listened for it it was gone. The nervous, deadly stab—stab—stab of the machine guns, like some gigantic woodpecker. The cannon booming like great bells, and the whistle of their shells. Boom—Pi-i-i-e-e-a-uuu! And that most terrible of all the sounds of war, shrapnel exploding. Crash—Whee-e—eaaa!!!

Like the juxtaposition of dreamy romanticism and brutal reality in this passage from his book *Insurgent Mexico*, John Reed's life represented a mixture of romantic and revolutionary elements. Born in 1887 in Portland, Oregon, Reed grew up a sheltered and wealthy young man. Until the age of sixteen or so, he was a thin and sickly boy. By the time he entered Harvard College in 1906, however, he had conquered physical weakness. He had also begun to write fiction.

At Harvard, Reed continued his writing, contributing stories and poems to the school's famous publication the *Lampoon*. He also took up with a group of young radicals and socialists. Among them was the future political writer and essayist Walter Lippmann. By the time Reed graduated, he had become an accomplished prose stylist, although certainly not the poet that his classmate T. S. Eliot was.

Like another famous Western writer of his day, Jack London, Reed thirsted for experience to give his prose the hard edge of realism. For a young man, the best way to find experience was in travel. Although he voyaged first to Europe, he quickly set his sights on New York, his "enchanted city."

Living in Greenwich Village, which was still a quaint, cheap backwater of the city, Reed plunged into the district's bohemian life, with its all-night discussions, passionate love affairs, and revolutionary politics. A friend of many of the century's young experimental painters and poets, Reed himself turned more and more to journalism. But this was not the typical journalism of his day. He insisted on being part of what he observed, on merging himself into revolutionary struggles, such as the one in Mexico, that seemed to be breaking out across the world.

So this poet and revolutionary trudged along the lines with Pancho Villa, the radical general of the Mexican Revolution, sending back dramatic articles describing the struggle. In 1917 Reed found himself in Russia, a participant in and recorder of the events of the communist revolution. This account he published in a famous and controversial book, *Ten Days That Shook the World*. In 1920 he died in Moscow, victim of an influenza epidemic, still a romantic—and a revolutionary—buried in the wall of the Kremlin as a hero of the Russian Revolution.

Picture: Culver Pictures

EUROPE AFTER WORLD WAR I (1925)

Countries created after World War I

CHRONOLOGY

1900 William H. Taft heads Philippine Commission. Secretary of State John Hay announces "Open Door" policy.

1901 Hay-Pauncefote Treaty signed by Britain and the United States.

March 1901 Filipino revolutionary Emilio Aguinaldo captured.

Fall 1901 Pacification efforts in Batangas province begin.

September 1901 Massacre of American soldiers at Balangiga, Philippines.

December 1901–January 1902 The ordeal of Samar.

1904 Treaty signed by United States and Panama.

1893 Frederick J. Turner presents his "frontier thesis." Grover Cleveland rejects annexation of Hawaii.

1850 Singer Sewing Machine Company founded.

1890	1892	1894	1896	1898	1900	1902	1904

February 1898 Battleship *Maine* explodes in Havana harbor.

April 1898 Congress declares war on Spain.

May 1898 American fleet sinks Spanish fleet in Manila Bay.

August 1898 American army seizes Manila.

August 1898 Spain sues for peace in war with the United States.

February 1899 Philippine insurrection.

1890 United States census marks end of frontier. Alfred T. Mahan publishes *The Influence of Sea Power upon History*.

1895 Cuban rebellion begins.

May 1902 Court-martial of General Jacob Smith.

July 1902 First Organic Act creating a colonial government in the Philippines.

1902 Pacification of the Philippines ends.

1903 Panama rebels against Colombia.

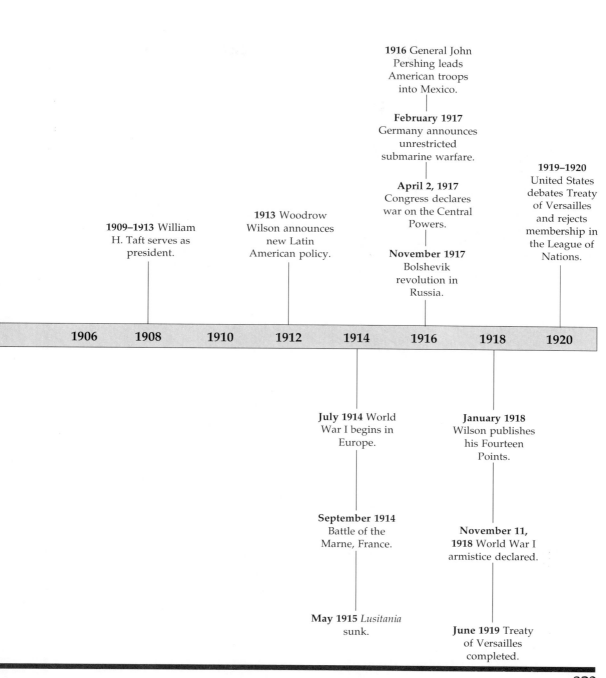

1916 General John Pershing leads American troops into Mexico.

February 1917 Germany announces unrestricted submarine warfare.

April 2, 1917 Congress declares war on the Central Powers.

1919–1920 United States debates Treaty of Versailles and rejects membership in the League of Nations.

1909–1913 William H. Taft serves as president.

1913 Woodrow Wilson announces new Latin American policy.

November 1917 Bolshevik revolution in Russia.

1906 1908 1910 1912 1914 1916 1918 1920

July 1914 World War I begins in Europe.

January 1918 Wilson publishes his Fourteen Points.

September 1914 Battle of the Marne, France.

November 11, 1918 World War I armistice declared.

May 1915 *Lusitania* sunk.

June 1919 Treaty of Versailles completed.

Woodrow Wilson riding to the 1921 inauguration.
Wilson, left, accompanying President-Elect Warren
G. Harding, right, to his inauguration in 1921, shows
the ravages of vascular disease. After his stroke in
1919, Wilson's participation in the day-to-day
functioning of government was minimal. (Library
of Congress)

refused to compromise on the League, and the
Senate refused to accept the treaty as written. The
dream of putting the world in order receded.

During his last year in office, Wilson rarely
appeared in public. Most decisions issued in his
name were made by advisers or his second wife
Edith, although for a confusing period in 1920,
he talked about running for a third term. By the
approach of the election, issues had degenerated
into considerations of personalities, and the winner of the race, Republican Warren G. Harding,
took no clear stand on the problems that most
divided the nation. Thus Wilson's final days
trailed off into helpless frustration. He even
spoke—plaintively—in the last year of his life of
accepting a college presidency again.

The political leader who had possibly best
understood the revolutionary new world that the
Spanish-American War and the struggle for the
Philippines brought had failed to persuade his
compatriots to follow his vision of a new, democratic world order. He had personally failed,
moreover, to understand the costs and pitfalls
for the nation in pursuing this elusive vision. He
had by his own definition failed as a leader.

Suggestions for Further Reading

DIPLOMATIC HISTORY

The field of American foreign relations at the turn
of the century has recently undergone a rich and
fruitful debate. The best early works in the field
established the outlines of American diplomatic history. Samuel Flagg Bemis, *The Latin American Policy
of the United States* (1943), is a classic study of the
intricacies of diplomacy. Dexter Perkins, *A History
of the Monroe Doctrine, 1867–1907* (1955), traces the
development of American attitudes toward other
Western Hemisphere nations. Charles S. Campbell,
*The Transformation of American Foreign Relations, 1865
to 1900* (1976), provides an excellent, balanced, and

updated account of American foreign policy in this
period.

Much of the dispute over the meaning of America's foreign relations was initiated after the publication of William Appleman Williams, *Tragedy of
American Diplomacy*, revised ed. (1962). This work
began a critical reevaluation of the motivations and
accomplishments of foreign policy. Another principal work in this vein is Walter LaFeber, *The New
Empire: An Interpretation of American Expansion, 1860–
1898* (1963), which explores the economic and ideological impulses that triggered the American quest
for empire. An excellent study in this tradition that

focuses on the Orient is Thomas J. McCormick, *The China Market: America's Quest for Informal Empire, 1893–1901* (1967). Robert H. Ferrell, *Woodrow Wilson and World War I* (1985), writes convincingly of the president's successes and failures. For a good discussion of domestic policy during the war, see David M. Kennedy, *Over Here* (1980). Edward Coffman, *The War to End All Wars* (1968, 1983), provides an excellent account of the American military experience in World War I.

IMPERIALISM

A key problem to emerge in the debate over foreign relations was the meaning of imperialism and the degree to which American policymakers shared imperialist ambitions. Thomas G. Paterson, ed., *American Imperialism and Anti-Imperialism* (1973), presents the writings of imperialists and anti-imperialists as they debated such questions as acquisition of the Philippines. The best examination of the leading participants in the debate is in Robert L. Beisner, *Twelve Against Empire: The Anti-Imperialists, 1898–1900* (1968). In connection with this issue, a fascinating and influential document is Alfred Mahan, *The Influence of Sea Power upon History* (1957). Ernest R. May, in his thoughtful *American Imperial-ism: A Speculative Essay* (1968), offers a different view of the origins and nature of the imperialism debate at the turn of the century. Kenton J. Clymer, *Protestant Missionaries in the Philippines, 1898–1916* (1986), explores the role and impact of the evangelicals. See also Stuart Creighton Miller's excellent *Benevolent Assimilation: The American Conquest of the Philippines, 1899–1903* (1982).

LATIN AMERICAN POLICY

American foreign relations in the progressive era related largely to Latin America. Theodore Roosevelt helped establish a new foreign policy toward America's southern neighbors. A good place to begin study of Roosevelt is John Morton Blum, *The Republican Roosevelt*, 2nd ed. (1977). A lively and interesting account of the Spanish-American War is Frank Freidel, *The Splendid Little War* (1958). P. Edward Haley, *Revolution and Intervention: The Diplomacy of Taft and Wilson with Mexico, 1910–1917* (1970), untangles the complicated and very important relations of the United States with Mexico prior to World War I. See also Arthur Link, ed., *Woodrow Wilson and a Revolutionary World, 1913–1921* (1982).

CHAPTER 19
MASS CULTURE
AND THE "JAZZ AGE"

THE EPISODE: *In 1926, a New York hotel manager offered a prize of $25,000 to the first person to fly an airplane non-stop from New York to Paris. During the next two years, four planes crashed making the attempt. And in those four crashes, six aviators died and several others were badly hurt.*

But there were still men and planes ready to dare for the celebrity and the money that would come to the first who succeeded. By May 1927, no fewer than three aircraft were poised at the edge of the dirt runway of Roosevelt Field on Long Island, New York, ready to make the attempt. Two of them were large, multi-engined craft, with crews of several men. The third, called The Spirit of Saint Louis, *was a small, single-engine plane that could carry only one man. His name was Charles A. Lindbergh, and he and his airplane were about to become the most adored objects of a decade that was hungry for celebrities and symbols. When the other crews were waiting for the weather to improve, Lindbergh decided to chance a difficult takeoff from a rainy and muddy field. He would make it to Paris. More importantly, he would make it into the minds and hearts of the first generation of Americans who had the means to confer instant media fame on the people they chose as their heroes.*

THE HISTORICAL SETTING: *Lindbergh's feat was in many ways a stunt and of no practical importance. Lindbergh had in fact been a barnstorming stunt pilot. For the historian, the significance of the flight does not lie in what it reveals about him or about the history of aviation. Instead, the significance of Lindbergh's flight lies in the terms in which it was celebrated, the ways the American public—the white, middle-class public, at least—transformed the stunt into a feat and transformed Lindbergh himself into a symbol of what they wanted to believe America was all about: youth and innocence combined with daring and technological mastery.*

Much of what makes up the romantic images of the 1920s—the notion of the "Roaring Twenties" or the "Jazz Age," or the idea of the "Lost Generation"— began to take shape in the progressive period. And the echoes of the 1920s lasted far beyond 1930. Nevertheless, the 1920s were the decade in which all the pieces necessary for the formation of a relatively homogeneous middle-class media "public" fell into place—the press, radio, motion pictures, and urban affluence.

The 1920s had another side, of course. Intellectuals produced a remarkable body of writing and art that was extremely critical of the so-called New Era. For the first time, a truly remarkable community of African-American artists and writers assembled in Harlem and generated what became known as the Harlem Renaissance. And white writers in centers like Chicago, New York, and Paris produced an equally impressive body of novels, poetry, music, and painting.

LINDBERGH'S FLIGHT

The captain was a little man, dapper and very French. But he sought a big prize: $25,000 for the first person to fly an airplane from New York to Paris. His name might sound somewhat strange—even funny—to American ears: René Fonck. But his reputation was formidable. He had been the youngest French air ace in the Great War (as World War I was known until World War II). Without being seriously injured himself, he had shot down at least seventy-five German planes. In a war that had turned the new aviators into overnight heroes, Fonck's reputation for skill, courage, and "dash" was probably greater than that of any other pilot. Now, in the summer of 1926, he was preparing for a flight that could make him an even greater hero, both in France and in the United States.

Compared with any of the planes Fonck had flown during the war, his new silver-colored craft was huge. Like most of the other large aircraft of the day, it had three engines and two pairs of wings—a biplane, it was called. Its large cabin was equipped for a crew of four: a pilot, a copilot, a mechanic, and a radio operator. The problem that Fonck faced was simply getting the plane off the ground with enough fuel to fly the 3,600 miles to Paris. All summer he tested the plane in New York, gradually increasing the gasoline load for each test.

At daybreak on September 21 Fonck's plane was pulled onto the east-west runway at Roosevelt Field, a small airport on Long Island. The wind was blowing from the west, as it almost always does after dawn on Long Island. So Fonck would take off from east to west. To get the plane off the ground, he and his crew would have to attain a speed of eighty miles an hour. One by one, the engines were turned up to their maximum power. The blocks were pulled away from the wheels, and the plane began to move. It lurched slightly, having over 2,000 gallons of gasoline aboard, and chased its own awkward shadow down the dirt runway.

When the plane passed the halfway point on the small airstrip, it did not have the speed needed for takeoff. The small crowd of onlookers waited for Fonck to cut power. But something had gone wrong, either with the pilot or with his controls. The plane simply roared on. The runway ended. The plane took a sharp, short drop into a gully, then exploded and burst into flames. Somehow Fonck got out, and so did his navigator. But the copilot and the radio operator burned to death.

Despite the crash, the man who had offered the $25,000 prize—Raymond Orteig, a Frenchman who managed two hotels in New York—announced that his offer still stood. For a while Fonck's crash made headlines and kept alive the idea of a New York–Paris flight. Late in February 1927 others began to announce that they would make the flight. It was soon obvious that a real contest was developing. It would not be merely a battle between one airplane and the ocean but a race among several aviators and their planes. The stage was set for what the public began to sense would be the greatest thrill of the decade.

By the end of March 1927 there were four serious contenders. One was the *America*, a plane piloted by Admiral Richard E. Byrd, who had gained fame as the first man to fly to the North Pole. Byrd was backed with over $100,000 from a wealthy New York merchant. His three-engined plane, with a wingspan of over seventy feet, was enormous by the standards of the day. It seemed to have the best chance.

A second entry was another trimotored craft, the *American Legion*, named after and supported by the veterans' organization. It too was backed with $100,000. Unlike Fonck's plane and Byrd's *America*, the *American Legion* carried only two men. A third entry was a plane known as the *Columbia*, a single-winged, single-engined craft. The *Columbia* would soon set the world endurance record by flying for over fifty hours. Finally, there was a French entry, a single-engined biplane called the *White Bird*. Its pilot and copilot, a pair of French aces from the Great War, planned to make the flight in reverse—from Paris to New York. The *White Bird* was said to have the most powerful gasoline engine ever put into an airplane.

By mid-April the weather had warmed up enough to make flight over the North Atlantic seem possible. On April 16 Byrd took his *America* up from a New Jersey airport for its first test flight. Byrd and three crewmen flew the plane for a few hours and then brought it down for its first landing. The heavy landing gear touched ground smoothly, but almost at once there was a sound of splintering wood and wrenched metal. The *America* flipped over and skidded to a halt on its back. All four men managed to escape. Byrd had a broken wrist, and two of the other crewmen were badly hurt. They would not be able to fly again for weeks.

Ten days later the *American Legion* was at Langley Field, Virginia, undergoing its last test flight. The plane had flown well in earlier attempts, but both its designers and its pilot knew it was too heavy. To find out whether the plane could make the Paris flight, the pilot and copilot decided to fly it from Virginia to New York with a full load of gasoline. The takeoff was slower than usual. For a moment it seemed as if the plane would not clear a line of trees at the end of the runway. To avoid them, the pilot banked to the right a few degrees. The slight turn was too much, upsetting the delicate balance of the plane. The *American Legion* slid downward into a wet marsh and turned over. The pilot and copilot were trapped inside the cabin that filled first with gasoline fumes and then with water. By the time rescuers came wading through the marsh, the two men were dead.

Four men had been killed and three others hurt, and the race over the Atlantic had not yet begun. On both sides of the ocean, in America and in France, newspapers stirred public excitement to a high pitch. Surely one of the planes would make it sooner or later. But no one knew what might happen next or who might be injured or killed. The race to Paris had the competitive excitement of a World Series or a heavyweight championship fight. And it had the danger and drama of war. In the United States the race gained as much importance in the public press as had the war of 1898, the sinking of the *Lusitania,* or even the declaration of war in 1917. In France the excitement was heightened by the memory of Fonck's crash. Moreover, the entry into the contest of two more young ace pilots, Charles Nungesser and Francis Coli, held great promise. Both had been wounded a total of twenty-six times in air combat. Between them they had won almost every medal that the French government could award.

At dawn on May 8, Nungesser and Coli took off for New York from Le Bourget airport near Paris. A great crowd gathered to watch the two heroes and their *White Bird.* Nungesser got the wheels off the ground, but too soon. The *White Bird* dropped back down onto the runway with a thud. Finally, it gathered speed and left the ground almost two-thirds of a mile down the long strip.

The next morning, American newspapers reported that the plane had been sighted over Newfoundland. Paris celebrated with an excitement that almost matched that of the day of the armistice. Nungesser and Coli had dropped their landing gear over the ocean to save weight and lessen wind resistance. New Yorkers watched the harbor where the Frenchmen hoped to land and keep afloat until they could be reached by waiting boats. But the *White Bird* was never seen again. In France the premature celebrations quickly came to a shocked end.

The death toll in the New York–Paris race had reached six in less than a year. The world's most experienced pilots—backed by large sums of money, flying the best airplanes that modern technology could provide, with the most powerful motors ever developed—had all failed.

The man who was finally going to win the race to Paris had been reading every newspaper report he could find on all the airplane tests, takeoffs, and crashes. When Fonck's plane burned, Charles Lindbergh was flying airmail between Chicago and St. Louis. When Byrd and the others announced they would enter the competition, Lindbergh was in San Diego supervising the construction of a new plane for himself. When Nungesser and Coli took off from Paris, he was waiting in San Diego for the weather to clear over the Rocky Mountains and the Great Plains, so he could fly east to St. Louis. From there he would go on to New York to make his attempt.

Lindbergh had only $2,000 of his own money, carefully kept for him by his mother in Detroit. He was only twenty-five years old. He looked even younger, so that almost everyone called him a boy. Worst of all, he decided on what struck everyone as a suicidal idea: to make the flight in a single-engine plane with only himself in the cockpit. He had been able to persuade some St. Louis businessmen to back him with $15,000. But this was a small sum compared to the support that Byrd's group and the *American Legion* had. Still, late in the summer of 1926, just before Fonck's crash, Lindbergh had come to an almost religious conviction that he could make the Paris flight.

At first Lindbergh had tried to negotiate with several large aircraft companies. He was turned down. No one wanted to risk a company's reputation on an insane stunt like flying from New York to Paris alone. Then Lindbergh sent a plain but daring telegram to Ryan Airlines, a small, little-known factory in California:

> RYAN AIRLINES, INC.   FEB. 3, 1927
> SAN DIEGO, CALIFORNIA
>
> CAN YOU CONSTRUCT WHIRLWIND ENGINE PLANE CAPABLE OF FLYING NONSTOP BETWEEN NEW YORK AND PARIS? IF SO PLEASE STATE COST AND DELIVERY DATE.

Surprisingly, the answer came quickly. The small company could build the plane, and it could do so for the amount of money Lindbergh had at his disposal. But it would take three months, the telegram said. Lindbergh answered:

> RYAN AIRLINES, INC.   FEB. 5, 1927
> SAN DIEGO, CALIFORNIA
>
> COMPETITION MAKES TIME ESSENTIAL. CAN YOU CONSTRUCT PLANE IN LESS THAN THREE MONTHS? PLEASE WIRE GENERAL SPECIFICATIONS.

Again the company answered quickly, making as much of a guess as a calculation. It could build a plane capable of carrying 380 gallons of gasoline at a cruising speed of 100 miles per hour, with an engine rated at only 200 horsepower. (This was less than half the power of the big engine that had taken the *White Bird* out over the Atlantic. It was also much less than the power supplied by the three engines of Byrd's great *America*.) Most important, the company promised to have the plane ready in time.

By the last week in February, Lindbergh was in San Diego working out the details on his plane. Neither Lindbergh nor the engineer who designed the plane even knew exactly how far it was to Paris. They drove to the San Diego public library to measure off the distance on a globe with a piece of string. Lindbergh remembered it this way:

> "It's 3,600 miles." The bit of white grocery string under my fingers stretches taut along the coast of North America, bends down over a faded blue ocean, and strikes the land mass of Europe. It isn't a very scientific way of finding the exact distance between two points on the earth's surface, but the answer is accurate enough for our first calculations. The designer was making quick calculations in pencil on the back of an envelope. "Maybe we'd better put in 400 gallons of gasoline instead of 380," he concludes.[1]

Lindbergh's project was simple, almost amateurish: hastily drafted telegrams, bits of string stretched across a globe, figures on the back of an envelope, and "maybe" calculations. But with no more detailed or expert plans, he decided to go ahead.

The mechanics and carpenters at Ryan started work at once on the plane that Lindbergh would call the *Spirit of St. Louis*. They built it almost literally around the

---

[1]Quotations from *The Spirit of St. Louis* by Charles A. Lindbergh are reprinted with permission of Charles Scribner's Sons, an imprint of Macmillan Publishing Company. Copyright 1953 Charles Scribner's Sons; copyright renewed © 1981 Anne Morrow Lindbergh.

Before the flight. This publicity photograph of Lindbergh and the *Spirit of St. Louis* was taken some time before the flight. Lindbergh may have been shy, but he fully understood the need to publicize his daring effort. And he knew how to emphasize the solitary nature of his flight by posing himself and his plane as though they were partners. (Culver Pictures)

pilot. The narrow, simple cockpit was just large enough to hold Lindbergh's tall, skinny body (and then only if the overhead ribs were hollowed out a little to make room for his head). In the end, the plane would be only about three feet taller than Lindbergh himself. Moreover, it would have a smaller engine than any of the other planes in the race. But this was the secret of Lindbergh's plane: simplicity. He would build the smallest, simplest plane possible, a machine designed with only one purpose: to carry enough gasoline for the trip. Everything else—comfort, safety, complicated navigating equipment—would be sacrificed to save weight, which could be translated into more gallons of gasoline.

On April 26, the day the two pilots of the *American Legion* were killed in Virginia, the *Spirit of St. Louis* was finished. Two days later Lindbergh was ready for his first test flight. He squeezed himself into his seat in the cockpit. He could touch the sides of the fuselage with his elbows. To the front, the cockpit was blind. Shiny metal sloped all the way up from the engine to the top of the wing. There were only two side windows and a glassed-in skylight overhead. For takeoffs and landings he had to lean out of one of the side windows. But the plane was designed for only one important takeoff and landing. The rest of the time, over the Atlantic, there would be nothing to see but ocean, clouds, sun, and stars.

Directly in front of Lindbergh's face was a small cluster of instruments: an air-speed indicator, a turn-and-bank indicator, a fuel-flow meter, a compass, and one or two others. The plane carried a pitifully small survival kit containing a rubber raft, a flashlight, a canteen of water, some matches, and string. Surrounding the cockpit were nothing but gasoline tanks. One tank rested in the nose between the pilot and the engine. Another lay behind the cockpit in the fuselage. And there were more tanks in the wings overhead. There was no radio, no heater to provide warmth at freezing altitudes, no sextant for navigational sightings, not even a parachute. The *Spirit of St. Louis* was built to carry only gasoline—over a ton of it, as it turned out, weighing more than the plane and the pilot put together.

But to Lindbergh, as he walked onto the sunny runway in San Diego, the *Spirit of St. Louis* was a thing of beauty and awe:

> What a beautiful machine it is, resting there on the field in front of the hangar, trim and slender, gleaming in its silver coat! All our ideas, all our calculations, all our hopes, lie there before me, waiting to undergo the acid test of flight. For me, it seems to contain the whole future of aviation.
>
> "Off! Throttle closed."
>
> I'm in the cockpit. The chief mechanic turns the propeller over several times.
>
> "Contact!"
>
> He swings his body away from the blade as he pulls it through. The engine catches, every cylinder hitting. This is different from any other cockpit I've been in before. The big fuel tank in front of me seems doubly large, now that I'm actually to fly behind it.
>
> I signal the chocks [blocks in front of the wheels of the plane] away. The *Spirit of St. Louis* rolls lightly over the baked-mud surface of the field.

The *Spirit of St. Louis* moved very quickly. Its tanks were almost empty for this first test flight.

> The tires are off the ground before they roll a hundred yards. The plane climbs quickly, even though I hold its nose down. There's a huge reserve of power. I spiral cautiously upward. I straighten out and check my instruments. I circle over the factory, watching little figures run outdoors to see the machine they had built actually flying overhead. I rock my wings and head across the bay.

During the next week Lindbergh tested the *Spirit of St. Louis* for speed, control, and, most important, takeoff under load. More and more gasoline was filtered by hand into the tanks for each run. With a load of slightly over 300 gallons, the plane took off easily. But continued landings with large loads were dangerous. Lindbergh decided to stop the tests.

The *Spirit of St. Louis* had needed a little more than 1,000 feet of runway to take off with 300 gallons. From this and other data, the Ryan designers made a theoretical calculation that, fully loaded with 400 gallons, the plane would need 2,500 feet of hard runway. Rather than tempt fate, as the crew of the *American Legion* had done by testing with a full load, Lindbergh decided to trust the plane and the designers' arithmetic. He was ready. And he knew Byrd's *America* had been repaired and was undergoing final tests. The *Columbia*, too, was ready. Both planes were poised on Long Island. Time counted more than tests.

But time seemed to work against Lindbergh. A big storm blanketed the western United States and was creeping eastward. Lindbergh had to wait several days until

Inside the *Spirit of St. Louis*. The cockpit of Lindbergh's plane was a model of stripped-down efficiency. The wicker seat may have been uncomfortable, but it was lightweight, and weight was Lindbergh's main concern. The plane had only side windows, so the pilot could not see much—for most of the flight, though, there was nothing to see. In any case, the most important thing Lindbergh had to watch for was ice on the wings. (National Air and Space Museum, Smithsonian Institution)

the rain and clouds had moved east. On the evening of May 10 he began the first leg of his trip, from San Diego to St. Louis. He flew the 1,500 miles in record time. It was the longest nonstop solo flight ever made. Then, after a night's sleep, he headed for New York.

Lindbergh arrived on Long Island May 12. He had set another record, for the fastest transcontinental flight in history. The crews of Byrd's *America* and the *Columbia* came over to shake his hand and wish him luck. A crowd gathered. Newspaper photographers and reporters pushed and shoved their way to Lindbergh, shouting for pictures and answers to their questions. A horde of people climbed to the roof of a small building next to the hangar where Lindbergh parked the plane. Their weight caused a wall to collapse. Something new and strange was happening to Lindbergh. The newspapers and the public were making him into a hero, almost a myth.

Even without Lindbergh, the New York–Paris contest had all the elements of an exciting publicity event: death, drama, and competition. But Lindbergh's entry into the race added new elements. He was going alone, thus he could become an object of hero worship in ways that the crews of the other planes could not. He was tall, thin, blue-eyed, and handsome in a boyish way. And along with his youthful good looks went other personality traits that soon endeared him to the newspapers. Above all, he was modest, shy, and simple.

All these traits combined to present a picture of an innocent young man ready to dare the impossible, alone. Lindbergh was the honest, plainspoken, cowboylike young man from the West. He was a modern David challenging the Eastern Goliaths, with their money, their experience, their financial backers, and their head start. In short, he was an underdog. The *Spirit of St. Louis*, too, was simple and seemingly innocent compared with the other planes in the race. It was a sentimental favorite.

Lindbergh could not leave his hotel room without being mobbed by people anxious to touch him "just for luck." And the newspapers played his story for all it was worth. They nicknamed him "Lucky," "The Flyin' Fool," or just "Lindy." (He had always been "Slim" to his friends.) All the hero worship that the Americans of the 1920s usually reserved for baseball players like Babe Ruth or movie stars like Rudolph Valentino was now showered on the twenty-five-year-old airmail pilot. The worship was made more serious by the fact that "The Flyin' Fool" was doing something real and dangerous, not merely hitting baseballs or posing for motion picture cameras.

In most ways this public personality created for the new celebrity was only a myth. Lindbergh may not have had Byrd's $100,000, but he had finally obtained solid backing from St. Louis businessmen. And even if the *Spirit of St. Louis* was smaller than the other planes, it was still a sophisticated piece of machinery, created by advanced technology. It was a little silly for newspapers to write of Lindbergh and his plane as though they were a cowboy hero and his beloved horse.

Nor was Lindbergh's background as simple as the newspapers tried to make it appear. He came from a well-to-do, educated family. His father had been a congressman. Lindbergh had been to college for a time and held a commission as captain in the Army Air Service Reserve and the Missouri National Guard. He had been chief pilot for the airmail company in St. Louis. He was, despite his youth, an experienced professional pilot, flying a state-of-the-art plane.

But there was just enough truth to the mythical picture to make it stick. It probably infected Lindbergh somewhat, too. He had always been a bit "wild," even though he was shy. Cars, motorcycles, ice boats—anything that involved speed—had always fascinated him. When he was just twenty he dropped out of college to learn to fly. He bought his first craft, a war-surplus plane, even before he had made a solo flight, and he almost crashed it on his first takeoff.

Lindbergh had barnstormed all over the West, crashing regularly and surviving only with luck. He had walked on airplane wings while in flight and done dangerous parachute jumps for one aerial circus after another. Four times he had been forced to parachute for his life from planes that had collided, run out of gas, or gotten lost at night.

All this, combined with Lindbergh's shyness and boyishness, his faith in himself and his plane, did smack of something faintly supernatural and mythical. So the hero worship that began almost as soon as he reached Long Island was probably inevitable. At times the publicity and the public attention irritated Lindbergh. Reporters went so far as to burst into his hotel room without knocking to discover what kind of pajamas, if any, he wore to bed. But the irritation could not overcome the excitement. Lindbergh was becoming, even before takeoff, a national hero.

The *Columbia* was scheduled to take off May 13, the day after Lindbergh reached Long Island. But the weather was closed in over New York and the North Atlantic. The same storm that had delayed Lindbergh in San Diego was making its slow progress north and east. So the *Columbia* had to wait. Lindbergh was able to test and tune his engine, to check and recheck every instrument. A noisy crowd that sometimes numbered over a thousand gathered around the hangar to watch him. By May 16 he was ready. As far as he could tell, Byrd was ready too. In the *Columbia* organization there was a legal quarrel over who would be the pilot. One of the men who had trained for the flight had secured a court order preventing the plane from taking off without him. But the court order could be lifted at any minute. So there seemed to be a real chance that two or possibly even three planes would take off from Roosevelt Field on the same morning.

The spring rains persisted for three more days. Then, on the evening of May 19, the forecast called for clearing skies. Though it was not clearing rapidly, Lindbergh made his decision. He would fly, even if it meant taking off into a rainy sky from a muddy field. He bought five sandwiches "to go." A few hours later the *Spirit of St. Louis* was towed to the west end of the Roosevelt Field runway. Lindbergh had decided to take off before dawn. Not far behind his plane was the scorched area, marked by a bent propeller stuck into the ground as a tribute, where Fonck's plane had burned.

Slowly, carefully, mechanics strained 5-gallon cans of gasoline into Lindbergh's plane. The oversize tanks had a capacity of 450 gallons instead of the 400 that the designers had planned earlier. Lindbergh decided to fill them to the brim, even though it meant a dangerous overload for the takeoff. In the hangars of the *America* and the *Columbia*, there was only darkness and silence. No one else was going to fly this morning.

As he looked over the situation, Lindbergh wondered whether he should go. He was overloaded with gasoline. The field was muddy. The wheels of the *Spirit of St. Louis* sank into the earth as though warning him that flight was out of the question. The wet weather affected the engine, which turned about thirty revolutions per minute slower than it should have at full power. Worst of all, the process of getting ready took so long that Lindbergh lost the dawn wind. By the time he was ready to fly, the breeze had shifted to his back, creating a tailwind of five or six miles per hour. This meant he would need even more speed on takeoff.

Lindbergh's only guidelines were the San Diego tests. They had demonstrated theoretically that with 400 gallons of gas he should be able to take off in 2,500 feet on a hard runway with no wind and with full engine power. But he had 450 gallons of gas, a wet field, a rough engine, and a wind at his back. At the end of the Roosevelt Field runway were a ditch, a parked tractor, some telephone wires and then a hill with a line of trees. He had to clear them all. He considered towing the *Spirit of St. Louis* through the misty rain and mud to the other end of the runway to get the help of the wind. He thought about postponing the flight altogether. But he decided to go.

Lindbergh looked around at the crowd that had gathered to watch. Nearby were the mechanics, the engineers, several policemen, all looking into the dark cockpit at his pale face.

Their eyes are intently on mine. They've seen planes crash before. I lean against the side of the cockpit and look ahead, through the idling blades of the propeller, over the runway's glistening surface. I study the telephone wires and the shallow pools of water through which my wheels must pass. A curtain of mist shuts off all trace of the horizon. Sitting in the cockpit, in seconds, minutes long, the conviction surges through me that the wheels *will* leave the ground, that the wings *will* rise above the wires, that it *is* time to start the flight.

I buckle my safety belt, pull goggles down over my eyes, turn to the men at the blocks, and nod. Frozen fingers leap to action. I brace myself against the left side of the cockpit and ease the throttle wide open.

The *Spirit of St. Louis* feels more like an overloaded truck than an airplane. The tires rut through mud as though they really were on truck wheels. Even the breath of wind is pressing me down. The engine's snarl sounds inadequate and weak.

A hundred yards of runway passes. How long can the landing gear stand such strain? I keep my eyes fixed on the runway's edge. I *must* hold the plane straight. Pace quickens—the tail skid lifts off ground—I feel the load shifting from wheels to wings. The halfway mark is just ahead, and I have nothing like flying speed.

The halfway mark streaks past. Seconds now to decide. I pull the stick back firmly, and—*the wheels leave the ground!* The wheels touch again. I ease the stick forward. Almost flying speed and nearly 2,000 feet ahead. The entire plane trembles. Off again—right wing low—pull it up—ease back onto the runway. Another pool, water drumming on the fabric [covering the fuselage]. The next hop's longer. I could probably stay in the air, but I let the wheels touch once more.

The *Spirit of St. Louis* takes herself off next time. Full flying speed. The controls taut, alive, straining—and still a thousand feet to the telephone wires. If the engine can hold out one more minute. Five feet, twenty, forty. Wires flash by underneath. Twenty feet to spare!

Green grass below—a golf links. People looking up. A low, tree-covered hill ahead. The *Spirit of St. Louis* seems balanced on a pinpoint, as though the slightest movement of controls would cause it to topple over and fall. Five thousand pounds suspended from those little wings. Five thousand pounds on a blast of air.

Now I'm high enough to steal glances at the instrument board. The earth inductor compass needle leans steeply to the right. I bank cautiously northward until it rises to the center line—65 degrees—the compass heading for the first 100-mile segment of my great-circle route to France and Paris. It's 7:54 A.M. Eastern daylight time.

Back in San Diego, when Lindbergh and the designer of the *Spirit of St. Louis* had measured the distance of the flight across a library globe, the string had made a straight line between New York and Paris. But on a flat map, where the lines of latitude are straightened out into parallels, the route had to bend into an arc known as a great circle. The route Lindbergh would take curved north and east from New York, up the coast over Cape Cod, then out over the ocean to Nova Scotia. Lindbergh planned to change his compass course every hundred miles (about one hour's flying time). He would head a few degrees farther south and east across the southern coast of New-foundland and then out over the North Atlantic.

As Lindbergh flew up the coast on this route, people waited on streets and housetops to watch him pass. Despite the fact that his navigating equipment was primitive, he managed to reach the Nova Scotia coast only a few miles off course. Every hour, excited messages were telephoned to New York giving details of his progress. In the twelfth hour of his flight, Lindbergh passed over St. John's, Newfoundland, then out over the ocean:

> I come upon it suddenly—the little city of St. John's—after skimming over the top of a granite summit. Farther ahead, the entrance to the harbor is a narrow gap with sides running up to the crest of a low coastal range. Twilight deepens as I plunge down into the valley. It takes only a moment, stick forward, engine throttled, to dive down over the wharves (men stop their after-supper chores to look upward) and out through the gap. North America and its islands are behind. Ireland is 2,000 miles ahead.

Throughout the flight, Lindbergh faced the ever-present dangers of engine failure, storms, and the possibility of a structural weakness in the plane itself. But between Newfoundland and Ireland there were two additional dangers. The first was sleep. Lindbergh had not slept at all the night before his takeoff. During the next night and the day after, as he flew over the ocean, he fought back the terrible temptation to close his eyes for just a few seconds of rest. Despite its virtues, the *Spirit of St. Louis* was not a very stable plane. Lindbergh knew that if he relaxed his hold on it for more than a moment, he might crash. He had to hold his eyes open with his hands. Once he even had to hit himself full force in the face to keep awake.

The second danger was ice. This hazard hit Lindbergh suddenly after he had climbed over 10,000 feet, trying to clear a bank of clouds about 200 miles east of Newfoundland. He was suddenly aware of being cold himself. (He had left the glass out of the side windows of the plane, hoping that the fresh air and engine noise would keep him alert.) Cold? He jerked himself wide awake. If *he* was cold, what about his plane?

> Good Lord! There are things to be considered outside the cockpit! How could I forget! I jerk off a leather mitten and thrust my arm out the window. My palm is covered with stinging pinpricks. I pull the flashlight from my pocket and throw its beam on a strut. The entering edge is irregular and shiny! *Ice!*
>
> I've got to turn around, get back to clear air—quickly!

But Lindbergh fought the urge to turn quickly. He knew that if he did, the ice on the wings might cause the plane to go out of control. Instead, he eased the *Spirit of St. Louis* around in a long, slow curve back toward Newfoundland.

> I throw my flashlight [beam] onto the wing strut. Ice is thicker! Steady the plane. Everything depends on the turn indicator working till I get outside the cloud. Just two or three more minutes.
>
> My eyes sense a change in the blackness of my cockpit. I look out through the window. How bright! What safety have I reached! I was in the thunderhead for ten minutes at most, but it's one of those incidents that can't be measured by minutes. Such periods stand out like islands in a sea of time.

Charles and Anne Morrow Lindbergh. In 1929 after he became famous, Lindbergh married the daughter of a wealthy stockbroker who served as the U.S. ambassador to Mexico. The Lindberghs never freed themselves from the publicity that had brought them together in the first place. This became an even more cruel fact in 1932 when a kidnapper murdered their infant son in one of the most celebrated crimes in American history. (Culver Pictures)

After this brief but dangerous encounter with the night sky, Lindbergh picked his way cautiously toward Ireland and dawn. (Since he was flying west to east, into the sunrise, he was experiencing the shortest night any person ever had.) He sipped cautiously at his quart canteen of water. The rest of the time, he just flew his plane, waiting for moonrise, then sunrise, then landfall. He later recalled the twenty-eighth hour of his flight.

I keep scanning the horizon through breaks between squalls. Is that a cloud on the northeastern horizon, or a strip of low fog—or—*can it possibly be land?* It looks like land, but I don't intend to be tricked by another mirage. I'm only sixteen hours out of Newfoundland. I allowed eighteen and one-half hours to strike the Irish coast.

But my mind is clear. I'm no longer half asleep. The temptation is too great. I can't hold my course any longer. The *Spirit of St. Louis* banks over toward the nearest point of land.

I stare at it intently, not daring to believe my eyes, watching the shades and contours unfold into a coastline. Now I'm flying above the foam-lined coast, searching for prominent features to fit the chart on my knee. I've climbed to 2,000 feet so I can see the contours of the country better. Yes, there's a place on the chart where it all fits—Valentia and Dingle Bay, *on the southwestern coast of Ireland!* I can hardly believe

Paris welcomes Lindbergh.   At 10 P.M., the *Spirit of St. Louis* came to rest on the runway at Le Bourget airport just outside Paris. A huge crowd gathered, ready to rush onto the field to greet the man who overnight had become the epitome of a "real American." (National Air and Space Museum, Smithsonian Institution)

it's true. I'm almost exactly on my route, closer than I hoped to come in my wildest dreams back in San Diego. What happened to all those detours of the night around the thunderheads? Where has the swinging compass error gone?

Intuition must have been more accurate than reasoned navigation.

The southern tip of Ireland! On course, over two hours ahead of schedule; the sun still well up in the sky, the weather clearing!

Now it was easy. So easy that Lindbergh himself fell into the temptation of making a myth out of his own achievement:

I'm angling slowly back onto my great-circle route. I must have been within three miles of it when I sighted Ireland. An error of fifty miles would have been good dead reckoning under the most perfect conditions. Three miles was—well, what was it? Before I made this flight, I would have said carelessly that it was luck. Now, luck seems far too trivial a word, a term to be used only by those who've never seen the curtain drawn or looked on life from far away.

The hero in New York. Lindbergh probably became a more famous celebrity, more quickly, than any American ever had. Here, in a nighttime parade in New York City, he is welcomed home among the crowds, the fanfare, and the flags that followed him everywhere. (Culver Pictures)

After Ireland the landmarks appeared rapidly—a lighthouse, the coast of England and the coast of France, "like an outstretched hand to meet me." For the first time, Lindbergh felt hungry. He ate one of the sandwiches, stale and dry now, that he had bought in New York. He picked up a series of beacons marking the route between London and Paris. Then the city rose before him. He circled the brightly lit Eiffel Tower and then turned northeast to look for Le Bourget. "You can't miss it," he had been told. He was like a tourist.

It was almost ten o'clock at night in Paris. Lindbergh was confused by an incredible number of lights around the dark spot where the airport ought to be. A factory, he thought. He did not know that he had suddenly become the most famous man in the world. Thousands of Parisians had rushed out to the airport to greet the American flyer. The roads leading to Le Bourget were jammed with cars with headlights blazing.

Finally, Lindbergh was able to pick out floodlights showing the edge of a runway. He "dragged" the field once, flying low over it to check for obstructions—a tractor or maybe some sheep let out to crop the grass, he thought. He brought the plane in as carefully as possible, as though he were teaching a student to fly. The plane felt sluggish. By his own guess he still carried a lot of gasoline. His own reflexes seemed slow. Lindbergh had never landed the *Spirit of St. Louis* at night. He glided in at an angle so he could peer out of his side window.

It's only a hundred yards to the hangars now. I'm too high, too fast. Drop wing. Left rudder. Careful. Still too high. I push the stick over. Below the hangar roofs now. Straighten out. A short burst of the engine. Over the lighted areas. Sod coming up to meet me. Careful. Easy to bounce when you're tired. Still too fast. Tail too high. Hold off. Hold off. But the lights are far behind. Ahead, there's nothing but night. Give her the gun and climb for another try?

The wheels touch gently. Off again. No, I'll keep contact. Ease the stick forward. Back on the ground. Off. Back, the tail skid too. Not a bad landing, but I'm beyond the light. Can't see anything ahead. The field *must* be clear. Uncomfortable, though, jolting into blackness. Wish I had a wing light, but too heavy on the takeoff. Slower now, slow enough to ground-loop safely. Left rudder. Reverse it. The *Spirit of St. Louis* swings around and stops rolling, resting on the solidness of earth, in the center of Le Bourget.

I start to taxi back to the floodlights and hangars. But the entire field ahead is covered with running figures!

SOCIETY AND CULTURE IN THE 1920s

When Lindbergh completed his ground loop at Le Bourget, about 100,000 French men and women broke through police lines to rush onto the field, almost hysterical over this new hero. All day, the transatlantic cables, the newspapers, and radio had been full of news of the flight. And for hours before Lindbergh landed, Parisians had been fighting heavy traffic to drive out to Le Bourget to greet this "Flyin' Fool."

As soon as the *Spirit of St. Louis* touched down, the crowd rushed the plane. Lindbergh was afraid (as he was to be for months, whenever he made announced landings anywhere in the world) that the overexcited people would run into his spinning propeller. When he tried to climb out of his cramped cockpit, the crowd grabbed him. For a long time, he could not even set foot on French soil, but was passed through the crowd, from shoulder to shoulder. In the din, he shouted for a mechanic, someone to protect the plane; but no one could hear or understand him.

In the log he kept of the flight, Lindbergh made this brief, slightly bitter entry: "May 20, Roosevelt Field, Long Island, New York, to Le Bourget Aerodrome, Paris, France. 33 hours. 20 min. Fuselage fabric badly torn by souvenir hunters." The first part of the entry, the flight, was what was significant to Lindbergh. But the second part, the half-crazed hero worship of the crowd, is just as important to understanding the full significance of what Lindbergh had done and

become. In Paris, but even more in New York and dozens of other American cities, Lindbergh was adored. From the time he landed at Le Bourget, his life was not his own. People crowded around wherever he went. They stole his hats in restaurants. He could not keep shirts, or even underwear, because laundry employees swiped them for souvenirs.

More than any other person of his generation, Lindbergh captured the imagination of his contemporaries. Newspapers printed more stories about him and his flight than they had about the death of President Wilson. More people—4 million, the police said—turned out to see him in a New York parade than had ever come out to look at any president. Something about Lindbergh and his feat touched a responsive chord in the America of the 1920s.

On the face of it, there was no overwhelming reason for Lindbergh's fantastic fame. As a matter of cold fact, his flight had proved nothing—except that a superb pilot, blessed by some luck, could fly a specially built airplane 3,600 miles. The *Spirit of St. Louis* could carry no passengers and no cargo. In fact, Lindbergh had refused to carry even one pound of mail, though he was offered $1,000 to do so. Lindbergh was not even the first man to fly the Atlantic. Eight years earlier, in 1919, a British dirigible had done it *twice*. That year, too, an American seaplane had crossed from New York to England, landing several times on the ocean. And in the same year, two pilots had made it nonstop from Newfoundland to Ireland, to win a prize of $50,000—double Lindbergh's prize. For a variety of reasons, when Lindbergh made his flight in 1927 almost no one seemed to remember these earlier feats, and "Lucky Lindy" quickly became a household word.

The causes of Lindbergh's incredible celebrity have to be found outside his actual accomplishment. They lie in deep changes that had occurred in American society. Americans were excited about Lindbergh for reasons that had more to do with them than with him. They projected more significance into the event than it really had. When masses of people experience such excitement, they tend to see historical actors as demons or heroes. They oversimplify the world and thus make some new kind of sense out of their own lives. This process often has very little to do with reality. Lindbergh became a symbol. His contemporaries saw in him what they wanted to see, making him into a sort of mirror for the technological and social changes that had transformed American society in the twentieth century.

Reaching a Mass Audience

One of the reasons for Lindbergh's rapid rise to fame was the publicity he received from the press and the radio. Since the 1890s the newspapers of the United States had been increasing in number and circulation. They competed fiercely for the attention of the public. This expansion of newspapers was only part of an important revolution in communications that began in the nineteenth century and still continues today.

One by one, new inventions brought people's lives closer together. These included the telegraph, the telephone, the phonograph, the cam-

era, the radio, and the motion picture. They created a world in which whole nations and continents could share almost simultaneously in distant events. Lindbergh's flight was covered intensely by the press, which transmitted its stories over telegraph and telephone lines. Lindbergh was also photographed mercilessly. His activities were recorded both in newspaper photographs and in the newsreels that accompanied the early silent motion pictures. Hour-by-hour reports of his famous flight were transmitted on the radio—an invention that had come into use only a few years before. As soon as Lindbergh landed in Paris, the news was flashed back to the United States by transatlantic telegraph cable.

In many ways, Lindbergh the hero was the creation of mass communication. He was the first celebrity to have the full advantage of every modern form of communication except television, which did not come into wide use until after World War II.

THE COMMUNICATIONS REVOLUTION

The revolution in communications began with the telegraph, which linked California and New York more than half a century before Lindbergh's flight. During the same period, newspapers began to attract a mass audience. The telephone, too, contributed to the rapid and widespread circulation of information. In the first part of the twentieth century the number of telephones in use skyrocketed, from a little over 1 million in 1900 to more than 10 million in 1915. By the time Lindbergh took off for Paris, practically every middle-class American home had its own telephone.

But the communications revolution did not gather full speed until the invention of the radio. The principle of wireless transmission of sound was almost as old as the telephone. In 1887 a German scientist had proved the existence of electrical waves in space. He speculated that they might be turned into signals. An Italian inventor, Guglielmo Marconi, applied the theory to wireless transmission of telegraph signals in

The power of communication. This Hood River County, Oregon, farm family instantly became closer to the nation through the radio. What once might have taken weeks to reach them—or dismissed as rumor—was now immediately available information. (The National Archives)

1896. From then on it was only a matter of assembling the appropriate tubes, transmitters, and receivers.

In 1920, Americans heard their first commercial radio broadcast. The station was KDKA in Pittsburgh, and the program was a news report on the 1920 presidential election. Soon after that, the winner of the election, Warren G. Harding, installed a radio set in the White House. Gradually, Marconi's invention was transformed from a toy into a commercial reality. By the time Lindbergh made his flight to Paris, an estimated 10 million sets were in use in the United States.

Two other inventions, the phonograph and the camera, furthered the revolution in mass communication. Thomas A. Edison found a way of capturing and re-creating sound that was to make music available to millions at an instant. George Eastman's perfection of the camera made it possible for newspapers to publish photographs on their pages.

All these changes allowed millions of people to participate indirectly in events they were not able to witness in person. In other words, these developing communications facilities had created a potential public that could take part in any happening, frown at any villain, worship any hero.

A MIDDLE-CLASS "PUBLIC" The new public that celebrated Lindbergh's flight with such enthusiasm should not be confused with the whole nation. Lindbergh's fame was primarily a middle-class phenomenon. He was, in some ways, a media creation, and the media that made him catered primarily to white, well-to-do citizens. Even newspapers were aimed primarily at a middle-class audience. Radios and telephones were the property of the middle class almost exclusively. In 1927 the phonograph and the camera were still alien novelties to many millions of poor Americans. Whole great subpopulations—blacks, many poor white farmers, millions of immigrants in the cities—were practically excluded from the new "public" that the mass media helped create.

Eventually, of course, the new inventions (and the television sets that completed the communications revolution) would become the common property of almost every American, rich or poor. But in the 1920s, and for some time after, they were still middle-class conveniences. If Lindbergh was a symbol of popular values, they were not necessarily values that belonged to all of America. They were the beliefs and hopes of white, middle-class citizens. At the time, it was easy and tempting for the members of this restricted "public" to believe that they *were* America. Most of them would have agreed quickly with the American ambassador to France, who said that Lindbergh represented "the spirit of our people." Similarly, the *New Republic*, a magazine with a small, highly educated audience, could say confidently that Lindbergh "is US personified." But the ambassador and the *New Republic* spoke carelessly. The "people" and the "US" they referred to were in fact only the public defined by the media.

As for the others, the majority—the poor, the blacks, the immigrants—there is no way to know what (if anything) they thought about Lindbergh. In all likelihood, if they noticed Lindbergh at all, it was only for a moment and with no special sense of identification with him or his feat. Like most of the cultural content of the "Roaring Twenties," the Lindbergh phenomenon occurred mainly within the very class from which he had come. In fact, he may have served the need of this class to believe that it really did possess the spirit of the whole nation.

The Machine and the Maverick in a Technological Society

Americans were fond of calling the period after World War I the New Era. Much of what they meant by the phrase was summed up symboli-

cally in Lindbergh's airplane. The New Era was above all a machine age, a triumph of advanced technology. Compared with a modern jet or a moon rocket, the *Spirit of St. Louis* was a very primitive machine. But to millions of Americans of the 1920s it was the final and glistening outcome of the industrial and technological revolution that had begun in the preceding century. It symbolized what they believed was happening in the United States: the creation of a new kind of civilization, a miracle of progress in which every barrier to human comfort and achievement would be broken by industry and invention.

The United States of the mid-1920s was much more thoroughly industrialized than it had been at the turn of the century. Total steel production, for example, quadrupled during the period between the death of McKinley and Lindbergh's flight to Paris. The total value of all manufactured goods increased about eight times in the same period. The number of people engaged in agriculture declined to about one-fourth of the total population. American cities grew at an astounding pace. By 1930, three years after Lindbergh's flight, 40 percent of the total population of the United States lived in twenty-five large metropolitan centers. In short, Lindbergh appealed to a society that was industrial and urban, and fundamentally dependent on machines and factories.

ELECTRIC POWER AND ASSEMBLY LINES

In some ways the New Era was an extension of the revolution in industry that had occurred after the Civil War. The factory system had continued to expand. New and more complex forms of machinery had been developed to produce more and more goods. But if the basic trends were the same, there were some new elements too. The New Era, to a far greater extent than the old, was powered by electricity and organized around assembly lines.

In 1870, when the industrial revolution was making its first powerful impact, steam and water were used equally to drive industry. Steam continued to be the main form of motor energy in

All in a day's work. The Ford plant in Detroit was a miracle of productivity. Assembly-line methods cut the time needed to produce these chassis from more than twelve hours each to less than two hours. The question was, who was going to buy all these cars? The answer, in part, lay in installment credit: Because of it, consumption rose much faster in the 1920s than the real incomes of working people. Sooner or later, there would be a reckoning. (The Henry Ford Museum & Greenfield Village)

industry until about 1917. But steam had its drawbacks. It was the introduction of electricity that made possible the extraordinary advances in industry that took place in the 1920s.

Again, the basic inventions belonged to the nineteenth century. Within the ten-year period from 1877 to 1887, the dynamo for generating electricity and the motor for converting it into motion were both perfected. This was largely the work of Thomas Edison. During these same years, Edison's incandescent light was introduced into homes and streets. In 1882 the first commercial electric power station, the Edison Illuminating Company, was built in New York.

While electric lighting brightened life in offices, houses, and streets, the electric motor helped transform industrial production. In 1900, electric motors provided only one-twentieth of the power used in American industrial plants. By World War I this figure had increased to about one-third. When Lindbergh flew to France, just ten years later, electricity provided almost two-thirds of the total industrial power in American factories and mills. Between 1870 and 1920 the amount of raw energy used by American industry, measured in horsepower, increased by well over 1,000 percent.

The development of the moving-belt assembly line also had far-reaching effects on industrial production. Assembly lines were first introduced on a large scale by Henry Ford at his automobile plant in Michigan in 1913. The principle was a simple one. Workers were placed in a row in the order of sequence of their jobs. As the product (in this case the automobile) moved past, each worker performed an assigned task. The idea might be simple, but the savings in time and motion were dramatic. Each worker, using a specialized tool to perform a small task, could now produce much more in a given day. Ford's assembly line was copied by dozens of other industries. By the middle of the 1920s it was a standard technique.

EFFECTS OF MECHANIZATION The industrial revolution continued. The changes brought about by the electric motor and the assembly line made the lives of most Americans in 1927 very different from a generation or two earlier. More and more, the ways in which people lived and worked were determined by machines and technological innovations. More and more, mechanical devices replaced human energy and skill.

This process of mechanization had two deep effects on American society. First, it made modern Americans more conscious of the efficient use of time and effort than any other people in the his-

AMERICAN IMAGES

People and Machines

During the summer of 1893, Henry Adams—historian, politician, essayist, and descendant of two presidents—traveled to Chicago to view the World's Columbian Exposition. Set in an artificial lagoon skirting the city's lakefront, the great fair presented the visitor with a unified vision, a "great White City" of display halls, fountains, and walkways. Adams was deeply moved by this unity of design and structure of molded and painted terra cotta and masonry. The fair proclaimed confidence, pride of accomplishment, and faith in the future. "Chicago," he wrote, "asked in 1893 for the first time the question whether the American people knew where they were driving."

Yet Adams foresaw a more uncertain future than the planners of the fair. As he pondered the exhibits of modern machinery, particularly the dynamo capable of generating electrical current, he sensed serious contradictions. For Adams, the dynamo was a symbol of power and force operating in ways that would drastically transform Amer-

Plate 1. In spite of its theme of progress and dedication to modern invention, the World's Columbian Exposition in Chicago in 1893 built a neoclassical city borrowing architectural styles from Europe but rendered on an American colossal scale. This, the Manufactures and Liberal Arts Building, fronted one of several canals designed to give the exhibition a Venetian look. (Culver Pictures)

Plate 2. The hand-held camera became commonplace and almost indispensable by the 1920s. For millions of Americans, it made possible a permanent record of family life and new leisure activities, such as depicted here. (The Bettmann Archive)

Energy Consumption, 1890–1940 (in thousands of horsepower)

	1890	1900	1910	1920	1930	1940
Work animals	15,970	18,730	21,460	22,430	17,660	12,510
Factories	6,308	10,309	16,697	19,422	19,519	21,768
Mines	1,445	2,919	4,473	5,146	5,620	7,332
Railroads	16,980	24,501	51,308	80,182	109,743	92,361
Merchant ships	1,124	1,663	3,098	6,508	9,115	9,408
Sailing vessels	280	251	220	169	100	26
Windmills	80	120	180	200	200	130
Electricity	447	1,350	6,228	17,050	43,427	53,542
Automobile	—	100	24,686	280,900	1,426,568	2,511,312

Source: U.S. Department of Commerce, Bureau of the Census, *Historical Statistics of the United States: Colonial Times to the Present*, Bicentennial ed. (Washington, D.C.: Government Printing Office, 1976), Vol. II, p. 818.

ican society—for better or for worse. But he could not be sure which it would be.

Adams's choice of the dynamo to symbolize the modern age was brilliant. Quietly transforming energy into power, the dynamo represented one of the most potent machines of the era. Likewise, Adams's uncertainty over the machine-dominated future was farsighted. During the next forty-five years, up to World War II, machines dramatically reshaped American life, work habits, transportation, the shape of everyday objects, even toys. They made consumer items available that previously had been only dreamed of. But in the midst of this amazing transformation, artists, writers, and ordinary citizens sometimes wondered where the machine was leading.

Part of the wonder of the new machine age of the 1890s derived from a special machine perfected during the era: the camera. In use during the mid-nineteenth century for portraits and posed public events, the still camera was gradually improved. In 1895, a miniature portable camera using roll film, the "Brownie," brought cameras out of the studio to become a permanent and indispensable part of the home. Motion pictures became practical after Thomas A. Edison invented the 35-mm camera in 1889. Further developments shortly thereafter made it possible to film and develop longer motion pictures. By the second decade of the twentieth century, a huge new industry had sprung up, first in New York and New Jersey, and then—after World War I—in Los Angeles.

Plate 3.   By the 1930s, photography was securely established as an art form and a means of social commentary. Margaret Bourke-White, one of the foremost photographers of the period, took this picture of flood victims in Louisville, Kentucky, in 1937—a startling and grimly ironic reminder that not all Americans reaped the benefits of the Machine Age. (Margaret Bourke-White, *LIFE* Magazine, © 1937 Time, Inc.)

The effect of the camera in refocusing America's vision and image of itself cannot be exaggerated. People and places—the faces of political leaders, celebrities, relatives, and friends; the silhouettes of national parks and monuments; the skylines of New York and Chicago—became familiar to everyone. By World War I, photography had also presented the nation with poignant pictures of the victims of exploitation and poverty, adding weight and authority to the proposals of the progressive reformers. By the 1930s, photography had earned a secure place as a public art form. Pictures carefully recorded the suffering of the Great Depression. Photographers such as Margaret Bourke-White became celebrities. Beginning in 1936, Life magazine provided millions of Americans with a weekly display of some of the finest contemporary photography.

One favorite subject of photographers and artists was machinery and objects transformed by machinery. With such images, they explored the contradictory attitudes of society toward machines. Machines provided the energy to tame nature and transform the countryside. They created great monuments like the Chicago skyscrapers. They transported people and commodities from shore to shore, from Canada to the Gulf, in only a few days. They increased productivity and made possible a multiplicity of new goods that transformed the home, the factory, the farm, and the workplace. For some, the machine was not just awe-inspiring, it was beautiful—a source of patterned motion that increasingly affected modern art and design.

Nonetheless, the machine (as it had in the nineteenth century) also represented darker forces: filth and pollution

Plate 4. Charles Sheeler's "Suspended Power," like much of the art of the 1930s, pondered the relationship of people and machines. Here the huge propeller dwarfs tiny figures of workers. Yet the painter has stripped away much of the detail of the machine, emphasizing the huge, potential motion—and beauty—of its shapes. (Dallas Museum of Art, Gift of Edmund J. Kahn)

Plate 5. This remarkable photograph, "The Steamfitter," by Lewis Hine, suggests a point that many artists and writers made during the 1920s. In order to work at his machine, the man is forced to bend his body to the contour of the wheel. Was it the fate of all people, social critics worried, to be shaped by machines? (International Museum of Photography at George Eastman House)

Plate 6. This experimental electric-driven GGI locomotive of the Pennsylvania Railroad (1934) was shrouded in metal to make it more aerodynamic. Two symbols emphasized its streamlined design: the five stripes on either shoulder symbolized an airstream and the central insignia, in the shape of a zig-zag rectangle, denoted lightning (electricty). (Altoona Area Public Library)

Plate 7. This 1930 "Beta" chair of tubular steel and upholstery fabric represented the extension of streamlining to furniture. Although designed for sitting, the chair—with its continuous wrap-around curves and its lack of visible support structure—stressed motion and activity. (The Brooklyn Museum, Gift of Nathan G. Horwitt)

Plate 8. These evening slippers in leather and stones sported the zig-zag design associated with electricity and mobility—an appropriate symbol for the grace and motion of a dance. (The Metropolitan Museum of Art, Gift of Mrs. R. C. Jacobsen)

Plate 9. This chrome-plated, enameled steel, brass, and glass table lamp, produced around 1935, rather than shading the light, broke it into planes at the top and then repeated the design on the stem and the base. (The Brooklyn Museum, H. Randolph Lever Fund)

and exploitation. Linked to an uncompromising search for profits, the machine seemed to empower the greedy and to condemn workers—including children—to long hours of alienating work and short, weary lives. Some social critics even wondered: Were human beings losing control of life to the machine? Were people becoming mere extensions of machines? These questions formed the subject of a good deal of literature, art, and photography throughout the period.

However the machine was evaluated, it changed every element of American life—from the shape of everyday objects like knives and forks, glassware, furniture, and clothing to the design of automobiles, trains, buildings, and ships. During the 1920s and 1930s, a great many ordinary objects were transformed by streamlining.

Trains, cars, smoothly curving buildings, rounded arches, graceful high-flying bridges—all testified to designers' dreams of a pleasant and completely functional future. By the time of the New York World's Fair of 1939, the stream-lined "World of Tomorrow" had anticipated future cities of glass and steel, with geometric shapes and machine-inspired designs. Unlike the Chicago Fair of 1893, the façades of buildings were themselves a kind of mechanical display. Gone were the ornate decorations of 1893, as well as the contradictory vision that Henry Adams had sensed. And yet the vision was contradicted—by the poverty and depression that plagued the late 1930s and by the approach of a second world war, just a few months away, in which mechanized force would contribute to the greatest destruction in human history.

Plate 10. Frank Lloyd Wright designed this wonderful house at Bear Run near Uniontown, Pennsylvania, in 1936. Perched over a waterfall in a woods, the house evoked geometric shapes and planes—not of light, but of water. (Hedrich-Blessing)

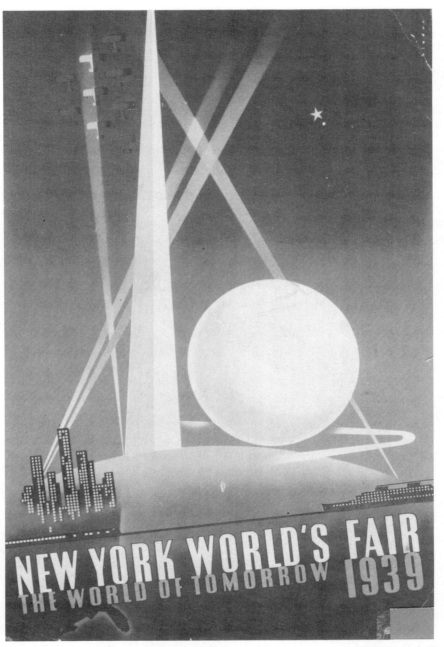

Plate 11. Perhaps the summation of machine-age design came at the 1939 New York World's Fair just as the popularity of this style began to ebb. There is an eerie futurism in this poster, as searchlights highlight overflying airplanes. When war broke out in Europe, this image would become a terrible and devastating reality as bombers roared over London and Berlin and anti-aircraft searchlights groped to find them. (Culver Pictures)

tory of the world. Second, it threatened to standardize life by reducing the area of imagination and individuality in people's daily working environment. The celebration of Lindbergh was connected to both these consequences.

In planning his flight, Lindbergh was almost ruthlessly efficient. The *Spirit of St. Louis* was a nearly perfect machine. It was designed to perform one simple task in the most effective way, with a minimum of wasted energy. Like a machine in a modern factory, the plane represented the harnessing of energy to a carefully designed instrument for the performance of a rigidly defined task. Much of what Americans admired in Lindbergh was precisely what they admired in their own society: technological achievement.

But there was another side to Lindbergh. He was a maverick. Some of the pet names the newspapers gave him, like "The Flyin' Fool" and "Lucky," made his daring seem more important than his technical skill. Lindbergh seemed to go against the trend toward standardization of life in the New Era. He represented individual imagination, as well as engineering and piloting skill. A large part of Lindbergh's fame probably rested on this contradiction. His flight was both a triumph of technology and a victory for individual daring.

Wheels and Wings: The Motor Age

The development of electricity had a powerful effect not only on industry but also on American home life. New inventions like the electric washing machine and refrigerator (which utilized small, inexpensive motors) changed the working and eating habits of American families. And a dozen other smaller electric appliances, from toasters to thermostats for home furnaces, helped usher in the American consumer's vision of a New Era.

PERFECTING THE AUTOMOBILE The largest change in American social life was brought about by the gasoline engine. The basic principle of the internal combustion engine was understood by the middle of the nineteenth century. The first was built and operated in the 1860s in France. Instead of burning fuel externally to convert water into steam, the internal combustion engine burned fuel in an explosive way inside a chamber. The force of the explosion was then used to drive a piston or a rotor. Power for the new engine was available in the form of gasoline, a "waste" product in the making of kerosene, the basic fuel oil of the nineteenth century.

It was only a matter of time, then, until someone perfected the engine, mounted it on a "horseless carriage," and so created the automobile. No one, however, could have begun to guess at the end of the nineteenth century just how rapid the development of the automobile would be. Nor could they foresee the range of consequences it would have on the ways Americans lived.

The first man in the United States to build a workable automobile powered by a gasoline engine was probably Ransom E. Olds. (His rickety machine was the forerunner of the present-day Oldsmobile.) Five years later, in 1895, Henry Ford began to put together his first car. The new machine was noisy, unreliable, and expensive. Still, a few Americans were willing to pay the price and stop their ears against the noise. By 1900 there were about 8,000 of the curious new machines operating in the country.

But Ford was not so much an inventor of the automobile as an inventor of a style and a method of production. In the early years of the century Ford began simplifying the automobile. He cut away every fancy decoration and convenience that had been adapted from the luxurious carriages of the day. Moreover, he reduced costs

Henry Ford

As much as any other single factor, automobiles caused the dramatic change in American life in the twentieth century. Yet the man who did the most to put the nation on wheels, Henry Ford, disliked the change. The older he grew, the more fondly he looked back on the America of his youth. He valued its rural base, Puritan work ethic, and simple pleasures.

Life began for Henry Ford on a farm near Dearborn, Michigan, on July 30, 1863. Early in his life two traits became apparent: He loved machinery, and he hated farming. He was a born tinkerer. By the time he was thirteen, he could disassemble and reconstruct a watch. He was forever fixing his father's farm machinery and his mother's household appliances. When he ran out of things to repair at home, he repaired the watches, clocks, and machinery of neighbors.

As soon as he could, he left the farm for Detroit to become a machinist. He quickly learned his trade and was soon a well-paid, highly skilled workman. In his spare time, he worked on a gasoline buggy in an old brick shed behind his home. By 1896 he was able to drive it through the hole he had knocked out of the shed wall. Mounted on four bicycle wheels was a two-cylinder, four-horsepower engine. Mounted on that was a buggy seat. To steer it

he used a curved stick like the tiller on a boat.

From this awkward beginning, Ford built a billion-dollar industry over the next fifty years. But as he grew from home-shop tinkerer to industrial tycoon, he never really changed his boyhood attitudes. They remained those of an agrarian Populist of the 1880s and 1890s.

As a result, Henry Ford was a mass of contradictions. While he professed a firm belief in the value of the individual worker and of hard and useful jobs, he developed an assembly-line process that was truly dehumanizing. He broke down each of the jobs involved in making a car into its tiniest steps. Consequently, a worker did only one thing—like tightening a single bolt—all day long. Ford was even proud of the fact that 43 percent of the jobs in his factories could be mastered in one day.

While he was an expert businessman, as his development of an enormous personal fortune and a vastly profitable corporation showed, Ford disliked many aspects of capitalism. He had an abiding mistrust of bankers and financiers.

And while he continued to turn out millions of cars, making America a highly mobile and rootless society, he romanticized stable, well-anchored small-town life. He so loved nineteenth-century rural America that he spent twenty years constructing a reproduction of the community he grew up in, Greenfield Village. There, skilled artisans worked at jobs that had long since been taken over by assembly lines.

Henry Ford died an unhappy old man of eighty-four, puzzled with the people and the world he had done so much to transform.

Picture: Detail of picture from the Henry Ford Museum & Greenfield Village.

by turning out standardized, mass-produced machines. The results were astonishing. In 1907 the average price of an automobile was over $2,000. The next year, Ford introduced a model selling at only $850. By 1914 he was able to cut the price to a little over $500. By the mid-1920s Ford was selling his assembly-line Model T for

less than $300. The car was similar in many ways to the *Spirit of St. Louis*. It was the simplest machine possible, designed to do a plain task in the most efficient way.

Other automobile makers began to imitate and compete with Ford. The result was an exploding new industry. By the 1920s the manufacture of automobiles was by far the largest consumer products industry in the United States. It employed tens of thousands of workers at large and growing factories centered in Detroit. The automobile had a remarkable impact on other industries, especially steel and rubber, which provided the raw products for the assembly lines. The oil industry also underwent a major expansion. The automobile turned gasoline into the main stock-in-trade of the petroleum companies.

LIFE IN THE MOTOR AGE The most obvious impact of the automobile was not on industry but on American social life. By 1927 Ford had made 15 million cars. About 20 million American families owned an automobile. The immediate result was that horses and other draft animals almost disappeared from the landscape and the streets.

But the automobile had other, less obvious and predictable effects. First, it encouraged Americans to move farther and farther out of the cities, into the suburbs. From about the time of Lindbergh's trip to Paris, the "lure of the suburbs" attracted more and more middle-class Americans. Second, cars and buses transformed American education, especially in small towns and farm areas. The school bus made it possible to consolidate school districts into larger units. Gradually, the simple one-room schoolhouse, with one or two teachers for all the grades, disappeared.

Finally, the automobile, the truck, and the bus began a process that would take another thirty years to complete: the near-destruction of the railroads—the principal technological innovation of the nineteenth century. At first, in the 1920s and 1930s, the car and the bus cut mainly into the railroads' local traffic. But as roads and engines improved, the competition became more and more severe. As for freight, the trucking industry began to compete for what had been almost a railroad monopoly. The train, with its mighty steam engine, had been the great symbol of the industrial revolution up to the 1920s. By the middle of the twentieth century, much of the railroad

industry was ailing and unprofitable, no longer able to survive as a private enterprise.

In the long run, the automobile proved to have unwanted as well as unpredicted consequences. Among these, the modern decay of central cities was the most serious. Gradually, large sections of cities like New York, Boston, and Chicago became the slums of the poor, who could not afford suburban homes. Also, although no one in Lindbergh's day could have predicted it, the automobile caused a major problem of air pollution. Smog resulted from the exhausts of millions of cars and trucks burning hundreds of millions of gallons of gasoline every year.

To most Americans, though, the automobile was an unquestioned miracle. To those who could afford it, it meant freedom to move at will through the city or the countryside. It also provided status, as manufacturers introduced more elaborate models, some costing ten times as much as Ford's Model T. And the automobile meant adventure. Middle-class Americans could get behind the wheel of a powerful, complicated piece of machinery—just as Lindbergh had climbed into the cockpit of his machine—and be off on an exciting journey of motion and speed every day. Like Lindbergh, too, Americans went beyond a concern with efficiency and practicality to a romantic affection for their machines. They polished them, paraded them, and gave them pet names like the "old bus," the "flivver," the "tin Lizzie," and the "merry Oldsmobile." Americans loved the car, despite its defects.

AIR TRANSPORTATION For the first quarter of the twentieth century, the automobile had the greatest social and economic impact on America. The development of the aircraft industry and airline passenger service did not become truly important until years after Lindbergh's flight. Like the automobile, the airplane depended on the small, powerful, and efficient gasoline engine. But the airplane was in many ways more thrilling than the automobile. (This was why Lindbergh and other pilots could make a living in the 1920s barnstorming across America in their aerial circuses.)

The first men to fly a real airplane were Orville and Wilbur Wright. In 1903 they camped at Kitty Hawk, North Carolina (a location they chose because it had strong and steady winds, plus a great expanse of beach), with a primitive biplane. It had a tiny gasoline engine, which turned two push-type propellers. The first successful test flight came in December, after a series of dangerous and frustrating failures. This first flight lasted a little less than a minute, and covered only about 800 feet. But the Wright brothers were soon experimenting with larger planes and engines. In 1909, after six years of work, they sold the first plane to the United States Army.

World War I brought about a dramatic spurt in design sophistication, not only in the United States but in Europe. The new planes had larger and better engines and a much more rigid construction than the Wrights' original. The war also romanticized flight and created a new type of military hero, the aviator. Lindbergh, then, was able to capitalize not only on advances in technology but on a new image of the heroic and daring "ace."

The main civilian use of the airplane was shipping mail. The government began service in 1918. Later, private companies (like the one Lindbergh worked for in St. Louis) took over the service. The operation was dangerous. A majority of the pilots were killed in crashes during the early years. But by the mid-1920s there was regular, all-weather airmail service between most major cities in America.

Lindbergh's flight, combined with the introduction of larger airplanes like Byrd's *America*, did more than any other single event to encourage the growth of air transportation. Lindbergh had faith in the future of aviation. Soon after his return to America in 1927, he began a flying tour of the country to promote airmail and air transportation. By 1930, just three years after his solo transatlantic flight, there were forty-three domestic airline companies, operating over 30,000 miles of flying routes.

New Manners and Morals

All these changes—the development of mass communication, the expansion of industry, the introduction of a new technology—brought about another revolution. This revolution marked a dramatic difference in the manners and morals of the American people. Americans of the 1920s knew they were living in a time when the world was undergoing rapid change. They coined new phrases, like the "Roaring Twenties," the "lost generation," and "flaming youth," to describe what was happening to them. Young Americans were adopting habits and moral standards that their parents found shocking and offensive.

A REVOLUTION FOR WOMEN At the center of the revolution in manners were women. The revolution that would change women's lives did not begin in the 1920s. During the first two decades of the twentieth century, many middle- and upper-class women had adopted new patterns of behavior (including divorce) that broke the traditions of nineteenth-century Victorian America. But because of the impact of World War I and the influence of books, radio, and advertising, the trend that had started at the turn of the century began to affect ever-widening circles of women. By the 1920s the revolution was in full bloom.

Politically, women *were* new creatures. After decades of agitation, they finally won the right to vote, with passage of the Nineteenth Amendment in 1920. But this new political role was only a small part of the emancipation of women. The new middle-class woman of the 1920s wanted to do everything. "Everything" included many more opportunities than her mother had had.

She was much more likely than her mother to attend college. She might go to work, too. By

Smoldering youth. Many Americans of the 1920s were intensely conscious of the changing ways men and women behaved toward each other socially and sexually. At the center of the supposed changes was the "flapper," the young woman scantily dressed, hatless, with bobbed hair, at home with alcohol, frankly provocative, and carefully posing in ways designed to seem altogether natural. In truth, the consciousness of change probably ran considerably ahead of the changes themselves. This cartoon of 1927 wildly exaggerates the degree of public naked-ness most women were willing to risk—or most men to accept. (Culver Pictures)

Simpering youth. Dancing was one of the main preoccupations of the popular culture of the 1920s. White people appropriated, and drastically modified, black dances just as they did black music. (They managed to do this, usually, with no apparent change in their racial attitudes.) Here a young couple are shown doing the Charleston. The effect they are striving for in this staged photograph is one that combines open sexuality with youthful innocence; their own highly patterned intimacy is mixed with an awareness that they are not so much dancing as they are performing for a public. (Culver Pictures)

1930, 10 million women were employed in the American labor force. This new experience of education and work increased the number of women who were likely to remain single, or, if they did marry, to get divorced. The divorce rate in 1930 was twice what it had been before the war. This did not mean that marriages were more unhappy but that women were less likely to put up with a bad marital situation. They would demand their freedom instead.

There was an even more obvious revolution in the way women dressed. The ideal that grad-ually emerged in the decade of Lindbergh's flight

was that of the "flapper." She wore her dress short—above the knees rather than at the ankle. And the dress was not only shorter, it was made of thin material, designed to move with her body as she walked or danced—designed, too, to give an occasional glimpse of thigh above the hemline. The flapper discarded the corsets that her mother had worn, and dispensed with the bustle, too. She put on much more makeup and perfume, and jangled with much more jewelry at her neck

Bessie Smith. One of the effects of the communications revolution was to turn previously obscure musicians into public celebrities, and art forms that had been folk music into commercial properties. This was particularly true for black artists and their music. Bessie Smith, shown here dressed in the ideal movie-queen costume of the period, made the blues into a form that managed to combine superb talent with commercial success. As a phenomenon, the celebrity was nothing new. But there were more of them than ever before, their variety was more striking, and their fame more instantaneous and widespread. (Bettmann Archive)

Like Lindbergh, though, the flapper and the "liberation" she symbolized were primarily a middle-class phenomenon. College, careers, divorce, and emancipated dress still touched only a minority of American women. Even though the right to vote now belonged to every woman, in practice that right was exercised primarily by middle-class women. For the rest, life continued to be quite confining. And when women did leave the home to take jobs, they still suffered from a systematic discrimination in wages and opportunities. In the final analysis, the flapper, like Lindbergh, had a significance that was more symbolic than real.

THE JAZZ AGE The new woman was part of a changing culture. A freedom of action and belief unheard of before seemed to go hand in hand with the triumph of industrial technology, with its prosperity and sense of unlimited possibilities for life. Both men and women listened to new music—jazz—and danced new steps. Instead of formal waltzes and other Victorian dances, they moved to the fast Charleston and the Black Bottom. They also danced close together in the slow fox-trot. Many older Americans were shocked by these changes. But these dances became part of the new culture, sweeping their way through high school gymnasiums and college campuses across the country.

and wrists. In advertisements and in movies, and in real life, too, she was likely to pose with a cocktail in one hand and a cigarette in a long holder in the other—the essence of a new "sophistication."

The sexual mores of Americans were changing, too. The ideas of the Austrian psychologist

Sigmund Freud on sex began to be discussed at the dinner table and in the polite magazines of the middle class. Words like *bitch* appeared in novels published by respectable publishers and read by respectable people. *Petting* and *necking* became part of the everyday vocabulary of magazine readers and even ministers. In the movies, sex became a major box-office attraction. Stars like Theda Bara and Clara Bow appeared on the screen in wispy clothing, locked in long, passionate embraces with their leading men. When Clara Bow was advertised as the "It" girl, hardly anyone needed to ask what "It" meant.

Americans drank more, too. Despite Prohibition (see Chapter 20), liquor was easy to obtain. And since liquor was illegal, millions of Americans became technically criminals on an almost daily basis. Probably half the respectable, middle-class families in the nation had their regular bootlegger. Terms like "bathtub gin" and "speakeasy" became part of the national language. Especially in colleges, drinking became a regular pastime of the "flaming youth" of the decade.

A BLACK RENAISSANCE The Jazz Age was a distinctly urban phenomenon. It was also an outcome of the greatest large-scale influence black music, dance, and style had ever had on white, middle-class Americans. And these two facts reflected two important changes in the African-American experience. The first of these changes was one of the most massive and significant migrations in American history. In 1910, nine out of ten African Americans still lived in the South, almost all of them in rural areas where they worked for meager wages as sharecroppers or day laborers. But blacks were beginning to leave the farms for the cities in great numbers. In the 1920s, 1.5 million African Americans moved into urban areas, most of them in the North.

The second great change in black experience was vocational. Those blacks who had managed to get an education during the decades after the end of Reconstruction had almost all been confined to careers as ministers or teachers in small

towns, or managed to get work as clerks in a special environment like Washington, D.C. In 1910 there was exactly one black judge and two state legislators in the entire United States. But things were changing. Black colleges were turning out hundreds of graduates every year, and a few blacks were able to graduate from old-line white colleges and universities. (The first black football players to be singled out as "All-Americans," in 1916 and 1917, played for elite, private white colleges, Brown and Rutgers, and each was the first black ever to play varsity sports.) The migration to Northern cities made it possible for ambitious young blacks to pursue careers—as lawyers, actors, singers, writers, editors—that would have been impossible in the rural South.

The place where these two changes came together to produce remarkable results was the part of Manhattan known by the old Dutch name of Harlem. The district, which ran north from 125th Street, had already become a black neighborhood by 1920. It was a neighborhood with real style, the place where every young black with ambition to be a doctor or a poet, a playwright or a lawyer took his or her dream.

W. E. B. Du Bois had brought his magazine, *The Crisis*, to Harlem at the beginning of World War I. After the war the National Association for the Advancement of Colored People (NAACP) moved its headquarters to Harlem (and at the same time replaced a predominantly white board of officers with a group of blacks headed by poet and lawyer James Weldon Johnson). Du Bois and Johnson were typical of the kinds of people who were going to lead black movements in the 1920s in one important respect: They were not just political men interested in social justice. They were also intellectuals, writers, and poets with an intense interest in art and culture. Soon they were joined in Harlem by a remarkable generation of black intellectuals and artists, many of them immigrants from the West Indies. Together they produced what they themselves referred to with justifiable pride as the Negro Renaissance or the Harlem Renaissance.

W. E. B. Du Bois

William Edward Burghardt Du Bois (1868–1963) had one of the most extraordinary and creative careers of any modern American writer or intellectual. During his nearly ninety-six years, Du Bois was a black student at Harvard, a poet, a novelist, a journalist, a reformer, a New York intellectual, a founder of the Pan-African movement, and, at the end, a communist and an expatriate.

Du Bois began his life in Massachusetts. Intellectually talented, he made his way through Harvard and did some graduate work in Germany to earn a prestigious Harvard Ph.D. His initial career choice was to be an academic. He taught at Wilberforce College in Ohio, at the University of Pennsylvania, and then at Atlanta University.

But his writing and his move to the South drew him gradually away from academic life and into the politics of race. His first book, *The Philadelphia Negro* (1899), was not only a superb exercise in academic sociology but a passionate recognition that the "Negro problem" could be solved only when blacks chose no longer merely to imitate whites but instead to cultivate a new attitude of respect for what they were as blacks.

In *The Souls of Black Folk* (1903), Du Bois pressed the point further. The prevailing program of reform among blacks had been devised by Booker T. Washington. But Washington's plan, as Du Bois saw it, proposed only that African Americans accept white society as they found it and seek gradually to work their way into it, from the bottom up. Du Bois believed this plan would not work—partly because of white resistance, which he viewed as determined and even violent. Washington's program was flawed in other ways as well. It did not recognize that blacks were different, that many of the black "souls" of which he wrote were kindly, gentle, and generous, and that it would be fatal merely to toss such souls into the white world of competition, materialism, and greed.

These ideas, combined with an increasing number of violent acts against blacks in all parts of the United States, led Du Bois into political activism. He was one of the founders of an organization called the Niagara Movement, dedicated to a more militant defense of African-American rights. Du Bois wrote a series of resolutions that voiced the sense of crisis that gave form to the movement, a sense of no progress. "Stripped of verbose subterfuge and in its naked nastiness, the new American creed says: fear to let black men even try to rise lest they become the equals of the white. And that in the land that professes to follow Jesus Christ. The blasphemy of such a course is only matched by its cowardice."

In 1910, in league with a large number of white reformers and intellectuals, Du Bois formed the Niagara Movement into a new organization, the National Association for the Advancement of Colored People. He was for many years the editor of the association's magazine, *The Crisis*. But Du Bois had been losing faith in the capacity of white society ever to accept blacks as blacks. He left teaching and moved into Harlem. He helped found the Pan-African Congress during the peace talks in Paris in 1918. And in his nineties he renounced his United States citizenship, announced his membership in the Communist party, and moved to the African state of Ghana, where he died.

The Crisis. In this twentieth-anniversary cover for *The Crisis*, artist Aaron Douglas brought together several themes and artistic techniques. The highly stylized female head is partly an assertion of pride in African origins, partly an allusion to the long-necked female figures of the great Italian painter Amadeo Modigliani (who had died nine years before), and partly an exercise in the newer vogue of abstract expressionism. The sun that is rising among the skyscrapers of New York is crowned with the letters NAACP. (The Schomburg Center for Research in Black Culture, The New York Public Library)

Langston Hughes. The artist Winold Reiss made this portrait of Langston Hughes about 1925. The portrait emphasizes Hughes's vocation as a New York writer, framed in ways that associate him with an emphatically avant-garde artistic modernism. The background is done in the style known as cubism, abstractly joining Hughes's bed and slippers, some random stairs to nowhere and jazz notes, with continuous clouds and curtains and the buildings of Harlem. (National Portrait Gallery, Smithsonian Institution, gift of W. Tjark Reiss, in memory of his father, Winold Reiss)

The literature of the Renaissance was varied in tone and manner. Langston Hughes's poetry moved easily from bitterness to gentleness, as did the poems of the Jamaican Claude McKay. Some writers explored the contemporary world. Some "discovered" the African past and its dense culture. Jean Toomer wrote a stunning collection of stories about black life in the 1880s in rural Georgia, *Cane*. But for all the differences in tone or subject matter, the writers of the Harlem Renaissance produced a body of work that had a recognizable unity.

This unity derived from the fact that the Renaissance was not just an intellectual flowering, it was an act of faith. The faith centered on a willingness to embrace black culture, history, and personality as something beautiful. The poet and essayist Langston Hughes put it simply: Creative blacks "intend to express our individual dark-skinned bodies without fear or shame." He would be glad, he went on, if whites were pleased with this kind of "expression," but if they were not, it would not matter. "We know we are beautiful."

Embracing an idea like this meant that black artists and intellectuals were doing more than producing art. They were making a political statement as well. In the 1920s the work of leading white writers and artists often ended in a repudiation of their culture and politics, questioning its vitality and authenticity. The Harlem Renaissance was attempting to do the opposite, to discover in the African-American experience sources of something that could be both authentic and vital, a basis for the emergence of what came to be called the New Negro. And for black intellectuals, this required not a separation of art and politics (as it did for an increasing number of white writers), but a fusion between the two. Deciding where you stood as an artist required you to decide where you stood as a black man or woman, both in relation to other blacks and in relation to white society.

The act of faith, the decision that to be black was a thing of beauty, did not translate into a single obvious political position. Out of the 1920s came a spectrum of proposed agendas. Perhaps the most conservative—though terms like *conservative* are of limited use in this matter—was the position of the NAACP. Under Johnson's leadership, the NAACP continued to struggle for legal equality and integration through the enforcement of the Fourteenth and Fifteenth Amendments. Du Bois and his followers continued to believe that black pride and black culture, not integration through legal means, was the solution. In this view, the work of what he called the "talented tenth" among blacks—the teachers, poets, and other intellectuals—was critical. An alternative vision was put forward by A. Philip Randolph, who brilliantly edited *The Messenger*. Randolph believed more in militancy than the NAACP leadership did. And he believed more in the crucial role of the black working class than Du Bois did. His solution centered on getting blacks to join aggressive unions, like the Brotherhood of Pullman Porters he organized. A very different kind of alternative was put forward by

the West Indian Marcus Garvey. Garvey was a black nationalist, whose vision involved promoting a return to Africa and the creation of a new black nation. In the meantime, he also urged the development of black capitalism in the United States as a way of making African Americans as free as possible from any necessary economic contact with whites.

Garvey's ideas had little appeal to the men and women who made the Harlem Renaissance. They were interested in finding ways to embrace their own racial culture, but they were also interested in being intellectuals. They wanted to reach into their own past—into slavery, into Africa, into rural poverty in the South—but they also wanted to reach out to the high culture of European and American whites. They traveled to England and to France. They attended parties in Harlem where they met their white counterparts. Many of them cultivated a new and fragile connection with white artists and writers who lived and worked downtown in Greenwich Village.

The connection did generate at least the beginnings of biracial culture in New York. The noted avant-garde playwright Eugene O'Neill wrote two plays with leading roles for a black man, *The Emperor Jones* (1920) and *All God's Chillun Got Wings* (1924). They were performed at the now-legendary Provincetown Theater in the Village, and *The Emperor Jones* had a brief run on Broadway. They even got some favorable notice in establishment papers like the *New York Times* and the *World*.

The Provincetown Theater was also the scene of a moment of great symbolic importance for the Harlem Renaissance. In 1925 a young and gifted singer, Paul Robeson, performed a concert of spirituals, or "sorrow songs." The moment was important partly because these songs were rooted in slavery and in the sufferings of poor blacks since emancipation. The small black middle class had usually preferred to forget about such music. It belonged to the past they were trying to leave behind. But for the Renaissance, it was important to see the black experience as something to be embraced, not left behind. And a brilliant singer like Robeson (with the help of some ingenious

TECHNOLOGY

A workable introduction to the new technology of mass production is Sigfried Giedion, *Mechanization Takes Command* (1948). Changes in business practice are treated exhaustively in Sanford M. Jacoby, *Employing Bureaucracy* (1985). Ford's career may be tracked in the exhaustive and sympathetic study by Allan Nevins and Frank E. Hill, *Ford* (three volumes, 1954–62). But the more interesting approach is through the writings of some of the molders of technological change, such as Henry Ford, *My Life and Work* (1922), and Wilbur and Orville Wright, *Papers* (1953).

POPULAR CULTURE

An elegant general book on the 1920s is William Leuchtenburg, *The Perils of Prosperity* (1958). Two classics from the period, the first charming, the second influential, are Frederick Lewis Allen, *Only Yesterday* (1931), and R. S. and H. N. Lynd, *Middletown* (1929). An interesting study of the definition of a generation is Paula Fass, *The Damned and the Beautiful: American Youth in the 1920s* (1977). William Henry Chafe, *The American Woman* (1974), is a plausible place to start reading on women in the 1920s. Interesting and usable books on mass entertainment are Harold Seymour, *Baseball* (two volumes, 1960–71); Edward Wagenknecht, *Movies in the Age of Innocence* (1962); and Robert Sklar, *Movie Made America* (1975). The social impact of the automobile is discussed in James Flink's fine *Car Culture* (1975). The development of the suburbs is the subject of Kenneth Jackson, *Crabgrass Frontier* (1985). Two useful treatments of the Harlem Renaissance are Nathan Huggins, *Harlem Renaissance* (1971), and David Levering Lewis, *When Harlem Was in Vogue* (1981). Manning Marable, *W. E. B. Du Bois: Black Radical Democrat* (1986), is thorough and sympathetic. The black experience in the cities is the subject of Ira Katznelson's fine *Black Men, White Cities: Race, Politics, and Migration in the United States, 1900–30, and Britain, 1948–68* (1976). A superb study of a great black artist and activist is Martin Duberman, *Paul Robeson* (1989).

INTELLECTUALS

Two classics of criticism from the period are Malcolm Cowley, *Exile's Return* (1934), and Edmund Wilson, *Axel's Castle* (1931). The two best general books on the literary history of the period—though both must be used very cautiously—are still Alfred Kazin, *On Native Grounds* (1942) and Frederick Hoffmann, *The Twenties* (1955).

CHAPTER 20
CAPITALISM IN
TRANSITION

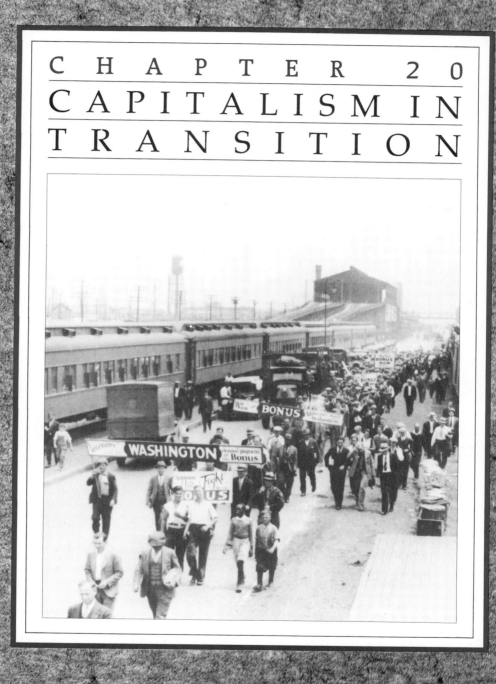

THE EPISODE: *In 1932, thousands of veterans of World War I began to gather in Washington, D.C., to demand immediate payment of a $1,000 "bonus" that Congress had scheduled to be paid to them in 1945. So they organized themselves into a "Bonus Army" and set up camps near the Capitol and at Anacostia Flats on the southeastern fringe of the city.*

During the spring and early summer, Congress debated the bonus. Finally, in June, the House passed a bonus bill, but the Senate rejected it—as thousands of angry bonus marchers waited on the Capitol steps. Even after the bonus failed, the Bonus Army did not leave the city. Some veterans were leaving, but others were coming to the capital every day to take their places in camps, rallies, and parades. Gradually, the government grew more tense. The president finally decided they were led by "radicals" and were a threat to the stability of the government itself. He ordered the army to clear the veterans from the District of Columbia, and soon the veterans faced bayonets and tanks of the same army in which they once had served.

THE HISTORICAL SETTING: *The Bonus March of 1932 occurred at the moment of deepest crisis the United States had experienced since the Civil War. After a decade of apparent prosperity in the 1920s, stock prices suddenly collapsed on Wall Street, and the economy entered the most severe depression in American his-tory. Within months, millions of people lost their jobs. Millions of others lost homes or farms or family businesses. So the desperation that drove the Bonus Army veterans to Washington was just one symptom of a much more widespread despondency.*

The administration that ordered troops to move against the Bonus Army was led by Herbert Hoover, the third in a succession of Republican administrations. But it was about to be replaced by Franklin Delano Roosevelt, who was promising a "New Deal." The marchers did not get their bonus, but the nation was about to get a seven-year tide of legislation that would permanently transform traditional assumptions about the relationship between the federal government and the American people.

The Great Depression, as people came to call it, was a world phenomenon that crippled the economies of all other industrial nations. All around the world, authoritarian leaders were gaining power over distressed and frustrated populations. The question posed by the Bonus March—and by the New Deal—was: Could industrial capitalism in the United States be saved within the framework of constitutional government, or was Hoover's use of the United States Army against freely assembled citizens the first step toward a major distortion of the American political system?

DEFEAT OF THE BONUS MARCHERS

The witness shifted nervously but stood his ground. Having waited a long time to testify, he was not going to be put off. Without formally addressing the committee or saying so much as a polite "Gentlemen," he began: "My comrade and I hiked here from nine o'clock Sunday morning, when we left Camden. I done it all by my feet—shoe leather. I come to show you people that we need our bonus. We wouldn't want it if we didn't need it."

The witness was Joseph T. Angelo, veteran of World War I. He was addressing a committee of the House of Representatives of the United States Congress in 1931. The committee was hearing witnesses testify about a controversial matter: the immediate payment of a "bonus" to all the veterans of the war. The country was in the second year of a depression, and the bonus would pay about $1,000 each to over 3 million veterans and their families. Congress had set up the bonus (a combination of life insurance and a pension) in 1924. It was not due to be paid until 1945, except to the heirs of veterans who died earlier. It would, in fact, be the greatest program of direct relief for the poor ever undertaken by the federal government.

For six days officials of the Republican administration testified. President Herbert Hoover was opposed to the bonus. The testimony of government officials reflected this opposition. A few congressmen and one or two officials of veterans' organizations spoke out for the bonus, but they were outnumbered by a long string of bank vice presidents, insurance executives, and other businessmen. The testimony was dull, full of statistics designed to prove that the bonus would bankrupt the federal treasury and bring about a dangerous inflation.

But now for the first time, an ordinary veteran, with no job, a hungry family, and a plain man's English, was testifying. Before Angelo had finished, the committee and the audience were stirred to a mixture of laughter, admiration, and stunned confusion.

> I have got a little home back there [in Camden, New Jersey] that I built with my own hands after I came home from France. Now, I expect to lose that little place. Last week I went to our town committee and they gave me $4 for rations. That is to keep my wife and child and myself and clothe us; and also I cannot put no coal in my cellar.

Here, in the poor grammar and tired face of the witness, was the whole meaning of the depression that had begun in 1929. Angelo said he spoke for hundreds like himself in New Jersey. But he spoke, too, for millions all over the country who had not worked for a long time, who stood in bread lines, and who built the shacks in the shabby little neighborhoods they wryly called Hoovervilles.

But Angelo was also a veteran. So he spoke from his experience of the two most important events in his time: the war that people still called the Great War and the depression they were beginning to call the Great Depression. There was no economic theory or political philosophy in his testimony. He was just a hungry man who had fought in France.

> All I ask of you, brothers, is to help us. We helped you, now you help us. My partner here has a wife and five children, and he is just the same as I am. He hiked down here at the same time with me, and our feet are blistered. That is all I have to say. And I hope you folks can help us and that we can go through with the bonus. We don't want charity; we don't need it. All we ask for is what belongs to us, and that is all we want.

Some of the congressmen were confused. Others were curious. Following the custom of congressional committees, they began to question the witness:

MR. FREAR: What is your business?

MR. ANGELO: Nothing. I am nothing but a bum.

MR. FREAR: You say you have not worked for two years?

MR. ANGELO: I have not worked for a year and a half. But there is no work in my home town.

MR. RAINEY: You are wearing some medal. What is it?

MR. ANGELO: I carry the highest medal in America for enlisted men, the Distinguished Service Cross.

MR. RAINEY: You have a Distinguished Service Cross? What is that for?

MR. ANGELO: That is for saving Colonel Patton.

George S. Patton was already a well-known Army officer. (In World War II he would become one of the most famous and controversial of America's generals.) Congressman Rainey continued the questioning and pressed Angelo for details. Angelo responded with a startling tale. He had been part of a 305-man unit attacked by German machine guns in the Argonne Forest in 1918. When the battle was over, he said, most of the men were dead. Colonel Patton was wounded, and only Angelo was left standing. Then Angelo showed the committee a tiepin made from a bullet he said was taken from Patton's leg in France. Neither the tiepin nor the medal had ever gone to "Uncle," Angelo's pet name for the pawnshop that had swallowed up most of his other possessions.

The afternoon was wearing on, but Angelo had roused the attention of the committee members and the audience as none of the other witnesses had. So the congressmen began to ask about his life. As Angelo answered, the audience sometimes laughed, sometimes applauded. He told them of working in a Du Pont plant, making munitions for the British before the United States entered the war. When Congress declared war in 1917, he enlisted at once. But he was almost rejected because he weighed a mere 107 pounds. Only after ten doctors had examined him and a general had watched him do a handspring and jump a table was he accepted.

Then, obviously agitated, Angelo wound up with another statement:

I can make money. I can make lots of money. Now, I could go bootlegging. It is just the same way I could have went to France and I could have run out on my outfit. Which is the best, to be a live coward or a dead hero?

When this was put on me, brothers, I wasn't worried when I went through. I don't have nothing to worry about. I wasn't married, and I got a wonderful sendoff when I went to France. My father throwed me out. [Laughter.] And when I came back, I went home to my father. I saw a big, fat woman sitting in the seat. I knowed her from next door. I said, "She is the last woman you want on earth. Pop, what is she doing here?" He says, "That is my wife." I says, "Oh, My God!" She says, "Get out of here," and that was my welcome home, and I got out. [Laughter.]

So, folks, I tell you all I will say to you is, help us through with the bonus. That is the best answer for you folks to give to the fellow at home. Don't forget me for a job. [Applause.]

Joe Angelo was three things: a veteran, a bum, and a victim of the most serious economic depression in American history. In each of these roles he was not just an individual grappling with purely personal problems; he represented over 4.5 million soldiers (about half of whom had actually been sent to Europe) suddenly discharged into civilian life in 1918 and 1919. These veterans organized, like other veterans in America's previous wars. More than a million joined the new American Legion and the Veterans of Foreign Wars. They thought of themselves as a special type of citizen, with a special claim on their country's gratitude.

As a bum, Angelo also spoke for countless people, many of them veterans, who had worked unsuccessfully at one job or another but mostly drifted through the 1920s. Naturally, the depression added millions of new "bums." Angelo, who had not been able to find work for a year and a half, was only one of a great, restless mass of unemployed. When he appeared before the congressional committee, at least 5 million men and women were classed as unemployed. Probably another 5 million were able to find only part-time work. Almost every second worker in America had his or her wages cut after the stock market crash of 1929. Few people could doubt in 1931 that unemployment was one of the most serious problems the United States had ever faced.

Joe Angelo's instinct was to turn to Washington for help. On his walk from Camden, he had met other small groups of veterans with the same idea. The unemployed, the veterans, and the bums (often one man, like Angelo, was all three) were looking more and more to the federal government for relief. They had one fairly good chance of getting help from a reluctant Congress and a stubborn president: payment of the bonus. This, in Angelo's words, was "the best answer for you folks to give."

Angelo wanted $1,000 immediately, instead of waiting until 1945 to collect a larger amount. This was the heart of an issue that was about to create the most dramatic crisis of the depression—the massing in Washington of a "Bonus Army." Behind the crisis lay the old task of writing a final chapter to the war and the new, complicated task of dealing with the depression. But for the marchers in the Bonus Army, the problem was quite simple: When and how would they be able to collect their bonus in full?

Veterans could already borrow money against the promise of the government to pay. Over 2 million had taken out loans that averaged $100 each—just enough to pay a back grocery bill, buy some coal for winter, or meet a medical emergency. But veterans everywhere were beginning to ask for ten times more, the payment of the entire bonus. And they found some sympathetic ears in Congress. Representative Wright Patman of Texas introduced a bill to authorize printing almost $2.5 billion in new paper money to pay the bonus. As time passed there was more and more talk of the bonus, not only in Washington but wherever knots of hungry veterans gathered.

In November 1931 a group of veterans left Seattle to ride freight trains to the capital. All over the country others were doing likewise. A movement had begun that would shake the Hoover administration.

For two years the president had been telling the nation that the depression was not so serious and would soon end. Administration officials had always played down unemployment statistics, portraying the crisis as a temporary economic slump that would cure itself. Meanwhile, Hoover kept to his principle that the federal government should not provide direct relief to poor individuals. The veterans who were hitchhiking and jumping freight trains headed toward Washington were not so sure of their principles. Certainly they lacked the president's political experience and skills. But they knew that they needed the bonus.

In May 1932, 300 men from Portland, Oregon, left for Washington in a group. They called themselves the Bonus Expeditionary Force—a play on the name of the American army in France, the American Expeditionary Force. They elected a leader, Walter F. Waters, once an Army sergeant, then foreman in a fruit cannery, now unemployed. They rode freight cars east and by late May reached East St. Louis, Illinois. There they tried to hop new trains going farther east. When railroad police told them to leave, they began to break up trains by uncoupling cars. They also soaped the rails in some places, making it impossible for engines to move.

The state called for its national guard to drive the veterans away. A scuffle occurred, but no one was hurt badly. The marchers were soon on their way again—in National Guard trucks that Illinois had provided in return for their promise to leave the state peacefully. But, most important, for the first time, the Bonus Army had won the attention of the newspapers and the public. Other veterans soon followed suit.

The scene was repeated everywhere. Merchants and mayors, railroad officials and governors, found it easier to supply trucks or boxcars than to stop the veterans. Thus a steady stream of bonus marchers was pouring into Washington. Each group had a leader or two, and their purpose was the same. They were in Washington to demand their bonus, even if they had to wait there until 1945 to get it.

One man deeply interested in the veterans' cause was Pelham D. Glassford, a West Point graduate and the youngest American in the war to become a brigadier general. In 1931 Hoover appointed Glassford superintendent of Washington's police force. He would have to deal with the Bonus Expeditionary Force in the capital.

Starting for Washington. In June 1932 this group of several hundred veterans from New York moved into the passenger yards of the Baltimore and Ohio Railroad in Jersey City, New Jersey. The men hoped to take over a train, which would carry them to Washington, where they could press their demand that the government pay them the bonus it had promised they would receive. (Wide World Photos)

Glassford hoped that the Bonus Army either would not come or would go home quickly. But when the marchers arrived, he became sympathetic and helpful. He regarded them as "his boys." He assigned them quarters in abandoned buildings on Pennsylvania Avenue, at the heart of official Washington, between the White House and the Capitol.

At Glassford's suggestion, also, the marchers made a muster, or list of their groups, to make it easier to track down criminals and keep out the "reds" and radicals. Gradually, the marchers formed companies and then regiments. They elected Walter Waters, leader of the Portland group, as their commander. He appointed junior officers and divided the men into companies named after states. Soon the Bonus Army had a structure of command like the regular army.

Glassford's original decision to let the marchers camp along Pennsylvania Avenue was based on his hope that few would come. Soon it was obvious that the Bonus Army was much too large and dangerous (and embarrassing to the administration) to be in the center of things. Glassford sent most of the marchers to a new campsite a few miles southeast of Capitol Hill, at Anacostia Flats, a muddy landfill near the fork of the Potomac and Anacostia rivers. There about 6,000 veterans built a shabby but orderly camp, with shacks and tents arranged in winding rows.

At Anacostia Flats the veterans tried to re-create their old army life. They woke to bugles, conducted roll calls, and had inspections. A company of men was assigned every day to KP. Waters exercised strict discipline.

In camp again. At their Washington campsites, the bonus marchers tried to maintain military order. Among other things, this meant setting up kitchens to cook and to serve large groups of men. Here, one ex-soldier ladles out a dish of food for another. The stove is a trench, covered by a steel beam, with a rude chimney at the cook's left. (Culver Pictures)

Other aspects of camp life were more relaxed. Some men had brought their wives and children. The Salvation Army set up a post office, a library, and a recreation room. Glassford managed to borrow some field kitchens and other equipment. He supervised the distribution of food donated by Washington citizens, American Legion posts, and others. At one point Glassford gave several hundred dollars of his own money to buy food. There was even a newspaper to keep the veterans informed about the progress of bonus legislation in Congress.

By June 6, 1932, the veterans were ready for their first direct action. About 7,000 left their separate camps around the city and lined up neatly in six "regiments" to parade through Washington. The men felt fairly hopeful as they moved along. The Patman bill, which was in the House, seemed as if it would pass soon. The rumors that they were controlled by communists, spread by some politicians to smear the Bonus Army, were not given much credit. Best of all, their parade had drawn a crowd of about 100,000, mostly Washington clerical workers. Every time another company with its American flag passed, the crowd applauded.

Shortly after dark the long line of marchers reached a circle near the Capitol. (They were forbidden to pass the White House or go to the Capitol itself.) Orders were given to fall out, and the marchers broke ranks to walk quietly back to Anacostia. They had heard that in less than a week the House would vote on the bonus bill. If it passed both the House and Senate and was signed by Hoover, most of the veterans could collect the $1,000 needed to get their hungry families through another depression year.

The parade was simply a beginning. Veterans kept coming to Washington—the police estimated 100 every hour. On June 15, when the House passed the bill, there were probably 15,000 veterans, plus some wives and children, scattered around Wash-

Veterans on parade. In July 1932 the Bonus Army held this shirtsleeve parade from the Washington Monument, shown in the background, to the Capitol. The marchers maintain their ranks and files in good order and are absolutely in step, in spite of the lack of a band. They are obviously trying to emphasize both their military skills and their patriotism. (UPI/ Bettmann Newsphotos)

ington. Anacostia Flats was crowded, but new shacks kept going up. By now the ex-soldiers had stripped half the city of every stray board and door, every spare piece of tin and canvas. One man moved a burial vault onto the flats and took up residence in it. The camp was about level with the river, and had to be protected by a levee. When it rained, mud was a foot deep. But the Bonus Army kept building.

~

Obviously, some kind of crisis might soon develop. Health officials predicted a typhoid epidemic. Waters predicted victory if 100,000 more veterans arrived. Hoover's advisers predicted that communists would take over the Bonus Army.

The Bonus Army and the administration were both waiting for the Senate to vote on the Patman bill. Hoover was sure he would win. The House elected in 1930 was Democratic. Since it was the first body of politicians to graduate from the depression, it was full of representatives who had recently promised their constituents direct action. But only a third of the Senate had been elected in 1930. The majority were still firmly Republican and loyal to the president. Both houses were striving for a July adjournment. (It was an election year, and everyone wanted to get home to campaign.)

The administration hoped that the Bonus Army would simply disappear after the Senate voted and Congress adjourned.

On June 17 the Senate would debate and vote on the bonus. Waters commanded his marchers to go to the Capitol and fill the galleries, steps, and grounds. By noon there were 10,000 marchers in and around the Capitol.

Inside, the Senate debated. Men would leave the galleries every few minutes to report to the marchers out on the steps. Opponents of the bill argued Hoover's position on what should be done about the depression: The government ought to cut spending, not spend more. Direct relief to individuals was not a federal responsibility. Recovery would come as large banks, businesses, and railroads regained their health. Then jobs would become available, and the economy would escape from radical tinkering.

Many senators supporting the bill argued that since the veterans were hungry and would be able to collect the bonus in thirteen years anyway, they should have it now. But one or two senators gave a more complicated justification for the bonus. In a depression, they insisted, the government should spend money, not save it. If the government printed 2.5 billion new dollars for the bonus, the money would swiftly circulate. The veterans would be only the first to gain. The stores where they spent their payments would get the money. These stores, in turn, would order more goods from wholesalers and manufacturers. So every bonus dollar would become a dollar in motion, moving through the economy and stimulating all business. Naturally, when the depression was cured, the government would stop deficit spending—that is, spending more than it raised in taxes. The economy would return to normal.

Though the debate went on, it soon became clear that only a political miracle could save the bonus. The Senate was much too conservative to experiment with such legislation. Even some of the liberal senators who usually opposed Hoover questioned the bill. What was needed, they said, was a general bill for relief of all the unemployed. Veterans should receive no special favors.

Finally, after 8 P.M., someone came from the galleries and whispered to Waters. The bill had lost decisively, sixty-two to eighteen. Waters climbed the steps and turned to face the largest body ever gathered in Washington to demonstrate for a cause. The marchers had been waiting for hours, and for a moment it seemed they might riot. Marines were stationed nearby, just in case. Members of the administration wanted to ready machine guns, but Glassford persuaded them not to. Waters shouted: "Comrades![1] I have bad news. Let us show them we can take it on the chin. Let us show them we are patriotic Americans." There was a muttering from the crowd. Then a gigantic roar came from 10,000 throats. Waters pleaded for calm:

> We are not telling you to go home. Go back to your camps. We are going to stay in Washington until we get the bonus, no matter how long it takes. And we are one hundred times as good Americans as those men in there who voted against it. But there is nothing more to be done tonight.

The situation was tenser than any in the capital since the Civil War. Ten thousand disappointed people, who had kept good discipline for weeks, were ready to break and mob the Senate. Waters played a final card to keep order: "I call on you to sing

───

[1]This was an old term from the war, not a communist greeting.

On the Capitol steps. The high point of the bonus march was probably this scene on the steps of the Capitol. Inside, while the veterans waited, the Senate was debating the Patman bill, which would have given them early payment of the bonus they had come to ask for. The bill's defeat nearly triggered an angry confrontation between the veterans and U.S. Marines, who had been called out to keep order. (Wide World Photos)

'America,'" he shouted. After a few false starts, the men obeyed. Gradually, the song gathered strength.

The emergency was over, at least for the moment. The singing died out, and bugles sounded assembly. The men milled about, looking for their outfits for the march back to camp. It was dark now, and the nervous men waiting inside the White House and the Capitol could take a deep breath. The bonus was dead, at least until Congress reconvened in December, after the presidential elections.

But the Bonus Army did not disappear. The government issued reports that the men were leaving, but the police reported that new recruits were arriving about as fast as old ones left. Estimates of the size of the group issued by the government, the police, the newspapers, and the Bonus Army itself varied widely. At its largest, the Bonus Army probably numbered about 20,000. Membership shifted constantly; perhaps as many as 50,000 veterans were in Washington at one time or another during June and July of 1932.

The government offered to lend the marchers train fare or gas money to leave town, plus seventy-five cents a day for other expenses. Many veterans simply took the money and stayed in town. Others used it to recruit new members. Thus a month after the Senate had defeated the Patman bill, there were about as many marchers as ever. The police estimated 15,000, two-thirds of them crowded into Anacostia Flats.

By late July, with no hope of a bonus from Congress, the veterans' mood soured. Their newspaper published more militant calls for action. Waters began to allow the small group of about 150 communists to eat occasionally at the Anacostia mess. (He had always thrown them out before.) He even began to talk about a permanent organization of veterans in politics, which he would call the "Khaki Shirts," in imitation of the Brown Shirts that Adolf Hitler had organized.

In the White House, too, opinions were getting stronger. After the Senate defeated the bonus, the president decided the marchers had no business squatting on government land. He also decided they were not truly patriotic veterans asking for relief. Instead, he believed they had been

> organized and promoted by the communists, and included a large number of hoodlums and ex-convicts determined to raise a public disturbance. They were frequently addressed by Democratic congressmen, seeking to inflame them against me.

The differences grew sharper, the summer hotter, and tempers shorter. On July 16 the most serious incident so far broke out at the Capitol. Congress was about to adjourn. Waters ordered his men to make one last symbolic demonstration. By midday, nearly 7,000 bonus marchers were at the Capitol. Their mood was much uglier than a month before, at the time of the Senate vote on the Patman bonus bill. Senators and congressmen crowded near every window to watch. Even Glassford lost his nerve.

Glassford ordered Waters taken into custody and moved to the basement of the Capitol. When the veterans saw what was happening, they stopped cheering Glassford and began to boo and jeer. "Waters! Waters!" they shouted. Glassford was forced to bring the Bonus Army's commander onto the platform. After a short, harsh exchange with Glassford, Waters tried to calm his people. Then he ordered them to move to the middle: "Use the center steps. But I want you to keep a lane open for the white-collared birds, so they won't rub into us lousy rats. We're going to stay here until I see Hoover!"

The demonstration was clearly dangerous. Several congressmen came out of the Capitol to speak to the demonstrators, trying to cool them off. Finally, the Speaker of the House, John Nance Garner, agreed to meet with Waters and a committee of his aides inside the building. Garner handled the situation well. He made a few empty promises of help and was photographed with Waters. When the conference was over, Waters went back outside and ordered his followers to their camps. For a second time, an extremely touchy and potentially violent situation had been controlled.

In the White House, however, tempers were also growing shorter. Hoover had just been renominated by the Republicans to run for a second term. The Democrats would meet soon to nominate Franklin D. Roosevelt, then governor of New York. Hoover knew the campaign would be rough. But he knew he would win if he could overcome the widespread idea that he was responsible for the depression.

A favorite tactic of Hoover's closest associates was to picture him as the firm opponent of all kinds of radicalism. Hoover had always opposed the bonus. Now he and his advisers decided to move firmly against the veterans. Some even hoped for an incident. Then it would appear that the government had to defend its very life against a radical insurrection.

The president's camp. Herbert Hoover opened a rest camp for himself in The Rapidan, Virginia, not far from Washington. To meet his new neighbors, Hoover held a lawn party, where he is shown chatting with one of the guests. (Culver Pictures)

A few days after Congress had adjourned, the administration decided to move. The tensest point in Washington was the two square blocks on the south side of Pennsylvania Avenue, just a block from the Capitol and a mile from the White House. The buildings here were part of a triangle of structures that had been condemned to make way for a government building program. All over the triangle, veterans had camped in and around vacant and half-demolished structures, eyesores that embarrassed the administration. On July 21, on instructions from the Treasury Department, the commissioners who governed the District of Columbia (and were directly responsible to the administration) ordered the veterans to evacuate the two blocks. For various reasons the order was not carried out at once. But Waters told his people to be ready to leave. Glassford was locating another site farther away, where they could take their few possessions and settle again.

Veterans and the police. A group of bonus marchers try to defend their tents against the advancing police. The Bonus Army was one of the few organizations in America that was more or less integrated racially, and the group shown here includes at least a couple of determined African Americans. The most intense struggle seems to concern whether the marchers or the police have a better right to the flag. (Culver Pictures)

Finally, at about 10 A.M. on July 28, treasury officials accompanied by Glassford and his police entered the area. The veterans began to evacuate the buildings and their makeshift shanties, leaving behind everything they could not carry or push along in small carts or baby carriages. Everything went peacefully, though a few veterans had to be taken out under arrest. Before noon the first building was empty. In the meantime, a large crowd of Washington citizens had gathered to watch. Their sympathies were divided between the police and the veterans.

Then, a little past noon, veterans from the other camps filtered into the area, mixing with the crowd. One group came to stage a formal demonstration. Paul Anderson, a journalist, described what happened next:

At noon, three bonus men, one carrying a large American flag, started across the block, followed by several hundred. When the leaders encountered a policeman, he grabbed the flag. There was a scuffle, and one of the marchers was hit on the head with a night stick. He wrested it from the officer and struck the cop, and there was a shower of bricks from the buddies in the rear. It looked like an ugly mess, but the cops kept their heads, and no shots were fired.

Glassford dashed into the heart of the melee, smiled when a brickbat hit him on the chest, and stopped the fighting. Within two minutes, the veterans were cheering Glassford.

For another half hour the police continued their work. The veterans were leaving the buildings, but they stood around outside, many on big piles of bricks. No one is certain what happened next. Some witnesses said a policeman tried to clear veterans out of a building that had not even been ordered vacated. They resisted. Another observer said that a policeman started climbing some makeshift stairs, lost his balance, and fell. In a panic he pulled his revolver and began to fire wildly into a crowd near him. Glassford gave what may be the most accurate account:

> I was about twenty yards away from the building when I heard a commotion. I went to the second floor. One officer had started up the steps, and near the rear, I heard some say, "Let's get him!"
>
> As he started up the steps, bricks started falling on him [Glassford was not certain whether the bricks were being thrown or were just falling], and as I leaned over the railing above, I saw him fall and draw his gun, firing two shots.

Other policemen also started shooting. Then veterans began to throw bricks at every policeman in sight. Again Glassford acted quickly to prevent a vicious riot. He ran outside, shouting, "Stop that shooting!" The firing ended, and the bricks stopped flying. Ambulances rushed to take away the injured. One policeman was hurt seriously by a brick. One bonus marcher was dead; another died later of gunshot wounds.

The battle of the Bonus Army might have ended here. Glassford had the situation in hand. The veterans were moving out of the buildings as they had been ordered. On the whole they were reluctant but still willing to cooperate. Waters had supported Glassford every step of the way. Within another hour or two, evacuation of the two blocks would have been complete. But the administration also had decided to act. Hoover had ordered the chief of staff of the army, General Douglas MacArthur, to bring troops into the city to restore civil peace.

The troops—about 500 at first, then later over 1,000—formed up behind the White House. They came armed with bayoneted rifles and heavy blue canisters of tear gas. There were cavalry with sabers, a machine-gun squadron, several infantry companies, and even a half-dozen tanks. MacArthur put the troops under the command of General Perry L. Miles. But as he later wrote, "In accordance with the President's request, I accompanied General Miles." With MacArthur was his aide, Major Dwight David Eisenhower. And in the cavalry was George S. Patton (who had no way of knowing that Joe Angelo had come back to Washington and was out in the troubled city with about 12,000 of his buddies, waiting).

At about four o'clock the cavalry led the way, the iron shoes of their horses clattering on the asphalt of Pennsylvania Avenue. Then came tanks, more cavalry, the infantry, and the mounted machine gunners. They rode, walked, and rumbled up to the triangle, pushing the crowds back and surrounding the buildings. Without any conference or hesitation, the troops (who wore gas masks and carried fixed bayonets) began to throw tear-gas bombs into the buildings. They were going to clear the entire area.

MacArthur and Eisenhower. The command of the military force that finally chased the Bonus Army out of Washington was in the hands of General Douglas MacArthur, shown here on the left, with his aide, Dwight David Eisenhower. MacArthur insisted that the bonus marchers were a fundamental threat to the government. (UPI/Bettmann Newsphotos)

The veterans did not resist. A few hung back and had to be jabbed at with bayonets. Mostly they stumbled out of the area and toward Anacostia. MacArthur, who also had tears streaming down his face from the tear gas, ordered most of his men to herd the veterans south. Another detachment moved west, to attack the small, separate camp of the communist group.[2] Suddenly, it became clear that the general intended to clear the entire District. In the triangle, smoke began to rise: The troops had set fire to the shacks, tents, and scattered belongings of the Bonus Army.

MacArthur's forces kept pushing the straggling veterans before them with bayonets and sabers. The sun was going down behind them. Ahead lay the drawbridge to Anacostia. The Bonus Army's rear guard hurried across the bridge at about sunset. Waters had already given the order to evacuate Anacostia and had sent word to MacArthur asking for time to move women and children out of the camp. On the flats about 7,000 men were scurrying around, trying to keep order in a forced retreat.

From the time the troops first appeared, the bonus marchers gave no resistance. They booed, they swore—but they moved. MacArthur left his tanks north of the river and paused before Anacostia Flats for an hour before sending the infantry. But when they went onto the flats, the soldiers threw gas everywhere. Stragglers were treated very roughly. The soldiers then set fire to the camp. (Many of the veterans had already put matches to their borrowed army tents.) Next they moved out of the camp to the

---

[2]Communists in this camp included James Ford, their candidate for vice president. On July 31 the *New York Times* ran a front-page article quoting the communists. "We agitated for the bonus and led the demonstration of the veterans in Washington." However, the communists were never the bonus force's prime movers.

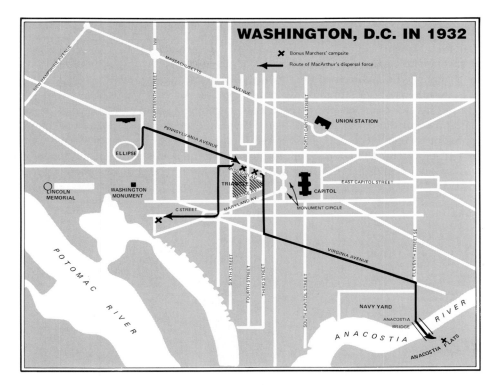

nearby area where many of the veterans still stood watching their shacks burn. As the troops rushed up the hill, which was not federal property, they continued to throw tear gas. One woman, whose baby had actually been born since the Bonus Army's arrival, told this story:

> The troops came up the hill, driving the people ahead of them. As they passed by the house [where the woman was staying], one of them threw a tear-gas bomb over the fence into the front yard. The house was filled with gas, and we all began to cry. We got wet towels and put them over the faces of the children. About a half an hour later, my baby began to vomit. I took her outside in the air and she vomited again. Next day, she began to turn black and blue.

A few days later the baby died—the third and last fatality of the battle of the Bonus Army.

The day after the action was a time for summing up. The White House and other administration officials issued statements. MacArthur gave his version in a press conference:

> That mob was a bad-looking mob. It was animated by the essence of revolution. They had come to the conclusion, beyond the shadow of a doubt, that they were about to take over either the direct control of the government, or else to control it by indirect methods. It is my belief that had the President not acted today, he would

have been faced with a grave situation. Had he let it go on another week, I believe
that the institutions of our government would have been severely threatened.

To this version of the threat posed by the bonus force, MacArthur added that it was
the veterans who had burned their own shacks in the triangle.

Another kind of summing up came from Joe Angelo, who told a newspaper
reporter his story. He was at Anacostia Flats, watching a group of infantrymen in gas
masks overrun the shack he had been living in. They were urged on by a tough,
confident cavalry officer. Angelo blinked the burning tear gas out of his eyes and
recognized George S. Patton. Then, like the rest of the Bonus Army, he ran. Soon he
was back home in Camden, where he had started his long hike to Washington a year
and a half before.

CRASH, DEPRESSION, AND A "NEW DEAL"

Most of the bonus march veterans who went to Washington were as politically innocent as Joe Angelo. Some of their leaders had a little political sophistication; but only the tiny fraction who were communists thought they understood the basic problems of American society and sought a revolutionary solution. The rank-and-file marchers were simply caught in a web of circumstances they did not understand or want.

The marchers' experience was defined by the two great events they had participated in, the Great War and the Great Depression. Between lay the decade of the 1920s, the "Jazz Age." But most of the marchers had experienced only a little jazz. Like most Americans, they had passed through a curiously contradictory decade. On the one hand, American society of the 1920s was characterized by tremendous innovations—some technological, others social. But alongside all the newness and experimentation, the 1920s had been a decade of profound, sometimes violent conservatism. Both in formal politics, centered in Washington, and in the informal politics of organized movements, the keynote had been not innovation but restoration.

Conservatism in politics received a kind of endorsement from the economy. The 1920s was a period of apparent prosperity. In some sectors, in fact, the economy virtually underwent a boom.

And this prosperity made it appear to many Americans that the country had returned from the distortions of progressive reform and war to what President Warren G. Harding called "normalcy." It took the depression to show that normalcy was an illusion, and that the 1920s had contained profound distortions of its own.

A Tide of Reaction

For millions of Americans, the uncertainties of modernity, the wave of progressive reforms, and the moral crusade of the war were all extremely unsettling. Even before the war was over, millions of people had already decided that change had gone too far, that the Republic was in desperate danger of losing its stability and virtue. For some, the threat was simple: The country was being overrun by foreigners and by foreign political ideas. For others, the problem was alcohol, and the loose life associated with it. Still others viewed blacks as the principal threat. For many, the danger lay in the growing number and power of Jews and Catholics. Some complained about the inroads new scientific ideas were making on traditional values and beliefs.

Not every American participated, by any means, but a large and very active segment of society—especially in the South and the Midwest—joined in a series of movements and organizations to save their country from what they saw as the perils of change. Sometimes the results were merely quaint, as when the sale of alcohol was forbidden by an amendment to the Constitution. Or when schoolteachers were prosecuted for explaining Charles Darwin's theory of evolution in their classrooms. At other times, however, the results were more serious, even tragic, as when dozens of African Americans were lynched by mobs, or hundreds of immigrant "radicals" were hounded in court and even sentenced to die for their supposed crimes. This was part of the character of "normalcy," the opposite and darker face of the Jazz Age.

THE RED SCARE The conservative reaction focused sharply on radicalism. The Russian Revolution of 1917, which had brought the communist government of the Bolsheviks to power, was followed by communist uprisings in Germany and Hungary. These developments created an atmosphere of fear in the United States. Many people, including a number of powerful leaders in federal and state governments, believed that a communist conspiracy was at work among them, ready to "radicalize" the country.

In 1919 a series of spectacular strikes and the outbreak of political sabotage fed the fear. In the spring of that year, two small groups of anarchists attempted to bomb the homes and offices of a number of government officials and businessmen. The bombs, most of which were sent through the mail, were probably the work of mentally unstable persons. Certainly they had nothing to do with the tiny organized Socialist and Communist parties of the country.

In fact, the bombers were incompetent. Many of the bombs were never delivered because they did not have enough postage. One bomb only damaged the house of its intended victim, but it blew the bomber himself, an Italian anarchist, to bits. Another, addressed to a Georgia politician,

was opened by his maid (a black worker, not a capitalist). She lost her hands as a result. But the bombings did convince many people that revolution was at hand.

One of the people who was most convinced was Woodrow Wilson's attorney general, A. Mitchell Palmer. Like Wilson, Palmer was a liberal and a strong antiradical. The attorney general also had his eye on the Democratic nomination of 1920. So he used the "red scare" to make his department the center of the action. He obtained a special appropriation for hunting down radicals. With the money, he formed a new antisubversive division of the Justice Department, headed by J. Edgar Hoover.

Beginning in November 1919, the Justice Department conducted a series of raids against radical groups, seeking out suspected communists at union meetings, at Communist party headquarters, and in their homes. The most spectacular of the raids, which came on New Year's Day 1920, resulted in the arrest of 6,000 people. In the end the Palmer raids led to the conviction of only a handful of citizens, most of them for minor crimes. Immigrant aliens, who were Palmer's main target, suffered more; about 600 were eventually deported, mostly to the Soviet Union.

Palmer's campaign created an atmosphere of near-hysteria among many Americans. It led to one episode that did more than any other single event of the 1920s to divide Americans of different political beliefs. In 1920 two Italian anarchists, Nicola Sacco and Bartolomeo Vanzetti, were arrested in Boston on a charge of robbing a shoe company and murdering two of its employees. Their trial soon became a political event, a test of the established authority against political radicalism.

The trial was unfair. But in the political climate of the red scare, Sacco and Vanzetti were convicted and sentenced to death. The appeals process was long and unsuccessful. Finally, in 1927, the year of Lindbergh's flight, both men were executed in the electric chair. To the small number of American liberals and radicals of the 1920s, Sacco and Vanzetti were the century's greatest

Sacco and Vanzetti. Here, in 1927, Nicola Sacco and Bartolomeo Vanzetti enter the courtroom to make their last plea for justice. Some recent evidence seems to show that at least one of them may have been guilty of the crime he was charged with. But no amount of new evidence can set aside the fact that they were unfairly tried and unfairly convicted. (UPI/Bettmann Newsphotos)

martyrs, modern counterparts of the victims of the Salem witch trials and the Haymarket affair. But to most Americans, they were just Italian radicals who had been properly punished.

The bonus marchers of 1932 had to contend with the lingering effects of the red scare. They were accused of being communists and serving as tools in a foreign conspiracy. When Douglas MacArthur marched on their camp at Anacostia, he did so in the belief that he was protecting the country from a powerful revolutionary movement. The irony was, however, that the marchers themselves accepted much of the ideology of "Americanism" that underlay the red scare. Their response to the charge that they were communists was to insist on their own patriotism, and to point proudly to their record of military service. Most of the marchers were probably just as devoutly anticommunist, just as insistent on their own "100 percent Americanism" as their critics.

The red scare also made it possible for those Americans who feared immigrants and their ethnic and religious differences to restrict immigration. In February 1921 (over the veto of President Wilson), Congress passed a law that limited immigration, especially from countries in southern and eastern Europe. According to the law, the number of immigrants from a country in any given year could not exceed 3 percent of the number of people of that nationality who were already in the United States in 1910. In 1924 the law was made even more restrictive. Quotas would now be based on resident population in 1890, immigration limited to 150,000 per year after 1927, and Asians totally excluded. The effect of the laws was to end, almost at once, the flow of immigration.

PROHIBITION AND REACTION Like the red scare and the movement for immigration restriction, the prohibition of alcohol in the 1920s had its roots in the progressive period. In 1919 the states had passed the Eighteenth Amendment, which empowered Congress to prohibit the sale of alcoholic beverages. The amendment marked the victory of a long campaign of "temperance." It provided another rallying point for conservative, small-town Americans. They divided society into the "drys" and the "wets" and opposed any politician who did not favor Prohibition.

The Prohibition movement failed to stop Americans from drinking. In most cities, people continued to drink whiskey in speakeasies. The sale of bootleg whiskey was controlled largely by organized gangs of criminals, like the one led by Al Capone in Chicago, which bribed public officials and policemen to cover up their operations. But for most conservative Americans, Prohibition was above all a moral crusade. It was an issue they could use to split their country into two camps: one composed of decent people, the other of riffraff.

Another conservative campaign of the 1920s was the attempt of many Protestant Americans—again, especially in the South and the Midwest—to prevent schools from teaching dangerous or "un-American" ideas. In several Southern states this crusade was aimed mainly at the idea of evolution. The notion of biological evolution was an old one. It became scientifically respected in the nineteenth century through the work of Charles Darwin. By the 1920s practically every scientist in the world believed that animals, including human beings, had evolved over a long period of time. But this seemed to many people to go against the fundamentals of their religion. They saw it as a challenge to the biblical story of creation.

Several state legislatures forbade their schools to teach the doctrine of evolution. In 1925 John Scopes, a schoolteacher in Dayton, Tennessee, decided to challenge the law. He was arrested, and his trial became almost as much a spectacle as the trial of Sacco and Vanzetti. Reporters from every major American newspaper—and several European papers—covered it.

Scopes was defended by the most famous criminal lawyer in the United States, Clarence Darrow of Chicago. William Jennings Bryan led the prosecution. Bryan, an aging but still powerful leader of millions of fundamentalists, stood ready to smite the forces of modernism. He was humiliated on the witness stand by Darrow.

But Scopes lost the case and was fined $100. The Tennessee law stayed on the books. After the Scopes trial, however, the direction of education in the South and elsewhere shifted away from Bryan's intellectual conservatism toward the acceptance of modern science. Bryan's crusade, like many other conservative movements of the 1920s, was only a temporary victory over twentieth-century ideas and social habits.

THE KU KLUX KLAN The most bizarre conservative movement of the 1920s was the Ku Klux Klan. The Klan, which had all but disappeared after Reconstruction, was reorganized in 1915 in Georgia. Its membership grew slowly until the war was over. Then, taking many of its cues from the red scare, the Klan began to gain support. Much of its strength still lay in the rural South and Southwest. But there was a new element in this second growth: Now, millions in the northern states, many of them city dwellers, joined the organization. At one time or another, about 5 million Americans took up membership and donned the white sheets that were the uniform of the Klan. The strongest Klan state was not in the South at all but Indiana, where the organization appeared for a time to control even the state government.

The Ku Klux Klan was a fringe organization, attracting only the most conservative citizens. The white robes and hoods, the secrecy and the rituals, the burning of crosses in the night demanded considerable dedication from its members. They had to be able to stomach a good deal of violence and torture. And they had to be able to tolerate a large element of the ridiculous, as in the titles of Klan officers, like "dragon," "kleagal," and "kludd." Nevertheless, the Klan was able to elect one of its dragons governor of Indiana, march openly in Washington in 1926, and influence the Democratic presidential nomination in 1924.

In the long run, the Klan—like the Prohibition movement and the fundamentalist attempt to prevent the teaching of evolution—was destined to lose. Blacks would not be lynched in great numbers forever, the freedom to drink alcohol would return, new scientific theories would get taught, eventually. But in the political atmosphere of the 1920s, it was possible for millions of Klansmen, and millions of other conservatives who did not join the organization, to convince themselves that their victory was close at hand, that the country would be saved, after all.

The KKK on the march. The Ku Klux Klan is shown here, in 1926, in one of its favorite kinds of moments. The robed Klansmen are marching publicly and openly, declaring to all the world their patriotic purposes and determination to save the country from a host of perils. And yet, even in this aggressively public setting, the marchers preserve the air of secrecy, mystery, and ritual that is so important to many of its members. ("Ku Klux" was an adaptation of the Greek *kuklos*, "circle" or "band." "Klan," of course, was an adaptation of *clan*.) (Culver Pictures)

The Politics of Conservatism

The political instrument of salvation, restoration, and "normalcy" was to be the Republican party. As the war ended, the Republicans could see as plainly as anyone else that there was a change in the atmosphere. The policies of reform and military crusade, on which Woodrow Wilson and the Democrats had built their success in national politics, were clearly falling into disrepute. The Republicans met at Chicago in their national convention of 1920 full of hope. They were still the majority party, they knew. And no Democrat on the horizon represented a real threat to the elec-

tion of a Republican president. Wilson's illness, the failure of the League of Nations, the doings of A. Mitchell Palmer—all had helped to disorganize the Democrats.

The only question seemed to be whether the Republicans could unite on a candidate. The convention deadlocked for six ballots. Then a few party leaders huddled in one of the most famous "smoke-filled rooms" in American history and chose a surprise candidate: Warren Gamaliel Harding, senator from Ohio.

WARREN G. HARDING Harding was a small-town newspaper publisher and politician, reminiscent of the Republican style of the late nineteenth century. He had risen carefully through the party system in Ohio to become a senator.

His political virtues were, primarily, loyalty to the organization and a discreet silence on most issues. A handsome but simple man, he was puzzled by complicated issues like taxation, the tariff, and foreign affairs. He was "one of the boys," who enjoyed a night of whiskey and poker with his cronies. He had never proposed an important law or policy, nor made an important speech, in his whole career. But he had a face that voters wanted to trust. And the people who ran the party knew they could trust him, too. He was a party regular. He would not have any strange ideas about regulating business or supporting labor unions, nor would he propose any odd reforms. He was, in a word, conservative.

For vice president, the Republicans nominated Calvin Coolidge, another small-town politician, who had first won a national reputation as a tough antilabor man during the strikes of 1919. Coolidge was governor of Massachusetts when Boston's police organized as an AFL local and went out on strike. Without attempting to settle the strike peacefully, he sent armed troops into Boston. The protest of Samuel Gompers, the AFL president, was met with one of Coolidge's most famous terse retorts: "There is no right to strike against the public safety, anywhere, anytime."

Coolidge was less a party regular than Harding, but he was even more conservative in matters of policy. Except for his odd flair for succinct statements, he was a lackluster man with a crabbed countenance, a striking contrast to Harding's open handsomeness. In any case, no one at the Republican convention thought that they were choosing anything but a vice president.

The Democrats nominated a lackluster candidate of their own, James M. Cox. However, they tried to spice up the ticket with a dashing young New Yorker, Franklin D. Roosevelt. Roosevelt had served as assistant secretary of the Navy under Wilson. The convention hoped the Roosevelt name would attract voters who remembered his cousin Theodore. But probably no Democratic ticket could have won in 1920. The voters wanted a change. Sixty percent of them voted for Harding. They also sent large Repub-

lican majorities to both the House and the Senate, making it one of the most complete victories in the history of American national politics. Harding carried every state outside the Democrats' solid South and cracked even that by winning Tennessee. The repudiation of Wilson's New Freedom seemed complete.

RETURN TO NORMALCY Harding took office with a slogan that coined a new word. He said the country needed a "return to normalcy." No dictionary defined *normalcy*, but almost every American probably knew what the president meant. Harding believed that there had been too much experimentation, too many attempts to regulate the economy and the working lives of Americans, too much speculation about new diplomatic arrangements such as the League of Nations. Normalcy meant letting things take their "natural" course—not interfering in the decisions of businessmen or in the complex affairs of other nations. Normalcy meant, in short, a return to simpler times and uncomplicated politics.

Harding's relaxed conservatism was not a well-defined policy. Rather, it was a wish for fewer policies and less activity by the government. For his cabinet, the president chose people sympathetic to the practices of industrial and business leaders. His most important appointment, in fact, was Secretary of the Treasury Andrew Mellon, a Pennsylvania industrialist who owned the only important company then making aluminum in the United States.

Mellon helped shape the small amount of legislation that the Harding administration presented to Congress. His pet bill was one cutting the maximum income tax on the wealthy from 65 percent to 25 percent. (Congress at first reduced the limit to only 50 percent, but Mellon later got most of what he wanted.) He also proposed, and got from Congress, much higher tariffs on imports, a policy that benefited American business and industry by limiting foreign competition.

THE OHIO GANG Specific legislation was less important in Harding's conservative administration than its general relaxation of federal controls over business. Harding did not try to tear down the established regulatory agencies, like the Interstate Commerce Commission or the Federal Reserve Board. Instead, he merely appointed persons to these agencies who were so friendly toward corporations that they administered the law gently or not at all. And Harding named as his secretary of commerce Herbert Hoover, who had made a fortune as a mining engineer and investor.

Hoover was clearly the most distinguished of Harding's appointments. He had made an enormous reputation during the war as head of the federal Food Administration. Unlike most of his colleagues in the Harding administration, Hoover was a thoughtful man, with a fairly clear-cut ideological position. He was a promoter of what he called "individualism." His central faith was that private enterprise, left to its own devices, could end poverty and usher in a "new era" of prosperity and progress.

To Hoover, the modern corporation was, ultimately, an instrument of social justice. Capitalism had, he believed, emerged from its nineteenth-century youth into a mature period of development. In this new maturity, corporations would be less concerned with sheer competition for profits and more determined to produce goods efficiently. In the process, the corporations would also contribute a great deal of what Hoover called "service" to society—technological innovation, education, the redistribution of income, and so on—until ignorance, poverty, and disease were banished.

The role of government, Hoover believed, should be to help this process along by providing information and assistance to businesses, not to hinder them through wasteful and inefficient regulation. This was the logic that Hoover applied as secretary of commerce. And this was the logic he would later bring to the White House.

Harding brought to Washington a group of friends who soon became known as the Ohio Gang. Some held seemingly harmless positions, like Old Doc Sawyer, a doctor in less than good standing with the medical profession. Old Doc became the White House physician, with the rank of Army brigadier general. Other gang members were given more important positions, such as attorney general and secretary of the interior.

After two years in office, Harding, who was personally honest about money, began to realize that his appointees were stealing and peddling influence. In the spring and summer of 1923, two administration officials committed suicide while being investigated. In June, Harding began a long vacation in the West. As he left, he complained to a journalist, "My God, this is a hell of a job. I have no trouble with my enemies. But my friends! They're the ones that keep me walking the floor nights!"

Two months later, in California after a trip to Alaska, Harding suffered what Old Doc Sawyer called food poisoning. Harding now had to pay personally for this political appointment, for Sawyer was wrong. The president had suffered a heart attack instead; on August 2 he died. In a way, Harding was lucky. He was mourned by his country almost as much as Lincoln had been. He was spared the knowledge of a new scandal that would later become almost synonymous with his name.

Albert Fall, Harding's secretary of the interior, had finagled Interior Department control of oil reserves set aside for the Navy. There were two large reserves, at Elk Hill in California and at Teapot Dome in Wyoming. Private oil interests were willing to pay almost any price to drill on the land. And they did.

Two oil company executives, Edward L. Doheny and Harry F. Sinclair, gave and "lent" Fall almost a half-million dollars in return for secret leases allowing them to drill on the reserves. The secret leaked out faster than the oil. The government managed to cancel the leases, but Fall went to prison for a year. He was the first cabinet officer in American history to be put behind bars.

Harding and Coolidge. Warren G. Harding (left) and Calvin Coolidge, president and vice president, were the personal symbols of the "return to normalcy" after World War I. Harding's style, as suggested by his clothing in this picture, was a trifle sporty for a president—but in keeping with the tone of the 1920s. Coolidge, on the other hand, was a man of unrelieved dourness, both of expression and of dress. (Library of Congress)

Coolidge and Business

When Harding died, Vice President Calvin Coolidge became president. Though privately a talkative man, "Silent Cal," as Coolidge was called, spoke very little in public. He kept most of Harding's appointees and basically followed his predecessor's policies for the rest of the term. As the 1924 election approached, there was little doubt about what the Republicans would do. Their convention enthusiastically nominated Coolidge.

The Democrats experienced a struggle between two wings of their party. One represented the rural South and West, the old Bryan supporters. The other wing, newer and based in the Northern cities, was made up mostly of "wets" (opponents of Prohibition) and depended heavily on the support of immigrants (many of them Catholics or Jews). After 103 ballots the convention settled on a compromise candidate, John W. Davis.

Coolidge was conservative. But so was Davis, who was associated with the financial firm of J. P. Morgan. Once more the time seemed right, as in 1912, to try a third party. The Progressive candidate was Robert La Follette, now nearly seventy but still a fiery opponent of business interests. He did well. Although Coolidge won the election easily, with 15 million votes, La Follette managed to get almost 5 million votes, and he carried Wisconsin's electoral vote. Davis and his badly split party could muster only 8.5 million votes, less than a third of the total.

Coolidge's second term in office was a continuation of the conservative policies of the earlier years, but without the scandals of 1921–23. Mellon and Hoover still exercised great influence. The new administration went on supporting high tariffs, low taxes on corporations and the wealthy, and a hands-off policy on trusts. It had an essentially do-nothing approach to farm problems and a negative attitude toward labor as well. The entire conservative politics of the 1920s was summed up in Coolidge's most famous statement: "The business of America is business."

Still, the president was popular, and doubtless he could have been nominated for a second full term and won. But his second most famous statement was: "I do not choose to run." Coolidge may have meant simply that he would accept a draft. But, for once, "Silent Cal" had spoken too soon and said too much. The Republicans took him literally and turned to Herbert Hoover, the most prestigious official in the administration.

THE DEMOCRATIC CHALLENGE OF 1928

The Democrats partially healed their old split, hoping for victory. Governor Alfred E. Smith of New York won the nomination easily. Smith and Hoover were almost perfect contrasts. Hoover was conservative, even gloomy. He dressed in neat blue suits and was the perfect representative of stability and efficiency. Above all, he opposed any extension of federal power over private enterprise (unless, as with tariffs, federal power could be used to help business).

Smith, on the other hand, was a happy, talkative, cigar-chomping Irish-American politician. He wore a brown derby and checked suits and talked with an urban twang. During the campaign, Hoover accused Smith of socialism because the New Yorker favored federal ownership of electric power-generating facilities.

However different their personalities and political backgrounds may have been, Smith and Hoover actually ran on similar platforms. To head his campaign, Smith chose a Republican executive from General Motors, a man who had in fact voted for Coolidge in 1924. And in a variety of other ways, the Democrats strained to capture the political center by hewing to a very conservative policy line. On the surface, at least, the election was a contest between personal styles and religious convictions.

Smith's Catholicism got most of the publicity. Some of the charges were merely nasty, as when the Methodist bishop of Virginia referred to Smith as "this wet Roman Catholic chamberlain of the Pope of Rome." But even literate, liberal Protestant newspapers and magazines were concerned. The *Christian Century*, one of the most popular Protestant journals, said that Smith's victory would be the victory "of an alien culture, of a mediaeval Latin mentality, of an undemocratic hierarchy and of a foreign potentate."

Smith's stand on Prohibition also alarmed many voters. Hoover called Prohibition a "noble experiment," and it may have been this stand, not Smith's religion, that won Hoover powerful support in the South and Southwest. Smith, on the other hand, was a publicly announced "wet," who believed that Prohibition was not only a failure but an act that unfairly deprived urban workers of their modest pleasures.

In the end, Hoover won what appeared to be a landslide. With 58 percent of the popular vote, he almost equaled Harding's record. In fact, because the turnout was unusually heavy, Hoover amassed 21 million votes—more than the combined votes of Coolidge and La Follette in 1924. In the process, Hoover cut deeply into the traditionally Democratic South, where he carried Virginia, Tennessee, North Carolina, Florida, and Texas.

But there was another side to the election, an aspect that was almost lost in the apparent landslide. Smith had made some gains, too. Although he had won fewer electoral votes than any Democrat since 1872, Smith had succeeded in taking two Eastern states, Massachusetts and Rhode Island. This was an indication of a powerful new source of support that the Democrats might be able to capitalize on later—support from immigrants and the children of immigrants in Eastern cities. In 1924 Coolidge had swept all twelve of the largest cities in the nation, and by a large margin. In 1928 Smith won more urban votes than Hoover.

Despite this straw in the wind, however, the Republican ascendancy was still in full swing. Hoover could look toward the inauguration and the future with confidence. The powerful and profitable industrial system, watched over at a discreet distance by a sympathetic government, did seem to be ushering in an era of unprecedented prosperity for millions. So it looked in the winter of 1928–29.

Boom and Bust

On the surface, at least, the 1920s was a decade of great prosperity. Progress seemed undeniable as more and more cars, radios, washing machines, and other goods poured off assembly lines. More workers were producing more goods than ever before. The United States seemed to have created an economic miracle.

American buyers and investors were confident. The New York Stock Exchange, where the economy's pulse seemed most vital, enjoyed an amazing boom period after 1923. Sales on the exchange quadrupled between 1923 and 1930. As sales increased, so did the prices of stocks. Americans were on an investment binge. The total amount of money kept in stocks and bonds increased faster than any other economic factor during the period (much faster, for example, than the actual production or sale of goods).

Much of the new investment was made on credit. According to the rules of the New York Stock Exchange, investors could buy stock by putting some money down and owing the rest to their brokers. These "brokers' loans" showed how little of the investment rush was real money and how much was pure speculation. By 1927 almost $4 billion was still owed on such loans. The whole structure of the stock market was rickety.

Such investment was really a form of gambling. If a stock cost ten dollars a share and an investor expected it to go up, he or she could buy a share and wait for the price to rise. In fact, for ten dollars the investor could buy ten shares, one for cash and the other nine on loan. When the stock went up, the investor could sell the shares at the new price, pay off the broker, and pocket the difference in cash. There would be a problem, though, if the stock went down. Then, when the broker's loan was due, the investor might have to sell not only the ten shares of stock but other assets as well. If the stock market fell too low, the person could be ruined.

Year after year, the gambles paid off. More and more ordinary people, with only small amounts of money to invest, began to play the market. The prospering economy appeared to justify their confidence.

A WARPED ECONOMY But this prosperity was very unevenly distributed through the population. There were large pockets of people who did not share in it at all. Blacks in both the South and the North did not benefit much. Nor did most farmers, whose lives had long been difficult.

The problems of farmers were especially pressing. In the second half of the nineteenth century, an agricultural revolution had provided the foundation for industrial expansion. Then, during the war, farmers had prospered because of high demand and government supports. The end of the war brought a sharp drop in the demand for exports, and an end to federal aid. At the same time, something odd happened in the domestic market. Improvements in diet slightly increased the demand for vegetables and fruit, but the demand for cereal grains dropped, partly because men released from heavy labor by machines needed fewer calories. In addition, the prevailing Victorian ideal of a sturdy, almost fat figure for men and women had given way to a new slender image of the ideal American.

Meanwhile, farmers were trapped by the high-volume, technologically sophisticated agriculture that had made many of them successful during the preceding two generations. In wartime, especially, they invested heavily in expensive machines, and they continued to do so even after the demand for their crops had fallen off. In the 1920s, in fact, the number of working tractors on American farms quadrupled.

The effect of these changes was to cause farm prices to drop and production to increase. In 1920 the income of farmers represented about 15 percent of the total national income. By 1929 this proportion had fallen to only about 9 percent. Several million farmers were driven off the land. They drifted to the cities or joined the ranks of the unemployed who made up the Bonus Army. Those who stayed in farming very often lost ownership of their land and had to become either tenant farmers or hired hands.

One solution to the problem was government intervention. Grain farmers, especially, supported a scheme that would guarantee farmers a "fair" price for their crop. The scheme involved two things. First, a tariff on imported foodstuffs was needed to prevent foreign producers from taking advantage of an "artificially" high price on the American market. Second, the domestic price of grain needed to be set at a level that was the average for the ten years preceding 1914. The result would be "parity," or a kind of rough equality of agricultural prices and other prices. Under the sponsorship of a senator from Oregon, Charles McNary, and a congressman from Iowa, Gilbert Haugen, a bill providing for parity for grain crops was introduced in the 1924 Congress, but it was defeated in the House.

Two years later, in a bid for Southern support, the McNary-Haugen bill was broadened to include cotton, tobacco, and rice. In 1927 it passed both houses of Congress but was turned back by a Coolidge veto that could not be over-ridden. The next year, 1928, Congress again passed the act, but President Coolidge once more exercised his veto power. The principle of parity would have to wait until well after the crash of 1929.

For industrial workers, the situation was a little better. Real wages—the actual purchasing power of earned dollars—rose during the decade by over 20 percent. And some corporations began to behave a little like Herbert Hoover's model, with programs of "enlightened" capitalism. Sanitary and safety conditions were improved in some of the more modern factories. Some companies started pension funds that gave workers a tiny share in the stock of the corporations that employed them. But the major purpose behind these "progressive" practices was to undercut the growth of industrial unionism. The AFL, meanwhile, pursued a cautious policy throughout the decade. The failure of strikes in 1919 and several succeeding years made many workers hesitate to join even a conservative union like the AFL. The outcome was a decline of about 15 percent in union membership, despite an increase in the total number of factory workers.

Those at the outer edges of the industrial system—blacks, most women, the many underemployed recent immigrants in the cities—simply did not participate in the prosperity of the decade. Such "soft" spots in the economy led to a very serious distortion. Technological innovation increased productivity rapidly. The question

was, simply, how would the increased production be absorbed? Who would buy the washing machines, the cars, the clothes, all the products of a sophisticated industrial system? The total quantity of goods for sale was increasing much faster than the population. Either wages would have to rise dramatically, so that workers would have more money to spend on all the things being made, or prices would have to fall, so that everyone could afford more. Otherwise, the gap between production and sales would grow until inventories were clogged with unsalable surpluses of consumer goods.

But business owners generally raised wages less than they should have. They also kept prices high. In the short run, their measures meant higher profits—and higher profits for corporations meant the price of their stock rose. They could either invest the profits in still larger factories and produce still more goods, or they could invest them in stock and heat up the stock market even more. Many corporations did both.

The result was a warped economy. The amount of goods being produced ran far ahead of the people's power to purchase them. Sooner or later an adjustment had to be made. Otherwise, factories would have to close until the surplus cars, clothes, tools, and other items could be bought. For a time the problem could be avoided in two ways. The surplus products could be sold, on credit, to people who could not really afford them. A family could pay for a car, for example, over two or three years. Or the surplus could be exported to foreign countries. But both credit and exporting could help a distorted economic system only briefly.

THE STOCK MARKET CRASH These facts were difficult to see. On the surface, the economy had never looked better, and Americans continued to bet on the future by speculating in stocks. In 1928 the average price of industrial stocks increased by about 25 percent. An investor who bought, say, $1,000 worth of stock in January could sell it in December for $1,250, then pocket the $250 profit or invest it in some new gamble. Most speculators did the latter.

Then, after a few rumblings and warnings, the bubble burst. The stock market was not a sure indicator of the country's economic health. In 1929, reality finally caught up with it.

In September the most popular index of stock prices stood at 452. Two months later it was 234. What this meant, in plain terms, was that the market value of stocks on the exchange had been halved. Most of the holders of the $4 billion in brokers' loans were ruined. So were many of the brokers. On the worst day of all, "Black Tuesday," October 29, the market index fell 43 points. Other days were almost as bleak and ruinous. Stock prices continued to slide. They reached bottom in 1932. Then, most stocks were worth little more than a tenth of their cost in September 1929. The Great Depression had begun.

It was difficult then, and still is, for people to understand why the panic on Wall Street should have had any effect on the real economy. The factories were still there, ready to roll out goods. The farms were still there, ready to produce food. All the hands willing to work before Black Tuesday were still there, still willing to work.

But month by month, the entire economic machine ground down. The stock market crash was the crucial link in the chain of events leading to this breakdown. It caused people to make the grim decision not to buy or invest. So storekeepers sold less. And factories produced less or closed down altogether. Many foreclosed on loans made to others because they needed money to pay off their own loans.

Farmers behind on their payments lost their farms as banks desperately tried to collect hard cash. The banks needed cash because millions of people with savings accounts, frightened now, lined up at tellers' windows to withdraw their money. The banks often could not produce the cash because they had invested or lent it. So even the banks began to fail.

Builders of houses and offices stopped construction because they could not borrow money to continue. Down at the bottom of this tangle were workers who, by the millions, received notices that they need not come to work any-more. Their jobs disappeared. Since they could not work, they could not buy; since they could not buy, others could not sell or make goods.

The jobless were not just the old-line poor. Many had been solid, middle-class citizens, such as bank tellers and factory foremen. Others were farmers, who had barely managed to survive through the rough decade. Now they had lost their farms forever. They moved to the cities, looking for food and work, or they began to drift, looking for migrant workers' jobs. People combed garbage heaps for food for their families. They made soup from dandelions. Mostly, however, they waited in a cold, gloomy fog of despair for something to happen.

HOOVER'S OPTIMISM The question posed by the depression and symbolized by the bonus march was simple. Could the federal government be used as a tool for dealing with economic disaster? In the past the answer had been no. Other depressions had been allowed to run their course without any federal attempt to bring early recovery or relieve human suffering. But the Great Depression was by far the worst ever. Now the industrial economy was so large and complicated that its collapse affected far more people. Countless millions were jobless; banks were failing by the hundreds; tens of thousands needed food. Something had to be done.

At first, the Hoover administration was optimistic. The stock market crash was called a needed "adjustment." The economy, Hoover announced, was fundamentally sound. Recovery would be natural and would come soon. Meanwhile, no federal action of any kind was needed.

Surprisingly, most Democrats agreed. In the congressional elections of 1930, the Democrats made Prohibition as big an issue as the depression. Nor did the voters heavily punish the administration for its failure to bring about recovery. The Democrats won the House, but the Senate stayed Republican. Hoover was still predicting that a return to prosperity was "just around the corner."

But things kept getting worse. In 1929 over 600 banks shut down; in 1930, over 1,000; in 1931, 2,000. For farmers, there seemed to be no bottom. Wheat in 1931 sold for 36 cents a bushel, compared to $1.03 in 1929. No one even knew how many people were unemployed by 1932, but guesses ran as high as 15 million. For those who still had jobs, pay envelopes grew smaller. By 1932, wages in industry were less than half what they had been in 1928.

As he faced all these facts—or, sometimes, tried not to face them—the president grew gloomy and confused. He tried to stay optimistic in public, believing business confidence was crucial to recovery. In private, however, he was trapped between two different beliefs. A humane man, he did not like to see people suffer. But he still thought government should not interfere in the economy. Free enterprise would bring the nation back to its feet.

Most important, Hoover believed that federal government must never give direct relief to the poor, unemployed, and hungry. Direct federal welfare, he thought, would destroy people's moral character, making them dependent instead of healthy, strong personalities. This set of attitudes, which he referred to as individualism, made Hoover seem insensitive and cruel. He became the target of bitter jokes. People named their shantytowns Hoovervilles and called an empty pocket, turned inside out, a Hoover flag. Reluctantly, Hoover decided that the government must act.

NEW FEDERAL POWERS Early in 1932 Hoover signed a law creating a new federal agency, the Reconstruction Finance Corporation (RFC). It could lend up to $2 billion to banks, insurance companies, and railroads. These loans, the administration believed, would be used especially by the banks to make other loans to businesses. Businesses would in turn use the money for new construction or to reopen factories. Their moves would create new jobs and save old ones. Thus RFC loans would eventually end up in the pockets of workers, who would then spend the money and create new demand, resulting in more new production, and so on, in a circle of recovery.

The president also went against his own beliefs by signing another law empowering the RFC to lend relief money to state governments. But the amount of the loans was too small to help much. Pennsylvania, for example, could borrow only enough to provide three cents a day to its unemployed workers. Also, the RFC loans to business were far too small to aid the economy effectively. Compared to previous government activity, Hoover's actions were bold experiments in the use of federal power. But measured against what was actually needed, they were too little too late, as the bonus marchers recognized.

The New Deal

THE ELECTION OF 1932 Herbert Hoover was not a cruel man. His reluctance to meet the crisis of the depression was not a result of hardheartedness but of confidence. He devoutly believed that the nation's economy was healthy and that it needed only "adjustment."

But the Democratic party was about to nominate a man who was altogether willing to define the depression as a crisis. Franklin Roosevelt had been working diligently for the nomination for months. By the time the party held its convention in Chicago during the summer of 1932, he had lined up the necessary support.

The contrast between Hoover and Roosevelt was striking. Hoover was methodical, somewhat gloomy, and calm. Roosevelt was cheerful, brash, and smiling. He had been stricken by polio in 1921 but had made a ten-year effort, with braces and canes, to look healthy and powerful. One of his main political tools was a wide, exaggerated grin. And he was ready to present himself as a leader who would not be bound by tradition. He

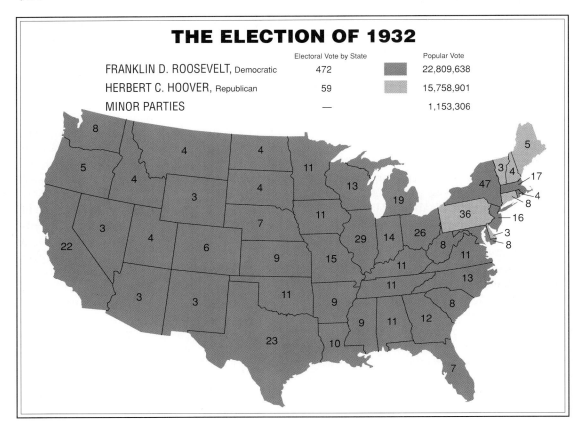

THE ELECTION OF 1932

	Electoral Vote by State		Popular Vote
FRANKLIN D. ROOSEVELT, Democratic	472		22,809,638
HERBERT C. HOOVER, Republican	59		15,758,901
MINOR PARTIES	—		1,153,306

broke precedent by going to Chicago to accept the nomination in person—and doing so in an airplane, not by train.

He quickly made it clear to the cheering delegates that his strategy would be simple and relentless: to define the depression as a real crisis and to flay the Republicans for their failure to meet it:

> Republican leaders not only have failed in material things, they have failed in national vision, because in disaster, they have held out no hope. I pledge you, I pledge myself to a new deal for the American people.

Roosevelt's campaign speeches never made clear just what his "new deal" would be. He made vague promises that he would relieve suffering, create jobs, and make the economy work again. And this, plus the fact that voters did blame Hoover for causing the depression, was enough to give Roosevelt a smashing victory. He received about 23 million votes, against about 15 million for Hoover. Just as important, the Democrats won large majorities in the House and Senate for the first time in modern history.

On March 4, 1933, Roosevelt took his oath of office with a ringing pronouncement that he would have both the courage to admit that a disaster had befallen the nation and the courage to deal with it. And he seems to have believed that courage was the key to the problem. "Let me assert my firm belief," he said in a bluff, confident voice, "that the only thing we have to fear is fear itself. This nation asks for action, and action *now*."

LAUNCHING THE NEW DEAL Roosevelt's inaugural proclamation was a little illogical. For men and women out of work, with hungry children, there was in fact plenty to fear. But what counted was not the accuracy of his statements but their bravery. And the statements had to be brave because there was a growing sense of despair and even panic in the nation. Millions of men were roaming the country looking for work. Radios played popular songs like "Brother Can You Spare a Dime?" Every city had its Hoovervilles and its bread lines. Middle-class Americans, who might still have their jobs and their houses, were frightened by the plague of bank failures, which seemed to be a sign that the economy had simply, perhaps finally, collapsed.

The banks were the most immediate problem Roosevelt chose to face. If they did not work, nothing else would. On his last night in the White House, Hoover declared: "We are at the end of our rope." After his inauguration, Roosevelt made it clear that he intended to pull the rope at once. He boldly declared a bank "holiday," shutting down all banks, sound and unsound, until further notice. At least a closed bank could not fail, and the money that was supposed to be in people's accounts would still be there. Then, five days after he became president, Roosevelt sent to Congress an Emergency Banking Relief Act, which empowered the federal government to buy stock in failing banks, providing the cash to pay off its depositors if they demanded their money. Astonishingly, the act passed through Congress in eight hours. The New Deal—whatever it was to be—had begun.

THE DEBATE OVER MEANING Ever since the 1930s, Americans have debated, sometimes in anger, the meaning of the New Deal.

For some, including both partisans and critics of Roosevelt, the New Deal was a kind of revolution. According to this view, Roosevelt's programs broke the normal patterns of politics and economics and brought radically new federal control and regulation of economic and social life.

For others, the New Deal did not represent much of a departure from the patterns of history. This argument claims that Roosevelt was, in essence, a conservative. His basic motive was to leave the Constitution and the capitalist economy intact. In fact, this picture of Roosevelt's administration is one of a program whose deepest wish was to preserve the American system from the kinds of convulsions and revolutions that had been occurring in Europe since the war.

Both pictures of the New Deal have a good deal of truth to them, depending on what kinds of comparisons are being made. Compared to other peacetime presidents, Roosevelt does seem something of a revolutionary. But when compared to the wartime presidencies of Abraham Lincoln and Woodrow Wilson, Roosevelt's administration seems much more "normal." Regarded as part of a progressive tradition reaching back to Populism, to Theodore Roosevelt's Square Deal, and to Wilson's New Freedom, the New Deal looks moderate, even tame. Finally, measured against the dramatic changes the Russian Revolution of 1917 had brought, or the kinds of changes that Benito Mussolini and Adolf Hitler were bringing to Italy and Germany, the New Deal can fairly be described as a program of preservation rather than of change.

The difficulty is that the arguments and the comparisons often assume the New Deal was a coherent, unified program based on a clear political and social theory. In fact, it was a loose bundle of laws and executive orders that were designed by many men and women. Most of the new policies were established as practical steps to solve immediate problems. There was only one crude idea behind it all: that the federal government's power should be used to meet any national crisis.

What held the New Deal together, in fact, was not a program but Roosevelt himself. And he was a curious, contradictory, and sometimes confused man.

Franklin D. Roosevelt at a CCC camp. The Roosevelt administration tried to help unemployed young men by creating the Civilian Conservation Corps, a quasi-military group that was supposed to plant trees, improve public land, and otherwise "conserve" the landscape. Here the president, third from right, takes lunch out of a mess plate with a group of uniformed members of the corps. Second from the left is Roosevelt's trusted adviser from the 1920s, Louis Howe. To the president's left is Henry Wallace, who would run for president in a controversial third-party bid in 1948. To Wallace's left is Rexford Tugwell, a member of the Brain Trust. (Franklin D. Roosevelt Library Collection)

FDR Franklin Delano Roosevelt was forty-seven years old when the stock market failed, and he was fifty-one when he won the presidency—young by American standards of the day. But he was old enough that his ideas about the world had already been formed, and there is little evidence that the depression changed any of those ideas very much.

He was, in many ways, a very traditional man. He came from a wealthy family of Hudson River aristocrats. He went to exclusive private schools and then to Harvard. He owned a great country estate, where he liked to play at being a gentleman farmer. In private life, he was a practicing, though not especially devout, Episcopalian. He was also a practicing, though not especially devout, capitalist. And he was a Democrat because his branch of the family were Democrats. Unlike some other great presidents—Jefferson, Lincoln, or Wilson—he was neither a scholar nor a gifted writer. All in all, he was a suave, smiling, public man; fond of dogs, children, and women; a man whose most striking characteristic was not his lameness but the intensity of his desire to be president.

On the other hand, Roosevelt's sense of personal confidence—combined perhaps with his determined victory over polio—made him open to experiment in a way Hoover could never have been. He was ready to try a variety of things and, if they did not work, to try others. He was also ready to appoint a large number of advisers with ideas of their own. The inner circle, composed heavily of academic economists and social sci-

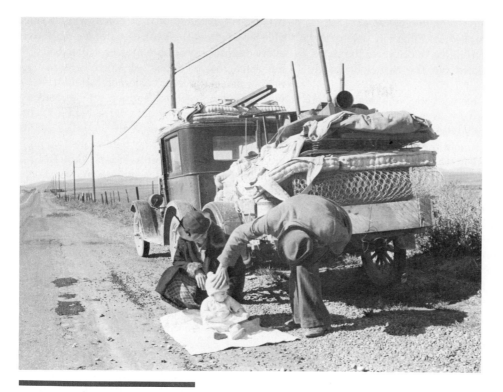

California rest stop. This family of uprooted farmers has stopped on a California roadside to rest and feed their baby. Everything they own—even a roll of chicken wire—has been strapped to their car and trailer. The photographer has posed them with their attention riveted on the baby, with its clean blanket and clothes, not on the empty road and barren landscape they are traveling along.

entists, became known as the Brain Trust. Some of its members did have theories of government and the economy. And some were much more radical than Roosevelt and worked to make the administration reflect their wishes.

But the president remained secretive, and even a bit coy, about what he had in mind. As it turned out, Roosevelt seemed to think always in very specific and concrete terms. He was willing to send to Congress a bewildering set of proposals for new agencies and programs, many of which became known by their initials. This gave rise to a popular joke that the New Deal was an alphabet soup. But the master chef—who was also popularly called by his initials, FDR—had no master recipe. This became obvious during

the first whirlwind weeks of his administration, which became known as the Hundred Days— after the Hundred Days of campaigning that followed Napoleon's escape from Elba and ended at Waterloo.

RELIEF AND STABILIZATION   The New Deal functioned on two very different levels. First, it involved direct efforts to feed people and to calm the economic panic, to achieve what people were calling relief and stabilization. Second, it included measures aimed at long-term reform. During the Hundred Days, and for some time afterward, relief and stabilization were the primary goals and concerns.

The simplest approach to relief was to distribute direct aid. The Federal Emergency Relief Act of 1933 distributed billions of dollars to the states, which in turn doled out the money to needy people.

But the most characteristic New Deal solution to hunger and poverty was not a dole but jobs. Roosevelt and his advisers were willing to make the federal government the employer of millions of men and women. The Public Works Administration (PWA), created in 1933, eventually spent over $4 billion, employing people to construct roads, public buildings, and other such projects. In 1935 the PWA was joined by a new agency, which scrambled the initials a bit. The Works Progress Administration (WPA) employed Americans in every kind of project, from construction to producing plays, concerts, paintings, and sculpture, to library work and scholarship.

The PWA and the WPA were designed to give people a steady income. But the New Deal was just as preoccupied with the other side of middle-class economic life: property. Some of its most important measures were designed to protect farmers from losing their land and homeowners from losing their houses because of unpaid debts or mortgages. In 1933 a Farm Credit Administration was created, with power to lend mortgage money to harassed farmers. In the same year, a Home Owners' Refinancing Act created a federal corporation to give government-financed mortgages to hard-pressed families threatened with foreclosure of their privately financed mortgages.

Direct relief meant much to the men and women who got jobs in the PWA or WPA, and to farmers who were able to save their land. But Roosevelt's administration was perhaps even more interested in getting the economy stabilized. Calling a bank holiday might help in the short run, but something more was needed to prevent bank failures in the future. Since banks failed because their depositors got frightened and suddenly withdrew all their money, the New Deal solution was simplicity itself. The Glass-Steagall Act of 1933 established a Federal Deposit Insurance Corporation (FDIC). This agency simply stood behind the banks, guaranteeing to pay every depositor his or her money—up to $10,000 for each account—if the bank failed. Presumably, neither banks nor their customers would have to worry any more about sudden and disastrous "runs" of withdrawals that left the banks' vaults empty.

The same sort of logic lay behind the two programs that were most central to the New Deal—both of which suffered heavily from attacks in the courts. The National Industrial Recovery Act and the Agricultural Adjustment Act, both passed in 1933, were aimed at regulating private industry and farming, respectively, without changing the basically private and capitalistic nature of either.

The National Industrial Recovery Act was, at its heart, simply a repeal of parts of the Sherman Antitrust Act. That law, which represented nineteenth-century confidence in the idea—if not the reality—of competition, forbade businesses to get together to set prices. It did not work, at least not very well. The new law recognized this fact and tried to build on it. It set up a National Recovery Administration (NRA), with the mission of encouraging corporations and businesses to work together to set and hold prices and production quotas.

For workers, the new law provided that the companies should agree on uniform wages and hours. And when some businesses were slow to cooperate, the NRA itself established wages and hours for industries. The companies that did cooperate won the right to fly a flag with the NRA's symbol, a blue eagle, as evidence of their civic conscience.

The Agricultural Adjustment Act attempted to deal with the farmers' peculiar problem: When prices fell, they were driven to produce even more food for the market. This simply sent prices further down, creating a spiral of oversupply and falling incomes. The act created the Agricultural Adjustment Administration, with the power to give farmers money *not* to plant crops. The AAA could also buy up "excess" amounts of crops like cotton and wheat and store them. The goal was to control production and marketing, to drive farm prices back up to the prosperity levels of 1909–14, a level of parity.

In the short run, at least, the AAA seemed to work, though some of its measures seemed misguided to the men and women rummaging in garbage heaps for scraps of food. The AAA plowed under millions of acres of potatoes and other crops. It also killed and dumped about 5 million pigs. But the result was apparently successful. In 1933, farm prices stood at about 55 percent of parity; in 1939, the ratio was 90 percent.

REFORMS OF THE NEW DEAL Programs aimed at direct relief and at economic stability made up the bulk of the New Deal, at least as measured in new laws. But Roosevelt and his advisers made efforts to introduce other, more fundamental and lasting changes in American life. These reform measures seem mild and timid in comparison to later exercises of federal power. But to many men and women of the 1930s, they seemed innovative, even radical or revolutionary.

One of the most visible of Roosevelt's measures was the Civilian Conservation Corps. The CCC set up camps for unemployed young men, put them into uniforms that looked military, and set them to cleaning up parks and planting countless trees all across the country, not only on federal property but on public lands of all kinds. Here was an astonishing, though short-lived, fact: a uniformed federal corps, not an army, working along hundreds of highways and lakefronts, doing things that were far removed from traditional notions of federal responsibility.

A more daring and enduring effort was the Tennessee Valley Authority. The TVA was established to build dams and generate electrical power in the backward, flood-ravaged valleys of the Tennessee and Cumberland rivers. But the responsibilities of the TVA went further: to reforest, to reclaim marginal land, to improve

health and recreation for the people of the valleys. Opponents charged that the plan was patterned on "Soviet dreams." But others saw the matter differently. For its supporters, the TVA was a magnificent effort to salvage some of the most economically and socially depressed areas of five states.

The National Labor Relations Act of 1935—popularly known as the Wagner Act, after a New York congressman—was another effort at social reform. The Roosevelt administration used the act to enable the federal government to intervene in relations between labor and capital in a more forceful way than in the past. The Wagner Act made it illegal for an employer to refuse to bargain with a union chosen by the employees. The Wagner Act also outlawed a list of "unfair labor practices" by employers, a list that could be extended indefinitely.

Partly as a result of the Wagner Act, union membership tripled between 1933 and 1939—from about 3 million to over 9 million. And the character of the unions changed too. The American Federation of Labor had organized workers by craft and trade. An employer could then negotiate—if willing to negotiate at all—with a series of separate organizations, each representing a fraction of the company's workers. Now a more radical vision of unionism gained force: industrial unionism, based on the idea that all the workers in a particular industry—steel, say, or automobiles—ought to be organized into one union rather than into a number of small craft unions. The most striking development of the 1930s in labor history was the emergence of the Congress of Industrial Organizations (CIO).

The organizing leadership of the CIO contained a number of labor radicals and even some communists. But its rank-and-file members were committed to the simple idea that collaboration was as necessary to workers as to corporations, that the only way to achieve fair bargains between workers and industrial giants was through wholesale solidarity among all the workers in an industry. Employers resisted, of course.

The Pickwick Dam. One of the proudest—and most controversial—achievements of the New Deal was the creation of the Tennessee Valley Authority. The agency built dams like this one in an attempt to control the waters that raged every year through the valleys drained by the Tennessee River. But the TVA also generated and sold electric power, hurrying a social revolution in the hill-country farms and towns of the area. The power-generating plant is at the end of the dam on the far side of the river. (Culver Pictures)

Bitter battles were fought. A massive sit-down strike at General Motors in 1936–37, in which the workers did not leave the plants but "sat down" at their places, ended in partial victory for the CIO. In 1937 the steel industry (notoriously anti-union for decades) was forced to submit to bargaining with the CIO.

In the perception of the New Deal, old people needed federal assistance even more than industrial workers. The Social Security Act of 1935 was an attempt to create an insurance and retirement system for American workers. It provided for small "contributions" from workers and their employers to be paid into a common fund. This fund could then pay a pension to men and women who retired, or benefits if they became disabled, or support for their children if workers died prematurely. The payments were small at first. But the Social Security Act was still a long first step in the direction of what critics of the New Deal referred to as a "welfare state."

There were a number of reform possibilities that the Roosevelt administration shied away from. There was no civil rights legislation. There was no attempt to massively redistribute income through taxation. In fact, there was no attempt to tamper with existing relationships between social classes, between races, or between men and women. His enemies might charge him with "Sovietism," but Roosevelt's own perception of the possibilities of federal action were far from drastic. Some of the young men and women who supported and worked in the administration might hope for more. But that "more" lay well over the historical horizon—beyond further years of depression and then years of total war.

THE TENNESSEE VALLEY AUTHORITY - 1933

Two-Thirds of a Nation

In one of Roosevelt's most memorable speeches, he said that one-third of the nation was ill-housed, ill-fed, and ill-clothed. His fraction may have been too high or too low, depending on the definition we might choose for "ill." But there is one fraction about which there can be no serious dispute. Two-thirds of the nation was unequally treated. This majority of Americans was deprived of fair access to work, education, medical care, recreation—to what many Americans liked to call their "way of life"—for the simple reason that they happened to have been born women or members of a particular racial or ethnic group. For such people, both the depression and the New Deal had special and sometimes contradictory meanings.

WOMEN At the outset of the depression, in 1930, over 10 million women held paying jobs. Most of these working women—about three out of four—were single. Some of them worked alongside men in fields and orchards as migrant farm labor and were not included in official statistics. Many others were part of an informal economy of domestic labor and thus were also left off the official rolls. In business, industry, and government work, where records were kept, women workers tended to be segregated into jobs that were considered appropriate as "women's work." In 1930, 98 percent of all nurses were women. So were 95 percent of all telephone operators, and 81 percent of all teachers. Jobs classified as "clerical" were about equally divided between men and women, though women usually held the jobs at the bottom of the ladder.

When the depression hit, it caused less unemployment among women workers than among men, because it struck hardest at manufacturing—steel and automobiles, for example. Nurses

The Marx Brothers

Like much of the best in American show business, the wisecracking, endlessly inventive, irreverent Marx Brothers brought to the stage and movie screen a comedy rooted in their immigrant heritage. Born to Simon and Minnie Marx, there were five brothers: Leonard, Arthur, Herbert, Julius, and Milton—better known as Chico, Harpo, Zeppo, Groucho, and Gummo. The father, a Jewish immigrant from Alsace, was a tailor with a widespread reputation for ineptitude. The mother was descended from a line of German performers and entertainers, and her brother Al Shean was part of a well-known and successful American vaudeville act.

Like other young boys in New York at the beginning of the century, the Marx brothers explored the new culture of the city streets with its gamblers, prostitutes, con men, its infinitely varied immigrant groups and working-class poor. From this rich culture came future movie producers and writers, singers and songwriters, romantic radicals, intellectuals, dancers, and politicians—and the Marx Brothers.

Chico, the first son, was a gambler (like his parents) and a pool hall hustler. Harpo, the father's favorite, learned his famous comic grimace by mimicking the expression of a local cigar roller. Groucho took after his mother and her habit of wisecracking. All the boys left school early, but only Groucho went directly into show business as a boy singer with his Uncle Al's act.

Pushed by their stage mother, various combinations of sons formed singing and comedy acts in the first decade of the century, until their repertoire began to jell. Each son developed a comic character reflecting his position in the family. Chico cultivated an immigrant personality, usually Italian, and played the piano in a fashion that became the rage of popular players. Harpo continued to strum the harp and developed a frenzied character born of a family incident where he donned a woman's wig. Groucho played a young "dirty old man," whose bushy eyebrows and cigar wildly exaggerated his leer. Zeppo often played straight man.

After a few very difficult years, the brothers began to pile one success on another, finally making it to Broadway with their 1924 hit, *I'll Say She Is*. Quickly thereafter, they repeated this success with *The Cocoanuts* and *Animal Crackers*. They also introduced Margaret Dumont, as a heavily corseted society lady who never quite seemed to understand the wicked barbs and insults thrown at her by Groucho. With writing by authors such as George S. Kaufman, Groucho, Chico, and Harpo developed routines that seemed entirely ad-libbed (many were). Their comedy was also pointed, with a sharp edge of social satire that was, nevertheless, always blunted by the comic anarchy that overwhelmed plot and situation.

Beginning in 1929, they translated their Broadway hits directly into films. At first, these were little better than filmed plays, cramped and limited by the primitive new sound technology. By 1931 when they went to Hollywood, however, large sound stages and better technology allowed for more cinematic experimentation. The result was, in rapid succession, four brilliant films: *Monkey Business* (1931), *Horse Feathers* (1932), *Duck Soup* (1933), and *A Night at the Opera* (1935).

The greatest of these, *Duck Soup*, was almost entirely devoid of the sentimental romantic interest that diminished some of their other work. But at the time, it was their least popular film. A satire of government bureaucracy and pompous nation-states and statesmen, the film ended with Margaret Dumont singing a patriotic anthem, "Fredonia," and being pelted with oranges by Groucho, Harpo, Zeppo, and Chico. Perhaps it was too much to expect Americans to laugh at anarchy or see much humor in tinhorn dictators in 1933, when they had just put their faith in the promise of a new deal. But audiences since then have recognized and applauded the zany mischief of the film's plot.

Later Groucho began a radio show, *You Bet Your Life*, which became a successful television quiz program in the 1950s. Thus over five decades and through four different forms of mass media, the Marx Brothers' work became part of the mainstream of American humor. But it was never better or sharper than in the 1930s, when its immigrant roots and irreverent respect for America were most obvious.

and teachers were less likely to be fired than male steel or auto workers. In fact, the number of women with paying jobs actually increased during the 1930s, from about 10 million to about 13 million. Women made up about 30 percent of the paid work force in 1930, but 35 percent in 1940.

As a result, there was a lot of uninformed talk about women taking jobs that ought to be held by male "breadwinners." Some states even passed laws against married women working in civil service jobs or as teachers. And the Roosevelt administration for five years of the depression refused to allow the federal government to employ more than one person from a family. If a husband and wife each held a government job, the woman usually was the one to quit, since she earned less money. But the truth was that women and men competed for very few jobs, and that most working women were single and needed to work to live.

For women who did not work, the depression was a tough experience. But because of sexual stereotyping, they may not have suffered as much as their husbands and brothers. In reality, women who did not have paying jobs were probably more intensely "employed" than they had been before 1929. They still had their jobs—cooking, mending, washing, and the rest of the daily round of domestic tasks. And the economic crisis actually increased the importance of this kind of unpaid work, as stretching family resources by skillfully making clothes and food last longer and go further became essential. But the depression did prove one thing: Most people, male and female, continued to believe firmly that men were the proper "head" of the family, even if they were unemployed and even if their wives had assumed a larger role than ever in enabling families to survive.

At least that is what most Americans *said* they still believed, when opinion polls asked them the question. But in thousands of families, men found it increasingly difficult to look their wives and children in the eye. The contradiction between belief and fact was hard to bear in a world where men were expected to be "providers" and family "heads." Not being able to be the first made it very difficult to continue to be the second. It is true that the divorce rate actually declined during the depression, but the birth rate went down even more sharply. The reasons for these trends are difficult for historians to know, since they involve forms of human intimacy that are often not understood even by people who experience them. But the declining divorce rate may only have been a reflection of an increase in the rate of desertion, in families where the legal idea of divorce had lost its practical meaning. Unemployed men do not normally pay alimony or child support. Also, poor people often did not take the trouble to get a divorce until they decided to marry someone else, and the depression made this decision less likely. The declining birth rate may have been the result of rational calculations about how many children a family could afford. But it may also have been the result of a more subtle and cruel process, a form of private, psychological depression that brought the ugly reality of the public, economic depression home. For people whose lives had become melancholy and pathetic, the idea of sex and new children may have been an increasingly unlikely assertion of hope.

One unemployed woman from Minnesota described her hours in an unemployment office this way: "So we sit in this room like cattle . . . unable to work, unable to get food and lodging, unable to bear children. Here we must sit in this shame looking at the floor, worse than beasts at a slaughter." She was convinced that the inability to find work had made her unable to have children, as though she had been made sterile and fit only for a "slaughter." There was an obvious rage in people who felt these things. But the rage was muted, translated into a sense of helplessness and shame. And this sense of things, which she shared with millions of other women and men, would have made the idea of divorce seem irrelevant, and the idea of sex and childbearing distant and forbidding.

Room in New York, 1932. No American artist was more gifted than Edward Hopper at capturing the kinds of personal depression that brought the Great Depression into people's daily lives. Here, he shows a childless couple framed in the window of an apartment that most people would have called "middle class." But the room is small, the furniture plain and almost shabby. The man is hunched over his newspaper, and the woman turns away, not to play the cheap piano but to toy with one key. They have lost touch with each other and with the world on the other side of their window. (F. M. Hall Collection, Sheldon Memorial Art Gallery, University of Nebraska–Lincoln)

AFRICAN AMERICANS The depression and the New Deal had mixed effects on African Americans. Most black people were much worse off to start with than whites. In 1930, infant mortality was twice as high among blacks as among whites. Black life expectancy was ten years below that of whites. And the depression made things worse. Unemployed whites were now willing to take jobs that had usually been filled by blacks, such as janitor or garbage collector. And governments and businesses were all too willing to replace black workers with whites. This pushed black unemployment up to rates as high as 50 percent in many industrial cities (compared to about 30 percent for whites).

Even some well-intended New Deal programs had negative effects on African Americans. One of the main agricultural programs was to encourage farmers not to produce "surplus" commodities like cotton. This was designed to help farmers by reducing supply and so raising prices. But the program helped only those farmers who *owned* their land. In the South, where more than half of black families lived in rural areas, most of them did not own land but worked it as sharecroppers. White landowners, paid by the gov-

No crop, no share. These sharecroppers have been evicted from their homes in Missouri. They told the reporter who took this photograph that they were sent away by their white landlords because the Agricultural Adjustment Administration government was paying land-owners not to grow crops. The picture was taken in January, 1939, and the stove will be badly needed when night comes. (UPI/Bettmann Newsphotos)

ernment not to plant crops, simply ordered sharecroppers (black and white) off the land. Between 1930 and 1940 the number of share-cropper families in the South fell by one-third.

Overall, the New Deal's modest efforts to redistribute wealth touched black families—and poor families in general—very little. Between 1929 and 1941 the share of the wealth owned by the richest 20 percent was cut a little, from about 54 percent to about 49 percent. But most of the loose money and property found its way into middle-class pockets. The middle 40 percent of Americans soaked up about four-fifths of this redistributed wealth. Not all poor people were black, but almost all blacks were poor people, so they benefited very little from the modest efforts of the Roosevelt administration to promote eco-nomic equality. Most blacks worked in jobs that

were not covered by Social Security and not pro-tected by any of the new labor legislation.

But there were fragile signs of promise and change. Some of the signs were merely symbolic. In 1939 the black opera singer Marian Anderson sought to give a concert in Washington. The Daughters of the American Revolution, which owned the Constitution Hall theater, refused to allow her to use their building. Eleanor Roose-velt, in a dramatic gesture, promoted a much larger concert by Anderson on the steps of the Lincoln Memorial. (But there were limits to even Eleanor Roosevelt's willingness to make such gestures. A year later, a similar problem was pro-voked by plans for a Washington benefit concert starring the great black singer Paul Robeson. The First Lady at first joined a committee to support the controversial concert, but she withdrew her name when she learned that the sponsors included an organization that was thought to be connected with the Communist party.)

The commitment of the president's wife, and of a few other prominent Democrats, to public support for blacks was very effective. In fact, most black voters seem to have become deeply convinced that however meager, or even damaging, the specific economic impact of the New Deal was on their lives, the Democratic party was their only political hope. In 1932, after three years of the depression, 80 percent of black voters were still loyal to the Republicans, the party of Lincoln and emancipation. In the next four years, an astonishing shift occurred. By 1936, 75 percent of the African Americans who voted chose Roosevelt. With the large number of "ethnic" voters who had shifted to the Democrats, blacks became part of a new Democratic coalition that was to play an important role in national politics for half a century.

Another fragile sign of promise and change for blacks grew out of an incident that at first seemed to offer only more proof of the power of racism. In the spring of 1931 a freight train pulled into the yards just outside the town of Scottsboro, Alabama. Riding the train were about twenty hoboes, black and white, male and female, part of the hungry and shifting debris of the depression. Armed sheriff's deputies were waiting for the train and arrested nine young blacks, accusing them of assaulting some white men on the train. Then two white women named Ruby Bates and Victoria Price stepped forward. They were probably just as scared and just as hungry as anyone else on the slow freight. After all, women like them were routinely arrested for prostitution, and raped in jail to reinforce their jailers' sense that public decency and order needed to be maintained. The two women also understood that poor white women had one defense against their powerlessness: They could accuse some black man of rape. Whatever their motives, the two women did claim that they had been sexually assaulted by the nine young blacks.

White justice was swift in Alabama. Before two weeks had passed, eight of the black youths had been convicted and sentenced to death. The ninth, who was twelve years old, was not found innocent by the twelve white male jurors; the jury was unable to agree on a verdict in his case.

But at least the boys and young men had not been lynched without trial. So there was a tiny crack in the system, the possibility of an appeal to the federal judiciary. In 1932 the United States Supreme Court ruled that the defense lawyers—court-appointed white men—had not presented a competent case for their black clients. The convictions were struck down, and Alabama had to choose whether to drop the charges or begin new trials. The prosecution chose new trials. But this time, the "Scottsboro Boys," as they had become known in the press, were defended by a skilled lawyer, Samuel Leibowitz. He had been hired by the International Labor Defense League, a Communist party affiliate. The local prosecutor sneered at Leibowitz in open court, and said, "Alabama justice cannot be bought and sold with Jew money from New York."

In the second trials, Leibowitz introduced medical evidence that clearly proved that Bates and Price had not been raped on the train. But the white jury still brought in a verdict of guilty against the first defendant. This time, the Alabama judge, James Horton, somehow found the courage to overrule the verdict. But the authorities found a new judge and held new trials. Again, the first defendant to be tried was found guilty. This time, the Supreme Court threw out the conviction on the ground that Alabama law excluded blacks from juries.

In 1936 a fourth round of trials took place. Only five of the nine original defendants were tried, but the five were convicted and sentenced, one to seventy-five years and the others to life. Only after fourteen more years were all five men free, four on parole and one by escape. For the thousands of African Americans who were carrying on the struggle for civil rights and social equality, there was not much to celebrate. But at least the Supreme Court had saved eight people from hanging, and set four of them free. The Court had also ruled, not for the first time, that state courts could not systematically exclude

The "Scottsboro Boys." Authorities in Alabama allowed a photographer to take this carefully staged photograph of Attorney Samuel Leibowitz and his clients. The picture was designed to assure the public that justice was being done, that the defendants were indeed represented by a lawyer and had access to them. But it was also designed to assure racially fearful whites that the conference was watched over by troopers, who only partially cover their pistols with their hands. (Brown Brothers)

blacks from juries. The stage was being set for new efforts to use the Constitution and the courts to protect the basic rights of black citizens—a struggle that would reach a climax after World War II, in the 1950s and 1960s.

For those who would not wait, there was one final consolation to be wrung from the New Deal. It came in 1941, when it was becoming increasingly clear that depression and the New Deal were about to give way to war. A. Philip Randolph, the brilliant and militant leader of the black union movement, decided that the time had come for blacks to demand justice from their government. He proposed a grand, all-black march on Washington. The Roosevelt administration was anxious to prevent "disorder" in the capital. And some officials were afraid that "communists" would "infiltrate" the movement. Roosevelt decided to negotiate. He told black leaders that

if they would call off the march, he would establish a Fair Employment Practices Commission, with at least some power to try to enforce equal treatment for black and white workers in the few industries where working conditions could be federally regulated. Randolph and his colleagues accepted the deal, and the commission was established in the summer of 1941, just a few months before the United States entered World War II. As one black newspaper put it, most African Americans thought they had little choice but to support Roosevelt and the Democrats, "until the real thing comes along."

MEXICAN AMERICANS A large influx of Mexican laborers into California and the Southwest, where most of them became migrant farm workers, had taken place in the 1920s. But the

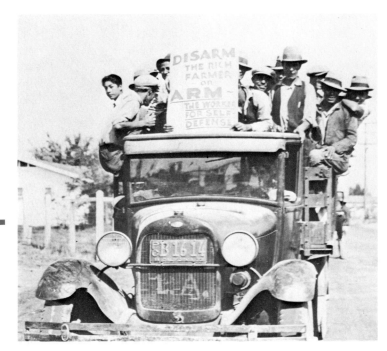

Mexicanos on strike. The striking braceros on this truck were unarmed. But they were threatening to arm themselves unless the landowners they usually worked for put down their own weapons and stopped hiring private armies of thugs to harrass striking workers. (Library of Congress)

irresistible forces of the depression turned on them severely. Hundreds of thousands of white farm families of the Southwest's Dust Bowl were losing their land or their sharecropping arrangements and heading west to California. The result was a dramatic reversal of the tides of migration. At the beginning of the crisis, only a small minority of the migrant work force on California farms had been North Americans. By the end of the decade, the North Americans—the "Okies" and the "Arkies"—made up nine-tenths of that labor force, doing the toilsome and low-paying jobs that had once been left to Mexicano "braceros."

The result was a huge outmigration of Mexicans and Mexican Americans. In the first five years of the depression, about half a million left. The U.S. census—woefully inaccurate when it came to minority groups—counted only half as many Mexican-born people in 1940 as it had in 1930. This drop was just about equal to the number of landless North Americans who had wandered into California looking for work. But the Mexicanos were not only discouraged by the economic crisis, they also were encouraged to go by governments like California's, which offered one-way tickets to Mexico, free of charge, to anyone willing to leave. And to offers like this, local police and bureaucrats often added harassment and ugly treatment. A government official in California said that "Mexicans are trash. . . . We herd them like pigs." (His command of English was weak. He was obviously trying to say that he thought Mexicans were like pigs. But his sentence could also mean "We herd them as though *we* were pigs.")

Some of the Mexicanos did resist, did refuse the free tickets "home," and did try to do something about their difficult jobs and miserable earnings. In the 1930s, Mexicano workers began to organize, to resist exploitation at the hands of Norteamericano landowners—and exploitation, too, at the hands of fellow Mexicans who organized work gangs and wrote contracts with the farmers. They organized a union, the Confederación de Uniones de Campesinos y Obreros Mexicanos (Confederation of Unions of Mexican Campesinos and Workers). There is no easy translation of *campesino*. It is sometimes translated as "peasants." But its meaning in Mexico and Central America covered a variety of forms of agricultural experience that included most of the rural poor, even those who owned small farms. The Confederación supported a number of bitter and sometimes bloody strikes during harvest seasons in the 1930s. In the largest strike, which took place in 1933, 18,000 Mexicano pickers refused to harvest the cotton crop in the rich San Joaquin Valley of California. But two strikers were murdered, and the violence eventually broke the strike. Still, during the next seven years, the Confederación promoted twenty-five major strikes.

By the end of the decade most landowners had shown that they preferred to hire North American workers, if they would work for the same low wages. The North Americans proved to be more docile than those Mexicanos who had stayed in the United States. As for the federal government, it tried to assist migrant farm workers by setting up camps run by the Farm Security Administration, camps that could provide decent temporary housing for laboring people. But the camps were established only in 1937, and the men who ran them, like the landowners, showed a definite preference for assisting North American migrant families. (John Steinbeck's famous novel about the sufferings of migrant workers in California, *The Grapes of Wrath*, was a moving and sympathetic book. But it did not have a single Mexican or Mexican-American character. His depiction of a Farm Security Administration camp is of an institution with no Mexicanos—or blacks, either.) Since agricultural workers were not covered by major New Deal programs like Social Security or the Wagner Act, and since only proven citizens were eligible for federal relief, the Mexicanos got little or no benefit from the New Deal.

NATIVE AMERICANS For Native Americans, economic depression was nothing new. For half a century Native Americans on reservations had lived in increasingly miserable conditions. Their main resource was land. But land ownership was governed by the rules of the Dawes Severalty Act of 1887 (see pp. 687–88). Under the terms of this law, land that tribes had once owned in common became the property of individual families. But with each passing generation, a fixed amount of land had to be divided among several children. The only alternative was for new generations to leave the reservations altogether, and try to cope with hardship and discrimination in towns and cities. So the inevitable long-term effect of the Dawes Act was to promote poverty and want.

The situation was perhaps worst in Oklahoma, which had once been the "Indian Territory." During the nineteenth century the federal government had crowded about thirty different tribes onto a skimpy expanse of land that was not very fertile in the first place. Increasing populations were unable to feed themselves adequately. Disease, especially tuberculosis, was epidemic. To Native Americans, the news that there was something called a "panic" on a street named "Wall" would have had a significance that was mainly ironic or bitter. And it appeared that help was not going to come to them any sooner than it was coming to the Mexican Americans. In 1929 the Hoover administration ruled that Native Americans living on reservations were not eligible for even the meager relief funds being provided by the federal government.

Then, in 1933, Roosevelt appointed a new commissioner of Indian affairs, John Collier, a former social worker. Collier made a number of decisions that were of real benefit to Native Americans who lived on reservations. Some of the decisions were of genuine symbolic importance. He ordered the bureaucrats who administered federal programs to respect Native American customs, language, and dress. He told them to stop doing what they had been doing for half a century, trying to force Indians to dress and talk and act like white people—or some-body's idea of the way white people ought to dress and talk and act. Other decisions were of more immediate and practical importance. Early in the New Deal, Collier persuaded Congress to fund the Indian Emergency Conservation pro-gram. It worked like the Civilian Conservation Corps, giving young men jobs building dams, planting trees, and improving roads. By the end of the 1930s about 90,000 Native Americans had worked in the program—nearly a third of the total Indian population. Paradoxically, life on the reservations during the Great Depression was probably better than it had been during the "pros-perity" of the 1920s.

But it was clear to most Native Americans that something more than "emergency" relief mea-sures was needed. Federal policy had to be changed. Tribal leaders worked with Collier to produce one of the decade's most significant pieces of legislation, the Indian Reorganization Act of 1934, which reversed many of the practices of the preceding fifty years. It recognized the basic concept of tribal ownership of land in common. It provided money—though never enough—for tribes to buy new land. The act also provided that tribes could write their own con-stitutions, which would be recognized as law by the federal government. And the act formally ended all restrictions on Native American cere-monies, dress, and language.

The Indian Reorganization Act did not touch the lives of those Native Americans who did not live on reservations, but some indirect assistance came to them through the Johnson-O'Malley Act of 1934. This law gave federal money to schools, hospitals, and other social agencies to encourage them to extend their services to Native Ameri-cans. Despite these measures, Native Americans probably remained the most impoverished of America's visible minorities—though the pos-sessors of one of its richest cultures. As with blacks and Mexican Americans, it would take one more generation for their pride in that culture to become a public fact of indisputable significance.

End of the New Deal

Franklin Roosevelt did everything he could to make the election of 1936 a test vote of the people's confidence in his efforts. And he won resoundingly. His Republican opponent, Gover-nor Alfred Landon of Kansas, took only Maine and Vermont. No American president had ever received such a ringing endorsement of such a controversial program of action.

But victory did not bring more of the New Deal. If anything, it brought less. For the New Deal now had to face a set of distressing realities.

The first problem, though minor, was noisy and irritating. A third-party candidate, Congress-man William Lemke, had polled almost a million votes in 1936. The vote itself did not matter, but it did seem to be the tip of an ominous political iceberg. Lemke had put together the votes of a number of critics of the New Deal who were demanding more radical action on a number of fronts. Senator Huey Long of Louisiana, an eccentric and fiery figure, was promoting a simple "Share Our Wealth" plan that held out the promise "Every man a king." A much quieter man, Dr. Francis Townsend of California, had created a movement for more adequate pensions for the elderly, a movement organized into thou-sands of Townsend Clubs. And an anti-Semitic Catholic priest, Father Charles Coughlin, had used the radio to generate a passionate belief in millions of people that Jews were responsible for the depression and that they controlled the Roosevelt administration. Hindsight makes it obvious that Long, Townsend, and Coughlin had little in common and no chance of success. But their movements raised serious doubts about the workability of the New Deal.

A much more trying problem for Roosevelt, however, was the failure of his efforts to end the depression. The gross national product would not budge. Federal deficits remained high, despite Roosevelt's personal commitment to a balanced budget. Unemployment refused to drop significantly. And no sooner was Roosevelt inaugurated the second time than a new wave of economic panic struck. The depression of 1937—a sort of depression-within-a-depression—shook the confidence not only of many voters but of many New Dealers themselves. The congressional elections of 1938 brought a coalition of Republicans and conservative Democrats to power, a coalition that made it virtually impossible to achieve any new legislative victories.

Finally, Roosevelt had to deal with an increasingly troublesome federal judiciary. In 1935 and 1936, parts of the Agricultural Adjustment Act and the National Industrial Recovery Act were ruled unconstitutional by the Supreme Court. Roosevelt became convinced that unless the Court could somehow be changed, the Wagner Act, the TVA, and the Social Security Act would not be safe.

He made a daring move. He proposed a scheme to "pack" the Supreme Court, suggesting that Congress empower the president to increase the size of the Court by one for every justice over seventy years of age.

What followed was a political fight lasting for months into Roosevelt's second term. In the end, he both won and lost. He won because some justices were frightened into retiring and others into shifting their votes. This change gave rise to one of the finest headlines of American history, "A switch in time saves nine." But Roosevelt also lost, in that public opinion seems to have turned markedly against him. Voters apparently disliked the idea of tampering with the Constitution (though the Constitution is in fact silent on the number of justices who sit on the Supreme Court). The Court fight virtually ended the New Deal. From that point onward, the attention of Roosevelt, and increasingly of everyone else, turned across the Atlantic and the Pacific, to fields of revolution and battle that would soon involve the nation in another world war.

Suggestions for Further Reading

THE BONUS ARMY

The two full-scale histories of the bonus march are Donald Lisio, *The President and Protest: Hoover, Conspiracy and the Bonus March* (1974), and Roger Daniels, *The Bonus March* (1971). The first is more concerned with what went on inside the Hoover administration, the second pays more attention to the marchers themselves. The *Reminiscences* of Douglas MacArthur (1964) are an interesting route into the mind of one important participant.

CONSERVATIVE REACTION

Robert K. Murray, *The Red Scare: A Study in National Hysteria, 1919–1920* (1955), is colorful and readable. The best place to begin reading about Sacco and Vanzetti is still Justice Felix Frankfurter's *The Case of Sacco and Vanzetti* (1962). It should be supplemented with William Young and David E. Kaiser, *Postmortem: New Evidence in the Case of Sacco and Vanzetti* (1985). The best account of Prohibition is Andrew Sinclair, *Prohibition: Era of Excess* (1962). The only book-length story of the Scopes trial is Ray Ginger, *Six Days or Forever? Tennessee v. John Thomas Scopes* (1958). Norman Furniss, *The Fundamentalist Controversy* (1954), is still a useful general treatment. The persistence of Christian conservatism can be followed in Leo Ribuffo, *The Old Christian Right* (1983). On nativism and the Klan, see John Higham, *Strangers in the Land* (1955); Kenneth Jackson, *The Ku Klux Klan in the City* (1965); and David M. Chalmers, *Hooded Americanism* (1965).

CHRONOLOGY

1924 Congress establishes veterans' bonus, to be paid in 1945. Immigration further restricted, Asians totally excluded. Ku Klux Klan plays prominent role in Democratic party convention. Coolidge defeats John W. Davis (Democrat) in presidential election.

1920 Warren G. Harding (Republican) defeats James M. Cox (Democrat) in presidential election. Nicola Sacco and Bartolomeo Vanzetti convicted of murder.

1928 Herbert Hoover (Republican) defeats Alfred E. Smith (Democrat) in presidential election.

1921 Federal law severely restricts immigration.

1925 "Monkey Trial" in Dayton, Tennessee.

1917 Russian Revolution.

1929 Stock market crash; Great Depression begins.

1916	1918	1920	1922	1924	1926	1928

1919 Red Scare begins. Eighteenth Amendment introduces prohibition.

1923 Harding dies, Calvin Coolidge becomes president. Teapot Dome Scandal. Stock market enters six-year boom.

1927 Sacco and Vanzetti electrocuted.

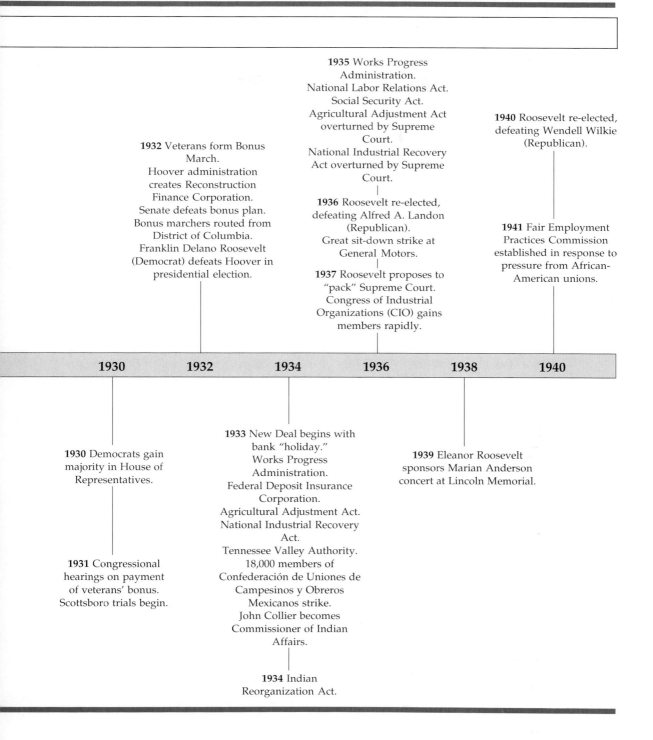

1935 Works Progress
Administration.
National Labor Relations Act.
Social Security Act.
Agricultural Adjustment Act
overturned by Supreme
Court.
National Industrial Recovery
Act overturned by Supreme
Court.

1940 Roosevelt re-elected,
defeating Wendell Wilkie
(Republican).

1932 Veterans form Bonus
March.
Hoover administration
creates Reconstruction
Finance Corporation.
Senate defeats bonus plan.
Bonus marchers routed from
District of Columbia.
Franklin Delano Roosevelt
(Democrat) defeats Hoover in
presidential election.

1936 Roosevelt re-elected,
defeating Alfred A. Landon
(Republican).
Great sit-down strike at
General Motors.

1941 Fair Employment
Practices Commission
established in response to
pressure from African-
American unions.

1937 Roosevelt proposes to
"pack" Supreme Court.
Congress of Industrial
Organizations (CIO) gains
members rapidly.

1930	1932	1934	1936	1938	1940

1933 New Deal begins with
bank "holiday."
Works Progress
Administration.
Federal Deposit Insurance
Corporation.
Agricultural Adjustment Act.
National Industrial Recovery
Act.
Tennessee Valley Authority.
18,000 members of
Confederación de Uniones de
Campesinos y Obreros
Mexicanos strike.
John Collier becomes
Commissioner of Indian
Affairs.

1939 Eleanor Roosevelt
sponsors Marian Anderson
concert at Lincoln Memorial.

1930 Democrats gain
majority in House of
Representatives.

1931 Congressional
hearings on payment
of veterans' bonus.
Scottsboro trials begin.

1934 Indian
Reorganization Act.

THE POLITICS OF CONSERVATISM

A fine general history of the Republican administrations of the 1920s—though an aging one—is John D. Hicks, *Republican Ascendancy* (1960). On the Democratic side, see David Burner, *The Politics of Provincialism* (1967), and Paula Elder, *Governor Alfred E. Smith* (1983). Two unusually sympathetic discussions of the most conservative presidents of the period are Robert K. Murray, *The Harding Era* (1969), and Donald R. McCoy, *Calvin Coolidge* (1967). An intriguing biography is *The Shadow of Blooming Grove: Warren G. Harding* (1968), by Francis Russell. Burl Noggle, *Teapot Dome* (1962), is excellent. Allan J. Lichtman's *Prejudice and the Old Politics* (1979) is a fine quantitative study of ethnic voting patterns.

BOOM AND BUST

The crash and what brought it can be approached best through John Kenneth Galbraith's fine little book, *The Great Crash, 1929* (3rd ed., 1972). A good treatment of the economic history of the 1920s and 1930s is Jim Potter, *The American Economy Between the Wars* (1974). Good discussions of Hoover's reaction to the onset of the depression are available in Joan Hoff Wilson, *Herbert Hoover, Forgotten Progressive* (1975); Martin Fausold, *The Presidency of Herbert Hoover* (1985); and William J. Barber, *From New Era to New Deal* (1985). Good firsthand accounts of the way the depression affected people are available in Richard Lowitt and Maurine Beasley, eds., *One Third of a Nation* (1981), and Robert McElvaine, ed., *Down & Out in the Great Depression* (1983). The victims of the crash speak eloquently in Caroline Bird, *The Invisible Scar* (1966), and Studs Terkel, *Hard Times: An Oral History of the Great Depression* (1970).

THE NEW DEAL

The literature on Roosevelt and the New Deal is vast. The most readable, though thoroughly biased, general account is the three volumes of Arthur M. Schlesinger, Jr., *The Age of Roosevelt: The Crisis of the Old Order, The Coming of the New Deal, The Politics of Upheaval* (1957–60). A useful and briefer account is Albert Romasco, *The Politics of Recovery* (1983). The Roosevelt administration's welfare policies are discussed in the early chapters of James Patterson,

America's Struggle Against Poverty (1981). Three excellent special studies of crucially important aspects of the New Deal are James Patterson, *The New Deal and the States* (1969); Ellis Hawley, *The New Deal and the Problem of Monopoly* (1966); and Barry Dean Karl, *Executive Reorganization and Reform in the New Deal* (1963). A fine, general, and brief book is William Leuchtenburg, *Franklin Roosevelt and the New Deal* (1963). The most ambitious study of Roosevelt is Frank Friedel, *Franklin D. Roosevelt* (4 vol., 1952–73). Two good studies of workers and unions are John Barnard, *Walter Reuther and the Rise of the Auto Worker* (1983), and Ronald W. Schatz, *The Electrical Workers: A History of Labor at General Electric and Westinghouse* (1983). A fascinating look at radical opposition to the New Deal is Alan Brinkley, *Voices of Protest: Huey Long, Father Coughlin, and the Great Depression* (1982).

WOMEN AND MINORITIES

The best study of women in the 1930s is Susan Ware, *Holding Their Own* (1982). Also useful are Alice Kessler-Harris, *Out to Work* (1982), and Winifred Wandersee, *Women's Work and Family Values* (1981). For the way the depression accelerated the transformation of Harlem into an African-American ghetto, see Gilbert Osofsky, *Harlem: The Making of a Ghetto* (1966). Gunnar Myrdal's classic study, *An American Dilemma* (1944), is still extremely useful. The relationship of the New Deal to black people is well treated in Nancy Weiss, *Farewell to the Party of Lincoln* (1983), and Harvard Sitkoff, *A New Deal for Blacks* (1978). The standard account of the Scottsboro trials is Dan T. Carter's very readable *Scottsboro* (1969). For the experiences of Mexican Americans and Mexicans in America, see Rodolfo Acuna, *Occupied America* (1981); Mark Reisler, *By the Sweat of Their Brow* (1976); Abraham Hoffman, *Unwanted Mexican Americans in the Depression* (1975); and Wayne Cornelius, *Building the Cactus Curtain* (1980). Kenneth Philip, *John J. Collier and the Crusade for Indian Reform, 1920–1954* (1977), and Lawrence C. Kelly, *The Assault on Assimilation* (1977), are both careful and thorough pieces of work on federal policies. Donald Parman, *Navajoes and the New Deal* (1976), is a specialized book, but it contains a fine summary of changes in federal policy toward Native Americans.

CHAPTER 21
A GLOBAL NATION

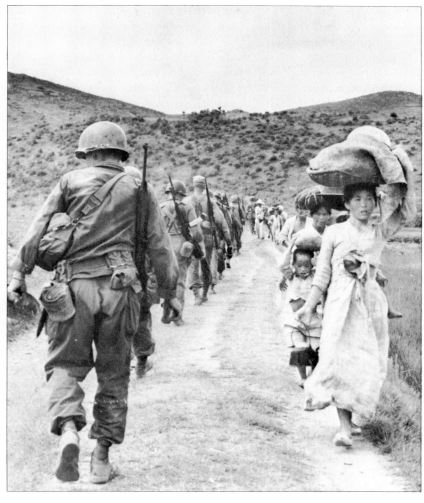

THE EPISODE: *There are few more dramatic events of the twentieth century than the explosion of atomic bombs over Hiroshima and Nagasaki, Japan. These terrible instruments of war convinced the already defeated Japanese to surrender. Exclusive possession of these weapons by the United States gave the nation an arms lead over the Soviet Union that remained decisive for several years after 1945. The atomic bomb also became a symbol for the cold war, the threat of a nuclear engagement that menaced the existence of humanity. Yet the atomic bomb and, particularly, the decision to build it in secrecy had a decisive impact inside the United States also, affecting relations between scientists and government, between research and funding and deployment of weapons. Atomic research helped to shape not just relations with the Soviet Union and the rest of the world, but the way the American government related to science in the postwar world.*

THE HISTORICAL SETTING: *The explosion of the atomic bomb seemed to signal the beginning of a new age. Indeed, there were dramatic changes in American foreign policy after 1945, as the nation emerged from the war at the head of a coalition determined to prevent the expansion of Soviet influence and the spread of communism. Among the exhausted participants of the war only the United States had the energy and capacity to undertake this crusade. Atomic weaponry was, necessarily, a major element in any such strategy. But development of the bomb occurred in the peculiar context of an alliance of enemies against the Germans and the Japanese during World War II.*

After almost a decade of appeasement, isolation, and fruitless negotiations, Britain, the United States, and the Soviet Union found themselves fighting a desperate war against Germany, Italy, and Japan. Their tenuous alliance, upon which the shape of the postwar world depended, fell apart rapidly after the war ended because of irreconcilable differences that emerged. Determined to enhance the influence of the USSR, Joseph Stalin gradually exerted control over vast areas of eastern Europe occupied by the Red Army. The United States organized its European allies into a military and economic coalition and undertook to rebuild Germany and Japan. As the sides hardened there were a number of dangerous flash points: jointly occupied Berlin, eastern Europe, and, in Asia—on the periphery of China—Taiwan, Korea, and, ultimately, Vietnam.

Yet, remarkably, the atomic bomb was not used again. Each side manufactured hundreds of atomic bombs and warheads for delivery by bombers or missiles. Each side spent billions, finally, on a weapon that by anyone's account had changed the rules of modern warfare forever.

HIROSHIMA

On a cold day in early spring 1955, a U.S. Air Force plane circled over Mitchell Field on Long Island, New York. Plunging into the turbulence, the aircraft landed and released its cargo: twenty-five young Japanese girls, "the Hiroshima maidens." Disfigured, some crippled, they huddled together, waiting to be taken to Mount Sinai Hospital for surgery to release their limbs, twisted by radiation and burns, and to smooth their swollen and distorted features. They were a fortunate few among the victims of the atomic bomb, brought to the United States by a group of religious workers and concerned citizens. It was a small, private gesture of reparation by Americans for the terrible destruction of Hiroshima.

Ten years earlier, shortly after eight o'clock on a warm August morning, a U.S. Army Air Force B-29 droned high over the center of Hiroshima, Japan. Most of the residents were only vaguely aware of its presence, reminded briefly, perhaps, of an earlier air-raid alert, which had then been followed by the all-clear signal. Most of the twenty-five girls were in the basement of their public school preparing erasers and chalk for classes. Most adults were on their way to work. Other schoolchildren were getting ready to resume their labor of clearing fire lanes in the city. This safety precaution, of pulling down crowded wooden houses and buildings in wide swaths across the city, had become necessary to prevent the fire storms from American incendiary raids that had obliterated whole square miles of Tokyo and other cities. Thus far, Hiroshima had been spared. Built on the flat delta of the Ota River, Hiroshima had become an important manufacturing center for the Japanese war effort. Most of its population lived along inlets connected by bridges, and most of the city was built of wood or other flimsy materials.

On the morning of August 6 the weather was clear. No antiaircraft fire or fighter planes met the American bomber, the *Enola Gay*, as it cruised smoothly toward its mission. Suddenly over target, the ship released its five-ton bomb and dived sharply to the right. The weapon drifted down slowly on a parachute, giving the plane forty-three precious seconds to escape. Then, shortly before it reached the ground, the bomb's altitude detectors triggered the device.

The burst flashed far brighter than the sun at midday. Waves of concussion pulverized everything at its center, and in an instant the enormous heat ignited the splintered debris. Inrushing winds thrust smoke and dust 40,000 feet into the atmosphere within two minutes. Still close by, but safe, the *Enola Gay* was buffeted by shock waves. One crew member looked back and remarked that it was "like boiling dust." The B-29 continued on its long trip back to base at Tinian Island. Built on a coral ridge, its six two-mile runways, constructed especially for heavy bombers, made it the world's largest airport. It had launched the *Enola Gay* and, with it, a new era in world history.

In Hiroshima, the devastation was instantaneous. About 80,000 people were killed or seriously wounded, most by burns, pressure from the blast, or falling buildings. Fires leaped out over the precautionary fire lanes. There was no way to fight them. The explosion had destroyed most firehouses, roadways were blocked, and scores of firemen were dead. Of the city's 200 doctors, 180 were killed or injured; of 1,780 nurses, 1,654 had died or were disabled. Some residents who survived, like Mrs. Futaba Kitayama, working about 2,000 yards from the blast, were terribly burned. Fearing that the bomb contained incendiary powders, she recalled, "I rubbed my nose and mouth hard with a *tenugui* [towel] I had at my waist. To my horror, I found that the skin on my face had come off in the towel." Farther out, people fell sick from radiation poisoning; many more died painfully within weeks. The Hiroshima maidens scrambled out of their collapsed school, some badly burned by fire or radiation. Nothing remained of their classrooms or schoolmates.

Of all the feelings experienced by Hiroshima survivors, perhaps the most universal was shock followed by a protective numbness. The single bomb, the single plane, surprise, and then enormous destruction—the combination wiped out all sense of proportion and disrupted the logic of cause and effect. It left only shock. As a Japanese poet wrote later:

> There is nothing for us to sing
> Whose eyes are closed,
> When we, in tears, gaze through
> The clear sky's depths.
> We find that all is lost and scattered;
> Suppose our brains have turned to ashes,
> Soaked in the River Ota, flowing in its blue;
>
> You people,
> Believe us;
> We find that all is washed away.
> What song is there for us to sing whose eyes are closed?
> But a song of tears?

Three days later, the United States dropped a second atomic bomb, this time over the city of Nagasaki. Although different in composition from the first, the device had an equivalent destructive force. But because of the hilly terrain and the greater prevalence of concrete buildings, the city sustained somewhat fewer casualties. Still,

Hiroshima. This picture of devastated Hiroshima captures the bewildering destructiveness of the atomic-bomb raids on Japan. (UPI/Bettmann Newsphotos)

the general effect was similar: a bewildered population, the breakdown of social services, and a landscape littered with splintered trees, twisted girders and towers, and the debris of what once had been a place of human habitation.

In August the Japanese had been on the verge of surrender—their cities shattered, their navy sunk, and their air force limited to defensive operations and suicidal kamikaze attacks against U.S. ships. Two days after Hiroshima, the Soviet Union declared war on Japan and marched rapidly into Japanese-held Manchuria. Against overwhelming odds on land, and facing extinction from the air, the Japanese sued for peace after Nagasaki. With their surrender, World War II ended on August 14.

The decision to drop the atomic bomb on two Japanese cities had been one of three key decisions relating to atomic energy that American policymakers had confronted during the war. The first decision was to build the bomb; the second, to use it; and the third, to try to maintain its secrets as an American monopoly during and after the war. None of these decisions was made lightly, for as the president, his

Nagasaki before atomic attack. Nagasaki, a port city and shipbuilding center, was the target of the second atomic bomb dropped on Japan at the close of World War II. Built on a series of hills, the city was devastated by the single blast on August 9, 1945. (The Bettmann Archive)

scientific advisers and administrators, and the few other officials brought into the process knew well, the shape of the postwar world depended on the wisdom of their deliberations.

The decision to develop an atomic bomb was, initially, made out of fear that the Germans would create this awesome weapon first. And there was no doubt that they would use it if they acquired it. Germany's blitzkrieg (lightning war) invasion of Poland in September 1939 had demonstrated the importance of technological superiority in winning battles. World War II was, as British Prime Minister Winston Churchill aptly called it, "a wizard war." By this he meant that inventions were decisive. The opposing nations spurred their scientists to develop weapons that would turn the tide of this desperate struggle. As Albert Speer, the German Reich's minister for armaments and munitions, said in 1946, even to the last moment the German population believed that some new "miraculous weapon" would save them from defeat.

The Americans and the British feared the potential of Germany's pure science and its sophisticated industrial plant. German military tactics, demonstrated in Poland and then in Belgium and France in the spring of 1940, underscored the advantages of a military strategy harnessed to science and industry. During the war, German science fielded several new weapons, including self-guided rockets and a new jet fighter plane. Had the jet been developed more quickly, it might have reversed Allied air supremacy in the last days of the war.

American and British science was also active in the development of weapons technology. A new radar system invented by the British helped deflect Hitler's effort to achieve air supremacy over England. Sonic systems to detect submarines, proximity fuses for mines, and a host of other engineering triumphs helped turn the tide of battle in favor of the Allies. None of these accomplishments, however, matched atomic power. Whoever tamed this energy first could command the gods of war.

The American scientific community, led by a distinguished group of European physicists who had fled German and Italian fascism, had good reason to fear German atomic science. In 1938, German scientists had demonstrated the possibility of nuclear fission, the basis for a chain reaction in radioactive material. The practical question was, could a chain reaction be harnessed and detonated as a bomb? In March 1939, physicist Leo Szilard (from Hungary) and Enrico Fermi (from Italy) directed successful fission experiments. Deeply worried that the Germans had made similar advances, Szilard went to the world-renowned scientist Albert Einstein. Einstein agreed to sign a letter to President Roosevelt warning him that Germany might be on the verge of developing atomic weapons: "It is conceivable," the letter concluded, "that extremely powerful bombs of a new type may be constructed."

Roosevelt undoubtedly knew little about the scientific basis of this prediction, but he was impressed enough by this warning to appoint a Uranium Committee inside the National Bureau of Standards. By early 1940 he had agreed to spend significant sums of money on atomic research, even though the United States officially remained at peace with Germany and Japan. Moreover, he determined that these activities should be pursued in secrecy; only a few scientists and only his closest political associates knew of the project.

In early summer 1941 Roosevelt appointed a larger committee to muster science in the cause of defense. Headed by Vannevar Bush, president of the Carnegie Institute and a noted engineer, this new National Defense Research Committee took over the work of the Uranium Committee. Bush reorganized the uranium group, adding more scientists and removing some of the military representatives. Then word reached Washington that the British had begun their own atomic program, dubbed MAUD in secret code. The British warned that a bomb was practical and could probably be built in two years.

Spurred to move faster by the British report, Roosevelt pushed through another reorganization during the fall of 1941, this time creating an advisory group called Section 1 and making it part of the recently formed Office of Scientific Research and

Enrico Fermi. One result of fascism in Italy and Germany was the flood of scientists and intellectuals who sought refuge in the United States during the 1930s. Some of these scientists, like Fermi, conducted crucial experiments that enabled America to construct the first atomic weapons. (UPI/Bettmann Newsphotos)

Development. Section 1 consisted of Bush; James B. Conant, president of Harvard University; Secretary of War Henry L. Stimson; Army Chief of Staff George C. Marshall; and Vice President Henry Wallace. In March 1942 Roosevelt turned the actual building of the bomb over to the War Department, which put Brigadier General Leslie R. Groves of the Army Corps of Engineers in charge of the project. By then, it had acquired a new name, the Manhattan Project, and a large, secret budget, hidden even from Congress.

Bureaucratic shuffling, agency reorganization, and new liaison committees were clues to the growing importance of atomic research. Roosevelt, by his actions, was also tightening federal control over the research, giving the military a dominant role in guiding it. By the time the project ended, it had spent about $2 billion. Over 100,000 people had worked on various aspects of the endeavor at thirty-seven military, scientific, and industrial installations—all to create a device that would cause about thirteen pounds of plutonium to release its energy. Yet this work had been accomplished with a degree of secrecy unknown in American history. Even many of the scientists did not know the precise objective of their research.

The project began in earnest in late 1942. General Groves appointed J. Robert Oppenheimer, a physicist from the California Institute of Technology, to direct the nuclear facility at Los Alamos, New Mexico, where much of the work was completed. In December, Enrico Fermi, working in an abandoned squash court at the University of Chicago, created the first self-sustaining chain reaction. Thus by early 1943, American scientists had acquired the basic knowledge and the facilities to develop a bomb. Ironically, at almost precisely the same time, German scientists concluded that an atomic weapon was not feasible. Yet no one knew of the Germans' decision for sure. In fact, Arthur Compton, a Manhattan Project participant, reported that the United States worried so much about German atomic progress that "when the Allies landed on Normandy [France] beaches on 6 June, 1944, certain of the American officers were equipped with Geiger counters," to detect traces of atomic weapons.

Secrecy, compartmentalization, and hierarchy characterized Groves's administration of the project. By dividing up the research and keeping any one scientist in the project from having access to more information than was required to answer a specific question, Groves prevented leaks of information. He possibly also slowed the progress of the project. More important, however, he stopped scientists from discussing the larger implications of their work: whether or not a weapon should be used and under what conditions. Furthermore, he angered a number of scientists with his security-conscious rules and bureaucracy.

Groves, however, was not the only policymaker who wanted to hide the project. Bush and Conant hoped to exclude the British, to prevent their gaining atomic weapons. At first, Roosevelt seemed to agree, but in the summer of 1943 he reversed himself. At an August conference with Churchill in Quebec, Canada, the president agreed to a full exchange of information. This left only the Soviet Union, America's other principal ally, out in the cold. In fact, the decision not to tell the Russians, while keeping the British informed, became one of the most momentous of the war, for it came to symbolize the lack of trust and cooperation between the opponents of Germany. Apparently, Roosevelt never seriously considered informing the Russians about the project or keeping them abreast of scientific developments. And, as Groves later declared, "There was never, from about two weeks from the time I took charge of this Project any illusion on my part but that Russia was our enemy."

Although atomic research always aimed at production of a usable bomb, its actual deployment remained uncertain and controversial. Depending on its completion date, a bomb could be dropped on Germany or Japan or both. If one or the other of the Axis powers was knocked out of the war—and by early 1945, Germany was rapidly crumbling—it would have to be used exclusively on the sole enemy survivor.

In 1944, as the bomb moved from the drawing board to construction, several scientists began to discuss the wider implications of atomic power. The resolve to use the bomb was implicit in its creation and in the momentum the Manhattan Project gained in 1944 and 1945. But the decision could have been reversed, and a few of the scientists working on the project or familiar with atomic energy desperately pressed for a reconsideration. They recognized that the bomb was more than just a new, powerful weapon. Its development and its use, they contended, would have vast implications in shaping the postwar world. This was a difficult position to take, for the bureaucratic structure governing the Manhattan Project was designed to prevent broad discussions of any sort—especially those that challenged the use of the bomb. Any halt to plans for deploying the bomb would have to come from the very top, from the few civilian leaders like Churchill and Roosevelt who knew the details of the weapon's development.

As the weapon became more of a likelihood in 1944, several scientists became uneasy about the choice of a target. Increasingly, it appeared that Germany would not be the victim. That country was rapidly falling apart under the massive attacks from west and east by Allied armies. That left Japan, a nation that could not develop a bomb of its own but that still clung tenaciously to its extended empire of Pacific conquests. Allied commanders estimated that to knock the Japanese out of the war would require a two-stage invasion of Japan—the first in November 1945 with a landing on the island of Kyushu, and a second, full-scale attack in the spring of 1946. Estimated Allied casualties in the two assaults were placed at somewhere around a million men. If this were the case, the atomic bomb could prove decisive. But it was also possible that the Japanese would give up before such a costly assault became necessary.

Other questions worried scientists as early as 1943. Niels Bohr, a Danish refugee and key theorist in the field of atomic science, firmly believed that atomic information should be shared among all the Allies, including the Russians. If not, he warned, an atomic arms race might develop after the war. In several memorandums to Roosevelt, he urged international control of atomic energy. And he asked the president to inform the Russians of the Manhattan Project. Scientists could help in promoting an

> understanding of how much would be at stake should the great prospects of atomic physics materialize, and in preparing an adequate realization of the great benefit which would ensue from a whole-hearted co-operation on effective control measures.

Roosevelt postponed taking any such initiatives, so Bohr tried to persuade Winston Churchill. The scientist traveled to England in the spring of 1944 with letters of recommendation and waited impatiently for a meeting with the prime minister. When it finally occurred, Churchill showed himself hostile to sharing atomic secrets with the Russians. Bohr left the meeting knowing he had failed: "We did not even speak the same language," he later remarked. Other scientists active in the project, such as Bush, eventually came to share Bohr's fears that attempting to maintain a monopoly on atomic secrets would stimulate an arms race between the United States and Russia. But by the end of 1944, Roosevelt clearly agreed with Churchill: The two allies would not share atomic knowledge with the Soviet Union.

By the spring of 1945 the Russian issue had even complicated the question of using the atomic bomb. And decision making became more difficult still in April. President Roosevelt died suddenly on April 12, leaving to Vice President Harry Truman the decision about dropping the first atomic weapon in history. War was racing to a climax in Europe. The new president had to face the hard task of designing a peace in an atmosphere of growing competition with the Russians. Truman had limited experience in foreign affairs; he had little sympathy for the Soviets; and he was not aware of the plans or promises Roosevelt had made. Most important, he did not even know about the atomic bomb.

At a White House meeting on April 25, Stimson and Groves informed the new president of the weapon about to be placed under his command. Secretly ushered into the president's office, Groves made several points: The United States would soon test an atomic device; the United States and Britain held a monopoly on the world's fissionable materials; the Russians were probably spying on the Manhattan Project. Stimson took a very different tack, warning the new president of the dangers atomic bombs presented to international diplomacy:

> In the light of our present position with reference to this weapon, the question of sharing it with other nations and if so shared, upon what terms, becomes a primary question of our foreign relations.

Truman's sole initiative at this meeting was to appoint an interim committee to choose targets in Japan.

Once the Germans had collapsed, in early May, Truman turned his attention to formulating a European peace and to ending the war in Asia. Increasingly, these two efforts became intertwined. The president was deeply distressed by news reaching Washington: The Russians, occupying Europe as far west as central Germany, were consolidating their hold on eastern European countries, including Bulgaria, Poland, Hungary, and Czechoslovakia. And the Japanese, he believed, were preparing to defend their island empire to the last inch. In both situations, the atomic bomb might be important. In Europe, exclusive American possession of a successful bomb might convince the Russians to cooperate with the United States on its plans for the shape of postwar Europe and Asia. In Asia, its use might save hundreds of thousands of American and Japanese lives.

Truman had both possibilities in mind when he scheduled a meeting at Potsdam, Germany, with Stalin and Churchill in July. The timing coincided with the first testing of the atomic bomb, the news of which Truman expected to reach him during the conference. As expected, on July 18 word flashed from Alamogordo Air Base, near Albuquerque, New Mexico: a successful explosion with "the brightness of several suns at midday." The president then proceeded to use the news. On July 25 he wrote in his diary:

> We met at 11 A.M. today, that is, Stalin, Churchill and the U.S. President. But I had a most important session with Lord [Louis] Mountbatten and General [George] Marshall before that. We have discovered the most terrible bomb in the history of the world. It may be the fire destruction prophesied in the Euphrates Valley Era, after Noah and his fabulous Ark.

The president then recorded his thoughts about using the bomb:

> This weapon is to be used against the Japanese between now and August 10th. I have told the Secretary of War, Mr. Stimson, to use it so that military objectives and soldiers and sailors are the target and not women and children. Even if the Japs are savages, ruthless, merciless and fanatic, we as the leader of the world for the common welfare cannot drop this terrible bomb on the old capital [Kyoto] or the new [Tokyo].

Truman believed that the bomb would save lives and that its use was inevitable, since the Japanese, even after warnings, would not surrender: "It is certainly a good thing for the world," he concluded, "that Hitler's crowd or Stalin's did not discover this atomic bomb. It seems to be the most terrible thing ever discovered, but it can be made most useful."

Truman's private musings contained at least three dubious assumptions or misapprehensions. The first was that the bomb incontestably had to be used. There were strong rumors at the time that the Japanese were on the verge of collapse. With Germany out of the war, Japan was isolated. On July 18 Stalin informed Churchill of a message from the Japanese emperor suing for peace. With the imminent prospect of a Soviet declaration of war on Japan, surrender—without the use of the bomb—was at least possible. Second, Truman had assured himself that the targets selected were primarily military. This was only partly the case, for both Hiroshima and Nagasaki were cities with large civilian populations. Finally, Truman believed the weapon could be useful. Perhaps he meant useful to end the war. But possibly he also meant that it would intimidate the Russians.

If making the Russians more cooperative was one purpose of the bomb, it did not entirely work. When Truman hinted to Stalin at Potsdam about the new weapon, the Russian leader replied calmly that he hoped it would be used against the Japanese. The conference resumed and eventually reached certain limited agreements about the shape of the postwar world. But as Truman later wrote:

> What a show that was! But a large number of agreements were reached in spite of the setup—only to be broken as soon as the unconscionable Russian Dictator returned to Moscow! And I liked the little son of a bitch.

By August, Truman had determined not to share any secrets with the Russians, and he was committed to dropping two bombs. Last-minute appeals of atomic scientists to reverse his decision failed to convince him. A committee of Chicago scientists had warned in early June that a surprise attack against the Japanese would initiate an arms race with the Russians. However, Truman's own Scientific Advisory Committee, made up of several eminent scientists, recommended using the weapon:

> We can propose no technical demonstration likely to bring an end to the war; we see no acceptable alternative to direct military use.

One last serious attempt to stop the bomb came from Chicago scientists on July 17. Leo Szilard authored a petition and gathered the signatures of sixty-eight other atomic scientists. The document urged President Truman not to drop the bomb:

> The development of atomic power will provide nations with new means of destruction. The atomic bombs at our disposal represent only the first step in this direction, and there is almost no limit to the destructive power which will become available in the course of their future development.

No nation, Szilard concluded, would ever be safe from destruction.

This petition, as well as other serious reservations expressed by other scientists, failed to reach the president. Project director Groves refused to pass them on because "no useful purpose would be served in transmitting either the petition or the attached

The crew of the *Great Artiste*. In this posed reenactment, Major Chuck Sweeney, commander of the B-29 that dropped the atomic bomb over Nagasaki, illustrates how he briefed his crew before taking off on the mission. (UPI/Bettmann Newsphotos)

documents to the White House." And besides, by the time the petition reached Groves, Truman was already in Potsdam. Having built this terrible weapon, and seeing its apparent multiple advantages—in ending the war immediately and in impressing the Russians—Truman, Stimson, and other policymakers were determined to use it.

On July 26 the United States, Britain, and China issued a new warning to Japan and a final demand for unconditional surrender. The proclamation threatened the "utter devastation of the Japanese homeland," but it did not mention the bomb. The Japanese rejected the call, still holding out for preservation of the power and status of the emperor. The decision to use the bomb had now become irreversible.

On August 6 President Truman in a dramatic report to the nation announced the explosion of the atomic bomb over Hiroshima. "Sixteen hours ago an American airplane dropped one bomb on Hiroshima, an important Japanese army base," he said. Then he described the size and power of the weapon. It was, he proclaimed, "the greatest achievement of organized science in history." It had been built in secret, and it would be continued in secrecy:

> It has never been the habit of the scientists of this country or the policy of this Government to withhold from the world scientific knowledge. . . .
>
> But under present circumstances it is not intended to divulge the technical processes of production or all the military applications pending further examination of possible methods of protecting us and the rest of the world from the danger of sudden destruction.

Truman's decision to maintain secrecy about atomic research and development was, like the decision to drop the bomb, very much the product of past decisions. Having already excluded the Russians, and believing that sole possession of the weapon by the United States would make them more amenable to American wishes for postwar Europe, Truman and his advisers were dubious about sharing America's scientific advantages. But any decision can be reversed, and there were some compelling reasons to do so in this case. In the first place, many scientists argued that there were no secrets. In the words of Albert Einstein, "There is no secret and there is no defense." Second, the administration recognized that Russian espionage was likely to penetrate American security anyway. This possibility was confirmed in September 1945, when the Canadian prime minister revealed details of an atomic spy ring operating in the United States and Canada. Furthermore, to hold scientists captive to the secrets they discovered in their research betrayed the very essence of free scientific inquiry. Finally, there was the possibility of an arms race. As a scientist at the University of Chicago put it in 1946:

> If we seek to achieve our own security through supremacy in atomic warfare, we will find that in ten years the whole world is as adequately armed as we, and that the threat of imminent destruction will bring about a "preventive" war.

These were grave risks: dependence on secrets that might not be safe, excessive government direction and interference in scientific research, and an arms race. Nevertheless, to Truman they were risks worth running. By late 1945 he had become convinced that a monopoly on the atomic bomb would allow the United States great flexibility in foreign policy without the cost of a large standing army. On October 27 he declared that American possession of the bomb was a "sacred trust" for humanity. Nonetheless, Truman made at least one serious effort in early 1946 to demilitarize nuclear energy. But the spring of that year was a tense time to formulate a treaty based on mutual trust. In February 1946, news of the Russian spy ring operating from Canada had been made public. And American and Russian foreign policies had both stiffened. Still, a committee in the State Department devised a plan for international control of atomic energy. The group was headed by David Lilienthal, former head of the Tennessee Valley Authority and future head of the Atomic Energy Commission. After serious debate, the committee suggested a scheme in March that would give the United Nations control over the mining, refining, and utilization of atomic raw materials. Each nation, under this plan, could retain control over the peaceful uses of nuclear energy.

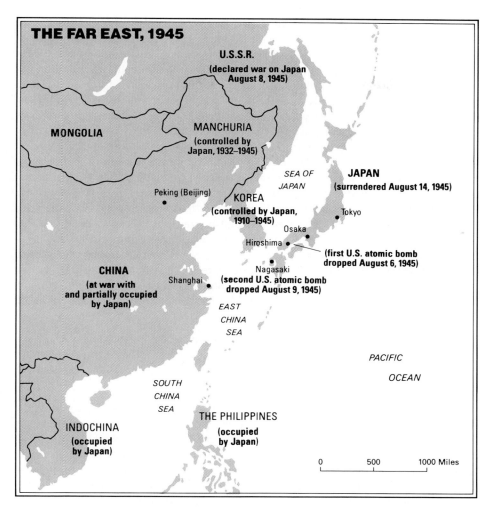

THE FAR EAST, 1945

U.S.S.R. (declared war on Japan August 8, 1945)

MONGOLIA

MANCHURIA (controlled by Japan, 1932–1945)

SEA OF JAPAN

JAPAN (surrendered August 14, 1945)

Peking (Beijing)

KOREA (controlled by Japan, 1910–1945)

Tokyo

Osaka

Hiroshima

(first U.S. atomic bomb dropped August 6, 1945)

Nagasaki

CHINA (at war with and partially occupied by Japan)

Shanghai

(second U.S. atomic bomb dropped August 9, 1945)

EAST CHINA SEA

PACIFIC OCEAN

SOUTH CHINA SEA

INDOCHINA (occupied by Japan)

THE PHILIPPINES (occupied by Japan)

0   500   1000 Miles

Truman endorsed the plan and appointed the elderly financier Bernard Baruch to present the plan to the UN Atomic Energy Commission. Baruch agreed to serve but insisted on the right to make changes. His modifications almost guaranteed a Russian refusal. He proposed total disarmament, not just control of nuclear weapons. His plan included dire punishments for nations who violated the agreement and private, not international, control of mining and manufacture. Finally, he proposed abolishing the Security Council veto in atomic energy matters. The Russians rejected the plan in the summer of 1946. Almost immediately, the United States resumed atmospheric nuclear bomb testing, and the Russians continued their drive to develop a bomb.

Public opinion—which might have contributed significantly to the extended debate about the bomb, atomic secrecy, and the role of science—was splintered, confused, and often anxious. A Gallup poll taken August 16, 1946, disclosed that about 85 percent of Americans approved the bombings, 10 percent disapproved, and 5 percent had no opinion. In the context of the war's end, this result is hardly surprising. Mixed into the approval were certain strong American beliefs: admiration for science and technology, a long-standing faith in air power as a kind of ultimate weapon, and a faith in progress. Shortly after the war, David Dietz captured this spirit in his book *Atomic Energy in the Coming Era*. Dietz predicted a plane that traveled more than 1,000 miles an hour and a moon rocket ship powered by atomic chain reactions. He also promised an automobile engine fired by "tiny explosions of Uranium 235." These, he proclaimed, were a few of the "miracles just ahead for mankind in the coming Era of Atomic Energy whose dawn was heralded Sunday, August 5,[1] when the first bomb of atomic energy exploded over the Japanese city of Hiroshima."

Nonetheless, many Americans worried about the bomb, especially after the initial euphoria of the war's end died down. They did not believe General Groves, who told a Senate hearing that radiation poison was "a very pleasant way to die." Church leaders in particular condemned the bomb. Roman Catholic spokesmen denounced the weapon because, contrary to expressed intentions, the explosion did not spare civilians. Thirty-four leading Protestant clergymen sent President Truman a petition calling the bomb an atrocity. In 1946 the Federal Council of Churches of Christ wrote of its anguish at the attack:

> As American Christians, we are deeply penitent for the irresponsible use already made of the atomic bomb. We are agreed that, whatever be one's judgment of the ethics of war in principle, the surprise bombings of Hiroshima and Nagasaki are morally indefensible.

It was not the moral outrage of churches that touched the American public so much as the book *Hiroshima*, written by novelist John Hersey. Hersey traveled to Japan in October and November 1945 and brought back material for an extended article for the *New Yorker* magazine. Ordinarily a witty and fashionable periodical known for its sardonic cartoons, the magazine suspended its humor for a single issue in August 1946. It printed no satire, cartoons, or verse, and even excised some of the more inappropriate advertising. The issue sold out four hours after it hit the newsstands. It was subsequently reprinted in fifty newspapers and then became a best-selling book.

Hersey wrote about the bomb in a way that most Americans could understand: through the eyes of six survivors. He clothed bare statistics with the details of the life and death of ordinary people. He captured the essential experience of surprise, nakedness, and numbness before a force that was incomprehensible. This approach cut through the depersonalized, abstract—often bigoted—way America had judged its enemy.

The effectiveness of Hersey's story aroused a response from the bomb's defenders. Hollywood produced a quick propaganda film in 1947, *The Beginning or the End?*, showing the president tormented by the fateful decision to employ the weapon. Some

---

[1]Because Japan is on the other side of the International Date Line, the blast occurred there on August 6.

of those who had helped guide the construction of the bomb, like Henry Stimson, wrote articles in popular magazines to defend its use. In the end, most Americans remained convinced that the bomb had been necessary. Neither guilt nor fear of atomic warfare translated into significant opposition to relying on a nuclear monopoly in foreign policy. On the contrary, the public increasingly worried about keeping nuclear weapons a secret.

In July 1945, just before the end of the war, Vannevar Bush had submitted a report titled *Science—The Endless Frontier* to the president, outlining his suggestions for a new relationship between science and the government. The war had created a new relationship and Bush wished to institutionalize it. The government should coordinate and support broad research programs, he wrote,

> but we must proceed with caution in carrying over the methods which work in wartime to the very different conditions of peace. We must remove the rigid controls which we have had to impose, and recover freedom of inquiry and that healthy competitive spirit so necessary for expansion of the frontier of scientific knowledge.

Bush's worries about government interference and rigidity were well founded, for three major groups were contending for the control of science and atomic research after the war. These included the scientists themselves, the civilian branch of the federal government, and the military. In the end, something of a compromise was worked out, and basic scientific research in the United States evolved into a partnership between scientists and the civilian and military branches of government. But to some researchers, this compromise severely limited their freedom to speak and publish and, above all, to determine the uses of their work. Research in peacetime remained too much like secret research under conditions of war.

In the next several years, three federal institutions were developed to direct and finance scientific research in the United States. The precedent of the Manhattan Project, the commitment to secrecy, and the desire to advance science in competition with the Soviet Union played a signficant role in their foundation. The first was the Atomic Energy Commission (AEC), established August 1, 1946, which guided and controlled the development and application of nuclear energy in a variety of military and non-military areas. The National Science Foundation, set up in 1950, became the major institution to fund and direct basic scientific research (some of it relevant to weapons development and much of it not). The third institution was the military administration and funding of large weapons projects by the Defense Department.

The AEC had many of the characteristics of the Manhattan Project. Its bylaws prevented international cooperation on atomic energy development, and its employees had to pass an FBI investigation. But tightly run as it was, the AEC represented a significant compromise. Scientists who had balked at tight security and Army interference on the Manhattan Project demanded freedom to do research. Some of them organized the Federation of Atomic Scientists in 1945 to oppose any efforts to impose direct military control of research. It successfully blocked legislation that would have placed military representatives in a dominant position on the commission.

The question of federal funding for basic scientific research ended in much the same sort of compromise. In his report on science, Vannevar Bush proposed a new agency to underwrite basic research. Run by civilians and scientists, it would direct research in a wide variety of fields, not just those related to military weapons. Although this proposal appealed to scientists, President Truman rejected the plan because it appeared to be independent from federal control. Thus in 1947, when a bill to create an independent National Science Foundation passed through Congress, Truman vetoed it. Lacking close executive branch supervision, Truman argued, the proposed foundation would be divorced from control by the people "to an extent that implies a distinct lack of faith in democratic processes." What he meant was that government would not have sufficient power to direct and focus the agency's activities.

Unable to agree on the shape of a new science foundation, the federal government still forged ahead with funding basic scientific and weapons research. Military planners pushed hard for weapons research. In particular, the Office of Naval Research, created in August 1946, funded large military research contracts. Many universities and corporations were initially skeptical about secret peacetime research, but by 1949 the office had spent more than $20 million on 1,200 projects at some 200 institutions. And most of this work was undertaken without public knowledge.

Militarily funded research met the immediate needs of a growing defense establishment, but it did not fill the place of a broader, federally funded science research program. This came, finally, in 1950 with the establishment of the National Science Foundation. The new agency would report directly to the president—a victory for Truman. Its purpose was to fund basic research in the sciences—a victory for scientists. Weapons development would remain primarily under the control of the military.

Thus by 1950, cooperation between scientists, the federal government, and the military had been established. Federal funds were lavished on research in ways hitherto unheard of in peacetime. A mode of operating in secret, yet with some latitude, had been established. Science had become the willing servant of federal policy. But there was a price.

In August 1949 the dream of scientific superiority over the Russians turned into an anxious nightmare, when American scientists detected traces of a Russian atomic blast experiment. The monopoly had been broken. The public and Congress demanded to know how the secrets had been lost. Scientists had often warned that there were, essentially, no secrets, but few had been willing to listen. This was even truer in 1949. In this atmosphere of recrimination and spy stories, President Truman pushed ahead to try for a monopoly on a new superweapon. In January 1950 he accelerated research into a hydrogen bomb. Two and a half years later the United States tested its first fusion devise. (Fission and fusion are, in some respects, opposite reactions. In the first, heavy nuclei are split; in the second, two lighter nuclei are combined.) By 1954 the Soviets had also tested a fusion bomb. American superiority had evaporated quickly in an arms race in which equality was probably the best that could be hoped for.

Rather than stimulating debate over fundamental issues, the growing stalemate in nuclear terror pushed concern about secrecy and security to a frenzied pitch. Ironically, the most important scientist of the Manhattan Project, J. Robert Oppenheimer,

The atomic army. During the 1950s, the United States and the Soviet Union carried on extensive open-air nuclear weapons testing. Frequently, as pictured here, American soldiers were stationed close to the test blast area for training purposes. The risks of such exposure to radiation were, at the time, rarely acknowledged. (UPI/Bettmann Newsphotos)

fell victim to this mood. From the very beginning, Oppenheimer, the physicist who had led the Los Alamos scientists to their triumph, had been viewed suspiciously by military and security experts. Some of his associates in the 1930s had been political radicals, including his wife and his younger brother. But during the years of the Manhattan Project, Oppenheimer always received security clearance. Moreover, Oppenheimer had supported using the bomb. Now, after the war, his independence of mind began to carry him away from established policy, and he started to question some of the assumptions of the arms race.

In 1948, shortly before the Russians exploded their first atomic bomb, Oppenheimer proposed making small tactical weapons. He wanted to develop atomic explosives suitable for use against military targets. He opposed building huge bombs to hold civilian populations hostage. Working for the AEC General Advisory Committee in 1949, he spoke against committing massive resources to developing the hydrogen bomb. Losing this debate, he also earned the suspicion and opposition of

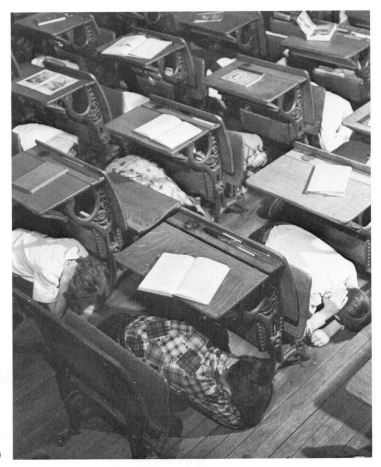

School children in 1951 duck for cover during a practice atomic bomb raid. Such experiences made the nightmare of World War III seem a plausible part of the waking world. (UPI/Bettmann Newsphotos)

scientists who were advocating the larger bomb, such as Edward Teller. Teller's opposition was well founded, for Oppenheimer had changed many of his views about atomic energy. Shortly after the decision to build a hydrogen bomb, Oppenheimer told a radio audience:

> The decision to seek or not to seek international control of atomic energy, the decision to try to make or not to make the hydrogen bomb, these are complex technical things, but they touch the very base of our morality. It is a grave danger for us that these decisions are taken on the basis of facts held in secret.

As Oppenheimer astutely saw, the decision to build the hydrogen bomb compressed almost every question surrounding atomic energy research into one momentous problem. Secrecy, international control—practically all the elements of the nuclear debate were involved. He decided he could not support such a decision.

Adolph Hitler in Nuremberg in 1935. A pretentious little man in an ill-fitting uniform and unkempt hair, Hitler inspired hysteria and obedience from his enthusiastic followers. (Library of Congress)

the Spanish fascists. In 1938 he annexed Austria and began to demand German ethnic areas inside Czechoslovakia. Despite treaties with France, the Czechs were forced to concede large areas of ter-

ritory—in effect, dooming that nation. Britain and France feared war and willingly appeased Hitler, hoping to satisfy his desire for expansion. But they miscalculated. After signing a Non-

Aggression Pact with the Soviet Union in August 1939, Hitler invaded Poland on September 1 and World War II began.

Here, for the first time, Hitler met resistance. The Poles refused to relinquish areas that Germany demanded. For the time being, the German leader had neutralized any potential interference by the Russians because the Non-Aggression Pact with them promised to respect Russian claims to territory lost to Poland in 1920. On September 1, German armored divisions and aircraft swept across western Poland while Russians moved into eastern areas of that nation. On September 3, France and England declared war on Germany. But Poland fell in less than a month.

The strategy of the Germans and their European allies in World War II was an extension of World War I plans, carefully revised to avoid failure. The Germans in studying their loss in 1918 realized the importance of mobility and logistics: the ability to deliver firepower rapidly and in massive amounts. Their strategy centered on tanks and mobile artillery with tactical air support.

The Japanese, Americans, and British during the 1930s also studied the successes and failures of World War I—in particular, the problems and potential of landing troops and materiel quickly, under fire, onto hostile shores. The Americans and Japanese also emphasized the aircraft carrier, which proved to be a superb attack weapon, superior to traditional naval vessels because of the striking force of the fighters and dive bombers it carried.

All of the major nations developed air power, but with varying success. Germany did not, at first, fully recognize the potential of long-range bombing and tended to use fighters primarily in aid of infantry. The British better understood the potential of long-range offensive air power as well as the need for an effective defense. The Americans also developed long-range weapons, culminating in the B-29 bomber, which dropped the atomic bombs on Japan.

As in World War I, Germany fought a war in two directions, but this time with far greater success. After a lull following the conquest of Poland, Hitler invaded Denmark and Norway. On May 10, 1940, German troops swept through Holland and into Belgium, conquering both nations by May 25. Hitler then sent his armored divisions into northern France. Facing a sometimes poorly equipped army and a divided Allied command, the Germans broke through. British troops pinned up against the English Channel were spared only because Hitler halted his armies to allow his air force to batter the British. The Allies were able to mount a desperate evacuation at Dunkirk while the Royal Air Force fought off the German Luftwaffe.

Hardly a victory, this evacuation saved 350,000 troops, but it left the French to fend for themselves. After only five days, German armored divisions were nearing Paris. The French military abandoned the city on June 13. On June 16 the French government—in disarray and retaining only a bleeding remnant of its army—surrendered. The Germans, to save themselves the costs of a total occupation, established a puppet government in southern France quartered at Vichy. Now Hitler aimed at Britain.

Hitler's strategy for the invasion of England hinged on establishing air superiority. Despite the new British radar system and a valiant defense, he almost succeeded. After sustaining days of bombardment, the British sent bombers to Berlin. Infuriated by this attack on their capital, the Germans shifted their attention to London and away from British defense installations. This decision allowed the British to concentrate their defenses, greatly raising the cost of air attacks. On September 30 the Luftwaffe made its last daylight raid. Hitler had to cancel plans to conquer England.

Throughout the spring and summer of 1941, the Germans and Italians moved against British positions in the Mediterranean and conquered Yugoslavia, Greece, and Crete. Germany's major objective, however, was the destruction of the Soviet Union. Hitler's divisions struck in June 1941, hoping to knock the Russians out of the war before winter. They almost succeeded, ad-

The Battle of Britain, 1940. St. Paul's Cathedral stands amid a Nazi air raid. The relentless bombing of London by the German Luftwaffe in the fall of 1940 failed to break the resistance of the population or secure Axis air superiority. The British fought back valiantly and gained the admiration and support of many Americans. (Library of Congress)

vancing hundreds of miles toward Moscow and Leningrad. To the very last, Stalin believed that Hitler would honor the Non-Aggression Pact. The Russians suffered over 1.5 million casualties, with a similar number taken prisoner. The Germans lost about 800,000 men. Despite superior equipment, training, and command, the Germans failed to deliver a decisive blow, and the Russians, with British and American aid, began to rebuild their armies. By December 1941 Hitler's empire was vast, but the short war he had anticipated had turned into a grueling battle of attrition.

JAPAN In Asia as in Europe, war began gradually through incidents of escalating aggression. Japan, which had long planned the conquest of China, moved against this weaker power beginning in the early 1930s. Japanese armies captured large areas of Chinese territory but could not eliminate the nationalist forces of General Chiang Kai-shek or the Chinese communists who controlled territory to the north. By 1940 the Japanese had turned toward conquest of the colonies belonging to European nations under occupation or attack: France, Britain, and the Netherlands. These areas held rich natural resources that the Japanese required to continue their war effort. The only significant powers standing in the way were Britain (now desperately fighting for survival in Europe) and the United States.

Japanese war planners realized the impossibility of outproducing or directly defeating the United States. Their plan called for surprise destruction of the American Navy, simultaneous seizure of Southeast Asia, and defeat of any counterattacks. They counted on the problem of maintaining long supply lines, and America's low level of preparedness, to discourage the United States.

The United States Enters the War

Roosevelt responded to these desperate events in Europe and Asia in two ways. He pushed for American rearmament and established close working relations with the British. And he approved plans to initiate research into building an atomic bomb. Although still officially neutral, the United States became the armorer for the opponents of Germany and Japan. In the summer of 1939 the United States informed Japan that it intended to terminate its trade treaties with that nation. Following the invasion of Poland, the president called Congress into session to repeal America's neutrality acts, which made it difficult to trade arms to belligerents. After extensive debate, Congress repealed some of the more stringent elements of these acts.

Following the fall of France, Roosevelt pushed harder for rearmament and direct aid to Britain. Moving around legal obstacles and obstinate public opinion, the administration agreed, in September 1940, to exchange destroyers for British bases in the Western Hemisphere. Most reaction to this agreement was favorable, but an America First Committee was formed to oppose U.S. participation in the war. Led by such celebrities as Charles Lindbergh, the committee galvanized the remaining opposition to war.

In early spring 1941 the United States took a giant step toward more direct involvement with passage of the Lend-Lease Act, which empowered the president to sell, lend, or otherwise dispose of defense materials to any country deemed strategic to American defenses. The original sum made available for this aid was set at $1.3 billion, but it quickly ballooned. As shipments to Britain increased, so did the risk to U.S. ships that had to cross the submarine-infested waters around the British Isles. Over the summer the United States began escorting convoys of merchant ships; by fall, the Navy had engaged in skirmishes with German submarines.

The Japanese decided the timing of America's actual entry into the war in dramatic fashion. Over the summer of 1941, Roosevelt announced that he would freeze the assets of the Japanese and end all trade in strategic materials if Japan proceeded to attack the French colonies in Indochina. When the Japanese imperial armies moved in this direction, the president acted. Although the Japanese continued to negotiate, they were secretly preparing a broad attack on U.S., British, and French possessions in Asia. During the summer of 1941, U.S. intelligence broke the Japanese diplomatic code. Intercepted messages pointed to an attack in early winter. On November 27, 1941, Washington warned commanders in the Pacific. Minimum defense steps were taken at the giant naval base at Pearl Harbor, Hawaii, including the fatal bunching together of fighter planes to prevent sabotage.

On December 7, again by decoding Japanese diplomatic messages, the United States learned of an impending attack. Washington sent out alerts to the Pacific, but these failed to reach the commanders in Hawaii on time. Even radar failed to detect the first wave of bombers and fighters that took off in early morning from the Japanese fleet lying secretly about 250 miles north of the Hawaiian island of Oahu.

Three waves of fighters and dive bombers plunged down out of the calm Sunday morning sky. The attack lasted about two hours. When it was over, the Japanese had devastated the Navy air force, killed 2,403 Americans (about 1,000 of whom died when the battleship *Arizona* exploded), and sunk or damaged the bulk of the U.S. Pacific fleet. Other U.S. bases and possessions came under attack. Wake Island fell, and

Salvage operations after the Japanese attack on Pearl Harbor, December 7, 1941. The tangled wreckage of two destroyers, the *Downes* and the *Cassin*, are in the foreground. Behind them is the battleship *U.S.S. Pennsylvania*, only lightly touched. Much of the American Pacific fleet was destroyed in the raid. (Franklin D. Roosevelt Library, Hyde Park, NY)

Roosevelt ordered General Douglas MacArthur to move his command from the threatened Philippines to Australia. By May the Philippines had fallen and the Japanese had taken most of the territory in their master plan. They now turned to menace Australia and India.

Despite these early successes, the Japanese had achieved a precarious victory at best. But their attacks exposed the weak defenses and inadequate planning of American forces in the Pacific. They also mobilized American public opinion. Roosevelt denounced the "sudden criminal attacks perpetrated by the Japanese in the Pacific" and asked for a declaration of war. On December 11, Hitler joined his Japanese ally and declared war on the United States.

Expansion of the armed services had begun before the United States entered the war. The

Army had reached 1.4 million men by July 1941. But after total mobilization, this number moved up rapidly. By 1945 over 8 million men were in the Army. (The Women's Army Corps—WAC—reached about 100,000 at this time.) The Navy experienced a similar expansion, reaching 3.4 million, with the Marines constituting about 500,000 of this total. The Air Force (administratively part of the Army) also expanded rapidly.

Military service touched all populations in America. By the end of the war about 1 million black Americans had participated in the various services, for example. The American armed forces in World War II mixed ethnic groups and social class, but in a curious way. Universal conscription threw together Northerners and Southerners, autoworkers and college professors. But if this necessitated a kind of melting pot culture in the barracks, it did not mean that democracy or racial harmony prevailed. For example, black soldiers were segregated into units commanded by white officers. Often they were relegated to stevedore or construction work. Japanese Americans were placed in special ethnic units such as the Nisei 442 Infantry Regiment that fought in Italy. Thus, despite the commitment to defeat Nazism—the most virulent racism of the twentieth century—few Americans saw anything paradoxical in establishing and maintaining racial segregation throughout the military. This is even more curious because American war films often pictured foxholes as representative democracies, and such films as *Bataan* (1943) even implied that racial integration existed where it clearly did not.

Once the United States had entered the war, Roosevelt decided on a strategy of attrition to defeat the Axis powers. He planned an enormous economic effort in which superior resources, supplies, productivity, organization, and scientific breakthroughs would overwhelm the enemy. This emphasis on weapons, he believed, would minimize American casualties. With this aim in mind, he authorized the secret building of the atomic bomb. His commitment made the factory assembly lines as important as the front lines of fighting men.

THE WARTIME ECONOMY The war buildup also meant new federal economic controls. After Pearl Harbor, Congress granted sweeping powers to the executive branch. On January 16, 1942, Roosevelt created the War Production Board, which had the power to channel civilian production into armaments manufacture and to contract for the construction of new defense plants. With the massive reorientation of production, the draft of millions of men, and a rise in employment, the United States suddenly faced labor shortages. War orders wiped away the huge unemployment left from the depression. The War Manpower Commission was organized to recruit new workers for the booming defense sector.

The largest pool of potential employees was women, and millions of them eagerly took over jobs in aircraft, shipbuilding, and munitions plants. They went to vocational schools and learned trades and skills that transformed their lives. They were crucial in building the vast array of weapons that poured from the factories. They constructed B-29 bombers like the *Enola Gay* that carried the first atomic bomb; they built the tanks and ships that shattered the Nazi armies and the Japanese navy.

While the employment of women in factories was expected to be temporary, it had profound and lasting effects. Several million women attended vocational schools. As early as 1942, over 35 percent of the American work force was female. By the end of the war, surveys revealed, a majority of these working women hoped to keep their positions. But telltale signs during the war suggested that "Rosie the Riveter" would eventually be pushed aside. Differential wages for men and women, hostility in the workplace, antagonism from unions, and, most of all, failure of the Roosevelt administration to support the Equal Rights Amendment to the Constitution (part of the 1944 Democratic national platform) suggested that gains made could be undone.

The other large group of potential workers were African Americans. At first, they were generally excluded from defense employment opportunities. But A. Philip Randolph of the

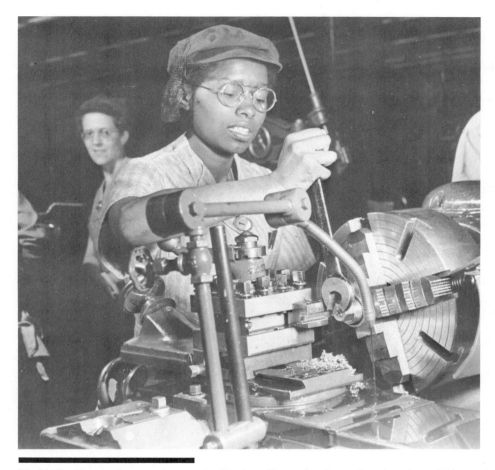

World War II opened economic opportunities to millions of underemployed workers. African Americans from the South joined the many women streaming into defense plants. (Franklin D. Roosevelt Library, Hyde Park, NY)

Brotherhood of Sleeping Car Porters threatened a protest march on Washington in the summer of 1941 unless equality of employment was offered. This helped persuade Roosevelt to order integration of defense industries. By the end of the war, hundreds of thousands of black workers had found jobs in war production. Despite these gains, however, they continued to suffer discrimination in the workplace and in housing. Racial tension often erupted when they took new jobs or moved into new areas to work in defense industries. Such was the case in Detroit in June

1943, when a bloody race riot broke out that had to be quelled by troops.

Eventually, full employment and shortages of consumer items like automobiles fueled inflation and labor unrest. The federal government stepped in here too, setting up the War Labor Board in January 1942 to prevent strikes and runaway wages. After several skirmishes with labor, the board established the "Little Steel" formula, worked out first for smaller steel-producing companies. This formula, which applied to other industries as well, placed a limit on pay hikes.

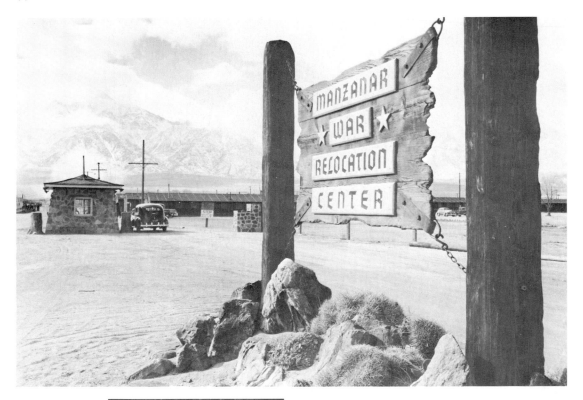

This simple, wooden sign, posted in the desert, marked the entrance to the Manzanar relocation center for Japanese families uprooted from their homes, primarily in the Los Angeles area. Other camps housed still more Japanese Americans, rounded up and deported from the coastal areas of the western United States. (Library of Congress)

Labor disputes did not disappear, but in general, the War Labor Board did much to ease the pressure on wages, and it allowed unions to raise their membership extensively.

Another new agency, the Office of Price Administration, tried to limit price rises by setting maximum prices for standard items. It also oversaw the rationing of scarce items such as coffee, canned foods (to save tin), shoes, and gasoline (to save rubber tires). Although many workers earned more money than before the war, there were few goods to spend it on; even a thriving black market could not supply them.

Extensive government control over the economy was matched by increased federal attention to shaping public opinion and preventing possible subversion. In this climate, civil liberties suf-

fered. Of course the military censored news from the front. There was little serious opposition to the war, but even so, the administration overreacted as demands for security and secrecy increased. For example, it brought a group of inconsequential American fascists and right-wing opponents of the war to trial.

JAPANESE-AMERICAN INTERNMENT

Much more serious was the treatment of Japanese Americans. In early 1942, American commanders on the West Coast argued that Japanese residents must be removed. This fear of sabotage scarcely concealed a long-standing racial antipathy toward the Japanese in California. (There was no corresponding internment of Japanese

Howard Y. Miyake, a Japanese American, receives the Silver Star from U.S. Army Colonel Lee D. Cady. Some Japanese Americans were allowed to participate in units in the European theater. (National Archives)

residents of Hawaii, where race relations were better.)

Thus, on February 19, 1942, President Roosevelt issued Executive Order #9066, which permitted removal of alien Japanese, Germans, Italians, and all persons of Japanese ancestry, whether citizens or not, from any "military area." These sensitive areas included California and parts of Oregon, Washington, and Arizona. In practice, exceptions were made for other groups so that only the Japanese were actually removed.

This policy may have had military considerations as its justification, but it also continued a history of exclusion and racial segregation. In 1924 Congress had denied further immigration to the Japanese, abrogating a "gentlemen's agreement" of 1907–08 between the United States and Japan in which Japan promised to restrict immigration. Despite the burden of this history and various local laws that discriminated, the Japanese community had achieved considerable

success in agriculture and small businesses. Their largest communities were centered largely around Los Angeles and Seattle, with much smaller contingents in San Francisco.

By June 1942 over 100,000 had been forcibly removed, their property and jobs stripped away. Most were placed in ten crude, dusty Army camps and provided with tarpaper barracks, cots, common toilets, and shared bathing and laundry facilities.

One internee recalled a camp set on a bleak plain behind Los Angeles:

There was a lack of privacy when we first went to Manzanar. The barracks were not actually completed. There were terrible wind storms that swept through the Owens Valley which brought dust through the cracks in the door. I think there were two months running where we suffered from diarrhea. The food was not properly prepared.

Many of the internees gained their release before the end of the war, but few ever recovered their farms, businesses, or homes. In 1988 Congress passed a law apologizing to Japanese Americans and promised $20,000 in compensation for each internee.

The War in Europe

While the administration worked to organize production, it defined its strategy to win the war. In practical terms, the United States had disagreements with both of its major allies. Roosevelt opposed Britain's desire to hold on to its vast colonial empire. And he was reluctant to allow the Russians to establish control over the invasion routes across eastern European nations. The president tried to circumvent potential friction through face-to-face encounters with Churchill and Stalin. Several conferences shaped the course of the war and established general principles for a peace settlement. In 1941, even before the United States entered the war, Churchill and Roosevelt met and signed the Atlantic Charter, a document that outlined international rights and responsibilities and promised self-determination, free trade, and the abandonment of force after the war. They also agreed to focus on defeating Germany first. Even after Pearl Harbor, this meant that a substantial portion of war supplies went to Britain and the Soviet Union; the Asian war took second place.

Churchill and Roosevelt made a second major decision at Casablanca, Morocco, in January 1943. There the two leaders agreed to demand unconditional surrender of the Axis powers in order to fix blame for the war on Hitler and Mussolini; no negotiated or partial peace with the fascist leaders would be tolerated.

For the Russians, the immediate and paramount problem was the opening of a second front—by an Allied invasion of France—so as to divert the German armies and relieve the enormous pressure that Hitler had brought to bear on the Soviet Union. The Russians were reeling before the German onslaught, sustaining huge casualties and losses of territory. A longer-range Russian desire was to gain control of those areas through which the Germans had twice invaded during the twentieth century.

Roosevelt and the U.S. Army commander, Dwight Eisenhower, agreed with the proposal for a second front, but Churchill twice convinced Roosevelt to postpone a landing, arguing that preparations remained incomplete. In August 1942 Churchill explained to Stalin why the United States and Britain had chosen to invade North Africa instead of France. Preparations for the attack advanced, and in November 1942, Allied forces landed in French North Africa. At first, French troops loyal to the Vichy government resisted, but Eisenhower negotiated a capitulation with Admiral Jean François Darlan. American and British troops pushed into Tunisia to engage German forces led by General Erwin Rommel ("the Desert Fox"). By May 1943 the battle for North Africa had ended. Rommel was defeated and a large contingent of his army captured. But Russia still stood alone with no second front in sight.

Once again, in the spring of 1943, the western Allies postponed the invasion of France. This time the United States and Britain decided to attack Sicily and knock Italy out of the war. Once again, the Russians were angered and suspicious that Britain and the United States wanted them to continue to bear the brunt of the European struggle. Nonetheless, the Allied command went ahead; troops landed in Sicily on July 9, 1943, and took thirty-eight days to conquer the island, although the bulk of the German army escaped into Italy.

This victory led to the fall of the Italian fascist leader, Mussolini. A provisional government signed a peace treaty with the Allies on September 3, and Italy switched sides in the war. On the same day, British and American troops invaded Italy itself, and gradually they pushed a

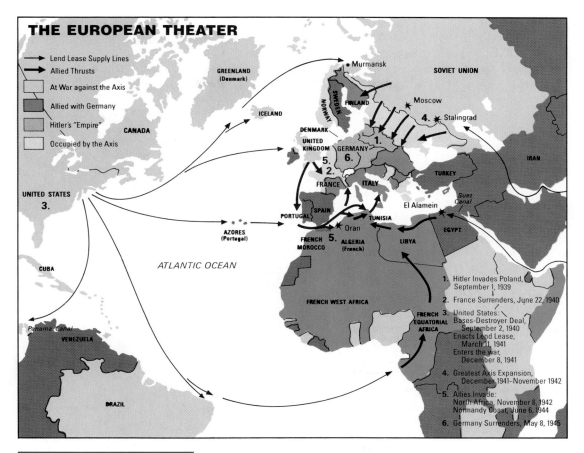

THE EUROPEAN THEATER

→ Lend Lease Supply Lines
→ Allied Thrusts
☐ At War against the Axis
■ Allied with Germany
▨ Hitler's "Empire"
☐ Occupied by the Axis

GREENLAND (Denmark)
ICELAND
CANADA
UNITED STATES
3.
AZORES (Portugal)
CUBA
Panama Canal
VENEZUELA
ATLANTIC OCEAN
BRAZIL
• Murmansk
SOVIET UNION
NORWAY SWEDEN FINLAND
Moscow
4. Stalingrad
DENMARK
UNITED KINGDOM GERMANY
5. 2.
1.
6.
FRANCE ITALY
PORTUGAL
SPAIN
FRENCH MOROCCO
5. Oran
ALGERIA (French)
TUNISIA
LIBYA
TURKEY
IRAN
El Alamein
Suez Canal
EGYPT
FRENCH WEST AFRICA
FRENCH EQUATORIAL AFRICA

1. Hitler Invades Poland, September 1, 1939
2. France Surrenders, June 22, 1940
3. United States: Bases-Destroyer Deal, September 2, 1940 Enacts Lend Lease, March 11, 1941 Enters the war, December 8, 1941
4. Greatest Axis Expansion, December 1941–November 1942
5. Allies Invade: North Africa, November 8, 1942 Normandy Coast, June 6, 1944
6. Germany Surrenders, May 8, 1945

The European theater. American strategy, once war was declared in Asia and Europe, necessitated a massive mobilization and military buildup. Since American productive supremacy in Asia was never in doubt, military planners emphasized the critical situation in Europe. Given their commitment to unconditional surrender, the Allies intended not only to defeat Germany and Italy but to destroy fascism. Their first object, however, was to relieve pressure at two critical points: on the Russian front and in northern Africa, where the Germans threatened to seize the Suez Canal.

fiercely entrenched German army toward the north. The British and Americans agreed to administer liberated portions of Italy jointly, excluding Russia from any significant participation in shaping postwar Italy. Stalin considered this a precedent for his treatment of eastern European nations liberated from the Germans by Soviet armies.

As German front lines in the east and in Italy receded, Hitler began the terror bombing of Eng-

land, using V-1 and, later, V-2 rockets. This belated attempt to terrify the British public did not, however, stanch German losses.

GERMANY CAPITULATES The western Allies finally launched the second front, in Operation Overlord, in early June 1944. When it came, it demonstrated masterly planning and execution. Although German defenders expected an

The landing by Allied troops in Normandy, France in 1944 required the huge movement of men and equipment and a mammoth effort of planning and coordination—one reason it came so late in the war. (Imperial War Museum)

attack, they misjudged its location. Allied troops established major beachheads in Normandy, designated by the Allied command as Utah and Omaha beaches. Landing massive amounts of materiel and troops, and protected by superior air cover, they fought their way inland. By late June the port of Cherbourg was liberated, then Caen in early July. A counterattack ordered by Hitler failed, and the Germans fell back rapidly. For the Nazis the war was over. The Russian armies, who had turned the tide of battle in late 1942, rushed toward Poland and eastern Germany. Paris was liberated on August 25, 1944, and the Germans retreated behind the Siegfried

Line along the German border. So hopeless was the war that a group of military officers attempted to assassinate Hitler on July 20 to hasten a German surrender.

In early 1945 Eisenhower ordered an offensive, moving into Germany and taking the Ruhr Valley during February and March. The Russians had entered Warsaw on January 17, and on April 13 they took Vienna. On April 30 Hitler committed suicide in his bunker in Berlin. At the last minute, German leaders offered to surrender to the United States, but Eisenhower refused. Germany had made war against all the Allies; Germany would have to surrender to all of them. Russian

The Tehran Conference, 1943. At meetings such as this one during the fall of 1943 in Tehran, Iran, Roosevelt (center) met with Russian Premier Joseph Stalin (left) and British Prime Minister Winston Churchill. Roosevelt hoped to use personal diplomacy to overcome the enormous differences in aims among the Allies. (Franklin D. Roosevelt Library, Hyde Park, NY)

troops took Berlin. Finally, on May 8, Germany surrendered. The Third Reich ended in flame and ruin. Allied troops finally stopped the murderous regime that in its frenzy had executed millions of Jews, Poles, gypsies, communists, and others.

Not only did Hitler prolong the war until every last pillbox and redoubt fell, his policy of exterminating Europe's Jews at death camps set up in eastern Europe continued methodically to the very end. When the holocaust ceased, this grotesque corruption of science, efficiency, and bureaucracy had eliminated 6 million men, women, and children, while the rest of the world, including the United States, did little to stop it or welcome Jewish refugees.

By May 1945, Allied armies occupied practically all of Europe—from France eastward through Poland and south through Italy. As the Allies had foreseen, this created immense political problems. Churchill, Stalin, and Roosevelt had tried to forestall some of these problems at

the Tehran Conference in 1943 and the Yalta meeting in February 1945. Roosevelt tried to restrain British hostility toward the Russians. (He had opposed Churchill's suggestions for an invasion of Germany through the eastern end of the Mediterranean to head off the Soviet forces.) Roosevelt hoped to accommodate Stalin and enlist his peaceful cooperation with the United States after the war. He had come to sympathize with the Russian desire to control the invasion routes of eastern Europe. And he encouraged Stalin to expect reparations to reconstruct his battered nation. In exchange, he hoped to secure Russian help against the Japanese in Asia. But Roosevelt did little to implement these policies and postponed hard decisions about redrawing European boundaries and reconstructing governments.

By the time of the Potsdam Conference, Germany had been defeated, Roosevelt was dead, and the new president, Harry Truman, had to make the decisions that Roosevelt had put off. Truman was more suspicious of Russian motives than Roosevelt had been, but more important, the United States now possessed a workable atomic bomb. But if the new president hoped this weapon would convince Stalin to compromise, he was mistaken. The most contentious issue was Poland. Occupying Russian forces changed the boundaries of that nation, incorporating eastern portions into the Soviet Union and pushing Poland's western boundaries to the Oder-Neisse line, thus giving them control over territory that had formerly been a part of Germany.

The issue of reparations also separated the Allies. Russia demanded huge compensation from Germany to restore some of the vast industrial losses it had suffered. But the amount and type of reparations could not be settled. Consequently, the Soviets dismantled factories in their zone of occupation and sent them eastward. On the issue of the occupation of Germany, the Allies agreed, after much dispute, to four zones: a Russian zone, including jointly controlled Berlin; a French zone, bordering on eastern France; an American zone in southern and central Germany; and a British zone to the north. But the alliance of convenience had degenerated swiftly into a contest between the United States and the Soviet Union, with each side blaming the other for blocking its legitimate aspirations, and with the atomic bomb playing a crucial role in the strategies of both sides.

The War in the Pacific

The war in the Pacific did not involve the Soviet Union until the very last days of the struggle. The chief burden of fighting the Japanese fell to the United States and China, with some aid from Australia and particularly from the British in areas like Burma. Although given a lower priority, the contest was bitter and protracted. American strategy, carried out by General Douglas MacArthur and Admiral Chester W. Nimitz, focused on seizing control of the air and the seas, retaking the Philippines, then moving from island chain to island chain toward Japan. This proved to be a brilliant strategy.

By midsummer of 1942 the Japanese advance in Southeast Asia had slowed. After furious fighting on land and sea, the United States held Guadalcanal in the Solomon Islands near Australia. By early 1943 the United States prepared to take the offensive. Gradually, American forces moved northward, skipping heavily fortified islands to outflank the Japanese. After several months of battle around the Philippine Islands, MacArthur finally retook Manila on March 4, 1944.

The island-hopping American forces, now superior against the crippled Japanese navy and air force, took Iwo Jima in early 1945 and Okinawa, near southern Japan, in April 1945. These conquests provided a final, crucial link in the American strategy: bases from which to bomb the Japanese homeland. From air bases on these islands and from Tinian and Saipan in the Marianas, new long-range B-29 bombers began to pound industrial and population centers in Japan. General Curtis E. LeMay took command of the bomber operations in late August 1944 and developed tactics that showed the terrible potential of the new planes. Using incendiary devices, LeMay began systematic attacks on Japanese cities designed to start fire storms. In March 1945, for example, B-29s destroyed about a quarter of the city of Tokyo. Still the Japanese refused to surrender and prepared for a desperate, even suicidal, defense of their island empire.

Air raids became more spectacular and punishing, culminating in the devastating attacks on Hiroshima and Nagasaki. Faced with obliteration from the skies and destruction of its armies by the Russians, the Japanese sued for peace on August 10. After maneuvering to save the Japa-

THE PACIFIC THEATER

INDIA
SINKIANG
TIBET
MONGOLIA
SOVIET UNION
ALASKA
CANADA

5.
MANCHUKUO
Beijing
SAKHALIN
KARAFUTO
BERING
SEA
ATTU
KISKA
ALEUTIANS
Dutch Harbor
Seattle
UNITED
STATES

BAY
OF
BENGAL
BURMA
Chungking
CHINA
KOREA
Vladivostok
KURILES

THAI-
LAND
INDO-
CHINA
Shanghai
Canton
Hong
Kong
FORMOSA
Nagasaki
6.
Hiroshima
JAPAN
Tokyo
OKINAWA

PACIFIC   OCEAN

San Francisco

SUMATRA
Singapore
Manila
PHILIPPINE I.
4.
LEYTE
IWO JIMA
MARIANA I.
SAIPAN
TINIAN
GUAM
YAP
2.
MIDWAY
HAWAIIAN I. (U.S.A.)
1.
Pearl Harbor
WAKE

BORNEO
JAVA
PALAU
CELEBES
TRUK
CAROLINE I.
ENIWETOK
MARSHALL I.
KWAJALEIN

INDIAN
OCEAN
Hollandia
NEW
GUINEA
SOLOMON I.
GUADALCANAL
GILBERT I.
HOWLAND I.
(U.S.A.)

Port
Moresby
3.
CORAL
SEA
NEW HEBRIDES
(Britain &
France)
FIJI I. (Britain)
TUTUILA
(U.S.A.)

AUSTRALIA

Sydney

NEW
ZEALAND

→ Allied Air Thrusts

➤ Allied Land or Naval Attacks

At War Against Japan, August 7, 1945

Japanese Empire, 1940

Occupied Areas, June 1942

◄---- Soviet Thrusts into Manchuria and Korea

◄······ Supply Lines

1. Japan Attacks Pearl Harbor, December 7, 1941

2. Greatest Japanese Expansion, June 1942

3. U.S. Forces Land on Guadalcanal, August 7, 1942

4. U.S. Forces Reoccupy the Philippines, October 1944

5. Soviet Union Enters the War, August 8, 1945

6. Atomic Bombs Dropped on Hiroshima and Nagasaki, August 1945

Japan Surrenders, September 2, 1945

nese emperor, the government capitulated August 14. Final surrender took place September 2 in Tokyo Bay, aboard the battleship *Missouri*.

The occupation and reconstruction of Japan remained principally an American task. The Soviets were not granted a share in the occupation, although by agreement they acquired important territory in northern China and on Sakhalin Island. By agreement also, Russian armies accepted the surrender of the Japanese north of the thirty-eighth parallel in Korea, while Americans administered the area to the south.

A more fundamental Asian problem was China. All Japanese troops in China were

Iwo Jima. This famous photograph of Marines raising the American flag on Mount Suribachi on February 23, 1945, marked the capture of the principal part of the island of Iwo Jima. Organized resistance collapsed on March 16. The battle, which was bitter and costly on both sides, gave the United States a major air base that was widely used in the last months of war. (The National Archives)

instructed to surrender to Chinese leader Chiang Kai-shek. But in northern China, communist rebel forces led by Mao Zedong took power from the Japanese and confiscated their war supplies. Troubled by conflict between these two Chinese factions during the war, the United States tried fruitlessly in 1945 to arrange a cease-fire while continuing to aid Chiang. But in late 1949 Chiang's corrupt and inefficient government was driven out of mainland China to the offshore island of Taiwan by the communists. Nothing short of full-scale intervention by the United States could have prevented this.

Demobilization and Postwar Allied Cooperation

Despite intensifying hostility between the United States and the Soviet Union in 1945, the United States proceeded rapidly to demobilize its war economy and armed forces. Even before Germany's surrender May 8, 1945, the Truman

The Japanese surrender. A party of Japanese officials surrenders to the Allies aboard the *U.S.S. Missouri* in Tokyo Bay on September 2, 1945, thus ending World War II. (Navy Department, in the National Archives)

administration began to cancel war orders and dismantle economic controls. By the end of 1945, most controls had been lifted and the economy was returning rapidly to civilian production. The American army demobilized under irresistible pressure from GIs and from their families at home. "Bring Back Daddy" clubs sprang up in the United States, and soldiers stationed abroad agitated for immediate release. Troops were hurried home and mustered out of the service as quickly as transportation could be arranged. Total personnel in the armed services fell from over 12 million in 1945 to 3 million in 1946 and 1.5 million in 1947.

But demobilization did not by any means imply that the federal government had suddenly ceased to intervene in the lives of Americans or in the economy. After a long debate, Congress agreed to the Employment Act of 1946, which pledged the government to maintaining an active role in directing the economy. Government officials also encouraged the shift of women out of the work force. The great and successful experiment in training and employing women was undone almost as fast as it had been achieved. Finally, defense spending and direction of scientific research in such fields as atomic energy required large expenditures and tight federal controls. Continued military production required that hundreds of decisions shaping the American economy be made in Washington. Even in the late 1940s, when defense spending was relatively low, it still consumed over 25 percent of the federal budget. And scientific research increasingly fell under the direction of federal agencies like the Atomic Energy Commission.

Young Mao Zedong, 1939. Chinese communist leader Mao Zedong found his greatest support among peasants and made them the basis for his opposition to the invading Japanese armies and the official Chinese government headed by Chiang Kai-shek. (UPI/Bettmann Newsphotos)

Other federal activities profoundly shaped the postwar world. To reward soldiers for their sacrifices, the U.S. government passed a generous bonus for returning soliders in the form of the Servicemen's Readjustment Act of 1944 (see p. 1002). State governments often added their own system of financial rewards and preferential hiring. Over 2 million soldiers used the GI Bill to attend college after 1946. The result was a significant democratization and expansion of American higher education.

Many Americans hoped that postwar peace could be maintained by the United Nations, a new institution organized around the wartime alliance against Germany and Japan. The UN Charter, signed in 1945, created two chambers: a Security Council and a General Assembly. The Security Council was made up of five permanent members (Britain, France, China, the United States, and the U.S.S.R.) and ten elected representatives of other nations. A permanent member could veto any Security Council undertaking. The General Assembly consisted of all member nations, each with one vote. But even in this peaceful endeavor, competition between the United States and Russia erupted. Finally, a compromise on membership was reached: The U.S.S.R. received three votes in the General Assembly (the Ukraine, Byelorussia, and the U.S.S.R.), and the United States secured membership for Argentina (a profascist power but counted as a friend of the U.S.) and ensured the legality of regional alliances like the Organization of American States.

On the trial of war criminals, the Allies remained united. After arresting German leaders in the summer of 1945 (those who had not committed suicide or escaped), the Allies opened trials in Nuremberg, Germany, in November. Four judges—one each from Britain, France, the

United States, and the U.S.S.R.—presided over the hearings. Prosecutors accused Nazi officials of crimes against peace (for undertaking aggressive war), breaches of accepted war conduct, and crimes against humanity in the death camps.

The first Nuremberg trial lasted 216 days; on October 1, 1946, 19 of 22 defendants were found guilty; 12 were sentenced to hanging, 3 to life imprisonment, and 4 to long prison terms. In addition, the judges declared 4 Nazi organizations to be criminal in character. In Japan much the same procedure was followed. When all the trials ended in 1949, 2,647 persons had been convicted, with 689 death sentences handed down. The purpose had been to stamp war guilt irrevocably on the German and Japanese leadership and to proclaim wars of aggression to be illegal.

Cold War in Europe

Despite agreements between the United States and the Soviet Union, a cold war quickly developed in international relations. On Roosevelt's death in 1945, Truman came into office ill prepared in foreign policy matters, yet facing urgent unfinished business. Sentiment to return to prewar neutrality was overpowered by the sense that the United States had to enforce its own interests and goals upon a turbulent world. This meant that the United States remained on a semiwar footing. Naturally, secret weapons research and development became a high policy priority. Just as inevitably, the federal government retained much of the power over research, allocation of resources, and direction of the economy that it had acquired during the war.

The impetus for military security also generated an atmosphere of suspicion. The arms race that had once been directed against the Germans now resumed against the Russians. But the growing sophistication of weaponry only increased the vulnerability that many Americans felt. Every

confrontation with the Russians stimulated the arms race and underscored the necessity for secrecy. More and more, these demands for control strained the assumption that a peacetime society ought to tolerate dissent and free scientific inquiry. The bitter conflict even convinced some Americans that they should try to define the purposes of their society more narrowly and perhaps exclude from it those who did not appear to agree.

Disputes between the United States and the Soviet Union at first focused on the restoration of Europe. The frightful destruction of war had created economic havoc in Germany, France, and eastern Europe. Political instability in France, Italy, and Greece brought local communists close to power. In Greece, civil war broke out in 1946 between British-backed royalist forces and communist-supported insurgents. But Great Britain was exhausted by the struggle against Germany and too feeble to play more than a minor role in Greece. Either the United States or the Soviet Union would fill the vacuum.

To exercise a decisive role in Europe, the Truman administration had to overcome several problems. One was traditional American reluctance to become involved in European politics. Truman eventually won the support of Republicans for a new activist policy in Europe. A second problem was the rapid disintegration of American military preparedness. The president could not rely on conventional military forces to oppose the Russians in Europe. As a result, the temporary monopoly on the atomic bomb and the defense potential of the American economy were crucial to foreign policy decisions.

At the war's end in Europe, the Soviet Union occupied Rumania, Hungary, Czechoslovakia, and Poland, and in these nations Stalin insisted on governments friendly to the U.S.S.R. Given the traditional bitterness toward the Russians in these areas, this often meant that only communists were willing to play such a role. And the placement of communists in power contradicted American desires for free elections and wholly independent nations in the area.

Federal Research and Development Funds, 1947–70
(in Millions of Dollars)

Year	Total for R&D	For Defense	For AEC*	For NSF†
1947	619.5	469.3	39.9	—
1953	3,106.0	2,577.3	309.9	2.3
1959	6,693.5	5,161.6	699.8	60.4
1965	14,614.3	6,796.5‡	1,240.7	187.2
1970	15,340.3	7,360.4‡	1,346.0	289.0

*Atomic Energy Commission.
†National Science Foundation.
‡After 1962, large amounts of research and development funds were funneled to the National Aeronautics and Space Administration (NASA). Some of these funds, because of their application to missile development, may be considered defense expenditures.

Source: U.S. Bureau of the Census, *Historical Statistics of the United States* (Washington, D.C.: U.S. Government Printing Office, 1975), Part 2, p. 966.

Acrimony between America and Russia broke out in a dispute over control of Iranian oil resources in early 1946. Russia had stationed several thousand troops in northern Iran but were eventually compelled to withdraw them. Negotiations at the United Nations over internationalization of atomic energy control failed in the early summer. And the United States rejected a Soviet request for a large loan to help rebuild its shattered economy. As prospects for a comprehensive peace receded, the United States and the Soviet Union began to create separate political and economic institutions in their German occupation zones.

In these trying times, Americans attempted to understand how the peace of 1945 had become so fragile. In a speech on March 5, 1946, Winston Churchill provided language that seemed to describe what had happened to the world. Speaking of Russian influence in eastern Europe, Churchill warned that "an iron curtain has descended" across Europe. Probably more influential in defining American policy toward the Soviet Union were ideas authored by George Kennan, counselor at the American embassy in Moscow. First in a long telegram in 1946 and then

in an essay published under the pseudonym "Mister X," Kennan provided a plausible rationale for American foreign policy. He argued that the United States had to "contain" Soviet influence and hope that this action would cause Russia to change internally. A number of American leaders were convinced by this notion of containment, although they often exaggerated its military aspects.

In early 1947, Kennan's principle of containment became a fundamental part of American foreign policy. This occurred in two ways. On March 12, 1947, the president announced the Truman Doctrine, which promised aid to Greece in its struggle against insurgents. Truman argued that the world was divided between two types of societies: Western democratic capitalist nations and Eastern communist nations. The outcome of the struggle between the two sides in Europe, he proclaimed, was "of grave importance in a much wider situation." Truman asked for military assistance for Greece and Turkey, and Congress obliged by voting funds on May 15.

Truman put forward the second stage of his policy in early summer. George Marshall—formerly a general, now secretary of state—pro-

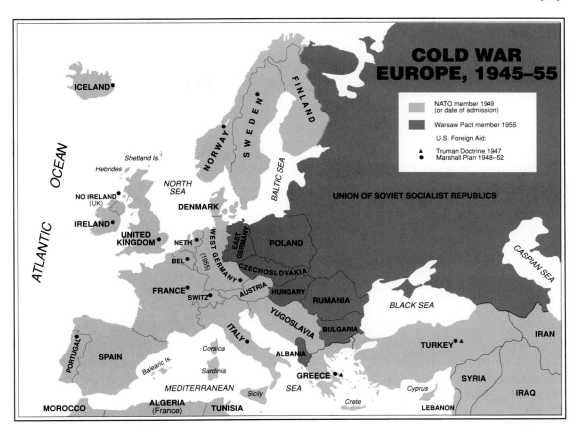

posed a plan of economic assistance for western Europe. The Marshall Plan, as it became known, promised to revive the economy of Europe and eliminate conditions that communist politicians could exploit. The program even offered economic assistance to the Soviet Union and its allies, but they refused. And Communist parties in Western countries like France demonstrated against the plan. Nonetheless, sixteen European nations eventually agreed to a joint plan for economic recovery, signed in September 1947. Congress funded the project in March 1948.

The Soviets responded to the growing integration of the western European nations by increasing their control of occupied territories such as Poland, Czechoslovakia, and Hungary. In 1948, with the United States and western European nations contemplating a military alliance,

with the Soviets' former ally Yugoslavia pursuing an independent course, and with the integration of the separate western zones of Germany to form one single political and economic entity, Stalin acted. After the United States introduced a single West German currency into West Berlin in late June, the Russians clamped a blockade on all ground and water entrances into the city. Truman had to make the next move: either abandon Berlin or force a reopening of supply routes.

The American president chose a third way. He initiated a massive airlift to supply the city. Finally, in the spring of 1949 the Russians lifted their ineffective blockade. Not only had Stalin's tactics failed, they had helped pressure Western nations into forming the North Atlantic Treaty Organization (NATO) in mid-1949. Britain, France, Belgium, the Netherlands, Luxembourg,

Berlin airlift: "Operation Vittles." Faced with the Russian blockade of Berlin, President Truman might have acquiesced in Soviet control over the divided city, or he might have forced open trade routes by military means. Instead, he chose a third alternative—the highly successful and dramatic supply of the American, French, and British sectors of the city by air. (UPI/Bettmann Newsphotos)

Portugal, Denmark, Norway, Italy, Iceland, Canada, and the United States joined. West Germany was admitted in 1954. This formal alliance became the mainstay of America's European policy and effectively prevented further deterioration of U.S. influence in Europe.

In September 1949, Truman announced that the Russians had exploded an atomic bomb. The short-lived American monopoly had been broken. The president ordered American scientists to begin serious development of hydrogen weapons to regain U.S. supremacy. In four short years, the peace of 1945 had degenerated into a new arms race and new entangling alliances.

The Korean War

The defeat of Chiang Kai-shek in 1949 touched off recriminations in the United States over who had "lost" China to the communists. In Asia, the victory of Mao Zedong created a major new revolutionary force. In this context, the Truman administration faced a serious crisis in June 1950. For two years the divided sections of Korea had glowered at each other with increasing hostility. Separated only by the thirty-eighth parallel as

A Korean War scene. A familiar sight during war on the Asian mainland in World War II and then the Korean conflict: Soldiers advanced to the front lines while civilians fled in the opposite direction, carrying what possessions they could. (UPI/Bettmann Newsphotos)

part of the postwar settlement, two nations had sprung up: North Korea, supported by the Russians, and South Korea, dependent on the United States. On June 25, 1950, North Korean troops plunged into the south. Truman had to decide quickly: stand and fight, risking a large-scale Asian war, or abandon an ally. Because of withering criticism of his foreign policy by Republicans and public doubts about the loyalty of some members of his government, Truman probably had no real choice.

The Korean conflict employed many of the weapons and tactics developed during the total war experience of World War II, but on a limited terrain and for limited goals. It was to prove a model for a series of later military encounters. This contradiction between potential means and narrow goals meant, for example, that the United States rejected use of the atomic bomb against

North Korea and communist China. It meant, also, that each side operated from privileged sanctuaries: the United States from naval and air bases in Japan, and the Chinese from behind their border at the Yalu River on the northern edge of North Korea. The battlefield in Korea, however, witnessed a war that was as bitter and bloody as World War II.

On June 27 President Truman called on Douglas MacArthur, commander of U.S. Armed Forces in the Far East, to support South Korea. The United Nations (with the Soviet Union absent because of a boycott) voted to demand North Korean evacuation and offered supporting troops. Eventually, small contributions came from France, Britain, Turkey, Greece, New Zealand, the Netherlands, Belgium, Ethiopia, and others. Most of the troops, however, were supplied by the United States and South Korea.

General Douglas MacArthur. General Douglas MacArthur was chief of Southwest Pacific operations in World War II, administrator of postwar Japan, and commander of United Nations forces in Korea. Because he disagreed with the limited American objectives in the Korean conflict—and said so publicly—President Truman removed him from command. (UPI/Bettmann Newsphotos)

Hemmed in by the continued communist offensive, American and South Korean troops retreated to the area in the extreme south around Pusan. But on September 15, 1950, the American army took the offensive. At the same time, a surprise amphibious landing near Seoul at Inchon, behind communist lines, broke North Korea's offensive and shattered its army. United Nations troops drove rapidly to the north and crossed the thirty-eighth parallel into North Korea, capturing the capital, Pyongyang, on October 20.

General MacArthur, after conferring with President Truman, drove farther north on two fronts toward the border of China. His purpose was to destroy the North Korean army. Disregarding warnings from the Chinese communists, he approached the Yalu River border. On November 25, Chinese troops, ferried across the river, attacked in force, compelling the UN troops to

retreat to the thirty-eighth parallel. MacArthur's brilliant victory at Inchon was thus undercut by his grave miscalculation.

Offensive and counteroffensive followed. MacArthur's outspoken advocacy of a wider war made his dismissal by Truman in April 1951 inevitable, if very unpopular. Costly battles pushed the front back and forth over the thirty-eighth parallel until July 1953, when a permanent armistice line was established somewhat north of the original line. For this eventual small exchange of territory there were perhaps 1.5 million casualties on the communist side and perhaps 450,000 on the UN side (including 33,710 Americans killed in action and several thousand more who died as prisoners of war). In terms of tactics and materiel, the United States Navy had completely dominated sea lanes and harassed North Korean coastal installations at will. The United States had

THE KOREAN WAR, 1950–53

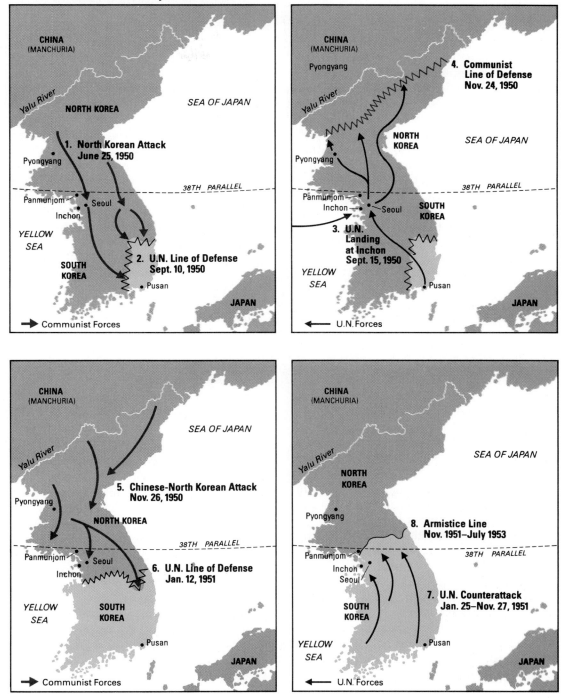

Map 1:
CHINA (MANCHURIA)
Yalu River
NORTH KOREA
SEA OF JAPAN
Pyongyang
38TH PARALLEL
1. North Korean Attack June 25, 1950
Panmunjom
Seoul
Inchon
YELLOW SEA
SOUTH KOREA
2. U.N. Line of Defense Sept. 10, 1950
Pusan
JAPAN
→ Communist Forces

Map 2:
CHINA (MANCHURIA)
Pyongyang
Yalu River
NORTH KOREA
SEA OF JAPAN
4. Communist Line of Defense Nov. 24, 1950
38TH PARALLEL
Panmunjom
Inchon
Seoul
SOUTH KOREA
3. U.N. Landing at Inchon Sept. 15, 1950
YELLOW SEA
Pusan
JAPAN
← U.N. Forces

Map 3:
CHINA (MANCHURIA)
Yalu River
SEA OF JAPAN
5. Chinese-North Korean Attack Nov. 26, 1950
Pyongyang
NORTH KOREA
38TH PARALLEL
Panmunjom
Seoul
Inchon
6. U.N. Line of Defense Jan. 12, 1951
YELLOW SEA
SOUTH KOREA
Pusan
JAPAN
→ Communist Forces

Map 4:
CHINA (MANCHURIA)
Yalu River
NORTH KOREA
SEA OF JAPAN
Pyongyang
8. Armistice Line Nov. 1951–July 1953
Panmunjom
38TH PARALLEL
Inchon
Seoul
7. U.N. Counterattack Jan. 25–Nov. 27, 1951
SOUTH KOREA
YELLOW SEA
Pusan
JAPAN
← U.N. Forces

also controlled the air over North Korea, although U.S. Saber Jet fighters met stiff resistance from Russian MIG planes stationed at bases inside China.

By the middle of 1953 the first armed confrontation between the United States and communist troops had finally ended. War had been confined to a small portion of the globe. The United States and the Soviet Union had avoided using the doomsday weapons that they now possessed in abundance. But the arms race and the cold war became, if anything, more serious in a divided and restless world. Peace was further away than it had been in 1945 when the war ended—and when American scientists had developed a weapon to end all wars.

Cold War at Home

At home, worry about military secrets and ideological purity increased. J. Robert Oppenheimer was not the only American to fall under scrutiny during this security-conscious era. In 1950 Julius and Ethel Rosenberg were arrested and convicted of passing atomic secrets to the Russians. They were executed in 1953. From 1949 to the mid-1950s, suspicion of communism focused on schools, teachers, books, and government workers. Charges of communist infiltration into the government and into the Democratic party became an effective campaign slogan, especially for opportunistic Senator Joseph McCarthy of Wisconsin. But McCarthyism became a corrosive element in politics because it also fed on the insecurities of Americans who were uneasy about rapid social change. Groups reluctant to accept the admission of labor unions or blacks into the American political consensus sometimes saw the hand of communist conspirators behind these

movements. It was no accident that segregationists charged that integration was a communist plot or that some Americans feared that the United Nations was communist-dominated.

In this charged atmosphere President Truman saw his task principally as defending the Democratic party against accusations of being "soft" on communism. This helps explain his swift, early action on federal employee loyalty. In 1946 he appointed a Temporary Commission on Employee Loyalty to design a security program. Following the commission's suggestions, he asked the attorney general to draw up a list of subversive organizations. He also established federal departmental loyalty boards that checked each employee. Five years later, about 20,000 federal workers had been screened: a little over half had been cleared, 3,000 cases were still pending, 2,500 employees had left service voluntarily, and 400 had been dismissed.

Despite Truman's extensive and overzealous scrutiny of federal workers, Congress, the Republican party, and a substantial part of public opinion remained skeptical. Between 1945 and 1952 over eighty congressional investigations of communism were held. Many of them explored federal agencies. The most important of these inquiries were held by the House Un-American Activities Committee (HUAC). Very little legislation emerged from this committee, but it did provide a forum to attack Truman. And some conservative Southerners on HUAC used the committee to charge that integration was un-American.

The principal anticommunist, antisubversive legislation of the era came in 1950 with the passage of the Internal Security Act. The bill required the Justice Department to register the names, finances, and membership of all communist or front groups. All literature from these groups passing through the mail was to be stamped "Communist." Known party members could not obtain passports. Most controversial was a provision to set aside internment camps for suspected disloyal Americans in time of emergency.

Edward R. Murrow

Radio, if it is to serve and survive, must hold a mirror behind the nation and the world. If the reflection shows racial intolerance, economic inequality, bigotry, unemployment, or anything else, let the people see it—or rather, hear it. The mirror must have no curves, and must be held with a steady hand.

With these words, Edward R. Murrow, shortly after World War II, explained the responsibilities of radio news reporting in America. However, the vitality and incisiveness of the news depended on who held the mirror. When it was Murrow, the result was bound to be brilliant and controversial.

Ed Murrow was born in rural North Carolina in 1908. In 1913 his family moved to Washington State. In high school he joined the debating team. In college, at Washington State University, he worked in the new field of radio. As a result of his election as president of the National Student Federation, he moved to New York City in 1930.

In 1935 CBS hired Murrow to be "director of talks"—that is, head of news features. Two years later, CBS sent him to England as its chief European correspondent. This job carried enormous prestige and responsibility. Murrow was the perfect reporter for the disintegrating world situation—from his trenchcoat, to the smoldering cigarette forever dangling from his lips, to a voice that conveyed worldliness and fatigue.

For many Americans, Murrow's was the grim voice of the war. He broadcast the retreat at Dunkirk; he recorded the blitz over London. He flew on a bombing mission over Berlin. When the war ended, he accompanied American troops into the Nazi concentration camp at Buchenwald. Throughout these trying times, his stand was clear. His trademark was informed opinion; his was no world for neutrals.

In 1946 Murrow returned to a desk job with CBS and then became producer of the news program *Hear It Now*. In November 1951 Murrow entered the new medium of television with *See It Now*. This enormously successful show established the general format for other television documentaries and news programs. Murrow appeared weekly, his film clips interspliced with critical commentary. In October 1953 he developed another new format, *Person to Person*, an interview program with celebrities such as Senator John F. Kennedy and movie star Marilyn Monroe.

In March 1954 Murrow ran a critical exposé of Senator Joseph McCarthy. Murrow spoke calmly but acidly about the senator's activities while showing him harassing witnesses at government investigations. McCarthy and his allies were furious. But Murrow's impact and continued popularity contrasted with McCarthy's sudden loss of popularity. In the contest for credibility, Murrow had won.

Nevertheless, CBS, its sponsors, and much of the mass media establishment began to frown on Murrow. As television evolved toward quiz shows and situation comedies like *The $64,000 Question* and *The Beverly Hillbillies*, Murrow's tough journalism seemed out of step. A symbol of war and cold war, with a critical roving eye willing to expose America's faults, Murrow lost influence after the early 1960s. He remained greatly admired for his integrity, but he was a man who belonged to an earlier age.

CHRONOLOGY

1940 United States begins serious atomic weapons research.

May 1940 Germans conquer Holland and Belgium.

September 1940 Destroyers-for-bases deal between FDR and England.

Fall 1940 Battle of Britain.

November 1940 FDR elected to third term as president.

1942 Manhattan Project commences.

May 1942 Philippines captured by Japanese.

June 1942 Japanese Americans interned in security camps.

August 1942 U.S. Pacific offensive begins with attack on Guadalcanal.

1944 United States begins construction of an atomic bomb.

June 6, 1944 Allied offensive forces land in Normandy.

August 1944 Paris liberated from Germans.

1945–46 Nuremberg war trials held.

1945–47 American armed forces demobilized.

1946 George Kennan calls for "containment" policy.

1946 Atomic Energy Commission established.

March 1946 Winston Churchill sounds alarm about "iron curtain."

August 1946 John Hersey publishes *Hiroshima*.

| 1939 | 1940 | 1941 | 1942 | 1943 | 1944 | 1945 | 1946 |

1931 Japan invades Manchuria.

1939 Hitler conquers Czechoslovakia.

August 1939 German-Soviet Non-Aggression Pact.

September 1, 1939 Hitler invades Poland; World War II begins.

September 3, 1939 France and Britain declare war on Germany.

1941 Britain begins atomic development program called MAUD.

March 1941 Lend-lease program enacted.

June 1941 Germany invades the Soviet Union.

August 1941 Atlantic Charter meeting between FDR and Churchill.

December 7, 1941 Japanese attack Pearl Harbor.

1943 Casablanca and Tehran Conferences held.

1943 Allies recapture North Africa.

June 1943 Detroit race riot.

September 1943 Italy changes sides in the war; Mussolini executed.

1945 United Nations founded.

February 1945 Yalta Conference held.

May 8, 1945 Germany surrenders: V-E (victory in Europe) Day.

July 1945 Atomic bomb successfully tested at Alamogordo, New Mexico.

July 1945 Potsdam Conference held.

August 1945 Atomic bombs dropped on Hiroshima and Nagasaki.

August 14, 1945 Japan surrenders; V-J (victory over Japan) Day.

1950 National Science Foundation established. Julius and Ethel Rosenberg convicted of espionage charges.

January 1950 Alger Hiss convicted of perjury.

February 1950 Senator Joseph McCarthy begins crusade against communism.

1948–49 Berlin blockade.

June 1950 Korean conflict begins.

1950–53 United States participates in Korean conflict.

1947	1948	1949	1950	1951	1952	1953	1954	1955

March 1947 Truman Doctrine announced.

1949 Nationalist Chinese flee mainland for Taiwan.

July 1953 Korean cease-fire signed.

1955 "Hiroshima maidens" come to America.

1947–48 Marshall Plan for western Europe enacted.

1949 North Atlantic Treaty Organization formed.

1953 The Rosenbergs executed.

1949 Russians test atomic bomb.

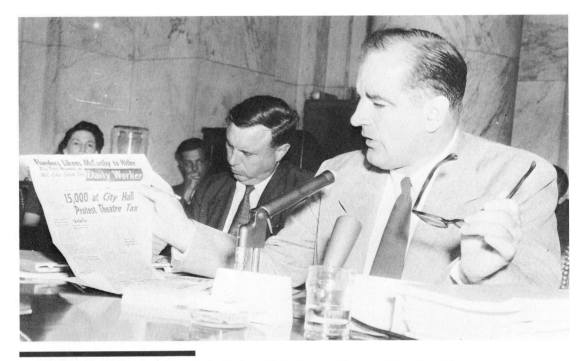

Senator Joseph McCarthy and the *Daily Worker*. McCarthy used Communist party publications such as the *Worker* during Senate hearings to cast suspicion on his opponents. Favorable mention in such a publication would often bring charges of disloyalty from the Wisconsin senator. (Wide World Photos)

Truman angrily vetoed the act, saying that it subverted elementary ideas of a free society. Congress thought otherwise and overrode his veto.

The Internal Security Act symbolized Congress's growing initiative on the anticommunist front. In 1948 Alger Hiss, a minor New Deal adviser and well-connected lawyer, had been charged with passing secrets to the Russians in the late 1930s. His accuser was Whittaker Chambers, a self-confessed spy, a man of many aliases, a writer and later an editor for *Time* magazine. Chambers accused Hiss before HUAC and then in public, on NBC's *Meet the Press*. Hiss sued for libel, but in 1950 he was charged with and convicted of perjury. HUAC investigators, led by

Congressman Richard Nixon, established a strong circumstantial case to fit Chambers's eyewitness accounts. Truman, Secretary of State Dean Acheson, and many liberals refused to believe in Hiss's guilt. But their attitude only increased the desire of some congressmen like McCarthy to expose communists in government. By 1952, issues of defense, secrecy, and spying threatened to overwhelm American political discussion. Under the circumstances, the commitment to building more bombs and maintaining secrets was hardly questioned. Only a few short years after the end of the war, fear and suspicion had invaded American policy at home and abroad.

Suggestions for Further Reading

HIROSHIMA AND THE ATOMIC BOMB

The effect on American society of building and deploying nuclear weapons is difficult to overestimate. Martin J. Sherwin, *A World Destroyed: The Atomic Bomb and the Grand Alliance* (1975), is an insightful account of the creation of the first atomic weapons. Gregg Herken, *The Winning Weapon: The Atomic Bomb in the Cold War, 1945–1950* (1980), details the role of nuclear weapons in policymaking. Of the many accounts describing the effects of the bomb, John Hersey, *Hiroshima* (1946), is the most personal and poignant.

WORLD WAR II AND ITS EFFECTS

For an accessible and comprehensive discussion of battles and strategies during the war, Richard Ernest and Trevor N. Dupuy, *Encyclopedia of Military History* (rev. ed., 1977), is indispensable. Alan S. Milward, *War, Economy, and Society, 1939–1945* (1977), and Richard Polenberg, *America at War: The Home Front, 1941–1945* (1968), are two excellent discussions of the effects of war on American society. Otis L. Graham, *Toward a Planned Society: From Roosevelt to Nixon* (1976), focuses on the role of federal economic planning during and after the war. In *Another Chance: Postwar America, 1945–1968* (1985), James Gilbert examines some of the long-range effects of the war. For a discussion of the failure to save the Jews, see David S. Wyman, *The Abandonment of the Jews* (1984).

A fine, brief discussion of the long-term economic effects of the war may be found in Harold Vatter, *The U.S. Economy in World War II* (1985). Paul Boyer, *By the Bomb's Early Light: American Thought and Culture at the Dawn of the Atomic Age* (1985), is a chilling appraisal of the effects of this new technology. Michael S. Sherry, *The Rise of American Air Power: The Creation of Armageddon* (1987), debunks the importance of air power in World War II.

THE COLD WAR

The origins of the cold war have been extensively debated. John Lewis Gaddis, *The United States and the Origins of the Cold War, 1941–1945* (1985), carefully and comprehensively explores the issues. An excellent account with substantial coverage of Soviet policy is Adam B. Ulam, *Expansion and Coexistence* (1968). Lloyd C. Gardner, *Architects of Illusion: Men and Ideas in American Foreign Policy, 1941–1949* (1970), sheds considerable light on the complex motivations of American policymakers. The central political figures of the cold war era have left excellent memoirs. In his *Memoirs* (2 vols., 1955–56), President Harry S Truman proves to be a marvelous storyteller and competent defender of his administration. George Frost Kennan, *Memoirs, 1925–1950* (1968), is a brilliant and intriguing account by a key policymaker and commentator. His new book, *Sketches from a Life* (1989), adds important material to this story. James MacGregor Burns, *Roosevelt: The Solider of Freedom* (1970), is a masterly description of the Roosevelt presidency during the war years. James B. Conant, *My Several Lives: Memoirs of a Social Inventor* (1970), is an account by one of the leading figures in the politics of wartime and postwar science. See also Walter LaFeber, *America, Russia, and the Cold War, 1945–1980* (5th ed., 1985).

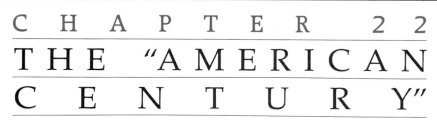

CHAPTER 22
THE "AMERICAN CENTURY"

THE EPISODE: *The extension of civil rights was not initiated by government act; civil rights were won through a long and bitter struggle of people determined to seize the citizenship that was their birthright. Deprived of political and business opportunities for a century, bright young black men and women turned to the black church to express their hopes, energies, and aspirations. This was particularly true in the segregated South. But during the 1950s the accumulation of change began to wear the edges of racial separation thin. When a young scholar, Martin Luther King, Jr., returned from Boston University to take up the ministry at Dexter Avenue Baptist Church in 1954 in Montgomery, Alabama, he had no hint that a nationwide civil rights movement would soon swirl around him or that his name would be linked with the great march on Washington of 1963 that would help open the floodgates of integration. What made King one of the most famous Americans of his day was the energy of a suppressed American culture, which he articulated into a momentous political and moral awakening. Its successes were his; its failures revealed his limitations and exposed the deepest barriers to equality in American life.*

THE HISTORICAL SETTING: *By reputation the 1950s (when the modern civil rights movement began) were politically conservative, perhaps even backward-looking. This representation is misleading. The 1950s were a time of consolidation in politics, when Republican President Dwight Eisenhower confirmed the welfare state and the broad tenets of guidance of the economy established during the New Deal and World War II. In fact, a variety of programs were expanded, even if the exuberant experimentalism of Roosevelt was relinquished. Beneath an apparently placid surface, American life was changing dramatically. The new consumerism of the era celebrated peace and prosperity and the virtues of the family—not the public—life. Centered around a dream of owning a home, raising children, and holding a good job, the new social ideal celebrated suburbs and their distance from old, urban problems.*

Even in these communities ringing American cities there were rebellions of sorts. The surprising demographics of the postwar period (steep rises in marriages and births, declines in divorce rates) crested about 1957. After a brief period, women began to return to the work force. Children increasingly explored new cultural forms emanating from the city ghettos, from working class and from African-American culture. The restive experimentalism in culture rampant in the next decade had its origins in this time. And the civil rights movement, which energized so much of what was to come, shimmered like an ebony ribbon through the period, transforming American life and culture.

MARTIN LUTHER KING, JR.: THE PURSUIT OF LIBERTY

At about one o'clock on the afternoon of Friday, May 3, 1963, the public safety commissioner of Birmingham, Alabama, Theophilus Eugene "Bull" Connor, stood next to the city's mayor, Arthur Hanes. Connor, a fleshy, heavy-jowled man, whose glass eye gave him a peculiar stare, watched the entrance to the Sixteenth Street Baptist Church. Nearby policemen, and farther on a line of police and firemen with high-pressure hoses, backed up by a dog squad with several German shepherds, also waited and watched. They were determined to prevent black civil rights demonstrators from marching. Connor, their commander, was a national symbol of old-style violent enforcement of race separation. Although this was just one more day in a series of rolling demonstrations that had continued for almost a month, it proved to be decisive. The Reverend Martin Luther King, Jr., leader of the demonstrators inside the church, had demanded "promises and action." "We are ready to negotiate," he claimed. "But we intend to negotiate from strength." Connor just as adamantly had promised to arrest every demonstrator, even if it filled every cell in the city jails. King, he scoffed, would "run out of niggers."

Hanes nudged Connor. "Here they come," he said. Connor's men swept back a crowd of about 100 jeering white onlookers and turned on the demonstrators. Police Captain G. V. Evans ordered the emerging group to halt and disperse: "Or you're going to get wet." The first 50 blacks continued to march. Most were young and carrying signs. Suddenly, the hoses squirted on. High-pressure water splattered the crowd. Some demonstrators fled. Some fell to the ground, upended by the force of the spray. Others skidded down the pavement, like debris in a gutter.

Now a large crowd of almost 2,000 blacks who had been waiting in nearby Kelly Ingram Park grew restless. Firemen turned their hoses on this more formidable group. Instead of dispersing, however, many in the crowd responded by hurling rocks, bricks, bottles, and chunks of concrete at the police. The situation had reached a breaking point. Connor signaled and his dog squad advanced. The enraged animals snapped at demonstrators, separating them into smaller groups, as other police moved in for arrests. But hundreds of demonstrators retreated into side streets, where they continued to pelt the advancing police. Finally, James Bevel, an assistant of King's, negotiated a quick truce. If the police called off the dogs and shut down the water cannons,

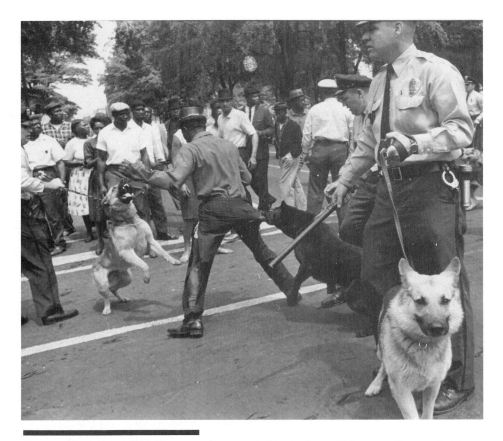

Force used against civil rights demonstrators. In Birmingham, Alabama, police resorted to the use of attack dogs to threaten participants in a demonstration pushing for civil rights. The ferocious animals (notice the destruction one has levied on a man's pants) were not enough to keep people from demanding what was rightfully theirs. (© 1963, Charles Moore, Black Star)

he would urge the demonstrators to go home. Gradually, the riot subsided, and Birmingham drew back once again from full-scale fighting. But the mask had fallen from Connor's segregation. The next day, in almost every newspaper in the country— and all over the world—one photograph told the story of Birmingham: a snarling police dog, scarcely restrained by an officer, lunging at the chest of a black demonstrator.

The violence in Alabama broke the impasse by escalating the confrontation. In Washington, Attorney General Robert Kennedy issued a sympathetic statement: "These demonstrations are understandable expressions of resentment and hurt by people who have been the victims of abuse and deprivation of their most basic rights for many years." Then he warned King against further marches. But quite clearly, the federal government had decided to intervene. Kennedy dispatched Assistant Attorney General Burke Marshall to Birmingham to negotiate a settlement between King and the local business community. Connor and Hanes were conspicuously left out of the talks.

Kennedy chose this tactic because of the chaos in Birmingham's government. Connor and Hanes were still in office only because of stubbornness and confusion. In November 1962 the voters of Birmingham had altered the old city government structure that was dominated by Connor. When the new structure went into effect in April 1963, Connor ran for mayor but lost to a milder segregationist, Albert Boutwell. Then, switching tactics, Connor claimed that he and Hanes could not be unseated, whatever the new frame of government. They would serve out their terms of office under the old system. Thus when the new mayor was sworn in on April 15, Connor and Hanes prevented him from taking office. The matter stood, in early May, before the courts.

Connor's use of police power to enforce segregation had pushed the situation to a crisis. Extremist elements in Birmingham and from the rest of the state, including the Ku Klux Klan, rallied to support Connor. Some of them pushed for further confrontations, in hopes of a declaration of martial law. To them, anything was better than integration.

In this explosive atmosphere, Burke Marshall began his negotiations with a group of city business leaders. From Washington, President Kennedy stepped up pressure as cabinet members persuaded corporate friends to ask Birmingham's business elite to support a compromise. What King and his forces demanded was not easy to grant: desegregation of lunch counters, restrooms, fitting rooms, and drinking fountains in all downtown stores; job placement for blacks as clerks and salespeople; release of prisoners arrested for demonstrating; and establishment of a permanent dialog between white and black leaders.

Marshall and his negotiating team raced against a short, sputtering fuse of racial violence, meeting in long sessions with white and black leaders. In the streets of Birmingham, the violence accelerated. King refused to call off demonstrators, even though confrontations with city police had escalated. Complicating matters, Alabama's governor, George Wallace, sent in reinforcements to aid Connor. By Tuesday evening, 575 riot-equipped state troopers were camped out around the city. On Tuesday night, however, Marshall hammered out a tentative agreement, and King and his forces canceled further demonstrations. The city waited . . . Wednesday, then Thursday, until the final details were worked out. Friday morning King announced the accord. Most of his demands had been met. The back of segregation was broken.

Nevertheless, segregationists tried to disrupt the agreement. Governor Wallace denounced the agreement with "lawless Negroes." He would never, he promised, compromise on segregation. On Saturday night, shortly after a joint Georgia-Alabama Klan rally in Birmingham, a car sped past the house of A. D. King, brother of Martin Luther King. Passengers tossed two dynamite bombs out of the car, blasting the house. Minutes later, four white men threw two more bombs at the Gaston Hotel, where King himself had been staying.

Although these bombings had caused no serious injuries, Birmingham's blacks poured into the streets. Picking up anything handy, they pelted policemen, smashed car windows, and beat up white bystanders. When police reinforcements arrived with the dog squad, the crowd became still more enraged. Even state troopers could not calm the situation. Finally, black leaders persuaded the crowd to disperse. The riot ended, but not before flames had consumed several white-owned businesses in the black section of town. Still, the agreement held. The events made King's words, uttered during the campaign, all the more prophetic: "I stand alone in the middle of two opposing forces in the Negro community. One is the force of complacency. . . . The other force is one of bitterness and hatred and comes perilously close to advocating violence."

Gradually, peace returned to Birmingham. The reign of Bull Connor ended May 23, when the Alabama Supreme Court unanimously certified Mayor Boutwell's election and right to office. The businessmen's agreement was implemented. But racial hatred and white resistance continued. On September 14 white terrorists hurled a dynamite bomb through a window of the Sixteenth Street Baptist Church. It exploded in a crowded Sunday school class, killing four young girls. Twenty other children were injured. In a eulogy sermon, King tried, as he always did, to channel sorrow and shock into something positive: "Their death says to us that we must work passionately and unceasingly to make the American dream a reality."

Birmingham was a grim and inevitable rendezvous for the Southern civil rights movement—a protest movement that had begun almost spontaneously in Montgomery, Alabama, in 1955. The success in Montgomery had been astounding, in no small measure because of King, who was thrust into leadership of the new movement. But Montgomery was also deceptive. It represented only one wall breached, the first battle in a war of attrition against Southern strongholds of segregation. One by one they fell, some in violence, some peacefully. But some strongholds, like Birmingham, held out.

King's generalship of this movement was crucial. His strategy was honed in failure and success. He recognized, where others did not, the great energy and moral force of Southern black religion. But he also understood the tenacity of segregation and the ultimate necessity of federal intervention. He realized that integration had to force its way into the American conscience, but without allowing fear to prevail in the white community. He knew that even Northern liberals had to be pushed into support for action. This line between vision and threat was a precarious one.

King was a new resident of Montgomery in 1955. He had arrived there just one year earlier—with a new Ph.D. and his wife, Coretta—to answer a call from the Dexter Avenue Baptist Church. King had grown up in Atlanta, where his father was a prominent minister at the Ebenezer Baptist Church. His mother was the daughter of Ebenezer's previous pastor.

An outstanding student academically, King entered public school and then switched to the private laboratory school at Atlanta University. From there he attended Atlanta's only black high school, Booker T. Washington. He skipped ninth grade and graduated at the age of fifteen. Like his father before him, he went on to Morehouse College. During this period he began to think seriously about the ministry. He began preaching at the age of seventeen and shortly thereafter became assistant pastor at Ebenezer.

But at this point, King's career diverged from his father's, which had always been limited to the black community and to the black educational institutions of Atlanta. Young King wanted a deeper, wider, more committed education. Thus in

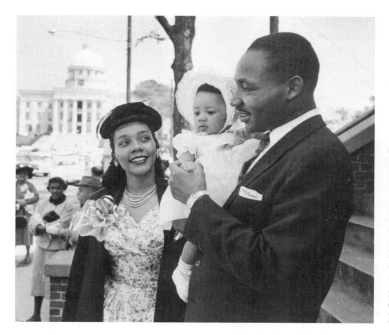

Martin Luther King, Coretta Scott King, and their first daughter, 1956. Despite his growing fame, King always depended on his wide family network for support and aid. Here he stands with his wife and first child on the steps of Montgomery's Dexter Baptist Church, his first pastoral position; the capitol building of Alabama is in the background. (Dan Weiner, Courtesy of Sandra Weiner/ Magnum)

1948 he enrolled at Crozer Theological Seminary in Chester, Pennsylvania, a predominantly white school. During his three years there, he also attended philosophy courses at the University of Pennsylvania.

In his studies, King immersed himself in the social philosophy of Marx, Hegel, and other Europeans, and in the writings of the American Protestant theologian Reinhold Niebuhr. He avidly studied the Social Gospel, an earlier theological movement that stressed working for social justice. He read deeply in the writings of Mahatma Gandhi, the pacifist leader of the Indian revolution against British colonial rule. King interwove ideas from these sources into the fabric of his experience. His developing philosophy brought together his understanding of the economic exploitation of his race, his admiration for nonviolent tactics, and the traditions of Southern black religion as he had experienced them. Could he, he wondered, transform the quiet and accommodating religion of Southern blacks into a force for change? And could he do this without inciting a violent backlash?

When King became a graduate student at Boston University, he did not yet know the answers. And being a young man, he was often concerned with matters other than philosophy and social change. While working for his doctorate in philosophy, he met a young woman, Coretta Scott, who was studying at the New England Conservatory of Music. He decided immediately that this was the woman he wanted to marry. After their first meeting, he said to her abruptly: "You have everything I have ever wanted in a wife."

For Coretta, the decision was difficult. As her affection for King grew, she was torn. Should she give up a promising career in music and marry a Baptist minister? She finally consented, and the couple wed in June 1953. Coretta joined the Baptist church and put aside her career. In 1954 the Kings accepted the call from the church in Montgomery. Within a year, King, only twenty-six years old, had become the leader of a bus boycott that initiated the modern civil rights movement.

On December 1, 1955, Rosa Parks, a black woman, exhausted from her shopping and her job as a seamstress, entered a crowded bus in front of the Fair department store in Montgomery to pay the driver. She then got off the bus and walked to the "colored "entrance in the rear, where she boarded the bus again. Finding most seats at the rear occupied, she moved forward and sat down in a row immediately behind the section reserved for whites. The bus resumed its route, stopping again at the Empire Theater. Six white passengers entered the front of the bus, paid and moved back. But there were not enough seats in the white section. Seeing this, the driver called on the nearest black passengers to vacate their places. All of them did—except Rosa Parks. Too tired, or perhaps mindful of earlier incidents of rudeness by white drivers, she refused. James F. Blake, the driver, left the bus and returned with a policeman, who arrested Mrs. Parks for violating Montgomery's segregation laws.

The incident was not entirely unexpected. Others had previously defied the law, and they had been arrested. But Mrs. Parks was different. She was a well-known figure in Montgomery's black community and a member of the city's National Association for the Advancement of Colored People (NAACP). The times were also different. The Supreme Court on May 17, 1954, in *Brown* v. *Board of Education*, had ruled school segregation unconstitutional: Separate could never be equal, the Court maintained. On May 31, 1955, the Court had ordered lower federal courts and school authorities to integrate schools "with all deliberate speed."

Yet nothing much had changed in Montgomery or the rest of the South. Few black citizens could vote, although the number of black voters was growing slowly. The "deliberate" speed of school integration was no speed at all. And the indignities of segregation continued to pervade private custom and public commerce. From birth to death, the races were separated. Hospitals, prisons, and graveyards were divided by race. Marriages across racial lines were strictly forbidden. Swimming pools, golf courses, movie theaters, and airport and railroad waiting rooms were segregated. So were drinking fountains and bathrooms. Stores often served blacks from a back or side door.

Mrs. Parks's arrest electrified the black community. Immediately after the incident, she telephoned E. D. Nixon and his wife, who went to the police station to seek her release. Nixon was head of the local NAACP and an official of the Brotherhood of Sleeping Car Porters. His wife was a member of the black Women's Political Council. In Mrs. Parks, the Political Council found a symbol they could organize around, and they quickly decided on a boycott of Montgomery's bus system. E. D. Nixon organized ministers' groups to support the boycott. Unable himself to assume leadership of the group because of his work for the union, he began to telephone local ministers searching for endorsements of the boycott. One of those whom Nixon called was Martin Luther King, Jr. On the afternoon of December 5, King accepted leadership of a new boycott group, the Montgomery Improvement Association (MIA).

Rosa Parks, the woman who defied the segregation laws of Montgomery and thus began the bus boycott of 1955, was able to take a front seat on a city bus a year later, after the Supreme Court banned segregated public transit in Montgomery. (UPI/Bettmann Newsphotos)

The initial demands of the group were cautious. They did not ask for an end to segregation. They asked only for courtesy from drivers, equal reserved seating (equal numbers of seats for blacks and whites), and black drivers on predominantly black routes. This modest plan would have made segregation work more harmoniously, not ended it. But after a fruitless meeting between the MIA, the City Commission, and the bus company, a lawyer for the company declared: "If we granted the Negroes these demands, they would go about boasting of a victory that they had won over white people, and this we will not stand for." The lines were drawn hard and fast.

By early winter both sides had stiffened their determination. But developments among the whites became ominous. The White Citizens' Council, a group devoted to preserving segregation, enlisted thousands of new members, including the mayor and the city commissioners. Abusive telephone calls frequently disturbed the King household. On the evening of January 30, 1956, a bomb blast on the front porch of the King residence split the porch and shattered windows in the house.

Faced with inflexible opposition to bus integration, the MIA decided to challenge segregation laws through the courts. On February 1, with help from the NAACP, Fred Gray, one of two black lawyers in the city, filed his case in federal court. At the same time, a group of white businessmen, the Men of Montgomery, began negotiations with the MIA. Sales in downtown stores had fallen, and the bus company was losing about $3,000 a day. Finally, in mid-February, elected officials and the MIA leadership met—but without results. The city was willing to back down, but it was too late for halfway concessions. Now Montgomery blacks demanded equality in bus transport. Weeks of struggle had led them to make bigger demands. In a shifting and increasingly explosive situation, King and other MIA leaders pressed for a more extensive program of integration. There was no other way to retain their leadership.

The city responded with tougher tactics. In late February, King and ninety others were indicted for breaking an old antiboycott law. Their trial began on March 19 before

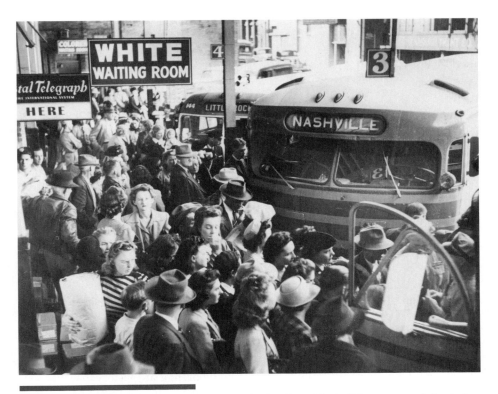

Segregated society in the South. Throughout the South, public facilities were carefully designated "white" or "colored." This custom persisted well into the 1960s. (Library of Congress)

Judge Eugene Carter. On March 22 King was convicted and fined $500 or thirteen months at hard labor. His lawyers appealed the decision. Meanwhile, the boycott continued. In mid-May a federal district court declared Alabama's bus segregation laws unconstitutional. The city immediately appealed to the Supreme Court.

As the boycotters stood firm through the spring and summer, they attracted more and more national and international attention. King spoke several times in the North, and funds raised by outside black congregations and white liberals began to flow into the city. Finally, on November 13, word came that the Supreme Court had declared Alabama's bus segregation laws unconstitutional. The boycott remained in effect until December, when the decision was implemented.

For King, the lessons of the fight had been painfully learned. He realized the crucial role of religious leadership in the black community. He recognized, too, the tenacious hatred of the segregationists. He understood that nonviolence, to be successful, would require outside intervention. King also gained insight into the problems of leading the currently inert but potentially explosive black population—a dangerous and volatile situation, given a constituency that was unpracticed in politics.

King's success in Montgomery elevated him to national leadership, but the movement remained unorganized, diffuse, and still without an articulate philosophy.

He was determined to change this. King knew the old answers and their modern equivalents: the accommodationism of Booker T. Washington, the legal integrationism of W. E. B. Du Bois and the NAACP, and the black separatism of Marcus Garvey. None of these strategies had deeply touched the masses of Southern black Christians. King's strategy was to organize his constituency around the black churches. He favored a philosophy that could transform the quiet strength of Southern blacks into an aggressive force for change. The ability of black men and women to suffer, to face indignities impassively, was the foundation on which he erected his program of nonviolence. And his ultimate goal was clear: integration of black Americans as equals into the full benefits of citizenship.

In early 1957, King, the Reverend Ralph Abernathy, and other ministers from the South met in New Orleans to organize the Southern Christian Leadership Conference (SCLC). The group, headquartered in Atlanta, selected King as head. One of King's first strategies was to capitalize on his national visibility to press for federal legislation. After leading a prayer vigil in Washington, he met with Vice President Richard Nixon in June. The result of this and other pressure was the Civil Rights Bill of 1957, a law that established a Civil Rights Commission to monitor voting rights violations.

King's general strategy was to force immediate change. Using nonviolence, he led masses of demonstrators into confrontation with segregationists. These nonviolent tactics had a special meaning in the American context. When Mahatma Gandhi led the nonviolent movement for Indian independence, he represented a majority of his society pitted against a small, vulnerable British colonial government. Once the Indian masses decided to be independent, probably nothing could have stopped them. But King had to use nonviolence in a society where blacks were only a minority.

Thus nonviolence depended ultimately on some form of national action—inspired either by agreement with the goals of integration or by fear of the social disorder that might be created by confrontation. King hoped it would be the former, for this would make ultimate accommodation between the races easier. It would also channel the raw anger of the black community. But there were great risks. King recognized that nonviolence would breed disenchantment among blacks who demanded speedy change.

This was precisely the complaint of the young integrationists who later challenged King. In February 1960 white and black college students began sit-ins in Durham and Greensboro, North Carolina, demanding service at the segregated lunch counters of Woolworth dime stores. The movement spread to fifty-four other cities in two months. By mid-April the Student Nonviolent Coordinating Committee (SNCC) had formed. King maintained cordial relations with the young leaders, but he eventually lost influence over the group.

In the next few years, the desegregation movement spread rapidly, and King struggled to maintain his leadership and a national vision of the goals. From 1961 through early 1962 he supported the "freedom rides" organized by another black group, the Congress of Racial Equality. These rides on integrated buses into the South called national attention to the problem of segregation, particularly in bus stations. The first ride left Washington in May 1961; its purpose was to integrate Southern transportation facilities. The trip was uneventful until the bus carrying the freedom riders was bombed and burned by whites near Anniston, Alabama, on May 14. Other groups that ventured out later were attacked in Birmingham and Montgomery. As these attacks grew, so did national concern. By the end of the month, a freedom ride that left for Jackson, Mississippi, was assigned an escort of the National Guard and Army helicopters. Responding to an intolerable situation, the Interstate Commerce Commission in December prohibited segregation aboard buses and in terminals.

A freedom ride to Albany, Georgia, in December 1961 to integrate a railway station marked the beginning of a newer, broader tactic employed by King, but one that also exposed the movement to counterattack and potential defeat. Black leaders in the city called in King to help organize a movement that had been stirred up by the freedom ride. The local SCLC leader hoped to focus protest on the entire race and caste system of the city. As in other Southern cities, public segregation was only symbolic of deeper divisions and exploitation in jobs, wages, social benefits, and political rights. On December 16 King and the Albany leadership organized a march to demand change in all of these areas. Over 700 demonstrators were arrested. King refused release on bond and called for more demonstrators to come to the city.

A temporary compromise was reached two days later. King left jail, and the railway station was integrated. Civil rights leaders were optimistic. But the city had not really budged. All of its parks, libraries, movie theaters, and buses remained segregated. So King and his allies decided to launch a selective boycott against white businesses and the bus company. The city struck back and reneged on an informal promise to integrate the buses.

By July 1962 King faced failure and mounting criticism of his leadership, so he turned to new tactics—civil disobedience to force Albany city leaders to grant SCLC demands. Groups of blacks fanned out across the city to integrate parks, lunch counters, bowling alleys. On July 20, however, a newly appointed federal judge granted the city an injunction against all demonstrations. Simultaneously, thousands of Ku Klux Klansmen gathered outside the city. Tension broke into angry rioting after a deputy sheriff brutally beat Mrs. Slater King in Camilla, Georgia. Mrs. King (no relation to Martin Luther) was the wife of an Albany civil rights leader. On the evening of July 24 a group gathered in Albany to protest the beating. Police moved in to break up the meeting. When they did, the long-suffering blacks of Albany reacted, just as King feared they might. Before long, thousands of demonstrators were battling police.

This outbreak of violence deeply distressed King. He had lost control of the movement; his nonviolent tactics had not worked. His first reaction was to pull back and avoid further demonstrations. The Kennedy administration in Washington was profoundly disturbed and embarrassed by events in Albany—but not enough to act. Scores of white Northerners who had poured into the city to bolster the movement were preparing to leave as fall approached. And the segregationists were holding firm. In September, with most white integrationists gone, they initiated selective revenge against local black leaders. Several churches were dynamited. Public facilities remained segregated or closed. The Albany movement had failed.

This setback represented a personal defeat for King. It resulted from poor planning, divided leadership, and inconclusive and uncoordinated tactics. Furthermore, he had failed to engage either national sympathy or, more important, federal support for his cause. He could either retreat or assault an even more dangerous citadel,

Birmingham. It was a risk that threatened the whole movement, for by 1963, Birmingham had become a symbolic center of resistance to integration. The new Alabama governor, George Wallace, elected in 1962, had vowed undying opposition to integration. Birmingham's tough police had a leader pledged to enforce laws that rigidly separated both the public and private lives of Birmingham citizens. As King described it:

> Birmingham is probably the most thoroughly segregated city in the United States. Its ugly record of police brutality is known in every section of the country. Its unjust treatment of Negroes in the courts is a notorious reality. There have been more unsolved bombings of Negro homes and churches in Birmingham than any city in this nation. These are hard, brutal and unbelievable facts.

King decided to risk failure and violence. He and the SCLC worked closely with local leaders headed by the Reverend Fred Shuttlesworth. They decided that their movement should be clearly focused, well planned and financed, and designed to elicit maximum sympathy from Northern liberals and the federal government. If the city used violence against demonstrators, this would only force outside intervention.

King and the SCLC planned Project C (for confrontation) to be launched during Easter week to disrupt the season's sales. This assault on business was designed to force economic leaders in the city to negotiate with integrationists. Several hundred volunteers worked to train black Birmingham in nonviolent tactics. B-day (the first day of protest) had to be postponed until April 3 to avoid disrupting the local mayoral election. B-day began twelve hours after Albert Boutwell's victory at the polls.

At first, it appeared that Bull Connor might also play by the rules of nonviolence. During the first few days, demonstrations and sit-ins occurred without serious incident. Then on April 10 a local judge issued an injunction against all further demonstrations. King decided to break the law and suffer the consequences. In itself, this was an important turning point. Jail meant national attention. But more important, King crossed a threshold by defying a court order. Until now, he had respected such orders. His defiance represented a deeper attack on segregation and the structure that supported it.

On April 12, Good Friday, King and several volunteers set out on an illegal protest march. Connor and his police allowed them to proceed several blocks and then moved in for arrests. Connor arrested King and held him in solitary confinement. He was allowed no calls or visitors. In Atlanta, his wife waited anxiously for word that did not come. Anything was possible in Connor's jail. So she telephoned Wyatt Walker, one of the Birmingham leaders. Together they agreed that she should call the president.

Mrs. King's call to Kennedy forced the president's hand. While Kennedy had expressed sympathy for integration, he had done little to push it publicly. But pressure in the North was building for action. Press commentary around the world sharply criticized government inaction in the face of brutality. Mrs. King tried several times to reach the president at the White House, without success. Then she tried Vice President Johnson, but he too was absent. Finally, a sympathetic operator, sensing her desperation, suggested that she telephone the president's aide Pierre Salinger.

He promised to notify Kennedy immediately. A short time later, Attorney General Robert Kennedy telephoned to promise his help. But he warned: "Of course, Birmingham is a very difficult place." Within fifteen minutes the phone rang again. It was King. He was safe.

King's eight days in the Birmingham jail were critical ones for him and for the fate of the integration movement. At first, he pondered the hope and despair of his situation. As he wrote: "You will never know the meaning of utter darkness until you have lain in such a dungeon, knowing that sunlight is streaming overhead and still seeing only darkness below."

What bothered King more, however, was the fate of the movement he headed. Had he led it into darkness, violence, and disarray? Were his tactics of challenge, which brought out the bitterest attacks from segregationists, inevitably doomed? Did the violence of Birmingham indicate that the doors to integration might remain forever shut? Was he going too far; was he in danger of losing the vision of racial justice that appealed to whites?

This last question was posed to him by eight white Alabama clergymen on April 12. In their "Public Statement Directed to Martin Luther King, Jr.," they wrote: "We are now confronted by a series of demonstrations by some of our Negro citizens, directed and led in part by outsiders. We recognize the natural impatience of people who feel that their hopes are slow in being realized. But we are convinced that these demonstrations are unwise and untimely."

King received the statement while in solitary confinement and almost immediately began his response. At first, he penciled his thoughts in the margins of a newspaper. When this proved inadequate, he continued his reply on sheets of paper brought in by a friendly black guard. Finally, he secured a pad of legal paper from his attorney. When finished, he dated and titled it: April 16, 1963, "A Letter from Birmingham Jail."

King answered the three charges of the clergymen: that he and his organization were outsiders, that he should be patient, and that his tactics endangered the whole community. His reply was careful but passionate. King realized from the tone of their letter that the eight clergymen defined him and all blacks as being outside the community of equal citizens. Thus in his response, he tried to find the language and symbols that would locate a place for Southern blacks in the community in which they had always lived but to which they had never belonged.

He bristled at the suggestion that he was an outsider. "We are," he said, "caught in an inescapable network of mutuality, tied to a single garment of destiny. Whatever affects one directly affects all indirectly. Never again can we afford to live with the narrow, provincial 'outside agitator' idea. Anyone who lives inside the United States can never be considered an outsider anywhere in this country."

As for the question of patience, King rejected the ministers' advice. "For years now," he recalled, "I have heard the word 'Wait!' It rings in the ear of every Negro with a piercing familiarity. This 'Wait' has almost always meant 'Never.'" How long, he retorted, while African nations had emerged into political sovereignty could American blacks remain "smothering in an airtight cage of poverty in the midst of an affluent society."

King did acknowledge the risks of violence. But he argued that only "creative tension" could push the white majority into negotiation. Breaking the law—the unjust and illegal law of segregation—was a duty, he continued. "In no sense do I advocate evading or defying the law as the rabid segregationist would do. This would lead to anarchy. One who breaks an unjust law must do it openly, *lovingly*."

If, as King believed, Birmingham represented the risk of failure and violent resistance from a closed community of bigotry, the march on Washington of August 1963 represented a chance to express, before a national audience, the vision of a new American community that King had sketchily defined in his Birmingham letter. The march, and King's dramatic speech there, represented a high point in the impulse to open America to all its citizens. It was so because he succeeded in making integration and equality for blacks the very center of a new sort of patriotism.

King had always recognized the limitations of a Southern movement and an all-black movement. He had long sought allies in the white community—among ministers, political liberals, and labor unions. His strategy was to force Americans to recognize Southern segregation as a national problem. In part, this was because the federal government tolerated the special status of Southern laws. The Democratic party allowed segregationists a veto over presidential nominees as well as over civil rights laws. To break the tentacles of power that radiated out from the South, King had forced federal intervention in Montgomery and then in the bloody situation in Birmingham. But the problem also required a national vision. Change would not come without firm civil rights laws and some national manifestation of solidarity. These were the goals of the march planned for the nation's capital.

Yet this was no easy task, for government at all levels of American society was often divided between reluctant sympathy to civil rights and aggressive hostility. This divided attitude even characterized the federal government. Thus in 1961, FBI chief J. Edgar Hoover instructed his agents to assemble a file on King that he hoped would discredit the black leader. At first, Hoover worried about some of King's radical supporters and advisers, but this concern soon faded, as Hoover began an intensive campaign to document King's extramarital affairs. This second operation culminated in 1964 when the FBI sent incriminating tapes to King's home with an anonymous note urging him to commit suicide: "You had better take it [your life] before your filthy abnormal fradulent self is bared to the nation." Thus King and his movement had to struggle at every level of society; there was no automatic refuge or sympathy anywhere.

At the center of national and international attention now (indeed, criticized for this by younger black leaders, who referred to him as "De Lawd"), King tried to turn the "creative tension" of Birmingham and its accompanying publicity into a broad national movement. President Kennedy had finally been forced to act—and not just to preserve peace in the South or to deal with a specific injustice. In early June the president spoke warmly of civil rights. New civil rights legislation in Congress was stalled by Southern opposition. Birmingham and the rest of the South seemed to be a powder keg, ready to explode. Arrests of civil rights demonstrators were shooting upward, totaling almost 14,000 during the year. In his speech, Kennedy reiterated the proposition that King had enunciated so forcefully in his Birmingham letter:

> We are confronted primarily with a moral issue. It is as old as the Scriptures and is as clear as the American Constitution. The heart of the question is whether all Americans are to be afforded equal rights and equal opportunities; whether we are going to treat our fellow Americans as we want to be treated.

Only passage of civil rights legislation, Kennedy concluded, could solve the crisis.

This was the commitment that King had long sought. But was it enough? Could the movement relent and wait outside the legislative halls for progress? King believed it could not, and together with other leaders—the aging A. Philip Randolph of the Brotherhood of Sleeping Car Porters and representatives from most of the other civil rights organizations—he planned the march on Washington for late August. As first conceived, demonstrators were to engage in civil disobedience and sit-ins on Capitol Hill. But planners rejected this idea. The march would be a simple demonstration of solidarity for "jobs and freedom" to stir the nation's conscience.

Yet from the beginning, the march was controversial. The president refused to endorse it, although he agreed to meet with civil rights leaders afterward. His wariness only underscored the risks. If there was violence or, worse, if only a small crowd assembled, the damage might be irreparable. But other political leaders were not so hesitant as Kennedy. Mayor Robert Wagner of New York City spoke in favor of the march and proclaimed August 28 "Jobs and Freedom Day." Support from some labor unions was strong: The United Auto Workers (a major contributor to the civil rights movement) and the International Ladies Garment Workers Union (ILGWU) sent representatives. Church leaders and rabbis endorsed the march. The National Council of Churches even prepared box lunches for sale at low prices during the march.

Other leaders and groups were reluctant or even hostile. Former President Truman deplored the demonstration, although he approved its goals. Governor Wallace tried to convince the Southern Governors Conference to denounce the march. A number of newspapers across the country warned of a possible backlash. They proposed that black Americans seek redress in Congress and in the courts, not in the streets. At the fringe, Robert Welch of the right-wing John Birch Society accused King of aiming to create a "Soviet Negro Republic," headquartered in Atlanta, with himself as president.

In the face of uncertainties and attacks, planning continued. At first, response was weak. Silence from the urban black ghettos and the rural South numbed the organizers. Then suddenly, in August, the headquarters of the march was swamped with requests for information and help. Special trains and buses had to be hired. Car caravans were organized. Some set out early on foot. In Washington, predictions of attendance went up and up. More marshals had to be recruited to control the crowd. The demonstration would be enormous.

August 28 was bright and hot, the sort of Washington summer day when humidity and bright light make the stark white government buildings and monuments shimmer in the glare. Marchers began pouring into the city, into Union Station near the Capitol, and into the Fourteenth Street bus terminal. Cars and chartered buses jammed the side streets around Capitol Hill. Diesel fumes and dust stirred up by hundreds of demonstrators hung over the gathering crowd as it moved toward the staging area at the Washington Monument for the march to the Lincoln Memorial.

By one o'clock a crowd of over 200,000 had assembled around the Reflecting Pool and the grassy approaches to the memorial. Most carried banners proclaiming "Freedom Now" or placards identifying the marcher with his or her hometown, church group, or labor union. The crowd had a look rarely seen at political gatherings in Washington: a sea of black faces set off by white shirts or made somber by the well-worn blue gabardine of Sunday-best suits. Sharecroppers, students, women with broad sun hats moved in an undulating mass. Fewer in number, but readily visible, were white faces—evidence of the racial solidarity that King had worked for.

The ceremonies began slowly. First, "The Star-Spangled Banner." Then a speech from Fred Shuttlesworth of Birmingham. Then words from Ralph Abernathy and greetings from 1,500 Americans abroad. Then a speech by A. Philip Randolph—a voice of continuity with old struggles and old battles. "We are," he proclaimed, "the advance guard of a massive moral revolution for jobs and freedom. This revolution reverberates throughout the land, touching every city, every town, every village where black men are segregated, oppressed, and exploited."

In the hot sun, the demonstrators shifted from foot to foot and swayed to catch the words carried out to them by loudspeakers. They had come to move and be moved, but so far the words had not done that. John Lewis, the new chairman of the Student Nonviolent Coordinating Committee, spoke angrily about the failure of government, the failure to achieve change. His remarks had been muffled by censorship: Patrick A. O'Boyle, the Catholic archbishop of Washington, had refused to appear at the march if Lewis directly attacked the Kennedy administration. But Lewis made his intent clear. Concerning the pending civil rights bill, he declared, "We support the bill with great reservations, for it is too little and too late." When he had finished, every black speaker shook his hand. Every white speaker on the platform ignored him.

As the speeches continued, some of the demonstrators began to drift back to their cars and buses. The march had been impressive, but they were tired or anxious to return home. Then the gospel singer Mahalia Jackson stood before the microphones. She began to sing an old hymn: "I Been 'Buked and I Been Scorned." As the words rolled out over the crowd, her familiar deep and resonant voice caught and stopped many of those who were departing:

> I'm gonna tell my Lord
> When I get home
> I'm gonna tell my Lord
> When I get home
> Just how *long* you've
> Been treating me wrong

When the echo of the song had died out, the crowd answered back, shouting, waving, screaming, moving tighter together around the memorial.

Then, finally, King rose to speak. When he mounted the rostrum, a burst of applause greeted him. He waited calmly for it to subside, showing no signs of fatigue and the late night he had spent finishing his speech.

The march on Washington. King addressed a huge crowd of civil rights supporters August 28, 1963. Standing on the steps of the Lincoln Memorial, he faced the Washington Monument, symbol of the foundation of the Republic, and the crowd roared approval as he proclaimed, "I have a dream." (©Bob Henriques/Magnum)

He began by invoking the memory and language of Lincoln—and of the emancipation that had been frustrated by a century of racism and segregation: "Five score years ago a great American in whose symbolic shadow we stand today signed the Emancipation Proclamation." He continued:

> When the architects of our Republic wrote the magnificent words of the Constitution and the Declaration of Independence, they were signing a promissory note to which every American was to fall heir. This note was a promise that all men—yes, black men as well as white men—would be guaranteed the inalienable rights of life, liberty, and the pursuit of happiness.

King directed these words at every American, but particularly at white Americans. He mentioned the three most famous documents of American history: the Gettysburg Address, the Declaration of Independence, and the Constitution—all of which defined freedom. And yet none of them had extended freedom to all Americans. King was demanding the payment of an old debt.

He then spoke of the question of caution. Was it time to be tranquil, to quiet the voice of protest? King firmly rejected this possibility. He called for new alliances, reaching out to those white Americans who would help. But he also warned that blacks would never be satisfied while "our children are stripped of their adulthood and robbed of their dignity by signs stating 'For Whites Only.'" As a leader, he would not rest until "justice rolls down like waters and righteousness like a mighty stream." And then he urged, "Go back to Mississippi, go back to Alabama, go back to South

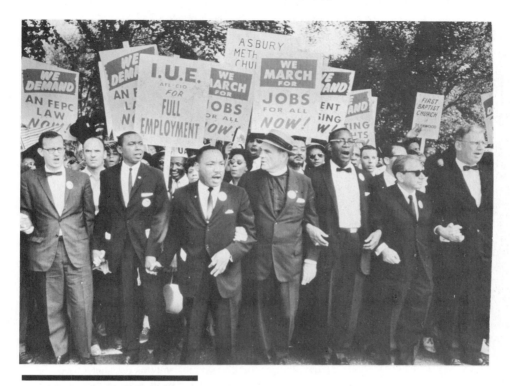

The first line in the 1963 March on Washington. This group of men suggests the broad base of support organized by Martin Luther King, Jr.: religious, political, and union leaders; black and white Americans. (Robert W. Kelley, *Life* Magazine, ©Time Inc.)

Carolina, go back to Georgia, go back to Louisiana, go back to the slums and ghettos of our Northern cities, knowing that somehow this situation can and will be changed."

From the beginning, the crowd had listened, straining to catch each word as it swept through the loudspeaker system. Most were now standing. A few murmured their approval. He had them with him as he returned to his opening words: "I still have a dream. It is a dream deeply rooted in the American dream. I have a dream that one day this nation will rise up, live out the true meaning of its creed: 'We hold these truths to be self-evident, that all men are created equal.'"

King could have stopped then. The speech had been a great one, evoking a vision of hope and the fulfillment of American ideals. The crowd was ready to burst into applause and movement. But he struck deeper. He also had a personal dream to confess: that his own "four little children will one day live in a nation where they will not be judged by the color of their skin but by the content of their character." "I have a dream," he repeated, that "right there in Alabama little black boys and black girls will be able to join hands with little white boys and white girls as sisters and brothers." The crowd roared its approval.

"I have a dream today," he continued, moving out and away from any specific reference to the civil rights movement or the march or his own family. "I have a dream," he continued, quoting words of biblical prophecy from Isaiah 40:4:

A King in the White House. Following the Civil Rights March, Martin Luther King, Jr., met with President John F. Kennedy and other important leaders, including (to King's right) Rabbi Joseph Prinz, chairman of the American Jewish Congress; A. Philip Randolph, director of the march; and (to Kennedy's right) Walter Reuther, vice president of the AFL-CIO. (UPI/Bettmann Newsphotos)

> I have a dream that one day every valley shall be exalted, every hill and mountain shall be made low. The rough places will be made plain, and the crooked places will be made straight. And the glory of the Lord shall be revealed, and all flesh shall see it together.

Every time he repeated the words "I have a dream," the crowd roared in response, moving with him as he revealed his vision. "I have a dream," he shouted again, this time quoting the words of the patriotic anthem "America" that someday "all of God's children will be able to sing with new meaning, 'My country, 'tis of thee, sweet land of liberty, of thee I sing.'"

As he finished, King wove these words into a final vision of America—an integrated America, in which the black experience would express the essence and meaning of the national experience:

> When we allow freedom to ring—when we let it ring from every city and every hamlet, from every state and every city, we will be able to speed up that day when all of God's children, black men and white men, Jews and Gentiles, Protestants and Catholics, will be able to join hands and sing in the words of the old Negro spiritual, "Free at last, Free at last, Great God a-mighty. We are free at last."

AN ERA OF PROMISE

The civil rights movement that Martin Luther King, Jr., led in triumph to Washington in the summer of 1963 was, in some regards, the culmination of a very old process in American history. Previous groups, such as labor unions and ethnic groups, had demanded and achieved legitimacy in American society. Now after nearly a century of struggle, it was the turn of black Americans to win the rights that others had been granted. Although this struggle was much harder and more bitter than any that preceded it, it nevertheless succeeded. If this was not what Henry Luce, editor of *Time* magazine, meant when he predicted an "American Century" in 1941, it was, nonetheless, a stunning victory for the nation.

King's triumph was possible because of a political consensus that gradually developed during and after World War II. This agreement was based on three fundamental assumptions about the nature of American society: (1) that an expanding economy would make it possible for all groups to share in the material bounty of the nation; (2) that a fundamental political program could be defined that would satisfy the diverse interests in American society; and (3) that government should be a major instrument to achieve these goals of bounty and social harmony.

The origins of this postwar liberal vision lay in the New Deal. In the 1930s, Franklin D. Roosevelt used the federal government to protect millions of forgotten men and women from the hardships of depression. He built a remarkable political consensus to support his programs, a consensus that included farmers, Catholics, urban workers, the solid South, and Northern ethnic groups. Broad as this group was, however, it did not fully embrace American blacks.

In 1944, when Roosevelt delivered his State of the Union message—what he called his economic bill of rights—he spoke of rights for all Americans, regardless of race or creed. These included the right to food, clothing, education, and a useful job. They included the right of every family to a decent home, medical care, and support in times of misfortune or old age. But these were words with little force or meaning for black Americans. Indeed, between Roosevelt's enunciation of a new program of rights and the beginnings of the civil rights movement in the mid-1950s, traditional phrases about liberty and equality had to acquire a new content. This was the point of Martin Luther King's speech; he created a new language of equality that really did include all citizens.

Had Congress enacted Roosevelt's economic rights with serious attention to racial, class, and ethnic equality, it would have initiated perhaps the greatest social revolution in American history. But legislators scarcely paid attention to Roosevelt's stirring suggestions. The Democratic majority in both houses had long since ceased to be a liberal majority. A coalition of Republicans and solid-South Democrats could veto any wide-ranging social legislation.

Yet Roosevelt's vision in his economic bill of rights was important. It promised an extension of the basic social programs of the 1930s. With its twin emphases on equality and inalienable social rights, it set an agenda that others—such as Martin Luther King, Jr., then only fifteen years old—would be able to seize upon and transform in the postwar period.

The Peacetime Economy

Roosevelt's immediate plans for postwar society concentrated on rapid conversion to peacetime production. Controls enacted by Congress generally had a time limit triggered by the end of the war. In late 1944 and early 1945 the economy was set to return to civilian production. There was little momentum to continue New Deal reforms or extend social planning. Yet one piece of legislation, passed to reward soldiers for their combat service and to prevent their reentering the labor force too quickly, profoundly affected the social status of millions of Americans. This was the so-called GI Bill.

This program, enacted in the Servicemen's Readjustment Act of 1944, provided federal subsidies for college attendance and home buying. The federal government would pay tuition charges as well as a small living allowance to any serviceman with two or more years of duty. And it offered low-interest mortgages for the purchase of houses and businesses. Veterans were also granted preference in federal and state employment. Together, the various federal and state programs to aid veterans amounted to a massive affirmative action plan that allowed millions of young men—men who might not otherwise have had the chance—to enter college, buy a house, or find a job in the public sector.

The GI Bill put millions of returning soldiers in school who otherwise might have joined the ranks of the unemployed. This, plus pent-up consumer demand for products that were scarce during the war, kept the economy booming. The favorable position of the United States in world trade also proved significant. Raw materials and energy supplies were cheap and easily available. Progress in aviation, television, and information systems, plus new inventions and materials, created whole new industries. These factors, along with constant federal intervention in the economy mandated by the Employment Act of 1946, guaranteed important gains in worker productivity, personal income, and gross national product.

What Roosevelt would have done to spread this bounty to the groups that did not yet share it will never be known, for he did not live to see the end of the war.

When the president announced he would seek reelection in 1944 for a fourth term, most voters fully expected him to serve four more years. In fact, he was already quite ill. Thus when he and the party leaders chose his running mate in 1944 they were, in effect, selecting the next president. Their choice, Harry S. Truman, senator from Missouri, proved a controversial one. Truman's qualifications for the vice presidency rested principally on his political support. Labor, represented by the CIO's Sidney Hillman, agreed that he was acceptable. As a border-state senator, he could count on backing from Southern Democrats. He also had a good reputation for his clearheaded and tough investigation of war industries. Most significant, his leading competitors, including the current vice president, Henry Wallace, all had serious liabilities.

TRUMAN'S FIRST ADMINISTRATION Like any vice president who graduates to the presidency in a crisis, Truman's first problem in the spring of 1945 was to establish command of the office. Although he pledged to pursue Roosevelt's policies, he did not. Nor could he. He lacked Roosevelt's consummate political skill.

Moreover, Roosevelt had not really defined a postwar policy except in the vaguest way. So Truman was on his own.

Much of what Truman did during the eight years of his presidency was dictated by his attempts to find and secure a political constituency. He had to hold onto the coalition that Roosevelt had assembled during the 1930s and perhaps try to extend it, particularly to strengthen it among African Americans who had migrated to Northern cities during the war in large numbers. Inevitably, he had to compromise among the conflicting interests of this coalition.

Like Roosevelt, Truman planned a rapid reconversion to peacetime production. In the last months of the war, he canceled hundreds of defense contracts. Only two days after V-J (Victory over Japan) Day, he modified controls over prices, wages, and raw materials. In November 1945 he terminated control of wage hikes exercised by the National War Labor Board. By the summer of 1946 he had reluctantly eliminated many controls over consumer prices. When the Republicans gained control of Congress in the elections of 1946, he eliminated the remaining price controls.

Deregulation of labor controls caused economic stress and brought serious political headaches to the new administration, which counted on unions for support. During the war, organized labor had rapidly increased its membership—from 10 million in 1941 to 14 million in 1945. Wage increases were modest during the war, but overtime and fringe benefits pushed up earnings. After the war, labor sought large increases, and management was just as determined to prevent them. The result was an outbreak of strikes as substantial as any in the twentieth century. Walkouts at General Motors and in the oil and steel industries involved hundreds of thousands of workers. In April 1946 the United Mine Workers went out. Finally, when railroad workers threatened a strike in May, Truman seized the railroads.

This rash of strikes fueled public hostility to unions and energized the successful Republican congressional campaign of 1946. When it met in 1947, the new Republican-controlled Congress

pledged to curb New Deal labor legislation. During the first four months of the session, members submitted seventy bills on this single issue. Finally, the Labor Committee chairmen in each house hammered out a compromise law. On the Senate side, conservative Robert A. Taft of Ohio provided leadership. In the House of Representatives, this was done by Fred A. Hartley, Jr., of New Jersey. The resulting Taft-Hartley Act outlawed the closed shop, in which every worker was required to join a union before employment. It required unions to file annual financial reports with the Labor Department. Right-to-work laws passed by states (that forbade requiring workers to join unions once on the job) were legalized, and the president was granted power to interrupt strikes with an eighty-day "cooling-off" period.

Passed by Congress on June 9, 1947, the bill went to Truman for his signature. Fully aware of the political consequences, he returned the bill with a sharply worded veto message. He denounced the legislation as contrary to the "national policy of economic freedom." It was, he continued, "a clear threat to the successful working of our democratic society." Congress thought so little of his arguments that it overrode his veto the following day. The bill became law.

In practice, the Taft-Hartley Act was not what either side claimed. It neither seriously limited the activities of organized labor nor destroyed democracy. In some ways, it represented the basis for a more permanent peace between management and labor, for while it trimmed the power of unions, it certainly did not seriously limit them. However, the controversy surrounding the act helped overcome suspicions of Truman in the union movement.

Truman's vigorous defense of labor in his veto was one key to his successful 1948 reelection campaign. Another was his overture to black voters. Trying to hold on to and expand Roosevelt's electoral coalition, Truman realized that he needed the support of blacks. The steps he took to win their votes were small but significant.

Following the Republican victory in 1946, Truman issued an executive order creating a special Civil Rights Committee headed by Charles E.

Wilson, president of the General Electric Company. Other members included representatives from labor organizations and the NAACP. The group was charged with writing proposals to improve the lives of American blacks. Several months later, on October 29, 1947, it submitted its suggestions. These included home rule for the largely black city of Washington, D.C., an end to racial segregation in the U.S. armed forces, protection of voting rights in state primary elections, an end to restrictive covenants in housing sales, a permanent commission on civil rights, and equal treatment in and access to facilities in interstate commerce.

Truman was certainly not prepared to push ahead on each one of these demands. Indeed, it took twenty years, the rise of new leaders like Martin Luther King, Jr., and a social convulsion of extraordinary proportions to realize most of them. But the president did include some of this agenda in his 1948 civil rights message to Congress. And by July 1948 he had started desegregation of the armed services, gradually phasing out all-black combat units. (It was not until October 1954 that the last segregated army unit was abolished.)

THE ELECTION OF 1948 Truman's initiative in civil rights earned him support from black leaders and from Democratic liberals, but it splintered his allegiances in the South. Bedrock Southern conservatives revolted against his nomination in 1948. When Northern liberals placed a strong civil rights plank in the party platform, a group of "Dixiecrats" bolted the party, met in Birmingham, Alabama, to found the States' Rights party, and nominated Governor Strom Thurmond of South Carolina for president.

The Republicans helped Truman hold on to what remained of his coalition by presenting a distinctly conservative alternative. Their nominee in 1948, Governor Thomas Dewey of New York, a candidate in 1944 against Roosevelt, had earned national praise for his attacks on orga-

nized crime and was known as a staunch conservative and a foe of the New Deal. As a campaigner, however, he left much to be desired. Dewey lacked the visible energy, humor, and humanity of Truman. The president's campaign was also aided by a splinter party to the left of the Democratic party. A new Progressive party nominated Henry Wallace, one-time vice president and then Truman's secretary of commerce. Running on a program criticizing Truman's cold war foreign policy and with Communist party support, Wallace actually deflected criticism away from the president. Truman could accurately claim that he represented the political center of the Democratic party—and perhaps the nation.

Truman relished nothing so much as a good fight. Once Congress had adjourned from a special session called during the summer, Truman began an energetic campaign trip by train across the nation. Punching away at the self-confident Republicans, he stressed the continuity between his presidency and the New Deal. The results of the November election proved how successful this strategy had been. He won 24 million votes to Dewey's 21 million. He had held the New Deal coalition together despite some defections in the South. He had also helped lay the political groundwork for federal support for civil rights.

TRUMAN'S SECOND ADMINISTRATION Truman began his second term in office with the promise of swift and extensive social reform. His rousing address in Congress on January 15, 1949, called for a "Fair Deal." His words and his program echoed many of Roosevelt's 1944 ideas. He began by defining the purpose of government: to use the nation's wealth "for the benefit of all." This definition implied intervention in the economy to maintain healthy production and regulation to ensure a fair distribution of goods and services. Specifically, Truman wanted a rise in taxes, repeal of the Taft-Hartley Act, a higher minimum wage, farm price supports, an increase

President Truman, during his "whistlestop campaign of 1948." This old-fashioned style worked one more time, but the Democratic coalition that elected him was seriously strained . . . and the railroads were already in severe decline. (Harry S. Truman Library)

in Social Security benefits and expansion of the system, a national prepaid medical insurance system, and government construction of more low-cost public housing units.

But the president failed to translate his surprise victory in November into legislative success. Despite a Democratic majority returned to the Senate and the House, the party remained divided over reforms. Medical insurance and Truman's agricultural program fell to intensive lobbying by doctors and farm groups. Repeal of the Taft-Hartley Act could not attain a majority, and the claims of racial minorities were ignored

despite the promises of the civil rights plank of the Democratic platform. Thus although civil rights had entered the legislative agenda, it had not yet become a compelling part of it. Only in the extension of Social Security coverage and in housing did the president achieve major successes. The 1950 amendments to the Social Security Act of 1935 extended coverage and raised benefits. The Housing Act of 1949 mandated construction of 810,000 low-cost units.

Spy convictions and Senator McCarthy's anti-communist crusade also helped weaken Truman in the last two years of his administration and

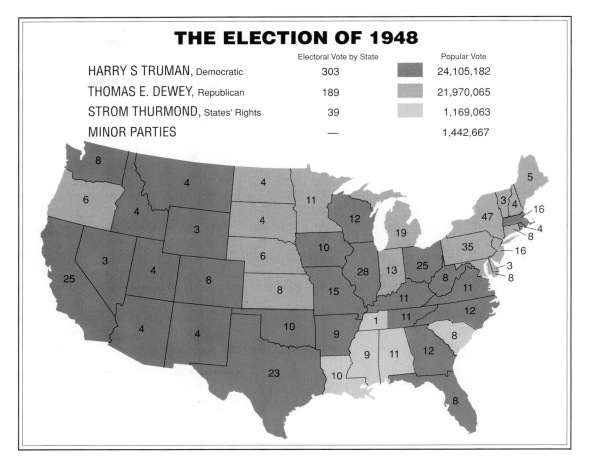

THE ELECTION OF 1948

	Electoral Vote by State		Popular Vote
HARRY S TRUMAN, Democratic	303		24,105,182
THOMAS E. DEWEY, Republican	189		21,970,065
STROM THURMOND, States' Rights	39		1,169,063
MINOR PARTIES	—		1,442,667

slow the momentum for reform. Nothing went well for the president. The war in Korea touched off a constitutional crisis when the commander of the U.S. forces, General Douglas MacArthur, openly criticized Truman's policy of limited warfare in 1951. In effect, MacArthur challenged the power of the president to set policy. As commander in chief of the armed forces, Truman had no choice but to remove the popular general if he wished to maintain civilian control of the military. In Congress, his Fair Deal failed to generate support. Scandals and accusations of communist influence surrounded the Democratic party. Clearly, Truman had become a serious liability.

The Eisenhower Years

THE SHIFT TO THE SUBURBS The disintegration of Truman's support came partly from opposition to his leadership and partly from shifts in social structure and demography that began after the war. New Deal rhetoric lost some of its power to galvanize voters, as memories of the depression faded and the new affluence of the 1950s took hold. Much of this affluence became visible in the suburbs that sprang up around cities. Of course, American cities had long had suburbs, but traditionally these were built out along commuter rail lines. In the 1940s and 1950s, suburbs were connected to central cities by means of new highways. Because of available loans and favorable tax laws, it was often cheaper to buy a new house than to refurbish or even rent an existing urban dwelling. As the suburbs proliferated, they tended to depend less on the central city and more on their own booming economies. In effect, suburbs had begun to compete seriously with central cities for industry, jobs, population, and political power.

The suburbs won a quick victory. After the war, most cities lost jobs in manufacturing and trade while gaining modestly in service industries. Employment in all three of these categories soared in the suburbs. By 1960 the central cities had lost almost 300,000 jobs. They were also left with diminished tax bases. Responding to this shrinking opportunity, increasing numbers of affluent or aspiring whites abandoned the central cities. Their places were taken by blacks and Hispanics. In 1950 the black population of central cities was about 12 percent of the total. Twenty years later, the percentage had doubled. (But the much smaller proportion of blacks in the suburbs remained about the same.) Political power followed affluence to the suburbs.

If the predominant image of the early 1950s was suburban life, the focus of that image was the family. Newspapers, magazines, radio, movies, and the new medium of television extolled the virtues of family life. Behind this publicity lay a surprising change in American demographics. After World War II, divorce rates fell sharply and the marriage rate (the percentage of eligible persons who in fact marry) rapidly increased. So too did the birth rate, which shot up from 20.4 births per 1,000 population in 1945 to 25.0 per 1,000 in 1955. This increase reversed decades of decline in the number of children born to American families.

Added to the family-centered and child-centered focus in popular culture and social mores

This elegant new television set was disguised to look like a piece of living room furniture. But the boy turning up the volume shows by his costume that television is his own window to an outside world of imaginary dramas and endless consumer delights. (Howard Frank)

was an emphasis on leisure living and informality inspired by California. During the war, the federal government had invested huge amounts of capital in industries there. By 1945, 9 percent of federal employees worked in the state. And this was only part of the boom. By the mid-1960s, California's population increased from 5 to 10 percent of the U.S. total. For those who did not live there, the state remained the most popular place to visit. Of all the states in the union, California exhibited an accelerated and exaggerated version of contemporary social trends. It was the most urbanized (and suburbanized) state. It had the most extensive freeway system. It had a huge

Diaper service in California. This obviously staged photograph is a picture of a 1950s dream: a bungalow project, a crowd of mothers and children, and diaper service at every door to suggest that it was all just beginning. (Ralph Crane, *Life* Magazine ©1958, Time Inc.)

modern aircraft and defense industry. Its lifestyles were the subject of countless Hollywood films and television shows—as well as the backdrop for most commercials. In a sense, California was America's future and a symbol of the new postwar economy and culture.

THE ELECTION OF 1952 Some of these changes began to register first in the 1952 election. The Republicans' vice-presidential candidate, Richard M. Nixon, was a congressman and senator from California. The mood of the electorate tended toward conservatism, reflecting in part the new priorities of suburban life. More important, the Democratic coalition reestablished by Truman in 1948 began to show some signs of age and strain, as the weight of political power shifted away from the central cities to the suburbs, and from the old industrial East to the new industrial West.

Both sides bitterly contested the 1952 election and, consequently, issues were sometimes lost in the flurry of flimsy and preposterous charges and countercharges. Republican chances appeared very good—but so had they in 1948. However, this time the party's choice of a candidate—General Dwight David Eisenhower—proved to be enormously popular.

Born in 1890, "Ike" grew up in Abilene, Kansas. From the time he entered the U.S. Military Academy in 1911, Eisenhower's life was defined by the Army. Mischievous, handsome, and athletic as a student, he rose, rank by rank, to become commander of the allied armies in Europe during World War II.

Women: The War and After

In 1945, House Beautiful *magazine addressed its female readers in an article on returning soldiers entitled "Home Should Be Even More Wonderful Than He Remembers It." As the author put it, "He's head man again. . . . Your part in the remaking of this man is to fit his home to him, understanding why he wants it this way, forgetting your own preferences."*

As this article suggests, the postwar years left women with an ambiguous experience that touched their identity and particularly their social image. During the war, they had been welcomed—and even encouraged—to enter the labor force to take the place of men drafted into the armed forces. Now they were encouraged—and sometimes forced—to leave. Many of them, however, did not leave; they simply could not afford to stop working. But most of these women took up jobs that were traditionally labeled "women's work," such as waiting on tables or nursing. Married women who remained in the work force found themselves shouldering a double burden: a job from nine to five and housework and cooking afterward. Statistics demonstrate that the percentage of working women shrank after 1945, but did not fall as low as prewar levels. In fact, after the initial drop, the number and percentage of working women resumed a steady increase.

These abrupt changes in women's activities gave rise to contradictory and conflicting pictures of the proper role of women in American society. During the war, the popular press, newspapers, and government publications stressed the contributions of women to the war effort. Of

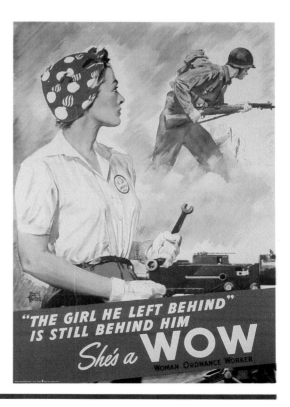

Plate 1. In this poster the female mechanic looks up from her workbench to dream of her husband in combat. There is nothing very ambiguous about this photo: The woman is making the weapon that the man is using. And the relationship is quite clear: She remains behind him. (Franklin D. Roosevelt Library)

Plate 2. This woman in a 1959 Sears ad is also working—but within the new context of do-it-yourself and fix-it-up domesticity. With her husband now home from the war, she manages to look both prim and seductive, as if the paint brush were only an afterthought. (The Nostalgia Factory)

Plate 3. With this circle of women in the doctor's waiting room, the artist has captured three important responsibilities of motherhood: nurture, companionship and comfort of children, and education. Keeping with this carefully gendered world, the doctor is a man and his nurse a woman. (Reprinted from The Saturday Evening Post © 1955 Curtis Publishing Company)

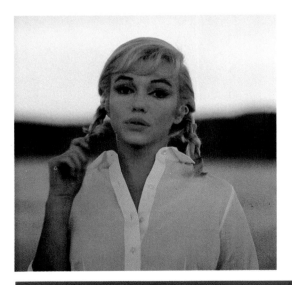

Plate 4. One image of women in the 1950s was epitomized by the movie star Marilyn Monroe: beautiful, sexy, fragile, and unapproachable—a goddess with a little girl's heart. What Monroe represented to the American male in the 1950s was re-examined by feminists (such as Gloria Steinem) in the 1980s, who found an unexpected strength of character struggling with her intuitive sense that she was ultimately a victim. Monroe's legend has continued to grow ever since her apparent suicide in 1962; despite arguments over how talented an actress she really was, by 1990 she attained the kind of status in our society that ancient Greeks reserved for minor gods. (Eve Arnold/Magnum)

The Saturday Evening

POST

September 19, 1959 - *15¢*

**Does it Help
to Swap Visits
With the Russians?**

Plate 5. This 1959 *Saturday Evening Post* cover picturing the dreams of the housewife and the career woman is intentionally asymmetrical. The secretary, surrounded by piles of work, dreams of a helpful, sharing husband. The housewife, whose husband lolls in front of the television while she contends with dishes and a cranky child, dreams of an unflustered day at the office. (Reprinted from The Saturday Evening Post, © 1959 Curtiss Publishing Company)

course, there were exceptions: In 1943, government and the press alike lamented the fate of "latch-key" children, working mothers' unsupervised progeny who returned from school to an empty house and "unfilled hours of loneliness." Generally, however, when women enlisted to work for the duration of the war, they were well received. Indeed, during the war, both major political parties endorsed an Equal Rights Amendment, which would have improved wages and job opportunities for women; however, both Secretary of Labor Frances Perkins and Eleanor Roosevelt, the president's wife, declined to support it.

After the war, government, business, and labor unions pressured women to return home. Women's magazines were filled with articles urging meticulous housekeeping, giving suggestions for improving domestic skills, or showering readers with new beauty and fashion tips. Eventually this pressure—and the desire of many women to live up to ideals of femininity derived from novels and movies— affected a wide range of behavior. It also led to a "family first" ideology that dominated American culture during

Women's Participation in the Labor Force

Married, with Children Under 6		With Children Under Age 1	
1950	11.9%	1976	31.0%
1955	16.2	1978	25.3
1960	18.6	1980	38.0
1965	23.3	1982	43.9
1970	30.3	1983	43.1
1975	36.6	1984	46.7
1980	41.5	1985	48.4
1985	53.4	1986	49.8
1987	56.8	1987	50.8

Source: *The New York Times*

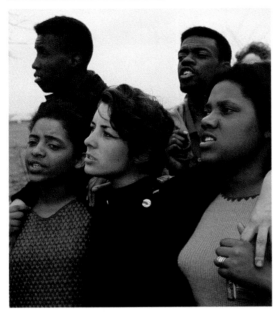

Plate 6. Women march for political freedom in Selma, Alabama (1965). Participating in the civil rights movement was, for some women, an exhilarating but troubling experience that helped spur the movement for their own equality. (Bob Adelman/Magnum)

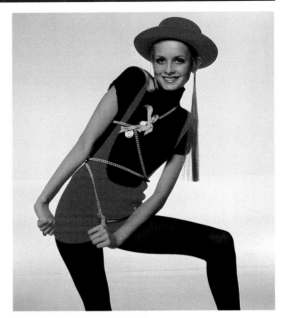

Plate 7. The British model Twiggy was extraordinarily popular in the 1960s. She represented the invasion of British fashion that came as a part of London's resurgence as a sophisticated international center. Note that the clothing she models has no obvious gender identity. (Bert Stern Photography)

the 1950s, giving that period a tone of orthodoxy and conservatism. According to the new domestic philosophy, women—whatever else they did—should put family above all else. As girls, their goal was marriage; as women, their duties revolved around caring for children and maintaining a home.

Statistics suggest that the revived ideology of domesticity was linked to changes in family-related behavior. From 1945 to the end of the 1950s, family stability increased. After a momentary postwar rise, the divorce rate in the United States fell until about 1960; thereafter, it increased sharply and then zoomed upward in the 1970s. After the war, the marriage rate also increased; not only were more persons of eligible age actually married, but the average age for marriage had also dropped. For women, this meant that about half married before the age of twenty. Most significant, the birth rate rose sharply after the war, reaching a peak in 1956. Simply put, more women were having more babies—thus reversing, temporarily, a twentieth-century American trend toward smaller families.

By the end of the 1950s, most of these trends began to shift. The marriage and birth rates declined, the divorce rate increased, the family appeared less stable, and the role of women was no longer clearly defined. Pressure to appear a model mother remained, but women increasingly found the role irrelevant. The suburban home, touted as the ideal environment in the 1950s, could be a barren place, where boring and empty days drove many women to various addictions (alcohol, barbiturates) in an effort to disguise their aimlessness. Perhaps more important, lifestyles were changing. Increasing accessibility of the means for birth control ("the pill" and intrauterine devices) made it easier for women to control reproduction. And economic necessity—the need to pay for the affluent lifestyles that modern families sought—often required women to work.

Plate 9. Despite real progress in legal rights and in the workplace, women were still considered by many men to be primarily sex objects. The Miss America pageant (pictured here in 1972) continued throughout the period to celebrate femininity as a blend of bathing beauty, charm, a movie-star smile, and a little bit of talent. (UPI/Bettmann Newsphotos)

Plate 8 (left). This march for the Equal Rights Amendment, at the Houston Women's Convention of 1977, may well have represented the high point of the women's movement, as well as the career of then-Representative Bella Abzug, wearing the hat that became her signature. (Stephen D. Northrop © 1977 Time Magazine)

Plate 10. The fact that this is a picture of a woman is the least important part of this ad. The copy recognizes that gender means less and less in the business world, and it is intentionally, even obviously, neutral. (Hyatt Corporation)

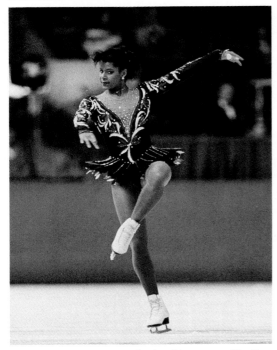

Plate 11. For women and minorities, every "first" is a visible triumph. Debi Thomas, runner-up in the 1988 Winter Olympics, became the first American black woman to achieve real prominence in figure skating. She is pictured here at the January, 1988, U.S. Figure Skating Championships (which she won) in Denver. (Wide World Photos)

Plate 12. Bishop Barbara Harris, the first woman bishop of the Angelican Church, in her ordination robes on February 11, 1988. Her elevation to this high role caused some consternation among conservatives but was hailed by others as opening the church to some of the more egalitarian and democratic forces at work in American society. (Wide World Photos)

Women in the Labor Force as a Percentage of Total Female Population, 1945–80*

1945	38.1
1950	33.0
1955	34.8
1960	37.7
1965	39.3
1970	43.4
1975	46.3
1980	51.6
1984	53.7

*Male participation in the labor force ranges from about 77 to 80 percent in this same period.

As women increasingly entered the job market in the 1960s, they encountered discrimination, the effects of inferior education, and sexism. Learning from the civil rights movement of the late 1950s and 1960s, some women organized to advance their cause. By 1966 the National Organization for Women (NOW) began to concentrate its efforts on passage of the Equal Rights Amendment (ERA) to the Constitution; the amendment passed Congress on March 22, 1972, but failed to win the necessary ratification by two-thirds of the states. In 1973, the Supreme Court in Roe v. Wade *assured the right of women to secure abortions.*

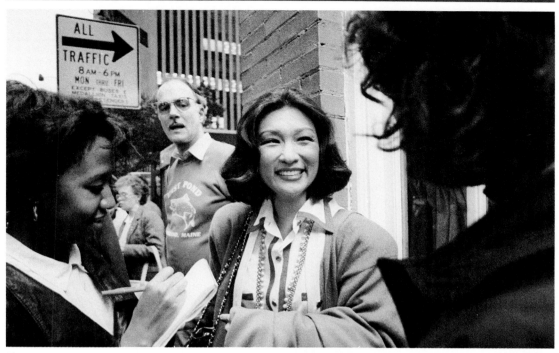

Plate 13. Connie Chung, NBC News anchor, finds herself the object of an interview in October, 1987, after a fire in the network headquarters in New York City. During the 1980s Chung became one of the best known, highest paid newspeople on American television. (Wide World Photos)

Plate 14. A massive demonstration in early 1989 in favor of maintaining the power of women to make their own reproductive decisions failed to prevent the Supreme Court from modifying those rights. But the "pro-choice" movement was energized by the court's decision. (A. Tannebaum/SYGMA)

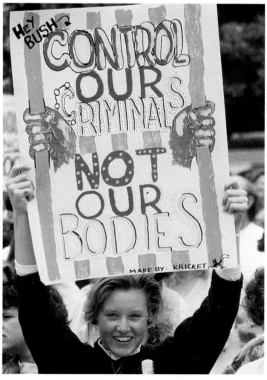

Enormous counterpressures developed despite these rulings. Many women did not wish to be "liberated" from traditional roles centering on the family; housewives often felt slighted by the career-oriented rhetoric of the women's movement. Many men resented the attack on their dominant position in the workplace. By 1982 the ERA had been blocked and its life as a proposed constitutional amendment ended. National agitation to end abortions, control contraception, and regulate sexual behavior of teenage girls grew quickly. As even more women entered the labor force, the conflict over their roles remained unsettled. New issues like child care and dual-track careers emerged. And in July, 1989, the Supreme Court, in Webster v. Reproductive Health Services *returned power to limit abortions to the states.*

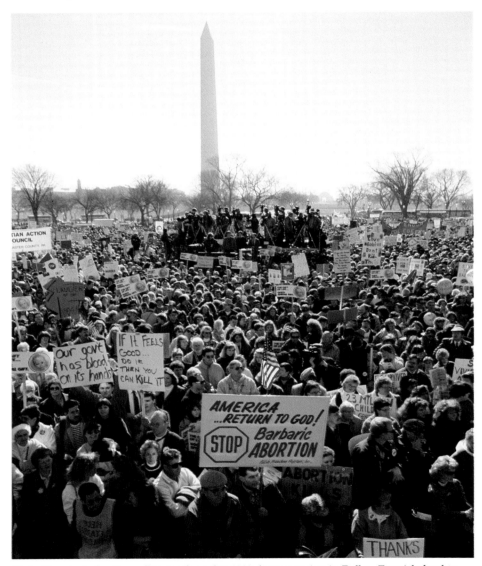

Plate 15. Anti-abortion rallies (such as this 1989 demonstration in Dallas, Texas) helped to inject the issue into national and state elections. Such groups won the battle of language, if nothing else, by persuading politicians, the news media, and even their opponents to refer to them as "pro-life." (David Woo/SYGMA)

The Baby Boom: Total Births and Rate per 1,000 Population

	Number of Births	Births per 1,000 Population
1935	2,377,000	18.7
1940	2,559,000	19.4
1945	2,858,000	20.4
1950	3,632,000	24.1
1955	4,097,000	25.0
1960	4,258,000	23.7
1965	3,760,000	19.4
1970	3,731,000	18.4
1975	3,144,000	14.6
1980	3,612,000	15.9
1984	3,697,000	15.7

Source: U.S. Department of Commerce, Bureau of the Census, *Statistical Abstract of the United States, 1986* (Washington, D.C.: Government Printing Office, 1985), p. 56.

Eisenhower's lack of civilian experience cost him very little in his political career. His position in the Army required the exercise of every skill needed by a politician. Furthermore, he owed no political debts. In fact, he had been approached earlier by the Democrats seeking him as a candidate. Thus when he declared his willingness to run as a Republican in 1952, he quickly became the front-running candidate. To heal any breaches in the party between moderates and conservatives, Eisenhower offered the vice presidency to Richard Nixon, a man known for his hard-line anticommunist views and popular with conservatives. The party adopted a relatively moderate platform, but the rhetoric of the campaign charged treason in high places and promised to crusade against communism, corruption, and the war in Korea.

For the Democrats, the choice was not easy. Truman realized his unpopularity but still wanted to play kingmaker. Adlai Stevenson, governor of Illinois, secured Truman's favor and the nomination, but he had an almost impossible task. He

had to endorse the previous twenty years of Democratic rule, yet declare his independence from Truman. He also had to hold onto the Democratic coalition that was increasingly divided on such questions as civil rights. Unfortunately for him, Stevenson's personality became an issue. Witty and elegant in his speeches, he earned loyal support from liberals. But to conservatives he appeared to be the incarnation of the suspect Eastern intellectual lambasted by McCarthy.

Despite a momentary shock when it appeared that Richard Nixon might have to withdraw because of charges that he had operated an illegal slush fund of campaign donations, the Republicans stayed on course. Nixon convinced most critics that the charges were groundless. After his famous explanatory "Checkers speech" (named for the pet dog his daughter had received as a gift), Nixon deflected criticism from the issue and convinced Eisenhower he was not a liability to the ticket. When Eisenhower promised to go to Korea, implying he would end the war, the outcome was all but decided. On November 4, Eisenhower won a landslide victory: 33 million votes to 27 million for Stevenson. The voters also swept Republican majorities into the House and Senate for the first time since 1946.

EISENHOWER'S FIRST ADMINISTRATION

Eisenhower's concept of government was a conservative one. He believed in balanced federal budgets and minimal intervention in the economy. But he did not seek to undo New Deal reforms. He hoped, instead, to create a harmonious partnership between business and government that would generate prosperity and opportunity. In large measure he succeeded—except in the area of civil rights. Within American society, the forces that touched off the Montgomery boycott and brought Martin Luther King, Jr., to national prominence proved to be irresistible. Over the rest of the world, the rise of former colonies to independence and the wholesale liberation of formerly subjected peoples brought issues of racial equality to the bargaining tables

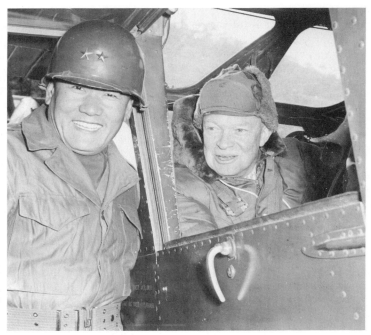

Ike in Korea. President-elect Dwight Eisenhower toured Korea in December 1952. His campaign for the presidency succeeded, in part, because of promises that he would be able to end the war quickly. (Wide World)

of international relations. Increasingly in the contest between capitalism and communism, the United States could ill afford to persist in old ways of racial injustice, for at least in part, the outcome of that contest lay in winning support in the Third World of black and brown peoples. By the beginning of the Kennedy administration in 1961, such issues had reached the flash point. Would American society finally accept its black members as equal participants? Or would the civil rights movement end in confrontation and violence?

Eisenhower's first priority on assuming the presidency was to defuse the anger and hostility in American society that his election had tapped. The president had to fend off Joseph McCarthy, whose attacks had become progressively wilder. At first, Eisenhower treated McCarthy with caution, although he personally disliked the senator's extremism. Eisenhower had caved in to pressure during the campaign and shied away from defending former Secretary of State George Marshall, an old friend, who was under attack by McCarthy. Once in office, he still refused to

challenge the senator. When McCarthy attacked "reds" in the Army in the summer of 1954, Congress—not the president—finally decided he had gone too far and voted to censure him.

On the issue of Korea, the new president did act decisively. Shortly after the election, in December 1952, Eisenhower visited Korea as promised. He renewed talks with North Korea and the People's Republic of China, and by summer, he had achieved an armistice. Thorny questions of repatriating soldiers were finally resolved. After three years of bitter struggle, peace was restored in 1953, but victory had eluded both sides.

In defense policy, the president developed what he called the "New Look" strategy to replace the large conventional military buildup pushed by Truman. This policy projected small, efficient defense budgets, allowing Eisenhower to redeem a campaign pledge to keep budgets balanced. Production would concentrate on sophisticated nuclear weapons and delivery systems—a strategy that would also provide deterrence against attacks from the Soviet Union.

The New Look plan had other implications. It concentrated on rearmament and self-defense for European nations, including West Germany. It did help the president maintain relatively low federal spending, with a balanced budget in three years and minimal deficits in two other years. It also enabled Eisenhower and Secretary of State John Foster Dulles to declare a policy of "massive retaliation." By this, Dulles meant that the United States would employ nuclear weapons against the Soviet Union in case of aggression.

Dulles's grand strategy based on U.S. nuclear superiority, however, had two flaws. First, it proved to be part bluster. The commitment to "roll back" communism turned out to be a hollow promise; twice, the United States stood by while the Soviets crushed popular movements in eastern Europe. Second, it was a policy that had minimal effect on turbulent Third World countries. Policies aimed at securing formal alliances against the Soviet Union had little to offer millions of people struggling to cast off colonialism, military dictatorships, and corrupt oligarchies. When revolutions occurred in the Third World, the American response was often worried and hostile. Lacking a flexible view of the dynamics of social and economic change, the United States frequently intervened secretly to retard or even overthrow such movements. Thus throughout the Eisenhower years, the Central Intelligence Agency (CIA) carried on clandestine operations in such countries as Iran, Guatemala, and Vietnam.

If some Republican conservatives hoped to undo the New Deal welfare state, they were not heartened by the president's domestic program. Eisenhower did agree to legislation that lowered farm parity supports from 90 percent to 70 percent on most commodities. These price supports were designed to guarantee a minimum living standard to farmers, but cutting them slightly did not in any way constitute a return to free market competition. Two other programs actually increased federal spending: a Social Security Act in 1954, which extended coverage to self-employed workers, and a new public housing program. In May 1954 Eisenhower signed a bill to construct the St. Lawrence Seaway, a waterway that would join the Great Lakes to the Atlantic Ocean via the St. Lawrence River. Two years later, the president signed an act to fund a system of more than 40,000 miles of interstate highways. It was the largest public works project in American history.

Inadvertently, Eisenhower initiated activism in an area where he had hoped to avoid change. Early in his administration, the president appointed California governor Earl Warren to be chief justice of the United States. But he did not anticipate that Warren would lead the Supreme Court into a period of social activism that would help redefine and broaden government guarantees of equality and civil rights. The Warren Court's most important decision came quickly, in the case of *Brown* v. *Board of Education* (1954). This unanimous decision revised the language of American democracy. Citing the evidence of experts, the Court rejected the prevailing and still legal school segregation on the grounds that any separation causes psychological damage. In addition, the *Brown* decision ratified the commitment of a growing number of Americans to equal rights. Like the GI Bill, it emphasized equality of education as the means to achieve equal citizenship.

For integrationists, the Supreme Court decision fixed their tactics. They could now confront local and state segregationists knowing that ultimately they could depend on the courts. Certainly this did not eliminate the risks they ran, but it did help determine the outcome of the struggle. This was the strategy that Martin Luther King, Jr., applied in the Montgomery boycott two years later and in Birmingham in 1963.

Warren's decision put Eisenhower in a difficult position. The president did not wish to push desegregation, although he had agreed to integration of the armed forces. During the remainder of his years in office, he refused to speak in favor of school desegregation and never affirmed his agreement—moral or otherwise—with the *Brown* decision. This excessive caution and lack

Central High School in Little Rock, Arkansas. The airborne troops, sent to ensure integration, watch as a few black students are escorted through a jeering mob of white students. (UPI/Bettmann Newsphotos)

of leadership encouraged some white Southerners to believe that the inevitable would never occur. But they were wrong. Even Eisenhower was finally forced to act. In 1957 he signed a weak but significant civil rights bill. More important, when Governor Orval Faubus of Arkansas tried to stop the integration of Little Rock Central High School in September 1957, the president was obliged to intervene. Faubus disobeyed a court order and installed the National Guard in front of the school to prevent black students from entering. After serious rioting, sparked by the governor's inflammatory remarks, Eisenhower dispatched federal troops to the city and appealed for calm. It was a small step, taken reluctantly. But it had enormous implications for

Jackie Robinson

If you do this you will be suspended from the league. You will find that the friends you have in the press box will not support you, that you will be outcasts. I do not care if half the league strikes. Those who do it will encounter quick retribution. All will be suspended and I don't care if it wrecks the National League for five years. This is the United States of America and one citizen has as much right to play as another.

The National League will go down the line with Robinson whatever the consequences.

With this firm statement, Ford Frick, president of the National Baseball League, squelched a strike planned by the St. Louis Cardinals in early 1947. The Cardinals, with support from players throughout the league, had decided to refuse to play on May 6, when the team faced the Brooklyn Dodgers for the first encounter of the season. The reason: the Dodgers had hired Jackie Robinson, a black man, to play first base.

Up to 1947 the National and American Leagues were lily white. Even the seating in some ball parks was segregated. The "national pastime" was a white man's sport. There were all-black baseball leagues with talented players, but none had made it yet into the majors.

Quite clearly, hiring Robinson was an experiment. Just out of the Army in 1944, Robinson joined the all-black Kansas City Monarchs. In August 1945 he was approached by a scout from the Brooklyn Dodgers. Branch Rickey, the Dodgers' president, had picked Robinson to be the first black player in the major leagues. Rickey hired Robinson and assigned him to the Montreal Royals farm club for the 1946 season. Then, early in 1947, he announced that Robinson would join the Dodgers for the coming season.

Both Robinson and Rickey had prepared for what happened next. Several Southern teammates protested the presence of a black man. Other players proclaimed that Robinson (and by implication all black men) lacked the talent to play baseball. Some opposing teams, like the Philadelphia Phillies, peppered him with obscenities from the dugout when he batted or fielded. Travel for road games proved to be very difficult because many hotels and restaurants refused to serve Robinson or seat him with his fellow players. Robinson had been coached by Rickey to cope with these taunts and insults.

In Boston, however, Robinson reached the breaking point. Fans shouted and cursed at him when he took the field. They also screamed at Pee Wee Reese, the Brooklyn shortstop. Reese was a white Southerner, and the fans taunted him for playing on the same team as a black man. When the shouting became more intense, Reese suddenly left his position. He walked over to first base and put his arm around Robinson. In a loud, clear voice, he shouted: "Yell. Heckle. Do anything you want. We came here to play baseball." The jeering died down.

Gradually, the heckling stopped all over the league. Robinson batted and fielded better than any of his detractors had predicted. His fiery hitting and base running helped the Dodgers to win the National League pennant for the first time in years. In the fall, Robinson was voted Rookie of the Year. Rickey's experiment in integration, and Robinson's talent, had made it possible for black players in sports to begin to compete as equals.

Picture: UPI/Bettmann Newsphotos

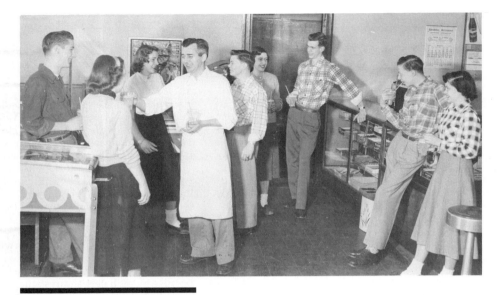

Teenagers in a snack bar. The teenage subculture of the 1950s provided endless fascination—and worry—for the rest of society. New dating customs, dancing, and music reflected the effects of postwar prosperity and new, more permissive methods of childrearing. (The Bettmann Archive)

the future pattern of civil rights agitation, for it put the federal government publicly on the side of the integrationists.

THE ELECTION OF 1956 AND THE DAWN OF THE YOUTH CULTURE Even though he delegated a great many tasks, Eisenhower's congenial and low-key administration focused attention and power on his own leadership. Thus his sudden heart attack on September 24, 1955, pointed up how fragile his administration was. He improved rapidly but then suffered a serious attack of ileitis in the spring of 1956, which required intestinal surgery. During neither illness was the president completely incapacitated, but attention nevertheless focused on Vice President Nixon. Viewing him with suspicion, some party regulars talked openly of a new vice-presidential candidate in 1956. But speculation quickly fizzled, and the Republicans renominated Nixon along with Eisenhower.

The Democrats turned once again to Adlai Stevenson, who then allowed the convention to select the vice-presidential candidate. Their choice was Estes Kefauver of Tennessee, a liberal senator with a reputation for racket and crime investigation. But he was unpopular with party bosses, whom he had offended in his investigations.

Another leading (but unsuccessful) candidate for vice president was John Fitzgerald Kennedy, senator from Massachusetts. Kennedy's rise to national attention in the late 1950s signaled the beginnings of a political and cultural transformation that came to fruition in the early 1960s. This new politics emphasized youth and activism, reflecting important changes in American lifestyles.

Beginning in the middle and late 1950s, American culture exhibited changes that began to disrupt the conservative, family-oriented assumptions of the immediate postwar period. The suburban culture that only a few years earlier had seemed to settle permanently on American society suddenly showed flaws. Beyond the books and articles that now criticized the smugness and conformity of the suburbs, many suburban children were defying those values. These young people absorbed a new youth culture that differentiated them seriously from their parents. While it too exhibited strong elements of conformism—its customs were organized around rituals of romance, "going steady," and marriage—the new youth culture also had a more restless side, reflected in the emergence of new popular heroes such as movie stars James Dean, Marlon Brando, and Natalie Wood. Dean, in particular, in such films as *Rebel Without a Cause* (1955), captured a mood that rejected the preselected social and sexual roles for youth. His sensitive and emotional acting challenged a stereotyped postwar image of the American male as a military figure complete with crew cut.

Also of immense importance to the burgeoning youth culture was rock 'n' roll, a new popular music that had sprung out of America's urban black ghettos. With dramatic and direct sensuality, this music expressed feelings of love, hate, and other emotions in ways that delighted teenagers and appalled their parents, teachers, and religious leaders. Although groups of white artists capitalized on the success and energy of the new sound, its creative origins in the black experience were never far from the surface. Moreover, with the appearance of Elvis Presley, the new music absorbed energy and inspiration from a long tradition of country music.

The mass media played a crucial role in developing and popularizing this distinctive new youth culture. Magazines such as *Seventeen* informed teenage girls of changing styles and customs. Recorded music became available to almost every young person because of the mass marketing of long-playing plastic records and because of a dramatic growth in radio stations aimed at the youth market. Hollywood films, once produced for the entire family, increasingly targeted specific audience segments, and often

Actor James Dean had a brief but brilliant screen career before his fatal auto accident in 1955. Dean evoked a good deal of sympathy from teenagers for his roles of anguished and misunderstood youth. (The Bettmann Archive)

the most lucrative of these seemed to be youth. Consequently, film companies produced scores of movies in the late 1950s featuring delinquency and rock 'n' roll, seen by teenagers packed into the drive-in theaters that dotted the suburbs.

In a more subtle way, this generation of teenagers (the first suburban generation and the older brothers and sisters of the postwar baby boom) seemed adrift and in search of belief. Many of them, although they could not vote, were attracted by John Kennedy, with his youthful political style and his glamorous wife. They were not as hesitant as their elders to face a new world of changing social and racial relations.

Senator John F. Kennedy and Jacqueline Bouvier.
Senator Kennedy's marriage to socially prominent
Jacqueline Bouvier in 1953 proved to be a great political asset. His political style, stressing action, youth,
and glamour, helped make him a strong presidential
contender by the late 1950s. (UPI/Bettmann
Newsphotos)

But in 1956 the political stage still belonged to
the moderate Republicans, and Eisenhower and
Nixon won a dramatic victory, garnering 35.5 million votes to Stevenson and Kefauver's 26 million.
This endorsement of Eisenhower's administration did not extend to Congress, where the Democrats held on to majorities in both houses. It
seemed that the American public wanted mod-
eration at the presidential level and continued
activism in Congress.

EISENHOWER'S SECOND ADMINISTRA-
TION Despite his great personal victory in the
election of 1956, Eisenhower faced serious problems in the remainder of his presidential years.
Beginning in 1957 and extending into 1958, a serious recession gripped the economy. Unemployment rose from about 4 percent to 7 percent, and
the gross national product fell back by about 1
percent. Eisenhower refused to apply federal
stimuli, and he rejected calls for a tax cut or public
works projects. He insisted that the best policy
was to allow the economy to correct itself. This
stance, added to an influence-peddling scandal
that forced the White House staff chief, Sherman
Adams, to quit, hurt Republicans in the 1958
congressional elections. After November, the
Democrats controlled the House by 283 seats to
153 and the Senate by 64 to 34. Then, on November 26, the president suffered a mild stroke. He
recovered quickly but was left with a slight
speech impediment.

Facing a revived Democratic party that
claimed to have uncovered a "bomber gap" in
1956 and a public that was shocked when the
Russians launched *Sputnik*, the first successful
space satellite, in October 1957, Eisenhower had
to struggle to maintain his modest defense budget strategy. Pressure to increase defense spending and invest in huge civil defense programs
came from all sides. But Eisenhower gave little
ground. He did, however, step up funding for
space programs and created the National Aeronautics and Space Administration (NASA) in
1958. In September 1958 he signed the National
Defense Education Act, which provided about
$1 billion in loans and scholarships for the study
of mathematics, the sciences, and foreign
languages.

In the last two years of his administration,
Eisenhower revived attempts to negotiate with
the Russians. After the new Russian premier,
Nikita Khrushchev, took office in March 1958, he
announced a suspension of open-air nuclear testing. The United States followed suit in late summer. Eisenhower's most astute move was an
invitation to the Russian leader to visit the United
States in the fall of 1959. Khrushchev and his
party toured the country, visiting farms, cities,
and Disneyland in California. Final negotiations
at Camp David, Maryland, set a spring summit
meeting for Paris in 1960. The Russian premier's
trip had been controversial, touching off scattered
demonstrations, but he impressed many Americans with his energy and self-confidence.

Despite its possibilities, the opportunity for rapprochement with the Russians was lost. Shortly before the Paris conference in the spring of 1960, the Soviets announced the downing of an American U-2 aerial reconnaissance plane deep inside their territory. On May 9, one week before the summit meeting, Eisenhower accepted responsibility for the overflight. When the conference began, Khrushchev seemed determined to disrupt it, demanding a personal apology from the president. When Eisenhower refused, the Russian premier left Paris, and negotiations ended.

Perhaps all of these troubles sobered Eisenhower's thinking. As he left office in 1961, he delivered an address to the nation that was more warning than farewell. He underscored the basic themes of his administration. He had tried to keep defense spending down. He had wanted to avoid acrimonious and divisive issues such as civil rights. He had hoped that a stable economy would satisfy those who preferred quick social change. But now he feared a push for larger budgets, more social legislation, and an adventurous foreign policy. He warned the nation of a "military-industrial" complex and a technological power elite that might destroy American democracy:

> In the councils of government, we must guard against the acquisition of unwarranted influence, whether sought or unsought, by the military-industrial complex. The potential for the disastrous rise of misplaced power exists and will persist. We must never let the weight of this combination endanger our liberties or democratic processes.

This final cautionary statement about a defense establishment growing out of control had little effect on the exuberant young politicians about to take office. It seemed misplaced and excessively conservative. The day belonged to a new generation of leaders, to the Kennedys and the Kings. They were determined to face with new strategies some of the social and economic questions that had been gathering force during the last eight years.

The Kennedy Years

THE RENEWED PROMISE In November 1960, American voters chose a president who exemplified change and action. But John F. Kennedy defeated Richard Nixon by only a slim margin. At first, the action he proposed aimed at ending the slump in economic growth of the late 1950s and the impasse in foreign relations that Eisenhower had reached. But the new administration quickly became the focus for social forces that were transforming American society. Young, photogenic, with a richly accented voice, Kennedy radiated self-assurance. As a Catholic of Irish origins, he personified an era of rising expectations and growing confidence among groups formerly defined as being outside the mainstream of American politics. Together with more and more Americans, he believed that government could bring the nation a fuller and more satisfying life. Government could help correct the injustices of the past and fulfill the aspirations of the present.

Kennedy was simultaneously a tough-minded practical politician and a man of legend. The myths that surrounded him came in part from his wealth and his highly publicized accomplishments. In part they were inspired by his heroism in the Navy during World War II. The second son of Joseph Kennedy, an Irish-Catholic millionaire who was a major contributor to the Democratic party, John grew up to live out the ambitions of his father. Able to move easily and gracefully in the public eye, he won the acclaim and political power that had eluded his father.

Kennedy's nomination and election in 1960 represented a departure in American politics, and it symbolized the growing political importance of groups once held at arm's length in presidential politics. He was the first Roman Catholic to be elected president—an issue heavily debated in some sections of the country. Some Protestants, like the leadership of the 9-million-member

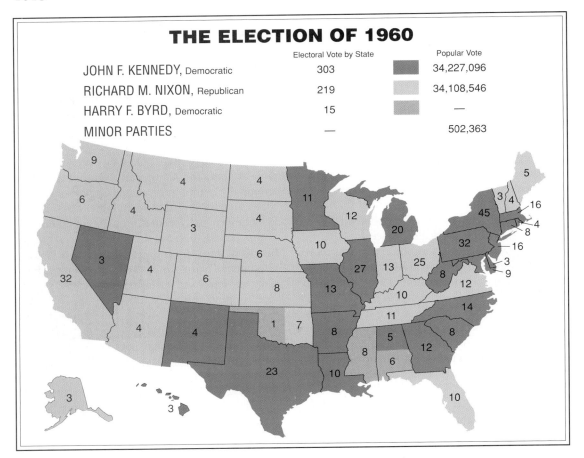

THE ELECTION OF 1960

	Electoral Vote by State	Popular Vote
JOHN F. KENNEDY, Democratic	303	34,227,096
RICHARD M. NIXON, Republican	219	34,108,546
HARRY F. BYRD, Democratic	15	—
MINOR PARTIES	—	502,363

Southern Baptist Convention, opposed him because of his faith. But his extraordinary proportion of Catholic votes (81 percent) neutralized most of this opposition.

The Catholic issue was just the first of many obstacles to Kennedy's nomination and victory. He also had to satisfy the various constituents of the Democratic party: liberals like Eleanor Roosevelt, labor leaders like Walter Reuther of the United Auto Workers, politicos like Harry Truman, and Southern conservatives. At best this road was tortuous, but Kennedy managed to neutralize his most serious opponents. His record as senator from Massachusetts had not been particularly distinguished, but he made up for

this weakness with political attractiveness and energy. Labor was reluctant to support him at first because of his tenacity in investigating the Teamsters Union for corruption. And liberals wondered aloud why he had never opposed Joseph McCarthy, a friend of Joseph Kennedy. Yet the political organization he built and the support he gathered helped swing the party to him and create an electoral majority.

During the campaign, Kennedy had pledged to get the American economy moving again. This meant, primarily, attacking the current recession, with its high unemployment and low productivity. Like Eisenhower, Kennedy could have waited for natural market forces to pull the econ-

Poverty in the Mississippi Delta. Poverty was not restricted to blacks in the 1950s and 1960s across the South. Nonetheless, some of the poorest Americans were blacks with small farms in the cotton belt. (©Danny Lyon/Magnum)

omy out of its lethargy. But he had promised action. Moreover, a major element among his advisers subscribed to the general theories of the British economist John Maynard Keynes. They believed that the federal government should, as required, intervene in the economy to expand or contract expenditures. These fiscal measures, based on enlarging or shrinking the federal budget in relation to tax revenues, might temporarily increase budget deficits, but they promised to touch off strong growth that would fill federal coffers later.

Kennedy's advisers were also convinced that the free market system inevitably left serious problems unresolved. Despite the successes of the Eisenhower years, 39 million Americans, or about 22 percent of the population, lived below the minimum poverty level set by government economists. Moreover, rapid changes in the economy had left residues of serious unemployment in rural areas of West Virginia, New England, and the South. In the cities, large numbers of working men and women had been left behind by technological unemployment (joblessness due to lack of the skills demanded by new industries). Underlying all these economic problems was a broad shift in the American economy away from farm and blue-collar employment into jobs in government and in the service, retail, and communications industries. The private economy,

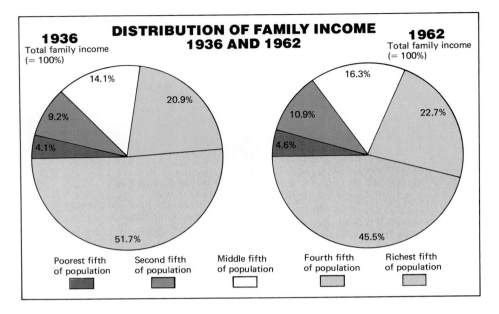

DISTRIBUTION OF FAMILY INCOME 1936 AND 1962

1936 Total family income (= 100%)

14.1% 9.2% 4.1% 20.9% 51.7%

1962 Total family income (= 100%)

16.3% 10.9% 4.6% 22.7% 45.5%

Poorest fifth of population | Second fifth of population | Middle fifth of population | Fourth fifth of population | Richest fifth of population

these advisers argued, excluded too many Americans. Only a large new spurt of growth stimulated by the federal government could sweep these eddies of poverty back into the mainstream.

The president was initially very cautious about adopting these ideas, but he eventually accepted the principles behind his advisers' suggestions. His first economic proposals in early 1961 focused on securing supplements to unemployment benefits, increased Social Security benefits, a higher minimum wage, and aid for seriously distressed areas. All these measures passed through Congress by September. But his proposals for withholding taxes on stock dividends and interest earnings and his attempt to narrow expense-account deductions met stiff resistance. He did succeed, however, in winning larger tax deductions for business investment in new equipment.

Nonetheless, business leaders were distressed by the Democratic administration. They distrusted Kennedy and the growing consensus among his inner circle of advisers that the federal government should intervene more decisively in economic and social matters. Kennedy was keenly aware of his unpopularity with business, and he tried to mend his fences. In early 1963 he

delivered several speeches designed to win business over to a new program of moderate tax reform. His major proposal, however, was a large individual income tax cut that would save taxpayers over $13 billion. Something of a gamble, it passed finally in 1964 and paid off handsomely by helping stimulate a burst of growth that actually increased tax revenues and narrowed the federal budget deficit.

KENNEDY AND CIVIL RIGHTS Kennedy's strategy for solving social problems rested on two tactics. He attempted to stimulate economic growth as a way of bringing underprivileged elements of the population into the mainstream. And he worked to maintain the political support of the diverse coalition that had elected him. But he remained reluctant to employ the power of the federal government to end segregation because of the political controversy it would stir.

During the campaign, Kennedy had called for Americans to dedicate themselves to high principles. This suggested his support for civil rights. But campaign hints proved difficult to translate into action. Initially, the president did little to reverse segregation. In fact, he appointed several men to federal judgeships who were unsympathetic to black rights. On the other hand, he chose several black Americans for ambassadorships. His brother Robert, responding to the Freedom Rides and other demonstrations and working quietly in the Justice Department, ordered desegregation of interstate transportation facilities in the South.

Still, pressure mounted to fulfill one specific campaign pledge: his promise to eliminate "with the stroke of a pen" the segregation maintained in federally financed housing projects. The president waited until June 1962 to act—partly because he hoped to create a new Department of Housing and Urban Development and appoint a black man, Robert Weaver, as head. Too much pressure, he reasoned, would raise the opposition of Southern congressmen and jeopardize his whole program.

Yet the idealism of which Kennedy spoke so often in public increased expectations that his administration would do something about the spreading confrontation between integrationists and segregationists. The president had to act in the fall of 1962 to protect James Meredith, the first black student to enter the University of Mississippi, from mob violence. When Governor Ross Barnett blocked a court order allowing Meredith to enroll, and used the threat of violence to intimidate Meredith, Kennedy federalized the Mississippi National Guard and ordered in federal troops. Before the confrontation ended, two persons were killed and almost 300 arrested. The young black student had to accept the protection of U.S. marshals for several months thereafter.

Kennedy had to intervene again in the spring of 1963, during the explosive Birmingham marches, to restrain police violence against demonstrators. These actions deepened resentment against the president in the white South. Gallup polls taken over the summer revealed profound national concern about integration, with a significant group of Americans worried that it was proceeding too fast.

Recognizing the growing momentum and importance of the civil rights movement, Kennedy believed that federal action on a broad scale had become necessary. In early June 1963 two black students tried to enroll at the University of Alabama in Tuscaloosa. George Wallace, governor of the state, stood defiantly in the doorway of the registration hall and read a proclamation denouncing federal interference in his state's business. Facing him, Deputy Attorney General Nicholas Katzenbach, sent by Kennedy, read a statement ordering the governor to end his obstruction of a court order to integrate the university. Confronted by federal power, Wallace stepped aside and the black students enrolled.

As Kennedy moved closer to acclaiming the goals of the civil rights movement, Martin Luther King, Jr., reached the height of his power and influence. During the massive march on Washington of August 28, 1963, King proclaimed a new meaning and content for the old promises of equality and freedom. These words, he declared, now meant for the first time equality and freedom for black men and women. Kennedy did not endorse or attend the march, but he invited its leaders to the White House afterward. A few weeks earlier, he had evoked his own vision of American citizenship and called for support of a new civil rights bill because, as he told a national television audience: "We face . . . a moral crisis as a country and as a people." Kennedy's bill proposed to end segregation in public accommodations, strengthen voting rights, and speed school desegregation.

Extensive reforms to aid other slighted populations in America made up Kennedy's 1963 legislative package: medical insurance for the elderly and subsidized care for the indigent, aid to education, and a new Urban Affairs Department of the federal government. Toward the end of the summer, he instructed his advisers to begin sketching out legislation for a concerted drive to end poverty. Kennedy thus proposed to move the federal government aggressively into the realm of social reform.

By the fall of 1963, the administration had embraced broad and ambitious new programs to expand the power of the federal government to guarantee the rights and well-being of minority, poor, and disadvantaged groups in America. It was a task worthy of the vision of Martin Luther King, Jr. But it was also, as King himself realized, a difficult task filled with great personal danger.

KENNEDY'S FOREIGN POLICY

As in domestic affairs, Kennedy promised activism in foreign policy. Unwilling to rely solely on nuclear weapons to preserve a stalemate between the United States and the Soviet Union, the new president believed that his country should intervene in Third World revolutions. Kennedy hoped that the United States could woo these nations into the Western camp. Or, failing this, he was willing to use military means to support wars against communist insurgents. Similarly, in January 1961 the Russian leader Nikita Khrushchev proclaimed his support for "wars of liberation." Thus both the Americans and Russians planned to increase their involvement in the unstable politics of the Third World.

Kennedy's policy was based on financial, technological, and economic aid coupled with military intervention. In March 1961 the president announced the Alliance for Progress for South America. This aid program promised assistance to Latin American nations for schools, roads, and health facilities. The president intended to strengthen middle-class elements in Latin America who were sympathetic to reform and who would steer their societies away from military dictatorship or Soviet influence. At the same time, the president announced the Peace Corps, a project to send young American volunteers into Third World countries to aid in agricultural efforts and community development.

Both these programs appealed to young Americans, who took them as symbols of a new and idealistic foreign policy. At the same time, however, Kennedy pushed readiness for military intervention. He encouraged the armed forces to develop plans for counterinsurgency, and he pushed creation of a new, sophisticated strike force for use against guerrillas, called the Green Berets.

Kennedy's first military intervention proved a fiasco. Toward the end of the Eisenhower administration, Cuban rebels led by Fidel Castro overthrew Fulgencio Batista, the ruthless dictator of the island. Castro was determined to secure agricultural reform, nationalization of foreign companies, and industrialization. His program brought harsh criticism from American business and the Eisenhower administration. During 1960 the CIA began planning Castro's overthrow, but Eisenhower decided to let his successor carry out the plans. Despite some hesitations, Kennedy approved a landing of American-trained and supplied counterrevolutionaries. When the landing party moved ashore at the Bay of Pigs, Castro's forces were ready. Most counterrevolutionaries were captured. Leaks to the press and circumstantial evidence linked the Kennedy administration with the invaders. Subsequently, Kennedy admitted U.S. involvement.

In October 1962, Cuba was once again the site of international conflict, but this time the incident involved a direct confrontation between the United States and the Soviet Union. On October 14, U.S. Air Force spy planes photographed missile sites being constructed in Cuba by Russian technicians. Both the Russians and the Cubans were convinced that Kennedy planned an invasion of the island. Thus Khrushchev ordered the installation of rockets capable of delivering atomic weapons to almost every corner of the United States. A number of warheads were already in Cuba and required only about five hours to install and fire.

Kennedy, of course, was gravely concerned. He could not allow deployment of these missiles, if only because of the intolerable political risks at home. But to destroy them would risk nuclear war with the Soviets. He chose, instead, a public confrontation, declaring a blockade of Cuba to prevent further Russian supply of the missiles. On October 28 the Russians finally agreed to dismantle their bases in exchange for an American pledge not to invade Cuba. This tangled web of

Mid-range ballistic missile site in Cuba. Aerial reconnaissance over Cuba on October 23, 1962, indicated that work was proceeding on Soviet-supplied missile sites in Cuba, despite the warnings of President Kennedy and the announcement, a day earlier, of a blockade around the island. On October 28 the Russians agreed to dismantle the bases in exchange for an American pledge not to invade Cuba. (Wide World Photos)

misunderstandings, incomplete reconnaissance, and inaccurate readings of motivations on both sides brought the world closer to nuclear war than at any other time.

Despite the risks incurred by intervention in Cuba, Kennedy approved stepped-up intervention in the more intricate affairs of Vietnam. At first, the president feared that communists would gain control of neighboring Laos, but his attention quickly focused on Vietnam. To Kennedy, Vietnam became a testing ground for his theories of nation building and counterinsurgency. The president recognized the complexity of the political and military situation in Vietnam. He understood that the division of the former French colony into two entities, one communist and the other supported by the United States, created instability. The communist-led insurgency that had driven out the French was now directed at expelling the Western-supported government in the south. But Kennedy believed that with United States support, the government of South Vietnam, headed by Ngo Dinh Diem, could survive.

Nonetheless, American intervention did not work as intended. The Diem government became more unstable than ever. Counterinsurgency could not stem government loss of control over the countryside. Diem spoke of reform, but he isolated himself from the political and religious majorities of the south. The military situation

CHRONOLOGY

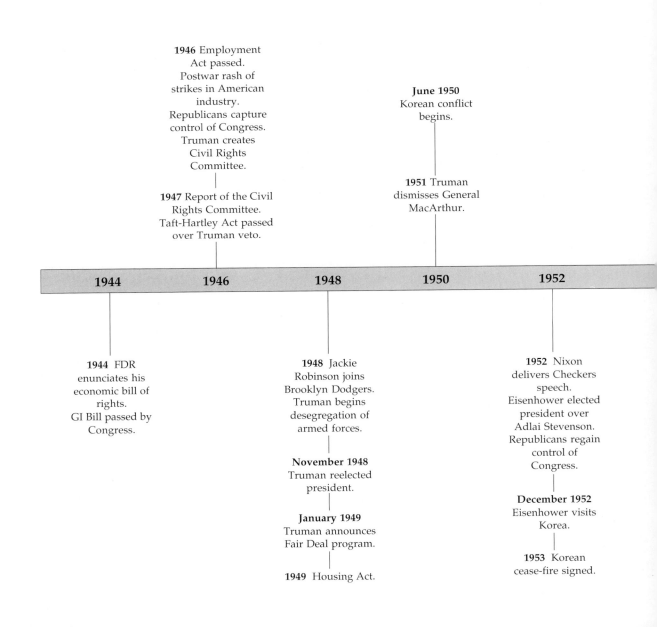

1946 Employment Act passed. Postwar rash of strikes in American industry. Republicans capture control of Congress. Truman creates Civil Rights Committee.

1947 Report of the Civil Rights Committee. Taft-Hartley Act passed over Truman veto.

June 1950 Korean conflict begins.

1951 Truman dismisses General MacArthur.

1944 **1946** **1948** **1950** **1952**

1944 FDR enunciates his economic bill of rights. GI Bill passed by Congress.

1948 Jackie Robinson joins Brooklyn Dodgers. Truman begins desegregation of armed forces.

November 1948 Truman reelected president.

January 1949 Truman announces Fair Deal program.

1949 Housing Act.

1952 Nixon delivers Checkers speech. Eisenhower elected president over Adlai Stevenson. Republicans regain control of Congress.

December 1952 Eisenhower visits Korea.

1953 Korean cease-fire signed.

1956 Montgomery bus boycott. Eisenhower reelected president over Stevenson. Interstate highway system funded.

1957 Southern Christian Leadership Conference formed. Eisenhower signs civil rights bill. Soviet Union launches *Sputnik* satellite.

September 1957 Eisenhower sends troops to Little Rock, Arkansas.

1960 U-2 incident ruins Paris summit meeting. John F. Kennedy elected president over Richard Nixon.

1961 Kennedy announces Alliance for Progress. Bay of Pigs invasion of Cuba fails. Cuban missile crisis.

April 1961 SNCC founded.

1961–62 Freedom rides in the South.

1954	1956	1958	1960	1962

1954 Congress censures Senator Joseph McCarthy. Construction of St. Lawrence Seaway begins. Supreme Court decides *Brown* v. *Board of Education*

1955 *Rebel Without a Cause* opens. Eisenhower suffers heart attack. Martin Luther King, Jr. accepts Montgomery ministry.

December 1955 Rosa Parks arrested in Montgomery.

1957–58 United States economy suffers recession.

1958 NASA established.

1959 Khrushchev visits the United States.

1962 Kennedy appoints Robert Weaver secretary of HUD. James Meredith enters University of Mississippi.

April 1963 King jailed in Birmingham, Alabama.

May 1963 Birmingham riots.

June 1963 Governor George Wallace tries to stop blacks entering University of Alabama.

August 1963 King leads civil rights march on Washington.

November 22, 1963 Kennedy assassinated in Dallas.

THE RANGE OF CUBAN–BASED SOVIET MISSILES

continued to deteriorate because the South Vietnamese army, despite its sophisticated equipment and training, proved unreliable in battle. Opposing revolutionaries—now called the Viet Cong—drew increasing support from the embattled rural population. The whole nation was becoming an armed camp.

By 1962, American advisers had approved more drastic policies: defoliants to destroy jungle cover, napalm, and a "stragetic hamlet" program to isolate revolutionaries by moving the peasantry into armed camps. Still, the internal political situation was shaky. Diem clung obstinately to unpopular dictatorial policies.

In the spring of 1963 Kennedy signaled his ambassador in Saigon that the United States would accept a replacement for Diem. However, when Diem was overthrown in November, the violence of the coup shocked the administration. Instead of a new order, corruption and brutality continued to rule South Vietnam. Insurgents operated freely and successfully despite 20,000 American troops and advisers. Kennedy himself was growing suspicious of optimistic military and intelligence reports from American military officials. The struggle had come to a crossroads. The president either had to increase American participation or slow it down and face Republican criticism. As in domestic policy, Kennedy was faced with serious choices. What he would have done will never be known, for he was assassinated on November 22, 1963, in Dallas, Texas.

Suggestions for Further Reading

MARTIN LUTHER KING, JR., AND CIVIL RIGHTS

Richard Kluger, *Simple Justice: The History of* Brown *v.* Board of Education *and America's Struggle for Equality* (1976), details the complex forces and events that converged on the Supreme Court when it delivered its landmark desegregation ruling. Richard Polenberg, *One Nation Divisible: Class, Race, and Ethnicity in the United States Since 1938* (1980), provides an interesting perspective for understanding some of the larger issues in American racial and ethnic attitudes. Coretta Scott King, *My Life with Martin Luther King, Jr.* (1969), is stirring and poignant. David Lewis, *King: A Biography* (1978), is far more critical, but ultimately it is a sympathetic portrait. Two superb additions to King scholarship are David Garrow, *Bearing the Cross: Martin Luther King, Jr., and the Southern Christian Leadership Conference* (1987), and Taylor Branch, *Parting the Waters: America in the King Years, 1954–63* (1988).

THE COLD WAR AT HOME

The issue of domestic anticommunism and the subsequent prominence of Senator Joseph McCarthy began during the presidency of Harry Truman. A good assessment of Truman is Alonzo L. Hamby, *Beyond the New Deal: Harry S Truman and American Liberalism* (1973). A controversial look at the effects of McCarthyism is David Caute, *The Great Fear: The Anti-Communist Purge Under Truman and Eisenhower* (1978). Richard H. Rovere, *Senator Joseph McCarthy* (1959), is a very readable account of the rise and fall of the senator from Wisconsin.

THE 1950s

An excellent economic history of the 1950s is Harold G. Vatter, *The United States Economy in the 1950s* (1963). The effects of prosperity during this decade were controversial. One book that set the tone for much of the subsequent criticism of 1950s lifestyles was David Riesman, *The Lonely Crowd* (1950). *The Affluent Society* (1956), written by the noted American economist John Kenneth Galbraith, details some of the problems of prosperity. On the other hand, David M. Potter, *People of Plenty* (1954), argues that abundance has had a generally positive effect on society. On suburban life, see Kenneth T. Jackson, *Crabgrass Frontier: The Suburbanization of the United States* (1985). An important corrective to the picture of a totally quiescent women's movement in the 1950s is Leila J. Rupp and Verta Taylor, *Survival in the Doldrums: The American Women's Rights Movement, 1945 to the 1960s* (1987).

THE EISENHOWER ADMINISTRATION

One good place to begin study of the Eisenhower presidency is Herbert S. Parmet, *Eisenhower and the American Crusades* (1972). More recently published material in *The Eisenhower Diaries* (1981), Richard H. Ferrell (ed.), reveals the president to be a very complex and thoughtful leader. Robert L. Branyan and Laurence H. Larson (eds.) have collected important public documents from the era in *The Eisenhower Administration 1953–1961: A Documentary History* (2 vols., 1971).

CHAPTER 23
LIBERALISM IN DECLINE

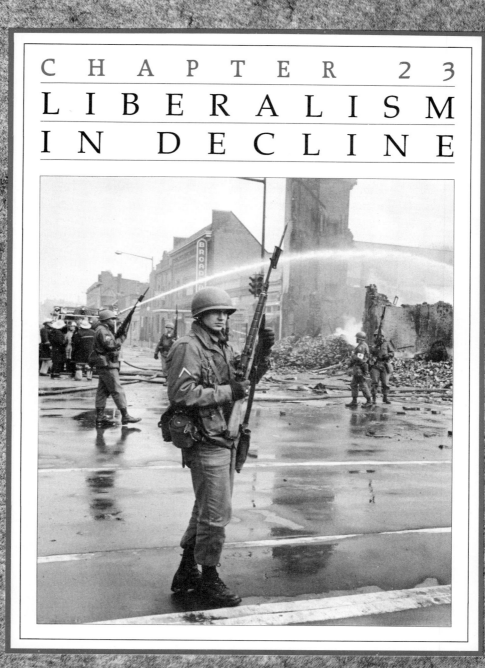

THE EPISODE: *Political convention sites in 1968 were chosen as much for security as to anchor a campaign in a particular section of the country. For the Democrats, Chicago seemed a safe place. Mayor Richard Daley controlled a political machine that delivered votes with perennial regularity. The Democrats had to be wary of demonstrations against the war in Vietnam. Practically driven from the presidency by rising discontent with the war, President Lyndon Johnson nonetheless maintained a tight grip on the Democratic Party. Opponents of the war were pushed to the periphery; leaders such as Senator Robert Kennedy and Martin Luther King, Jr., were both dead. Under the circumstances, political dissenters had to make either what seemed like unreasonable compromises or take to the streets. The choice for many was easy because opponents of the war already felt at home in the arena of public protest. Elements of the new left, the civil rights movement, and the counter culture had transformed pickets, marches, and street theater into a new language of politics perfectly suited to the age of television. Mayor Daley, on the other hand, commanded an old-fashioned force of tough and angry policemen with no sympathy for the protestors or interest in their right to demonstrate. The stage was set for an extraordinary confrontation.*

THE HISTORICAL SETTING: *The pitched battle between anti-war demonstrators and Chicago's police was the cul-minating moment of the presidency of Lyndon Johnson, a major turning point in America's determination to continue the war in Vietnam, and a crucial step in the decline of the Democratic party. It also marked a shift of the new left and the counterculture in a more ideological, and ultimately self-destructive, direction. The year 1968 also marked the victory of a new sort of political movement, as yet vaguely conceived and clumsily organized, but important nonetheless. This was a new conservatism based upon growing hostility to demonstrations, civil rights marches, protests, urban riots, crime, and upon hostility to the liberal legislative agenda.*

Of course, one event—even a year—cannot account for such shifts. Changes happen over time and flow from a wide variety of causes. Nonetheless, the political riots of Chicago, 1968, and the election of Richard Nixon (which in no small way depended upon this political debacle) confirmed a serious reorientation in American life. Significant developments in lifestyles, popular culture, and social relations continued. Demographic changes in the labor force and in family life continued to alter the shape of institutions. The sexual revolution did not falter, and integration, while it did not achieve all its goals, gradually eliminated the most overt and distasteful elements of racism in American life. Nonetheless, the riots of 1968 tested the limits of political liberalism.

CHICAGO, 1968

Giants lived here once. It was that kind of town, thirty years gone, that made big men out of little ones. It was grand for great deeds then, as it is grand for small deeds now.

—Nelson Algren

Dear Students for a Democratic Society:

I'm twelve years old, and I wish to join the society. Because of the conditions at school your hair must not be two inches above the eyebrow. You must wear white socks. If you wore any other color you'd be punished and this is the reason I want to join the society.

—Letter to the Editor,
New Left Notes, 1968

SURREALISM IN CHICAGO
—Dallas Morning News

Jerry Rubin mounted the stage at the Grant Park bandshell in Chicago shortly after 4 P.M. on August 28, 1968. His arms circling a large, squirming pig, he shouted out to the delighted crowd of 10,000 student and other demonstrators: "Today is a historic day for America—we are proud to announce the declaration of candidacy for the presidency of the United States by a pig." The crowd roared its approval of Pigasus.

Rubin, with his shaggy hair and unkempt beard, was well known to police guarding the edges of the park. So friends had smuggled the pig through the crowd in a burlap bag from a nearby car. (Earlier in the week, Rubin had tried the same stunt at Chicago's Civic Center, but police had arrested him before he could start his speech.)

Milling around in anticipation, the crowd had already listened to several speakers. Whiffs of tear gas rose from the grass or drifted across from the nearby flagpole area. Only a short time before, police had charged into a group of demonstrators trying to haul down the American flag. Tear gas exploded and police waded through the group, flailing nightsticks. Volunteer medics dragged the injured to safety.

David Dellinger, longtime peace advocate and leader of the National Mobilization Committee to End the War in Vietnam, a group that helped organize the demonstration, now rose to address the crowd. He announced a march out of the park, across Chicago's Loop (the business district), to the Amphitheater, where the 1968 Democratic convention was in session. There was no permit for the demonstration, but Dellinger insisted the march was a question of free speech. "This is a peaceful march," he cried. "All those who want to participate in a peaceful march, join our line. All those who are not peaceful, please go away and don't join our line."

A few small groups, some wearing helmets, their eyes smeared with Vaseline to protect against the chemical Mace and tear gas, broke off. But most of the demonstrators followed Dellinger up Columbus Drive at the edge of the park until they ran up against a solid line of Chicago policemen. The demonstrators stopped and sat down. Dellinger went off to negotiate with the police. But the officials refused to budge: no march would be permitted. Hearing this, the crowd began to clump into thick knots, which then moved around the police line and toward the bridges that led from the park, hoping to make their way over the railroad tracks and into the heart of the city. National Guardsmen standing on the bridges prevented this by firing tear gas. But the demonstrators quickly discovered one unprotected bridge toward the north and raced across it. They poured down Michigan Avenue to the Conrad Hilton Hotel, headquarters for several candidates and a symbol of the Democratic convention. The stage was set for a violent battle between police and demonstrators— a battle that shocked the nation and shook the Democratic party to its foundations.

YOUTHS FRUSTRATED, BITTER
—*Boston Evening Globe*

The origins of the confrontation in Chicago lay in opposition to the war in Vietnam. The brutal course of this war had battered the presidency of Lyndon Johnson. Early in 1968 a Viet Cong insurgent attack against South Vietnamese and American troops (the Tet offensive) had brought the war into the streets of every city in South Vietnam. Although the Viet Cong fell back with severe losses, the campaign was a debacle for American homefront support for the war. Many Americans concluded, as they watched the nightly accounts on television news, that the war was neither winnable nor worth the rising casualties.

The Tet offensive was just one element of a growing political crisis that forced President Johnson out of the race five months before the convention. Johnson had staked his reputation and fate on winning the civil war in Asia. But after three years of heavy escalation and commitment of American resources to the war, casualties

Robert F. Kennedy. In 1964 "Bobby" Kennedy ran a successful campaign for election as a U.S. senator from New York: here he is overwhelmed by upstate admirers. During the presidential primaries of 1968, Kennedy attracted equally enthusiastic crowds and growing support. Acceptable to some Democratic party bosses as well as much of the antiwar movement, he was, perhaps, the only candidate who might have held the party together. But he was assassinated in June 1968. (©Cornell Capa/Magnum)

were still mounting with no end in sight. Opposition, particularly within the Democratic party, was growing rapidly. At first, it gathered around Senator Eugene McCarthy of Minnesota, who came close to defeating Johnson in the March 12 New Hampshire presidential primary. Predictions for the upcoming primary in Wisconsin were even bleaker for the president. So Johnson, in a surprise national television broadcast on March 31, announced his withdrawal from the race.

Nonetheless, Johnson had no intention of bowing out of politics. He remained determined to choose his own successor. He believed that McCarthy was only a marginal threat; the real danger to the continuation of his policies was Robert Kennedy, who could rally antiwar support and win approval from Democratic party regulars. As his candidate, Johnson pushed Hubert Humphrey, his vice president. But he made his support contingent on Humphrey's firm commitment to pursuing the war in Vietnam to victory.

In late spring, Kennedy's chances for the nomination mounted, as support for McCarthy dwindled and Humphrey failed to attract much popular support. On June 4 Kennedy won the crucial California primary and seemed well on his way to unseating Humphrey, the party front-runner. Then in the early morning of June 5, at a victory celebration in Los Angeles at the Ambassador Hotel, shots suddenly rang out. An Arab immigrant, Sirhan Bishara Sirhan, fired at Kennedy from close range. The candidate died twenty-five hours later. This second murderous attack on the Kennedy family removed the only viable antiwar candidate from the race. Humphrey was as good as nominated.

The Republican party proved even less hospitable to antiwar sentiment, counting on polls that showed a majority of Americans still supporting the war. When Republican conventioneers gathered in Miami, Florida, they had no trouble agreeing to nominate Richard M. Nixon. Nixon opened his campaign to the center and the right—to gather up critics of Johnson and the Democrats, and to take advantage of a growing backlash against civil rights and antiwar demonstrations. He was vague and noncommittal on the issue of Vietnam. He promised to end the war but declined to say how.

For those who opposed the war—and significant numbers of Americans did—there was no place to go: no political haven, no believable candidate, and no welcome from either party. Nor was there a meaningful third-party alternative. Thus when the Democratic party shut its doors to the antiwar movement, it almost inevitably pushed that movement out onto the streets of Chicago.

CHICAGOANS AWAIT PROTESTORS WITH TEETH, FISTS CLENCHED
—Los Angeles Times

Although many voters disapproved of the war in Vietnam, it was young people who took to the streets to manifest their opposition. Two groups in particular organized and led the Chicago demonstrations: the Yippies and student radicals.

The Youth International Party (YIP), founded in early 1968, dedicated itself to a world revolution led by youth. During late 1967 and early 1968, student protests against the war escalated across the United States. Student movements and crippling strikes also rocked France, West Germany, and other European nations. Many young Americans concluded that they were part of a rising generation destined to change the world. The Yippies capitalized on this sentiment and wove together diverse elements of youth culture: political protest and experimental lifestyles associated with the hippies living in San Francisco and around large university campuses like Berkeley. As Allen Ginsberg, poet and troubadour of the movement, described it, it drew together

> younger people aware of the planetary fate that we are all sitting in the middle of, imbued with a new consciousness and desiring of a new kind of society involving prayer, music, and spiritual life together rather than competition, acquisition, and war.

The Yippies formed originally from a group of ex–college radicals living on New York's Lower East Side. They worked at shelters for runaway teenagers and held music festivals and street theater for the growing hippie community and drug culture of that area. During a large antiwar protest march October 21, 1967, on the Pentagon in Washington, two future Yippie leaders, Jerry Rubin and Abbie Hoffman, demonstrated their genius for combining politics, culture, and humor. They built the protest into a media event and urged the crowd to circle the huge building to "exorcise" the evil inside. They astutely recognized the enormous importance of such symbolic gestures. Photographs and newsreels of demonstrators planting daisies in the gun barrels of troops guarding the building brought more attention to the march than did speeches, lobbying, or slogans.

The tone of Yippie protests was mocking and antiestablishment, but it was not entirely unfamiliar. Indeed, the exploits of Rubin and Hoffman belong to the anarchic

Yippie political theater in Chicago. Yippie demonstrations against the Vietnam War were dramatic, outrageous, and effective. Marching under the symbol of death, Yippies marked the "Unbirthday" of President Johnson on August 27 during the Democratic convention. (© 1969 Roger Malloch/Magnum)

vein of American humor exemplified by the Marx Brothers in their best political films, such as *Duck Soup*, shot in the 1930s (see p. 912 about the Marx Brothers). In a gesture that might have fitted such a film, Hoffman and a group of friends burst into the New York Stock Exchange in August 1967. Standing on the balcony above the bustling exchange floor, they threw dollar bills over the side. Some of the brokers below them jeered and shook their fists; others scrambled for the bills that floated downward. Those demonstrators who escaped arrest rushed to the front entrance of the building and chanted "Free! Free!" while they shredded and burned dollar bills.

The Yippies decided to organize as a political movement in February 1968. As Hoffman related:

> There we were, all stoned, rolling around the floor. . . . Yippie! . . . Somebody says oink and that's it, pig, it's a natural, man, we gotta win. . . . Let's try success, I mean, when we went to the Pentagon, we were going to get it to rise 300 feet in the air. . . . So we said how about doing one that will win.

The purpose of the Yippie organization was to turn the Chicago Democratic convention into a protest. The tactic was to organize a "Festival of Life"—a giant counterculture rock concert to be held at the same time the Democrats nominated a candidate for president. As singer and Yippie member Phil Ochs said, "They wanted to be able to act out fantasies in the street to communicate their feelings to the public."

On March 17, at the Americana Hotel in New York, Hoffman, Rubin, Ochs, singer Arlo Guthrie, and others announced further details of their Festival of Life. It would feature a concert with Guthrie, Judy Collins, the Fugs, Country Joe and the Fish, and other popular music groups. Leaders promised to cooperate with Chicago officials, to secure proper permits for the concert and permission for the audience to sleep in the city parks. But Mayor Richard Daley of Chicago refused to grant permits for the festival, believing that a tough line would restrict the numbers who came to the city during the convention.

Without permits, several performers withdrew. But the obstinancy of the city suited Yippie purposes. As one flyer put it, YIP was a "National disorganization whose sole purpose would be the Theater of Disruption." Accordingly, the Yippies revised their plans. They still planned a concert, but the highlight of their mock celebration would be the nomination of Pigasus for president. This act had a special significance. *Pig* was urban ghetto slang for policeman. By nominating a pig for president, the Yippies were proclaiming that the United States was a police state.

Through the summer the Yippies tried, without success, to persuade Chicago officials to grant a permit for their festival—although they made no effort to hide their purpose of disrupting the convention. And the list of demands they released was designed to shock, rather than to form the basis for any negotiations. They insisted on an end to the war in Vietnam, legalization of marijuana and other psychedelic drugs, freedom for prisoners, the disarming of police, and the abolition of money. As for events of the festival, they "predicted" activities in Chicago that would disrupt the entire city: an "unbirthday" party for President Johnson on August 27, a plan to dump LSD into the Chicago water system, a stall-in on city traffic arteries, the release of greased pigs throughout the city, and the recruitment of "230 hyper-potent hippie males into a special battalion to seduce the wives, daughters, and girlfriends of convention delegates." As the Yippies and their supporters began to converge on Chicago in late August, Hoffman proclaimed: "I use guerrilla theater as a medium for creating what I call blank space. Blank space is where you use media so that the observer, the audience, becomes a participant, becomes involved." But for Mayor Daley and the police and convention officials, the Yippies' agenda was not theater but political warfare, not humor but a threat.

Far larger than the Yippie group was the contingent of demonstrators that came to Chicago from the more subdued and serious student antiwar movement. The largest of the political action groups, the Students for a Democratic Society (SDS), founded in 1962, refused to participate officially. Its leaders believed demonstrations to be ineffective, and they feared violence from the police. They also wanted to remain separate from any movement that might support the candidacy of Senator McCarthy. Nonetheless, two former SDS leaders, Tom Hayden and Rennie Davis, played leading roles in Chicago. And the days of protest had a profound effect on radical organizations like SDS.

The National Mobilization Committee to End the War in Vietnam (MOBE), headed by David Dellinger, was an umbrella organization that included most of the important student radical groups. It was MOBE that had organized the 1967 demonstration at the Pentagon. Its leaders occasionally worked with the Yippies, but the Yippies never officially joined it. Their strategy was theater, not serious politics.

In February 1968, MOBE opened a Chicago office and chose Davis and Hayden to coordinate activities. Their first job was to secure demonstration permits from the city for a march on the convention. At a planning session held in late March, Hayden and Davis defined their aims. They wanted peaceful, legal demonstrations during the convention. But they anticipated police violence that would "dramatize to the world the large numbers of people who feel unrepresented, and in fact disgraced and used, by our government's policies on the crisis of Vietnam and racism and the mockery that democracy has become." Hayden hoped that demonstrators would converge on Chicago:

> The final funeral march on the Democratic Convention, beginning as the first ballot is taken, should bring a half a million people demanding a choice on the issues of peace and justice; citizens who have come to "make the democratic process work" by pinning the delegates in the International Amphitheater until a choice is presented to the American people.

MOBE leaders agreed that the final march to the Amphitheater would be their central aim. But Johnson's announcement in March that he would not seek reelection put these plans on hold. The violent response of Chicago police to the ghetto riots that erupted after Martin Luther King's assassination in April also gave pause. Mayor Daley had encouraged the police to take stern measures against looters and arsonists. Observers warned that he would also be very tough on demonstrators.

Nonetheless, MOBE leaders meeting in Cleveland in mid-July decided to proceed. They appropriated money for the Chicago office and organized a legal group to help out with arrest and bail problems. Medical groups, including the Committee on Human Rights and the Student Health Organization, were asked to set up first-aid support services. MOBE expected trouble.

During the summer, Davis and Hayden still hoped for official permission to march. After several fruitless phone calls and letters, they finally set a meeting with city officials in early August. When the officials stalled on a permit, MOBE pressed for a court injunction. But the judge ruled on August 21 that the city was not obligated to issue a permit. The city did make one counteroffer—a location for a march at least ten miles from the Amphitheater and well away from the business heart of the city. MOBE refused this. Finally, during the convention, the city did issue one permit, for the afternoon rally at the Grant Park bandshell on August 28.

Quite clearly, the city intended to frighten protesters from coming to the convention by making marches and demonstrations illegal. In part, they succeeded. Chicago officials put MOBE leaders in an awkward position. By planning illegal demonstrations, were they not inciting to riot? On the other hand, did they not have a duty to exercise their right to assembly and free speech? The MOBE leadership chose to proceed, believing that if violence occurred, it would be initiated by the police. This in turn would discredit the Democratic party and the presidential nominee. David

Dellinger promised: "We are not going to storm the convention with tanks or Mace. But we are going to storm the hearts and minds of the American people."

Other protest groups decided to come to Chicago during the convention, but they played a minor role. The Black Panthers did not officially join the demonstrations, but their representatives sometimes spoke at meetings. The Panthers, founded in Oakland, California, in 1966 by Huey Newton and Bobby Seale, were a black power group that advocated self-defense and political coalition with white radicals. Shadowed closely by police agents, Panther leader Seale spoke in Chicago, but the organization generally kept in the background. The black leader who participated most actively in the demonstrations was comedian and civil rights advocate Dick Gregory.

Chicago also attracted large numbers of young McCarthy supporters, who came to demonstrate for their candidate. Originally, they did not intend to join the Yippies or MOBE, but many of them crossed over to the radical lines after the first bloody encounters with police. And finally, Chicago drew several literary celebrities, including novelists Norman Mailer, Terry Southern, and William Burroughs, poet Allen Ginsberg, and French playwright Jean Genêt.

CHICAGO: CITY OF MUSCLE, IN INDUSTRY AND POLITICS
—New York Times

The Democratic party had chosen Chicago as a convention site partly because of the tough reputation of Mayor Richard J. Daley. One of the last old-time city political bosses, he ran Chicago as his own personal fiefdom. Labor unions, the police, and city employees all marched to his tune. If anyone could maintain an orderly city and keep control over local arrangements, Daley seemed the one.

With one firm hand on the convention site in Chicago, the Democratic party was ruled by another firm hand in Washington. Johnson's power in the party remained strong, and he was determined to prevent the convention from adopting either a platform or a candidate that questioned American participation in the war in Vietnam. Thus Johnson prevented Humphrey from accommodating the antiwar forces in the party. He made sure that the credentials committee did not lean toward antiwar delegates in deciding disputed seats. He also insisted that the platform committee write a prowar plank. All these moves were successful, but they stripped Humphrey of power and a separate identity. In fact, Humphrey had so little influence that when he wrote to ask Daley to grant parade permits to demonstrators, his request went unanswered.

From the beginning, Mayor Daley and his police advisers prepared for a confrontation. They took Yippie "predictions" seriously. In January the city established a joint planning command with the police department, the mayor's office, the fire department, the U.S. Secret Service, and military intelligence. This committee met every two weeks until August, when it stepped up the tempo of its conferences. One function of the committee was to assess intelligence gathered by agents assigned to infiltrate MOBE and Yippie meetings or taken from publications in the underground press. The committee paid special attention to possible participation by Chicago's black citizens. After the violent riots in April, Daley feared renewed outbreaks. Should white radicals enlist support from the black ghetto, the mayor feared he might not be able to control the city.

Daley channeled his antiriot efforts through the police task force, which in April had been the backbone of the crackdown on demonstrations and riots in the ghetto. This agency borrowed a large tear gas dispenser from the U.S. Army, which it mounted on a city sanitation truck. And it organized police helicopter surveillance of routes leading to the convention center.

Squads of police were assigned to the two major city parks: Lincoln Park on the north side, which became the demonstrators' headquarters, and Grant Park, across from Michigan Avenue and the railroad tracks, facing the Hilton Hotel. All leave was canceled for the period, and twelve-hour shifts were instituted. The fire department was put on special alert. Police officials also issued special riot equipment to officers: nightsticks, helmets, service revolvers, and disabling Mace spray. A number of officers, on their own, purchased plastic face shields to attach inside their helmets. Instructions issued to officers stressed the need to maintain calm, especially while making mass arrests:

> Mass arrests made by police in a helter-skelter manner will serve absolutely no purpose as far as maintaining law and order is concerned. However, arrests made in an orderly and well-planned manner indicate a trained force prepared for such emergencies and will help convey to the demonstrators and the rest of the city that they are dealing with a superior force.

Mayor Daley also asked for support from the Illinois National Guard. Following several weeks of negotiations with the guard, the governor's office, and the U.S. Fifth Army, the governor announced that the guard would be activated. Approximately 5,000 guardsmen were stationed in armories around Chicago by August 23. In addition, 6,000 federal riot-control troops were brought to the city (U.S. Air Force C-141 jet cargo planes were assembled to ferry the troops). With about 11,000 reinforcements, Daley and his police force probably outnumbered the demonstrators who planned to come to Chicago.

Security around and inside the convention hall was tight. Barricades prevented any unauthorized persons from approaching the entrance. Police assigned to the inside of the Amphitheater were supplemented by Andy Frain, Inc., ushers generally on duty during Cubs baseball games at Wrigley Field. Entrance would be by ticket only, and delegates would receive new tickets each day. Any delegate or any newspaper or television reporter without proper identification would be removed from the floor or the galleries of the hall.

Mayor Daley also increased security around the city's water system in view of the Yippies' warning that they might dump LSD into the reservoirs. Special police were assigned to the two main pumping stations. Elements of the canine section of the task force guarded filtration plants.

Demonstrators and the Illinois National Guard. During the Democratic convention, Chicago city police were supplemented by 5,000 National Guardsmen activated by the governor of Illinois. Scenes such as these persuaded many observers that the war in Vietnam was tearing apart American society. (© 1969 Roger Malloch/Magnum)

Daley apparently took one further step to control the protest. An International Brotherhood of Electrical Workers strike, begun prior to the convention, remained unsettled. (It was settled immediately after the convention ended.) Daley intervened enough to ensure that live television coverage would come from the convention itself, but networks were not allowed to set up live coverage facilities around possible demonstration focal points. They could still film, but the film had to be carried to network facilities at the Amphitheater for processing. A story in *Television Digest* on August 26 explained the problem:

> Networks encountered several new labor disputes last week and were told by Chicago police they couldn't park videotape vans on streets outside major hotels. They also are prohibited from locating cameras outside hotels or in windows overlooking streets.
>
> New difficulties brought back into prominence earlier charges that Democrats were deliberately attempting to curb TV live coverage outside Convention Hall. CBS News President Richard Salant saw difficulties as part of "a pattern well beyond simple labor disputes, logistics, and security problems."

The news media also made special preparations for the convention, partly because of these obstacles. Besides the large contingent of reporters and camera operators assigned to the Amphitheater, the major networks, new services, and newspapers like the *New York Times* assigned about 300 reporters and photographers to follow the demonstrators. Each major news service was handed a special introduction to Chicago published by the police department. It opened: "Welcome, Newsmen! Welcome to Chicago, the City of 'The Front Page,' with an outstanding tradition of competitive journalism. Another tradition has been the excellent rapport between the Chicago police and newsmen." The news services, however, did not anticipate excellent rapport. In fact, they prepared for the worst. The *Washington Post*, for example, issued the following warning in its list of instructions:

Tear Gas Protection. Reporters traveling in areas that have been heavily gassed have encountered significant problems. Each of the cars is now being equipped (in the trunk) with small containers of oxygen, and with watersoaked cloths. The cloths, enclosed in plastic bags, should be used to sponge out eyes and remove the gas from the skin. An additional small supply of oxygen containers will be kept in the radio room cabinet. This style of tear gas protection was decided upon since the Army-type of gas masks would tend to make reporters targets, and are quite uncomfortable to users who are not accustomed to their use.

IN THE HALL: BLACK CREPE AND ANGER
IN THE STREETS: TEAR GAS AND CLUBS

—Washington Post

Despite the overwhelming force of the city and its troop reinforcements, and with the press anticipating trouble, the Yippies and the MOBE leadership refused to retreat. The city's unwillingness to grant a march permit anywhere near the Amphitheater or to allow demonstrations, plus police refusal to allow anyone to sleep in the parks, meant that almost any action was, by definition, illegal. Thus in the tightly surveyed and tense city, any act of political protest threatened to become a confrontation.

Neither the MOBE nor the Yippie leadership (even if they desired it) had much control over the thousands of young people who began to assemble in the city over the weekend of August 24. MOBE did train several hundred marshals to control crowds during marches, but they proved totally ineffective in the chaotic conditions of police confrontation. Communications between leaders and followers were spotty and often tardy, carried by word of mouth or by flyers pasted to walls. Moreover, the two principal wings of the protest, MOBE and the Yippies, had different aims. MOBE had a more traditional belief in the effectiveness of demonstrations and protests to attract attention to their message of opposition to the war. The Yippies also opposed the war, but their vehicle for protest was any public event that brought attention—by shock, anger, or amusement. Under such circumstances, the initiative belonged to the police. They determined the nature and extent of the pitched battles that followed.

The police had the further advantage of an informer close to Jerry Rubin. Posing as a member of the motorcycle gang the Headhunters, Robert L. Pierson, a private investigator employed by the Chicago Police Department, met with Rubin and Hoffman and secretly relayed information about demonstration plans back to police headquarters. In order to convince the Yippies of his loyalty, Pierson had to be active in the demonstrations. As one newsman reported:

> One such hell-raiser—Robert L. Pierson—has indiscreetly told the *Chicago Tribune* (as published August 31) how he gained Rubin's confidence and, to confirm his

Days of rage. After the failure to end politics as usual at the Democratic convention, some elements of the new left decided upon a strategy of continuing disruption. In this picture, Tom Hayden addresses a crowd of activists in Lincoln Park in October, before they marched into Chicago's loop to try to interrupt business as usual. (UPI/Bettmann Newsphotos)

credentials, threw rocks and bottles, hurled epithets at the police and even participated actively in lowering the American flag and raising a red flag in Grant Park—an action that touched off a police assault.

Those demonstrators who were prepared to brave what they realized could be physical danger headed for Lincoln Park, about two miles from the city's center. There, in a large area that separated Lake Michigan from Old Town—Chicago's bohemian center—the Yippies set up their headquarters. Many of the demonstrators planned to take advantage of housing offered by nearby residents, but others brought sleeping bags to spend the night in the park.

At about the same time, convention delegates began to stream into town and fill the hotels in downtown Chicago. The media set up to report on two simultaneous events: the opening of the convention and the first confrontations between police and demonstrators. The two stories became point and counterpoint in the nomination process. As Humphrey's selection moved inexorably forward, it was increasingly punctuated by events outside the Amphitheater, by the growing tension and violence between police and demonstrators.

Yippie and MOBE strategists hoped to keep media attention focused on their protests, and to build support and momentum for the large (illegal) march on the convention center Wednesday evening, the time of the nomination vote. During the weekend and first two days of the convention, television and newspapers were filled with pictures of Yippies—camping in the parks, holding rock concerts and news conferences, practicing *washoi* (linked-arm marching tactics borrowed from Japanese radicals)—and of Allen Ginsberg chanting Indian mantras. On Tuesday, they reported the mock "unbirthday" party for Lyndon Johnson, featuring music by the Holocaust No-Dance Band, songs by Phil Ochs, and speeches by writers opposed to the war.

Yet the high jinks of the Yippies were gradually overshadowed by the violence that occurred nightly in a battle for the parks. The city insisted on closing the parks in the evening. Thus each night, as police swept through Lincoln Park, spraying tear gas and exploding smoke bombs, the atmosphere became more ominous. Demonstrators increasingly fought back and, when forced out of the park, continued their harassment of police from nearby streets. More and more, the police struck and arrested first, and asked questions later. And increasingly, reporters were caught in the middle and then on the side of the demonstrators. By Tuesday, many of the reporters and their parent news services were convinced that they were watching a police force riot out of control.

The convention floor was also a battlefield of sorts. Dissenters and antiwar delegates faced the same unfavorable odds. The convention's rules and credentials committees, which had convened a week earlier, evidenced the first sharp encounters. Antiwar delegates pledged to McCarthy challenged Humphrey's forces in an effort to demonstrate that the convention was boss-ridden. They were only partly successful. Surprisingly, Humphrey delegates joined to push through several dramatic changes in the rules relating to Democratic party conventions. They agreed to abolish the unit rule, whereby a state could require all its votes to be cast for the same candidate. And they voted to ask the convention to reexamine its manner of selecting delegates. A Reform Commission was chosen to suggest how these changes might be implemented. But of course, these reforms would not apply to the 1968 convention.

On the question of the platform, however, Humphrey's forces were unbending. They wrote a plank praising Lyndon Johnson's conduct of the war. The minority of the platform committee that wanted to commit the party to a quick end to the war vowed to carry their fight to the convention floor.

CHICAGO NOTEBOOK:
TERROR IN THE STREETS
BILLY CLUBS AND BLOOD
IN A NO-MAN'S LAND

—Seattle Times

On Wednesday, although the convention had not yet nominated a presidential candidate, one outcome of the contest had already been decided. As predicted, Yippie tactics had brought enormous publicity. Action shots, music, wild dress, and extravagant statements were far more interesting than the droning speeches inside the convention. None of this theater of the absurd, however, blunted the point of the demonstrators: They were there to protest the continuing war—and the police were determined to stop them.

As police violence mounted, the nation watched in astonishment. Reporters and television commentators increasingly sided with the students. Their photographs and video clips showed police beating protesters. And police attacks on reporters only increased their partiality. By Tuesday night, protests from major news organizations like CBS began to pour into Chicago city headquarters, demanding that Mayor Daley control the police. Even several Chicago aldermen, usually quiet on such matters, denounced police brutality. As Frank Sullivan, press officer of the Chicago police, bitterly put it: "[the demonstrators] are a pitiful handful. They have almost no support. But, by golly, they get the cooperation of the news media."

On Wednesday the spirit of confrontation even entered the Amphitheater. For a brief time, the convention itself was threatened. As the press increasingly criticized Daley, he and his aides packed the spectator section of the hall with city workers who waved American flags and signs supporting Daley. On the floor, with the Illinois delegation, Daley watched the proceedings in sullen silence. Late in the afternoon, the convention began debate on the majority (Humphrey) and minority (McCarthy) Vietnam planks. The peace delegates fervently cheered speakers who called for a speedy, negotiated end to the war. But Humphrey's forces were too numerous. When the votes were tallied, the Humphrey–Johnson position on Vietnam had won: 1,567¾ to 1,041¼. The democratic party was now pledged to support President Johnson's position on the war. This accomplished, the convention adjourned until evening. But many of the delegates remained in their seats. New Yorkers broke into peace songs. The convention band, in reply, blared out the tune "This Will Be the Start of Something Big." Several California delegates moved over to the New York standard and joined in the singing. The band retorted with "California Here I Come" and "Happy Days Are Here Again." Strains of music overlaid shouts of "Stop the war!" as the last stragglers filed off the floor.

At about this time, the Grant Park bandshell demonstration broke up and David Dellinger tried to lead protesters out of the park. He and other leaders, however, lost all control when the crowd discovered the unguarded northern bridge, swarmed over to Michigan Avenue and then ran down the avenue toward the Conrad Hilton. Now about 3,000 strong, the crowd approached a police line across Michigan Avenue at East Balboa Drive blocking their route. Another police line stretched west of the Hilton on Wabash Avenue. Guardsmen, reporters, and television trucks waited in front of the hotel.

When they encountered the police line on Michigan Avenue, several demonstrators began shouting and chanting slogans and insults. Blue-helmeted officers repeatedly ordered the crowd to leave the street. A few demonstrators tried to flank police lines by heading west and then south toward the Amphitheater. Most were turned back after brief, violent scuffles. They rejoined the growing crowd blocked on Michigan Avenue.

Then, at about 7:30, a small contingent of black demonstrators following a mule train tried to make its way through the crowd south on Michigan Avenue and past the Hilton. To do so it had to pass through the demonstrators and the police lines. This group, led by the Reverend Ralph Abernathy of the Southern Christian Leadership Conference and including old people and children, had a legal permit to march.

A police wedge allowed them through and they continued south on Michigan and then west away from the hotel.

By this time, the corner of Balboa and Michigan had become an undulating mass of confusion. Segments of the crowd tried to push forward, shouting "Pig!" at the police who blocked them. Others tried to sneak through police lines behind the SCLC demonstrators. The protesters were determined to continue their march toward the Amphitheater. And the police were determined to stop them. Where the two groups

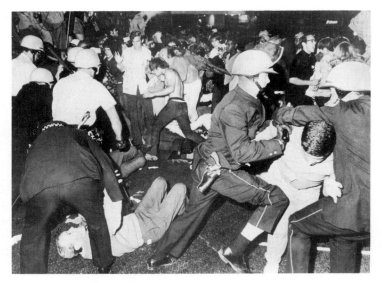

The battle for Michigan Avenue. During the short, violent confrontation in front of the Conrad Hilton hotel on August 28, 1968, enraged police charged into crowds of demonstrators. The major casualty, however, was Hubert Humphrey, whose nomination was associated with violence and riot. (UPI/Bettmann Newsphotos)

butted against each other, violent incidents flared. In the twilight, police and television floodlights cast an eerie and ominous glow.

Police again tried to warn the crowd to leave Michigan Avenue. But in response, a large number of young people sat down in the street. Another group split off and headed west on Balboa until they ran into an advancing phalanx of officers with clubs in their hands. The protesters retreated, shouting epithets and throwing rocks and bottles. Police guarding the front of the Hilton were struck by objects hurled down from the front windows of the hotel.

At about 7:57, police advancing along Balboa neared the main body of demonstrators on Michigan Avenue. Suddenly, they charged into the crowd, trying to clear the street and grabbing at random to make arrests. Nightsticks flying, they trapped a mass of demonstrators that was so large and hemmed in, it couldn't move. Part of it pressed up against the police line on Michigan Avenue, and these officers, too, began to swing their clubs. Rocks and other thrown objects thudded onto the helmets of police as they advanced.

Reporters and news cameras focused on incident after incident of brutal beatings by the police. Even the deputy superintendent of the police department rushed into the crowd to stop his officers from their attacks. One witness testifying at later hearings on police violence reported a typical beating by police:

> When they caught him, they began to beat him with their nightsticks until he fell to the pavement. They continued to beat him briefly after he fell. Then they dragged him about 30 feet to a paddy wagon.

As the police drove demonstrators back up Michigan Avenue, away from the hotel, a group numbering about 200 pushed through police lines and raced toward the entrance of the Conrad Hilton. Officers attacked the edges of this group using Mace spray. They pushed the bulk of the group up against the hotel and the plate-glass windows of its Haymarket Lounge. Suddenly, a shattering noise burst above

THE LIMITS OF POLITICS

The young protesters who clamored to enter the Democratic party convention of 1968, those who shouted their defiance at symbols of authority, were assaulting the foundations of the postwar political consensus. The target of their ire, Hubert Humphrey, the candidate nominated by the party to run against Richard Nixon, was a man of impeccable liberal credentials. His record on civil rights stretched back to the 1948 Democratic convention, when he engineered a strong plank on black rights. Throughout the 1950s and 1960s he had championed the cause of organized labor. He stood behind most of the social reforms passed by the Kennedy and Johnson administrations. Yet the Chicago protesters dismissed him with contemptuous cries of "Dump the Hump!" They demanded, instead, a very different sort of politics than that practiced by men like Humphrey.

In the brief eight years between the election of John F. Kennedy and the Chicago convention, much had happened to fragment the consensus in American society and to convince a variety of interest groups to repudiate political compromise. The result by the end of the decade was growing acrimony, confrontation, and violence. In 1968 it appeared as if the political center could no longer hold and that politics would splinter into competing ideological groups.

To some extent, the breakup of the liberal coalition of the 1960s resulted from the rising and unfulfilled expectations of social reform, and the rising costs and unfulfillable aims of the war in Vietnam. The promise of the civil rights movement foundered on white resistance and splits in the black movement. Reformers and elected officials pledged more than they could deliver. And from the middle of the Kennedy administration, through the five years of Johnson's presidency, the war in Vietnam was a constant drumbeat. At first only audible as a kind of background noise, the war eventually drowned out the voices still calling for social reform. By 1968, opposition to the war in Vietnam had all but consumed the impulse to reform, as the war frustrated the expectations aroused in the early years of the decade.

The march on Washington of 1963 represented the high point of hope that the ideals of King and the practical political sense of Kennedy could be intertwined to achieve major civil rights legislation. It was not optimism, however, but violence and tragedy that eventually persuaded Congress to pass the Civil Rights Act as well as Kennedy's other reform projects.

Late in the fall of 1963, most of the president's program was stalled in Congress. The Civil Rights Bill, toughened and amended, languished despite Kennedy's support. The centerpiece of his economic program, an extensive tax cut designed to stimulate production and jobs, remained unpassed. Work had begun in earnest to develop a program to fight large poverty pockets in rural states and urban areas, but hopes for passage of such a program were not bright.

Partly as an effort to win support for his faltering legislation, partly to shore up his presidency for the election one year away, Kennedy embarked on a speaking tour in late November. One of his stops was Dallas, Texas, a center of opposition to his programs. On November 22, Kennedy rode through the center of the city in an open car. Suddenly, rifle fire exploded and the president slumped forward. Two bullets had shattered his skull and throat. John Connally, governor of Texas, who was sitting in front of Kennedy, was also wounded. The driver of the car sped to a nearby hospital, but the president's wounds were fatal. His administration had begun in a burst of enthusiasm and media attention. Now millions of Americans watched on television the last scenes of its tragic ending: the murder of the accused assassin, Lee Harvey Oswald, and then the Kennedy funeral.

Johnson as President

It was Lyndon Baines Johnson's genius to turn this tragic moment into triumph. Assuming the presidency, Johnson stood back from the rituals of bereavement, acting to consolidate his power. In many ways this was a difficult task, for Johnson represented a different constituency of the Democratic party. He was a Texan, boisterous and crude in manner. He had mastered the clubroom politics of the U.S. Senate, which had brought him enormous legislative influence during the late 1950s. But most of the Kennedy entourage of advisers and cabinet officers considered him an outsider. Now, suddenly, he was president.

SOCIAL PROGRAMS On the other hand, Johnson believed even more strongly than Kennedy in the power and duty of the federal government to guarantee the rights of marginal or poor citizens. Seizing the stalled legislative program of the Kennedy administration, Johnson vowed to win its passage as a memorial to the slain leader and, perhaps, as testimony to his own right to the presidency. But there was an irony to this. Johnson succeeded in pressing reform legislation through Congress that dwarfed Kennedy's accomplishments. Yet he could never elicit the enthusiasm that his predecessor had.

Johnson grasped the wheel of government firmly. Five days after the assassination he addressed Congress, pledging to continue the policies of Kennedy. By early 1964 his efforts bore fruit. Congress enacted bill after bill: a major tax cut to stimulate the economy; the Economic Opportunity Act, setting up the structure for a "war on poverty"; and, most significant, a major civil rights act. To push civil rights legislation through Congress meant overcoming strong Southern opposition. Johnson built a majority by calling in debts owed him by other senators. Particularly important was the Republican support he gathered. Convincing the Republican leaders, Everett Dirksen of the Senate and Charles Halleck of the House, ensured victory.

Johnson also did what neither Eisenhower nor Kennedy had done: He adopted the language of the civil rights movement itself. On March 15 he appeared before Congress to speak for civil rights. The United States, he demanded, must "overcome the crippling legacy of bigotry and injustice." Delay, hesitation, and compromise were intolerable. Then he paused and repeated slowly and deliberately the most important slogan of the civil rights movement: "And . . . we . . . shall . . . overcome."

The new Civil Rights Act did not end discrimination, but it strengthened voting rights, outlawed segregation in public facilities, increased federal capacity to enter desegregation cases, and bolstered the Civil Rights Commission. When the

Three Democrats. In the early 1960s, John F. Kennedy (left), Eleanor Roosevelt, and Lyndon Baines Johnson represented three versions of Democratic party liberalism and the continuity between the New Deal of the 1930s and the pragmatic liberalism of the 1960s. (Library of Congress)

new tax-cut legislation passed, it worked as anticipated, although part of the stimulus may have come from the escalation of the war in Vietnam. Economic growth rates increased rapidly in 1964, 1965, and 1966. Unemployment shrank, and the federal budget hovered almost in balance. This economic growth, in turn, helped improve the ratio of black to white family income from .55 in 1960 to .64 in 1970.

The Office of Economic Opportunity (OEO) was largely Johnson's project. The Economic Opportunity Act of 1964 centralized federal antipoverty activities into one comprehensive executive agency. It created a job training corps, agricultural loan programs, incentive loans to hire the hard-core unemployed, and education benefits, plus later education programs such as Head Start and Upward Bound. While some of this amounted to sleight-of-hand transfers of existing programs to a new agency, a substantial portion of the OEO represented an innovative, broad-scale attack on poverty.

THE ELECTION OF 1964 By mid-1964, Johnson had clearly established legitimate claims to

the office of president. His renomination was assured. The only question was a running mate. The Democratic convention, meeting in Atlantic City, New Jersey, in August, chose liberal Senator Hubert Humphrey of Minnesota. Campaign strategy centered on defending Johnson's legislative record and turning the conservative Republican opponent, Senator Barry Goldwater of Arizona, into an issue.

Goldwater attacked the Johnson administration on domestic and foreign policy. Goldwater's grass-roots campaign in the Republican party represented a temporary triumph over political professionals. He aroused considerable enthusiasm among voters who opposed Johnson's use of the federal government to redress social and economic inequalities. Much of his support was concentrated in the rapidly growing sunbelt, the South and Southwest, where opposition to integration and social programs was strongest.

In some ways, the Goldwater movement was premature. His campaign was troubled by public distrust of some of his right-wing supporters. And he did not completely capitalize on growing hostility to civil rights demonstrations and liberal legislation. Governor George Wallace of Alabama had illustrated the significance of this backlash

Comparison of White and Black Family Income (in constant 1975 dollars)

	White Families	Black Families	Ratio
1950	$7,702	$4,178	.54
1955	9,271	5,113	.55
1960	10,604	5,871	.55
1965	12,370	6,812	.55
1970	14,188	9,032	.64
1975	14,268	9,321	.65
1980	20,502	12,380	.60

Source: U.S. Department of Commerce, Bureau of the Census, *Statistical Abstract of the United States, 1981* (Washington, D.C.: Government Printing Office, 1981), p. 436.

vote in primary elections in Wisconsin, Maryland, and Indiana. But Goldwater could not build a movement strong enough to block the Johnson landslide.

THE WAR IN VIETNAM   One relatively unimportant campaign issue was the war in Vietnam. During his year in office, Johnson had proceeded cautiously, without calling attention to the implications of his actions, but he moved the United States toward far greater involvement in the war. Early in 1964 he made several important decisions. He approved plans for covert harassment of North Vietnam, and he agreed to bombing missions against the north in the event of provocation. He also appointed General William Westmoreland to head military operations. These moves rested on two assumptions: first, that North Vietnam was responsible for and could control the insurgent Viet Cong in the south; second, that American intervention in the form of air strikes and ground troops could be decisive. Johnson and his advisers did not believe that American actions would increase the fighting in the south or cause an uncontrollable infiltration of troops and arms from the north.

The pretext for full-scale intervention came in late July 1964. On July 30 South Vietnamese PT (patrol torpedo) boats attacked bases in the Gulf of Tonkin inside North Vietnamese waters. Simultaneously, the *Maddox*, an American destroyer, steamed into the area to disrupt North Vietnamese communication facilities. On August 2, possibly seeing the two separate missions as a combined maneuver against them, North Vietnam sent out several PT boats to attack the destroyer. The *Maddox* fired, sinking one of the attackers, then radioed the news to Washington. Johnson ordered another ship into the bay. On August 3 both destroyers reported another attack—although somewhat later, the commander of the *Maddox* radioed that he was not sure. Nonetheless, the president ordered American planes to retaliate by bombing inside North Vietnam.

Johnson then sought congressional support and justification for his action. He quickly received it. Senator William Fulbright guided a resolution through his Foreign Relations Committee and then through the Senate in less than a week. Fulbright's action was perhaps related to his fear that Barry Goldwater might use the Vietnam issue in the forthcoming election. Neither he nor anyone else in the Senate had been told all the facts about the Gulf of Tonkin skirmish, and later critics would question whether or not an attack had actually occurred.

The War on Poverty: Education, Employment, and Training Funds, 1960–80

	1960	1965	1970	1975	1980
Percentage of federal budget	1.1	1.8	4.4	4.9	5.3
Amount (in billions of dollars)	1.0	2.1	8.6	15.9	30.8

Source: U.S. Department of Commerce, Bureau of the Census, *Statistical Abstract of the United States, 1981* (Washington, D.C.: Government Printing Office, 1981), p. 248.

Like the Korean War and the cold war, the origins of the war in Vietnam lay partly in unresolved questions left over from World War II. American participation in the struggle was by accumulation, some of it public and some of it secret. This made it a process and a cause that few Americans understood very well.

The fighting in Vietnam began in 1945, at the end of Japanese occupation, and terminated in 1975, when North Vietnamese and Viet Cong soldiers marched into Saigon, the South Vietnamese capital, thus putting an end to the last American-supported government. This thirty-year struggle by communist-led forces sought to eliminate first French and then American influence in Vietnam. Essentially a civil war, it was complicated by French colonialism, by international agreements, by encouragement and aid from outside nations, and by a massive effort of the United States to thwart the communists.

When the French reconquered most of their former colony of Vietnam after World War II, communist forces inspired by Ho Chi Minh began an uprising that eventually defeated the French in 1954 at the battle of Dien Bien Phu. From 1950, the United States supplied the French but refused direct intervention. During the Eisenhower administration, the president and his advisers sympathized with the French, gave them aid, and hoped to prevent the further spread of communist influence in Asia. But Eisenhower also understood the extreme risks of direct involvement in another Asian war after the unpopular conflict in Korea.

Exhausted and defeated after Dien Bien Phu, the French agreed to a peace conference in Geneva, Switzerland, in July 1954. The Geneva Accords provided for French withdrawal and temporarily divided Vietnam into two administrative areas: the north, occupied by the communist Viet Minh, and the south, organized by pro-French Vietnamese. Reunification elections were mandated to decide the permanent fate of the nation. The United States sent observers to the Geneva conference but did not sign the accords. In fact, the Central Intelligence Agency worked secretly to undermine the agreements, to disrupt the economy of the north, and to install a pro-American ruler in the south. This last goal was accomplished when Ngo Dinh Diem became prime minister of the south. Diem asked for and received advice and aid from the United States. And he refused to participate in reunification. Partly to counter this, Diem's opponents, aided by the north, turned to insurgency.

From this time onward, American financial and military support poured in as five American presidents, from Eisenhower to Ford, attempted to salvage American interests in the area. For the United States, however, intervention had no really distinct beginning. War was never officially declared, although the Gulf of Tonkin resolution

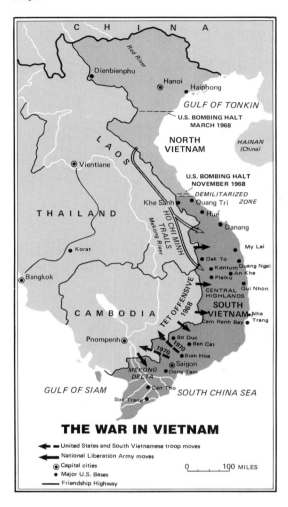

THE WAR IN VIETNAM

← United States and South Vietnamese troop moves
← National Liberation Army moves
◉ Capital cities
● Major U.S. Bases
— Friendship Highway

0 _____ 100 MILES

authorized the president to protect American forces and interests in the area. American participation grew in small increments, sometimes openly and sometimes secretly. By 1965 there were 181,000 American troops in South Vietnam; by 1968 there were 536,000.

Like the Korean War, the war in Vietnam was fought within serious constraints. The ultimate suppliers of war materiel—the United States, the U.S.S.R., and China—were not attacked, and supply lines into Vietnam remained open on both sides for most of the war. The victory the United States sought was the permanent establishment of a Western-oriented government in South Viet-

nam. But the means to achieve this were, from the beginning, controversial.

The nature of warfare in Vietnam was determined by the jungle terrain and by the sympathy of many South Vietnamese for the rebels. In the absence of fronts or battle lines, the Viet Cong (South Vietnamese rebels) and North Vietnamese troops could choose the time and place of engagement. After a battle, they could slip into dense jungles or hide among supporters in the peasantry. Their weapons were sometimes crude— they used booby traps and captured arms—but they also possessed more sophisticated Russian and Chinese equipment. The United States, adapting to jungle warfare, relied most heavily on helicopters, which gave great flexibility to troop movements. After 1964, American tactics focused on preventing supplies from reaching rebels in the south. Intensive bombing and defoliation of jungle foliage with herbicides disrupted supply routes, but eventually intensive bombing of North Vietnam was undertaken to cut supplies off at the source.

In his first year in office, Johnson prided himself on the consensus he had achieved in domestic and foreign affairs. In dealing with Vietnam he appeared to be a moderate. And in some respects he was. But he locked himself in by three assumptions that gradually convinced him to commit more men and more resources to the Indochina war. The first of these beliefs was the "domino theory," originally propounded by Eisenhower. This notion assumed that if South Vietnam fell to the communist-supported insurgents, other Southeast Asian nations would topple into the communist camp. The second assumption was that gradual escalation, covert action, and misinformation could hide the war from the American people and thus preserve consensus. (The war would be over before anyone realized its extent or cost.) Finally, Johnson wanted to save face. He believed that the United States could not afford to withdraw or back down without inviting a barrage of accusations that he had sold out to the communists. Having lived through one period of McCarthyism, he was determined to prevent another.

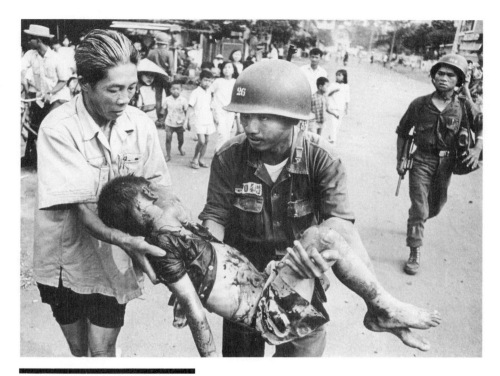

A Vietnamese casualty. Both sides in the Vietnam War inflicted heavy casualties on innocent civilians. Photographs such as this one, featured in American newspapers and on nightly television newscasts, convinced many Americans that the fight could never be won without a savagery and brutality that they would not support. (©Philip Jones Griffiths/Magnum)

Believing the optimistic appraisals of his military advisers and the "hawks" in his administration, he gradually committed American troops and prestige to the jungle war. He cut himself off from the "doves" (war opponents) in Congress. Planning strategy and defending his decisions against mounting public criticism became his preoccupations. By pursuing this policy, he convinced many Americans that the Democratic party had fallen to the control of a narrow group of professional politicians who could not understand why any reasonable person might oppose the war.

The Vietnam War was only one factor that undercut support for the liberal consensus on which Johnson depended. There were growing numbers of critics of the federal activism of the Kennedy and Johnson administrations. Opponents of integration and conservatives in general rejected the notion that government should intervene in the economic and social order to guarantee a fair distribution of opportunity and rewards. From the opposite point of view, students, the civil rights movement, the poor, and then the growing women's movement criticized the federal government for delaying social reforms.

The New Right

Large numbers of disaffected Americans joined the "new right." Born in the troubled 1950s from the marriage of traditional conservatism and a new, vociferous right wing, this movement captured the Republican party temporarily in 1964

A helicopter swoops into battle to pick up a wounded American soldier. The helicopter gave troops great mobility and the sound of choppers was a link to the safer world of American bases outside the confusing and gruesome battlefields in the countryside. (AP/Wide World Photos)

and exercised a strong influence on the direction of the party thereafter.

REACTION TO THE WARREN COURT The new right originated in dissatisfaction with the Eisenhower administration and, in particular, with the Warren Court decisions that liberalized American society. Besides *Brown* v. *Board of Education*, the Warren Court in *Watkins* v. *United States* (1957) upheld the rights of witnesses testifying before a congressional committee. In effect, this decision made future McCarthy-like hearings less likely. Another decision, *Reynolds* v. *Sims* (1964), ruled that state legislative districts had to be apportioned evenly according to population. This decision deprived rural (and generally conservative) areas of much of the political power they had exercised in state government. A later case, *Miranda* v. *State of Arizona* (1966), ruled that a person apprehended for a crime must be informed of his or her rights—including the right

to remain silent—before any statement relating to the crime could become legal evidence.

These Court decisions, together with many others—on civil rights, definitions of obscenity, protection of free speech—greatly strengthened minority civil rights. They opened the federal courts to a wide variety of lawsuits brought by groups claiming discrimination. The Warren Court thus took the lead in expanding the rights of citizens and the power of the federal government to intervene in the lives of every American. Because of this activism, the Court also became the target of extensive and angry criticism.

The John Birch Society was founded in 1958 by candy manufacturer Robert Welch from Massachusetts. The society (named after an anti-communist missionary who died in China) became the most strident center of criticism of the Warren Court. Welch had been deeply disappointed by Eisenhower's refusal to undo New Deal reforms. He concluded, in fact, that the Republican party had been infiltrated by communist agents. Welch discovered support for his views across America and particularly in southern California and the nation's Eastern suburban areas. In 1960 the Birch society launched an "Impeach Earl Warren" campaign. By 1964, Birch members controlled a significant portion of the Republican party—enough to ensure the nomination of Goldwater.

INTELLECTUALS AND EVANGELISTS A growing number of right-wing intellectuals were among those who attacked government-mandated egalitarianism. One of the most important among them was William F. Buckley, whose *National Review* magazine, founded in 1955, became a center for opposition to the liberal postwar consensus.

Other conservative forces, which were at first less clearly focused or politically motivated, centered around Protestant revivalism. The early leader of this movement was the Reverend Billy Graham. Beginning in the early 1950s, Graham led successful revival crusades in cities across the nation. Although the political message of his sermons and books was sometimes muted, he preached salvation by individual redemption, not by government regulation. He appealed to elements in society who were disturbed—or left behind—by rapid social change. Praising "rugged individualism," he criticized social legislation and labor unions while remaining silent on questions like integration. This stand captivated a strong element of white Southerners, who were most affected by the turbulence of civil rights.

SEGREGATIONISTS In fact, the gains of civil rights caused consternation among many white Americans, and not just those of the South. Repeatedly, Gallup polls in the 1950s and 1960s demonstrated white America's divided conscience on this issue. Gradually, most white Americans, even in the South, accepted at least a limited version of the goal of integration. But most at the same time feared the means used to accomplish it, such as marches and demonstrations.

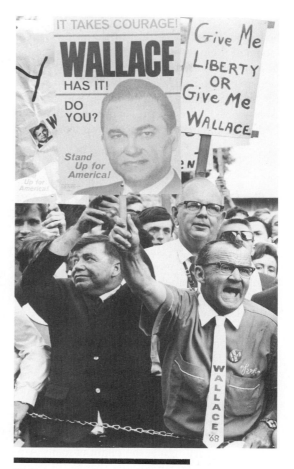

Wallace supporters, Lansing, Michigan. Confusion in the Democratic party and the moderate line taken by Republican candidate Richard Nixon in 1968 bolstered third-party presidential hopeful George Wallace of Alabama. Wallace also ran in 1964. He gained support from disgruntled conservatives frustrated with the limited war policy in Vietnam, demonstrations, and racial integration. (©Hiroji Kubota/Magnum)

Some of the opposition to integration rallied around Governor George Wallace of Alabama. Defeated in several local showdowns with federal officials over Alabama's segregation policies, Wallace became a symbol of resistance to federal erosion of local power. In 1964 he gathered significant support as a presidential candidate inside the Democratic party, although not enough to win the nomination. In 1968 he ran for president on the ticket of the American Independent party and won about 13 percent of the popular vote (some of them former Democrats), coming close to forcing the election into the House of Representatives. He campaigned on a platform calling for "law and order" (thinly veiled anti-integration code words)—the suppression of urban rioting and protest marches against the war in Vietnam.

Splintering of the Left

The most important element to break away from the liberal consensus was the civil rights movement. In some respects, this break was only partial. Organizations such as the NAACP and the Urban League continued to work closely with the Democratic party and the federal government. Black voters repeatedly demonstrated their allegiance to Democratic candidates. Congress and the courts still played a major role in enforcing and extending the rights of minorities. But what Martin Luther King, Jr., had feared might happen did occur after the summer of 1963 and the passage of the 1964 Civil Rights Act. Despite the progress in legal rights, the plight of many African Americans remained little changed. Integration proceeded slowly; job opportunities especially remained scarce. In order to gain support, the civil rights movement had aroused the expectations of every black American. Inevitably, these expectations were frustrated.

King was cautious (many in the movement said too cautious) about exhausting white tolerance for civil rights progress. During the summer of 1964, before the presidential election, a voter registration drive in Mississippi led by SNCC and the NAACP brought hundreds of college students to the state. After three of them were murdered in Philadelphia, Mississippi, King became so worried about such incidents of violence and the possibility that Republicans might successfully exploit them to focus hostility on civil rights

that he called for a temporary moratorium on demonstrations. But other groups like SNCC and CORE refused.

BLACK UNREST Lack of visible progress toward either racial equality or improved living standards became apparent in Northern cities during the mid-1960s. Fed by mass migration from the rural South during and after World War II, the black population in northeastern cities more than doubled between 1950 and 1970 while the white population actually fell in the same areas. Consequently, urban tax bases eroded, and city social services were overburdened. At the same time, discrimination in hiring, poor schools, and inadequate training kept much of the black population unemployed or underemployed. The network of federal social services could not fill every gap. Inflamed by incautious police enforcement and violent incidents, urban ghettos exploded into rioting in 1964–67 and particularly in 1968.

Increasing violence precipitated a split in the unwieldy civil rights movement that Martin Luther King, Jr., had tried to guide. The African American community had never been entirely unified. Enormous regional and class gulfs split the black population. Generational differences divided leadership. Gradually, a gulf widened between proponents of alliances with white liberals and the federal government and advocates of all-black organizations. The charismatic Black Muslim leader Malcom X, for example, preached a separatism that appealed to many urban blacks. Although Malcom X was assassinated in 1965, his position continued to attract the more radical elements of the Northern ghettos.

The first major urban riot occurred in the summer of 1964 in Harlem. Then violence exploded in the Watts section of Los Angeles the following summer. Other cities were struck in 1965–68. Most of these disturbances followed the same pattern. An incident in the ghetto would bring police action. Unable to control the situation, police would call for reinforcements. Then ghetto residents would pour out of tenement buildings, attacking and looting stores and setting fires. As the conflagration spread, snipers sometimes appeared. Police and, finally, the National Guard would isolate a riot area, proclaim a curfew, and arrest thousands of residents. Frequently, the police and guard put down riots with excessive force. During 1967, a year in which seventy cities were besieged by riots, more than eighty people died—most of them black—and thousands were arrested.

King still clung to nonviolence in the midst of this disorder. But groups like SNCC were less hesitant about condoning violence. In 1966 Stokely Carmichael, the leader of SNCC, advocated self-defense for blacks. He also popularized the term "black power," which implied cutting ties with white liberals and pushing for gains using exclusively black organizations.

After 1967, relations between black civil rights leaders and the administration deteriorated sharply. In the spring, Martin Luther King, Jr., broke with the president over the war in Vietnam. For the civil rights leader, this was an anguished moment. In 1965 King had briefly criticized the war, but Johnson had applied enormous pressure, and King had reversed himself. Now, however, he believed that the war could not be ignored. Its incessant funding demands had cut into poverty programs. The draft and college deferments (primarily exercised by young white men) placed a disproportionate percentage of black soldiers on the Asian front lines. Despite the company of white radicals and black power advocates that an antiwar stance placed him in, King sharply attacked the war. The United States, he declared, was "the greatest purveyor of violence in the world today." Carl T. Rowan, a black journalist, wrote: "By urging Negroes not to respond to the draft or to fight in Vietnam, he has taken a tack that many Americans of all races consider utterly irresponsible." King's decision of conscience speeded a process of alienation that took civil rights off the federal agenda. But the leader had already begun to falter and the movement he headed was deeply divided over goals

and strategies. The doors to the house of reform were, indeed, being shut.

The black civil rights movement endured one further, and perhaps fatal, loss in the spring of 1968. King was planning a "poor people's campaign" and demonstration in Washington to rekindle the smoldering movement. He also participated in a strike of black garbage workers in Memphis, Tennessee. The strike was a bitter one, called after two workers were accidentally killed on the job. The strikers demanded better wages and working conditions. King worked hard to prevent violence. On the evening of April 4, as he prepared to leave his Memphis motel for dinner, King stepped out on the balcony for a moment to speak to his driver below. A rifle cracked and King fell, mortally wounded.

The news of King's death blew through the ghettos of American cities like a ravaging wind. Riots erupted in over 100 cities. Buildings burned, businesses were looted. The National Guard and police once more moved in with force. Mayor Daley of Chicago, which suffered one of the worst riots, spoke of a need to "shoot to maim or cripple" looters if riots broke out again. When the soldiers and police finally withdrew, the civil rights movement, and much of the sympathy it had engendered, had been gutted.

STUDENT RADICALS King and other black civil rights leaders had, by their example, inspired the country's white student radicals. Young white Americans had been among the most enthusiastic supporters of President John Kennedy. His New Frontier appealed to a generation that rejected the secure and smug middle-class world they associated with their parents and the suburbs where they lived. Kennedy's inaugural address in early 1961 struck a responsive chord. The new president dedicated his administration to reviving America's traditional mission in the world: the protection and extension of political freedom. To the "tempered," "disciplined," and "proud" new generation of Americans he addressed, he promised an endeavor whose glow would be a beacon for the world. He

The aftermath of the urban riots in black ghettos in 1968 transformed the cores of American cities into war zones occupied by troops (the National Guard). (©Burt Glinn/ Magnum)

asked of others only what he required of himself: "not what America will do for you," but "what together we can do for the freedom of man." But these were words of warning as well as promise, for implicit in their fervent rhetoric of sacrifice lay the seeds of the confrontational policies that led to intervention in Cuba and escalation in Vietnam.

Such lofty goals as Kennedy articulated were inevitably compromised in the real and hard world of politics. Like civil rights advocates, with whom they shared much in common, young white Americans had rising expectations for their society. They desired not only civil rights for blacks but a much greater voice for themselves in the direction of society. Their goals consisted of a patchwork of radical reforms—of politics, of culture, of universities and schools, and of social and sexual relationships. These aims were eventually focused in two related movements: the "new left" and the "counterculture." At first, student radicals found themselves in alliance with the Kennedy and Johnson administrations.

Pleased by some of the reform legislation and inspired by the stirring rhetoric, the new left and the counterculture nonetheless gradually moved away from the political center of American society. By 1968 they were in open confrontation with it.

The new left and the counterculture originated in the 1950s. The more politically minded students were profoundly dissatisfied with the politics of the Eisenhower era. The slow pace of integration, the tense standoff between the United States and the Soviet Union, McCarthyism, and widespread poverty and social discrimination inspired a group of university students in 1962 to found a new sort of political organization, the Students for a Democratic Society (SDS). Unlike the "old left," which they dismissed as ineffectual and conservative, these student radicals wanted to break with the prevailing liberal consensus—or at least to stretch it far beyond its current dimensions. With other young radicals, Tom Hayden, a student at the University of Michigan, wrote the "Port Huron

The Beatles (John, Ringo, Paul, and George) early in their careers. Their conservative dress more than anything else reveals their working-class origins. The group, their music, and their styles evolved enormously during the 1960s. (Howard Frank)

Statement," a document that proposed a new political system of "participatory democracy" and called for an end to racial discrimination and the cold war.

By the early 1960s, SDS was only part of a larger political stirring on campuses across the country. Much of this movement took its inspiration from and some of it participated in the civil rights marches and demonstrations. Northern white students joined in picketing national corporations such as Woolworths that practiced discrimination in their Southern branches. Or they joined in freedom marches and voter registration drives in the South, particularly during the "Mississippi Summer" of 1964. Other students became politically active around opposition to the investigations of the House Un-American Activities Committee. By 1964 the radical movement had organized on several large university campuses: Michigan, the University of Chicago, Wisconsin, and, particularly, the University of California at Berkeley.

Berkeley became the center of national attention during the fall of 1964. The centerpiece of the prestigious California system of higher education, Berkeley enjoyed a reputation for liberal regulations and a distinguished faculty. But as an institution it was also large, impersonal, and bureaucratic. In 1964 the administration altered rules governing campus areas set aside for student political meetings and recruitment drives. Students reacted quickly and angrily. They organized a Free Speech movement and held large demonstrations and sit-ins. Eventually, they took over administration buildings. Most of these tactics were borrowed from the civil rights movement.

Frightened by the rising anger and organization on campus, and pressured by state officials, the university called in the police. Now the students declared a general strike and shut down most of the campus. Eventually, the new restrictions were lifted. But the student movement remained strong. Indeed, Berkeley set an example for students across the country, who in turn began to protest unwanted rules and restrictions on their own campuses. At the same time, student radicalism became an issue for conservative political campaigns. Ronald Reagan's successful quest for the governorship of California in 1966 gained energy and focus from his promise to deal firmly with Berkeley.

The counterculture. During the 1960s, two symbols represented the counterculture: a V sign, meaning peace in Vietnam, and the word LOVE. Both signified the desire of many young Americans to revise the nature of sexual, social, and political relationships. (©Burt Glinn/Magnum)

THE COUNTERCULTURE Whatever coherence the radical student movement attained depended in part on a growing network of counterculture. The counterculture was not necessarily political in orientation, but it was opposed to many of the practices of adult culture. It traced its origins to the 1950s and rock 'n' roll music, which at first was almost entirely a teenage phenomenon.

By the 1960s this youth culture had spread and deepened. The antiestablishment character of the youth rebellion became more and more explicit. The youth culture acquired advocates like writers Allen Ginsberg, Jack Kerouac, and Paul Goodman—whose book *Growing Up Absurd*, published in 1960, explored the anguish of the younger generation. Also by the 1960s the counterculture had absorbed more sophisticated versions of rock'n'roll in the music of the Beatles and the protest songs of Bob Dylan. Equally important, many young people had begun to experiment with illegal drugs: marijuana, hashish, and LSD.

The young people who experimented with drugs and new sexual relationships were seeking a congenial and hospitable environment. Their lifestyles represented a sharp contrast to the daily grind of work shifts and overtime. So some of them "dropped out" or sought comradeship in communal living on farms or in rural areas. This emphasis on a return to nature and a rejection of modern industrial life, materialism, and artificiality eventually became a strong element not just of the counterculture but of the rest of American society as well.

By the mid-1960s many young people had begun to reject the liberal consensus of Kennedy and Johnson, largely because of the war in Vietnam. Not only did the war starve social programs that many young radicals supported, it weighed heavily on their own lives because of the draft. Many of them received deferments while in college or graduate school. But this special status, which exempted them from duty in the jungles of Asia, only increased their uneasiness with their privileged positions in society.

Increasingly, the war split America. It cut off students, the civil rights movement, and intellectuals from the established consensus. And it divided those who believed the war could not be won from those who believed it must be won at all costs. Justification for the war, however, rested on the basic assumptions of post–World War II American foreign policy. Thus failure either to win the battle in Asia or to convince the American public to support it wholeheartedly frayed the fabric of faith in politics that had been unchallenged for twenty years.

Percent of Black Voting Age Population Registered in Eleven Southern States, 1960–80

	Total	Ala.	Ark.	Fla.	Ga.	La.	Miss.	N.C.	S.C.	Tenn.	Tex.	Va.
1960	29.1% (White—61.1%)	13.7	38.0	39.4	29.3	31.1	5.2	39.1	13.7	59.1	35.5	23.1
1975	58.3% (White—60.8%)	55.8	52.2	53.1	69.5	58.8	60.7	49.2	44.0	64.2	61.9	49.8
1980	57.7% (White—79.4%)	57.5	59.9	61.4	51.9	61.3	64.1	55.3	55.8	66.7	54.8	54.1

Source: U.S. Department of Commerce, Bureau of the Census, *Statistical Abstract of the United States, 1981* (Washington, D.C.: Government Printing Office, 1981), p. 495.

Johnson's Presidency

After his electoral triumph of 1964—now president in his own right—Johnson believed he had created a durable political consensus for further domestic reforms. He was aware of opposition from the political right and left, but he was also sure of his mastery of government. Consequently, in 1965 and 1966 he placed before a heavily Democratic Congress an astonishing program of reform legislation. Congress passed and funded Medicare insurance for the elderly and Medicaid to provide free medical services for those unable to afford them. An important Voting Rights Act of August 1965 eliminated literacy tests and other obstacles to participation in elections by minority voters. In the same month, Johnson fulfilled Kennedy's promise to establish the Department of Housing and Urban Development (HUD). Other legislation poured out of the hopper: a Clean Air Act, highway beautification, federal funding of urban transit. Each act testified to the president's legislative skill.

Nonetheless, many of these "Great Society" programs lacked coordination and adequate funding. Legislation sometimes promised much more than it could deliver. Johnson himself seemed more interested in passing laws than in administering them. Bureaucratic inertia and local opposition slowed implementation. Most ominous, however, was the war in Vietnam, which by 1965 and 1966 had begun to divert funds away from social programs into the bottomless pit of an Asian land war.

THE WAR ESCALATES Although the Gulf of Tonkin resolution gave Johnson a mandate to protect American lives and interests in Vietnam, its implications were not clear until early 1965. Then, on February 6, Viet Cong rebels attacked an American base at Pleiku. In response, the president ordered sustained bombing of the north. He also authorized search-and-destroy sorties by American troops and, by the end of the year, had approved the dispatch of nearly 180,000 American personnel to Vietnam. A stepped-up strategic enclave policy was also initiated. During the summer of 1965, the president added to the bombing by approving regular B-52 saturation raids on enemy strongholds in the south and increased strategic raids on the north.

By the beginning of 1966 a seemingly unchanging pattern had been established in which several interlocking factors relentlessly escalated the war. American bombing and added troop strength (which mounted to 486,000 in 1967 and 536,000 in 1968) destabilized South Vietnamese society and increased northern infiltration. And northern infiltration further destabilized the south and led to even greater U.S. intervention.

Johnson did not present the issues or the costs of the war to the American public in a forthright manner. He underestimated costs in 1966 and declined to ask for increased war taxes until early 1968. (Eventually, the war cost the United States about $100 billion, with defense spending rising 16 percent in 1966, 15 percent in 1967, and 3 percent in 1968.) He responded to his critics with scorn, sarcasm, and charges of unpatriotic behavior. Nonetheless, he tried to give the impression of flexibility. On several occasions—December 1966, February and December 1967, and March 1968—he ordered a halt to the bombing and suggested negotiations. But neither North Vietnam nor the Viet Cong would agree to his terms, which were intended to guarantee the independence of South Vietnam.

Because the war remained unresolved and promises of an early victory proved false, Johnson faced mounting opposition. The burgeoning student radical movement, intellectuals, civil rights groups, Republicans angry that the war dragged on without victory, and many others chided the president. A Gallup poll revealed profound public division and confusion about the war. American goals seemed unclear. In part because of his inability to articulate clear and believable aims, the president's popularity plummeted. His carefully constructed consensus, built around fulfilling the idealism of the Kennedy years, disintegrated.

LBJ AND CIVIL RIGHTS Meanwhile, continuing summer outbreaks of riot in American cities took their toll on Johnson's civil rights achievements. Not only split over the war in Vietnam, the United States was quickly becoming more seriously divided than ever over racial questions. Johnson attempted to prevent this polarization and to preserve the ties of the civil rights movement with his administration. In 1967 he appointed a National Advisory Commission on Civil Disorders, headed by Governor Otto Kerner of Illinois. The report, when issued in 1968, warned of the degeneration of American society into two warring racial cultures. The commission also blamed "white racism" for the urban riots. But a Gallup poll found that only a third of Americans accepted this conclusion.

Following the disorders of 1967, Johnson also secured passage of a new civil rights act in early 1968 that barred discrimination in most American housing. But while he recognized the need for quick action to correct social injustice, Johnson opposed riot and confrontation as a means of attaining such goals. After the riots of 1967 he declared: "Violence must be stopped, quickly, finally, and permanently."

The president faced still other political problems because of a backlash against his social programs. After midterm Democratic congressional losses in 1966, a more independent-minded and stronger opposition confronted him. Funds for some of his projects, such as the War on Poverty, dwindled. Yet Johnson continued to advocate reform, if only to hold the sympathy of his liberal constituency.

JOHNSON BOWS OUT A disastrous turn of events in Vietnam during early 1968 effectively ended Johnson's presidency. Beginning in January and extending for more than a month, the Viet Cong challenged American and South Vietnamese forces everywhere: in defended hamlets, in the countryside, in the cities, even in front of the American embassy in Saigon. This Tet offensive (so named because it coincided with the Tet lunar new year) marked a turning point in the war. Although the Viet Cong eventually lost most of their gains and, in fact, suffered enormous losses of personnel, the gruesome battle convinced many Americans that the war could not be won.

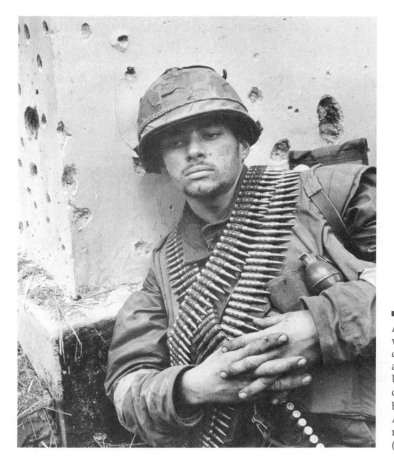

An American in Vietnam. Why were these boys dying? It was a question the politicians were unable to answer persuasively. This U.S. soldier was photographed during the Tet offensive in 1968, a battle so overwhelming that many Americans were convinced of the need for their country to withdraw. (Donald McCullin/Magnum)

This growing doubt registered in Johnson's disappointing showing in the New Hampshire Democratic primary. Young people by the hundreds flocked to the state to organize support for Senator Eugene McCarthy, who had declared his opposition to the war. Their efforts led to a near-defeat of the president. Johnson realized that even if he won renomination, his candidacy would rip apart the Democratic party. Thus on March 31, he surprised the nation by announcing his withdrawal from the race.

Yet Johnson's withdrawal could not stop the escalation of either the war or the dissension at home. Nor did it prevent the president from intervening in the convention to ensure that his policies would be defended by the party platform and by the candidate it chose. The expectations that he had helped to arouse had now soured. His administration, as versatile and innovative as any in the twentieth century, was about to be condemned on the overriding issue of the war. Civil rights, economic progress, the peace of American society—all seemed to hang in the balance of a struggle thousands of miles away. That struggle and the war came home in the summer of 1968. The stage was set for its reenactment as Yippie theater in the streets of Chicago.

CHRONOLOGY

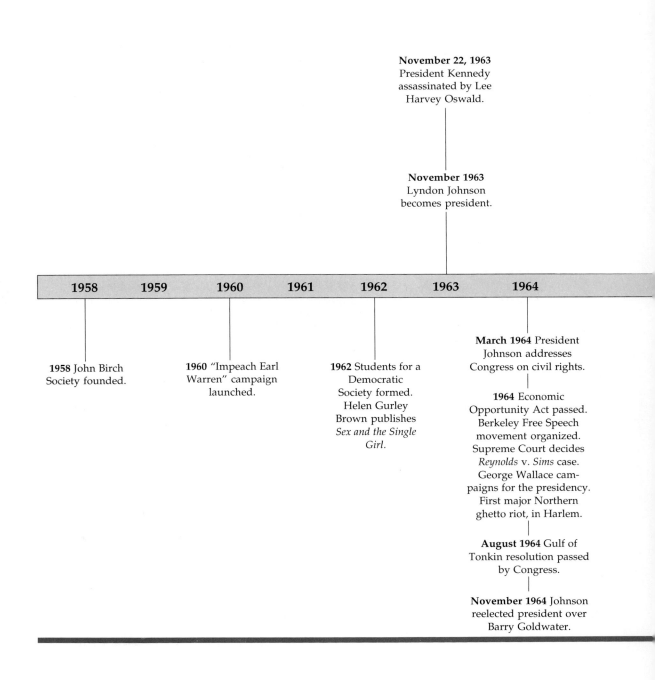

November 22, 1963
President Kennedy assassinated by Lee Harvey Oswald.

November 1963
Lyndon Johnson becomes president.

1958 | 1959 | 1960 | 1961 | 1962 | 1963 | 1964

1958 John Birch Society founded.

1960 "Impeach Earl Warren" campaign launched.

1962 Students for a Democratic Society formed. Helen Gurley Brown publishes *Sex and the Single Girl.*

March 1964 President Johnson addresses Congress on civil rights.

1964 Economic Opportunity Act passed. Berkeley Free Speech movement organized. Supreme Court decides *Reynolds* v. *Sims* case. George Wallace campaigns for the presidency. First major Northern ghetto riot, in Harlem.

August 1964 Gulf of Tonkin resolution passed by Congress.

November 1964 Johnson reelected president over Barry Goldwater.

1965 181,000 American troops committed to South Vietnam. Johnson orders bombing of North Vietnam. Malcolm X assassinated in New York City. Watts riot in Los Angeles.

August 1965 Voting Rights Act passed by Congress.

1965–66 "Great Society" programs passed.

1968 536,000 American troops in South Vietnam. Youth International party (Yippies) founded. New civil rights act bars discrimination in housing. National Advisory Commision on Disorders (Kerner Commission) reports.

January 1968 Tet offensive begins in South Vietnam.

1967 Martin Luther King, Jr., speaks out against the war in Vietnam.

Summer 1967 Seventy cities experience black riots.

1969 Senator George McGovern appointed chair of Democratic party reform commission. Several youth leaders indicted for inciting Chicago convention riot.

| 1965 | 1966 | 1967 | 1968 | 1969 | 1970 | 1971 | 1972 |

March 12, 1968 Senator Eugene McCarthy comes close to defeating Johnson in New Hampshire primary.

1966 Black Panther party founded. Supreme Court decides *Miranda* v. *State of Arizona* case.

March 31, 1968 Johnson renounces plans for reelection.

June 5, 1968 Robert Kennedy assassinated by Sirhan Sirhan.

July 1968 Republicans nominate Richard Nixon for president.

August 24, 1968 Thousands of protesters assemble in Chicago.

August 28, 1968 Chicago Democratic convention riot erupts.

August 28, 1968 Democratic party nominates Hubert Humphrey for president.

November 1968 Nixon elected president over Hubert Humphrey and George Wallace.

1970 Judge Julius Hoffman sentences Chicago defendants to prison.

1972 Judge Hoffman's sentences reversed by appeals court.

Helen Gurley Brown

I think marriage is insurance for the worst years of your life. During your best years you don't need a husband. You do need a man of course every step of the way, and they are often cheaper emotionally and a lot more fun by the dozen.

These words, in the opening pages of Helen Gurley Brown's *Sex and the Single Girl* (1962), announced the death of America's faith in the marriage ideology of the 1950s and declared the sexual liberation of single women. Brown's aggressive and unrelenting defense of sex for the unmarried girl won her book a prominent place on the best-seller list of 1962. It also earned her the status of a celebrity. Answering letters of appreciation and requests for advice, she marketed her responses as a column, beginning in 1964, called "Woman Alone," distributed to fifty magazines and newspapers. In March 1965 she assumed editorship of *Cosmopolitan*, a women's magazine with a long history and a rapidly declining readership. By 1969 she had rebuilt its circulation to over a million copies monthly, sold almost solely from newsstands and grocery stores, making it one of the most successful commercial periodicals. In 1967 she launched a television interview show, *Outrageous Opinions*.

Helen Gurley was born in Arkansas in 1922, neither rich, beautiful, nor cosmopolitan. She suffered an impoverished childhood. After World War II she attended business school in Los Angeles. Between the ages of eighteen and twenty-five, she held eighteen different secretarial jobs, until she found a position in an advertising firm in 1948. Picking up the trade as she went along, she became first a copy editor and then an advertising executive. In 1959 she married David Brown, a director and story editor at 20th Century-Fox Studios. After reading some of her old love letters to a former boyfriend, her husband suggested that she write an advice book for single women. The result was her best-seller and a new career.

Although *Sex and the Single Girl* declared sexual freedom for women, it did so in a curious fashion. In one sense, Brown only articulated major changes occurring in American culture: the open and explicit discussion of sex; the increasing use of birth control measures such as the intra-uterine device and "the Pill"; and the growing respectability of soft-core pornographic magazines such as *Playboy*. But Brown's advice was strongly tempered with traditional attitudes. If marriage was out, dependency on men was not. In fact, the single girl as Brown described her lived for nothing so much as multiple sexual encounters. Everything about her—job, diet, friends, apartment—was designed to attract men. Men were still the aggressors; women always temptresses. By comparison, it might be argued, the narrowest suburban housewife, confined by babies, house and garden, husband, and PTA, had a rich and busy life next to the ever-aging single girl trying to market her attractions.

Brown's celebration of casual sexual encounters deeply upset traditional moralists, who upheld the sanctity of marriage. She helped make explicit the changing mores of American society. She assured women that extramarital sexual behavior was acceptable and desirable. She could not, however, provide any answers to women who wanted fulfillment in ways other than a "man-loved kind of life."

Suggestions for Further Reading

SOCIAL UPHEAVALS

Even if the promise of the Kennedy-Johnson years remained unfulfilled, the 1960s was nonetheless a decade of fascinating social changes. One of the most important documents of that change and an influential book in its own right is Betty Friedan, *The Feminine Mystique* (1963). Another such influential work is Michael Harrington, *The Other America: Poverty in the United States* (1963). This work by a leading American socialist helped inspire the antipoverty programs of the 1960s. Explanations for such reforms have abounded. One of the most challenging interpretations is by William G. McLoughlin, in *Revivals, Awakenings, and Reform* (1978), which places the 1960s in the context of other periods of intense moral reform in American history. Charles A. Reich, in *The Greening of America* (1970), argues that Americans developed a wholly new consciousness of themselves, their environment, and their society. David Farber, *Chicago '68* (1988), traces in rich detail the events of the convention riot from a variety of points of view. Kirkpatrick Sale, *SDS* (1973), is an indispensable guide to the largest student radical group of the decade. In *The Sixties: Years of Hope; Days of Rage* (1988), Todd Gitlin adds personal experience to his fascinating narrative of the events of that decade. At the other end of the political spectrum, George H. Nash, in *The Conservative Intellectual Movement in America Since 1945* (1976), explores the decade's growing conservative challenge to American liberalism.

KENNEDY AND JOHNSON

During the 1960s, American presidents inspired both admiration and profound disillusionment. Consequently, the evaluation of Kennedy and Johnson has been marked by controversy. In the first of several incisive books on American elections, Theo-dore White, *The Making of the President, 1960* (1961), provides a very readable account of the issues and personalities in the election that brought John Kennedy to the White House. Several memoirs by Kennedy aides have offered insights into Kennedy's style of governing. Among the best is Pierre Salinger, *With Kennedy* (1966). A much more critical account, which stresses the failures of the administration, is Henry Fairlie, *The Kennedy Promise: The Politics of Expectation* (1973). A more recent appraisal is by Herbert S. Parmet, *JFK: The Presidency of John F. Kennedy* (1983). Lyndon Johnson's presidency was, if anything, more controversial. Doris Kearn, *Lyndon Johnson and the American Dream* (1976), is a loving portrait of an unlovely man. Jim F. Heath, *Decade of Disillusionment: The Kennedy-Johnson Years* (1975), is a readable critical history of the 1960s. Robert Caro, *The Years of Lyndon Johnson*, Vol. I (1982), is an unfriendly but fascinating account of Johnson's early life.

THE WAR IN VIETNAM

Of all the issues that divided Americans during the 1960s, the Vietnam War was probably the most important. George C. Herring, *America's Longest War: The United States and Vietnam, 1950–1975* (1979), is a thorough history of the struggle. David Halberstam's brilliant *The Best and the Brightest* (1972) recounts the ultimate failure of the generation of promising political advisers who counseled involvement in Vietnam. Godfrey Hodgson, *America in Our Time* (1976), is a delightful general history of the era in which Vietnam became the single most important issue. A splendid and provocative collection of essays on Vietnam is John Schlight, ed., *The Second Indochina War: Proceedings of a Symposium* (1986). Also see the fascinating *American Myths and the Legacy of Vietnam* by John Hellman (1986).

Three Mile Island. This photograph shows the nuclear power plant, with its large cooling towers, on Three Mile Island in the Susquehanna River, before the partial meltdown. (UPI/ Bettmann Newsphotos)

turbine system nothing happened. The three emergency pumps churned furiously, but no water flowed through the pipes. During a previous maintenance operation, the emergency pump valves had been shut—and left shut. In effect, phase one of the accident had already passed before anyone had had time to react. The first set of safety devices failed. Now the second line of defense went into operation.

Although the accident had begun in the turbine system, the emergency shifted to the reactor unit. As pressure fell there, two auxiliary pumps kicked on, pushing hundreds of gallons of water into the core. This was sufficient to keep the core covered and cool until the open emergency relief valve was discovered.

In the control room, lights on the horseshoe panel began flashing and several of the plant's alarms sounded. The overnight operators, Craig Faust and Edward Frederick, and supervisor William Zewe knew the company procedures handbook well. They paid special attention to the warning "Never take the plant solid." What that meant, simply, was not to let the reactor system get too much water in it. If it did, then any shock to the system might break it open. Protection against this sort of accident was maintained by keeping air in the pressurizer chamber below the emergency relief valve. Without this pillow of air to absorb changes in pressure, the reactor system would be in danger.

From the information available in the control room, this is precisely what appeared to be happening. The water level in the pressurizer moved up, indicating that the whole system was becoming superflooded. Thus the operators shut down the flow of emergency water into the reactor. At eight minutes into the incident, Faust discovered that the valves of the turbine system were closed. He turned them on and water began to flow back into that system. Once again the plant seemed to stabilize. The operators had followed instructions exactly.

But the operators had gravely misinterpreted the problem. Instead of being awash with coolant, the core system was still rapidly leaking through the broken relief valve. Water had risen in the pressure tank, but it had been forced there by steam now forming over the reactor and throughout the system. As pressure inside the system fell, the water began to boil, bubbling steam to the top of the reactor and then into the pipes that ran in and out of the core, blocking them and preventing cooling water from flowing through. The water level in the core began to drop dangerously. If the atomic pile uncovered, it would start to melt.

In the control room, the crew began to realize that a serious malfunction had occurred. Lights flashed and new alarms sounded. The computer reported problems throughout the plant, but in helter-skelter fashion. It was hours before it finally recorded the malfunction in the broken pressurizer valve. The third and last system of defense was about to be called into operation.

This system, unlike the first two, was designed to contain a nuclear accident. Should radioactivity escape from the plant, it could seriously endanger the lives of millions of people in its wake. However, the Three Mile Island containment building, which held the reactor system, was designed to prevent such an occurrence. This twenty-story high, two-foot thick concrete-and-steel enclosure was built to withstand the force of a jet airliner crashing into it at full speed. More important, it could tolerate large increases in the pressure of gases that might build up inside. The only possible leakage from the containment building was through the sump pump system that took water off the floor of the building and into a storage tank in the unshielded auxiliary building. But the sump pumps were protected by a cutoff that stopped them if radio-activity was detected in the water.

At about twenty minutes into the accident, operators called Gary Miller, the station emergency director, who arrived at Unit 2 about an hour later. Operating crews believed that they had the plant under control. They knew that overflow water was gushing onto the floor of the containment building and then moving through the sump pump system into tanks in the auxiliary building. But they believed this was turbine water. As Frederick said, "We decided it was a nonradioactive leak, therefore it must be the steam system and not the reactor coolant system. The symptoms are identical except for the radiation alarm." That alarm had malfunctioned, however, and did not sound until 6:50. By that time, hundreds of gallons of radioactive waste had poured into the auxiliary building, some of it spilling out and venting small amounts of radioactive gas into the building and out into the atmosphere.

In the control room, operators followed accident procedures precisely, but they were puzzled by new alarms and flashing lights. Since they could not see inside the reactor system, they did not realize that their emergency responses had actually inten-sified the accident. The atomic core in shutdown position was still creating considerable decay heat. This, in turn, was increasing the steam trapped at the top of the reactor core and pushing more steam into the intake and outflow pipes. Steam bubbles shot through the system and the regular cooling pumps began to shudder and vibrate. At about 5:20, one set of pumps had to be shut off. At 5:41, a second pair shut down automatically. This further diminished the flow of water over the reactor. With the pressure emergency valve still trapped open, the system continued to leak. The nuclear core was about to be uncovered and no one knew it.

As the core water level fell, it exposed the nuclear fuel, causing three serious reactions. Radioactive discharges from the system increased rapidly, contaminating the coolant water and, eventually, the containment building. The very high temperatures, together with the continuing chain reaction, caused some of the oxygen in the water to combine with metals in the core, giving off highly flammable hydrogen gas as a byproduct. Most dangerous, the exposed fuel heated rapidly, melting the tubes that held it, and increasing the reaction. The 100 tons of uranium fuel, arranged in stacked pellets, began to fuse together, touching off a larger chain reaction. The plant now clearly risked a meltdown, in which fuel would fall into a searing radioactive heap at the bottom of the reactor. The intense heat—over 5,000° F—would melt through the twelve-inch steel encasement of the reactor, and uranium would tumble onto the floor of the containment building. Then it might melt through the cement base, cracking the building open and allowing the deadly release of gases and radioactive sludge.

However, neither the officials from Metropolitan Edison nor the plant operators worried about this risk, because they did not realize that the core was uncovered. Their only measurements of water in the system were indirect—and these indicated, falsely, that the reactor was brimming with water. Shortly after 6 A.M., Brian Mehler, the Metropolitan Edison shift supervisor, arrived. At 6:22, after checking through other systems, he recognized that the emergency relief valve above the pressurizer had jammed open. He immediately ordered it shut. The leak in the reactor finally stopped, but no one started the emergency pumps. The core remained uncovered.

Starved of coolant, the reactor smoldered and crumbled. The damping rods overheated, swelled, and ruptured. Tubes containing the uranium pellets melted. Over the next sixteen hours or so, about one-third of the core fell into a superheated, poisonous mass. Hundreds of gallons of radioactive water flowed into the auxiliary building and gases escaped into the air.

Finally, at 6:50, radiation alarms in the auxiliary building sounded. Miller, the emergency director, declared a "site emergency" and began notifying authorities of a "slight problem at Three Mile Island." He also called the Pennsylvania Emergency Management Agency, the Bureau of Radiation Protection, and the regional headquarters of the U.S. Nuclear Regulatory Commission (NRC). Shortly thereafter, he declared a general emergency. The public was about to receive its first news of a nuclear accident that experts at the plant had yet to understand.

For the next several days, misleading statements, misinformation, confusion, and rumor clouded public understanding of what had happened. This is not surprising. Confusion had always surrounded the atomic power industry and issues of regulation and safety. In part, this came from the extraordinary complexity of the technology. The public understood very little of how this complicated plant worked, yet they had to make decisions that deeply affected their lives on the basis of what they expected to happen. There could be no more dramatic proof of the distance between modern science and the population at large. The accident also revealed an astounding inability to communicate: a panicky press, and government agencies and private corporations that distorted or misinterpreted what had happened. In the rush to protect groups that had an important stake in atomic energy, truthfulness and genuine accountability were lost.

In large industrial accidents, it is sometimes possible to assemble "paper trails"—that is, memos, letters, and reports that warn of weaknesses in a system that eventually fails. In the case of Three Mile Island, there were several of these trails, but none had led to any action. Each warning about the reactor system was sidetracked by bureaucracy, special interests, and communications breakdowns. Ignorance, ineptitude, and fear of upsetting the economically precarious nuclear industry combined to block warnings of impending problems.

One reason for the breakdown of Unit 2 lay in the design of the reactor–heat transfer system, its installation, and its operation. All these areas concerned the manufacturer and designer of the reactor, Babcock and Wilcox. Metropolitan Edison, the generating company, operated the equipment according to B & W instructions. Modifications in procedures continually flowed from B & W headquarters as the company monitored the operations at the generating plants it designed.

Just such a monitoring process led Joe Kelly, a B & W engineer, to ask the company in November 1977 to change its instructions for dealing with a depressurization incident (like the one at Three Mile Island). The company worried most about too much coolant entering the reactor system and so instructed operators to shut down emergency pumps if the system suddenly lost pressure. But Kelly argued that instructions should be changed to read that emergency pumps should never be turned off except during a normal shutdown. If operators had received this advice, the Three Mile Island accident would have ended without danger.

Kelly reached his conclusions after investigating an incident at the Davis-Besse generating plant near Toledo, Ohio. Using a B & W system, the Davis-Besse plant was operating at about 9 percent capacity in September 1977 when a loss-of-coolant accident occurred. With safety and measurement equipment giving confused signals, the plant operators responded according to B & W instructions and shut off the emergency cooling system. Had the reactor been operating at full capacity, Kelly reasoned, these actions might have caused major fuel damage and a dangerous meltdown.

In November 1977 Kelly collected his suggestions and submitted them in a memo to B & W executives concerned with safety procedures and customer relations. He enlisted others in the emergency–safety management service division. New guidelines were drawn up, but the department failed to send them out to B & W equipment operators. Kelly, however, did not realize this.

The company also had warnings from another source. In September 1977 Carlyle Michelson, a Tennessee Valley Authority engineer and consultant for the Nuclear Regulatory Commission, submitted a report on B & W equipment. He concluded that in a loss-of-coolant accident, the pressurizer gauge would mislead operators as to the amount of water in the system. Michelson submitted his report to the NRC. Nothing happened. So several months later, he shook the bureaucratic tree again to stimulate action. No decisions were taken. Babcock and Wilcox also received a copy of the report, but the company merely filed it away. Michelson sent two letters to B & W headquarters; the second arrived in February 1979, but the company did not respond—or warn its customers.

The Nuclear Regulatory Commission was aware of these warnings about B & W equipment. The Michelson report had been pushed into the agency paper flow in

1977. More important, however, the NRC had done its own investigation of the Davis-Besse incident, and their investigator agreed with Kelly and Michelson.

James S. Cresswell, an NRC reactor inspector, worried about the Davis-Besse incident. After studying the problem there, he concluded that all B & W systems were susceptible to such incidents, and he tried to spur the NRC to action. He talked to a number of NRC officials, who generally rejected his conclusions. Finally, on January 8, 1979, he issued a formal memorandum on Babcock and Wilcox plants, in effect leapfrogging the immediate bureaucracy and making his findings public. But the company continued to reassure the NRC that their systems were safely insulated against accidents and that their instructions were appropriate.

Frustrated in his efforts, Cresswell went to the top of the agency in the spring of 1979 and finally got a meeting with two NRC commissioners. Both were impressed with his evidence, and one of them sent a request to the agency to act on the information. The commissioner's request arrived at the agency March 29, one day after the Three Mile Island accident began.

The company and the NRC acted slowly on these warnings for several reasons. For one thing, NRC "nugget" files (records of operating problems) showed hundreds of incidents in the operation of nuclear plants. It was not immediately clear that this particular problem with B & W equipment was any more dangerous than scores of others. Also, changes in equipment and operating procedures were expensive. Caught in a serious price squeeze, the nuclear industry was trying to save itself, and the NRC wanted to help.

Furthermore, the history of regulating nuclear electrical generation was an ambiguous one. The industry began in 1953 with the announcement of President Eisenhower's Atoms for Peace program. Atomic power plant construction began a year later, and the first generating unit was completed in 1958. From the beginning, the federal government subsidized the industry by allocating funds for research and development. The Atomic Energy Commission acted both as advocate for the industry and as regulator—a contradictory mission. In addition, Congress passed the Price-Anderson Act of 1957, which limited to $560 million the total liability of a nuclear generating plant in the case of accident. In effect, the government declared that victims of a serious accident would have to pay for most damages themselves.

Protected, encouraged, and screened by the government, the nuclear industry boomed during the 1960s. Low costs for uranium fuel (below seven million dollars a ton in 1970), rapid rises in demand for electrical power (about 7 percent a year), and increasing unreliability of oil and gas supplies, plus pollution and accident problems associated with coal burning and mining, made nuclear energy seem a perfect replacement. Over seventy plants had ben constructed by 1979, and they produced about 13 percent of the nation's electrical energy.

Nonetheless, by the mid-1970s the industry was facing hard times. Uranium ore prices had shot up. Construction costs in plants had risen astronomically, due in part to stricter regulation—some directives were as thick as a telephone book. General inflation had also pushed construction costs upward, so that nuclear-generated electricity cost about ten times as much in 1979 as it had in 1970. Cost overruns in plants like Three Mile Island were huge. The original expense was projected to be about $130 million, but Unit 2 cost $700 million when completed.

The 1970s also raised problems because of a sudden drop in energy requirements. The huge increase in oil prices after 1973–74 did not result in a switch to nuclear alternatives. Instead, sluggish economic growth and conservation cut demands for electricity. Optimistic predictions about a 50 percent nuclear future proved to be very wide of the mark. As *Business Week* commented in December 1978: "One by one, the lights are going out for the U.S. nuclear power industry. Reactor orders have plummeted from a high of 41 in 1973 to zero this year."

The federal government in 1974 had tried to reorganize the industry through better regulation. Recognizing the contradiction between advocacy and regulation, Congress abolished the Atomic Energy Commission and created the Nuclear Regulatory Agency. Nonetheless, many AEC employees, most of them nuclear enthusiasts, transferred to the new agency.

The NRC proved unwilling to tighten regulations at a time when the industry was beginning to nose-dive. Expensive safety retrofitting of reactors was not ordered. The NRC hesitated to issue instructions that would make operations more costly. And it had to contend with opponents of nuclear power plants. With the industry in crisis and with growing public clamor to shut down plants, the NRC was reluctant to interfere with the operation of new plants such as Three Mile Island.

Another paper trail to the accident in Pennsylvania existed in consumer opposition to nuclear energy. Headed by consumer advocate Ralph Nader, antinuclear forces significantly slowed the licensing process of plants, at hearings and through lawsuits. Nader's objections rested on several grounds. He cited evidence that any increase in radiation was a health and genetic danger to plant workers and nearby residents. Since all nuclear plants emitted some radiation, he concluded that this constituted technological victimization. Nader also worried about possible theft of radioactive fuels, sabotage, unresolved waste disposal problems, and the credibility of the government and the nuclear industry.

In his book *The Menace of Atomic Energy*, published in 1977, Nader cited AEC tests of 1970 and 1971 that showed the malfunctioning of emergency systems in a loss-of-coolant accident. These tests, he concluded, demonstrated that water pumped into the system at low pressure would turn to steam and block the intake and outlet pipes to the reactor. The core would then become exposed and melt. In such an event, the containment floor would also fail, and the "China syndrome" would occur: The molten mass of uranium fuel would burn through the building, into the ground, and downward toward the earth's core, polluting groundwater as it went.

Nader's use of the term "China syndrome" to describe a meltdown accident was nothing more than the adoption of industry slang—a kind of joke, that the molten mass would pass through the earth and come to rest in China on the opposite side of the globe. But the seriousness of such an accident was no joke. A secret AEC report, pried out of the agency in 1973, predicted that in the worst possible accident, 45,000 people would die, 100,000 would sustain injury, and an area that "might be equal to that of the state of Pennsylvania" would be devastated.

This same reference to Pennsylvania occurred in the film *The China Syndrome*, produced by Michael Douglas and released in March 1979, about two weeks before

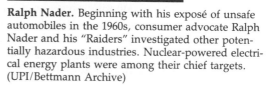

Ralph Nader. Beginning with his exposé of unsafe automobiles in the 1960s, consumer advocate Ralph Nader and his "Raiders" investigated other potentially hazardous industries. Nuclear-powered electrical energy plants were among their chief targets. (UPI/Bettmann Archive)

the accident at Three Mile Island. This was no mere coincidence—but only another paper trail based on a prediction that came true.

In 1976 Mike Gray, a documentary filmmaker, approached Douglas with a completed film script about a near-accident at a nuclear generating plant. Gray had studied AEC reports and investigated minor incidents at plants near Detroit and Chicago. The results of his study went into the script. Douglas liked the idea and approached actress Jane Fonda about joining the venture. She agreed but changed the script, writing in a character for herself to play—a television news commentator trying to find out about and then report honestly on a dangerous incident at a nuclear plant. Douglas hired nuclear engineers to provide expertise on plant operations. The film also incorporated testimony from hearings on nuclear plants.

Melodramatic though it was, the film accurately portrayed the sequence of events in a near-meltdown accident. And the drama confronted the larger issue of credibility. The action begins when Kimberly Wells, a commentator on the evening news, accidentally films a serious incident at the Ventura, California, power plant while doing a feature story. After showing the film to a nuclear engineer, she becomes convinced that she has witnessed a near-accident. The engineer explains:

LOWELL: If that's true, then we came very close to the China Syndrome.
KIMBERLY: The what?
LOWELL: If the core is exposed for whatever reason, the fuel heats beyond core heat tolerance in a matter of minutes. Nothing can stop it. And it melts right down through the bottom of the plant, theoretically to China, but, of course, as soon as it hits groundwater it blasts into the atmosphere and sends out clouds of radioactivity. The number of people killed would depend on which way the wind is blowing [and] render an area the size of Pennsylvania permanently uninhabitable.

A plant engineer named Godell (played by Jack Lemmon) recognizes that the welds supporting cooling pumps are faulty, and he tries to prevent the plant from going back into operation. Holding the control room at gunpoint, he demands a live interview on television. Kimberly, eager to get the story, rushes to the plant with her crew. But when Godell tries to explain, he fails completely:

> GODELL: I mean, that happened, but that's not why I'm here. It's—I'm not making any sense.
> KIMBERLY: No, it's all right.
> GODELL: It's so complicated, but there . . . there's something else. There's this— see, it's so complicated . . . yet so simple . . . simple . . . it's terribly complex . . . and it's very difficult.

Action piles on action: Godell is shot by a special police squad; the plant shuts down safely; and Kimberly files her story. As Godell realized, nuclear technology is too complicated to explain to the public, which must depend on the credibility of government and industry. When that fails, only a feature reporter's chance persistence saves California from disaster.

Predictably, the nuclear industry attacked the film. In a public letter dated nine days before the opening of the film and two weeks before Three Mile Island, Southern California Edison charged that the movie had "no scientific credibility and is in fact ridiculous." But if anything, the film underplayed the danger.

One final trail led to the accident. This was the short but troubled history of Unit 2 operations. After a long and expensive construction period, the second reactor at Three Mile Island "went critical" (began operation) on March 28, 1978. At ceremonies in September, Metropolitan Edison representatives, the lieutenant governor of Pennsylvania, and U.S. Deputy Secretary of Energy John F. O'Leary dedicated the new facility. O'Leary addressed the assembly and called for keeping "the nuclear option open." He urged even more: "Our goal is to achieve a balance of 50 percent coal and 50 percent nuclear." The facility, he concluded, was "a sort of a miracle in many ways."

Residents of the area generally accepted this view. The plant pumped thousands of dollars in construction jobs into the region and employment for the "nukes," as permanent employees called themselves. But there was scattered opposition, centered primarily in a small group, the Three Mile Island Alert, which published a small underground tabloid, the *Harrisburg*.

The utility company replied to all adverse publicity with soothing words about safety, stressing the nuclear industry's exemplary record. They cited the industry motto: "Defense in depth—backup systems to back up backup systems." They noted that half the investment in Unit 2 was for safety devices. As a Metropolitan Edison flyer, called "Your Personal Radiation Inventory," said: If the worst conceivable accident "were to occur at the Three Mile Island nuclear station, because of safeguards, a man could remain at a spot less than a half-mile from the reactor for 24 hours a day for an entire year and be exposed to only 2 mrems of radiation." (*Mrem* stands for *millirem*, or one-thousandth of a rem. Exposure of 600 rems is generally a fatal dose.) This was a negligible amount compared to the 100 mrems that all Americans received each year from natural causes.

Although utility officials exuded public confidence, Unit 2 proved unreliable and accident-prone. The emergency relief valve stuck open more than once, and operators installed an indirect gauge to determine its position—but even this gauge sometimes malfunctioned. And the valve leaked slightly. Other problems flared up in the complicated cooling and heat transfer systems. Employees complained that the alarm system was too extensive and hence meaningless in an emergency. Nonetheless, Metropolitan Edison put the plant on line on December 30, 1978. They did so for two reasons. The company wanted to take advantage of tax breaks for 1978. And they were seeking a rate increase to help cover operating expenses. This was granted in March 1979. However, the flawed system remained out of operation for much of the time.

Plant operators, the utility company, and the NRC did not suspect the gravity of the Three Mile Island accident in its early stages. Communications between the plant and the NRC in Bethesda, Maryland, near Washington, were confused and difficult. When the utility did begin to realize the problem of a partial meltdown, it refused to admit so publicly. At first, the NRC accepted Metropolitan Edison assurances. As a result, the credibility of information flowing through the media from the plant and from the NRC degenerated. The local population was restrained by meaningless assurances and then panicked by rumors.

At 7:30 Wednesday morning, once the general emergency had been declared, the most immediate problem was whether or not to evacuate the nearby residents. This decision depended on accurate information. With the coolant system out of control—it remained so for about twelve more hours—the risk of total meltdown and radiation discharge increased. Plant operators, utility experts, B & W scientists, and the NRC only gradually realized the extent of the damage. But they could not advise state officials about evacuation until they knew what was happening on site.

At the plant, emergency director Gary Miller tried to establish control of the reactor and also coordinate public communications. But he recalled, "I was constantly pulled to the phone by senior persons in the state government, the NRC, and my own management. . . . The phone, the pressure, the fact that the plant was in a state that I had never been schooled in combined to make it almost intolerable."

Those in charge of evacuation had even less information. The Pennsylvania Emergency Management Agency (PEMA), headed by Lieutenant Governor William Scranton, was charged with directing emergency procedures. Evacuation plans existed, but they had not been made public for fear of arousing anxiety. PEMA, located in a radiation-proof building in Harrisburg, prepared to act, but it had to have facts. And the man who would instruct it to begin, Governor Richard Thornburgh, had received contradictory advice from Metropolitan Edison and the NRC.

The public first heard of the accident at about 8 A.M. A local broadcaster discovered that local civil defense authorities had ordered fire equipment on alert. He called Metropolitan Edison, and the company reported a "minor problem" at Three Mile Island. Later in the morning, the company released its first public statement:

> The nuclear reactor at Three Mile Island Unit 2 was shut down as prescribed when a malfunction related to a feedwater pump occurred about four A.M. Wednesday. The entire unit was systematically shut down and will be out of service for about a week while equipment is checked and repairs made.

Three Mile Island reactor. The top portion of nuclear reactor Unit 1 at Three Mile Island. Had a complete meltdown of Unit 2 occurred, the blistering hot, radioactive pile would have fallen through the reactor floor (not visible here). (UPI/Bettmann Newsphoto)

Metropolitan Edison continued to maintain for several days—against all evidence—that less than 1 percent of the fuel in the reactor core had been damaged. By underestimating the problem, the company quickly lost credibility with government officials and the public. While company experts worked to correct what they knew was an increasingly dangerous situation, they continued to reassure the public that no danger existed. By Wednesday afternoon, Lieutenant Governor Scranton publicly criticized the company for misrepresenting the extent of the accident. The company had "given you and us conflicting information."

Communications between the plant and the NRC offices were difficult to establish. Although NRC inspectors arrived at Three Mile Island at 10 A.M., phone lines to headquarters did not function well. Accurate information about the accident remained sparse in Washington. President Carter had been notified at 9:00, but he let the NRC monitor the problem.

At about 11:30 A.M., plant operators tried to reestablish the blocked flow of coolant into the reactor by depressuring the system, bleeding more steam out through the pressurizer. Their strategy failed. Indeed, it may have uncovered the core even further. Then at 1:50 P.M., the computer recorded an unnoticed pressure spike (a sudden rise in pressure in the containment building). Almost simultaneously, containment spray turned on and emergency liquid shot into the building to neutralize radioactive iodine. Operators shut off the spray. They did not realize, until later, that a bubble of escaped hydrogen, produced in the core, had exploded. This event, when recognized, became the source of fear that hydrogen might explode inside the reactor, creating the worst devastation imaginable and a total meltdown.

Finally, in late afternoon, plant operators attempted to repressurize the system. Gradually, they succeeded. Steam began to dissipate, and by 7:50 that evening, coolant water again began to flow through the system. The core was re-covered. It was now time to assess the damage.

To do this, a sample of core coolant water had to be taken and analyzed for radioactive discharges that would indicate fuel damage. Results of this test became available at 6 P.M. the next day. At last, officials understood the seriousness of an accident they could not see or measure directly. On Wednesday evening, however, the most immediate problem was how to eliminate the radioactive water and gas trapped in the containment and the auxiliary building. Whether they wanted to or not, company officials decided they had to discharge some of this into the air and into the Susquehanna River.

On Thursday morning, plant officials decided to dump mildly radioactive water into the river. If they did not, it would spill out anyway because storage tanks were completely filled. At about 2:45 P.M., technicians started to empty this pollutant into the Susquehanna. State officials strenuously objected, and at 6 P.M., the NRC ordered a halt to the dumping. But by midnight, all parties had agreed to resume the discharge. All day, conflicting stories reached the news media about releases of gas and water. Joseph Hendry, chairman of the NRC, briefed Congress, reporting that there might be some minor cracks in "perhaps about 1 percent" of the fuel rods, but he assured Washington that there was no serious risk.

Reporters and television crews began to flood the Harrisburg area. But unlike other sorts of accidents, this one attracted no spectators. The possibility of a deadly release of radiation kept bystanders at home. All of the media attention did little to improve the flow of information or restore credibility. The technological and scientific aspects of the accident were difficult to understand, and scientists themselves disagreed sharply about the accident. News reaching the governor remained contradictory. But by 11 P.M., he knew how serious the incident was: Core samples confirmed a partial meltdown.

Friday was the most confused day yet. Communications among civil authorities concerning evacuation became scrambled. The public believed less and less of what it heard. Serious amounts of radioactive gas still had to be vented. And technicians realized that a large hydrogen bubble was building in the reactor. It seemed only a matter of time before a fatal explosion.

The population around Harrisburg was obviously jittery. A quick telephone survey revealed that most area residents feared another nuclear accident even if this one ended uneventfully. Other residents confided their deep-seated fears about radiation to reporters. Paul Holowka, a dog breeder living near the reactor, claimed: "Last year I lost twelve dogs. They died of cancer. That never used to happen."

By the end of the day, the area was in turmoil. Phone circuits were jammed, schools were closed, and lines had formed in front of gasoline stations. Toll booth operators on the Pennsylvania Turnpike noted a sudden spurt of heavy traffic, with most cars filled with families. A general exodus that eventually reached almost 140,000 people had begun. One of those fleeing said frankly: "The main reason we're leaving is I don't trust the information they are giving us. No one really knows what happened Wednesday morning."

Even Governor Thornburgh admitted as much. "I am very skeptical of any one set of facts," he told a sweltering news conference in the capitol building (the air conditioning had been shut off to prevent circulation of radiation). At 12:30 P.M., Thornburgh ordered a partial evacuation. Radio broadcasts throughout the morning had warned of such an eventuality. After NRC officials received news that vented radioactivity had reached 1,200 mrems per hour, they phoned the state and suggested a general evacuation. Then they rescinded the suggestion. But Thornburgh advised all pregnant women and preschool children within five miles of the plant to leave. Other residents were asked to stay indoors.

Thornburgh, the NRC, and President Carter (more involved now in watching the crisis) grew increasingly worried about the hydrogen bubble. Operators now realized that the earlier pressure spike represented a small hydrogen explosion. If, as many scientists warned was possible, the bubble continued to grow and if oxygen in the core reached sufficient levels, the reactor and the entire containment might explode. Metropolitan Edison officials declared that there was little danger of this—but no one listened. Instead, newspapers and television blared the news. Areas close to the Three Mile Island plant, such as the King River Haven mobile home park, became ghost towns.

Imagining a hydrogen explosion translated the accident into an occasion for venting people's worst fears. Some residents recalled stories of the terrible, fiery crash of the German dirigible, the *Hindenburg*, in New Jersey in 1937. A child told reporters of a dream she had had: "It was a big ball, and you know the way things glow? It glowed just like that. And then there was a witch and the big ball killed everybody. And all the cats and dogs and rabbits were all dead." To some residents, the hydrogen bubble represented the beginning of the end of the world—the first stage in a chain reaction leading to the Last Judgment. Yet there were some local residents who knew almost nothing about the accident or the danger. These were the Amish, the "plain people," who lived on nearby farms, not using automobiles, tractors, modern plumbing—or electricity.

After the confusion over evacuation, and because of scrambled stories coming from the facility, President Carter designated Harold Denton as chief and sole spokesman on the accident site. His first task was to restore the public's faith in the information it was receiving. Denton arrived at Three Mile Island about 2:30 Friday afternoon and quickly took charge. He also stepped into what seemed like the most critical moment of the accident.

During the next day, Denton worked to keep control of news coming from the plant. He warned Governor Thornburgh of a possible general evacuation of the area. For the next harrowing hours, he oversaw attempts to determine the danger of a hydrogen explosion. In Washington, Secretary of Health, Education, and Welfare Joseph Califano advised Carter to order a general evacuation. But the president insisted

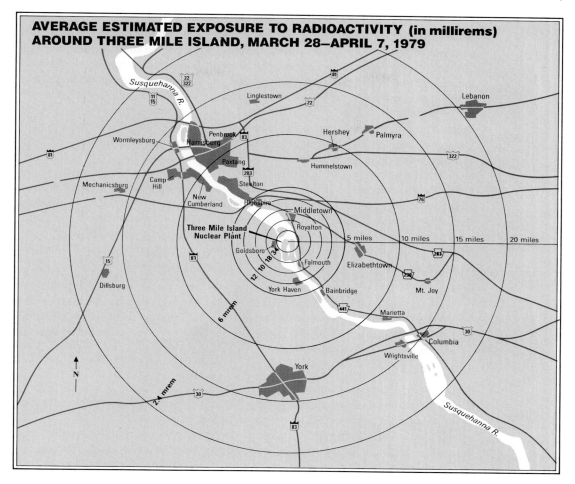

AVERAGE ESTIMATED EXPOSURE TO RADIOACTIVITY (in millirems) AROUND THREE MILE ISLAND, MARCH 28–APRIL 7, 1979

that Denton make such decisions. Nonetheless, the federal government took precautions to order massive amounts of potassium iodide shipped to the area. This drug, if taken before exposure to severe nuclear radiation, saturates the thyroid gland to prevent any absorption of radioactive iodine.

By late Saturday evening, Denton and experts working on the accident realized that the danger had passed. The bubble had begun to shrink. The site would be safe enough for President Carter to visit the next day. Quite clearly a publicity gesture, the visit would signal that the crisis had passed. Denton informed the media: The president would visit the plant the next afternoon.

On Sunday the president flew to Harrisburg and then went to the plant for an inspection. Mrs. Carter stopped to visit local residents. Shortly after the visit, scientists at Three Mile Island recognized that they had miscalculated the quantities of hydrogen and oxygen in the reactor. Late that night they confirmed that the bubble was disappearing. By midday on Monday, April 2, it had all but dissipated. The most dangerous phase of the accident had ended.

The Three Mile Island accident ended when operators recovered control over the reactor at 7:50 P.M. on April 4, but the radioactive pollution it released will probably outlast civilization. The reactor came, perhaps, within a half hour of complete meltdown. Although eventually contained, the event had serious and lasting effects on the utility company, the industry, the federal and state regulatory agencies, the local population—and on the credibility of government and the scientific establishment.

Gradually, the Three Mile Island plant was cleaned up. During the operation to extract the radioactive poisons and permanently remove the nuclear core, the core remained covered by cooling liquids. Worker safety, locating a dump site for wastes, and constant monitoring of the plant presented difficult problems. Over the four years of decontaminating the site, about 1,000 workers were employed and close to a billion dollars had to be spent. If the costs of Metropolitan Edison's purchase of replacement electricity are added in, the total price is about $3 billion—over three times the initial cost of Unit 2 and almost twenty-five times the original estimated cost of the unit.

In the years following the accident, local residents continued to worry about periodic radioactive releases into the air and into the Susquehanna. In March 1980, for example, a citizen living three miles from the plant told the NRC:

> Met Ed's alleged concern for my safety insults me. . . . I have been blitzed by their PR campaigns and their charts and their fancy numbers and their smiling assurances that the levels of radiation to be vented are within Federal safety limits. But who knows if the Federal safety limits are safe?

Bruce Smith, chairman of the board of supervisors in Newberry Township near the site, declared: "I am so angry about Three Mile that I have become one of the leaders in the movement to close TMI forever as a nuclear plant."

Plant workers received far higher doses of radiation during the accident than most area residents. Many of them absorbed the maximum safe yearly amount in a few moments. Measured in millirems, a level of 500,000 causes immediate death in 50 percent of a population; 100,000 mrems causes radiation sickness in most. Standard yearly maximums for plant employees had been set at 8,000 mrems. As Joe Hipple, a health physicist, told the press during the accident: "I was the hottest I've been in a long time. I hit the frisker [the radiation counter] and it went boing! I probably got half my year's exposure in a day, probably in four minutes."

This exposure to high radiation caused a shortage of technicians. To fill the gap and attract new employees, Metropolitan Edison ran a want ad in the *New York Times*: "Immediate ground floor opportunities for dedicated scientists and engineering personnel who want to be in the forefront of emerging technologies."

Public reaction in the United States and the rest of the world to the accident was strong. Antinuclear sentiment mounted in the United States, as evidenced by a large rally in Washington on May 6, 1979. Local opposition to bringing new plants on line, or to planning for the future expansion of facilities, stiffened. In Europe, antinuclear opinion emerged as a strong force in countries like West Germany. During the accident, 35,000 West Germans marched, chanting, "We all live in Pennsylvania." Added to hugely mounting costs, delays, and new regulations, this growing skepticism hurt an already crippled industry.

No-nukes rally, 1979. Following the accident at Three Mile Island, sentiment against nuclear power plants mounted. At this rally in Washington on May 6, 1979, Tom Hayden (former leader of SDS and coordinator of the demonstrations at the 1968 Democratic convention in Chicago) and Jane Fonda, star of *The China Syndrome*, addressed the crowd. (AP/Wide World Photos)

The accident and the ensuing communications failure at Three Mile Island also undercut the faith of many Americans in their political, scientific, and economic institutions. Several congressional investigations faulted the NRC for its lack of leadership and candor. A separate presidential report criticized information provided to the public by the NRC and Metropolitan Edison. Exaggeration, ignorance, and rumor had dominated reporting of the event, at least until Harold Denton took control of communications. When the accident was at its most dangerous stage, the public received the advice that nothing was wrong. After the crisis had passed, the media and even state safety officials exaggerated the danger and incited a mass exodus.

Revelation of the existence of paper trails leading to the accident fueled public suspicion that the government and the nuclear industry had conspired to conceal atomic power plant dangers. Regulators did not regulate sufficiently, and companies cut corners to sustain a sick industry. Publication in 1979 of a report on a nuclear disaster in the Soviet Union added to the controversy. A Russian emigré scientist described an accident that had occurred in 1957 in the Ural Mountains at a nuclear dump site. He maintained that it had caused devastation of thousands of square miles and killed hundreds of people—and that U.S. government officials had known about the accident for two decades. They had not reported it to the public for security reasons and, he speculated, to protect America's nuclear industry from public criticism. Even when the terrible meltdown occurred at Chernobyl in the Soviet Union in April 1986, public officials in the United States and in European countries with heavy commitments to nuclear power played down the incident.

The accident at Three Mile Island was, in the final analysis, a disaster that did not really happen. The worst predictions did not come true. The third line of defense in the containment building held. The core did not melt down completely, and the China syndrome was avoided. And yet the accident had a profound effect. It spread a further cloud of doubt over American society at a time when many Americans were asking agonizing questions about social, economic, and political institutions that also did not function as they were designed.

THE CREDIBILITY CRISIS

The accident at Three Mile Island and its aftershocks of disbelief and doubt epitomized the growing problem of accountability in American society during the 1970s. As the economy, technology, government bureaucracy, and social issues became more complex, Americans wanted to know who was responsible. Often, it was impossible to find a straightforward answer to this question. In the case of Three Mile Island, the war in Vietnam, Watergate, the Iranian hostage crisis, and other major events of the decade, it was difficult to find a person, an agency, or an institution that would take responsibility. Increasingly, companies, government bureaucrats, and officials of all sorts masked their activities behind public relations, the object of which was to convince and persuade the public, but not necessarily to inform it.

American Society at a Crossroads

Ironically, this reliance on credibility and persuasiveness came at a time when private and public institutions were growing ever larger and more complex. The world of computers, nuclear plants, and space travel could not be translated into simple explanations. The technology of nuclear power plants performed remarkable tasks—in silence, out of sight, and beyond the comprehension of most Americans. There were no familiar spinning gears, whirling belts, or clanging machines in such new industries. They performed marvels of production, but they also sometimes released deadly—and invisible—pollutants. Their operation in the public interest demanded knowledge, skill, and honesty. The public had no other choice but to trust its experts.

Trust was also crucial for the success of government. During the 1970s the federal government took up difficult—perhaps impossible—tasks. Special-interest groups increasingly demanded that government redress grievances and balance old inequalities in social relations. Rising expectations about what government could do to solve problems transformed complex social, economic, and even personal and family issues into political issues. And the federal government also had to confront new and contradictory economic crises such as rising inflation, low productivity, and energy shortages.

In this complicated and difficult world, institutions and bureaucracies often used public relations and the mass media to maintain their credibility. Indeed, *credibility* became a widely used political word in this decade, although the

1092

problem was certainly older. It meant the ability to inspire confidence in a government official, a company spokesperson, a labor union representative, a consumer advocate. But it did not necessarily mean truthfulness. Inevitably during the 1970s, times of crisis were also credibility crises. The accident at Three Mile Island became a credibility crisis because the public began to doubt official statements and reports, to distrust experts, and to question the intentions of elected representatives. More than ever, Americans wanted government to solve problems—and more than ever, they feared it could not.

The 1970s were also years of limitation and readjustment. Many of the institutions whose stability a generation of Americans had taken for granted suddenly appeared weak and ineffectual. The period from 1945 to about 1968 had been exceptional in American history because of its sustained economic growth and dramatic social progress. Thus Americans had come to accept such successes as normal. But prior to World War II, the nation had experienced prolonged depressions as well as booms, bitter social struggles, and political crises. The 1970s served to remind Americans that economic progress is erratic. This was not a welcome lesson to a nation that had come to expect uninterrupted expansion.

ECONOMIC PROBLEMS

Economic problems in the 1970s were complex and interrelated. The delayed impact of expenditures for the war in Vietnam pushed inflation higher. Small rises in productivity rates after 1966 indicated that many American industries were falling behind Japanese and western European competitors in adopting modern technology. Profligate use of cheap energy made energy shortages and steep price hikes painful to absorb. In time, the energy crisis fueled inflation and slowed economic growth. And the shrinking margin of competitiveness of American goods destabilized the dollar and turned the international balance of payments against the United States. Large budget deficits, high interest rates, and inaction often

compounded these problems. The economy did grow during this period, and real wages for most workers did increase—but not at the pace set in the 1960s.

Social change, too, tested the resilience and credibility of American institutions. Political demonstrations and violence occurred sporadically in the early 1970s. As reported, crime rates seemed to rise relentlessly: Between 1968 and 1978, aggravated assaults increased by about 60 percent. Larceny and theft rates increased at about the same rate. Heavily concentrated in cities, these crimes were well publicized and visible. There seemed to be a direct link between the size and congestion of a city and its crime rate.

Other indicators suggested a transformation in the family—once the most stable of institutions and now split by divorce and altered by changing relationships between men and women in American society. After a low point in the mid-1950s, divorce rates almost tripled by the end of the 1970s. The size of American families shrank as the postwar baby boom ended. This in turn affected the age structure of the population. America was growing older, and this older population was becoming increasingly active politically.

WOMEN

Perhaps most important in terms of lifestyles was the change in women's roles. Masked by the domestic ideology of the late 1940s and 1950s, rapid change had in fact affected women's lives after World War II. Most significant was the increased participation of women in the work force. In 1947 only about 27 percent of workers in the labor force were women. In 1981, women constituted about 43 percent of the labor force. Put another way, in 1947 about 30 percent of women worked. In 1981 almost 50 percent worked. Many of them joined the labor force to maintain their family's standard of living. Together with increasing recognition of their past treatment as second-class citizens, this new economic power convinced many women to challenge the customs of family and society that had

Violent Crime Rates in Fourteen American Cities, 1977

Rate per 100,000 Population	
Detroit	1,829
Baltimore	1,726
New York	1,629
Washington	1,427
San Francisco	1,409
Los Angeles	1,209
Dallas	1,019
Chicago	935
Memphis	784
Indianapolis	744
Philadelphia	635
Phoenix	630
San Diego	560
San Antonio	491

Source: U.S. Federal Bureau of Investigation, *Crime in the United States*, annual, 1986.

Marriage and Divorce Rates in the United States

Year	Total Divorces	Divorce Rate per 1,000	Marriage Rate per 1,000
1965	479,000	2.5	9.3
1970	708,000	3.5	10.6
1975	1,036,000	4.9	10.0
1980	1,182,000	5.3	10.6

Source: U.S. Department of Commerce, Bureau of the Census, *Statistical Abstract of the United States, 1981* (Washington, D.C.: Government Printing Office, 1981), p. 56.

restricted their roles. Women demanded equality, respect, and an end to formal and informal restrictions on opportunities and careers. Many of their endeavors were highly visible: more women elected to public office, increased interest in women's sports, and perhaps equally important, the discovery of a hidden history of past achievements.

However, a change of this magnitude could not occur without challenges. Increasingly during the 1970s, disputes over women's roles focused on the proposed Equal Rights Amendment to the Constitution. Little more, in fact, than a ratification of the rights to equal treatment that many women already enjoyed and that most Americans supported, the ERA came to symbolize those changes in modern society that more conservative Americans opposed. In this dispute, both sides viewed the government as the ultimate arbitrator. Although the amendment failed in 1982, public opinion supporting it did not diminish.

MINORITIES Much of the same sort of struggle prevailed in questions of race relations. Increasing ethnic and racial self-confidence in the late 1960s gave rise to strong pressure groups, but it also fed resentment and controversy over the gains of minorities through legislation and court mandate. Many Americans came to believe that the federal government operated in favor of special-interest groups—whether racial minorities, the poor, and women, or the oil companies and the nuclear industry.

This kind of thinking fed a general tendency toward less political participation that began in the mid-1960s. Percentages of eligible voters who cast ballots—despite the increased ease of doing so—declined. Political scandals, corruption, and favoritism disillusioned and alienated voters, convincing many that their votes did not count.

A deep crisis of faith in government surfaced in an abrupt way during 1973 in the unlikely rendezvous of Native Americans and federal forces at Wounded Knee. The civil rights movement had promised to redress old wrongs. Not unexpectedly, its energies touched Native Americans, who by the 1970s lived for the most part in terrible poverty and dependence. A third of the population on reservations survived on welfare; life expectancy was only forty-six years; and rates of alcoholism and suicide were astoundingly high.

Representative Shirley Chisholm. During the 1960s and 1970s, an increasing number of blacks and women were elected to local, state, and federal office. Shirley Chisholm of New York City was a pioneer. The first black woman elected to Congress, she served in the House of Representatives from 1969 to 1982. (©Lee Goff/Magnum)

Years of Indian policy designed to suppress Native American culture had, contrary to expectations, not created a population willing or able to assimilate.

Almost inevitably, this policy of neglect and cultural aggression created an explosion. With no little irony was it focused at Wounded Knee in the Pine Ridge reservation in South Dakota. There in the late winter and spring of 1973, the American Indian Movement and the Oglalla Sioux, protesting the terrible conditions on the reservation, violence by whites against Native Americans, and the hostile and inept leadership of the designated tribal chief, took over the town. Surrounded by FBI agents and local vigilantes,

the group held out until May. Few of their demands were met; several were killed in gun battles; and other leaders became enmeshed in lengthy, dispiriting court battles.

Publicity about the plight of Native Americans did, however, result in increased federal funding for education and housing, at least up to the Reagan administration. A far more important result, however, came after various lawsuits before the Indian Claims Commission, in which Native Americans sued for compensation for tribal lands illegally seized by white settlers. Created to compensate tribes for lost territory, the commission and its rulings often engendered more controversy than it settled as tribes realized that accepting cash payments would lose them their territory forever. This prompted some groups to demand return of their ancient lands.

The general transformation of political and social change into stalemates such as these was partly generated by a new individualist ethic. This new morality of unlimited self-expression prompted satirist Tom Wolfe to dub the 1970s "the Me decade." The term refers to a decline of belief in community, of working together to solve problems, and an emphasis on the private individual. In some cases, this celebration of the self led to an increasing frankness about sexuality and lifestyles that would have been unthinkable ten years earlier. Movements of personal liberation included such groups as the handicapped, gay men and women, and children's rights advocates. Whether or not this development benefited society, however, became an increasingly disputed question.

Above all else, the war in Vietnam was the catalyst in creating the tone of political and institutional crisis in the 1970s. President Johnson's decision not to seek reelection in 1968—and Richard Nixon's defeat of Hubert Humphrey for the presidency—reflected public opposition to continuing the war. But paradoxically, Americans did not wish to lose in Vietnam. Thus it took five more painful years before the United States finally extricated itself from the war.

Nixon and Southeast Asia

The career of Richard M. Nixon was marked by recurrent controversy, triumph, and defeat—or as he put it, "crises." Born into a Quaker family in 1913 in Yorba Linda, California, Nixon earned a law degree at Duke University. He set up a law practice in Whittier, California, shortly before the beginning of World War II. During the war he served as a naval supply officer in the Pacific. Afterward, he returned home to California and began his rapid rise in national politics—from representative to senator to vice president. From the first, his campaigns, if not actually dishonest, were marred by political smears and innuendos about the patriotism of his opponents. He served in Congress and achieved prominence for his pursuit of Alger Hiss while a member of the House Un-American Activities Committee. Loyal to the party and hardworking, by 1952 Nixon represented the best compromise candidate for the vice presidency.

During his eight-year tenure in Eisenhower's shadow, Nixon worked hard to build his leadership of the Republican party. In 1960 he was an easy winner of the presidential nomination and only a narrow loser in the election. Back after defeat in a race for governor of California, Nixon won the Republican nomination in 1968, again by occupying the center of his party. In the campaign, he benefited from growing dismay over the war and the social strife that it was causing at home. He promised to resolve the Vietnam conflict but refused to say how.

Nixon's attitude toward government was a curious blend of admiration, suspicion, and hostility. He enjoyed the power and pomp of office. But because of long-standing enmities with the press and the Democratic party, he saw himself as an outsider—a representative of those who distrusted government. This sort of division showed up in his political appointments. Most members of his cabinet were men with Washington connections, or they were well-known in Republican circles—like Henry Kissinger, his special assistant for national security. But Nixon's personal staff was made up of men who distrusted the Washington political establishment. The White House inner circle was ruled by H. R. (Bob) Haldeman, the chief of staff, and, to a lesser extent, John D. Ehrlichman, domestic council chief.

VIETNAMIZATION Promising an open government, Nixon in fact shut many of his most important decisions away from public scrutiny. He and Henry Kissinger were both convinced that the United States had to maintain credibility in opposing the Soviet Union and still end American participation in the Vietnam War. To achieve this contradictory purpose, the president decided to withdraw American forces from combat and yet deny victory to the Viet Cong and North Vietnam through air power. This tactic was named "Vietnamization." Over the next two years, he withdrew almost 500,000 American troops until only 50,000 remained in late 1972. American soldiers straggled back to their lives in the United States, neither heroes nor victors. Many of them were victims of low morale, drug dependency, and bitterness. At the same time, Nixon stepped up air raids and approved the invasion of Cambodia and Laos to cut off enemy supply lines.

In bombing Cambodia, early in his administration, Nixon altered the rules of the war. The president had ordered an attack on a nation that was officially neutral. He wanted to keep the intervention a secret, especially from the American public. When news of the raids leaked to the *New York Times*, Nixon and Kissinger were furious. The White House ordered wiretaps on the telephones of five newsmen and several employees of the National Security Agency to find out who had told the press. In effect, Nixon's crisis of credibility had begun.

FIGHTING THE WAR PROTESTERS The president's anger at the press and television did not prevent him from using the media to try to defuse protests against his Vietnamization policy. During the summer of 1969 he attacked demonstrators in speeches and news conferences. But his efforts proved ineffective. On October 15 thousands of Americans demonstrated against the war in several cities. An even larger coalition, supported now by important members of Congress and newspapers, began to solidify around the peace issue.

Nixon and his aides concluded that if the American public believed the criticisms of the administration appearing in the media, then it was time to attack the integrity and objectivity of the media. Thus the president approved Vice President Spiro Agnew's accusing the press and the major television networks of biased reporting. The president also approved Agnew's bitter denunciation of student protesters as an "effete corps of impudent snobs who characterized themselves as intellectuals." Both tactics, the administration hoped, would split the nation and polarize opinion. If antiwar opinion could be isolated, it might also be quieted. As Agnew put it, "it is time for a positive polarization."

Nixon's policy of diverting war casualties to the Vietnamese and deflecting criticism at home had achieved some success by early 1970. On April 4 a large group of prowar demonstrators congregated in Washington. The overthrow of neutral Prince Sihanouk of Cambodia and his replacement by the pro-American Lon Nol made it possible to take more drastic action to cut off supplies reaching the Viet Cong through that country. In late April, Nixon authorized an invasion of Cambodia. But he miscalculated the domestic effects of this action. The antiwar movement suddenly sprang to life with demonstrations and strikes on college campuses throughout the nation. Police and the National Guard were called out to restore order in a number of places. At Kent State University in Ohio, National Guard troops opened fire on a crowd of students on May

4, killing four of them. Shortly afterward, at Jackson State University in Mississippi, two black protesters were shot and killed. In his angry comments on such incidents, the president appeared to blame the demonstrators for their fate. In Cambodia the result was a civil war with hundreds of thousands of casualties and no real settlement for twenty years.

With pressure mounting for an end to the war, Nixon tried to enlist the country's "silent majority" to turn back war opponents. His chance came during the fall congressional elections, but the results were inconclusive. The Republicans gained two Senate seats, but lost nine places in the House and eleven governorships. Rather than isolating war critics, the president had begun to isolate himself.

In early 1971, Nixon showed a more conciliatory mood, but this dissolved in the wake of further serious opposition to the war. A South Vietnamese invasion of Laos with American air support brought little vocal opposition. But two events riveted national attention on war critics. The first was a large, disruptive demonstration in Washington on May 2 and 3 by the "Mayday Tribe," which resulted in 10,000 arrests. Much more serious was publication of the "Pentagon Papers," beginning June 13 in the *New York Times*. This history of U.S. involvement in Vietnam, culled from secret government files by Daniel Ellsberg, a former Kissinger aide, showed the extent of covert American involvement in Southeast Asia and exposed the intrigue and deception of three administrations.

Nixon tried to stop publication of these damning government documents, but the Supreme Court ruled in favor of the public's right to know. No documents implicated the Nixon administration, but the history of America's secret and growing involvement in Southeast Asia undercut the reputations of three previous presidents. Nixon did not dispute the truthfulness of the history. His charge was that publication of the Pentagon Papers would undermine the credibility of government.

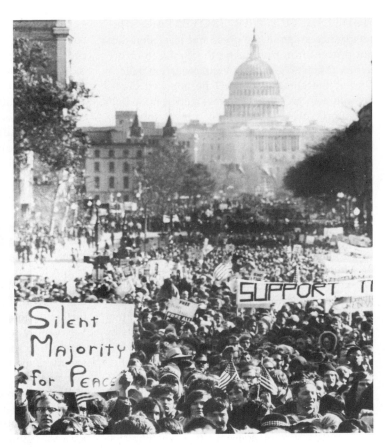

This huge march for peace in Vietnam, November 15, 1969, expressed the desire of millions of Americans for an end to the war. Because the American electorate was deeply divided, however, in the short run such demonstrations only increased the bitterness of political debate. The war ruined the careers of two eminent Democratic leaders, Lyndon Johnson and Hubert Humphrey, and deeply compromised the presidency of Richard Nixon. (AP/Wide World Photos)

DÉTENTE As the war in Vietnam continued its bloody course, Nixon and Kissinger pursued another, different goal in foreign policy. Both leaders were convinced that the United States must recognize the rising power of other nations. Europe, Japan, the Soviet Union, and China all represented separate poles of power. With Europe taking a more independent course, the president believed the time was ripe to upgrade relations with China. He also wished to reach a limited arms control agreement with the Soviet Union.

The president initiated his policy secretly, in part because he did not wish to stir criticism from the right wing of his own party, which vigorously opposed détente (conciliation) with the Chinese

communists and the Russians. Nonetheless, signs of a thaw with the Chinese were unmistakable. In April 1971 a U.S. table tennis team traveled to mainland China for a series of matches. In July the president announced to a surprised nation that he would visit China, a result of negotiations carried out by Henry Kissinger.

Inevitably, these moves seriously compromised support for America's staunch ally nationalist China, which still occupied Taiwan. On October 12 Nixon announced a similar trip to the Soviet Union. Both these initiatives represented major changes in American policy because they softened U.S. opposition toward an accommodation with the two major communist powers.

Nixon in China. Richard Nixon, his wife Pat, Chinese Deputy Premier Li Hsien-nien and his wife, and Secretary of State William Rogers at the Great Wall of China in February 1972. Customary visits by politicians to this enigmatic boundary suggest the two extremes of Chinese policy—excluding foreigners or welcoming them in. (UPI/Bettmann Newsphotos)

After the president's dramatic, weeklong visit to China in February 1972, the United States began to normalize relations with that nation. Warmer relations with the Chinese, in turn, convinced the Soviet Union to seek closer ties with the United States.

The results of bargaining with the Russians bore fruit in the spring and summer of 1972. When Nixon returned from the Soviet Union in late May, he had cemented two major agreements. The first was a Strategic Arms Limitation Treaty (SALT I), signed with Soviet leader Leonid Brezhnev on May 26 and limiting U.S. and Soviet deployment of antiballistic missile systems. The second was a large Russian purchase of American grain, announced in July.

THE END OF THE WAR But the president failed to persuade either China or the U.S.S.R. to abandon North Vietnam. Indeed, the Vietnam crisis worsened. The South Vietnamese government made no real advance in winning the support of its population. Militarily, the situation remained bleak. With diminished numbers of American troops in the country, U.S. power relied more on air strikes. And time obviously favored the insurgents. Domestic support for the war continued to crumble. In a symbolic but ominous act in 1971, the Senate rescinded the Gulf of Tonkin resolution. During the spring and summer and into the fall of 1972, the United States and North Vietnam conducted peace negotiations in Paris. To influence the 1972 presidential

Norman Lear

At 9:30 P.M. on January 12, 1971, CBS television inaugurated a new series by warning its viewers that the contents of the program might seem offensive or inappropriate to some viewers. What followed was the first showing of Norman Lear's *All in the Family*, in which the leading character, Archie Bunker, vented his petty prejudices against "hebes," "spics," "greasers," and "coons." This offensive language decorated equally offensive opinions. Archie Bunker represented bigotry. His wife, Edith, however, was naive and goodhearted; and his son-in-law, Mike ("Meathead"), was a liberal. The sparks that flew between family members illuminated serious tensions in American society, but the program was always lighthearted and satiric. Archie Bunker lost each week's battle, although he was never at a loss for expressing a new prejudice in the next episode. Audiences did not flinch from this tough satire; they loved it. By May, Lear's series had become the most popular show on television and CBS moved it to an earlier time.

Lear's fertile imagination quickly concocted other shows. One spinoff was *Maude*, which first aired in September 1972. In this production, the heroine was a liberal counterpart of Archie Bunker, and as stubborn and rigid in her opinions as he was in his. Other shows inaugurated by Lear included *Good Times*, the story of a black family living in a housing project, and *Mary Hartman, Mary Hartman*, a send-up of afternoon soap operas. In each of these programs, Lear's touch was obvious. The worlds he created and satirized were those of stereotypes—in politics, popular culture, and American society.

In some respects, Lear wrote his own past into his best productions. Archie Bunker was based on his father, an ineffectual entrepreneur who often shouted at his mother, "Stifle yourself!" and, at Norman, "You're the laziest white kid I ever saw." Lear fought his way into show business as a comedy writer. During the late 1950s he became a regular television scriptwriter, and during the 1960s he dabbled in film writing and production. After working out the story idea and writing sample scripts for *All in the Family*, he tried to sell the program to ABC-TV. The company praised the idea but rejected it as too controversial. So Lear turned to CBS, which accepted the proposal.

CBS, however, did not always support Lear. In-house program censors sometimes tried—unsuccessfully—to cut potentially offensive material. In late spring of 1975, CBS, ABC, and NBC created a "family hour" to run from 7 to 9 P.M. (6 to 8 in the Midwest). This special time segment, it was agreed, would limit violence and present programming suitable for everyone in the family. *All in the Family* was not considered by CBS to be suitable for this time period, so the network rescheduled the program for a later hour. Lear was furious and brought suit against the network. In late November 1976 a federal judge decided in Lear's favor, and the "family hour" agreement was rescinded. Lear won this battle, but he ultimately lost the war for American audiences. By the late 1970s several of his newer productions had disappeared. Lear's social sitcoms gave way to sexcoms like *Charlie's Angels*. By 1980, Lear had, by and large, abandoned his innovative role in American television.

Picture: UPI/Bettmann Newsphotos

election, Kissinger announced during the fall that a peace treaty was imminent. But negotiations faltered, and the president ordered new, saturation bombing of the north. Finally, in January 1973 a treaty was signed. American prisoners of war were to be released, and the South Vietnamese regime was to remain in power. But North Vietnam was allowed to keep troops in the south. In effect, the United States had abandoned the south for which it had fought so long.

Although it ratified a military reverse of major proportions, the treaty was in one sense a positive accomplishment. Nixon had ended the war and yet had avoided the right-wing backlash that had paralyzed two presidents before him. Added to the rapprochement with the Chinese and the Russians, ending the war represented a significant turning point in American foreign relations and a major accomplishment for the president. He had also manipulated foreign policy to win a landslide re-election against Democrat George McGovern in 1972.

Nixon's Credibility at Home

In domestic policy, President Nixon faced two obstacles: a Congress dominated by the Democratic party and a government bureaucracy unresponsive and unsympathetic to his policies. These stumbling blocks constituted a major impediment to the conduct of his administration. The president focused on four issues, but each of them proved highly resistant to change: He attempted to strengthen legal weapons against crime and political violence. He sought a major overhaul of social welfare policy. He attempted to cope with a serious bout of economic stagnation, inflation, and energy shortages. And he tried to reorganize the executive branch of the government.

Elected partly because he had promised decisive action against social disorder, Nixon secured a tough new criminal justice law in the District of Columbia. His attorney general, John Mitchell, sought to isolate student and radical groups by infiltrating their ranks with agents and prosecuting them under an antiriot law passed in 1968. Since many administration members as well as voters believed that civil rights was a major source of social unrest, he also tried to slow federal desegregation actions. Attorney General Mitchell testified against extending the Voting Rights Act, due to expire in August 1970. But Congress renewed the act anyway.

Striking at another institution that had loosened social restraints, Nixon tried to transform the Supreme Court. Early in his administration, the president had his first opportunity to make a change when the position of chief justice fell open. Nixon appointed Judge Warren Burger to the post. The next vacancy occurred in 1971. In this case the president nominated first one, then another, undistinguished, conservative Southern appeals court judge. The Senate rejected both on the grounds of incompetence and because of their extreme views on race relations. Stung by these defeats, Nixon appointed Judge Harry Andrew Blackmun. His last appointment did lay the groundwork for a conservative court when he appointed William Hubbs Rehnquist as Justice. Nixon had hoped to affect the complexion of the Court immediately, but it still continued to advance integration, and in 1973, in the landmark *Roe* v. *Wade* decision it declared constitutional a woman's right to have an abortion.

The issue of welfare payments to nonworking mothers and children was part of the larger question of providing social services and income maintenance to the poor and elderly. Some Americans believed that the poor should suffer the consequences of their fate and that the federal government should provide only minimal assistance. The president did not share this harsh view, but he did oppose the tangle of agencies and programs left over from the Great Society. His first plan to correct this confusion was the Family

Assistance Plan—a plan to provide a guaranteed income of $1,600 for a family of four (plus $820 in food stamps). Twice passed by the House, the act failed in the Senate, and Nixon abandoned it in 1971.

Taking a different tack, the administration did succeed in shifting some federal social programs to the states in the 1972 State and Local Fiscal Assistance Act. This law created "revenue sharing" for the states. In effect, it provided block grants to state authorities, with general standards set but wide discretion left to local administration as to how the money should be spent.

THE ECONOMY Some of the president's difficulties in passing new social legislation lay in the sluggish economy. As the leader of a political party that ritualistically proclaimed its faith in the private sector, Nixon used federal fiscal and monetary instruments to fight economic problems. To explain this economic activism, at one point he even declared himself a follower of Keynesian economics. But his administration lacked an overall, consistent policy.

Shortly after entering the White House, Nixon had promised to nudge the lethargic economy with increased federal expenditures. But by mid-1971, fighting inflation took top priority. In the summer the president acted on several fronts. Calling this Phase I of his economic program, he froze wages and prices for ninety days, slapped a 10 percent surcharge on imports, and devalued the American dollar.

A second phase began in the summer of 1973, when the president reimposed a price freeze for sixty days. After these controls were relaxed, prices soared again. One reason for this sudden, uncontrollable inflation was the steep increase in imported oil prices. By 1973 the United States was importing about one-third of its total crude oil. More than half that total came from OPEC—the Organization of Petroleum Exporting Countries. These nations, among them Saudi Arabia, Kuwait, Libya, Iran, Iraq, Nigeria, and Venezuela, had jointly raised oil prices about 400 percent above 1970 prices. In addition, during the winter of 1973–74, Arab members of OPEC embargoed all shipments of oil to the United States and other Western nations that supported Israel during the 1973 Yom Kippur War against Egypt and Syria. Spot shortages appeared in the United States, with long lines of automobiles snaking around filling stations.

DOMESTIC SPYING Unable to develop a consistent and effective economic program, Nixon also discovered enormous inertia in government itself. Of all the problems he faced, none frustrated the president as much as his lack of control over the federal bureaucracy. Twice, Nixon and his advisers tried to reorganize the executive branch. But both efforts, in 1970 and in 1973, failed. In particular, his attempts to subordinate cabinet heads to the White House staff met spirited opposition.

Finding himself stalemated in several directions, and feeling besieged by the press and Congress, the president tried to undermine the institutions that blocked him. In doing so, he created a submerged, secret branch of government that depended on intrigue and conspiracy. The first such instance was the phone taps used after the bombing of Cambodia. He took a more serious step in the fall of 1970. Tom Huston, a White House aide, prepared a program of domestic spying to be implemented by the president's staff. J. Edgar Hoover, head of the FBI, refused to agree, in part because it would undercut his own agency. When this proposal failed, the administration created the White House investigation unit known as "the plumbers," whose job it was to plug information leaks.

Losses in the election of 1970 and continued criticism of his Vietnam policy convinced the president to act. After publication of the Pentagon Papers, the White House approved plans to break into Daniel Ellsberg's psychiatrist's office to search for material that might discredit him.

The operation was financed with money received in a secret donation from the milk industry, given in return for administration support of higher milk price supports.

WATERGATE   In 1972 the administration plunged deeper into illegal activities. Many of these originated in the Committee for the Re-election of the President (CREEP). CREEP hoped to shape the election of 1972 to Nixon's advantage. It willfully misinformed the public and broke the law. Using secret contributions solicited from corporate donors, the group employed "dirty tricks" that injected false issues into Democratic party primaries. CREEP also broke into Democratic party headquarters in May 1972 to install wiretaps and to photograph documents. When the group returned in mid-June to obtain more material, a night watchman alerted the Washington, D.C., police. They arrived quickly at the Watergate complex that housed the headquarters and arrested several of the burglars. A few were Cuban refugees, but two were ex-employees of CREEP.

The Democratic party denounced the break-in, but administration spokesmen dismissed it as a "third-rate burglary attempt." Watergate never emerged as an election issue. The Democratic candidate, George McGovern, tried to galvanize his party around opposition to the Vietnam War and promises of social reform. But his own credibility was compromised when he supported Senator Thomas Eagleton of Missouri for vice president and then dropped him after information about the senator's history of mental illness surfaced. This was less important, however, than his inability to rally the Democratic party. Much of McGovern's early support fell away, and traditional sources of Democratic power in urban political machines and in the labor movement refused to work for him. Nixon's campaign stressed his accomplishments: dramatic changes in foreign policy and a revived economy. Evidently, the voters believed him. He won every

state but Massachusetts and the District of Columbia. But the Democrats retained their majority in Congress.

In his second inaugural address, the president spoke words that came to have a bitter irony for his next years:

> From this day forward let each of us make a solemn commitment in his own heart: to bear his responsibility, to do his part, to live his ideals.

At the beginning of 1973, Nixon moved to assert firmer control of the executive branch and to dismantle the Great Society. Even though he impounded funds (refused to spend appropriated money), he made little headway. Instead, he found himself increasingly mired in explanations of the Watergate break-in and other campaign irregularities.

The Watergate scandal hinged on the question of credibility. For Nixon and all his advisers, the problem of truthfulness was rarely an issue. Rather, the Watergate defendants tried again and again to create credible explanations for their behavior, willfully mixing truth with invention and misinformation. As they retreated, more and more of the real story emerged from the paper trail they left behind them. The administration's problems began when Judge John Sirica, presiding over the trial of the burglars in Washington in early 1973, pressed the defendants. One of them, James McCord, implicated high administration figures in the planning of election espionage. He accused John Mitchell and White House staff members Jeb Magruder and John Dean. *Washington Post* reporters picked up loose ends of evidence that emerged in the trial and began weaving together the story of a painstaking plot to cover up ties between the Watergate burglars and the White House.

When John Dean testified during June hearings before the Presidential Campaign Committee, set up in the Senate, he used this forum to escape what he believed was a White House decision to make him a scapegoat for Watergate. He

Watergate Roster

	Position	Role in Watergate	Sentence	Amount of Sentence Served
Richard M. Nixon	President of the United States	Unindicted co-conspirator	Pardoned	
Dwight L. Chapin	Presidential appointments secretary	Convicted of lying to a grand jury	10 to 30 months	8 months
Charles W. Colson	Special counsel to the president	Pleaded guilty to obstruction of justice	1 to 3 years; fined $5,000	7 months
John W. Dean III	Counsel to the president	Pleaded guilty to conspiracy	1 to 4 years	4 months
John D. Ehrlichman	Domestic Council chief	Convicted of conspiracy to obstruct justice, conspiracy, and perjury	Concurrent terms of 20 months to 8 years	18 months
H. R. Haldeman	Chief of the White House staff	Convicted of conspiracy and perjury	30 months to 8 years	18 months
E. Howard Hunt	White House aide	Pleaded guilty to conspiracy, burglary, and wiretapping	30 months to 8 years; fined $10,000	33 months
Herbert W. Kalmbach	Personal attorney to the president	Pleaded guilty to violation of Federal Corrupt Practices Act and promising federal employment as a reward for political activity	6 to 18 months; fined $10,000	6 months
Richard G. Kleindienst	Attorney General of the United States	Pleaded guilty to refusal to answer pertinent questions before a Senate committee	30 days; fined $100	Sentence suspended
Egil Krogh, Jr.	White House aide	Pleaded guilty to conspiracy	2 to 6 years (all but 6 months suspended)	4½ months

Watergate Roster *(continued)*

	Position	Role in Watergate	Sentence	Amount of Sentence Served
Frederick C. LaRue	Assistant to John Mitchell	Pleaded guilty to conspiracy	1 to 3 years (all but 6 months suspended)	5½ months
G. Gordon Liddy	White House aide	Convicted of conspiracy, burglary, and wiretapping	6 years and 8 months to 20 years; fined $40,000	52 months
Jeb S. Magruder	White House aide	Pleaded guilty to conspiracy, wiretapping, and fraud	10 months to 4 years	7 months
John N. Mitchell	Attorney General of the United States	Convicted of conspiracy and perjury	30 months to 8 years	19 months
Donald H. Segretti	"Dirty tricks" specialist	Pleaded guilty to campaign violations and conspiracy	6 months	4½ months
Maurice H. Stans	Finance director of Committee for the Re-Election of the President	Pleaded guilty to misdemeanor violations of the Federal Elections Campaign Act	Fined $5,000	
Bernard L. Barker	Watergate burglar	Pleaded guilty to conspiracy, burglary, wiretapping, and unlawful possession of intercepting devices	18 months to 6 years	12 months
Virgilio R. Gonzalez	Watergate burglar	Pleaded guilty to conspiracy, burglary, wiretapping, and unlawful possession of intercepting devices	1 to 4 years	15 months

Watergate Roster *(continued)*

	Position	Role in Watergate	Sentence	Amount of Sentence Served
James W. McCord, Jr.	Watergate burglar	Convicted of conspiracy, burglary, wiretappping, and unlawful possession of intercepting devices	1 to 5 years	4 months
Eugenio R. Martinez	Watergate burglar	Pleaded guilty to conspiracy, burglary, wiretapping and unlawful possession of intercepting devices	1 to 4 years	15 months
Frank A. Sturgis	Watergate burglar	Pleaded guilty to conspiracy, burglary, wiretapping, and unlawful possession of intercepting devices	1 to 4 years	13 months

even implicated the president in the cover-up. With this new evidence, the investigation intensified. A grand jury began to weigh evidence against a mounting list of accused conspirators. Other material surfaced through efforts of a special prosecutor, Archibald Cox, appointed to oversee the investigation in the attorney general's office. Surrounded, and with his own defenses crumbling, the president worked publicly with the investigation while he privately tried to impede it. As he instructed John Mitchell:

> I want you all to stonewall it, let them plead the Fifth Amendment, cover-up or anything else, if it'll save it—save the plan.

One by one the president's close advisers resigned. In October 1973 Vice President Agnew left office, pleading no contest to charges of income tax fraud after a grand jury discovered that he had accepted bribes and payoffs while governor of Maryland. The most startling discovery, however, came when a White House aide told of hundreds of tapes of recorded conversations between Nixon and his advisers made secretly over the previous two years. These could establish the president's guilt or innocence.

Nixon's refusal to submit any of the tapes to Cox, the grand jury, or the Senate committee further damaged his credibility. He tried every means to keep the material secret, invoking "executive privilege," and fighting with lawsuits and delays. He even fired prosecutor Cox on October 20, 1973 in the infamous "Saturday Night Massacre," when Attorney General Elliot Richardson and Deputy William Ruckelshaus resigned rather than do the president's bidding. But Cox's replacement, Leon Jaworski, persisted in demanding the evidence. Finally, in April 1974, Nixon released edited versions of the tapes. Even

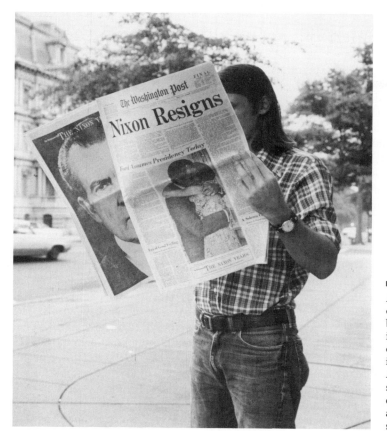

An American disgraced. The first chief executive driven from office by scandal and the threat of impeachment, Richard Nixon succumbed to this last, largely self-inflicted crisis of his political career. Americans, although relieved, were stunned by the magnitude of the crisis; their faith in the presidency as an institution might never be the same. (© Alex Webb/Magnum)

in abridged form, the documents revealed that the president was deeply involved in the Watergate cover-up. They also uncovered the private Nixon—a man who was as ruthless and vulgar in private as he was cautious and well spoken in public. The House Judiciary Committee began hearings on impeachment.

As Nixon was forced to release more tapes, impressions of his guilt became firmer. Two new groups of tapes released over the summer disclosed the president's direct participation in the cover-up of the Watergate burglary. On August 8, after his administration had almost ceased to govern—and facing impeachment—the president resigned. But he would admit no wrong-

doing, only "bad judgment." As Nixon boarded a plane for California, Gerald Ford, Vice President Agnew's replacement, became president.

The turmoil of Watergate and the dramatic exposures of corruption in government convinced many Americans that most politicians were either inept or immoral. True, the system had worked to replace a government that had subverted some of the most important institutions of democracy. But the process was so wrenching that it undercut faith in government itself. New revelations in the media about kickbacks and other scandals and stories of CIA and FBI illegal activities added to the growing credibility gap.

Consumers Lose Faith

Gerald Ford and the Failure of Leadership

The reputations of private institutions were also tarnished in the early 1970s. The consumer movement carried on a spirited attack on private corporations for their shoddy and dangerous practices. Consumerism had had an active history in the early decades of the twentieth century and was reborn in the mid-1960s. Critics such as Ralph Nader and Barry Commoner wrote exposés of dangerous flaws in automobile design, adulteration of foods, pollution, and, especially, nuclear hazards. They helped stimulate a wave of consumer protection legislation, such as the Consumer Product Safety Act of 1972, which established a five-member regulatory agency. These laws aided the removal of dangerous products from the market.

Nader's efforts coincided with an important social movement of the early 1970s—a movement that grew out of the counterculture. Many Americans began to lead what they believed was a less artificial life, stressing vegetarian diet, natural childbirth, communal and rural living, a more natural sexuality, less differentiated sex roles, and the use of solar energy. Many of the thousands of participants in this movement rejected competitive, urban living. They were wary of the great technological feats of the era, such as the U.S. moon landing in July 1969 and the generation of nuclear power. They viewed industrial and scientific progress with deep suspicion.

Perhaps most symbolic of this new mood was a change in automobile design. To increase fuel efficiency and compete with Japanese and European imports, American auto makers shortened and lightened their cars. They lopped off the titanic fins, chrome strips, and long hoods and trunks that had added weight, horsepower, and expense. The dream of owning a shiny new car did not end, of course, but it did take a more practical bent.

Gerald Ford, the new president-by-appointment, had the difficult task of restoring belief in American institutions in a moment of deep crisis. A well-liked congressman from Michigan, Ford had almost no national reputation and little experience with the difficult administrative tasks of his new office. He faced a leadership crisis that was intensified by a serious recession, continuing energy shortages, and the final, bleak days of the government of South Vietnam. Of his inherited administration, he kept Henry Kissinger, but he replaced most of the White House staff. To fill the vacant vice presidency, he appointed Nelson Rockefeller, who was governor of New York. The choice proved politically damaging. Rockefeller was without a significant following in the Republican party—disliked by the large and growing right wing and with little vocal support from moderates.

Soon after taking office, Ford made his most controversial move. He granted a general pardon to ex-President Nixon. As he said, "My conscience tells me that only I, as president, have the constitutional power to firmly shut and seal this book." But his act sealed only the lips of Richard Nixon, who did not reveal or admit the extent of his involvement in Watergate. Many Americans believed that Ford had struck a deal for the presidency with Nixon—although there was no evidence to support this suspicion.

Despite the damage of the pardon, Ford benefited from his reputation for honesty and openness. His wife, Betty, strengthened this impression of candor by speaking openly of a breast cancer operation she underwent in late 1974 and by supporting her own political causes, such as the Equal Rights Amendment. But Gerald Ford also had a reputation as a bumbler and a man not up to the intellectual rigors of the office.

Astronaut Edwin E. Aldrin, Jr., photographed by Neil Armstrong on July 20, 1969, while both men stood on the surface of the moon. Aldrin's sharp shadow falls across footprints left by the two moonwalkers. Although it occurred decades ago, this endeavor represents the most spectacular success of the American space program. (NASA)

This impression of ineptness continued for the next two years, fed by the merciless satire of the popular television program *Saturday Night Live*.

The new president inherited the final debacle of Vietnam. Now prevented by law from committing any American forces to this Asian conflict, Ford could do nothing when the North Vietnamese army routed the forces of the south and drove toward Saigon in the spring of 1975. An emergency airlift rescued remaining Americans and thousands of South Vietnamese officials linked to the United States. The longest war in American history ended in scenes of hasty and confused retreat.

However, there were few domestic recriminations. And America's reputation for decisive action was partly restored when Ford achieved the rescue of an American merchant ship, the *Mayaguez*, seized by the Cambodians in May. Ford ordered ships, planes, and men into action. Although the expedition was costly in terms of lives lost, the thirty-nine-man crew was recaptured. Congress and much of the press applauded the president's attempt to restore credibility, although they realized the action might have been unnecessary.

On the domestic front, Ford had few successes. His antirecession plans failed to pass

Congress. Infighting and indecision in the administration convinced the public that weak leadership persisted. On questions of energy, conservation, and the environment, Ford relinquished leadership to Congress. Increasingly, he vetoed measures, only to see them passed again over his objections.

THE ELECTION OF 1976

In early 1976, Ford announced that he would seek election to a full term as president. He possessed the significant advantage of incumbency, but he had few concrete accomplishments. His party split into two factions, with the most vocal and highly organized portion supporting former governor of California Ronald Reagan. Reagan challenged Ford in primaries across the country, attacking his foreign policy, détente with the Russians, and the continued influence of Henry Kissinger. He filled his speeches with old-fashioned homilies and invited nostalgia for a vaguely remembered American past. This strategy almost succeeded. In a closely divided convention, Ford had to accept a "morality in foreign policy" plank that, in effect, criticized his own foreign policy. Nonetheless, Ford narrowly won the nomination.

The Democratic party in 1976 was, if anything, more deeply divided than the Republican. The multiple leadership of the party and the new rules for delegate selection made it difficult for any one candidate to emerge. The most obvious choice was Senator Edward Kennedy of Massachusetts. But Kennedy's chances remained seriously compromised by an accident that had occurred on Chappaquiddick Island, Massachusetts, on July 18, 1969. A woman companion riding in his car had been killed, and Kennedy could never satisfactorily explain the circumstances of the accident. Other candidates lacked national support. As a result, the most persistent candidate, James (Jimmy) Carter, former governor of Georgia, won the nomination.

Carter won a narrow victory in November after a campaign highlighted by televised debates. Carter's margin was provided by an exaggerated turnout of two traditional Demo-

The Bicentennial. Celebrations of the two hundredth anniversary of the Declaration of Independence took place across the United States during 1976. Here, President Gerald Ford and his daughter Susan wave to crowds in front of Independence Hall in Philadelphia on July 4, 1976. (AP/Wide World Photos)

cratic constituencies: the South (proud of its native son) and black voters. But beneath the surface, this coalition was shaky. Blacks and blue-collar whites could be split apart, as George Wallace's campaigns over several years had proven. Labor unions, once the backbone of the Democratic party, had declined in membership and prestige during the 1970s. They had also lost power in the party as a result of the new rules that gave proportional representation to women and minorities.

The South might have been solid in electoral votes for Carter, but the region had become increasingly diverse and Republican. While the Voting Rights Act had enfranchised large numbers of black voters, industrialization, large population increases, and traditional conservatism had brought a strong resurgence of Republicanism. Other, traditionally strong Republican areas also gained strength during the 1970s, particularly the Southwest and the West. The census of 1980 confirmed a massive trend in population flow after World War II, out of the North and East to the South and West. For the first time, the population center of the nation crossed the Mississippi River.

The election of 1976 demonstrated another long-term trend in American voting patterns, away from voter participation. Registration was easier, and whole new populations were enfranchised, but the percentage of persons voting continued to decline. So did party identification. The effect of this nonparticipation was to increase the power of special-interest groups and small, well-organized segments of the population. Furthermore, the mass media exercised an increased power in the campaign, with advertising and pollsters largely determining the issues and answers for candidates. But apparently, as Americans learned more of the intimate details of politics, they were less keen to participate.

The only substantial exception to this trend appeared among America's growing elderly population. During the 1970s the average life expectancy increased more than two and a half years, continuing a tendency to longevity that added millions to the number of retirees. Among older Americans, issues of cuts in Social Security or medical benefit programs were a matter of life and death. So not only did the elderly vote in large numbers, they also organized pressure groups such as the Gray Panthers.

Jimmy Carter appealed to many disaffected voters. His campaign criticized the Washington establishment and the lingering problems of Watergate. He promised never to deceive the American public. And he stressed traditional values and honesty in government. He made char-

acter the issue of the campaign. His strenuous and persistent campaigning paid off.

Born into a Georgia farm family, Carter attended the U.S. Naval Academy and, after World War II, worked in the new nuclear submarine fleet. Retiring from the Navy, he returned to Plains, Georgia, and started a successful peanut warehouse and distributing business. He entered Georgia state politics in 1962 and won the governorship in 1970. Widely known as a representative of the "new South"—that is, a South that accepted racial integration—Carter in 1976 also had strong ties to the old South, with its tradition of evangelical Protestantism. The tone of his campaign stressed the personal virtues he could bring to the office: truthfulness, family values, decency, and principle. He promised nuclear disarmament, open and competent government, and a restoration of faith in America.

Jimmy Carter and the Credibility Crisis

The new president appointed several Washington professionals to his cabinet, including Cyrus Vance as secretary of state and Joseph Califano as secretary of health, education, and welfare. He appointed Patricia Harris, a black woman, as secretary of housing and urban development. And large numbers of lower-level administrative appointments went to women and African Americans. By appointing two women, he had almost as many women in his cabinet as all previous presidents combined. Nonetheless, Carter's White House staff was headed by his campaign manager Hamilton Jordan, with other Georgians occupying leading roles—among them Bert Lance as head of the Office of Management and Budget and Andrew Young as U.S. ambassador to the United Nations. This group was known as the "Georgia Mafia."

Energy Source by Type (in quadrillions of BTU's)

	1960	1970	1980	1984
Refined petroleum	19.9	29.5	34.3	31.0
Natural gas	12.4	21.8	20.4	18.0
Coal	10.1	12.7	15.7	17.2
Nuclear	—	.2	2.7	3.5
Hydroelectric	1.7	2.7	3.1	3.5
Other	—	—	.1	.2
Total	44.1	66.9	76.3	77.5

Source: U.S. Department of Commerce, Bureau of the Census, *Statistical Abstract of the United States, 1986* (Washington, D.C.: Government Printing Office, 1985), p. 557.

Almost from the beginning, Carter's inexperience in national politics and his indecisiveness (perhaps reflecting the conflicts in his electoral majority) hurt his relations with the Democratic-controlled Congress. In a sense, Carter's personality and politics reflected each other. He was both liberal and conservative, a Southerner with important ties and dependencies in the North, a born-again Christian with sophisticated views of moral and social problems. This was also the nature of his coalition and political support, and it was an inherently unstable one.

ENERGY POLICY Energy took priority with the new president. Personally rejecting the extravagant style sometimes associated with the presidency, Carter urged all Americans to conserve energy and live simpler lives. His major energy legislation, introduced in April 1977, was designed to ease American dependence on OPEC oil and induce domestic conservation. Sections of the proposed program encouraged a return to coal use and mandated energy savings in automobile design.

By August 1977 the energy bill had sailed through the House, practically intact. But it stalled in the Senate, primarily over the issue of deregulating natural gas. Although a new Department of Energy began operating in October 1977, Carter's principal energy legislation did not pass until a year later. In five linked acts, Congress approved measures to encourage home energy conservation, to enforce the use of coal in electrical generating, to encourage auto efficiency, and to increase natural gas prices. Several key questions remained unanswered, however, such as the timing and extent of oil price deregulation and the fate of the nuclear industry.

Carter called the energy crisis the "moral equivalent of war." For his presidency, at least, this slogan proved to be apt. The president recognized that because of recurrent gasoline shortages, many Americans did not trust the oil companies. Were they withholding gasoline from the market in order to raise prices, as many suspected? The president declared that this might be the case. Yet he did not act. A long, bitter coal strike over the winter of 1977–78, in which the president did not intervene quickly, also added to the impression of his inability to show leadership on the issue of energy.

Energy policy reached an impasse in the spring of 1979. Political turmoil in Iran in late 1978 and 1979 cut that country's oil production to almost nothing. Although Iran supplied only about 5 percent of U.S. needs, the cutoff was significant. Rapid price hikes and serious shortages resulted by spring. Particularly in California and in Washington, D.C., long lines formed

Imported Energy by Type (in quadrillions of BTU's)

	1960	1970	1980	1984
Crude oil	2.2	2.8	11.1	7.3
Refined petroleum	1.8	4.7	3.4	4.1
Natural gas	.2	.9	1.0	.9
Percentage of supply imported	9.2%	12.1%	19.8%	16.4%

Source: U.S. Department of Commerce, Bureau of the Census, *Statistical Abstract of the United States, 1986* (Washington, D.C.: Government Printing Office, 1985), p. 557.

around filling stations. Many Americans believed the oil shortage to have been deliberately engineered, but there was little conclusive evidence, and the government failed to confirm or deny this speculation. Carter's response was a limited decontrol of oil prices and a windfall oil profits tax passed in 1980.

The Three Mile Island catastrophe in early spring 1979 compounded Carter's energy worries. Although, after the incident, he spoke enthusiastically about preserving the U.S. commitment to nuclear power, the nuclear industry did not recover. Alternative energy sources, such as gasohol, solar, wind, and geothermal, did not prove as promising as originally hoped. The conservation that did occur in this period came from increased auto efficiency and a lower use of energy dictated by rapidly rising costs.

THE ECONOMY AND "MALAISE" Carter's energy problems were matched by difficulties elsewhere. Fueled by expensive oil, large budget deficits, administered prices (prices not determined by the market), and high wage demands, inflation shot upward in 1978, to 7.7 percent. The stock market registered its lack of confidence in the president's economic program by declining sharply in the spring. The economy was hit by "stagflation"—the double bind of inflation and slow growth.

Carter's leadership in these circumstances faltered. His difficulties with Congress, bickering among his staff, and allegations of improper campaign and banking practices by Bert Lance, which led to his resignation in late 1977, compounded the president's problems. The implications of growing national frustration with government and with mounting taxes became apparent in California, where voters approved Proposition 13, cutting property taxes by more than 50 percent. Carter's reaction to this mood of disenchantment was to reorganize his cabinet and try to work more closely with Congress. Yet part of his response was quixotic—he mused in public about "a national malaise" that he should have recognized as partly attributable to his own lack of leadership.

FOREIGN AFFAIRS Foreign relations questions provided the president with several accomplishments—and his final undoing. In part, his troubles stemmed from appointing two competing advisers: Cyrus Vance, a traditional, cautious diplomat, as secretary of state, and Zbigniew Brzezinski, a more aggressive anticommunist, as head of the National Security Council. At first, Carter tried to listen to both sides, to receive conflicting advice and then exercise his best judgment. It seemed as if this strategy would open a much-needed debate over foreign policy. But after some initial successes Carter relinquished

Sadat, Carter, and Begin. This portrait, taken at the beginning of the ceremony marking the signing of the Camp David accords, symbolized the achievement of President Jimmy Carter (center) in negotiating a peace treaty between President Anwar Sadat of Egypt (left) and Israeli Prime Minister Menachem Begin in March 1979. (UPI/Bettmann Newsphotos)

some of his caution and pursued a more confrontational policy.

The weakness of the dollar, huge energy price increases, and controversial problems forced the president to make unpopular choices. His foreign policy of emphasis on human rights, while commendable, was very difficult to pursue. It proved disruptive to American alliances to insist that friendly nations respect an internal climate of political freedom in order to receive American aid. But on the question of disarmament, Carter negotiated a new agreement with the Russians—SALT II, limiting weapons systems—on June 18, 1979. The Senate, however, refused to ratify it. Passage of the Panama Canal treaties, although bitterly opposed in Congress, returned the Canal Zone and eventual control of the American-built canal to the government of Panama. And the United States also established formal ties with the People's Republic of China in 1979.

The president's most lasting achievement was a negotiated settlement between Egypt and Israel in March 1979. Intense negotiations between President Anwar Sadat of Egypt and Prime Minister Menachem Begin of Israel, urged on by Carter, took place in late 1978 at Camp David, Maryland, the presidential vacation retreat. For eleven days, Begin and Sadat and Carter debated the outstanding issues between Israel and Egypt. When the conference finally ended, Egypt and Israel, after years of hatred and intermittent war, were at peace. The Camp David agreement cemented the gradual peacemaking process that had begun in the aftermath of the Yom Kippur War of 1973. It increased hopes for a final settlement of the explosive antagonism in the Middle East between Israel and its neighbors.

Relations with the Soviet Union, despite SALT, cooled. Expansion of Soviet power and influence in Africa, especially in Angola and

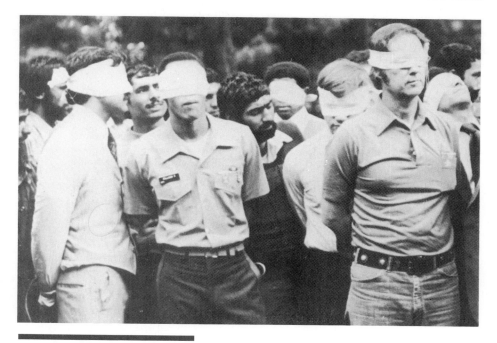

American hostages in Iran. In early November 1979, Iranian militants seized the American embassy in Tehran and took its occupants hostage. Photographs such as this one infuriated the American public and increased their frustration with Jimmy Carter's foreign policy. (UPI)

Ethiopia, and—even more—the Russian invasion and occupation of its neighbor Afghanistan brought American-Soviet relations to a low point. Many Americans also believed that the Russians were near to achieving military superiority over the United States. Pressure built for increased defense expenditures, and Carter responded in 1979 with a larger defense budget and plans to install the complex MX missile system and to develop a neutron bomb. By this time, Carter had ceased to waver between his two major policy experts; Brzezinski had won the war of advisers.

Frustration over foreign policy intensified in November 1979, after angry Iranians stormed the U.S. embassy in Tehran and held the American staff hostage until January 1981. Early in 1979, the Ayatollah Khomeini had returned from exile to lead a Muslim fundamentalist revolution against the American-supported shah of Iran. The hostage crisis was precipitated when the deposed shah, then in exile, was granted entry into the United States to receive cancer treatment. Carter believed that an old friend of the nation must be welcomed to the United States despite the risks. The student captors, with the support of the Iranian revolutionary government, demanded the return of the shah to Iran. President Carter refused this demand and froze Iranian assets. He did, however, persuade Panama to allow the shah to settle there, although this act did nothing to soften the anger of the Iranians. Then Carter cut off imports of Iranian oil into the United States. But there was little else he could do to force the Iranians to release the hostages—short of war. An ill-planned and ill-executed rescue mission in April 1980 only increased the public's sense of the president's impotence. Cyrus Vance, who had opposed the raid as well as much of Carter's recent foreign policy, resigned. Nightly news broadcasts, which amounted to

CHRONOLOGY

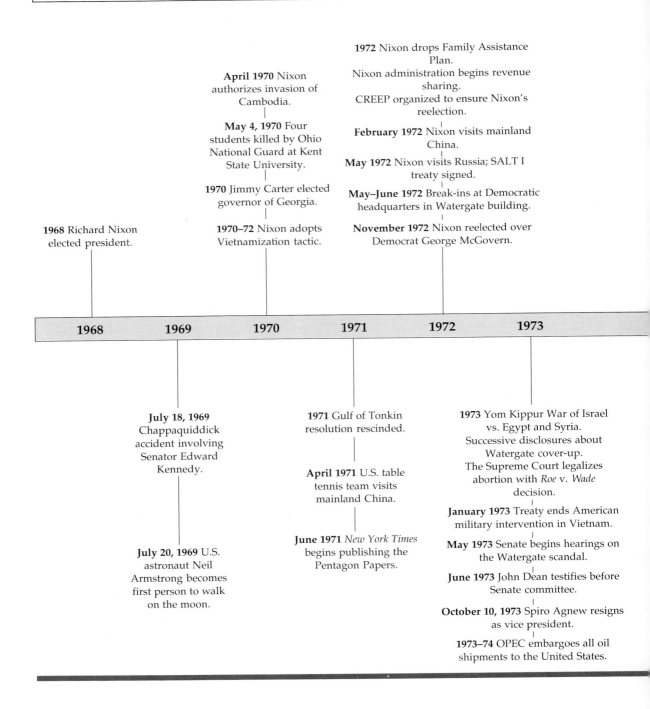

1968 Richard Nixon elected president.

April 1970 Nixon authorizes invasion of Cambodia.

May 4, 1970 Four students killed by Ohio National Guard at Kent State University.

1970 Jimmy Carter elected governor of Georgia.

1970–72 Nixon adopts Vietnamization tactic.

1972 Nixon drops Family Assistance Plan.
Nixon administration begins revenue sharing.
CREEP organized to ensure Nixon's reelection.

February 1972 Nixon visits mainland China.

May 1972 Nixon visits Russia; SALT I treaty signed.

May–June 1972 Break-ins at Democratic headquarters in Watergate building.

November 1972 Nixon reelected over Democrat George McGovern.

1968	1969	1970	1971	1972	1973

July 18, 1969 Chappaquiddick accident involving Senator Edward Kennedy.

July 20, 1969 U.S. astronaut Neil Armstrong becomes first person to walk on the moon.

1971 Gulf of Tonkin resolution rescinded.

April 1971 U.S. table tennis team visits mainland China.

June 1971 *New York Times* begins publishing the Pentagon Papers.

1973 Yom Kippur War of Israel vs. Egypt and Syria.
Successive disclosures about Watergate cover-up.
The Supreme Court legalizes abortion with *Roe* v. *Wade* decision.

January 1973 Treaty ends American military intervention in Vietnam.

May 1973 Senate begins hearings on the Watergate scandal.

June 1973 John Dean testifies before Senate committee.

October 10, 1973 Spiro Agnew resigns as vice president.

1973–74 OPEC embargoes all oil shipments to the United States.

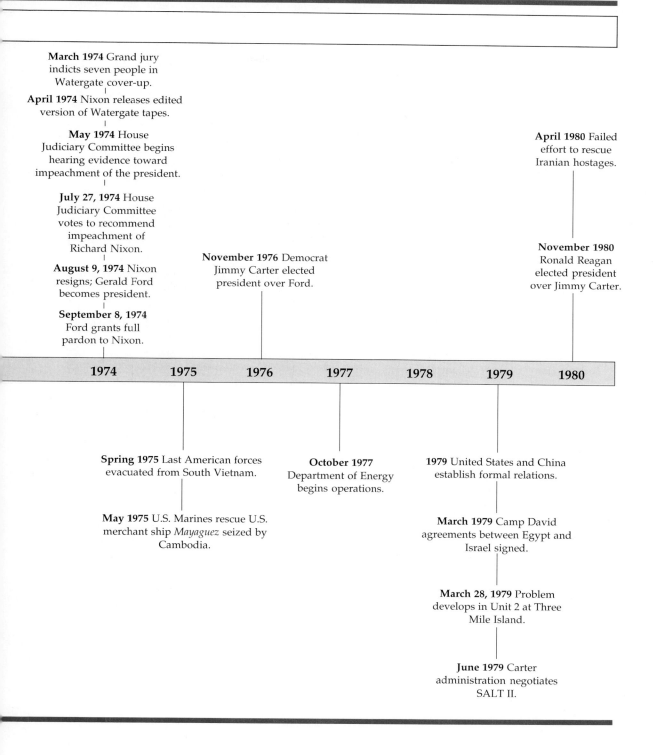

March 1974 Grand jury indicts seven people in Watergate cover-up.

April 1974 Nixon releases edited version of Watergate tapes.

May 1974 House Judiciary Committee begins hearing evidence toward impeachment of the president.

July 27, 1974 House Judiciary Committee votes to recommend impeachment of Richard Nixon.

August 9, 1974 Nixon resigns; Gerald Ford becomes president.

September 8, 1974 Ford grants full pardon to Nixon.

November 1976 Democrat Jimmy Carter elected president over Ford.

April 1980 Failed effort to rescue Iranian hostages.

November 1980 Ronald Reagan elected president over Jimmy Carter.

1974   1975   1976   1977   1978   1979   1980

Spring 1975 Last American forces evacuated from South Vietnam.

May 1975 U.S. Marines rescue U.S. merchant ship *Mayaguez* seized by Cambodia.

October 1977 Department of Energy begins operations.

1979 United States and China establish formal relations.

March 1979 Camp David agreements between Egypt and Israel signed.

March 28, 1979 Problem develops in Unit 2 at Three Mile Island.

June 1979 Carter administration negotiates SALT II.

some of the most persistent coverage of any event in American history, cut away Carter's support and credibility.

THE ELECTION OF 1980 By the spring of 1980 the president's popularity had sunk. Senator Kennedy challenged Carter in presidential primaries. The president pursued a "Rose Garden strategy," refusing to campaign away from the White House (and hence its Rose Garden) so long as the hostages remained in Iran. While this worked to focus attention on Kennedy's weaknesses, it also increased public attention to the imprisoned Americans, who had become almost an obsession for the administration. After months of acrimonious and inconclusive campaigning, Carter won the nomination. But the damage of this skirmish was enormous. The president was unable to create a workable electoral coalition around the programs he supported, such as the Equal Rights Amendment, or around his accomplishments in foreign policy.

Indeed, many of these accomplishments were turned against him by Ronald Reagan, who captured the Republican nomination. Reagan, a former movie star, a favorite of the Republican party right wing, and a longtime presidential aspirant, ran a remarkably well-focused and well-financed campaign. He capitalized on the antagonism to Carter and to government in general. Among a minority of voters, he inspired fervent support with his promises of a huge tax cut, a balanced budget, sharp increases in defense spending, and a much reduced federal commitment to social legislation. To a number of other voters, he simply represented the possibility of change—and of leadership. Despite the third-party candidacy of Republican moderate John Anderson of Illinois, Reagan won a decisive victory in November 1980. More significant, the Republicans gained control of the Senate and achieved an effective majority

President Ronald Reagan. Ronald Reagan's successful campaigns for the presidency and his achievements in office partly depended upon his ability to evoke patriotic feelings in the American public. Many of his speeches conspicuously appealed to such symbols as the American flag. George Bush recreated this strategy in the 1988 election. (UPI)

in the House—with the help of conservative Southern Democrats.

By the late months of 1980, Ronald Reagan prepared to assume office, heading a conservative reaction to the political and social liberalism that had dominated much of American life since World War II. He promised to restore faith in institutions by reaffirming traditional American values and myths and releasing the energy of individualism and private enterprise.

Suggestions for Further Reading

THREE MILE ISLAND, ECONOMICS, AND ENERGY

Some of the specific economic and energy problems that contributed to the political instability of the United States during the 1970s are explained in Lester C. Thurow, *The Zero-Sum Society: Distribution and the Possibilities for Economic Change* (1981). Tad Szulc, *The Energy Crisis* (rev. ed., 1978), is a useful explanation of the oil shortages of the mid-1970s. The consumer movement, which cast doubt on the quality of American production, began with Ralph Nader's exposé of the auto industry, *Unsafe at Any Speed* (1965). An excellent and thorough description of the bureaucratic tangles that aggravated the crisis at Three Mile Island is Daniel Ford, *Three Mile Island* (1982).

THE SEVENTIES

The 1970s was a complex period in which economic issues, problems of political leadership, and foreign relations assumed critical importance. An excellent account of the interrelationship of these problems is Richard Kirkendall, *A Global Power: America Since the Age of Roosevelt* (2nd ed., 1980). Gaddis Smith, *Morality, Reason, and Power: American Diplomacy in the Carter Years* (1986), is a very good description of this complex foreign policy. Richard J. Barnet, in his essay *The Lean Years: Politics in the Age of Scarcity* (1980), examines the impact of diminished productivity and scarcity of resources on the politics of the 1970s. Jonathan Schell's very readable *The Time of*

Illusion (1976) stresses the impact of the Vietnam War on American society.

THREE PRESIDENTS

As in the previous decade, there was a rapid turnover of presidents and administrations during the 1970s. Nonetheless, the central figure of the decade was Richard M. Nixon. An excellent place to begin further reading about Nixon is his own *Memoirs of Richard Nixon* (1978). Fawn Brodie, in her controversial *Richard Nixon: The Shaping of His Character* (1981), suggests psychological explanations for the president's complex and sometimes quixotic behavior. Patrick J. Buchanan, in *The New Majority: President Nixon at Mid-Passage* (1973), outlines the basis of a new conservative electoral majority inspired by Nixon. Stephen E. Ambrose, *Nixon* (1987), is a fascinating, major biography of the early career of the former president. Of several books on Watergate, the most intriguing remains the account by the two *Washington Post* reporters who uncovered much of the story: Carl Bernstein and Bob Woodward, *All the President's Men* (1974). On the interim presidency of Gerald Ford, John Osborne, *White House Watch: The Ford Years* (1977), is one of the best works. Henry Kissinger, secretary of state under Nixon and Ford, offers interesting insights in *Years of Upheaval* (1982). Jimmy Carter, *Keeping Faith* (1982), is a readable, if self-justifying, appraisal of his one-term presidency. Carter's last hectic year of administration is well documented in the very readable *Crisis: The Last Year of the Carter Presidency* (1982) by administration insider Hamilton Jordan.

THE EPISODE: *Early in 1986 a baby was born in New Jersey. Before she was a year old she had become famous, under a name given her by a judge. "Baby M" was the daughter of a married man and a woman who had been hired to conceive the man's child by artificial insemination and then to turn it over to him and his wife after delivery. But the man and the "surrogate mother" came to fight over who really was entitled to the baby, and their dispute achieved national attention that divided and disturbed the American people.*

Public opinion hinged on the way people saw the nature of the contract that brought Baby M into being. The key questions were these: Had her natural mother sold her services? Or was she selling the baby itself? At the beginning of the trial, most people probably framed the issue in terms of the first question, and for that reason a majority were ready to accept the legality of the contract. But by the trial's end, many people had come to sense that the second answer might be the true one—and they found this prospect disturbing.

THE HISTORICAL SETTING: *The fight over Baby M occurred on a stage of intense moral and political drama in the 1980s. A personal, intimate story became, for a time, the property of politicians and the mass media. The expansion of the mass media into a larger place in daily life was one of the significant marks of the postwar world. Television and tabloid journals dared, with little hesitation,* *intrude where historically they had once feared to tread.*

More important, a broad shift in the style and content of American politics gained strength from such events. Some observers claimed that America was being swept by a wave of Puritanism. But the pivotal place of moral issues in politics had a more complex explanation. During the 1980s—centered around, but not confined to, the presidency of Ronald Reagan—a new political coalition emerged. Traditional Republican conservatives were joined by millions of Americans reacting to very troubling events. To them, moral issues appeared more important than the continuation of politics as usual. Many of these voters were troubled by threatened or real status changes among such groups as African Americans or women.

The American family was changing. With increases in divorce and remarriage, illegitimate children, single-parent families, and nonmarital cohabitation arrangements, as well as legalized abortions, many Americans concluded that social morality was rapidly declining. Finally, there was a growing fear that American economic policy was inadequate.

The major conservative political movements of the day, led by Ronald Reagan, appealed to this constituency by promising a return to unregulated capitalism and a much more regulated moral and social order.

THE CASE OF "BABY M": PRIVATE LIVES AND PUBLIC MORALS

Dear Friends:

We welcome you to The Infertility Center of New York. We know this is an emotional step for you—but one that is filled with new hope. The Center provides professional assistance for prospective parents who are seeking a realistic alternative to being childless. . . . No one who hasn't had the experience can presume to understand the agony of the long and frustrating search for fertility.

We believe it is every couple's right to experience the fulfillment, joy and challenge of parenthood. The Infertility Center offers childless couples a practical alternative— surrogate parenting. The advantages are clear: the husband is the biological father, the couple is involved in selecting the surrogate mother-to-be, and there is no prolonged waiting period.

We are anxious to help you. Please contact us.

These were the reassuring opening words of an advertising brochure issued by The Infertility Center of New York. But the actual process of "surrogate parenting" was rather something that many people would find a little disturbing, even to picture: sex without sexual intercourse, sex for money—but not for pleasure. Sex not in a bed or on some bearskin rug, but at a sperm bank, performed by a man and a woman who did not even meet for the act.

This is how it was done: In a small room, alone, the man masturbated, ejaculating into a receptacle provided for the purpose. His semen was stored. Later, when the woman ovulated, it was her turn to visit the sperm bank. She lay down on a table, her feet in a pair of stirrups. Using a medical instrument, a physician released a small portion of the stored sperm into the woman's vagina. The woman went home and waited to see if she had become pregnant. If not, she came back to the sperm bank each month until the procedure worked.

The crucial link between the advertisement and the act was a legal contract, arranged through a surrogacy center. The man and the woman would have signed a contract in which the woman agreed to bear the man's child but to give it up immediately after birth and to surrender all parental rights. In return for her services, she would receive a fee from the man—typically $10,000 plus expenses. The agency would also receive a fee for its services—typically an additional $10,000. All in all, counting expenses, the arrangement would cost the man about $25,000.

Surrogate motherhood was a sign of changing times. Unknown in America before the mid-1970s, by the mid-1980s at least 500 contracts had been fulfilled, with the number steadily increasing. There were several reasons. One couple in ten was not able to have children at all. More and more married couples were choosing to delay having children, only to discover that they had waited too long and could not produce offspring. Traditionally, such couples had only one recourse: adopting some-one else's child. But adoption was itself becoming more difficult, and the waiting period was often as long as five years. At the very time that demand was rising, fewer and fewer children appeared to be available for adoption, because of other changes during the 1970s and 1980s. These included women's access to birth control and legal abortion, and a moral climate that was making it much easier for unmarried mothers to choose to keep their babies.

So in the 1980s, surrogacy agencies were set up, and by 1985 the largest of them, The Infertility Center of New York, was arranging about six conceptions each month. As the brochure noted, surrogacy was much faster than adoption, and also closer to "real" genetic parenthood. And it seemed to pose few ethical problems. If it was legitimate for a man to sell his sperm, then why should not a woman be allowed to "rent" her womb? Anyway, if the practice was banned, most people thought, it would simply move underground, or else to places like Puerto Rico, where women had once gone to have abortions before they became legal in 1973.

And so by 1984, surrogate childbearing had quietly taken its place among the publicly acknowledged sexual practices of Americans. In some ways, it was just a small part of an astonishing revolution in which millions of people suddenly came into the open with things that had once been hidden behind clothing, behind closed doors, underground, or "in the closet": nonmarital sex, abortion, homosexuality, por-nography, birth control.

This was the setting for surrogacy. And this was the setting for the conception and birth of the little girl who became known as "Baby M." Eventually, this child became the center of a remarkable trial that riveted the attention of many millions of people. But when she was conceived, nothing seemed unusual. After all, as the man who arranged for the birth of Baby M put it, "You are not going to stop the drive of an infertile couple to have a genetically related child."

William Stern and his wife Elizabeth were a couple with this strong drive. Bill Stern was a child of the Holocaust, a Jew born in Berlin, the capital of Hitler's Third Reich, only a year after the end of World War II. His father had once been a banker, but had been forced to go into hiding from the Nazis. Somehow, he and his wife managed to survive, the only members of either of their families to live through the war. Soon after Bill's birth in 1946, the family migrated to the United States. They settled in Pittsburgh, where his parents found menial jobs—his father as a short-order cook and his mother working in a window factory. Bill was their only child. Genetically speaking, he was the end of the family's line. He would later say that he felt "com-pelled" to see his "genes" continued.

Education came first, though—and a lot of it. Stern stayed in school until he was twenty-eight. Then, in 1974, he received his Ph.D. in biochemistry. He married the woman he had been dating for five years. She also received a Ph.D. the same year, in human genetics. But Betsy Stern soon decided that she wanted to become a physician, not a geneticist. The Sterns were a caring couple, supportive of each other's needs, and so, like many couples in their position, they decided to delay having a baby until Besty had completed her medical training, seven years later. She would be thirty-five years old.

Then health intervened. At about the time Betsy Stern was finishing medical school, she began to experience some worrisome symptoms—blurred vision and a numbness in her toes and legs. She diagnosed these symptoms as the early signs of a dread disease, multiple sclerosis. And while the symptoms soon faded and did not recur, she was fearful, and her concerns intensified when she learned that getting pregnant might bring her symptoms back. However much they had looked forward to having a baby, the Sterns now decided that pregnancy was simply not worth the risk. Adoption was one alternative, but the Sterns rejected it, since an adopted baby would not carry on Bill's genes, and it was likely to take four or five years, anyway. Surrogacy seemed the perfect solution. It would be fast, and it would continue *his* family line without risking *her* life.

In the fall of 1984 the Sterns sent for a brochure from The Infertility Center of New York. By December they had signed an agreement with the center giving them the right to look through the files of the women who had offered their services as surrogates. They soon decided on a likely prospect, a twenty-eight-year-old married woman with two children of her own. The woman's name was Mary Beth Whitehead, and like the Sterns, she lived in New Jersey, within easy driving distance of their own house.

First, the Sterns wanted to see what the Whiteheads were like. In January 1985 the two couples arranged to meet at a restaurant halfway between their two houses. The meeting went well, and Mary Beth Whitehead seemed eager to come to terms on the spot. But the Sterns needed to be sure she would not change her mind and decide she wanted to keep the baby. Whitehead assured the Sterns on that point: "She had no interest in keeping a baby. . . . She said she would not come to our doorstep. All she wanted from us was a photograph each year and a little letter on what transpired that year." The Sterns were delighted. As William Stern later recalled: "We got back to the car, kissed each other, and said, 'This is perfect.' She was the perfect person. We didn't want to give her up. She was too good to be true."

That February, Mary Beth Whitehead signed a contract agreeing to be insemi-nated by William Stern, and to give up her rights to the baby she would deliver. It took Whitehead four months, four trips to the sperm bank, to get pregnant; she conceived in late June. The pregnancy went well. Tests revealed that the fetus seemed healthy, and that it would be a girl. The two couples sometimes got together socially, joined by the Whiteheads' own children, Ryan and Tuesday, and were soon on a first-name basis. Meanwhile, the Sterns prepared their house for the new arrival: The baby would have a second-floor bedroom, newly decorated in wallpaper with teddy bear patterns. The Sterns even had the baby's name picked out. They would call her Melissa. On March 27, 1986, in a hospital in Long Branch, New Jersey, she was born.

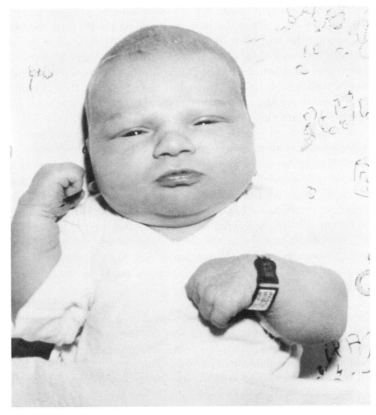

Baby M. This official hospital photograph was taken within a few hours of the baby's birth—a standard procedure designed as a form of identification to ensure that one baby was not mistakenly exchanged for another by the hospital and given to the wrong mother. (The plastic band on Baby M's left wrist was used for the same purpose.) Unfortunately, the problem of Baby M's correct "identity," and that of her parents, could not be solved by anything as simple as a wristband or a photograph. (Ricki Rosen/The Picture Group)

It is hard to know just when Mary Beth Whitehead began to have second thoughts. Almost a year before she met the Sterns, a psychological profile prepared by the Infertility Center reported that she was likely to have "strong feelings against giving up" a baby. (The Sterns were not shown this profile.) Richard Whitehead, Mary Beth's husband, said he knew that "toward the end of the pregnancy, she was getting very attached. I knew she was getting torn." But Mary Beth Whitehead herself insisted that it was only after she delivered the baby that she changed her mind: "At the end, something took over. It overpowered me. I had no control." Moments after the birth, the obstetrician placed the baby on Whitehead's stomach. Within five minutes she was breast-feeding. The doctor would remember that "she was crying a lot," and that "she felt the baby looked exactly like her." He did not know that Mary Beth Whitehead had arranged to give up the baby. In fact, on the birth certificate she had given it a name of her own choosing, Sara Elizabeth. The birth certificate also said that the baby's father was her own husband, Richard Whitehead.

The Sterns quickly sensed that there was trouble, but the baby was two days old before Mary Beth Whitehead confirmed their fears: "She said she didn't know if 'I could go through with it,'" Elizabeth Stern later remembered; "I felt this pit in my stomach." A day later, the Whiteheads took the baby home with them. The situation was utterly confused.

The next day, March 30, was Easter Sunday. The Sterns drove to the Whitehead house in Brick Township to get their baby. They knew that Mary Beth had not actually reneged on the deal; she had only said she was having second thoughts. Whitehead was uncertain of her own intentions: "I didn't want to give her to them, but I felt an obligation to them also." She was sobbing when the Sterns arrived at her house. William Stern recalled: "It was an unbelievable situation. I really didn't know what to do. I don't think anybody would have known what to do." But after about two hours, the Sterns prevailed and took the baby home with them. It was late afternoon. As soon as they had left, Richard Whitehead later said, his wife "broke down. She was crying hysterically. She couldn't believe what she had done. She said, 'Oh, my God, what have I done?'" Mary Beth Whitehead herself put it this way: "I just sobbed for hours and hours and hours. It was like somebody had cut off my arm."

A few hours later, Whitehead phoned the Sterns and told them "she didn't know if she could live anymore." That night, according to her husband, she kept waking up "crying and screaming." Things got so bad that Richard Whitehead talked about leaving the house. But eventually, in desperation, he said simply: "Let's go get the baby."

At 7:30 the next morning Mary Beth Whitehead again phoned the Sterns. She asked to come by. She and Rick arrived sometime before noon at the Sterns' house in Tenafly. Her behavior during this visit was something the Sterns would soon come to recognize. First, she told them how she had "woken up screaming in the middle of the night," and added that her husband was threatening to leave her. Then she repeated her suicide threat, how she had considered "taking a bottle of Valium." But over and over, what Mary Beth Whitehead kept telling the Sterns was that only one thing would help: Let her take the baby. Not forever, she added quickly—just for a few days. "I just want her for a week and I'll be out of your lives forever."

The Sterns did their best to calm her down, but they were also moved. Elizabeth Stern said later: "Bill was crying, I was crying, Mary Beth was crying." Finally, the Sterns gave in and let the Whiteheads leave with the baby. William Stern explained the decision this way: "We thought she was suicidal. She said she couldn't live without the baby." Elizabeth Stern put it like this: "She'd done this wonderful thing for us, and we couldn't have lived with ourselves if she went home and did something to herself."

As the Whiteheads left, Betsy gave Mary Beth some of the baby's things to take along, and Bill spoke to her with sympathy as she got to the front door: "He told me something nice I had done," Mary Beth Whitehead recalled. "He shared with me the death of his father and his mother. He told me I would get over the feeling of loss and that if I gave it time I'd be OK."

What Mary Beth Whitehead actually did with the baby was to go into hiding. She took a plane to Florida, staying with her parents. The days wore on. Every time Bill Stern phoned for news, it was Rick Whitehead who answered the phone, and it was plain that he was stalling. Finally, after almost two weeks, Mary Beth came back to New Jersey and gave the Sterns the news they had come to dread. She would not let them have the baby—not then, not ever.

Feeling manipulated and betrayed, William Stern finally took action. He consulted a lawyer, and within a few weeks he and his wife received a judge's order granting them temporary custody. On Monday, May 5—the baby was now five weeks old—the Sterns arrived at the Whitehead house. This time their compassion for Mary Beth had withered. They were accompanied by five policemen, who handed the Whiteheads an official document ordering that "Melissa" be handed over to the Sterns. But Mary Beth was prepared. She insisted that there was no baby named Melissa in the house. Standing in the living room, Richard Whitehead showed the police the birth certificate, on which the baby was listed not as "Melissa" at all but as "Sara"— the name Mary Beth had given her in the hospital. The policemen did not know what to do. In the confusion, Mary Beth went to a rear bedroom and passed the baby through the window to her husband, who was waiting outside. Eventually, the policemen went away.

The next day Mary Beth Whitehead once again fled to Florida with the baby, this time accompanied by her husband and the two other children. She was now a fugitive, in violation of a court order, and she was prepared to hide as long as necessary. Some of the time she stayed at her parents' house, but she knew that it was one of the first places the authorities would come looking. So she was mostly on the road with the baby, moving from one motel to another, never telling anybody who she was or why she was there, always trying to avoid the police or the detectives she knew would be coming for her and her child.

By July, after two months as a fugitive, Mary Beth Whitehead was getting desperate. She was out of money. Her husband had left his job when the family went to Florida. Even more serious, she had lost control of her remaining financial resources. In the effort to force her out of hiding, the Sterns had managed to get all her assets legally frozen. That meant she could not sell her house, or even withdraw money from her New Jersey bank account.

On Monday, July 15, Mary Beth Whitehead made a risky and dramatic gesture. She phoned Bill Stern at his office. Her purpose was to persuade him to give up his pursuit of her—or, at the very least to call off the freeze on her assets. They talked for forty-five emotional minutes. What she did not know was that he was recording every word, and that the conversation would eventually be published in newspapers and magazines around the country.

Her tactics included a plea—and a threat. The plea was simple. The baby was now more than three and a half months old, and she had come to know and to need the mother with whom she had spent almost all her life:

> Who do you think she's going to want more? Her own mother? And I've been breast-feeding her for four months. Don't you think she's bonded to me? . . . Bill, she knows my smell, she knows who I am. You cannot deny that. . . . She's bonded to me, Bill. She won't even sleep by herself. You tell me, what are you going to do when you get this kid screaming and carrying on for her mother?

The threat was simple, too. It was of suicide—and murder. Yes, Whitehead told Stern, he had been able to take away her property: "You took my house. I mean, we don't even have a car anymore. I can't even afford the car payments. You took everything away from me." It was true, too, that Stern had the law on his side, and that she herself was a fugitive. "I'm telling you right now, Bill, you think you got all the cards. You think you could do this to people." But there was one card Stern did not hold: He did not have the baby. It was Whitehead who had her, and as long as she did, she could do whatever she wanted. First, she asked him ambiguously whether "me and Sara should just vanish off the face of the earth?" When Stern said, "I want my daughter back," Whitehead responded with ominous words: "Well, Bill, how about if there's no daughter to get back?" And a little later she said simply: "I'd rather see me and her dead before you get her."

Later came this exchange:

WHITEHEAD: I gave her life, I can take it away. If that's what you want, that's what I'll do.
STERN [*frantic*]: Mary Beth, no! Mary Beth, wait!
WHITEHEAD: That's what I'm going to do, Bill.
STERN: Please . . .
WHITEHEAD: You've pushed me.

Stern did not panic at this threat, but he did concede one point. When he told Whitehead, "I don't want to see my daughter hurt," she rejoined: "My daughter, too. Why don't you quit doing that, Bill, OK?"

STERN: OK, OK. All right.
WHITEHEAD: It's *our* daughter. Why don't you say it, *our* daughter?
STERN: All right, our daughter. OK, Mary Beth, our daughter.
WHITEHEAD: That's right.
STERN: OK, Mary Beth, our daughter. . . .
WHITEHEAD: Why do you keep on saying 'my, my, my, my'? She's mine, too.
STERN: OK, Mary Beth, OK. She's our daughter.

The next day, Whitehead called Stern again. (Once again, he recorded the call.) This time she made a different threat, even more bizarre than the first: She would tell the judge in New Jersey about an occasion—in the happier days when the two families got together socially—when Stern had tried to sexually molest the Whitehead's eleven-year-old daughter. (Whitehead was simply making up this episode. Months later, she would admit as much. She made the threat because, as she put it flatly, "It was the last low blow I could think of.")

Actually, Mary Beth Whitehead was at the end of her rope. Less than two weeks after making the threatening pair of phone calls, suffering from exhaustion and a urinary tract infection, she entered a Florida hospital, leaving the baby behind at her parents' house. So it was there, on the last day of July, that the Sterns' private detectives found the baby and took her back to New Jersey. "Baby M," as she was now officially called, was four months old. Whitehead would not see her for another five weeks— and then for only a few hours each week, under strictly supervised conditions that resembled prison visits: The visits were held in a home for "wayward" youths, and in the presence of an armed guard. The rest of the time, the baby stayed with the Sterns.

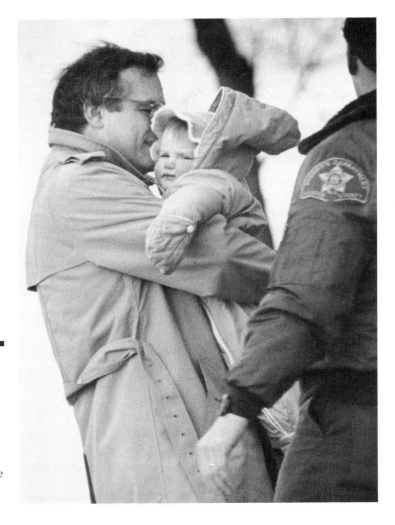

Baby M during the trial. After September, 1986, Mary Beth Whitehead was permitted to visit Baby M for only a few hours each week, in the presence of a uniformed guard. Here, in the midst of the trial, William Stern has just picked up Baby M after one of those visits and is about to return her to the Sterns' house, where she stayed the rest of the time. (UPI/ Bettmann Newsphotos)

By the time the case of Baby M came to trial early the following January, her plight was becoming well known to the public through coverage in the press and on television. As a "human interest" story, the case was irresistible. The only problem lay in how to interpret it. The dilemma was this: Who was trying to take whose baby?

Many people found it easy to identify with the Sterns, and to think that the couple had behaved reasonably and even generously. Mary Beth Whitehead, on the other hand, had lied about her intentions, kidnapped the baby, and even threatened to kill her. Above all, from a legal point of view, she had broken a *contract*. Whitehead had agreed in writing that she was not the real mother, but only a substitute (or "surrogate") for the real mother. (As one expert would put it at the trial, she was a "surrogate uterus.") The people who held this position argued, in effect, that Whitehead had rented the use of her womb to the Sterns, just as a man might sell his sperm to a woman who wished to conceive by means of artificial insemination. If

Whitehead could now claim that the baby was really hers, then what was to prevent a sperm donor from demanding parental rights over an artificially conceived child?

For people who were sympathetic to the Sterns' position, the implications of this argument reached even further. What was to prevent a group of workers in an automobile factory, for example, from claiming ownership of a car they had been hired to produce on the assembly line—and then driving off with it? After all, in both the case of the auto worker and that of the surrogate mother, one party to the contract had provided the raw materials, while the other party had actually performed the "labor." Yet most Americans deeply respected such free labor contracts and believed them to be at the heart of the system of free enterprise. Few would have felt that the auto worker was entitled to drive off with the manufacturer's car. What, they could ask, entitled Mary Beth Whitehead to keep the Sterns' baby? For those people who believed that Whitehead had signed a normal contract to perform a "service," there could be only one answer: The baby was not hers.

But there *was* one thing that seemed to make a difference between Whitehead and the auto worker. Auto workers generally did not fall in love with the cars they made—but mothers did fall in love with their babies, contract or no contract.

One way of understanding the fascination generated by the Baby M case is to see how it brought into conflict two of the most deeply held values in American culture: the special sanctity of contracts and the special sanctity of family life. The two concepts had rarely come into such direct conflict before. Contracts had belonged to a public realm of business and paid work that involved mostly men. Family life had belonged to a private realm of unpaid work in which women played the central role. But all this was changing in the 1970s and 1980s. More and more women were entering the public world of paid work, and men were taking a more and more active part in the private world of the family. And now, it seemed, even motherhood might become a business. The story of Baby M seemed to bring to the surface the deep contradictions involved in that change. As one commentator put it, women who "fall in love with their babies" have "no business" becoming surrogates—"no business at all."

One way to avoid at least some of these contradictions was to try to maintain at all costs the old distinction between contract and family life, between business and motherhood. The attempt to maintain these traditional distinctions took several forms. Some people—especially conservative Roman Catholics and Orthodox Jews—argued that *any* "artificial" interference with "natural" sexual reproduction was wrong: surrogacy, artificial insemination, abortion, or even most forms of birth control.

Other people (and also many Catholics as well) took another tack. They argued that because surrogate mothers received money for giving up the babies they bore, surrogacy amounted to nothing less than baby selling. As one psychiatrist put it, "You can't sell babies." Responding to this argument, surrogacy advocates insisted that the surrogates were not selling babies, but only the *services* they provided by carrying the babies—a womb rental fee, in effect. The lawyer who had arranged the birth of Baby M made an additional claim: "I can say that most of the volunteers who want to be surrogates don't do it for the money aspect but because they wish to share the gift of a child with a childless couple." (Whitehead's own actions seemed to confirm the lawyer's point: She had refused to accept a penny of her $10,000 fee. But the lawyer was wrong. Almost all the women who had agreed to be surrogate mothers said they would not have done it without receiving their payment.)

The argument that surrogacy amounted to baby selling was a powerful one to many people. As word of the Baby M case spread through the United States, politicians in many state legislatures introduced bills that would effectively ban surrogacy by prohibiting would-be surrogates from receiving any significant payment for their services. The sponsor of one such bill defended it by saying: "This [bill] recognizes that surrogate parenthood is not a business deal. I don't think we should be doing things that encourage surrogate motherhood as the newest cottage industry."

But underlying this argument lay an even deeper concern. It was the fear that if surrogacy was left unchecked, many couples would soon come to use it for the sake of *convenience* rather than *necessity*—not because they were incapable of having their own children, but because, for one reason or another, they did not wish to do so. For the people who had such fears, it was one thing for truly infertile couples to employ surrogate mothers, but it would be quite another for women who feared that pregnancy would interrupt their careers or spoil their "looks."

This anxiety was rarely expressed in public, but it had deep roots among tradition-minded Americans who were distressed at the new freedom many women suddenly seemed to be exercising—the freedom not to marry, or to combine marriage with an ongoing commitment to a career, or to retain their "single-girl" sexual identity after marriage (by not having children at all, or by looking and acting as if they had none). It was the power to control the reproductive use of their own bodies that permitted women to exercise this freedom. For many people who would have called themselves conservatives, the prospect of surrogacy for the sake of convenience—much like the prospect of abortion for convenience—seemed to symbolize and encourage everything that was going wrong with American society.

Nobody was willing to suggest in public that the Sterns themselves had acted out of convenience. The fact that William Stern's family had been killed off in the Nazi genocide made it easy to appreciate his special desire for a biologically related child. Similarly, his wife's fear that she was suffering from multiple sclerosis made it easy to understand her reluctance to become pregnant.

But there were some things that could cause anyone who was suspicious of surrogacy to be suspicious of the Sterns. It came out that the Sterns had decided not to have a child years earlier—well before Elizabeth Stern had her self-diagnosis confirmed by another physician. (In fact, the disease—a mild case in any event—was not diagnosed by anyone except Betsy Stern herself until after the beginning of the dispute over Baby M.) Also, there was no clear medical evidence that pregnancy would have aggravated the illness.

To those who feared that surrogacy might become a matter of mere convenience, these small points were unsettling. What if Betsy Stern's real concern had been only that a pregnancy might damage her career? How, a critic of surrogacy could ask, did *that* square with William Stern's professed wish to reproduce his genes?

To someone already inclined to be skeptical, there was an obvious and disturbing explanation. It would have run this way: The Sterns had postponed having a child in order to allow Betsy Stern to establish herself in a career. To begin with, there had been a long, five-year engagement while she earned her Ph.D. Then had come another seven-year delay while she completed medical training. The multiple sclerosis seemed to have had no serious effect on her life. It had not prevented her from completing

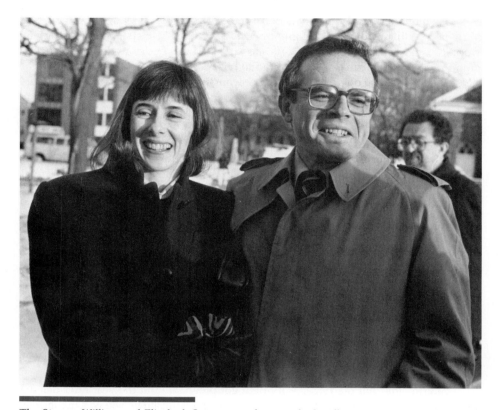

The Sterns. William and Elizabeth Stern were photographed walking arm in arm as they arrived at the Bergen County, N.J., courthouse for their first day of testimony, January 6, 1987. Despite the tension they must have been experiencing, both the Sterns managed to flash engaging smiles for this waiting newspaper photographer. (UPI/Bettmann Newsphotos)

her medical studies, or from winning and working at a coveted full-time position as professor of pediatrics at the Albert Einstein College of Medicine in New York. By the time Baby M was born, Betsy Stern was earning $48,000 a year. If she had gotten pregnant, she would have had to take at least a short maternity leave from her professorship. And even after she returned to work, the memory of her pregnancy would cause her colleagues to think of her as a mother instead of as a professional colleague. So, at least, a skeptical critic might reason.

From Betsy Stern's point of view—a point of view many other people shared—such suspicions were misguided and irrelevant. It was true that she cared about her career—she planned to continue working full-time after the child's birth. But what was wrong with that? Was it really fair for women to surrender their professional aspirations simply because they had children? Men were not obliged to do that. And what did it matter if William Stern had always wanted a child and Elizabeth Stern was unwilling to bear it? Was not surrogacy an ideal strategy—one that resolved their dilemma and satisfied the primary wishes of each of them?

As matters turned out, Betsy Stern did not continue working full-time. After Mary Beth Whitehead began to fight for custody of Baby M, Betsy Stern reduced her work load to twenty hours a week. As she explained this decision during the trial, "I didn't realize how much time is required to raise a child."

Mary Beth Whitehead was the kind of woman who thought that mothers should not hold full-time jobs. When she learned, seven months into her pregnancy, about Betsy Stern's plans, she got upset: "I didn't like the idea of Sara in the care of a baby-sitter. I thought Betsy wanted to be a *mother*."

This disagreement about whether mothers ought to "work" was only one of the many things that divided Mary Beth Whitehead and Elizabeth Stern, and the White-heads and the Sterns as couples. In 1972, when the Sterns were in their mid-twenties and still in graduate school, fifteen-year-old Mary Beth Messer decided to drop out of high school at the end of her sophomore year. Her father was a schoolteacher himself, and he was angry about her decision. But Mary Beth never enjoyed school, and she wanted to earn some money for herself.

She got a job working at a delicatessen owned by her brother, and, later on, another job at a local pizzeria. Early in 1973 she met a young man eight years her senior, and in December of that year, when she was sixteen, the two were married. Rick Whitehead was a policeman's son, who had been drafted soon after graduating from high school and sent to Vietnam, where he saw combat in the Mekong Delta. He was a pleasant and unaggressive young man, but without any of the skills that would allow him to get ahead in 1970s America. And after his return to the United States, he was injured in an accident that blinded him in one eye. Futhermore, like many other Vietnam veterans, Rick Whitehead developed a drinking problem.

Shortly after her marriage, Mary Beth got pregnant, and the year after her son was born she got pregnant again. Before her nineteenth birthday, she was the mother of two young children and had quit her job in order to be with them. (Betsy Stern was thirty at the same time, and still near the beginning of her medical studies.) Rick Whitehead was eking out enough money in his job driving a truck for a local construction company to keep the young family afloat.

The Whiteheads' precarious life took an ominous turn at the end of 1978. Rick's drinking problem had gotten worse. One day he fell asleep while driving and his car crashed into three telephone poles. He was convicted of drunk driving and lost his license—and, with it, his job. Mary Beth was now forced to be the sole support of the family. Once again she looked for a job, and found one as a barroom dancer and bartender. (The bar was owned by one of her sisters, just as the delicatessen in which she had worked years earlier was owned by her brother. She had six siblings in all, and most lived in the general area.) Speaking afterward about this job, Mary Beth Whitehead insisted: "I never did anything to embarrass my husband or my children."

Rick Whitehead joined Alcoholics Anonymous and abstained from alcohol for about a year. But when Mary Beth found him drinking again, she was furious. The couple had a shoving match, and she even had him arrested. Then Rick was convicted a second time of drunk driving. The marriage was on the rocks, and the couple separated for about half a year. But they had a reconciliation and moved back together again. Mary Beth Whitehead was twenty-two years old.

The Whiteheads. Mary Beth and Richard Whitehead are pictured here with their daughter Tuesday (age 10) and son Ryan (age 11, wearing a New York Mets baseball cap and a shirt with an alligator logo). Mary Beth Whitehead was proud that she chose the clothing that her children would wear each day. To complete this portrait of her family, Whitehead holds the hospital photograph of newborn Baby M (her "Sara"). (S. Tell/SYGMA)

During these years the Whiteheads were living on the edge of poverty. They had never been able to buy a house of their own. Because the late 1970s and early 1980s was a period of high inflation, they were forced to move from one rented house to another, from one blue-collar town to another along the New Jersey shore, as rents went up faster than their ability to pay. By 1981 they had moved at least twelve times, sometimes living in the houses of other family members.

Rick Whitehead held seven different jobs in the course of the marriage, and he was sometimes unemployed. Mary Beth supplemented the family's meager income by working in a series of temporary, part-time jobs: cleaning houses, working at coat-check counters in restaurants, selling ski equipment during the Christmas season in a department store. Through it all, she was unwilling to take a full-time job, even though that would have brought in substantially more money. Doing so would have taken her away from her two children when they came home from school each day. "I wanted to be home with them," she insisted. "I felt that was more important than making money."

Mary Beth Whitehead's priorities, combined with the economic recession of the early 1980s and with her husband's ongoing difficulty with alcohol, proved too much for the family's precarious finances. The Whiteheads had gone deeply into debt. In 1983 they filed for bankruptcy.

One day late that winter, as Mary Beth Whitehead was scanning the classified ads in a local newspaper, trying as always to find some new source of additional money, she read the following notice:

> SURROGATE MOTHER WANTED. Couple unable to have child willing to pay $10,000.00 fee and expenses to woman to carry husband's child. Conception by artificial insemination. All replies strictly confidential.

Ten thousand dollars! It seemed like some television game show. For years, Mary Beth Whitehead had been constantly buffeted by the conflict between money and motherhood, between her urgent need for cash and her cherished belief that mothers should not hold full-time jobs. Now, suddenly, she might be able to get the cash—lots of it—without "working" at all. She could get paid for doing the one thing she knew well: having babies. As she said of herself, "I don't have an education. I don't have a skill. The only skill that I know I do well is being a mother." If surrogacy seemed a good solution to the Sterns' problem, for Mary Beth Whitehead it was perfect.

Within a week she had answered the advertisement. (It had not actually been placed by a "couple unable to have child," but by The Infertility Center of New York.) In April 1984, after submitting to a series of interviews and tests, Whitehead was accepted as a candidate for surrogacy. The very next month she was contacted by a married couple who wished to engage her services. Over the next eight months, she was inseminated regularly with the man's sperm, but each time, she failed to conceive, and the couple finally gave up on her in December 1984. Several weeks later, she was contacted by William and Elizabeth Stern. This time things went better.

Her luck had turned. If all went well with the pregnancy, the Whiteheads could count on receiving a check for $10,000 the following March. With this prospect, they might finally be able to settle down in a house of their own. Once again, Mary Beth's siblings came to her assistance. One of her sisters was planning to move out of her own house, and now she and her husband agreed to sell the house to the Whiteheads for $65,000, a price well below its market value. They even offered to lend the Whiteheads $33,000 to help them finance the purchase. As one of the terms of the arrangement, the Whiteheads would repay $8,000 of the loan at the end of March 1986. That was when the baby was due, along with the Sterns' check for $10,000.

Late in 1985 the Whiteheads moved into their new house. It was in a decent neighborhood, a ranch-style house with three bedrooms. All the Whiteheads had to do now was wait for the baby. Then the most elusive piece in the puzzle of their lives—money—would fall into place. They were on their way to security.

There is a simple term that describes many of the differences between the Whiteheads and the Sterns. The term is *class*. When Baby M was born, William Stern was working as a biochemist at a salary of $43,500 a year; Richard Whitehead was a garbage collector, earning $28,500—when he worked. Elizabeth Stern earned $48,000 as a professor of pediatrics; Mary Beth Whitehead was a full-time wife and mother who had no regular income at all. The Sterns were together making $91,500—more than three times the Whiteheads' income.

Closely related to this disparity were differences in education and family structure. Bill Stern was his parents' only child; Mary Beth Whitehead was the sixth of eight children. Both the Sterns continued their schooling into their thirties and received advanced degrees; both the Whiteheads ended theirs in their mid-teens, and only Rick graduated from high school. The Sterns delayed having children until they were forty; Mary Beth Whitehead was the mother of two when she was eighteen.

That is not to say that the Sterns were rich, or that the Whiteheads were impoverished members of some alienated American underclass. Ninety thousand dollars is not all that much money for a couple living in the suburbs of New York City, and the Whiteheads' house in Brick Township did not look all that different from the Sterns' house in Tenafly. For her part, Mary Beth drove a new Honda; for theirs, the Sterns were no doubt paying off medical school debts and a large mortgage. It was possible for the two couples to meet in the restaurant in New Brunswick, to socialize, and to be on a first-name basis—even (as they once did) to cry together. If Mary Beth Whitehead had been a true member of the American underclass, she would almost certainly have been screened out of the surrogate process—if she had ever thought to apply. It might be fair to say that the Sterns were living on the margins of wealth, where they could hope for an even better life, and that the Whiteheads were living on the margins of poverty, always fearful that they would fall through some invisible line that somehow seemed reassuringly to connect them to the world of William and Elizabeth Stern. In truth, both couples (like most Americans) would no doubt have thought of themselves as members of the "middle class." But it was a class with two broad frontiers, one facing toward true wealth and the other toward true poverty. The Sterns lived on one of these frontiers, the Whiteheads on the other.

It was therefore no coincidence that it was William Stern who hired Mary Beth Whitehead as a surrogate, and not Richard Whitehead who hired Elizabeth Stern. Only the Sterns had the financial means with which to pay for a surrogate mother, and only the Whiteheads badly needed the money.

But the class difference between the Whiteheads and the Sterns involved something more than money, or jobs, or education. It also involved power. For example, even though Bill Stern and Mary Beth Whitehead each approached The Infertility Center of New York freely, and as legal equals, it was Stern who had the power to look through the files of surrogate volunteers containing Mary Beth Whitehead's name and telephone number, her personal history, and her photograph. It did not work the other way around. (The Infertility Center's promotional brochure promised that "surrogacy files tell you so much about the women who want to help you. You can see their pictures and read their own descriptions of their lives.") And it was Stern who held the power to select Whitehead from the files and contact her—just as he could have contacted any of the other would-be surrogates whose files he had read. The only thing any of these women could do was to sit and wait for a phone call from whichever stranger decided he liked what he had learned about her background, her attitude, or her looks.

Mary Beth Whitehead was used to being excluded from this kind of power, just as Bill Stern was used to having access to it. From her early years, she had come to feel alienated from the professional people who controlled the institutions she came in contact with. Her characteristic reaction was to fight for her independence by staying away from them. There was the school system, for example. Whitehead had dropped out of school at fifteen, and even when she was herself a parent, she chose to remove her own son from school rather than to follow his teacher's insistence that he be held back in the previous grade. After the birth of Baby M, when the Sterns won temporary custody of the infant, Whitehead responded by simply "kidnapping" her and running to Florida.

It is difficult to imagine William Stern doing what Mary Beth Whitehead did. That is partly because his personal style was so different from hers: calm and methodical rather than high-strung and risk-taking. But it is also because he expected to win the *cooperation* of the same authorities that she saw as her adversaries. That is a difference in class as well as personality. It was experience that helped make Stern personable and easygoing, and helped make Whitehead rebellious and abrasive. He had learned to achieve his goals through understatement; she had learned to assert hers through overstatement. *She* acted impulsively and by manipulating other people's emotions; *he* acted cautiously and by manipulating the structures of American power.

So it was the difference in their social class that had brought the Sterns and the Whiteheads together in the first place. The same class difference had shown itself clearly in the way the conflict between the two families took shape. Now it was another aspect of class—the difference in their expectations and styles of behavior—that would determine the course and outcome of the conflict over Baby M.

The class differences between the Sterns and the Whiteheads had already begun to play an important role in legal matters as early as April 1986, when Mary Beth Whitehead had refused to give up her "Sara." The Sterns' response had been to turn at once to the institutions of power. They made a series of telephone calls, trying to identify the *best* lawyer for their case. They used their professional connections in making these calls: one was to a high official of a national organization, Planned Parenthood Federation of America. The lawyer they had settled on was Gary Skoloff, known in New Jersey legal circles as "Mr. Family Law."

Skoloff accepted their case and went right to work. His first move was to take the case to a judge. What Skoloff needed from the judge was an order granting temporary custody of the baby to the Sterns. Up to now, Mary Beth Whitehead had just as much legal right to the baby as William Stern did (perhaps even a greater right, since Richard Whitehead's name, not Stern's, was listed on the birth certificate as the baby's father). If Stern tried to take the baby from the Whiteheads against their will, *he* could be charged with a crime. But an official custody order would place the power of the state on the Stern's side. Once presented with such an order, it was Mary Beth Whitehead who would become a criminal if she refused to turn the baby over to the Sterns. The word of a judge, and not the mere actions of the principals, would determine who was a criminal and who was a good citizen.

The judge readily granted Skoloff's request and signed the temporary custody order. Ordinarily, there would be a five-day waiting period before such an order went into effect. But Skoloff persuaded the judge to take the unusual step of waiving this waiting period and allowing the order to take effect immediately. It was not for nothing that Gary Skoloff was known as "Mr. Family Law."

When Whitehead violated that court order by taking her baby to Florida, she was acting the way people do for whom lawyers and courts always mean trouble and costs. She had not even consulted a lawyer. And when she telephoned Stern two months later and threatened to kill the baby, she still had no lawyer.

One legal scholar underlined the importance of this difference:

> The Sterns achieved a major legal advantage in the case by getting [temporary] custody in the beginning. They painted her [Whitehead] as unstable. If she had been a middle-class person, she could have gotten a lawyer to call up [before the Sterns arrived on May 5 with the police and a court order] and say, "Don't do anything until I show up."

Stern was fully aware of how he had gained his advantage. In the middle of the dramatic July 15 phone conversation, he even *asked* Whitehead why she had not relied on a lawyer's advice instead of impulsively taking the baby to Florida. In her tearful reply, she showed poignantly that she was more conscious than he of the real social and economic differences between them.

> STERN: You know, you just had to get a lawyer [all you needed to do was to get one], and he would have said to the judge, hey—
> WHITEHEAD [crying hysterically]: With what, Bill? With what, Bill? . . . You hold all the cards, Bill.

In fact, Mary Beth Whitehead *had* tried to hire a lawyer while she was on the run in Florida, but none was willing to take her case without a cash advance. She had no cash to offer, because Stern had frozen all her assets. Under the circumstances, Stern's comment about her getting a lawyer was at best naive. And Whitehead's pained reply came from a true understanding of her plight. The "cards" of power that William Stern held were made of money, and the social habits it supported.

After she returned from Florida, Whitehead finally did manage to hire a lawyer. But he dropped the case after asking for a $5,000 lien on her house. Then she retained a second lawyer, but he, too, dropped the case. Finally, when Baby M had become a national celebrity, a third lawyer entered the case. His name was Harold Cassidy. When Cassidy took the case in December 1986, the trial was scheduled to begin in a mere three weeks. He would have very little time to prepare.

Neither New Jersey nor any other state had laws pertaining to surrogate motherhood. On the one hand, that meant the original contract between the Whiteheads and the Sterns was not *illegal*. But it also meant that the contract was not necessarily *enforceable*. It was not even clear just what kind of law should apply to the case. Was it a matter of contract law? Or a matter of family law? And if it was family law, what kinds of rules should apply? Was it like a contested divorce in which the two parents argued over which one received custody of the children? Or was it closer to an adoption case in which the biological mother changed her mind and felt like keeping the child after all? Those were questions that would soon be decided by legislation in many states, but the judge in the Baby M case was on his own. (The case would be heard by the judge alone, without a jury.)

Judge Harvey Sorkow was in charge of the Bergen County branch of the State Superior Court's Family Division. It was Judge Sorkow who had originally granted the Sterns temporary custody back in May. The fact that the case was being tried in family court probably determined the answer to the first question: The case of Baby M would be treated primarily as a family dispute; the contract issue would be secondary.

The answer to the other question—was this like a contested divorce or an adoption that had gone awry?—would go a long way toward determining the outcome of the trial. In one way, it resembled a divorce case: Baby M was the biological child of both William Stern and Mary Beth Whitehead, and the two "parents" knew each other (though only in a limited way). But it resembled an adoption case even more. The biological mother, after all, had decided before the baby's birth not to keep her baby, and she had arranged the exchange through a special agency. Then, immediately after the baby's birth, she had changed her mind. But it if was adoption law that applied to this case, then permanent custody of Baby M would almost certainly be awarded to Whitehead. The reason was simple: In New Jersey (and almost every other state), the biological mother was entitled to a grace period after the baby's birth in which she could decide to keep her baby after all.

Judge Sorkow ruled that adoption law did *not* apply. The case would be tried like a divorce. Custody of Baby M would be awarded to whichever couple was likely to do the best job of raising her. The sole criterion was the baby's own "best interests." The judge added that "all other concerns . . . constitute commentary."[1]

Gary Skoloff—"Mr. Family Law"—specialized in winning just this sort of case, and he knew very well what his strategy had to be. Skoloff bluntly described the strategy to reporters: "It is my intention to show instability in the Whitehead family. That's what custody litigation is all about."

For his part, Whitehead's lawyer, Harold Cassidy, chose not to pursue such a strategy. His decision may have been based on very practical considerations: Cassidy had only three weeks to prepare his case, not enough time for private detectives to investigate the past lives of the Sterns. But his decision may also have been based on Whitehead's own reluctance to win custody by attacking the Sterns. Whitehead insisted throughout the trial that she did not want her lawyer to use such tactics. As far as Whitehead was concerned, she was entitled to custody for just one, compelling reason: *She was the baby's mother.* When a reporter covering the trial asked her if she could give any reason why Betsy Stern would be an unfit mother, Whitehead replied, "No—other than she's not her mother."

---

[1]The "best interests" doctrine was relatively new. Until the mid-1970s, mothers generally received custody under the doctrine of "tender years," which presumed that mothers were best suited to raise young children. But as custody rulings became more gender-neutral, "tender years" was gradually replaced by the doctrine of "best interests."

But Whitehead and her lawyer were on shaky ground here. For one thing, by 1987, custody disputes were no longer routinely settled in favor of mothers. The feminist movement had persuaded many courts that such routine settlements only reinforced the traditional sex roles that kept women in the home, tied to their children. In any event, the baby herself had now been living with the Sterns for half a year—more than half of her ten months of life. When Whitehead had phoned Stern back in July, she had pleaded with him that the baby needed *her* ("She's bonded to me, Bill!"), but now the tables were turned. It was the Sterns who could, and did, argue that Baby M was now bonded to *them*. William Stern touchingly described the relationship:

> When I come home . . . she starts crawling across the floor as soon as I come in. If I don't pick her up right away, she starts crying. . . . You know, I never understood when friends talked on and on about their kids. It's hard to describe that feeling, but I know now. . . . She looks at every little thing I do. That's the really amazing thing. When I measure out her cereal in the morning—four tablespoons—she watches. When I open the refrigerator door, she tries to stick her head in. If there's a single thing in the middle of the room, she crawls to it. . . . When she grabs my shirt, I feel so special. When she smiles, I see her beaming. It makes me feel very happy. It makes me feel worthwhile. [Going on, in tears and scarcely audible] I always hope people will forget there's a Baby M, and she can be normal like other children.

Betsy Stern made the same point:

> She's the cutest thing around. She's always pulling at the clothes in Bloomingdale's [a fashionable New York department store], trying to get them off the rack. I feel I am Melissa's mother. I've been with her the past six months. I feed her. I bathe her. And I take care of her. Psychologically, I *am* the mother.

Attorney Cassidy was in a bind. He could not attack the Sterns. He could not argue that Baby M was "bonded" to Whitehead. So he was left with only one strategy, and it was defensive. He had to try to convince the judge that the Whitehead household was a good place for a child to grow up. He had Mary Beth describe the family's social activities: sledding, swimming, fishing, digging for shellfish at an ocean beach near their house. Mary Beth and Rick Whitehead always attended their kids' soccer games, and she was enthusiastic when describing how good her husband was with children: "This Halloween he had twenty-five kids trailing behind him. He does all the corny things kids like. I love him with all my heart." Other witnesses testified that the Whitehead children were unfailingly polite and well-groomed. (Mary Beth chose their clothing every day and even blow-dried their hair herself.) One of the Whiteheads' neighbors, a policeman, was apparently expressing the general opinion of people like those who lived in the neighborhood when he said of her, simply, "She's as good a mother as anyone can be."

But on point after point, the Sterns' lawyer was able to cast suspicion on the Whitehead family. For example, when one member of Cassidy's legal team tried to argue that the large Whitehead clan functioned as a "warm" and supportive "extended family," Skoloff was prepared with a rebuttal: His private investigators had discovered that one of Mary Beth's sisters had once been arrested on a bad check charge, and that her brother had pulled a shotgun on his wife during a marital fight. Skoloff also revealed that the sister who had so generously arranged for the Whiteheads to buy their house was now foreclosing the mortgage because the Whiteheads had not paid their debt on schedule.

Skoloff even tried to discredit Whitehead's treatment of her own older children. He brought up the episode in which she removed her son from school, and he disclosed that her daughter had once contracted frostbite when there was no heat in a small house the Whiteheads were renting. And over and over, he brought up the impulsive and even illegal way she had acted in the dispute over Baby M.

Skoloff had prepared his case thoroughly and presented it effectively. But it may have been Judge Harvey Sorkow himself who did the most damage to Whitehead's cause. Back in August, soon after Baby M had been "found" in Florida, the judge had appointed a lawyer, Lorraine Abraham, to represent the baby's own interests. To help her determine Baby M's best interests, Abraham consulted three mental-health experts whose assessments were expected to provide unbiased testimony. All three experts agreed that Mary Beth Whitehead displayed symptoms of emotional "instability" so serious that she should be denied all access to Baby M for at least five years.

One of the experts, Dr. David Brodzinsky, testified that Whitehead suffered from an "immature personality structure." The second expert, Dr. Judith Greif, spoke of "serious deficits" in Whitehead's parental ability. The third expert, Dr. Marshall Schechter (a distinguished professor emeritus of child psychiatry), presented the most damning diagnosis of all. Dr. Schechter had observed Whitehead during one of her two-hour visits with Baby M. As he looked on, the two played a game of "pattycake." When the baby clapped her hands together, Whitehead had responded by calling out "Hooray!" That was inappropriate, Dr. Schechter testified. The proper response would have been the word "pattycake." Schechter also criticized Whitehead for giving Baby M a stuffed panda, when a bowl, a spoon, or some other kitchen utensil would have been more suitable for a child her age.

A careful examination of Whitehead's history, Schechter argued, confirmed that these small mistakes were part of a larger pattern of inadequacy—a pattern of impulsive and self-destructive behavior, unstable personal relationships, suicidal and homicidal gestures, lack of empathy for people, a preoccupation with grooming, a constant craving for novelty, and chronic feelings of "victimization." The doctor concluded that Whitehead was suffering from a mental illness known to psychiatrists as "mixed personality disorder," and he stated that there was "clear and convincing proof that the mental disability which I have described . . . will continue indefinitely regardless of medical treatment."

In an effort to refute this bleak assessment, Harold Cassidy brought to the stand Dr. Donald Klein, the psychiatrist who had actually *written* the textbook chapter about "mixed personality disorders" on which Dr. Schechter had based his diagnosis. Dr. Klein pointed out that "Mrs. Whitehead is in a real fix right now," and he insisted that no diagnosis of personality disorder should ever be made on the basis of the way someone behaves in a time of intense conflict. If she was *feeling* victimized, it was because she was *being* victimized.

When the time came for Judge Sorkow to issue his decision, few people had much doubt what it would be. He had sustained almost every one of Skoloff's objections, and overruled almost every one of Cassidy's. He had refused to permit Cassidy

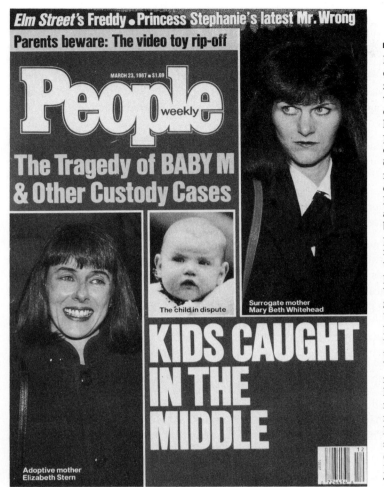

Media coverage. This is how the cover of *People*, a popular magazine, chose to represent the two women contending for possession of Baby M. Mary Beth Whitehead looks suspicious and vindictive, perhaps even somewhat out of control. (Because of the placement of the individual pictures on the magazine cover, she appears to be eyeing Elizabeth Stern and Baby M.) In contrast, Elizabeth Stern appears to be smiling—at the baby—with radiant good will. The photographer almost certainly took many pictures of these two women, and in some of these other pictures Whitehead almost certainly was smiling and Stern looking grim. The editors of *People* decided to use these particular pictures, placing them where they appear on the cover. The editors also chose the language of the captions: Whitehead is labeled the "surrogate mother" (she could as accurately have been dubbed the "natural mother" or the "biological mother"). Media coverage like this helped persuade many people to sympathize with the Sterns. (Reprinted by special permission of PEOPLE Weekly Magazine; © 1987, Time, Inc.)

to introduce important witnesses, and even chided him for being unprepared. On March 31, 1987, Sorkow issued the decision. It held few surprises.

Sorkow determined that living with the Sterns would be in the "best interests" of Baby M. He granted them permanent custody and denied Mary Beth Whitehead all further rights of visitation.

In explaining his decision, the judge berated Whitehead for the way she had coped with the difficult events of her life. He attributed her behavior to some great personal failing, a flaw in her character. Never did he recognize the possibility that her problems were not of her own making, or that she had dealt with them as well as most people in her position might have done. Over and over, Judge Sorkow used a curiously familiar set of adjectives to describe Mary Beth Whitehead: *"dominating,"* *"impulsive,"* *"manipulative,"* *"exploitative,"* and *"self-centered."* The adjectives were familiar because they were the clichés men had used so often, for so many years, to describe women they did not like.

First, Sorkow concluded that Whitehead was too *dominating*: "Mrs. Whitehead dominates the family. Mr. Whitehead is clearly in a subordinate role . . . [and] permits his wife to make most of the important decisions in their family." She was "the controlling parent" of her older children, and she would be likely to dominate Baby M as well. (The judge seemed to be assuming that there was something repugnant about the role Mary Beth Whitehead played in her family, and he never asked what would have happened to it if she had *not* made the "important decisions.")

Second, Whitehead was *impulsive*:

> Mrs. Whitehead is . . . impulsive, especially in crisis circumstances. . . . She doesn't think of the consequences: at age fifteen and a half she drops out of school, she withdraws her son from second grade for what she perceives to be an affront to him without first inquiring of the teacher or principal, she elopes to Florida in direct violation of a court order, without considering the economic and emotional consequences.

(The judge did not ask whether dropping out of school, or having trouble with the authorities, might just be an understandable reaction for people who could expect only second-class jobs and had no hope of getting ahead.)

Third, "clear and convincing proof" had shown her to be *"manipulative* and *exploitative."* The proof consisted of the murder threat she had made during her phone call to William Stern. If this threat was not a real one, it showed that Whitehead was "certainly manipulative." She was even willing to "use her children for her own ends":

> Witness the bringing of her older daughter to court, where the child was terrorized by the crush of media, by her fawning use of the media to her own narcissistic ends.

(The judge raised no question about the way quite normal people behave when they are convinced that all the cards are stacked against them.)

Fourth, Whitehead was *self-centered*. She mistook her own needs for those of her children:

> She exhibits an emotional overinvestment. It was argued . . . that Mrs. Whitehead loved her children too much. This is not necessarily a strength. Too much love can smother a child's independence. Even an infant needs her own space.

Even her love for Baby M was a sign of Whitehead's selfishness:

> Mrs. Whitehead has been found too enmeshed with this infant child and unable to separate her own needs from those of the child. She tends to smother the child with her presence. The court doubts Mrs. Whitehead could or would subordinate herself for the child's benefit.

(The judge never mentioned the fact that he himself had forbidden Whitehead from seeing the child except for a few intense hours each week, nor did he acknowledge how common it was in many American working-class and ethnic families for mothers to "enmesh" themselves in the lives of their children.)

On only one issue did Judge Sorkow treat the difference between the Sterns and the Whiteheads as a difference between the social groups they belonged to. That issue was education, and the judge attributed this contrast to what he called the

Whiteheads' "milieu"—a word taken from the French that meant, roughly, "surroundings," or social "place":

> The Sterns have demonstrated the strong role that education has played in their lives. They both hold doctoral degrees in the sciences. Mrs. Stern is a medical doctor. Mrs. Whitehead dropped out of the tenth grade in high school. Mr. Whitehead graduated high school doing enough, as he said, "to get by." . . . Education plays a subordinate role in the Whiteheads' milieu.

The judge did not even believe Whitehead when she assured him of her willingness to provide Baby M with the good education she herself had failed to get:

> Mrs. Whitehead has interposed herself in her son's education, denying the finding of a professional child study team and rejecting their recommendations. . . . Dr. Metnick, the school psychologist, testified that in seven years only ten parents out of hundreds of students tested have rejected the child study team recommendations.

Finally, Sorkow pointed to the Whiteheads' difficult marriage, "plagued with separations, domestic violence, and severe financial difficulties requiring numerous house moves." (Once more, the judge seemed to assume that the Whiteheads' difficulties were caused by the personal failings of Mary Beth and Richard Whitehead, and not by a "milieu" that would have made millions of woman "unfit" to be mothers.) He contrasted the Whitehead marriage with the Sterns' "strong and mutually supportive" relationship, their "private, quiet and unremarkable life, which augurs well for a stable household environment."

> They have shown an ability to make rational judgments in the face of the most trying emotional circumstances. They have obeyed the law. . . . They have shown no difficulty coping with crisis.

The Sterns themselves had presented their case sympathetically in the courtroom and in interviews with the media. Bill Stern always said the judicious and generous thing. "I feel very bad for *all* of us that what started out as a beautiful experience should end like this." Stern even promised that if the judge awarded custody of Baby M to Whitehead, he would accept the decision so that the baby herself would not become a "ping-pong ball":

> I'd prefer she just not know about me. I'd be an outside force in her life. For her to see me once a month and be told I'm her biological father—I don't think that's doing her any good. I just don't want to be in a position to start wondering, "Who's daddy? Who's mommy?" If I found she wanted to see me, that would be OK. But I don't want to come knocking at her door. I just don't want to intrude on her life.

And when Betsy Stern was asked whether she had been concerned about the ethics of "taking" the baby from Whitehead, she responded by using Judge Sorkow's favorite phrase: "Yes. In a sense I knew it would be very painful, but I was thinking in Melissa's best interests."

Responding to the same question, Mary Beth Whitehead spoke defiantly: "I don't care what they do. I will not surrender my child." She even denied that Stern should be regarded as the baby's father, dismissing him contemptuously as "Mr. Sperm."

It was clear that Judge Sorkow disliked Whitehead and felt comfortable with the Sterns. But his decision was based on something more than a personal reaction. At the heart of his legal logic lay his fundamental belief that everyone had the right to have children, and that this right was so basic that it must be protected from government interference, as an aspect of a general constitutional right to privacy in sexual matters. Sorkow quoted from a 1972 decision of the U.S. Supreme Court that had guaranteed Americans the right to use birth control:

> "If the right of privacy means anything, it is the right of the individual, married or single, to be free of unwarranted governmental intrusion into matters so fundamental affecting a person as the decision whether to bear or beget a child."

The judge went on:

> It must be reasoned that if one has a right to procreate coitally [through sexual intercourse], then one has the right to procreate noncoitally. If it is the reproduction that is protected, then the means of reproduction are also to be protected. The value and interests underlying the creation of family are the same by whatever means obtained.

The traditional recourse of childless couples who wanted to create a family was that of adoption. But Judge Sorkow pointed to the acute "shortage" of what he called "adoptable children." It was this "dearth of adoptable children" that had led to the need for surrogate mothers. To restrict or outlaw surrogacy "would constitute an unconstitutional interference with procreative liberty, since it would prevent childless couples from obtaining the means with which to have families."

Judge Sorkow also addressed another antisurrogacy argument: that surrogacy entailed the exploitation of poor people by more prosperous ones. He acknowledged that some people were arguing that "an elite upper economic group of people will use the lower economic group of woman [sic] to 'make their babies.'" But he found that argument to be "insensitive and offensive to the intense drive to procreate naturally and when that is impossible, to use what lawful means as [sic] possible to gain a child." He pointedly added: "This intense desire to propagate the species is fundamental. It is within the soul of all men and women regardless of economic status."

But Sorkow also used a second argument to deny that surrogacy constituted class exploitation. It was that William Stern and Mary Beth Whitehead had dealt with each other as equals in a free marketplace:

> Here neither party has a superior bargaining position. Each had what the other wanted. A price for the service each was to perform was struck and a bargain reached. One did not force the other. Neither had expertise that left the other at a disadvantage. Neither had disproportionate bargaining power. . . . The bargain here was for totally personal service. It was a very scarce service that Mrs. Whitehead was providing. Indeed, it might even be said she had the dominant bargaining position, for without her Mr. Stern had no other immediate source available. Each party sought the other to fulfill their needs.

Judge Sorkow did not even see surrogacy as a matter of "baby selling" but as the "gift of life" to an infertile couple:

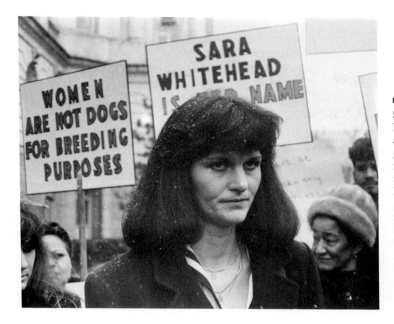

Support for Mary Beth Whitehead. By March 1987, as the Baby M trial approached its end, Whitehead had gained the sympathy of many feminist women (although other feminist women supported the Sterns). In this photograph Whitehead is shown with these supporters, holding placards in front of the courthouse. ("Sara" was the name Whitehead had given to Baby M.) As was so often the case, this photographer chose to capture an image of Whitehead looking grim and unmotherly. (Tannenbaum/ SYGMA)

The Whiteheads have two children. They did not want any more. Theirs was the perfect family, Mrs. Whitehead testified. . . . Mr. Stern wanted progeny, a child. Mrs. Whitehead wanted to give the child she would bear to a childless couple. His sperm fertilized her egg. A child was born.

It was that simple.

Just before Sorkow issued his decision, a public opinion poll indicated that Americans would agree with him by a large margin—three to one. But their opinions varied with their income and education. People without a high school diploma were more likely to favor giving custody to Mary Beth Whitehead than people who had attended college. Those with annual incomes under $15,000 favored Whitehead in far greater proportion than did those with incomes over $50,000.

The case also caused many middle-class Americans who were originally prepared to side with the Sterns to reconsider their views. For some, it was a question of the way the Sterns had handled the problem. If the Sterns were really concerned with the "best interests" of Baby M, why had they put her in a situation in which, *whatever* the outcome, she would inevitably go through childhood under a public spotlight? After all, the Sterns *could* have backed off when Whitehead first let them know she had changed her mind. What William Stern wanted was a genetically related child— but only Mary Beth Whitehead had fallen in love with an actual newborn baby. The Sterns could have returned to the Infertility Center, looked through its files again, and hired another surrogate. Giving in to Whitehead would not have been easy—but perhaps it would have served the baby's best interests.

For other people, there was an even more troubling aspect to Judge Sorkow's decision. At several points he had referred to an "adoptable child shortage," to a "dearth of adoptable children." Everybody knew what he was talking about. But he was incorrect. There were, around the world and in the United States itself, thousands of babies who were available for adoption, babies who otherwise faced lives of extreme poverty, hunger, and disease. Most of these babies, however, were not white babies: They were black or yellow, brown or red. But few white American couples wanted to adopt these babies. Judge Sorkow knew that. When he spoke of a "dearth of adoptable children," what he surely meant was a dearth of adoptable *white* children.[2] If the judge had given the question a moment's thought, he would as surely have realized that his statement—an assumption, really—was, in the most literal sense of the word, racist. And he would have realized that if surrogacy could be justified only on the grounds that adoption was not a practical option for infertile couples, then surrogacy could be justified only with a racist assumption.

～

In July 1987 two groups filed separate but similar briefs opposing surrogate motherhood with the New Jersey Supreme Court, to which the Baby M case was being appealed. There was nothing surprising about the group filing the first brief: It consisted of the Roman Catholic bishops of New Jersey. In their brief, the bishops argued that surrogacy "promotes the exploitation of women and infertile couples and the dehumanization of babies. . . . In short, it trafficks for profit in human lives. . . . To put it bluntly but truthfully, were it not for the fee, Baby M could not have existed at all." Surrogacy puts pressure on poor women to support themselves by selling the use of their bodies. It constitutes "a new form of prostitution."

The second brief was filed by a very different group, a group containing many of the best-known feminist women in the United States. The feminists and the bishops were bitter opponents on many controversial questions (the right to abortion, for instance, against which the Catholic church was waging an aggressive political campaign, but which was a centerpiece of most feminists' ideology). Yet, on *this* issue of reproductive technology, the feminists' position was remarkably similar to that of the bishops. The feminists, too, argued that surrogacy involves "trafficking in human lives, particularly the buying and selling of infants and children." And they argued as well that it leads to the exploitation of poor women. What might have looked like freedom to Mary Beth Whitehead actually amounted to the very degradation identified by the bishops: "She has been dehumanized and has been reduced to a mere 'commodity' in the reproductive marketplace."

There were differences between the two briefs. For example, the bishops emphasized that it was the *babies* who were dehumanized by surrogacy, whereas for the feminists it was the surrogate mothers themselves. And the bishops had reached their position easily; they had been insisting on it all along. For the feminists, on the other hand, the brief was the result of a real struggle. As one admitted, "It was difficult, because for years we have been saying it's wrong to tell women what they can or

---

[2]For their part, many minority people in the U.S. were reluctant to see children of color raised in white households.

After the verdict. Here Mary Beth and Richard Whitehead were photographed with their daughter Tuesday as they left the Bergen County courthouse soon after the verdict was announced by Judge Harvey Sorkow. In explaining his verdict, Judge Sorkow criticized Mary Beth Whitehead for exposing the girl to "the fawning use of the media." (UPI/Bettmann Newsphotos)

can't do with their bodies." Before the Baby M case, most of the opposition to surrogacy had come from conservative people who feared women's new sexual and economic freedom. But now many feminists were beginning to look with suspicion on the new reproductive technologies, and even to defend some of the values associated with traditional family life—for example, the right of a biological mother to her child. The convergence of feminists and conservatives over the Baby M case may have represented an important new development of the mid-1980s.[3]

By the beginning of 1988 the antisurrogacy movement had taken the political offensive. Bills intended to ban or restrict surrogacy had been introduced in the legislatures of nearly half the states as well as in Congress. By the middle of the year, four states had passed laws that prohibited surrogate-mother contracts from being legally enforced, and two others (Michigan and Florida) had actually made it a felony, punishable by years in prison, to arrange a surrogate-mother contract that involved money.

---

[3]Some Catholics and feminists had come together before in the early 1980s, in joint opposition to the sale of pornography.

Back in New Jersey, the state supreme court acted in February 1988 on Mary Beth Whitehead's appeal of the Baby M decision. The court decided unanimously that surrogacy contracts were illegal in the state, and that Whitehead's contract with the Sterns was null and void. The court restored Whitehead's legal status as Baby M's mother and granted her extensive rights to visit with her child. But at the same time the court also allowed the Sterns to retain permanent custody of Baby M. The ambiguity of the court's decision indicates how difficult it was—and continues to be—to bridge the gap between the public world of contract, work, and business and the private world of sex, motherhood, and family.

But by this time, Mary Beth Whitehead had made some important changes in her own life, changes that made her new "victory" (like her original defeat) less urgent. Late in 1987 Whitehead publicly announced that she was divorcing her husband and that she was planning to get married again. Her prospective husband, Dean R. Gould, was a twenty-six-year-old accountant who worked in New York City, a professional man who belonged more to the world of William Stern than to that of Richard Whitehead, and who promised to offer his new wife the solid middle-class comfort and security that Rick Whitehead had never provided. Even before the divorce was made final, she had become pregnant again, by Dean Gould. A year later the Goulds had a second child together.

Mary Beth Whitehead-Gould (as she would henceforth be known) had changed in another way as well. The battle over Baby M had made her a well-known national figure. And it had given her a new sense of purpose. She was becoming a prominent representative of the emerging antisurrogacy movement, a public woman who was speaking out about her views at press conferences and rallies. She even testified before Congress.

By 1989 she had written a book about the Baby M case and the surrogacy question, and to publicize it she traveled across the country in high style. Here was a mission that promised to be as important, perhaps as time-consuming, as motherhood itself. At the age of thirty-one, Mary Beth Whitehead-Gould finally held within her grasp something that many other American women would have envied—the prospect of both private security and public acclaim. If she was lucky, the future might be hers.

THE EIGHTIES AND BEYOND

Like a handful of sensational public trials in this century and the last, the Baby M case bore the burden of contemporary political problems. It reflected a growing confusion in America between public and private spheres of life. Although the U.S. Supreme Court had greatly expanded the legal content of the word *privacy* during the 1970s and 1980s, in a contradictory sense, many of the most intimate questions facing any individual or family became grist for politics or the mass media.

The Baby M case also suggested some momentous consequences of new medical technologies that redefined sexual life, birth, and even death. The trial pointed up some of the implications of privilege and social class in America. And it expanded the national debate over the roles of women, men, and marriage. It evoked questions about the uses and abuses of mass media. But more fundamentally, the case also pitted two notions against each other, notions that as much as anything else during the 1980s defined much of American thinking about society and politics. The first was faith in the primacy of economic values and the private marketplace. Just as strong was the faith that society's highest values were family, religion, and individualism—nonmaterialist values. In the Baby M case, the judge and the public were forced to choose between a contract transacted between two adults and an age-old idea about motherhood. The judge was obliged to honor one of these ideals in a situation where, perhaps, neither was really appropriate.

Like previous court cases—the Dred Scott decision, the Lizzie Borden case, the Scopes trial, the trial of the Rosenbergs, and Watergate—that pitted conflicting interpretations of fundamental American institutions against each other, the Baby M case brought problems to the surface that seemed too complex or too explosive to be settled by political debate. Thus a small custody case, of limited impact, nonetheless provides a glimpse into the polarized heart of contemporary history.

New Lifestyles

As the Baby M case suggests, much of the visible social change during the late 1970s and 1980s affected the American family. Whatever the persistent strength of the old ideal of a working father, a housewife-mother, and two or three children, reality became infinitely more complex. Perhaps the most striking trend was the rapid evolution of living arrangements. As an illustration, divorce and remarriage figures increased slightly during this time, but the greatest growth was in the number of unmarried couples who lived together, rising from 523,000 in 1970 to 1,983,000 in 1985. Added to increased numbers of other nonfamily types of households, non-married groups made up 30 percent of all living arrangements in 1985. Put another way, this meant that the proportion of Americans over eighteen who were married in 1985 had declined by 10 percent from 1970.

By themselves, these statistics explain little, but journalists, sociologists, and even politicians worried about an apparently growing reluctance to marry. Indeed, marriage during the 1980s, although still predominant, was only one of several possible and acceptable social relationships in which men and women, adults and children, and single-sex couples or groups could live. As always, confirmation of the acceptability of these arrangements could be found in the mass media, which quickly recognized, mirrored, and focused on these groups as a potential new market. In part, this explains the rash of TV situation comedies in which an unusual living arrangement was the situation: *Kate and Allie* (two divorced women and their children), *The Golden Girls* (four older women), and *The Cosby Show* (remarkable because it featured a mother, father, and children).

Attention to evolving social relationships could scarcely overlook the yuppies—young urban professionals. This group, including men and women, whites, blacks, and Hispanics, was perhaps more an advertiser's dream than a reality, but it expressed an aspiration that immediately became a popular stereotype. Fresh from law or business school, these middle-class strivers purportedly stepped into $35,000-a-year professions, bought prestigious imported cars, and viewed human relationships as secondary to career. While the press and moralists treated such stereotypes with amusement or scorn, others celebrated their new materialism as a welcome relief from the angry and politically tumultuous 1960s and 1970s, a refreshing change from the counterculture that took everything seriously, from popular music to diet. Of course, yuppies and

even most Americans were profoundly changed by that earlier age. For example, job opportunities for middle-class women certainly owed much to the women's movement of the 1970s. Experimental lifestyles, so much a part of the expectations of the 1980s, had evolved during the embattled previous decades. And freer sexual practices owed much to the postwar period, and especially to the invention and acceptance of new contraceptive devices.

Other groups with more controversial lifestyles believed themselves now free of the heavy hand of social disapproval and repression. They too declared their presence and independence. This was especially true for homosexual men and women who made a visible and sometimes public move "out of the closet." Men and women from all walks of life openly declared their sexual preferences; many organized politically to encourage local officials to rescind sodomy laws and outlaw discrimination in hiring and housing. Gay groups achieved some initial successes, but encountered strong opposition, led particularly by the hierarchy of the Catholic church and evangelical Protestant groups.

THE NEW POOR Freer lifestyles and more fluid family arrangements inevitably had a negative side. The rise in divorce rates, decline in marriage rates, and increase in children born out of wedlock became more and more the burden of single women. The income of these female householders in 1986 was less than half that for married couples. With black and Hispanic families earning only 60 and 67 percent of white household income, poverty was concentrated especially among black and Hispanic women and children. Thus 45 percent of black children in America were born into poverty and one in five of all children lived in poverty in 1986. Undoubtedly, the decline of structure and stability in family life was a major cause for an accompanying sharp rise in reported cases of child abuse and neglect. Between 1978 and 1985, these dreary figures more than doubled, although some of the increase was undoubtedly due to better statistics.

The concentration of poverty among women and children represented, in some sense, the negative side of a striking success story: declining poverty among older Americans. In 1970 about a quarter of Americans over the age of sixty-five lived in poverty. By 1987 this figure shrank by more than half, to 12.2 percent. This remarkable change vividly highlighted a shift in national priorities and confirmed a transfer of national resources and social welfare funds from one group to another, from one generation to another, from one increasingly disorganized and dispirited underclass to an increasingly visible and politically astute interest group of retired Americans.

While the number and percentage of poorer Americans slowly increased during the 1970s and then accelerated in the 1980s, the political clout of this population shrank. Participation in presidential elections by people living in urban poverty centers declined by one-half over the period. By 1984 three-quarters of the immense group of Americans who did not vote were from the blue collar and service work force. This spiral of poverty and marginalization increasingly meant that the poor were viewed as objects of charity, not a potentially strong political bloc of organized voters. Victim to its own powerlessness, this growing population lost dignity as well as a sense of participation in society.

Surging Subcultures

Shifting opportunities and rewards did not always follow the fault lines of race and ethnicity. Despite the bleak and despairing black slums in American cities, a new African American middle class became particularly evident in and around such cities as Atlanta, Georgia, Washington, Chicago, and Los Angeles. Resulting in part from freer access to government employment and better-paying service jobs, this important group acquired both economic and political visibility.

Moreover, the explosive growth and maturity of newer immigrant groups such as Hispanics and Asians profoundly affected the shape of the income structure. Like the 1890s, the last two decades of American history have seen a fundamental shift in the sources of immigration. Although the flow to the United States from Asia and Latin America is not new, vastly increasing numbers precipitated visible changes in this period. Like immigrants before them, these newcomers entered for a variety of reasons: pushed by political repression and poverty and pulled by opportunity. As before, they also brought strikingly different skills, education, and status which helped or hindered their adjustment to American life.

ASIAN AMERICANS In particular, education was a vital badge of success. By the mid-1980s, whereas 16 percent of all native-born Americans had graduated from college, Asian groups including Filipinos, Koreans, Chinese, Japanese, Indian, and Taiwanese had substantially higher education levels. Only the Vietnamese had lower than average education levels. Their education and professional experience, which they either brought with them or acquired here, translated directly into earnings as Asian immigrants, except the Vietnamese, earned wages higher than or equal to those of the native born.

Given the significance of education to these groups, it is not surprising to find a nationwide movement of second- and third-generation Asian Americans into higher education. The impact has been striking. At the University of California, Berkeley, about one-third of the enrollment in 1989 was Asian American (based on a state population of 7%), while the native-born white contingency fell to less than half. As a consequence of such scholastic skill and ambitions, charges were leveled at several elite institutions of maintaining discriminatory quotas against Asian Americans.

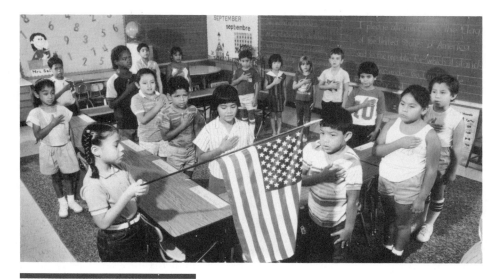

A bilingual second-grade class. Although bilingual education provoked controversy, its purpose was accepted even by its critics: to speed the integration of foreign-language speaking children into the mainstream. Bilingual education fostered this process by teaching basic skills in the child's own language. (Bob Daemmric)

HISPANICS The same factors of class and education also influenced the lives of millions of Latin Americans who came to the United States in this period. Of foreign-born Hispanic Americans, only Argentineans had a significantly higher education level and average income than the United States norm. Cuban Americans tended to approximate both American education and income levels, but many other nationalities, especially the largest group, Mexican Americans, had low education and income.

Concentrated especially in Florida, Arizona, New Mexico, Texas, and California, but with large offshoot populations in cities such as Chicago and New York, Hispanics played an increasingly significant role, transforming some cities into bicultural and bilingual centers. With a huge population growth in neighboring Mexico, and revolutionary wars in Central America from which thousands sought refuge in the United States, legal and illegal immigration expanded rapidly. By 1985 over 17 million people of Hispanic origin lived in the United States, making this the fastest-growing population group in the

nation. Like previous immigrant groups, Hispanic Americans tended to congregate in lower-paying service, manufacturing, and agriculture jobs.

As so often had happened with other immigrant groups, Hispanics were welcomed by employers who wanted cheap labor but resented by other elements of the population. In 1986 this sentiment spilled out into movements in sixteen states to declare English the official language. Some states, such as California, passed such ordiances, ending the use of Spanish in courts, on legal documents, and on ballots. To curb illegal immigration, particularly from Mexico, Congress passed the Immigration Reform and Control Act of 1986. This act granted amnesty to immigrants who had been living illegally in the United States since 1982. But to close off further immigration, the act criminalized hiring workers who lacked official documents, and imposed fines on employers from $250 to $10,000 for doing so.

This bitterly contested legislation made audible a problem of growing intensity: opposition to increasing Hispanic immigration into the

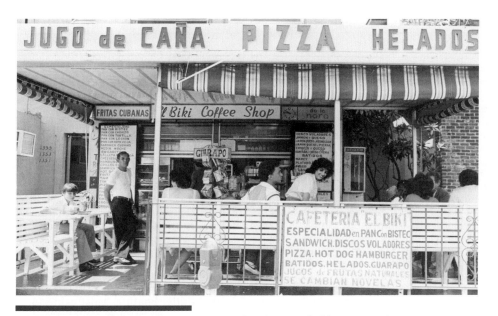

Una cafetería en Miami Latino. This small coffee shop typified businesses that sprang up in major American cities with large Latino populations. Its bill of fare, although primarily Cuban, features typical American food—that is, food brought to the United States by other immigrants. (R. Taylor/SYGMA)

United States, particularly across the lengthy and porous Texas-Mexico border. The fight over language in various state legislatures, in turn, gave testimony to increasing debate over the effectiveness of bilingual education. Encouraged by federal government grants since 1968, bilingual education proposed to ease the transition of Spanish-speaking students into English by beginning instruction in their native language. But the programs were costly and, to critics, ineffective.

Both of these outbreaks of political controversy revealed, in turn, a major shift in the nature and impact of Hispanic immigration. Before the 1970s the relatively open borders of the American Southwest brought a steady source of labor for farms and ranches. Some of these temporary immigrants remained in the United States, but their numbers were relatively slight. With the weakening of the Mexican economy and the chronic violence, poverty, and civil war in Central America during the 1970s and 1980s, refugees who had no intention of returning home began

to pour across the Mexican border, many from El Salvador, Guatemala, and Nicaragua. As these groups spread out across the United States, they congregated, as a century of immigrants had before them, in cities where they found relatives, compatriots, or the hope of employment.

Like other immigrants before them, Hispanic Americans lived in two cultures, their adopted North American world and the strong remnant of the cultural inheritance they brought with them. Divided by national cultures and strong rivalries, Hispanic Americans were torn between old loyalties and new identities. Like other immigrants, their transition to becoming an American meant giving up the extreme parochialism of loyalty to town and province in the old country, and even their identity as Mexicans, Salvadorans, or Cubans. Ironically, they became Hispanic Americans in part because other Americans, in dealing with them, disregarded complex questions about national origins. A Hispanic was someone who came from a Spanish-speaking culture.

Miami

In 1910 the city of Miami was little more than a real estate developer's dream imposed on a swamp and a strip of pristine beach. Nonetheless, such dreams often become realities in the hands of speculators. By the 1920s a causeway bridge had been built linking city and beach; plantings of coconut palms created a tropical skyline; watery sinkholes and bayous were drained and filled; and a city of modest accomplishment and great pretensions had appeared. Hotels sprang up and land changed hands quickly in this newly adorned utopia; real estate values soared as celebrities like William Jennings Bryan preached the virtues of south Florida.

Unfortunately, there were setbacks—a devastating hurricane in 1926, for example. And some of those who wintered in the area brought too much notoriety, such as Chicago gangster Al Capone. Still, it was a city that sought its identity in everything out of the ordinary and as a respite from cold, industrial America. Its architecture affected a Spanish or Mediterranean look; its most distinctive theme was art deco, an international, industrial style softened by motifs of curving waves, flamingos, and full moons. An exotic, almost foreign-looking place, Miami was unlike other cities that had a distinct Spanish heritage. Miami's earliest settlers were a mixture of blacks, whites, Native Americans, and some Spanish.

Yet Miami's (and Florida's) links to Latin America were obvious. In 1898, during the Spanish-American War, the state became an important staging point for the invasion of Cuba. More important, in the 1920s Pan American Airways—the great air link to Central and South American cities, hotels, and commerce—made Miami the hub of its operations.

After World War II and almost two decades of uneven growth, the city prospered and changed with the arrival of new immigrants. Miami Beach threw up huge new hotels, each the fulfillment of a wish for leisure and comfort. The city itself served the hotels and its temporary guests, while its airport increasingly became the center for travel to points south. And a new, dark twin resort was erected in Cuba by American mobsters who ran its hotels and gambling establishments.

By the late 1950s and 1960s Miami was, in fact, several cities: gateway to Latin America, mecca for American tourists and retirees, a Southern city with strict segregation and black ghettos called Liberty City and Overtown, and a center of a new population of Cubans fleeing a revolution that, among other things, had shut down American-owned resorts. The deciding factor occurred in 1980 when Cuba's premier Fidel Castro allowed the departure of about 120,000 refugees via the Mariel boatlift: Most came to Miami. Next came a brief but significant wave of Haitian immigrants seeking to escape the extraordinary poverty and violence of that island nation.

By the 1980s the city was transformed again. As in many other American cities, Spanish was frequently spoken on the streets. But there was a difference, because the city's Cuban Americans had achieved an extraordinary economic success and rise in political power. With 56 percent of the population, they elected a mayor and a majority of the city council.

Still, the city maintained its reputation for intrigue, violence, and crime. The CIA used the city to mount its anti-Castro and anti-Nicaraguan operations. Major drug dealers with South American connections were naturally attracted to its transportation and banking facilities. Two serious racial conflicts erupted in 1980 and 1989. A new wave of refugees from Nicaragua inundated the city in late 1988.

Thus Miami continued its curious place in American life—underscored by the film *Scarface* in 1983 and in the TV series *Miami Vice*. Behind this picture was, of course, another story: the substantial success of a coherent and ambitious group of Hispanic immigrants who had succeeded in a city, like other American cities, that was divided by poverty and wealth and race.

As the numbers of Hispanics increased, this culture became more visible. With millions of potential buyers, the Hispanic community attracted specialized advertising in Spanish. Radio and television stations sprang up to cater to these large groups of consumers. Among the favorite programs were broadcasts of Latin American soccer matches and *novelas* (Latin American soap operas).

A more controversial impact of Hispanics was on the American Catholic church. A hierarchy dominated by Irish and other older immigrant traditions, the church seemed cold, formal, and inhospitable to the huge numbers of Hispanic Catholics. With their emphasis on cults of the Virgin Mary, festivals, and other locally important traditions, Hispanics often found themselves either clashing with or avoiding the American Catholic church. Thus when the union leader César Chavez organized Mexican farm workers and marched behind the banner of the Virgin of Guadeloupe, he found little support initially from the established Catholic church in California.

This distance underscores two important trends in Hispanic-American religion. One is the significant inroads made by Protestant evangelicals like the Jehovah's Witnesses and Baptists, who offer a service and religious culture sometimes more compatible with Hispanics' desires. The second trend will bring Hispanic membership in the American Catholic church to a dominant position sometime before the year 2000. By that time, about one-half of all American Catholics will be of Hispanic origin.

With enormous numbers of immigrants, refreshed by new recruits, and a culture made tenacious by the Spanish language and a host of specially created media, merchandising, and business institutions, the question that the immigration act and the fight over bilingualism posed was whether this new immigrant culture, unlike so many others, might resist melting into the great, confusing sea of American ethnic groups. Since there was no way to know, the argument and its manifestations ensure that the controversy will remain.

The Eighties Economy

In their complex and multiple effects, these changes in family and demography reflected a deep but slow change in the American economy that first became visible in the early 1970s. This was a slight increase in the inequality of American income distribution. In an ominous-sounding book, *The Great Depression of 1990*, Ravi Batra, an economist at Southern Methodist University, noted the growing disparity in income between the top one-fifth of the population and the bottom one-fifth. Other economists contended that changes in income distribution were not unusual or permanent; there had always been waves of greater or lesser equality. But many of them conceded that from the 1970s onward, the opportunities for social mobility were fewer. With a shrinking industrial sector that still paid high wages, and a burgeoning low-skilled service sector, the economy during this period generated a great many new jobs. Some of these were in high-paying finance and high-technology fields. But many of them—close to half of those from 1980 to 1985—paid at or less than the minimum wage of $3.35 per hour and $7,000 per year. Just this sort of difference in income and social class emerged as one of the most telling distinctions between the Whiteheads and the Sterns in the Baby M trial.

Despite greater optimism among middle-class Americans, particularly after 1980, this group also faced somewhat diminished opportunities. The median income of all American families fell slightly after the 1970s and would have turned down more precipitously except for the new earnings of millions of women who entered the labor force during those years.

These were slight but significant economic changes, and they had immediate effects. One was the rise of homelessness in American cities, numbering perhaps three million in 1988. Additional factors, of course, helped thrust these people onto the streets. Thousands of mental

Homeless in America. Homelessness affected poor people in every segment of American society in the 1980s. This growing population, with nowhere else to go, shared public spaces with residents and commuters in the city, making them visible to everyone. (Bill Viggiano, Photographer)

patients were released from hospitals and found nowhere else to go; there was a rapid increase in various drug addict populations. But a growing share of the homeless lived over heat grates or in makeshift city shelters simply because housing cost too much and social welfare programs were inadequate. Some of the homeless even had full-time jobs.

Homelessness in America became a national cause in the 1980s, particularly after Americans became aware of terrible famines in East Africa. An international rock concert in June 1985, "Live Aid," raised funds to feed famine victims and focused attention on the terrible plight of starving families in eastern Africa. In 1986 a project modeled after this event, "Hands Across America," solicited money for the homeless. It momentarily raised national consciousness of the problem, but failed to deliver significant funds to ameliorate it.

THE GLOBAL ECONOMY   In linking the cause of the homeless in the United States to

starvation in the Third World, Americans were only underscoring a fact of postwar life: the interconnection of the economies and societies of the whole world. Economic development throughout the world exhibited some of the same tendencies appearing in America. The dominant few economies of the industrialized world—the European Economic Community, Japan, and newly expansive Taiwan, Hong Kong, South Korea, and Singapore, as well as the United States—continued to grow, although competition dramatically shifted the relative shares of production within this group. For the undeveloped and developing world, there were fewer success stories. In some cases, countries with strong initial growth, such as Mexico, Brazil, and Nigeria, fell into debt and stagnation. The very indebtedness of these nations gave them a kind of reverse power over the most prosperous lenders, for the threat to default on loans from private American and European banks became a way to squeeze out new loans or reduce the interest paid on old ones.

This human immune system cell is pictured under attack by much smaller HIV viruses responsible for Acquired Immune Deficiency Syndrome (AIDS). The infected cells reproduce the HIV virus and no longer function normally. (Courtesy of Lennart Nilsson, Boehringer Ingelheim International GmbH)

Other Social Changes

AIDS Another area of internationalization was health. One of the greatest accomplishments of modern medicine was achieved during the 1980s, when the disease smallpox, one of history's deadliest killers, disappeared from the human community. At almost the same time, however, a new and equally frightening infectious disease was discovered, AIDS (acquired immune deficiency syndrome). A viral disease diagnosed in the early 1980s, but common before that time in certain parts of Africa, AIDS spread rapidly in America, particularly among male homosexuals and intravenous drug users. By the late 1980s the disease, with no known cure or vaccine, appeared to have jumped beyond these two groups to spread generally, although very slowly, among other sectors of the population. Increasingly, AIDS became concentrated among poorer occupants of American cities.

By 1987, AIDS had become one of the leading infectious diseases, certainly the most deadly. Like surrogate motherhood, abortion, and contraception, AIDS became a political issue tangled in moralism, with positions sometimes taken based on disapproval of the victims. Because homosexuals and drug users—groups traditionally shunned by the majority—formed the greatest percentage of patients, the United States declined, at first, to take fighting the disease seriously. Prevention programs were often stymied because of fears that contraceptive devices and sex and drug education designed to prevent transmission of the disease would, in fact, encourage promiscuity.

THE MEDIA EXPLOSION The problems and possibilities of these complicated social changes of the 1980s formed a vast source material for commentary and dramatization in American culture. For example, the Baby M case, homelessness, and AIDS became the subjects of made-for-TV movies and countless newspaper and magazine stories.

In part, the acceleration of change had to do with media technology itself. For example, the manufacture and sale of videocassette recorders spiked in the mid-1980s. Only 1 percent of American households owned a VCR in 1980; almost 40 percent had purchased one only five years later. Feeding the enormous and diverse appetite for home viewing were films rented through video outlets, special children's presentations, and rock videos. Cable television, available in millions of homes, also featured multiple entertainments aimed at special population segments. Even commercial television began to feature rock videos.

The vast increase in the number of programs available through cable television and the home rental of films and specially made videos opened a wider window on the world for most American households. The proliferation of television talk shows and radio call-in programs no doubt increased a sense of connectedness and even intimacy between audiences and celebrities. The other side of this development, however, may well have been a decline of public participation and a rootlessness in American society. Consequently, soap operas, idiosyncratic confessions on talk shows, celebrity quirks, and prolonged media dramas such as the Baby M trial appeared to replace older networks of family and community.

More important, all of these media began to incorporate whatever was new in the cinematic and cultural values of each form, erasing distinctions between types of entertainments. For example, the television program *Miami Vice* adapted many of the values of other media: rock videos, fashion, and changing architectural tastes. The long-running program, shot in subtle hues of pink and blue against the striking art deco architecture of Miami, Florida, moved along skimpy plots punctuated by violence, drug busts, and sentimentality. Most interesting, however, was the studied ambiguity of the actors' racial and ethnic identities.

This ambiguity was also typical of rock videos. Shot in hostile-looking urban settings, pulsating with montages of images and dancers, these videos produced a new crossover culture, a visual blending of white, black, and Hispanic elements that became as various and eclectic as the music itself. Of all modern performers, perhaps Michael Jackson exemplified this trend best, as he strutted his sexual and racial ambiguities, appealing to millions of American youth.

New York's AT&T Building. This brilliant example of postmodern architecture self-consciously borrowed styles from other eras and forms. The result is a good-natured, witty facade that disrupts the monotony of glass and steel boxes so familiar in urban areas. (Reproduced with Permission of AT&T)

To describe this new culture of ambiguous styles, multiple sources, and fractured meanings, social commentators borrowed a word already used in architecture: postmodernism. The term seemed to fit a great many developments in high culture. Among them were movements in art and literature that borrowed freely from previous

One hundred fifty West Side stories. New York developer Donald Trump poses with a model of his latest enterprise: Trump City. Like many of his schemes, this one promised to be the biggest, the best, and the most extravagant. It also aroused heated opposition that blocked its construction. (UPI/Bettmann Newsphotos)

styles and even from cinematic practices. But it was in architecture that the term had its most visual, obvious implications. A famous example is the brilliant and influential architect Philip Johnson, who discarded his own earlier designs to upstage the dominant minimalist styles and functionalism of the 1960s. Rejecting the cold but clean lines of functionalism, his buildings began to sport columns, arcades, atriums, balconies, and arches, while new materials and pastel colors replaced glass boxes for a softer and more fanciful look. One of his most controversial skyscrapers, the AT&T building in New York, was built to resemble a Chippendale cabinet, a witty act of borrowing that eliminated the distance between art forms and blurred the history of architecture.

MATERIALISM In this eclectic cultural context, mass culture celebrated some peculiar forms of individualism, materialism, and celebrity. In the mid-1980s, the popular singer Madonna recorded a song, "Material Girl," whose lyrics, whether satiric or serious, were a hymn to the newly approved materialism of the era, a paean to "living in a material world," where "the boy with the cold, hard cash is always Mr. Right." Another hero created by the new materialism was Wall Street arbitrageur Ivan Boesky. Riding a wave of publicity in 1985 generated by his breathtaking gains in the corporate takeover frenzy sweeping Wall Street, Boesky instructed an audience of business students: "Greed is all right, by the way. I think greed is healthy. You can be greedy and still feel good about yourself." Boesky's speech became a model for the amoral entrepreneur played by Oscar winner Michael Douglas in the film *Wall Street*.

This raw materialism did not pass without condemnation. In a thoughtful and disturbing book, *Habits of the Heart*, published in 1985, five prominent sociologists and philosophers explored the cultural resources that Americans brought to their world of the 1980s. Their conclusions were sobering. The American ideal of freedom had stimulated initiative and creativity, even toleration. But it had left "Americans with a stubborn fear of acknowledging structures of power and interdependence in a technologically complex society dominated by giant corporations and an increasingly powerful state. The ideal of freedom makes Americans nostalgic for their past, but provides few resources for talking about their collective future."

VIGILANTISM What these sociologists feared seemed to come true in an ominous event in the

Crime Rates in the United States, 1957–86

	Murder	Rape	Robbery	Burglary
		(Rate per 100,000 Inhabitants)		
1957	5	8	39	355
1960	5	10	60	502
1965	5	12	71	653
1970	8	19	171	1,071
1975	10	26	218	1,526
1980	10	37	251	1,684
1985	8	37	209	1,287
1986	9	38	225	1,345

Source: Federal Bureau of Investigation figures.

closing days of 1984. Terrified by a previous mugging, a middle-class white man, Bernhard Goetz, shot four black youths in a New York City subway when one of them asked him for five dollars. Admitting his guilt and unrepentant for having paralyzed one of the group, Goetz became both a hero and a villain: the "subway vigilante." By his old-fashioned act of taking the law into his own hands, he symbolized the failure of efforts to end urban crime and the resulting frustration of citizens driven to protect themselves. Yet Goetz was an inappropriate symbol and a reluctant hero, undeserving either of the praise or animosity directed to him. Acquitted by a jury of attempted murder, he sought to "fade into the woodwork and lead a normal life again."

EVANGELISM Unsettling and extreme reactions of the sort that flared up in the Goetz case symbolized the desire of many Americans to reaffirm old-fashioned notions of heroism, to revive "traditional values." An important minority of Americans found this aspiration best expressed among evangelical Protestant television ministers who crusaded for a restoration of conservative lifestyles. Although in the period from 1960 onward church membership by percentage actually fell slightly in America, the nature of religious experience changed dramatically. The number of Americans who considered themselves "born again," with a profound experience of religious conversion in their lives, almost doubled to about 40 percent of the population.

While individual religious experience was significant, its cultural expressions proved more important. Television evangelists such as Oral Roberts, Jim and Tammy Bakker, Jerry Falwell, Pat Robertson, and Jimmy Swaggart used the mass media with astounding skill to spread their message, raise money, and organize politically. They gathered a congregation of worshipers and consumers who bought books and pamphlets, purchased a huge variety of goods produced by affiliated companies, or traveled to the Bakkers' Heritage Park USA, a combination amusement park and didactic display that in the mid-1980s outdrew all other American theme parks except Disney World and Disneyland. Designing their programs to resemble talk shows, variety shows, dramas, and political and news events, television evangelists persuaded millions of Americans that they could live in the modern world, use the most advanced communications devices and consumer items, and yet cling to traditional values.

The politics of this movement also had an immense impact. Although not all television evangelists or born-again Christians belonged to the political right—and certainly not all were

The Language of Race and Gender

In postmodern theory, the act of naming something and the "discourse" of describing something or someone were given important political weight. Thus the most elementary act of labeling a group became a debatable issue. For Mary Beth Whitehead to claim the title of *mother* to the child she had promised to give away to another woman won her immediate public sympathy. So too on larger issues of gender and race, the accepted names of groups could evoke sympathy or scorn. They could also reveal profound assumptions about social equality or the lack of it and the democratic aspirations of minority groups in America.

Since the 1960s the public discourse around issues of race and gender has changed dramatically. Rather than accept traditional words, coded with implications of inferiority applied by powerful groups to the less powerful, both women and minority groups have demanded the privilege to rename themselves. Of course, they could not wipe out the slang terms that pervade American culture. But they could demand that public discourse change.

For example, many women demanded important revisions in language that would recognize their social equality. In part, this meant insisting on visibility, which involved replacing the terms *man* and *mankind* (to indicate men and women as a species) with *humankind*. *Chairperson* replaced *chairman* because the latter presumed male leadership. In another sense, women pressed for less visibility. Instead of the titles *Miss* and *Mrs.*, which indicated their marital state, they wanted one term, *Ms.*, to correspond to the neutral term *Mr.* for men.

The changing terminology of race and ethnic groups was, if anything, more complex. American Indians insisted on being called Native Americans. For people of African descent, the question was more changeable and complicated. Popularly used terms like *colored* gave way in the 1950s and 1960s to *Negro*. Then, with the explosion of civil rights and cultural pride, the preferred term became *black*, and to a lesser degree, *Afro-American*. By the late 1980s, however, there was another shift to *African American*, suggesting the mixed cultural identity of every citizen.

Other groups also insisted on changes. People of Asian descent rejected the word *Oriental* and called themselves Asian Americans, or more precisely, Japanese Americans, Chinese Americans, and so on. The same process was true of immigrants from Central and South America, who referred to themselves as Hispanics or Latinos, or more narrowly, Mexican or Cuban Americans.

This shifting language reflected both the imperfect operation of cultural pluralism in America and a desire to make it work better. And it offered a striking answer to the old question "What's in a name?" By seizing the privilege of naming, minority groups and women in America gave a forceful answer.

Protestant or white—the majority impulse held to a vision of America that was Protestant and conservative. Using a nostalgic conservatism to judge the culture and politics of the 1980s, evangelical political groups blamed government for stimulating dangerous social change. Yet the same groups demanded government action to restore the paternalistic family and prayer in public schools, and to end abortion and other forms of sexual and social liberation. Jerry Falwell, founder of the Moral Majority, and Pat Robertson hoped to harness these sentiments as a permanent force inside the Republican party. Robertson ran in Republican presidential primaries in 1988.

CONSERVATISM   Although liberals continued to publish and even to dominate the academic world, conservatives of various persuasions increasingly defined public policy debates. This about-face has many explanations: for example, lucrative appointments in right-wing think tanks located in Washington, D.C., and other key cities across the country. Several influential opinion journals such as the *New Republic* modified their enthusiasm for liberalism. The most audible defection sounded when an important group of New York liberals embraced neoconservatism, a philosophy that had been developing for several decades but now received brilliant statement by old masters of polemics such as Norman Podhoretz of *Commentary* magazine. Aggressively anticommunist, deeply discouraged by perceived failures of President Johnson's Great Society, and totally opposed to schemes of engineered egalitarianism like affirmative action, school busing, and racial and gender hiring quotas, they turned against the welfare state to celebrate the old ideal of individual social mobility.

Important books such as Charles A. Murray's *Losing Ground*, published in 1984, dissected postwar welfare programs and found that government subsidies, food stamps, and other forms of transfer payments actually increased poverty, broke up families, and encouraged forms of behavior that deepened dependency. Only if the poor faced the consequences of their failures, he concluded, would they become strong enough to resist the calamity of poverty.

Developing alongside this movement was a different sort of conservatism, represented by Congressman Jack Kemp of New York and economists Arthur Laffer, George Gilder, and Milton Friedman, and articulated most persuasively by governor and presidential candidate Ronald Reagan of California. While this group of thinkers and politicians developed different strategies for releasing the energy of the American economy, all united behind another major idea of the 1980s: an almost mystical faith in the restorative power of the marketplace. Several corollaries followed from this belief. The first was that economic growth, and no other force, could end poverty

and create a good society. The only true engine of economic growth was the private market. Its liberation from regulation and consequent freedom of individuals from excessive taxation would propel the American economy out of the doldrums of the 1970s. Of course, government had to intervene in the economy in profound ways: defense spending, regulation of banking and money, and so on. So some taxes and expenditures were acceptable. But this market philosophy demanded dismantling the welfare state, from Head Start programs to Social Security—from cradle to grave.

Creating a new right-wing politics, however, was no simple task. Two distinct impulses had to be blended: traditional moralism and the ideology of a marketplace test for economic, social, and cultural ideals. Before 1980, this was only a potential coalition with a very divided constituency. And as the Baby M case so poignantly demonstrated, the free market could be a destructive enemy of traditional ideas about family and marriage. The validity of a contract in this case deeply undercut strong beliefs about motherhood. Indeed, throughout American history, economic change and market values have consistently challenged tradition. The force of capitalist enterprise transformed men, women, children, races, and ethnic groups as it imbedded their destinies in the fate of an even larger and more complex world.

Yet one political appeal did seem to work: a call to a return to the past, when market and morality appeared to operate in tandem. It was the genius of Ronald Reagan to articulate this vision and provide a platform that combined the desires of born-again, poor, and middle-class populists with the interests of some of the wealthiest corporate leaders in America behind a program that could appeal to a majority of voters now convinced that government regulation sapped the strength of American enterprise. He was also fortunate to follow one of the most unpopular presidents of the twentieth century, Jimmy Carter.

The Election of 1980

The election of 1980 was momentous, not because it initiated a sharp realignment of regions, races, ethnic groups, and social classes but because it brought profound political change without any radical transformation of the electorate. In the long run, this inertia acted to retard and then stop conservative attempts to dismantle the welfare state, exposing the contradictions inherent in the Reagan alliance. Yet in January 1981, when Ronald Reagan assumed the presidency, the Democratic party, the dominant political force in the postwar period, hung its head in stunned silence. The new president, whatever the depth or clarity of his mandate, moved quickly to translate his ideas into action.

In 1980 the bruising fight for the Democratic nomination between President Carter and Senator Edward Kennedy was matched by splits among Republicans. Before the Republican convention in Detroit in the summer of 1980, Reagan had defeated all his opponents, although George Bush, former head of the CIA, gamely contested the nomination. Liberal Republican Congressman John Anderson of Illinois declared he would run as an independent. This defection of Republican liberalism clinched the victory of conservatives in the Republican party. They declared a far-reaching program of change.

RONALD REAGAN Although no newcomer to electoral office—Reagan had served as governor of California for two terms, from 1967 to 1975— he represented a fresh force in politics. Despite his advanced age of seventy in 1981, he symbolized much that was contemporary in American life. He was the first president to have been divorced, and he shared with many other Americans the problems of two families and two generations of children. Practically his whole life had been spent working in the entertainment industry, first as a sports newscaster, then as a film actor, and finally as a professional lecturer. He fulfilled the revised myth of American social mobility, based not on hard work but on celebrity, achieving his success in the most mythic place in America, Hollywood. Rising from an impoverished Illinois family, he made his way with force of personality rather than diligence. His career in films was solid if not distinguished; he had two glamorous marriages to actresses. Completely at home in the world of celebrities, Ronald Reagan promised a Hollywood ending for the problems of the American economy and foreign policy.

Along the path of this ascent, Reagan gradually relinquished a once strong allegiance to the Democratic party, although he never outgrew his deep admiration for President Franklin Roosevelt. Looking for milestones in his conversion to conservatism, journalists Rowland Evans and Robert Novak argue in their book *The Reagan Revolution* that the future president was jolted by the high income taxes he suddenly had to pay in 1939. Others cite the influence of his militantly conservative second father-in-law, Loyal Davis. Unfriendly critics point to a movie career that never really advanced and consequent scapegoating of Hollywood liberals and communist sympathizers. Reagan himself emphasized his struggle inside the Screen Actors Guild against communist influence in the 1940s.

None of these explanations, however, quite captures the emotional quality of Reagan's conversion to conservatism. For one thing, it did not take the form of the dour first principles of fiscal conservatism and isolationist foreign policy advanced by Ohio Senator Robert Taft in the 1950s. Instead, Reagan's conservatism had more theatrical flourish. He found sources of belief, for instance, in the film heroes he played, such as George Gipp, the legendary Notre Dame halfback, or the amputee hero from *King's Row*. Both these figures triumphed over enormous odds. Both provided inspiring examples of the modern American success story. Both illustrated the myth-making power of Hollywood's melodramas.

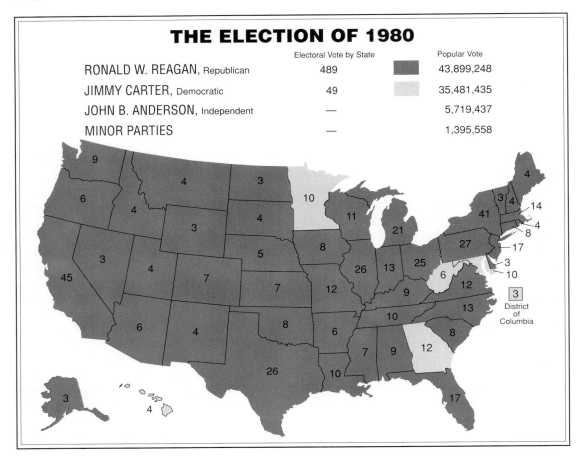

THE ELECTION OF 1980

	Electoral Vote by State		Popular Vote
RONALD W. REAGAN, Republican	489	▨	43,899,248
JIMMY CARTER, Democratic	49	▨	35,481,435
JOHN B. ANDERSON, Independent	—		5,719,437
MINOR PARTIES	—		1,395,558

This same anecdotal approach to American individualism defined Reagan's political vision. The success of an individual, like that of a nation, he believed, depended on each person striving, without the interference of government. And he cited not just laudatory anecdotes, but shocking ones: stories of "welfare queens" chauffeured in Cadillacs to pick up government checks or young men who used food stamps to buy liquor. These riveting parables supported Reagan's beliefs and provided a simple, plausible explanation for distressing social problems. They offered a smooth transition between contradictory ideas. And they gave flesh to complex economic and social ideas.

Ronald Reagan actively sought the presidency between 1968 and 1976, but finally won the Republican nomination in 1980. He did so partly by persistence and partly with an upsurge of conservative voters in the party. But only in 1980 did he finally develop a program that appealed beyond his limited ideological base to a generally frustrated and disillusioned electorate.

The greatest cause of that disillusionment was President Carter's reaction to the cold, hard facts of America's relative decline in world economic and political status. From almost any perspective—trade, manufacturing, finance, and military power—the United States was a less potent world force in 1980 than in 1945 or even 1960. One index illustrates it all: In 1945 the United States' share of world manufacturing was 60 percent. By 1985 this had fallen to 30 percent. Weak economic growth, sluggish productivity, slack investment, low savings rates, and inattention to human resource problems like education and training explained half this decline. The other half was competition from the bustling economies of western Europe, Japan, and the industrialized Pacific Rim nations like Taiwan and South Korea.

Over these long-term developments lay the immediate crisis of the terrible inflation rate of 12 percent. In a famous speech in July, 1979, Carter warned Americans that they courted a deep spiritual crisis. But searching inwardly for solutions sounded like retreat and only intensified the growing sense that American leaders cowered helplessly before a hostile world. In 1978 the Soviet Union engineered a coup in neighboring Afghanistan, and throughout 1979 stepped up military aid to fight opponents of the new regime. In response, President Carter canceled American participation in the 1980 Moscow Olympic games and imposed an embargo on sales of grain to the Soviet Union. Whatever the intent of these moves, many Americans believed that Carter suffered foreign policy problems much like a penitent, welcoming adversity, rather than as a leader. During the Iran hostage crisis of 1980, the president seemed to lose direction and self-confidence.

Ronald Reagan restored that confidence, and began a program to rejuvenate the American economy. In some respects, this was a seamless web of contradictions, woven together only by the candidate's political energy and charisma. In economics, Reagan urged a tight monetary policy (already begun under Carter) to squeeze inflation out of the economy. At the same time, he was a convert to "supply side" economics. This theory, called, in an unusual moment of candor, the "trickle-down" strategy by his budget director David Stockman, proposed large tax cuts especially for affluent Americans to encourage savings and investment. This would, theoretically, stimulate economic growth and, therefore, tax revenues. Another aspect of the program was to severely pare down social programs and pour huge amounts into defense spending. As further

measures to liberate individual initiative, Reagan proposed abolishing or curtailing environmental, work-related, and other business regulations. This would be accompanied by the privatization, wherever possible, of all government services.

Yet while promising to get government "off our backs" in economic matters and let the values of the marketplace prevail, Reagan proposed a contradictory program of moral activism, using the office of the presidency and the federal government to restore traditional values to American society. He opposed the Equal Rights Amendment to the Constitution; he opposed abortion; he favored prayer in public schools and public funding of religious and private schools; he opposed affirmative action and quota systems of hiring. Most important, he denied the validity of "entitlement" politics, wherein groups of Americans, bound by some common interest, sought funding or programs from the government. Reagan denounced this as a subversion of the interests of democracy.

Thus Reagan's program promised that less could be more. By curbing the welfare state, restoring national moral standards, a firm foreign policy, and liberating the private market, the United States could reassert its claim to a unique and special destiny. By November the 1980 election had become no contest at all. A series of debates showed Reagan a confident, witty, and congenial man. Reagan and vice-presidential candidate George Bush won 489 electoral votes. Carter and Walter Mondale took only 49, and John Anderson none. In popular votes cast, Reagan garnered 51 percent, but this far exceeded Carter's 41 percent. As important as the size of the presidential victory was the Republican triumph in the Senate where, for the first time since 1952, the party won a majority. Significant gains in the House of Representatives meant that with expected support from conservative Southern Democrats, the Republican party could pass its program.

On January 20, 1981, Ronald Reagan promised a new beginning, to preserve "this last and greatest bastion of freedom." Even by the standards of most inaugural addresses, this one promised more. With a sweeping declaration that "government is not the solution to our problem; government is the problem," Reagan proposed to use his office, Congress, and the courts to restore America to the pinnacle of power and self-confidence.

If there were sharp contradictions in promising to strengthen the positive power of government by limiting its size, collect more revenues by lowering taxes, balance the budget by decreasing revenues, and end government interference in individual lives by pressing for morals legislation, the contradictions only reflected the different priorities of the Reagan coalition. Not organized around political compromises, Reagan voters existed as independent groups, ready to marshal media support, campaign funds, and votes for a specific cause. With their broad, even utopian aims, these groups did not operate as a traditional political party. By running against Congress and the bureaucrats of Washington, D.C., Reagan promised not to play traditional interest-group politics. He would, he noted, go over the heads of politicians to appeal to the American people.

Reaganomics

The new president and his advisers quickly moved to institute their economic program while postponing serious and potentially unpopular attempts to achieve the moral reform so fervently demanded by their evangelical constituencies. Appointing conservatives to cabinet posts, such as James Watt, an anticonservation activist, to Interior and Caspar Weinberger to Defense, Reagan instructed David Stockman of the Office of Management and Budget to scrutinize and trim funds from each federal agency except defense. Hoping to achieve large cuts in bureaucracy and regulations before cabinet officers became advo-

cates for their agencies, Stockman, with Reagan's blessing, tried to eliminate the departments of education and energy and to slash funds from programs targeted at health, education, housing, agriculture, income maintenance, and unemployment. As Stockman later noted, "My blueprint for sweeping, wrenching change in national economic governance would have hurt millions of people in the short run." Stockman even proposed to squeeze the fat out of defense budgets, but the president remained adamant about a rapid and expensive arms buildup.

Alongside budget cutting blossomed a far more important and achievable goal: the promised tax cut. The president repeatedly accused the Democrats of a demoralizing policy of tax and spend. He proposed to prune federal income taxes by as much as 30 percent across the board. In justification, the president promised that a tax cut "would provide incentive and stimulate productivity, thus reducing inflation and providing jobs for the unemployed." This pledge prompted substantial popular support, in part because of the growing hostility to the way some federal funds were spent and its recipients. Moreover, "bracket creep" up the rate ladder of the progressive income tax tables meant that every income earner in America, in this time of fast-rising prices and wages, became more and more alert to their escalating income taxes.

Although liberals in the House of Representatives resisted a major tax cut, a group of Southern Democrats dubbed the "Boll Weevils" offered hope for decisive action. Just as pressure mounted to pass the legislation, on March 30, 1981, the president was leaving a Washington hotel following a speech when he was suddenly shot by a single gunman, John Hinckley. Pushed into his limousine and rushed to George Washington University Hospital, he easily survived the assassination attempt. Just as important, his joking manner and irrepressible good humor in a terrifying situation gained him enormous public sympathy. This he skillfully turned into support for his economic program.

Increases and Decreases in Percent of Federal Budget Allocations, 1980–86

Increases	1980	1986	Decreases	1980	1986
Defense	22.68	27.13	International affairs	2.15	1.75
Social Security	25.49	27.43	Income security	14.64	12.05
Agriculture	1.49	2.64	Health	3.93	3.64
Interest on federal debt	8.8	14.56	Veterans	3.59	2.71
			Education & training	5.38	3.13
			Commerce	1.59	.39
			Transport	3.69	2.77
			Environment	2.35	1.32
			Energy conservation	1.73	.45
			Commercial development	1.91	.81
			Science	.98	.91
			Justice	.78	.69
			Government expenses miscellaneous	.74	.64

Source: U.S. Department of Commerce, Bureau of the Census, *Statistical Abstract of the United States, 1987* (Washington, D.C.: Government Printing Office, 1986), pp. 293–94.

Facing an inevitable defeat, the Democrats offered up an alternative plan, but Reagan won his battle. The bill passed Congress and became law on August 13, 1981. Graduated rates were lowered in three stages: 5 percent the first year and 10 percent in each of two succeeding years, making for a total reduction of 25 percent. In simplest terms, this meant that a taxpayer who owed $2,000 in federal income taxes in 1981 would eventually save $500 a year. For the taxpayer who owed $20,000 in 1981, the annual savings would be $5,000. Some economists deplored the unbalanced impact of this equal treatment; a few warned of an abrupt decline in federal revenues. Coupled with new tax savings for corporations, the income tax reduction eliminated $41 billion in revenues during the first year alone.

The president, however, had a compelling answer: He would balance the federal budget by reducing federal expenditures; tax revenues would rise with economic expansion. This promise, however, turned into an annual ritual of evasion. Despite Stockman's dogged attacks on a whole range of government beneficiaries, from Amtrak to farm subsidies, Medicare to science and health projects, not nearly enough was cut to offset either increases in defense spending or declining revenues. In negotiations with Congress over the budget, pet local projects inevitably crept in. Moreover, recognizing a growing public furor, Congress balked at cutting Social Security benefits. Areas of the budget without strong constituencies lost more than those with powerful lobbies.

This significant shift in priorities had the greatest impact on the poor, who were growing in number over this entire period. Thus a decreasing share of funds fell to an increasingly large group of needy people. At the same time, some forms of entitlements shared by the middle class, such as Social Security, actually increased. Thus the income redistribution inherent in the Reagan administration budget and taxation programs marginally accelerated inequality in the United States. Ironically, the attempt to cut the budget across the board solidified support for some social programs, with real cuts made only in those aimed at the bottom of society.

Because the 1981 tax act and the annual budgets worked at cross purposes, a huge increase in the federal deficit threatened. It became inevitable when tight money strategies to fight inflation touched off a recession. By mid-1982 the United States found itself in the midst of the most severe downturn since the 1930s. As production declined, revenues shrank. The deficit increased rapidly from around $60 billion in 1980 to over $200 billion a year in 1986.

To fund this massive debt, the government borrowed money from its citizens and from foreigners attracted by an overvalued dollar and high interest rates. In turn, the high dollar and a wave of consumer optimism after the end of the 1982 recession fueled a huge imbalance of trade that rose to over $170 billion a year in 1987. Over the seven years of the Reagan presidency, the United States fell from being the greatest creditor to the greatest debtor nation in the world.

By 1982, David Stockman, Treasury Secretary James Baker, and other cabinet members recognized that the push-me, pull-you economic program of stimulus and restraints demanded quick repair. Their solution, with the acquiescence of Congress, was a new tax act in 1984, the largest single increase in revenue in history. But this only slowed the growth of the deficit. President Reagan refused to lower defense spending or raise further taxes, and the administration, recognizing public sentiment against cuts to Social Security and veterans' payments, withdrew from the battlefield of the budget. The only rainbow among the deficit clouds was the supply-side theory that economic growth would solve all problems.

The election of 1984 proved to be something of a referendum on economics. With inflation down, consumption up, and the deficit having no visible impact, the administration won handily. The Democrats, led by former Vice President Mondale and Representative Geraldine Ferraro (the first woman nominated for such a position by a major party), advocated higher taxes and more social programs with restraint in defense spending. Reagan and Bush confidently defended their record. Their landslide victory confirmed that a majority of the Americans who voted approved of the policy of borrow and spend over the Democrats' tax and spend.

Returned to power with a somewhat diminished hold over the Senate and fewer representatives in the House, the Republicans (with the support of key Democrats) nonetheless won a further tax reform in October 1986, which all but ended the progressive income tax. While abolishing most tax shelters and deductions used by wealthier people, it lowered tax rates for 1988 to 15 percent below $29,750 and 28 percent above that figure. Billed as a fairer, simpler system, it was not immediately clear how its provisions would affect the average American family.

Although the growing deficit carried no political liabilities and provoked few hesitations in the consumer shopping spree of the mid-1980s, it lay like a terrorist bomb inside the economy. On October 19, 1987, the stock market registered a huge shock: Values sank almost 500 points a day. The giddy rise of prices and paper fortunes of the previous years was dashed by a decline as severe as the first days of the 1929 crash. Belated efforts to wean America of dependency on foreign borrowing and purchase of imports by lowering the value and foreign purchasing power of the dollar had failed. Foreign investors and governments quickly blamed U.S. economic policy for what became a world-encircling wave of stock declines and currency fluctuations.

Until 1987 this underlying distortion had a marginal impact on the president's popularity, although economic experts remained dubious. Despite an overall slowdown in economic growth since the 1970s and no substantial reversal of the relative decline of America's world economic standing, the administration maintained its popularity. In spite of strident words about budget cutting, Reagan was stymied by entrenched interests after 1982 and a gradually diminishing power base in Congress. More important, immediate benefits outweighed the intangible threat of future problems. Tax cuts put money into the

Newspapers used their largest type to announce it and social commentators hauled out comparisons with the Crash of 1929, but the Stock Market plunge of 1987, while sobering, did not induce a depression or even a recession. (Andrew Popper/The Picture Group)

pockets of wage earners. Inflation fell sharply, and the spending binge of the government merely validated the buying binge of consumers. Finally, the various Reagan policies had differential effects on Americans. If the poorest fell through wide tears in the "safety net" of social services, they were a constituency that rarely voted and possessed little power. Those who gained in these flush years had ample reason to celebrate fewer regulations and lower taxes.

Reagan and Social Issues

The strategy of flourish and postponement that the president pursued on the budget also framed his actions on social issues. In this area he disappointed many of his fervent admirers, who proposed a menu of moral demands including an end to legal abortions, reinstating school prayer, and funding private schools with public money. What the president could accomplish by speaking at evangelical conferences and before right-wing think tanks, he did. What he could accomplish by appointing conservative judges and revising government guidelines, he did. Several of his cabinet members—for example, William Bennett, secretary of education in 1985—urged a revival of "family values," and blasted sex education in the schools. In civil rights cases, Attorney General Edwin Meese and Assistant Attorney General for Civil Rights Bradford Reynolds often entered court cases as friends of those accused of civil rights violations. Reagan also appointed a Civil Rights Commission with several members openly hostile to previous federal attempts to reverse patterns of discrimination.

But in this area, too, Reagan recognized the pitfalls of radical change. For one thing, as the Baby M case revealed, some of the most fundamental beliefs of the Reagan coalition could sharply contradict each other. The path of least

Sandra Day O'Connor, appointed to the Supreme Court by President Reagan in 1981, was the first woman to hold this position. Her tenure was more important for creating a conservative majority than in providing any special or distinct representation for women's issues. (UPI/Bettmann Newsphotos)

political resistance, therefore, seemed to be the Supreme Court. Having denounced the activist Court of Justice Earl Warren and the Burger Court which followed it, the president tried to use appointments to the Court to reverse decisions on abortion, privacy, affirmative action, and separation of church and state. His first appointment, of Sandra Day O'Connor in 1981, had little immediate impact. In fact, his appointment of the first woman to the Supreme Court was hailed as a breakthrough in women's rights. With his next opportunity, he elevated William Rehnquist to chief justice and filled his vacant position with Antonin Scalia, another conservative. But in 1987, when a further vacancy occurred, one that might have drastically shifted the Court, the president blundered in proposing Judge Robert Bork.

Given his eccentric theories and controversial writings, Bork attracted the bitter opposition of civil rights and women's groups. He was also opposed by a sizable segment of the judicial and legal professions. The Senate soundly defeated his appointment.

This rebuke came partly because the Democrats had seized control of the Senate in the 1986 elections. But a second nominee, Judge Douglas Ginsburg, fared no better. Ginsburg also professed highly controversial beliefs about the functions of the Court and the meaning of the Constitution. But before battle lines could be drawn, he withdrew his candidacy after revelations that he had smoked marijuana some years before. Reagan's third (and successful) candidate was Anthony M. Kennedy, a conservative jurist with orthodox views of the Court. He was no overt advocate of the president's social agenda but his appointment decisively shifted the court to the right.

In fact, by 1987 the president's most conservative supporters were in disarray, torn by warfare over succession, growing dislike for his foreign policy, and split by scandals that ripped the television evangelical ministry, the mainstay of the constituency crusading to restore "traditional values."

The enormous growth in sophistication by the evangelical right during the 1980s had had a seismic impact on American politics. Sending delegates to nominating conventions, winning concessions in party platforms, and altering the tone and language of campaigns, the evangelical right forced its issues onto the national agenda. Ronald Reagan encouraged this development. He visited the PTL Club of Jim and Tammy Bakker and addressed the National Association of Evangelicals and other such religious organizations. On March 8, 1982, before the NAE, he dramatically denounced the Soviet Union as an "evil empire." The struggle with the Russians, he warned, was between "right and wrong and good and evil."

Despite this crusading rhetoric, the president kept his distance from the religious right. This policy proved wise when in 1987, an evangelical schism opened between the Bakkers, Jimmy Swaggert, Jerry Falwell, and others. The falling-out involved charges of misappropriation of funds and sexual philandering by Bakker. When Bakker confessed to serious misdeeds and a lurid sexual affair, his financial and religious empire collapsed with a crash that resounded throughout the evangelical world.

But the evangelical right was dismayed by Reagan's subsequent about-face in foreign policy. In this arena, his conservative following found both its greatest victories and worst defeats. As the president wavered between ideology and compromise and realism, he provoked hope and controversy.

Foreign Policy

From the beginning, Ronald Reagan never left doubts about his basic foreign policy values. In countless speeches during the 1970s, he had hammered away at American defense weakness and Soviet aggression. He had fervently supported the war in Vietnam and scorned détente with the Russians. Speaking in 1982, he recalled with approval the words of a fellow actor: "I would rather see my little girls die now, still believing in God, than have them grow up under communism and one day die no longer believing in God." In such moments, he imagined the final titanic struggle between the superpowers as the beginning of Armageddon, the fiery end of the world described in the Bible. Accommodation with the Soviet Union, as he told the Foreign Policy Association in 1977, meant retreat: "Détente to the Soviet Union became not a sign of compromise, but a victory for the U.S.S.R. and a growing sign of Western weakness caused by the internal contradictions of capitalism."

This searing anticommunism balanced another deeply held belief in the moral superiority of American society. "In a world wreaked [sic] by hatred, economic crisis, and political tension," he said in late 1982, "America remains mankind's best hope." A theme gilding all of his speeches, this faith in America as a morally redeemed society revived the strong nationalism characteristic of the cold war period. This nationalism had been muted in the 1970s by the loss of the war in Vietnam, by Soviet achievement of nuclear arms parity, and by the increasingly competitive world market. Haunted by fears that the nation might not maintain its military, political, and economic preeminence in this complex world, some Americans found Reagan's nostalgic vision comforting. And if the exercise of power provoked warlike metaphors, better to talk of risks than accept decline without a struggle.

THE ARMS BUILDUP Bolstered by accelerating defense expenditures and tough-minded advisers—Secretary of State Alexander Haig, CIA Director William Casey, and National Security Adviser Richard V. Allen—Reagan began to implement his foreign policy. The cornerstone was arms superiority over the Russians—negotiating from strength, as the president called it. Claiming that the Soviets led in nuclear strike forces, the president pushed a huge nuclear arms buildup and then announced a revolutionary new defense strategy. In part a response to a growing antinuclear peace movement in the United States and western Europe and continued deployment of missiles in eastern Europe, the Strategic Defense Initiative (SDI) aimed through exotic outer space weapons such as laser beams to cripple any attacking rocket force. Portrayed as a shield against nuclear war, this "Star Wars" scheme promised survival from a nuclear attack and the ability to retaliate. But the Russians claimed that it would allow the United States to launch a first strike and then survive any retaliation.

The SDI assured two benefits for America. Huge government investment in computer, laser, and other weaponry guaranteed new inventions and technological breakthroughs for industry. Given American technological superiority, it would force the Soviet Union to direct even larger funds into an already bloated defense budget, thus intensifying the severe economic problems of that nation.

Finally, Reagan assembled an able group of arms negotiators that was wary of making any agreement with the Soviets. Backed by Defense Secretary Caspar Weinberger, such men as Richard Perle, assistant secretary of defense and a leading arms control expert, made it clear that the Reagan administration was reluctant to sign any treaty at all.

The Reagan administration's anticommunism also led it into active attempts to roll back Soviet influence in the Third World. Thus the United States supported antigovernment forces in Afghanistan, Cambodia, Angola, Ethiopia, and Nicaragua, countries either dependent on or directly influenced by the Soviet Union.

To justify this policy, the administration accepted United Nations Ambassador Jeane Kirkpatrick's distinction between authoritarian and totalitarian states. While certainly reprehensible, the former type, she declared, deserved qualified U.S. support because they could evolve in democratic directions. Translated into policy, this implied toleration for the apartheid regime of South Africa and dictatorships in the Philippines and South America. But in the world of political realities, this distinction proved elusive. Bitter opposition inside the United States prevented any closer ties with South Africa. In fact, college students forced universities to divest themselves of South African stock holdings. And when dictator Ferdinand Marcos finally fled the Philippines after losing an election to Corazon Aquino in early 1986, the United States could take some credit for this outcome.

TERRORISM Terrorism was another matter that evoked intense views. Terrorism had several definitions, depending on the context. It meant kidnapping and hostage taking, as when Iran seized the American embassy in 1979. It applied to the tactics of the Libyan government, which encouraged clandestine attacks on American officials, soldiers, and tourists in the Middle East. It applied to Palestine Liberation Organization assaults on Israeli soldiers and civilians. In general, it described the tactics of indirect military confrontation practiced by states or groups hostile to the United States but far too weak to risk a direct confrontation.

Some of the president's advisers encouraged the belief that the Soviet Union and its allies secretly sponsored terrorism. This theory received an inconclusive test in the long trial of several Bulgarians in Italy for their alleged participation in a plot to assassinate Pope John Paul II. An Italian court eventually acquitted them in 1986. But some members of the administration continued to implicate Russians, Cubans, and eastern Europeans in the training of terrorists for hit-and-run warfare against American allies.

Standing tall in the Middle East unfortunately made Americans a target precisely because of the unorthodox tactics of guerrilla warfare in the region. When Lebanon erupted into civil war and threatened to disintegrate under pressure from neighbors Israel and Syria, the Reagan administration sent a peacekeeping force of Marines to Beirut. In October 1983 a truck filled with explosives slammed into an American bivouac at the Beirut airport, killing 241 Marines. Despite the folly of placing American troops at such risk, there were few recriminations. But the administration quickly withdrew remaining troops to offshore ships.

INTERVENTION The administration did win applause for its invasion of the Caribbean island of Grenada in October 1983. Beset by internal struggles and growing Cuban influence, Grenada seemed a perfect place to pursue the Reagan doctrine of turning back Soviet influence in the Third World. The brief skirmish between 10,000 American troops and a ragtag collection of Cuban militia advisers was hailed by Reagan as a major turning point in American policy. Many Americans were sure he was right.

A much more intractable problem was Nicaragua. Its history, like that of much of Central America, was written in economic misery, instability, dictatorship, and periodic United States interventions. When rebel forces known as the Sandinistas overthrew the ruthless Somoza regime in 1979, there was optimism for Nicaragua. But as the new regime swerved left politically, it aroused internal opposition and American hostility. Support for revolutionary groups in neighboring countries convinced some American policymakers to oppose the new Nicaraguan government and even finance its overthrow. Others, however, were willing to tolerate a nation friendly to the Soviet Union, provided it did not try to export revolution.

After the Reagan administration took office in 1981, however, it gave secret military assistance to the Contras, an army of old Somoza loyalists aided by Nicaraguans disenchanted with the Sandinistas. But CIA implication in mining the Nicaraguan harbor of Managua in 1983, and, in particular, a CIA training manual advising rebels to "neutralize" Nicaraguan officials with "selective use of violence" exposed the operation. In the same year, Congress passed the Boland Amendment, forbidding the administration to supply funds to the Contras.

THE IRAN-CONTRA AFFAIR It was the genius and folly of President Reagan's leading advisers, William Casey, Robert McFarlane (head of the National Security Council), and Admiral John Poindexter (McFarlane's replacement), and Poindexter's assistant Lieutenant-Colonel Oliver North, to compound problems in the Middle East and Nicaragua by linking them together. In the process, they helped rescue two American hostages held by pro-Iranians in Lebanon, but the events shattered confidence in the president's leadership and competence.

The complicated intrigue known as the Iran-Contra affair began in the context of a long and bitter war between Iran and Iraq. Fought around the periphery of the world's richest oil reserves, the war was intensified by superpower interference. Iraq received arms from the Soviet Union and several Western countries. Because of Iran's extreme hostility to its pro-American neighbors and bitterness to the United States, it had difficulty securing arms.

Catching the ear of North and McFarlane, several shadowy Iranian and Israeli arms dealers proposed a complicated transaction. If the United States agreed to sell arms to Iran, the Iranians would help secure the freedom of several American hostages held in Lebanon. In their defense, it is possible that North, McFarlane, Reagan, and other administration officials convinced themselves that they were, in fact, encouraging opponents of the militantly hostile Iranian leader, the Ayatollah Khomeini.

To execute this arrangement required presidential approval, particularly since it represented a dramatic contradiction of stated refusals to deal with terrorists. Hoping to keep the affair a secret, in early 1986 the president signed a "finding," or a document legitimizing this policy change. Congress and the American people were not informed, and Secretary of State George Shultz and Defense Secretary Weinberger distanced themselves from a policy they disapproved of but declined to fight.

The second phase of the affair emerged when North, Casey, and others determined to send profits from arms sales as secret aid for the Contras. Although such transactions clearly violated the Boland Amendment, the administration had already waded deeply into operations in the gray areas of this prohibition. North and others also used their contacts with wealthy conservative supporters to solicit private funds for the Contras. Other administration officials engineered Contra contributions from friendly foreign powers such as Saudi Arabia, Israel, Taiwan, and Brunei.

Unfortunately for these secret operations, a small Beirut weekly, *Al Shirra*, acting on a tip from the Iranians, published a story on November 3, 1986, disclosing the Iranian leg of the operation. Two days later, the story splashed across American newspapers, and the administration moved quickly to control political damage. At first, the president issued denials that the United States had swapped arms for hostages. On November 13, 1986, Reagan declared, "We did not—repeat—did not trade weapons or anything else for hostages—nor will we." Whatever the administration called the deal, however, after the Reverend Lawrence Jenco was freed on July 26, 1986, the United States had delivered Hawk missile spare parts to the Iranians on August 3. When David Jacobsen was released November 2, 1986, the Iranians received 500 TOW missiles.

But there was more. On November 15, 1986, Attorney General Meese revealed that funds from the arms sales had been secretly credited to Nicaraguan Contra bank accounts. Moving to protect the president, the administration fired North and replaced Poindexter. Since October, however, North had been using his office paper shredder to destroy incriminating documents. Nonetheless, a great deal of evidence remained, enough to infuriate Congress and raise nagging doubts about the president's denial that he knew of the deal.

Eventually, four investigating bodies sprang up to explore the enormously complex events: two congressional committees, a special commission headed by former Senator John Tower of Texas to explore the workings of the National Security Council, and a special prosecutor, Lawrence Walsh, to prepare whatever criminal indictments might be warranted.

As evidence accumulated over the spring and summer of 1987, it became clear that the Iran-Contra affair was both comic opera and a miserable misjudgment. Tales of escapades ranging from U.S. officials carrying a chocolate cake and a Bible inscribed by President Reagan on a secret trip to Iran, to deals with shady arms merchants revealed an administration drawn into plotting with men craftier than they. American foreign policy was being conducted in secret, by private citizens, sleazy gun runners, and fake experts and profiteers. Still, Colonel North defended his actions before Congress in the summer of 1987: "I saw the idea of using the Ayatollah Khomeini's money to support the Nicaraguan freedom fight-

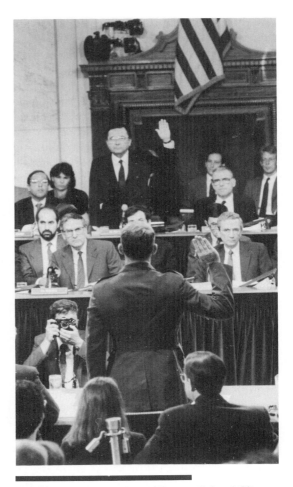

Who is swearing in whom? Witness Colonel Oliver North is sworn in by Senator Daniel Inouye at the Iran-Contra hearings during the summer of 1987. North's testimony was so successful that it seemed to place the Senate itself on trial. (Wide World Photos)

ers as a good one. I still do. I don't think it was wrong. I think it was a neat idea."

It was also an idea that threatened the presidency itself. The Tower commission, when it reported in February 1987, criticized Reagan's "personal management style" and faulted Casey, Shultz, and Weinberger, as well as Poindexter and North. Finding no firm evidence that the president knew about the secret funding of the

Contras, it chided him for *not* knowing, for not exercising more control over foreign policy.

Senate and House hearings over the summer exposed even more dreary details. But they also provided Poindexter, North, and others with a forum to preach their pro-Contra cause. North in particular proved to be a difficult witness. Claiming a higher purpose to justify his actions, he disarmed the legislators, becoming a momentary television celebrity. Although this success proved fleeting, it dampened the enthusiasm of Congress for the investigations. There would be no repeat of Watergate. Despite a severely critical report issued by the committees in the fall of 1987, there were no answers to what everyone wanted to know: What did the president know and when did he know it? Even the trial and conviction of Oliver North on three felony counts in early 1989 only provided tantalizing hints that the president and Vice President Bush had known far more than they admitted.

SUMMIT WITH GORBACHEV As several presidents before him had, Reagan gained immensely from successful negotiations with the Soviet Union. A summit conference, held in December, brought Mikhail Gorbachev, general secretary of the Soviet Communist party, to Washington to sign the Intermediate Nuclear Forces Agreement (INF treaty) reducing mid-range nuclear missiles. Both Gorbachev and Reagan used this meeting to reinforce their shaky personal power. For different reasons, both needed a foreign policy success. But the compromise also meant reversal of long-standing policies. The Russians dropped their opposition to on-site arms inspections enforcing the treaty. They agreed to destroy many more missiles than the United States. They dampened their strong opposition to SDI research and deployment. Reagan paid the price of cutting his ties to the extreme right wing, replacing a large number of very conservative members of his administration with moderates.

This ideological winnowing had already begun shortly after the Iran-Contra affair. The day after the Tower commission released its report in February 1987, White House Chief of Staff Donald Regan resigned, and former Republican Senator Howard Baker, a moderate, replaced him. William Casey also quit the CIA in February, and in early March the acerbic and combative Patrick J. Buchanan resigned as communications director. Shortly before the Washington summit, other advocates of a rigid line toward Soviet negotiations, including Weinberger and arms expert Richard Perle, left the administration. Their departure and the summit aroused an acrimonious split on the Republican right, with such former allies as political commentator Howard Phillips calling Reagan a "useful idiot" of Soviet propaganda.

Reagan's new, more moderate attitude to the Soviet Union seemed to betray his crusading anticommunist career. But the summit could also be considered a success of that stubborn position. Faced with the impossible predicament of increased arms competition with the United States, severe economic problems, and a desire to liberalize Soviet society, the Russians under Gorbachev wanted a compromise. They found a president willing to change.

There were other foreign policy successes. In May 1988 the Soviet Union, under immense pressure, finally agreed to withdraw its troops from Afghanistan. Rising casualties, drooping troop morale, and persistent, deadly attacks by guerrillas supplied with American weapons persuaded the Soviet Union to call its soldiers home. In South Africa, a fragile peace was negotiated between Angola and South Africa in a very complex war. In April 1988 the Sandinistas of Nicaragua agreed to negotiate with the rebel Contras. Although the Reagan administration opposed some of the terms of this slippery cease-fire, it remained bound by congressional purse strings to uphold them. Finally, in the summer of 1988, Iran and Iraq signed a cease-fire to end their bloody eight-year war. Again, the United States had at least an indirect hand in this settlement.

After the American election of 1988, General Secretary Gorbachev of the Soviet Union, President Reagan, and President-elect Bush, met in New York. In the last years of his second term, Reagan established a close relationship with Gorbachev. Bush, in the photograph, still seems the outsider. (Jean Louis Atlan/SYGMA)

The Reagan Record

Whatever the immediate reasons, the president's flexibility was entirely in character, for he often compromised in the face of difficulties. Determined in 1980 to dismantle the welfare state, he only chipped away at its weakest points and probably galvanized support for certain programs like Social Security. Pledged to revolutionize the American economy, to make it freer and more competitive, he contained inflation but presided over the worst budget and trade deficits in American history. Promising to restore morality and traditional family values, he shrank from the serious political battles that might have advanced the program of the evangelical right. Determined

to fight communism, he recognized the great power stature of the Soviet Union.

Hoping for a major political realignment, the president built no great new coalition. Unlike Roosevelt and Eisenhower, two previous popular presidents, his elections did not bring out increasing numbers of voters. Participation in national elections hovered at around 50 percent of eligible voters in 1980 and 1984. In effect, this confirmed a growing trend in American politics for potential voters to drop out and for the electorate to consist of special groups, tied to a candidate but not a party. In a curious way, the electorate had become like an audience and the old parties operated more and more according to the dictates of the mass media.

Most ironic of all, the president did nothing to lower the expectations of Americans for their

The Vietnam Memorial in Washington, D.C.—captured here on Memorial Day, 1987—evoked strong emotions and tearful reunions of veterans grieving for lost comrades. (J.L. Atlan/SYGMA)

national government. By succeeding with intangibles, by allowing Americans to feel better about themselves and their national stature, without substantial reasons, Reagan continued and even exaggerated the affirmative bluster of his boyhood hero, Franklin Roosevelt, with his promises to awaken the American spirit. Yet difficult problems remained: the economy, the arms race, global competition, and the poor fit between

morality and social change, poverty, problems of race and class. Scandal after scandal washed over the administration, the most serious and persistent involving the attorney general, Edwin Meese, and his lax behavior toward friends seeking special favors.

And as the case of Baby M demonstrated in microcosm, the changing possibilities of technology and evolving sexual and social mores undercut tradition. Aggravated by the discrepancy between unequal power of individuals and abstract equal rights, this case tested the ability of Americans to come to terms with a new world of possibilities and risks. Was belief in the marketplace or traditional morality adequate to cope with the emerging world of the 1980s? Neither helped very much in this complex case between two very different families, the Whiteheads and the Sterns. Such questions remained for the newly elected president, George Bush, to face.

The Election of 1988

After a bitter and uninformative presidential campaign, with image makers vying to diffuse any substantial issues between the Democratic candidates, Michael Dukakis and Lloyd Bentsen, and the Republican candidates, George Bush and Dan Quayle, Bush and Quayle were elected. Their margin of victory was substantial in total and electoral votes, although the Reagan coalition appeared considerably weakened from 1984. And Democrats increased their majorities in both the House and the Senate. Despite the contentious campaign—or because of it—participation continued to slide, with a majority of potential voters choosing to stay away from the polls.

If there was an obvious issue in the campaign, it was contained in Bush's various promises not to raise taxes, even though surveys indicated that most Americans did not believe him. This paradox suggests that voters were astute about real prospects for dealing with crushing budget deficits and burgeoning costs of government, but not quite ready to relinquish the aura of optimism that had characterized the Reagan years, when a majority of Americans had seen economic improvement. Thus they voted for continuity knowing full well that it was doubtful.

Yet the presidency of George Bush began with an almost overt repudiation of Reagan's style of government. Stepping away from the long

Jesse Jackson campaigns during the Iowa presidential primary of 1988. Attempting to assemble a "Rainbow Coalition"—reflecting a union of genders, races, ethnic groups, and social classes—the candidate dons a farm cap and jacket to court rural voters. (Jim Heemstra/The Picture Group)

shadow of his mentor, Bush promised a "kinder and gentler" society—presumably by contrast with the harsh social policies of the previous eight years. The new president also filled his cabinet with insiders, lawyers and business people familiar with Washington politics. Congress was elated at this indication that the new government would proceed by negotiation and not ideology. Bush even acknowledged a serious crisis in savings and loan banks nationwide and in one of his first acts as president suggested an extensive and

George Bush, elected president in 1988, with his wife Barbara. (J.L. Atlan/SYGMA)

costly plan to reorganize and regulate their activities.

In his first budget message he proposed small increases in federal spending for some education programs, solving the huge drug problem, environmental threats, and several other popular programs. But, overall, these gestures did not reverse the longer-term federal divestiture of social responsibilities pursued during the Reagan years. Indeed, the new president's call for renewed volunteer work and individual charity underscored this. Nor did the budget come to terms with the accumulation of economic problems left over from the consumer boom of the 1980s: the balance of payments in trade budget deficits, low growth in productivity of American workers, inflation, and the crises in housing and education. The solution to these problems would test the feasibility of the bipartisan, negotiated presidency that George Bush proposed.

Suggestions for Further Reading

BABY M

The Baby M case is very recent history. The trial can be followed in the files of any big newspaper in and around February, 1987, and most national newsmagazines also ran cover stories on the case. The best discussion of the general issues raised by the Baby M case is Martha A. Field, *Surrogate Motherhood* (1988). Mary Beth Whitehead tells her story in *Mother's Story* (1989). A feminist critique of the surrogate motherhood is Phyllis Chesler, *Sacred Bond: The Legacy of Baby M* (1988); see also Rochelle Sharp, *The Case of Baby M: And the Facts of Life* (1989). In the

CHRONOLOGY

January 1981 Iran
hostage crisis ends.
Ronald Reagan
assumes presidency.

March 30, 1981
Assassination attempt
against Reagan.

August 14, 1981 Tax
reform act cuts income
taxes by 25 percent.

1983 Strategic Defense
Initiative announced.
Boland Amendment
prohibiting military aid to
Contras passed.

October 1983 Attack on
Marines in Beirut.

October 1983 Invasion of
island of Grenada.

1981   **1982**   **1983**   **1984**

June 1984 Tax act
raising $50 billion in
revenues.

December 1984
Bernhard Goetz shoots
four black youths in New
York subway.

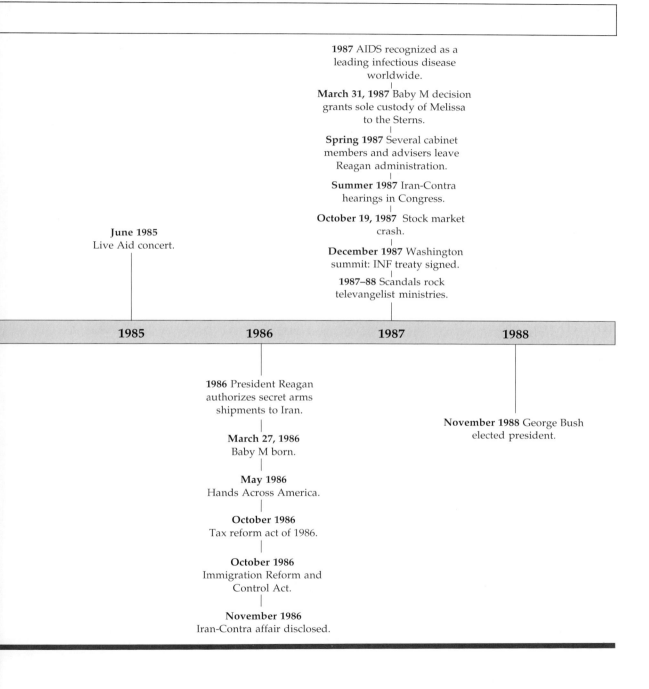

1987 AIDS recognized as a leading infectious disease worldwide.

March 31, 1987 Baby M decision grants sole custody of Melissa to the Sterns.

Spring 1987 Several cabinet members and advisers leave Reagan administration.

Summer 1987 Iran-Contra hearings in Congress.

October 19, 1987 Stock market crash.

December 1987 Washington summit: INF treaty signed.

1987–88 Scandals rock televangelist ministries.

June 1985 Live Aid concert.

1985   **1986**   **1987**   **1988**

1986 President Reagan authorizes secret arms shipments to Iran.

March 27, 1986 Baby M born.

May 1986 Hands Across America.

October 1986 Tax reform act of 1986.

October 1986 Immigration Reform and Control Act.

November 1986 Iran-Contra affair disclosed.

November 1988 George Bush elected president.

aftermath of the Baby M case, two other surrogate mothers have published books about their experiences: Patricia Adair, *A Surrogate Mother's Story* (1987) and Elizabeth Kane, *Birth Mother: The Story of America's First Legal Surrogate Mother* (1988). Five years before Baby M was born, the broker who owned the company that arranged her birth (The Infertility Center of New York) published a book promoting surrogate motherhood: Noel P. Keane with Dennis L. Breo, *The Surrogate Mother* (1981); see also Lori B. Andrews, *New Conceptions: A Consumer's Guide to the Newest Infertility Treatments* (1984).

THE EIGHTIES AND BEYOND

Inevitably, the literature for the 1980s, particularly the social and cultural history of the decade, is incomplete. One book that touches all the aspects of this period, William Chafe, *The Unfinished Journey: America Since World War II* (1986), provides a beginning. *Habits of the Heart: Individualism and Commitment in American Life* (1985) by Robert N. Bellah and others is a fascinating exploration of the moral resources of Americans in the 1980s.

RONALD REAGAN

Two books on Ronald Reagan offer particularly interesting discussions of culture and politics in contemporary society. They are Michael Rogin, *Ronald Reagan, the Movie, and Other Episodes in Political Demonology* (1987), and George Will, *The Morning After: American Success and Excess, 1981–1986* (1986).

Of two older biographies of Ronald Reagan, the best is Lou Cannon, *Reagan* (1982). Robert Dallek in *Ronald Reagan: The Politics of Symbolism* (1984) explores the relationship of the president with political symbolism. Perhaps the best and most persuasive inside story of Reagan's early successes is Rowland Evans and Robert Novak, *The Reagan Revolution* (1981). To catch a flavor of the president's words, it is instructive to read collections of his speeches. One such is *The Triumph of the American Spirit* (1984), edited by Emil Area and Gregory J. Pamel. A fine analysis of the crucial election of 1984 in an interesting collection of essays is Theodore Lowi, "An Aligning Election, A Presidential Plebiscite," in Michael Nelson, ed., *The Elections of 1984* (1985). Two liberal appraisals of the Reagan years are Joel Krieger, *Reagan, Thatcher, and the Politics of Decline* (1986), and Robert Lekachman, *Visions and Nightmares: America After Reagan* (1987).

Undoubtedly there will be more books from former aides and administration officials. Several of these "kiss and tell" memoirs have painted a curious, often acrimonious White House. So far the best of these is David A. Stockman's very self-serving, very interesting *The Triumph of Politics: How the Reagan Revolution Failed* (1986). Presidential assistant Michael K. Deaver in *Behind the Scenes* (1987) and former chief of staff Donald T. Regan, *For the Record: From Wall Street to Washington* (1988), reveal a good deal of the infighting in the administration—from their perspective.

THE DECLARATION OF INDEPENDENCE

In Congress, July 4, 1776. *The unanimous Declaration of the thirteen United States of America.*

When in the Course of human events, it becomes necessary for one people to dissolve the political bands which have connected them with another, and to assume among the powers of the earth, the separate and equal station to which the Laws of Nature and of Nature's God entitle them, a decent respect to the opinions of mankind requires that they should declare the causes which impel them to the separation.—

We hold these truths to be self-evident, that all men are created equal, that they are endowed by their Creator with certain unalienable Rights, that among these are Life, Liberty and the pursuit of Happiness.—

That to secure these rights, Governments are instituted among Men, deriving their just powers from the consent of the governed,—

That whenever any Form of Government becomes destructive of these ends, it is the Right of the People to alter or to abolish it, and to institute new Government, laying its foundation on such principles and organizing its powers in such form, as to them shall seem most likely to effect their Safety and Happiness. Prudence, indeed, will dictate that Governments long established should not be changed for light and transient causes; and accordingly all experience hath shown, that mankind are more disposed to suffer, while evils are sufferable, than to right themselves by abolishing the forms to which they are accustomed. But when a long train of abuses and usurpations, pursuing invariably the same Object evinces a design to reduce them under absolute Despotism, it is their right, it is their duty, to throw off such Government, and to provide new Guards for their future security.—

Such has been the patient sufferance of these Colonies; and such is now the necessity which constrains them to alter their former Systems of Government. The history of the present King of Great Britain is a history of repeated injuries and usurpations, all having in direct object the establishment of an absolute Tyranny over these States. To prove this, let Facts be submitted to a candid world.—

He has refused his Assent to Laws, the most wholesome and necessary for the public good.—

He has forbidden his Governors to pass Laws of immediate and pressing importance, unless suspended in their operation till his Assent should be obtained; and when so suspended, he has utterly neglected to attend to them.—

He has refused to pass other Laws for the accommodation of large districts of people, unless those people would relinquish the right of Representation in the Legislature, a right inestimable to them and formidable to tyrants only.—

He has called together legislative bodies at places unusual, uncomfortable, and distant from the depository of their public Records, for the sole purpose of fatiguing them into compliance with his measures.—

He has dissolved Representative Houses repeatedly, for opposing with manly firmness his invasions on the rights of the people.—

He has refused for a long time, after such dissolutions, to cause others to be elected; whereby the Legislative powers, incapable of Annihilation, have returned to the People at large for their exercise; the State remaining in the mean time exposed to all the dangers of invasion from without, and convulsions within.—

He has endeavored to prevent the population of these States; for that purpose obstructing the Laws for Naturalization of Foreigners; refusing to pass others to encourage their migrations hither, and raising the conditions of new Appropriations of Lands.—

He has obstructed the Administration of Justice, by refusing his Assent to Laws for establishing Judiciary powers.—

He has made Judges dependent on his Will alone, for the tenure of their offices, and the amount and payment of their salaries.—

He has erected a multitude of New Offices, and sent hither swarms of Officers to harrass our people, and eat out their substance.—

He has kept among us, in times of peace, Standing Armies without the Consent of our legislatures.—

He has affected to render the Military independent of and superior to the Civil power.—

He has combined with others to subject us to a jurisdiction foreign to our constitution, and unacknowledged by our laws; giving his Assent to their Acts of pretended Legislation:—

For quartering large bodies of armed troops among us:—

For protecting them, by a mock Trial, from punishment for any Murders which they should commit on the Inhabitants of these States:—

For cutting off our Trade with all parts of the world:—

For imposing Taxes on us without our Consent:—

For depriving us in many cases, of the benefits of Trial by Jury:—

For transporting us beyond Seas to be tried for pretended offences:—

For abolishing the free System of English Laws in a neighbouring Province, establishing therein an Arbitrary government, and enlarging its Boundaries so as to render it at once an example and fit instrument for introducing the same absolute rule into these Colonies:—

For taking away our Charters, abolishing our most valuable Laws, and altering fundamentally the Forms of our Government:—

For suspending our own Legislatures, and declaring themselves invested with power to legislate for us in all cases whatsoever.—

He has abdicated Government here, by declaring us out of his Protection and waging War against us.—

He has plundered our seas, ravaged our Coasts, burnt our towns, and destroyed the lives of our people.—

He is at this time transporting large Armies of foreign Mercenaries to compleat the works of death, desolation and tyranny, already begun with circumstances of Cruelty & perfidy scarcely paralleled in the most barbarous ages, and totally unworthy the Head of a civilized nation.—

He has constrained our fellow Citizens taken Captive on the high Seas to bear Arms against their Country, to become the executioners of their friends and Brethren, or to fall themselves by their Hands.—

He has excited domestic insurrections amongst us, and has endeavoured to bring on the inhabitants of our frontiers, the merciless Indian Savages, whose known rule of warfare, is an undistinguished destruction of all ages, sexes and conditions.

In every stage of these Oppressions We have Petitioned for Redress in the most humble terms: Our repeated Petitions have been answered only by repeated injury. A Prince, whose character is thus marked by every act which may define a Tyrant, is unfit to be the ruler of a free people.

Nor have We been wanting in our attentions to our British brethren. We have warned them from time to time of attempts by their legislature to extend an unwarrantable jurisdiction over us. We have reminded them of the circumstances of our emigration and settlement here. We have appealed to their native justice and magnanimity, and we have conjured them by the ties of our common kindred to disavow these usurpations, which, would inevitably interrupt our connections and correspondence. They too have been deaf to the voice of justice and of consanguinity. We must, therefore, acquiesce in the necessity, which denounces our Separation, and hold them, as we hold the rest of mankind, Enemies in War, in Peace Friends.—

We, Therefore, the Representatives of the united States of America, in General Congress, Assembled, appealing to the Supreme Judge of the world for the rectitude of our intentions, do, in the Name, and by the Authority of the good People of these Colonies, solemnly publish and declare, That these United Colonies are, and of Right ought to be, Free and Independent States; that they are Absolved from all Allegiance to the British Crown, and that all political connection between them and the State of Great Britain, is and ought to be totally dissolved; and that as Free and Independent States, they have full Power to levy War, conclude Peace, contract Alliances, establish Commerce, and to do all other Acts and Things which Independent States may of right do.—

And for the support of this Declaration, with a firm reliance on the protection of divine Providence, we mutually pledge to each other our Lives, our Fortunes, and our sacred Honor.

John Hancock
(MASSACHUSETTS)

New Hampshire
Josiah Bartlett
William Whipple
Matthew Thornton

Massachusetts
Samuel Adams
John Adams
Robert Treat Paine
Elbridge Gerry

Delaware
Caesar Rodney
George Read
Thomas McKean

New York
William Floyd
Philip Livingston
Francis Lewis
Lewis Morris

New Jersey
Richard Stockton
John Witherspoon
Francis Hopkinson
John Hart
Abraham Clark

North Carolina
William Hooper
Joseph Hewes
John Penn

Maryland
Samuel Chase
William Paca
Thomas Stone
Charles Carroll of Carrollton

South Carolina
Edward Rutledge
Thomas Heywood, Jr.
Thomas Lynch, Jr.
Arthur Middleton

Rhode Island
Stephen Hopkins
William Ellery

Connecticut
Roger Sherman
Samuel Huntington
William Williams
Oliver Wolcott

Pennsylvania
Robert Morris
Benjamin Rush
Benjamin Franklin
John Morton
George Clymer
James Smith
George Taylor
James Wilson
George Ross

Virginia
George Wythe
Richard Henry Lee
Thomas Jefferson
Benjamin Harrison
Thomas Nelson, Jr.
Francis Lightfoot Lee
Carter Braxton

Georgia
Button Gwinnett
Lyman Hall
George Walton

THE CONSTITUTION OF THE UNITED STATES OF AMERICA

We the People of the United States, in Order to form a more perfect Union, establish Justice, insure domestic Tranquility, provide for the common defence, promote the general Welfare, and secure the Blessings of Liberty to ourselves and our Posterity, do ordain and establish this Constitution for the United States of America.

The preamble establishes the principle of government by the people and lists the six basic purposes of the Constitution.

ARTICLE I LEGISLATIVE DEPARTMENT

Section 1. All legislative Powers herein granted shall be vested in a Congress of the United States, which shall consist of a Senate and House of Representatives.

Section 2. The House of Representatives shall be composed of Members chosen every second Year by the People of the several States, and the Electors in each State shall have the Qualifications requisite for Electors of the most numerous Branch of the State Legislature.

Representatives serve two-year terms. They are chosen by those electors (that is, voters) who are qualified to vote for members of the lower house of their own state legislature.

No Person shall be a Representative who shall not have attained to the Age of twenty-five Years, and have been seven Years a Citizen of the United States, and who shall not, when elected, be an Inhabitant of that State in which he shall be chosen.

The number of representatives allotted to a state is determined by the size of its population. The 14th Amendment has made obsolete the reference to "all other persons"—that is, slaves.

Representatives and direct Taxes shall be apportioned among the several States which may be included within this Union, according to their respective Numbers, <u>which shall be determined by adding to the whole Number of free Persons, including those bound to Service for a Term of Years, and excluding Indians not taxed, three-fifths of all other Persons.</u> The actual Enumeration shall be made within three Years after the first Meeting of the Congress of the United States, and within every subsequent Term of ten Years, in such Manner as they shall by Law direct. The Number of Representatives shall not exceed one for every thirty Thousand, but each State

A census must be taken every ten years to determine the number of representatives to which each state is entitled. There is now one representative for about every 470,000 persons.

Source: House Document #529. U.S. Government Printing Office, 1967.
Note: The Constitution and the amendments are reprinted here in their original form. Portions that have been amended or superseded are underlined. The words printed in the margins explain some of the more difficult passages.

shall have at Least one Representative; <u>and until such enumeration shall be made, the State of New Hampshire shall be entitled to chuse three, Massachusetts eight, Rhode Island and Providence Plantations one, Connecticut five, New York six, New Jersey four, Pennsylvania eight, Delaware one, Maryland six, Virginia ten, North Carolina five, South Carolina five, and Georgia three.</u>

When vacancies happen in the Representation from any State, the Executive Authority thereof shall issue Writs of Election to fill such Vacancies.

The House of Representatives shall chuse their Speaker and other Officers; and shall have the sole Power of Impeachment.

Section 3. The Senate of the United States shall be composed of two Senators from each State, <u>chosen by the Legislature thereof,</u> for six Years; and each Senator shall have one Vote.

Immediately after they shall be assembled in Consequence of the first Election, they shall be divided as equally as may be into three Classes. The Seats of the Senators of the first Class shall be vacated at the Expiration of the second Year, of the second Class at the expiration of the fourth Year, and of the third Class at the Expiration of the sixth Year, so that one third may be chosen every second Year; and if Vacancies happen by Resignation, or otherwise, <u>during the Recess of the Legislature of any State, the Executive thereof may make temporary Appointments until the next Meeting of the Legislature, which shall then fill such Vacancies.</u>

No Person shall be a Senator who shall not have attained to the Age of thirty Years, and been nine Years a Citizen of the United States, and who shall not, when elected, be an Inhabitant of that State for which he shall be chosen.

The Vice President of the United States shall be President of the Senate, but shall have no Vote, unless they be equally divided.

The Senate shall chuse their other Officers, and also a President pro tempore, in the absence of the Vice President, or when he shall exercise the Office of President of the United States.

The Senate shall have the sole Power to try all Impeachments. When sitting for that Purpose, they shall be on Oath or Affirmation. When the President of the United States is tried, the Chief Justice shall preside: And no Person shall be convicted without the Concurrence of two thirds of the Members present.

Judgment in Cases of Impeachment shall not extend further than to removal from Office, and disqualification to hold and enjoy any Office of Honor, Trust or Profit under the United States: but the Party convicted shall nevertheless be liable and subject to Indictment, Trial, Judgment and Punishment, according to Law.

Section 4. The Times, Places and Manner of holding Elections for Senators and Representatives, shall be prescribed in each State by the Legislature thereof; but the Congress may at any time by Law make or alter such Regulations, except as to the Place of chusing Senators.

The Congress shall assemble at least once in every Year, <u>and such Meeting shall be on the first Monday in December,</u> unless they shall by Law appoint a different Day.

Section 5. Each House shall be the Judge of the Elections, Returns and Qualifications of its own Members, and a Majority of each shall constitute a Quorum to do

"Executive authority" refers to the governor of a state.

The Speaker, chosen by and from the majority party, presides over the House. Impeachment is the act of bringing formal charges against an official. (See also Section 3.)

The 17th Amendment changed this method to direct election.

The 17th Amendment also provides that a state governor shall appoint a successor to fill a vacant Senate seat until a direct election is held.

The Vice President may cast a vote in the Senate only to break a tie.

The president *pro tempore* of the Senate is a temporary officer; the Latin words mean "for the time being."

No President has ever been convicted on charges of impeachment. In 1868 the Senate fell one vote short of the two-thirds majority needed to convict Andrew Johnson. Thirteen other officials—eleven federal judges, one senator, and one secretary of war—have been impeached; five of the judges were convicted.

Elections for Congress are held on the first Tuesday after the First Monday in November in even-numbered years.

The 20th Amendment designates January 3 as the opening of the congressional session.

Business; but a smaller number may adjourn from day to day, and may be authorized to compel the Attendance of absent Members, in such Manner, and under such Penalties as each House may provide.

Each House may determine the Rules of its Proceedings, punish its Members for disorderly Behavior, and with the Concurrence of two thirds, expel a Member.

Each House shall keep a Journal of its Proceedings, and from time to time publish the same, excepting such Parts as may in their Judgment require Secrecy; and the Yeas and Nays of the Members of either House on any question shall, at the Desire of one fifth of those Present, be entered on the Journal.

Neither House, during the Session of Congress, shall, without the Consent of the other, adjourn for more than three days, nor to any other Place than that in which the two Houses shall be sitting.

Section 6. The Senators and Representatives shall receive a Compensation for their Services, to be ascertained by Law, and paid out of the Treasury of the United States. They shall in all Cases, except Treason, Felony and Breach of the Peace, be privileged from Arrest during their Attendance at the Session of their respective Houses, and in going to and returning from the same; and for any Speech or Debate in either House, they shall not be questioned in any other Place.

No Senator or Representative shall, during the Time for which he was elected, be appointed to any civil Office under the Authority of the United States, which shall have been created, or the Emoluments whereof shall have been encreased during such time; and no Person holding any Office under the United States, shall be a Member of either House during his Continuance in Office.

Section 7. All Bills for raising Revenue shall originate in the House of Representatives; but the Senate may propose or concur with Amendments as on other Bills.

Every Bill which shall have passed the House of Representatives and the Senate, shall, before it become a Law, be presented to the President of the United States; If he approve he shall sign it, but if not he shall return it, with his Objections to that House in which it shall have originated, who shall enter the Objections at large on their Journal, and proceed to reconsider it. If after such Reconsideration two thirds of that House shall agree to pass the Bill, it shall be sent, together with the Objections, to the other House, by which it shall likewise be reconsidered, and if approved by two thirds of that House, it shall become a Law. But in all such Cases the Votes of both Houses shall be determined by Yeas and Nays, and the Names of the Persons voting for and against the Bill shall be entered on the Journal of each House respectively. If any Bill shall not be returned by the President within ten Days (Sundays excepted) after it shall have been presented to him, the Same shall be a Law, in like Manner as if he had signed it, unless the Congress by their Adjournment prevent its Return, in which Case it shall not be a Law.

Every Order, Resolution, or Vote to which the Concurrence of the Senate and House of Representatives may be necessary (except on a question of Adjournment) shall be presented to the President of the United States; and before the Same shall take Effect, shall be approved by him, or being disapproved by him, shall be repassed by two thirds of the Senate and House of Representatives, according to the Rules and Limitations prescribed in the Case of a Bill.

Margin notes:

Each house of Congress decides whether a member has been elected properly and is qualified to be seated. (A quorum is the minimum number of persons required to be present in order to conduct business.) The House once refused admittance to an elected representative who had been guilty of a crime. The Senate did likewise in the case of a candidate whose election campaign lent itself to "fraud and corruption."

Congressmen have the power to fix their own salaries. Under the principle of *congressional immunity*, they cannot be sued or arrested for anything they say in a congressional debate. This provision enables them to speak freely.

This clause reinforces the principle of separation of powers by stating that, during his term of office, a member of Congress may not be appointed to a position in another branch of government. Nor may he resign and accept a position created during his term.

The House initiates tax bills but the Senate may propose changes in them.

By returning a bill unsigned to the house in which it originated, the President exercises a *veto*. A two-thirds majority in both houses can override the veto. If the President receives a bill within the last ten days of a session and does not sign it, the measure dies by *pocket veto*. Merely by keeping the bill in his pocket, so to speak, the President effects a veto.

The same process of approval or disapproval by the President is applied to resolutions and other matters passed by both houses (except adjournment).

These are the *delegated*, or *enumerated*, powers of Congress.

Duties are taxes on imported goods; *excises* are taxes on goods manufactured, sold, or consumed within the country. *Imposts* is a general term including both duties and excise taxes.

Naturalization is the process by which an alien becomes a citizen.

Government *securities* include savings bonds and other notes.

Authors' and inventors' rights are protected by copyright and patent laws.

Congress may establish lower federal courts.

Only Congress may declare war. *Letters of marque and reprisal* grant merchant ships permission to attack enemy vessels.

Militia refers to national guard units, which may become part of the United States Army during an emergency. Congress aids the states in maintaining their national guard units.

This clause gives Congress the power to govern what became the District of Columbia, as well as other federal sites.

Known as the *elastic clause*, this provision enables Congress to exercise many powers not specifically granted to it by the Constitution.

This clause concerns the slave trade, which Congress did ban in 1808.

Section 8. The Congress shall have Power to lay and collect Taxes, Duties, Imposts and Excises, to pay the Debts and provide for the common Defence and general Welfare of the United States; but all Duties, Imposts and Excises shall be uniform throughout the United States;

To borrow money on the credit of the United States;

To regulate Commerce with foreign Nations, and among the several States, and with the Indian Tribes;

To establish an uniform Rule of Naturalization, and uniform Laws on the subject of Bankruptcies throughout the United States;

To coin Money, regulate the Value thereof, and of foreign Coin, and fix the Standard of Weights and Measures;

To provide for the Punishment of counterfeiting the Securities and current Coin of the United States;

To establish Post Offices and post Roads;

To promote the Progress of Science and useful Arts, by securing for limited Times to Authors and Inventors the exclusive Right to their respective Writings and Discoveries;

To constitute Tribunals inferior to the superior Court;

To define and punish Piracies and Felonies committed on the high Seas, and Offenses against the Law of Nations;

To declare War, grant Letters of Marque and Reprisal, and make Rules concerning Captures on Land and Water;

To raise and support Armies, but no Appropriation of Money to that Use shall be for a longer Term than two years;

To provide and maintain a Navy;

To make Rules for the Government and Regulation of the land and naval Forces;

To provide for calling forth the Militia to execute the Laws of the Union, suppress Insurrections and repel Invasions;

To provide for organizing, arming, and disciplining the Militia, and for governing such Part of them as may be employed in the Service of the United States, reserving to the States respectively, the Appointment of the Officers, and the Authority of training the Militia according to the discipline prescribed by Congress;

To exercise the exclusive Legislation in all Cases whatsoever, over such District (not exceeding ten Miles square) as may, by Cession of particular States, and the acceptance of Congress, become the Seat of the Government of the United States, and to exercise like Authority over all Places purchased by the Consent of the Legislature of the State in which the Same shall be, for the Erection of Forts, Magazines, Arsenals, dock-Yards, and other needful Buildings;—And

To make all Laws which shall be necessary and proper for carrying into Execution the foregoing Powers, and all other Powers vested by this Constitution in the Government of the United States, or in any Department or Officer thereof.

Section 9. The Migration or Importation of such Persons as any of the States now existing shall think proper to admit, shall not be prohibited by the Congress prior to the Year one thousand eight hundred and eight, but a tax or duty may be imposed on such Importation, not exceeding ten dollars for each Person.

The privilege of the Writ of Habeas Corpus shall not be suspended unless when in Cases of Rebellion or Invasion the public Safety may require it.

No Bill of Attainder or ex post facto Law shall be passed.

No capitation, or other direct, Tax shall be laid, unless in Proportion to the Census of Enumeration herein before directed to be taken.

No Tax or Duty shall be laid on Articles exported from any State.

No Preference shall be given by any Regulation of Commerce or Revenue to the Ports of one State over those of another; nor shall Vessels bound to, or from, one State, be obliged to enter, clear, or pay Duties in another.

No Money shall be drawn from the Treasury, but in Consequence of Appropriations made by Law; and a regular Statement and Account of the Receipts and Expenditures of all public Money shall be published from time to time.

No Title of Nobility shall be granted by the United States: And no Person holding any Office of Profit or Trust under them, shall, without the Consent of the Congress, accept of any present, Emolument, Office, or Title, of any kind whatever, from any King, Prince, or foreign State.

Section 10.   No State shall enter into any Treaty, Alliance, or Confederation; grant Letters of Marque and Reprisal; coin Money; emit Bills of Credit; make any Thing but gold and silver Coin a Tender in Payment of Debts; pass any Bill of Attainder, ex post facto Law, or Law impairing the Obligation of Contracts, or grant any Title of Nobility.

No State shall, without the Consent of the Congress, lay any Imposts or Duties on Imports or Exports, except what may be absolutely necessary for executing its inspection Laws: and the net Produce of all Duties and Imposts, laid by any State on Imports or Exports, shall be for the Use of the Treasury of the United States; and all such Laws shall be subject to the Revision and Controul of the Congress.

No State shall, without the Consent of Congress, lay any duty of Tonnage, keep Troops, or Ships of War in time of Peace, enter into any Agreement or Compact with another State, or with a foreign Power, or engage in War, unless actually invaded, or in such imminent Danger as will not admit of delay.

ARTICLE II   EXECUTIVE DEPARTMENT

Section 1.   The executive Power shall be vested in a President of the United States of America. He shall hold his Office during the Term of four Years, and, together with the Vice President, chosen for the same Term, be elected, as follows.

Each State shall appoint, in such Manner as the Legislature thereof may direct, a Number of Electors, equal to the whole Number of Senators and Representatives to which the State may be entitled in the Congress: but no Senator or Representative, or Person holding an office of Trust or Profit under the United States, shall be appointed an Elector.

The Electors shall meet in their respective States, and vote by Ballot for two persons, of whom one at least shall not be an Inhabitant of the same State with themselves. And they shall make a List of all the Persons voted for, and of the Number of Votes for each; which List they shall sign and certify, and transmit sealed to the Seat of

---

The writ of habeas corpus permits a prisoner to appear before a judge to inquire into the legality of his or her detention.

A *bill of attainder* is an act of legislation that declares a person guilty of a crime and punishes him or her without a trial. An *ex post facto* law punishes a person for an act that was legal when performed but later declared illegal.

The object of Clause 4 was to bar direct (per person) taxation of slaves for the purpose of abolishing slavery. The 16th Amendment modified this provision by giving Congress the power to tax personal income.

States are hereby forbidden to exercise certain powers. Some of these powers belong to Congress alone; others are considered undemocratic.

States cannot, without congressional authority, tax goods that enter or leave, except for a small inspection fee.

Federal officials are ineligible to serve as presidential electors.

the Government of the United States, directed to the President of the Senate. The President of the Senate shall, in the Presence of the Senate and House of Representatives, open all the Certificates, and the Votes shall then be counted. The Person having the greatest Number of Votes shall be the President, if such Number be a Majority of the whole Number of Electors appointed; and if there be more than one who have such Majority, and have an equal Number of Votes, then the House of Representatives shall immediately chuse by Ballot one of them for President; and if no Person have a Majority, then from the five highest on the List the said House shall in like Manner chuse the President. But in chusing the President, the Votes shall be taken by States, the Representation from each State having one Vote; a quorum for this Purpose shall consist of a Member or Members from two thirds of the States, and a Majority of all the States shall be necessary to a Choice. In every Case, after the Choice of the President, the Person having the Greatest Number of Votes of the Electors shall be the Vice President. But if there should remain two or more who have equal Votes, the Senate shall chuse from them by Ballot the Vice President.

The Congress may determine the Time of chusing the Electors, and the Day on which they shall give their Votes; which Day shall be the same throughout the United States.

No person except a natural born Citizen, or a Citizen of the United States, at the time of the Adoption of this Constitution, shall be eligible to the Office of President; neither shall any Person be eligible to that Office who shall not have attained to the Age of Thirty-five Years, and been fourteen Years a Resident within the United States.

In a Case of the Removal of the President from Office, or of his Death, Resignation, or Inability to discharge the Powers and Duties of the said Office, the same shall devolve on the Vice-President, and the Congress may by Law provide for the Case of Removal, Death, Resignation or Inability, both of the President and the Vice President, declaring what Officer shall then act as President, and such Officer shall act accordingly, until the Disability be removed, or a President shall be elected.

The President shall, at stated Times, receive for his Services, a Compensation, which shall neither be encreased nor diminished during the Period for which he shall have been elected, and he shall not receive within that Period any other Emolument from the United States, or any of them.

Before he enter on the Execution of his Office, he shall take the following Oath or Affirmation:—"I do solemnly swear (or affirm) that I will faithfully execute the Office of the President of the United States, and will to the best of my Ability, preserve, protect and defend the Constitution of the United States."

Section 2. The President shall be Commander in Chief of the Army and Navy of the United States, and of the Militia of the several States, when called into the actual Service of the United States; he may require the Opinion in writing, of the principal Officer in each of the executive Departments, upon any subject relating to the Duties of their respective Offices, and he shall have Power to Grant Reprieves and Pardons for Offenses against the United States, except in Cases of Impeachment.

He shall have Power, by and with the Advice and Consent of the Senate, to make Treaties, provided two thirds of the Senators present concur; and he shall nominate, and by and with the Advice and Consent of the Senate, shall appoint Ambassadors, other public Ministers and Consuls, Judges of the supreme Court, and all other

Officers of the United States, whose Appointments are not herein otherwise provided for, and which shall be established by Law: but the Congress may by Law vest the Appointment of such inferior Officers, as they think proper, in the President alone, in the Courts of Law, or in the Heads of Departments.

The President shall have Power to fill up all Vacancies that may happen during the Recess of the Senate, by granting commissions which shall expire at the End of their next Session.

Without the consent of the Senate, the President may appoint officials only on a temporary basis.

Section 3.   He shall from time to time give to the Congress Information of the State of the Union, and recommend to their Consideration such Measures as he shall judge necessary and expedient; he may, on extraordinary Occasions, convene both Houses, or either of them, and in Case of Disagreement between them, with Respect to the Time of Adjournment, he may adjourn them to such Time as he shall think proper; he shall receive Ambassadors and other public Ministers; he shall take Care that the Laws be faithfully executed, and shall Commission all the Officers of the United States.

The President delivers a "State of the Union" message at the opening of each session of Congress. Woodrow Wilson was the first President since John Adams to read his messages in person. Franklin D. Roosevelt and his successors followed Wilson's example.

Section 4.   The President, Vice President and all civil Officers of the United States, shall be removed from Office on Impeachment for, and Conviction of, Treason, Bribery, or other high Crimes and Misdemeanors.

ARTICLE III   JUDICIAL DEPARTMENT

Section 1.   The judicial Power of the United States, shall be vested in one supreme Court, and in such inferior Courts as the Congress may from time to time ordain and establish. The Judges, both of the supreme and inferior Courts, shall hold their Offices during good Behaviour, and shall, at stated Times, receive for their services, a Compensation, which shall not be diminished during their Continuance in Office.

Federal judges hold office for life and may not have their salaries lowered while in office. These provisions are intended to keep the federal bench independent of political pressure.

Section 2.   The judicial Power shall extend to all Cases, in Law and Equity, arising under this Constitution, the Laws of the United States, and Treaties made, or which shall be made, under their Authority;—to all Cases affecting Ambassadors, other public Ministers and Consuls;—to all Cases of admiralty and maritime Jurisdiction;—to Controversies to which the United States shall be a Party;—to Controversies between two or more States;—between a State and Citizens of another state;—between Citizens of different states;—between Citizens of the same State claiming Lands under Grants of different States, and between a State, or the Citizens thereof, and foreign States, Citizens or Subjects.

This clause describes the types of cases that may be heard in federal courts.
The 11th Amendment prevents a citizen from suing a state in a federal court.

In all Cases affecting Ambassadors, other public Ministers and Consuls, and those in which a State shall be Party, the supreme Court shall have original Jurisdiction. In all the other Cases before mentioned, the supreme Court shall have appellate Jurisdiction, both as to Law and Fact, with such Exceptions, and under such Regulations as the Congress shall make.

The Supreme Court handles certain cases directly. It may also review cases handled by lower courts, but Congress in some cases may withhold the right to appeal to the highest court or limit appeal by setting various conditions.

The trial of all Crimes, except in Cases of Impeachment, shall be by Jury; and such Trial shall be held in the State where the said Crimes shall have been committed; but when not committed within any State, the Trial shall be at such Place or Places as the Congress may by Law have directed.

The 6th Amendment strengthens this clause on trial procedure.

Section 3.   Treason against the United States, shall consist only in levying War against them, or in adhering to their Enemies, giving them Aid and Comfort. No

Treason is rigorously defined. A person can be convicted only if two witnesses testify to the same obvious act or if he or she confesses in court.

Person shall be convicted of Treason unless on the Testimony of two Witnesses to the same overt Act, or on Confession in open Court.

The Congress shall have Power to declare the Punishment of Treason, but no Attainder of Treason shall work Corruption of Blood, or Forfeiture except during the Life of the Person attainted.

ARTICLE IV   RELATIONS AMONG THE STATES

Section 1.   Full Faith and Credit shall be given in each State to the public Acts, Records, and judicial Proceedings of every other State. And the Congress may by general Laws prescribe the Manner in which such Acts, Records and Proceedings shall be proved, and the Effect thereof.

Section 2.   The Citizens of each State shall be entitled to all Privileges and Immunities of Citizens in the several States.

A Person charged in any State with Treason, Felony, or other Crime, who shall flee from Justice, and be found in another State, shall on demand of the executive Authority of the State from which he fled, be delivered up, to be removed to the State having Jurisdiction of the Crime.

No Person held in Service or Labour in one State, under the laws thereof, escaping into another, shall, in Consequence of any Law or Regulation therein, be discharged from such Service or Labour, but shall be delivered up on Claim of the Party to whom such Service or Labour may be due.

Section 3.   New States may be admitted by the Congress into this Union; but no new State shall be formed or erected within the Jurisdiction of any other State; nor any State be formed by the Junction of two or more States, or parts of States, without the Consent of the Legislatures of the States concerned as well as of the Congress.

The Congress shall have Power to dispose of and make all needful Rules and Regulations respecting the Territory or other Property belonging to the United States; and nothing in this Constitution shall be so construed as to Prejudice any Claims of the United States, or of any particular State.

Section 4.   The United States shall guarantee to every State in this Union a Republican Form of Government, and shall protect each of them against Invasion; and on Application of the Legislature, or of the Executive (when the Legislature cannot be convened) against domestic Violence.

ARTICLE V   AMENDING THE CONSTITUTION

The Congress, whenever two thirds of both Houses shall deem it necessary, shall propose Amendments to this Constitution, or, on the Application of the Legislatures of two thirds of the several States, shall call a Convention for proposing Amendments, which, in either Case, shall be valid to all Intents and Purposes, as part of this Constitution, when ratified by the Legislatures of three fourths of the several States, or by Conventions in three fourths thereof, as the one or the other Mode of Ratification may be proposed by the Congress: Provided that no Amendment which may be made prior to the Year One thousand eight hundred and eight shall in any Manner affect the first and fourth Clauses in the Ninth Section of the first Article; and that no State, without its Consent, shall be deprived of its equal Suffrage in the Senate.

Margin notes:

Punishment for treason extends only to the person convicted, not to his or her descendants. ("Corruption of blood" means that the heirs of a convicted person are deprived of certain rights.)

States must honor each other's laws, court decisions, and records (for example, birth, marriage, and death certificates).

Each state must respect the rights of citizens of other states.

The process of returning a person accused of a crime to the governmental authority (in this case a state) from which he or she has fled is called *extradition*.

The 13th Amendment, which abolished slavery, makes this clause obsolete.

A new state may not be created by dividing or joining existing states unless approved by the legislatures of the states affected and by Congress. An exception to the provision forbidding the division of a state occurred during the Civil War. In 1863 West Virginia was formed out of the western region of Virginia.

A *republican* form of government is one in which citizens choose representatives to govern them. The federal government must protect a state against invasion and, if state authorities request it, against violence within a state.

An amendment to the Constitution can be proposed (a) by Congress, with a two-thirds vote of both houses, or (b) by a convention called by Congress when two-thirds of the state legislatures request it. An amendment is ratified (a) by three-fourths of the state legislatures or (b) by conventions in three-fourths of the states. The twofold procedure of proposal and ratification

ARTICLE VI   GENERAL PROVISIONS

All Debts contracted and Engagements entered into, before the Adoption of this Constitution, shall be as valid against the United States under this Constitution, as under the Confederation.

This Constitution, and the Laws of the United States which shall be made in Pursuance thereof; and all Treaties made, or which shall be made, under the Authority of the United States, shall be the supreme Law of the Land; and the Judges in every State shall be bound thereby, any Thing in the Constitution or Laws of any State to the Contrary notwithstanding.

The Senators and Representatives before mentioned, and the Members of the several State Legislatures, and all executive and judicial Officers, both of the United States and of the several States, shall be bound by Oath or Affirmation, to support this Constitution; but no religious Test shall ever be required as a Qualification to any Office or public Trust under the United States.

reflects the seriousness with which the framers of the Constitution regarded amendments. Over 7,000 amendments have been proposed; only 26 have been ratified.

The *supremacy clause* means that if a federal and a state law conflict, the federal law prevails.

Religion may not be a condition for holding public office.

ARTICLE VII   RATIFICATION

The Ratification of the Conventions of nine States shall be sufficient for the Establishment of this Constitution between the States so ratifying the Same.

DONE in Convention by the Unanimous Consent of the States present the Seventeenth Day of September in the Year of our Lord one thousand seven hundred and eighty-seven and of the Independence of the United States of America the Twelfth. In Witness whereof We have hereunto subscribed our Names.

The Constitution would become the law of the land upon the approval of nine states.

G° WASHINGTON
Presid^t and deputy from
VIRGINIA

Attest: *William Jackson*, Secretary

Delaware
Geo: Read
Gunning Bedford, jun
John Dickinson
Richard Bassett
Jaco: Broom

Maryland
James McHenry
Dan: of St Thos Jenifer
Danl Carroll

Virginia
John Blair
James Madison Jr.

North Carolina
Wm Blount
Richd Dobbs Spaight
Hu Williamson

South Carolina
J. Rutledge
Charles Cotesworth Pinckney
Charles Pinckney
Pierce Butler

Georgia
William Few
Abr Baldwin

New Hampshire
John Langdon
Nicholas Gilman

Massachusetts
Nathaniel Gorham
Rufus King

Connecticut
Wm Saml Johnson
Roger Sherman

New York
Alexander Hamilton

New Jersey
Wil: Livingston
David Brearley
Wm Paterson
Jona: Dayton

Pennsylvania
B Franklin
Thomas Mifflin
Robt. Morris
Geo. Clymer
Thos. FitzSimons
Jared Ingersoll
James Wilson
Gouv Morris

AMENDMENTS

[The date following each amendment number is the year of ratification.]

AMENDMENT 1 (1791)

Establishes freedom of religion, speech, and the press; gives citizens the rights of assembly and petition.

Congress shall make no law respecting an establishment of religion, or prohibiting the free exercise thereof: or abridging the freedom of speech, or of the press; or the right of the people peaceably to assemble, and to petition the Government for a redress of grievances.

AMENDMENT II (1791)

States have the right to maintain a militia.

A well regulated Milita, being necessary to the security of a free State, the right of the people to keep and bear Arms, shall not be infringed.

AMENDMENT III (1791)

Limits the army's right to quarter soldiers in private homes.

No Soldier shall, in time of peace, be quartered in any house, without the consent of the Owner, nor in time of war, but in a manner to be prescribed by law.

AMENDMENT IV (1791)

Search warrants are required as a guarantee of a citizen's right to privacy.

The right of the people to be secure in their persons, houses, papers, and effects, against unreasonable searches and seizures, shall not be violated, and no Warrants shall issue, but upon probable cause, supported by Oath or affirmation, and particularly describing the place to be searched, and the persons or things to be seized.

AMENDMENT V (1791)

To be prosecuted for a serious crime, a person must first be accused *(indicted)* by a grand jury. No one can be tried twice for the same crime *(double jeopardy)*. Nor can a person be forced into self-incrimination by testifying against him- or herself.

No person shall be held to answer for a capital, or otherwise infamous crime, unless on a presentment or indictment of a Grand Jury, except in cases arising in the land or naval forces, or in the Militia, when in actual service in time of War or public danger; nor shall any person be subject for the same offence to be twice put in jeopardy of life or limb; nor shall be compelled in any criminal case to be a witness against himself, nor be deprived of life, liberty, or property, without due process of law; nor shall private property be taken for public use, without just compensation.

AMENDMENT VI (1791)

Guarantees a defendant's right to be tried without delay and to face witnesses testifying for the other side.

In all criminal prosecutions, the accused shall enjoy the right to a speedy and public trial, by an impartial jury of the State and district wherein the crime shall have been committed, which district shall have been previously ascertained by law, and to be informed of the nature and cause of the accusation; to be confronted with the witnesses against him; to have compulsory process for obtaining witnesses in his favor, and to have the Assistance of Counsel for his defense.

AMENDMENT VII   (1791)

In suits at common law, where the value in controversy shall exceed twenty dollars, the right of trial by jury shall be preserved, and no fact tried by a jury, shall be otherwise reexamined in any court of the United States, than according to rules of the common law.

A jury trial is guaranteed in federal civil suits involving more than twenty dollars.

AMENDMENT VIII   (1791)

Excessive bail shall not be required, nor excessive fines imposed, nor cruel and unusual punishments inflicted.

AMENDMENT IX   (1791)

The enumeration in the Constitution, of certain rights, shall not be construed to deny or disparage others retained by the people.

The listing of specific rights in the Constitution does not mean that others are not protected.

AMENDMENT X   (1791)

The powers not delegated to the United States by the Constitution, nor prohibited by it to the States, are reserved to the States respectively, or to the people.

Limits the federal government to its specific powers. Powers not prohibited the states by the Constitution may be exercised by them.

AMENDMENT XI   (1798)

The Judicial power of the United States shall not be construed to extend to any suit in law or equity, commenced or prosecuted against one of the United States by Citizens of another State, or by Citizens or Subjects of any Foreign State.

A state cannot be sued by a citizen of another state in a federal court. Such a case can be tried only in the courts of the state being sued.

AMENDMENT XII   (1804)

The Electors shall meet in their respective states and vote by ballot for President and Vice-President, one of whom, at least, shall not be an inhabitant of the same state with themselves; they shall name in their ballots the person voted for as President, and in distinct ballots the person voted for as Vice-President, and they shall make distinct lists of all persons voted for as President, and of all persons voted for as Vice-President, and of the number of votes for each, which lists they shall sign and certify, and transmit sealed to the seat of the government of the United States, directed to the President of the Senate;—The President of the Senate shall, in presence of the Senate and House of Representatives, open all the certificates and the votes shall then be counted;—The person having the greatest number of votes for President, shall be the President, if such number be a majority of the whole number of Electors appointed; and if no person have such majority, then from the persons having the highest numbers not exceeding three on the list of those voted for as President, the House of Representatives shall choose immediately, by ballot, the President. But in choosing the President, the votes shall be taken by states, the representation from each state having one vote; a quorum for this purpose shall consist of a member or members from two-thirds of the states, and a majority of all the states shall be

Revises the process by which the President and Vice President were elected (see Article II, Section 1, Clause 3). The major change requires electors to cast separate ballots for President and Vice President. If none of the presidential candidates obtains a majority vote, the House of Representatives—with each state having one vote—chooses a President from the three candidates having the highest number of votes. If no vice presidential candidate wins a majority, the Senate chooses from the two candidates having the highest number of votes. The underlined portion was superseded by Section 3 of the 20th Amendment.

necessary to a choice. <u>And if the House of Representatives shall not choose a President whenever the right of choice shall devolve upon them, before the fourth day of March next following, then the Vice-President shall act as President, as in the case of the death or other constitutional disability of the President:</u>—The person having the greatest number of votes as Vice-President, shall be the Vice-President, if such number be a majority of the whole number of Electors appointed, and if no person have a majority, then from the two highest numbers on the list, the Senate shall choose the Vice-President; a quorum for the purpose shall consist of two-thirds of the whole number of Senators, and a majority of the whole number shall be necessary to a choice. But no person constitutionally ineligible to the office of President shall be eligible to that of Vice-President of the United States.

AMENDMENT XIII (1865)

Abolishes slavery.

Section 1. Neither slavery nor involuntary servitude, except as a punishment for crime whereof the party shall have been duly convicted, shall exist within the United States, or any place subject to their jurisdiction.

Section 2. Congress shall have power to enforce this article by appropriate legislation.

AMENDMENT XIV (1868)

This section confers full civil rights on former slaves. Supreme Court decisions have interpreted the language of Section 1 to mean that the states, as well as the federal government, are bound by the Bill of Rights.

Section 1. All persons born or naturalized in the United States, and subject to the jurisdiction thereof, are citizens of the United States and of the State wherein they reside. No state shall make or enforce any law which shall abridge the privileges or immunities of citizens of the United States; nor shall any State deprive any person of life, liberty, or property, without due process of law; nor deny any person within its jurisdiction the equal protection of the laws.

A penalty of a reduction in congressional representation shall be applied to any state that refuses to give all adult male citizens the right to vote in federal elections. This section has never been applied. The underlined portion was superseded by Section 1 of the 26th Amendment. (This section has also been amplified by the 19th Amendment.)

Section 2. Representatives shall be apportioned among the several States according to their respective numbers, counting the whole number of persons in each State, excluding Indians not taxed. But when the right to vote at any election for the choice of electors for President and Vice-President of the United States, Representatives in Congress, the Executive and Judicial officers of a State, or the members of the Legislature thereof, is denied to any of the male inhabitants of such State, being <u>twenty-one</u> years of age, and citizens of the United States, or in any way abridged, except for participation in rebellion, or other crime, the basis of representation therein shall be reduced in the proportion which the number of such male citizens shall bear to the whole number of male citizens twenty-one years of age in such state.

Any former federal or state official who served the Confederacy during the Civil War could not become a federal official again unless Congress voted otherwise.

Section 3. No person shall be a Senator or Representative in Congress, or elector of President and Vice-President, or hold any office, civil or military, under the United States, or under any State, who, having previously taken an oath, as a member of Congress, or as an officer of the United States, or as a member of any State legislature, or as an executive or judicial officer of any State, to support the Constitution of the United States, shall have engaged in insurrection or rebellion against the same, or given aid or comfort to the enemies thereof. But Congress may by a vote of two-thirds of each House, remove such disability.

Section 4.   The validity of the public debt of the United States, authorized by law, including debts incurred for payment of pensions and bounties for services in suppressing insurrection or rebellion, shall not be questioned. But neither the United States nor any State shall assume or pay any debt or obligation incurred in aid of insurrection or rebellion against the United States, or any claim for the loss or emancipation of any slave; but all such debts, obligations and claims shall be held illegal and void.

Makes legal the federal Civil War debt, but at the same time voids all Confederate debts incurred in the war.

Section 5.   The Congress shall have power to enforce, by appropriate legislation, the provisions of this article.

AMENDMENT XV   (1870)

Section 1.   The right of citizens of the United States to vote shall not be denied or abridged by the United States or by any State on account of race, color, or previous condition of servitude.

Gives ex-slaves the right to vote.

Section 2.   The Congress shall have power to enforce this article by appropriate legislation.

AMENDMENT XVI   (1913)

The Congress shall have power to lay and collect taxes on incomes, from whatever source derived, without apportionment among the several States, and without regard to any census or enumeration.

Allows Congress to levy direct taxes on incomes.

AMENDMENT XVII   (1913)

The Senate of the United States shall be composed of two Senators from each State, elected by the people thereof, for six years; and each Senator shall have one vote. The electors in each State shall have the qualifications requisite for electors of the most numerous branch of the State legislature.

Provides for election of senators by the people of a state, rather than the state legislature.

When vacancies happen in the representation of any State in the Senate, the Executive authority of such State shall issue writs of election to fill such vacancies: *Provided*, That the legislature of any State may empower the executive thereof to make temporary appointments until the people fill the vacancies by election as the legislature may direct.

This amendment shall not be so construed as to affect the election or term of any Senator chosen before it becomes valid as part of the Constitution.

AMENDMENT XVIII   (1919)

Section 1.   After one year from the ratification of this article, the manufacture, sale, or transportation of intoxicating liquors within, the importation thereof into, or the exportation thereof from the United States and all territory subject to the jurisdiction thereof for beverage purposes is hereby prohibited.

Legalizes prohibition—that is, forbidding the making, selling, or transporting of intoxicating beverages. Superseded by the 21st Amendment.

Section 2.   The Congress and the several States shall have concurrent power to enforce this article by appropriate legislation.

Section 3.   This article shall be inoperative unless it shall have been ratified as an amendment to the Constitution by the legislatures of the several States, as provided in the Constitution, within seven years from the date of the submission hereof to the States by the Congress.

AMENDMENT XIX   (1920)

Gives women the right to vote.

The right of citizens of the United States to vote shall not be denied or abridged by the United States or by any State on account of sex.

Congress shall have power to enforce this article by appropriate legislation.

AMENDMENT XX   (1933)

The "lame duck" amendment allows the President to take office on January 20, and members of Congress on January 3. The purpose of the amendment is to reduce the term in office of defeated incumbents—known as "lame ducks."

Section 1.   The terms of the President and Vice-President shall end at noon on the 20th day of January, and the terms of Senators and Representatives at noon on the 3d day of January, of the years in which such terms would have ended if this article had not been ratified; and the terms of their successors shall then begin.

Section 2.   The Congress shall assemble at least once in every year, and such meeting shall begin at noon on the 3d day of January, unless they shall by law appoint a different day.

Section 3.   If, at the time fixed for the beginning of the term of the President, the President elect shall have died, the Vice-President elect shall become President. If a President shall not have been chosen before the time fixed for the beginning of his term, or if the President elect shall have failed to qualify, then the Vice-President elect shall act as President until a President shall have qualified; and the Congress may by law provide for the case wherein neither a President elect nor a Vice-President elect shall have qualified, declaring who shall then act as President, or the manner in which one who is to act shall be selected, and such person shall act accordingly until a President or Vice-President shall have qualified.

Section 4.   The Congress may by law provide for the case of the death of any of the persons from whom the House of Representatives may choose a President whenever the right of choice shall have devolved upon them, and for the case of the death of any of the persons from whom the Senate may choose a Vice-President whenever the right of choice shall have devolved upon them.

Section 5.   Sections 1 and 2 shall take effect on the 15th day of October following the ratification of this article.

Section 6.   This article shall be inoperative unless it shall have been ratified as an amendment to the Constitution by the legislatures of three-fourths of the several States within seven years from the date of its submission.

AMENDMENT XXI   (1933)

Repeals the 18th Amendment.

Section 1.   The eighteenth article of amendment to the Constitution of the United States is hereby repealed.

Section 2. The transportation or importation into any State, Territory, or possession of the United States for delivery or use therein of intoxicating liquors, in violation of the laws thereof, is hereby prohibited.

States may pass prohibition laws.

Section 3. This article shall be inoperative unless it shall have been ratified as an amendment to the Constitution by conventions in the several States, as provided in the Constitution, within seven years from the date of the submission hereof to the States by the Congress.

AMENDMENT XXII (1951)

Section 1. No person shall be elected to the office of the President more than twice, and no person who has held the office of President, or acted as President, for more than two years of a term to which some other person was elected President shall be elected to the office of the President more than once. But this Article shall not apply to any person holding the office of President when this Article was proposed by the Congress, and shall not prevent any person who may be holding the office of President, or acting as President, during the term within which this Article becomes operative from holding the office of President or acting as President during the remainder of such term.

Limits a President to two full terms or one term plus two years of a previous President's term.

Section 2. This article shall be inoperative unless it shall have been ratified as an amendment to the Constitution by the legislatures of three-fourths of the several States within seven years from the date of its submission to the States by the Congress.

AMENDMENT XXIII (1961)

Section 1. The District constituting the seat of Government of the United States shall appoint in such manner as the Congress may direct:

By giving the District of Columbia three electoral votes, Congress enabled its residents to vote for President and Vice President.

A number of electors of President and Vice-President equal to the whole number of Senators and Representatives in Congress to which the District would be entitled if it were a State, but in no event more than the least populous State; they shall be in addition to those appointed by the States, but they shall be considered, for the purposes of the election of President and Vice-President, to be electors appointed by a State; and they shall meet in the District and perform such duties as provided by the twelfth article of amendment.

Section 2. The Congress shall have power to enforce this article by appropriate legislation.

AMENDMENT XXIV (1964)

Section 1. The right of citizens of the United States to vote in any primary or other election for President or Vice-President, for electors for President or Vice-President, or for Senator or Representative in Congress, shall not be denied or abridged by the United States or any State by reason of failure to pay any poll tax or other tax.

Forbids the use of a poll tax as a requirement for voting in federal elections.

Section 2. The Congress shall have power to enforce this article by appropriate legislation.

AMENDMENT XXV   (1967)

Outlines the procedure to be followed in case of presidential disability.

Section 1. In case of the removal of the President from office or of his death or resignation, the Vice-President shall become President.

Section 2. Whenever there is a vacancy in the office of the Vice-President, the President shall nominate a Vice-President who shall take office upon confirmation by a majority vote of both Houses of Congress.

Section 3. Whenever the President transmits to the President pro tempore of the Senate and the Speaker of the House of Representatives his written declaration that he is unable to discharge the powers and duties of his office, and until he transmits to them a written declaration to the contrary, such powers and duties shall be discharged by the Vice-President as Acting President.

Section 4. Whenever the Vice-President and a majority of either the principal officers of the executive departments or of such other body as Congress may by law provide, transmit to the President pro tempore of the Senate and the Speaker of the House of Representatives their written declaration that the President is unable to discharge the powers and duties of his office, the Vice-President shall immediately assume the powers and duties of the office as Acting President.

Thereafter, when the President transmits to the President pro tempore of the Senate and the Speaker of the House of Representatives his written declaration that no inability exists, he shall resume the powers and duties of his office unless the Vice-President and a majority of either the principal officers of the executive department or of such other body as Congress may by law provide, transmit within four days to the President pro tempore of the Senate and the Speaker of the House of Representatives their written declaration that the President is unable to discharge the powers and duties of his office. Thereupon Congress shall decide the issue, assembling within forty-eight hours for that purpose if not in session. If the Congress, within twenty-one days after receipt of the latter written declaration, or, if Congress is not in session, within twenty-one days after Congress is required to assemble, determines by two-thirds vote of both Houses that the President is unable to discharge the powers and duties of his office, the Vice-President shall continue to discharge the same as Acting President; otherwise, the President shall resume the powers and duties of his office.

AMENDMENT XXVI   (1971)

Lowers the voting age to eighteen.

Section 1. The right of citizens of the United States, who are eighteen years of age or older, to vote shall not be denied or abridged by the United States or any state on account of age.

Section 2. The Congress shall have the power to enforce this article by appropriate legislation.

INDEX